PRESSURE DROP

DROP

REGGAE IN
THE SEVENTIES

PRESSURE DROP

REGGAE IN THE SEVENTIES

JOHN MASOURI

OMNIBUS PRESS

London / New York / Paris / Sydney / Copenhagen / Berlin / Madrid / Tokyo

Cover design by Darren Rumney
Cover image © Adrian Boot
Picture research by the author

HB ISBN: 978-1-9131-7284-8

A catalogue record for this book is available from the British Library.

Typeset in Kalix by
Palimpsest Book Production Ltd, Falkirk, Stirlingshire

Printed in Poland

www.omnibuspress.com

CONTENTS

PREFACE

When writing this book, I didn't set out to make it wholly comprehensive or to shoehorn in every artist, producer and recording I could find. The aim wasn't completeness but to give an overall picture of how reggae music developed in the seventies, who helped to shape it, how it was impacted by events and how it was received. It's a story rich in adventure, controversy, resilience and imagination, and has its origins in the indomitable spirit of the Jamaican people.

My qualifications for attempting to tell it are rooted in honesty and, to me, that's what matters. Like many others of my generation, I grew up with the music as it unfolded. I remember watching Millie sing 'My Boy Lollipop' on black and white television and being thrilled at the sheer vivaciousness of what I saw and heard. I was 11 and became smitten with her and Jamaican music ('Blue Beat') from that moment onwards. By the age of 15 I'd experienced my first Caribbean house party or shebeen – we called them 'blues' – and added Prince Buster and Desmond Dekker to my list of favourite singers. I'm often asked how someone like me, a white Englishman, got into reggae, but the answer didn't involve any great feat of discovery or even crate-digging. During my school years, reggae music was mainstream – it wasn't unusual for Jamaican records to appear in the national charts, or to see artists like Desmond Dekker, Jimmy Cliff and Bob & Marcia performing their latest hits on *Top Of The Pops*. Their songs played on national radio, just like those by black American artists such as the Temptations, Stevie Wonder and Johnny Nash.

1

It was some skinheads' violent behaviour that stopped all that in its tracks, because their association with Jamaican music brought shame to the genre. I remember being in blues parties when gangs of skinheads gathered outside, shouting abuse and smashing windows. I also recall being at a club where hippies congregated when the doors burst open and maybe a dozen skinheads rushed inside and began attacking people with fists, boots, broken bottles and bicycle chains. Not all skinheads behaved in this way, but I was still relieved when the Wailers' *Catch A Fire* marked the end of early reggae (which the skinheads liked) and the start of the roots era (which most of them didn't).

My involvement with the music at that time was restricted to buying records and going to concerts. Early UK tours by Dennis Brown, Toots and the Maytals, Bob Marley, Gregory Isaacs and Burning Spear brought the music and culture of Jamaica into focus like never before, and while we no longer saw or heard the same number of reggae records on national TV or radio, specialist publications like *Black Music* and *Black Echoes* had appeared by then. Thanks to Island Records and Virgin's Front Line label, we could also buy albums by Jamaican artists in high street shops – a development that made all the difference to fans living outside of London and other major cities with sizable Caribbean communities, which is where most of the import shops were. Brighton, where I lived then, was close enough to London for me to see shows, buy records and visit places like Brixton or Dalston, where you could buy a draw of high grade ganja and hear the music played on a sound system. That was the ultimate listening experience, and although London dances weren't so welcoming as those in Nottingham, that wasn't reason enough to stay away.

It wasn't until 1988, when I started writing for *Black Echoes* (by then retitled *Echoes)* that I began meeting people connected to the reggae industry. Two years later I threw caution to the wind and became a full-time music journalist specialising in reggae and dancehall – a position I still hold today, more than thirty-five years later. From that point onwards I made the transition from ardent fan and occasional DJ/radio presenter to a participant of sorts – one with a mission to help share an appreciation of the music far and wide, and with as much professionalism as I could muster. Apart from making regular trips to Jamaica and supplying *Echoes* with a never-ending supply of articles and reviews, I wrote promotional material and liner notes for a host of reggae labels, before being commissioned to write books by Omnibus Press.

Over the years, I've interviewed countless reggae artists, musicians, producers, managers, label owners and soundmen, many of whom are quoted in this book. Before the advent of Zoom calls and WhatsApp, the majority of these interviews were held in person – either backstage, on tour buses, at rehearsals or in studios, hotels, record company offices and people's homes, including my own. I am grateful to each and every one of the people who've granted me the time and opportunity to ask them endless questions about their work, the times they've lived through and the conditions they sometimes had to endure in bringing their music to the world. If I can pass on even a fraction of the spirit and determination that it took for them to become recognised, or the passion and sincerity they felt when outlining their feelings about society and their hopes for humanity, then I will have gone some way towards doing them justice.

That ten-year period we call the seventies is now considered to be a golden age for reggae music. It was a time when musical landmarks came thick and fast, and reggae artists like Bob Marley, Peter Tosh and Burning Spear earned legendary status. From the mid-seventies onwards there was an over-riding sense that something significant was happening, and those of us living outside of Jamaica could do no more than hang on to its coat-tails, there was no mistaking the heady scent of change in the air. The music told us this, and many of these artists and musicians were genuinely intent on raising people's consciousness and igniting a social and cultural revolution that would finally sweep away the colonial construct they termed 'Babylon' – a form of mental and actual slavery upon which western society is based, and that Jamaica's griots sought to replace with a 'one love' philosophy forged from sufferation and Biblical prophecy.

The story of these soul rebels wasn't the sum total of the seventies' reggae narrative, but it was easily the most compelling part – not just because of the larger-than-life characters, the way they looked and spoke, their cultural differences and the events they were caught up in, but also because of what their songs could teach us about human existence. Everywhere we looked, such artists were triumphing over adversity and turning their lives around while seeking to uplift their listeners. I still find that extraordinary, and marvel at the courage and perseverance needed to make that happen. That's a large part of the story I wanted to write when working on this book, because a great deal of my thinking and understanding about life has been shaped by reggae music and its cultural framework. I was taken on the journey of a lifetime, because it was during the seventies that Jamaica introduced the world to toasting, dub, Rastafari and rockers, whereas Britain rallied by contributing punk, lovers rock and 2 Tone. I've included all of these different forms in the following chapters, along with political and societal factors that provided an essential backdrop to the music.

Some of the featured artists were deejays capable of talking a mile a minute about literally anything at all. They were part of an influx of entertainers providing thrills and amusement, while others aimed for crossover recognition or hoped to please ordinary folk wanting to hear something they could dance and sing along to. Certain singers, like Gregory Isaacs and Beres Hammond, used their voices and lyrics to tug at our heartstrings. Their songs could make us weep just as easily as making us feel like a million dollars. And we haven't even mentioned dub magicians like King Tubby and Lee 'Scratch' Perry, mystical figures such as Augustus Pablo, or flamboyant characters like Bunny Lee and Niney The Observer, whose quick-witted antics brought humour and creativity to the genre. It's to all of the above that I dedicate these pages, covering the decade in which their talents shone most brightly.

INTRODUCTION

Before embarking on the story of the seventies, let's remind ourselves of what happened leading up to that period. The previous decade had been the most prolific in musical history, fuelled by the public's hunger for new releases and the advent of transistor radio and home hi-fi equipment. Jamaicans had grown accustomed to jukeboxes blasting the latest hits in bars all across the island, while sound systems competed against one another to spin the most exclusive acetates and play them loudest. Mythical characters emerged from that world like Arthur 'Duke' Reid the Trojan, an ex-policeman who wore guns on both hips and a crown perched on his head. His competitors included Tom the Great Sebastian and King Edwards, but Reid's greatest rival was Clement 'Coxsone' Dodd – a jazz and rhythm and blues fan who hung out with musicians and wasn't averse to reasoning with the Rastafarians he met in Trench Town's tenement yards.

Early soundmen like these were the bedrock of the Jamaican music industry, but to keep ahead of the competition they had to visit different parts of the US and search out the best records to play at dances back home. There was no local music to speak of that could rival American rhythm and blues for excitement, especially when hyped up by MCs like Count Machuki, Sir Lord Comic and King Stitt, whose jive talking would ring out in the night air even before the stylus bit into the shellac.

Prince Buster was one of Coxsone's strongarm guys who helped ward off Duke Reid's thugs when they tried to sabotage Coxsone's equipment or frighten away his followers. The day he was born, his parents had been caught up in street battles between striking workers and police. They were on their way to the hospital when policemen opened fire on the strikers, witnessing trade union leader William Alexander Bustamante pushing his way to the front, shouting, 'shoot me and save the innocent people of Jamaica!' Buster's parents were so impressed they named their newborn son Cecil Bustamante Campbell in his honour.

Like his namesake, who went on to become prime minister and oversee Jamaican independence, Buster was fiercely ambitious. He was a champion runner at school and used to practise boxing under the streetlight outside the Caribbean restaurant on Drummond Street in downtown Kingston. The owner named him 'Prince Buster', although he was also known as 'Wild Bill' for a time because of his daredevil behaviour. He claims to have been the catalyst for Jamaican soundmen like Dodd and Reid starting to record local talent rather than remain in hock to the Americans.

'When I was growing up I used to listen to singers like Frank Sinatra, Billy Eckstine, Sarah Vaughan and Ella Fitzgerald,' he told me. 'Those were early days, but then the music changed and I started listening to artists like Fats Domino. I was in love with rhythm and blues but, at the same time, I had to fight it, because that was Coxsone and Duke Reid's power. What you must understand is that I was within Coxsone's camp, and the records he was playing were all bought from America. He'd just scratch off the label and not let anyone know what he was playing. For instance, Sir Coxsone had a number one tune he called 'Coxsone's Hop.' He played that tune for seven years without Duke Reid finding a copy, but it was an American rhythm and blues song by Willis Jackson called 'Gator's Tail' and there was nothing Jamaican about it! Well, I was there studying what was going on and whenever we were playing the sound system, I'd be listening to the records and watching how the crowds reacted. They wouldn't know the artist who was singing. All they heard was somebody saying it's an exclusive, y'know?

'Well, Count Machuki wasn't feeling too good about Coxsone by this time, so he come and complain to me about it. He say that him never see too much cash yet, and why don't I start up a sound system of my own? I think about it and that's when I decide to go and get a farm work ticket, so I can leave for America to buy some rhythm and blues and get the money to start up a sound system. Well, I pass every test, and then the morning I was supposed to leave there was a line extending down to the quay and a man come up to me and say, 'open your hands.' He said my hands were too soft to cut cane, and so I can't go. It was like everything come down on me, and I later find out it was Coxsone's father-in-law who say that to me, because they were afraid of me going there. After that now, I go and find a drummer named Arkland Parks – we call him 'Drumbago' – and he said I can't turn back, so we rehearse every day for about three weeks straight before going into the studio and making some tracks. If I'd have got that farm work ticket, then I would have come back with rhythm and blues just like the rest of them. But because I didn't get it, I went to Drumbago and there it was, the birth of ska!'

That first session yielded tracks like 'Little Honey' and an instrumental, 'Buster's Shack', credited to Buster's All-Stars. The latter was issued in the UK on a subsidiary of Melodisc called Starlite, owned by Emil Shalit, who'd been selling folk music from around the world, including calypso from Trinidad. Shalit would later become Buster's mentor and business adviser.

'I named my sound system Voice Of The People, and I overthrew them by playing the new sound, which was ska. But what I was really overthrowing was rhythm and blues. We had this song called 'They Got To Go' but I wasn't just speaking about Coxsone, Duke Reid and King Edwards – I was referring to rhythm and blues as well. That song was a big hit in Jamaica, but then I change the lyrics around, saying they must come my way because ska was the biggest thing happening at that time, and the others had to adapt to it to stay alive in the business. It gave the people something that represented their own culture and it bring them joy, but it also cause problems because Coxsone and Duke Reid had been making a lot of money bootlegging rhythm and blues and when ska came, it killed it for them. That caused a lot of trouble, but it felt so good to know that Duke, Sir Coxsone and King Edwards had been vanquished. After I demolish them now the three of them became friends and that shocked Jamaica, because how could that happen? Except they do it to try and overthrow Prince Buster, and they all turned against me.'

Buster's speaker boxes were even bigger than those of Duke Reid and Coxsone, and aptly named 'Houses Of Joy.' He also introduced the concept of having separate amplifiers for the bass, mid-range and treble, but it was the fervour created by his own recordings – released just prior to Jamaican Independence and dubbed 'Jamaica's first national sound' – that stirred up the most excitement. Buster previewed his new sound system in Salt Lane and promptly challenged Duke Reid to a clash, although the latter failed to turn up. Shortly afterwards, both men held dances just a block apart. Reid hired Forrester's Hall, and Prince Buster the Jubilee Tile Gardens on King Street.

That night Buster's friend Pama Dice ran a length of speaker cable all the way down North Street and set up a treble horn in a tree right near where Reid was playing. Buster turned his sound up full blast, but then a man from Duke Reid's camp called Tassie cut the wire. Buster raced to reconnect it, defeated Tassie in a knife fight and then leapt onto a nearby wall and urged the crowd to come to his dance instead. It was a defining moment in the history of Jamaican music, and Buster would explore every avenue open to him from thereon. He opened Prince Buster's Record Shack on the corner of Luke Lane and Charles Street and also invested in jukeboxes prior to making his first-ever stage performance at the Glass Bucket. The Prince Buster phenomenon hadn't yet extended beyond central Kingston, but his next move would have the most far-reaching repercussions of all: persuading Count Ossie and his

Rastafarian drummers to record a couple of tracks with him at local radio station JBC in 1961.

'I wasn't a Rasta,' says Buster. 'I grew up in a Rastafarian street and there were Rastas where I stayed in the country for a while, but my family were Christians, and so I couldn't go in front of them with locks in my hair. They were Garveyites as well, though, so they had nothing against Rastas, even though Rastafarians were under serious pressure at that time. No one would check for them, but I decided to take them into the studio so that I could stay one step ahead of Duke Reid, Coxsone and the rest. The only way I could do that was to keep coming different all the time, and leave no space for monotony, y' understand?

'Like I say, I grew up amongst Rastafarians. When I was a little boy, I used to climb up a tree on Salt Lane whenever Count Ossie would come down from Wareika Hill on his way to a Rasta gathering, or I'd be running alongside them as they played. Ossie and I later became friends, long before we did any recording together. When I was on top with 'They Got To Go', my mind went back to Count Ossie, so I decided to use him on a record. A friend said that couldn't happen because of the way things were with Rastas back then but they hadn't seen Ossie play as a child like I had, and so they couldn't imagine what I had in mind for him to do, y' understand? So I went up Wareika Hill one night and Ossie thought I wanted him to play as a member of my band. But I said, "no, that's not what I want. I just want the band playing like you used to in Salt Lane." He said he didn't want to play with a bass or regular drummer, and I agreed but that delayed our arrival, and so Duke Reid took over my session. There was a big uproar about that when I arrived, but a man from the radio station calmed me down and said not to worry about it. He told me there was another room we could make into a studio, so we went upstairs, put a partition in there and it just so happen that it had exactly the right acoustics for the Rasta drumming. It was perfect. But then, after I released those songs, the radio stations wouldn't play them! I couldn't believe that, y' know? My sound system push them for a while, and then I start to cut some copies onto soft wax for people like Lloyd the Matador so he can play them, until eventually things start to happen. I knew I was going to be challenged for using Count Ossie, but his band was full of great players and the night we do those recordings the man's fingers were burning, I tell you! That was the night we did 'Oh Carolina', and it was a song that had only existed in my imagination before then.'

Buster recorded Bunny & Skitter's 'Chubby' during that same session, but it was 'Oh Carolina', sung by the Folkes Brothers, that stood out with its chanted, folksy melodies and mesmerising hand drumming. Though Rastas were still vilified by the establishment, according to Buster, the radio stations didn't necessarily ignore 'Oh Carolina' because it promoted Rastafari or sounded radically different from everything else, although such factors surely played a part.

'It was because the DJs had private agreements with some of the manufacturers to push certain things,' he said, with disdain. 'They were getting payola, so it took them about three or four months before they played 'Oh Carolina', and then only because they were forced to play it due to public demand. People just loved it from the minute they heard it, and that in turn helped the Rasta movement to grow, because they had a song to represent them at last, and something to hold onto.'

After the release of 'Oh Carolina', Buster and Emil Shalit entered an exclusive agreement to issue Buster's productions on the Blue Beat label, distributed by Melodisc. 'Blue beat' was the name given to the West Indian-style rhythm and blues as popularised by Laurel Aitken and Higgs & Wilson. With help from Siggy Jackson, Shalit had been quick to capitalise on blue beat's popularity in England by releasing records, selling merchandise and booking weekly slots at London's Marquee club.

'Mr Shalit was a very intelligent man,' says Buster. 'He was my teacher, because before I met him Jamaica was my world and everything I had was there, but Mr Shalit turned me from someone with an island mentality into someone with a worldview. I learnt so much from that man. I was just an island guy, singing for my supper and green to the world, but he saw something else in me. He told me to park up the sound system, go into the studio and make records, and then he would distribute them for me, and I'm sure glad that I followed his advice.'

During this time with Blue Beat, Buster produced records by Owen Gray, the Mellow Larks, the Maytals, Eric 'Monty' Morris, Basil Gabbidon, Rupie Edwards, Hortense Ellis, Lord Creator and numerous other local artists. his was in addition to issuing a string of wonderfully diverse hits under his own name. Buster recorded songs about everything – love, sTex, outlaws and Rasta, you name it. All human life was there in his sixties' recordings and he also voiced some of the first talking records ever committed to vinyl, well before King Stitt and U-Roy made their debuts and the Last Poets and Gil Scott-Heron laid the foundations of hip-hop in America. There's also a strong case for crediting Prince Buster with having been the first-ever dancehall artist, since he had all the characteristics associated with that genre: he was boasty, had sharp dress sense and a vocal style that blurred the lines between singing and rapping. He also wrote ditties about explicit sex that predated 'slackness', and made some thrilling gangster records that bristled with bravado and outrageous theatricality. For proof, listen to 'Al Capone', which opened with the immortal phrase, 'don't call me scarface...' The rhythm then started up and one of the all-time great dance records began hurtling down the grooves like a runaway train. It was only much later that most of us learnt it was King Sporty's voice on that intro and not Buster's, but no matter, because the flip side – 'One Step Beyond' – was pretty impressive, too.

In 1964, he accompanied Byron Lee, Jimmy Cliff and Monty Morris to the World's Fair in New York. Buster was unstoppable, although his thunder would soon be stolen by 16-year-old Millie Small, who was still starry-eyed after being flown to London a year earlier by Island Records' Chris Blackwell. The latter had started his record label back in 1959 after travelling back and forth to the US and buying records to sell to Jamaican sound system owners. One of his earliest productions, Laurel Aitken's 'Boogie In My Bones', has been called Jamaica's first indigenous pop record, but the urbane Blackwell nearly chose a career in film rather than music after working as location manager on the James Bond film, 1962's *Dr No*. It was a visit to a fortune teller that persuaded him otherwise, after she advised him to carry on making records. In 1962 the 25-year-old Blackwell left for London where, always the entrepreneur, he began licensing records from Jamaican producers like Leslie Kong and selling them to independent shops out of the back of his Mini.

'I thought that in view of my complexion I'd be better off in England than in Jamaica,' Blackwell admitted, 'Jamaica had just become independent and every problem it had was considered to be associated with white folk and colonial oppression. It was a changed situation. People who had no money and no influence were saying they'd been oppressed by the British and they wanted to get theirs now. Their time had come...'

When Blackwell first started licensing and selling records, his main customers were people from the Caribbean living in the UK. But that would soon change with the release of 'My Boy Lollipop.'

'The business expanded so quickly,' Blackwell said. 'There were so many producers in Jamaica, you see. Many of the guys who had sound systems were also producers, and they made some great records. Coxsone Dodd was a great example of that, and it was him who first produced this little girl called Millie. I heard her sing and thought she was incredible, so I brought her over to England and was looking for a song that would be a hit for her. I found this old song [by Barbie Gaye] called 'My Boy Lollipop' that I'd found ages ago during the days when I would go up to New York to buy records. That record changed my life, because up until that point I'd just been driving around the periphery of London, going into all the shops and selling them records... I absolutely loved it and 'My Boy Lollipop' was a hit *everywhere*. I didn't put it out on Island though, because I'd seen what could happen when small independent labels had a hit. They'd generate a huge amount of revenue and then, when their next record came out, it wouldn't hit and they'd crash back down again. So I licensed 'My Boy Lollipop' to Fontana.'

Millie Small's family were from Clarendon, where her father worked as an overseer on a sugar plantation. She had twelve brothers and sisters and, after entering local talent competitions and winning first prize on Vere Johns' popular radio show *Opportunity Knocks*, she auditioned for Coxsone, who thought that she sounded like Shirley Mae Goodman of Shirley & Lee. Small's earliest recordings were duets with Owen Gray and Roy Panton, but the London pop scene – then dominated by the Beatles, the Dave Clark Five and Dusty Springfield – would provide a sterner test.

Once she'd arrived in the UK, Blackwell arranged for Small to have dancing lessons and enrolled her in speech-training classes. He then booked her to play West Indian social clubs throughout the country, where people from the Caribbean communities welcomed her with open arms. Millie's voice had a shrill upper register, but it was her appealing personality and upbeat cheeriness that they liked – qualities that 'My Boy Lollipop' showcased in abundance. Astute as ever, Blackwell had asked Millie to voice the song in a cupboard so that her delivery would have additional resonance, and the resulting take was irresistible. Rarely had so much fun and vivacity been squeezed into a song lasting under two minutes, and once 'My Boy Lollipop' entered the UK national charts in March 1964 there would be no stopping it. It reached number two in Britain and the US and would ultimately sell over seven million copies worldwide. Despite Prince Buster's best efforts, it was Millie who introduced Jamaican music to mainstream Britain and America. But her follow-up, 'Sweet William', flopped and she would never come up with another smash hit like 'My Boy Lollipop'.

Like Buster, Millie had also performed at the World's Fair in

New York during August 1964, by which time ska had been hailed as the latest dance craze – even First Lady Jackie Kennedy was photographed doing it. Millie returned to Jamaica soon afterwards and thousands lined the streets as she was driven into the city in an open-top limousine. She headlined Independence anniversary shows at the Sheraton Hotel and National Stadium during that visit and also shared a bill with Otis Redding at May Pen's Capri Theatre. What an amazing night that must have been, with Otis singing his hits 'Respect', 'My Girl', 'Shake' and 'I've Been Loving You Too Long' and Millie performing a comeback show in her home parish after conquering Britain and America!

A few months later, *Ready Steady Go* broadcast a television special called *Millie In Jamaica* featuring Jimmy Cliff, Count Ossie, Prince Buster, Roy Panton and Louise Bennett. That black and white film was a revelation for fans in the UK, some of whom fell under the spell of the music's Caribbean roots and never recovered. Why Fontana then followed the show with the corny 'See You Later Alligator' was anyone's guess, since it missed this important new demographic by a country mile. Meanwhile, billed as 'the Pint-Sized Hurricane', Millie breezed through Australia, New Zealand, Hong Kong, Singapore, Japan and the US before heading for Central and South America.

Small was Jamaica's first musical jetsetter. Still riding on the crest of 'My Boy Lollipop', she and Jackie Edwards toured Africa, performing in countries like Kenya, Uganda, Tanzania, Ghana and Liberia long before any other Jamaican acts did. American film star Marlon Brando, whose girlfriend, Esther Anderson, was Millie's chaperone, joined them briefly on that trip, although by 1966 and the release of her album *Ska At The Jamaica Playboy Club* – with a cover-photo of Millie wearing a swimsuit and Bunny Girl ears – the zest and vitality of her early time in the spotlight had largely dissipated. She wasn't yet 20 years old and must have felt exhausted, although the music of her homeland had only just begun its own incredible journey.

Prince Buster was the second Jamaican artist to capture the imagination of British audiences when 'Al Capone' was reissued in February 1967 and raced up the UK national charts, peaking at number thirteen. The previous year, shortly after witnessing Emperor Haile Selassie I's triumphant state visit to Jamaica, Prince Buster had travelled to London, where he met heavyweight boxer Muhammad Ali, who was about to fight Henry Cooper for a second time. Ali was going through major changes at the time and, like Buster, was unafraid to stand up for what he believed in. After embracing Islam and discarding the name Cassius Clay, he'd alienated a great deal of his popular support and would soon have his world titles taken from him after announcing that he wasn't going to fight in Vietnam. Black men weren't encouraged to assert their racial and cultural identity, as the Rastafarians had discovered in Jamaica, and Black Muslims and Civil Rights' activists had found to their cost in America. Led by the firebrand Malcolm X, the Black Muslims preached self-empowerment and offered a sense of pride that wasn't all that far removed from what Marcus Garvey had advocated back in the twenties. It's therefore hardly surprising that Buster – who assumed the name Mohammed Yusef Ali and started a new label called Islam – felt drawn to them, although he remained a fighter at heart and wasted no opportunity to attack his rival producers, both on record and otherwise whenever things got heated. Coxsone was the target on 'Thirty Pieces Of Silver', and then Duke Reid came in for a mauling on 'Big Fight', as Buster brought all the excitement and drama of being ringside at a boxing match into the studio with him. According to legend, Buster had voiced 'Madness' after taking his revenge on one of Duke Reid's thugs, and eye witnesses said the assault was so brutal they thought that he'd gone crazy. (Remember that name 'Wild Bill'?) Another time his skull was fractured after someone hit him on the head with a paving slab, and he was also stabbed with an ice pick at some point during those early sound wars.

'I was fighting against people who were prisoners, criminals and thugs, like you'd find out in the road,' he said. 'I had a broken skull thanks to them, so I had to be wild and vicious myself and that's why I called one of my labels Wild Bells because it represented a dangerous part of my life, when I had to be wild to survive.'

Fellow singer Derrick Morgan, who'd previously recorded for Buster, hardly qualified as a serious opponent, but quitting Buster's camp for Chinese-Jamaican businessman Leslie Kong's brought a wealth of scathing invective down on his head. Morgan's battle with Prince Buster quickly became the talk of Jamaica and provided welcome publicity for both of them. Buster's opening retort to Morgan's defection was 'Black Head Chiney', which was racism, laced with humour. Derrick countered with 'Blazing Fire', using the rhythm of 'Madness', but then Buster insinuated Derrick was working for nothing on 'Praise Without Raise' and, in a reference to Morgan's blindness, accused him of being 'too blind to understand.' Buster then told Derrick to 'rest in his nappy,' on 'Creation.' Relations between the pair somehow remained cordial despite these skirmishes, but their supporters didn't always realise this.

'It was just a musical war,' Derrick assured me. 'I wrote 'Blazing Fire' off him, and then, when him come back with 'Praise and No Raise', I say that when I was recording with him I wasn't even taking praise, much less raise... Ah, so it start, the rival thing, and it went on and on and on. When I come with 'Tougher Than Tough', he then came with those Judge Dread songs, but it get big and bad in Jamaica after a while. Gangs start to fight one another over Buster and I, and man and man would cut up one another in bars. That's when the government step in and asked us to do something about it. I can't remember whether it was Buster's plan or not, but [Jamaican MP Edward] Seaga tell us to go to [Jamaican newspaper] the *Gleaner* so they can take pictures of us together and that's how it all got calmed down...'

Several other acts, jealous of all the attention that Buster and Morgan were getting, tried to join in, but without success. Coxsone even talked Delroy Wilson into singing against Buster, but he refused to pay the youngster any mind. Meanwhile, groups of disaffected youths called 'rudies' were causing trouble in Kingston's inner city communities, and also at the dances.

'Rudies were young men aged between 14 and 30 who had joined the migration from country to Kingston,' explained French filmmaker Stefan Paul. 'With no skills and West Kingston's chronic 30 per cent unemployment, the rudies redefined the street life, hanging out, suffering, flicking deadly ratchet knives, trolley-hopping, purse-snatching, occasional muggings... petty theft and insolence, singing and general hooliganism became lifetime careers, most of which ended very early. For the rudie, the only way out of West Kingston, Trench Town, Tivoli Gardens, Ghost Town, Jones Town or Denham Town was via a hit single or a police bullet.'

The island's two main political parties were the JLP and PNP, and as they struggled for power, gangs had formed around them in different parts of the city. One such gang leader, Zackie The High Priest, was the inspiration for Buster's brilliantly conceived 'Judge Dread', on which he acts as Judge Four Hundred Years and presides over a court involving such fabulous names as George Grab And Flee and Emmanuel Zechariah Zackeepom. It was an inspired piece of social commentary, but there was humour in it too, like when Buster turns to one of the prisoners and tells him to hush up, asking if he was going to shoot him as well. The follow-ups in this series included 'Barrister Pardon', aka 'Judge Dread Dance', voiced on the same rhythm as 'Judge Dread' and 'The Appeal' featuring a lawyer from Europe called Judge Dread Locks, who Buster sentences to life imprisonment for 'racial injustice and slave trading.'

'We knew a lot of good Rastamen who believed in what they were doing,' he said, 'but then it became a fad and everybody became a Rasta. After that, some of these people started to do criminal things, even whilst talking about Jah, and let me tell you, that upset me greatly – it bugged me so much that I make this song 'Judge Dread' and sentence them all to four hundred years! But if the Jamaican government had taken my advice they could have nailed the problem right there and then...'

Prime Minister Hugh Shearer needed to look no further than his own cabinet – and Edward Seaga, minister for welfare and development, in particular – for answers. In late 1966, Seaga invited an overseas circus to Jamaica for the Christmas holidays. During their stay in Kingston they were based at the George VI Memorial Park, where a large crowd came to see the lights, listen to carols and hear the band of the First Battalion of the Jamaica Regiment. The evening's entertainments then ended with a fireworks display 'which delighted children and grown-ups alike and sent a thrill of joy through all hearts for the season,' according to a report in the *Gleaner*, which then complained that 'the noise from the circus nearby made some of the singing almost inaudible.' Legend has it that this circus was the catalyst for much of the gun violence that followed. It's said that guns had been hidden in the large teddy bears given as prizes on many of the stalls, and this was why children carrying these bears were stopped as they left the park and had their prizes taken off them. We can only imagine the upsets this caused, but why else would anyone do that?

Most old-timers agree that 1967 was the year that the Kingston gang wars became more prevalent, and also more violent. The main gangs affiliated to the JLP in that era were the Skulls and Zackie The High Priest's Phoenix gang. Their key rivals included the Vikings, led by Dillinger, and the Spanglers, who controlled the Regent Street area. Dudley Thompson marshalled the PNP troops, and Seaga did the same with gangs supporting the JLP. Apart from their usefulness in causing mayhem and division, these gangs' primary purpose was to ensure that people in their neighbourhoods voted to keep certain politicians in office. This ultimately resulted in a network of no go areas spread across the city that neither party could row back from, since their hands were too bloody. Seaga then compounded the problem by giving the order to flatten a shanty town called Back O' Wall so he could build apartments there instead, which were then let to JLP supporters. This new power base was called Tivoli Gardens, but hundreds of squatters, Rastafarians and impoverished people were made homeless by the destruction of Back O' Wall; many of them watched on helplessly as their make-do shelters were razed to the ground. Those who didn't and chose to protest instead were chased away and beaten by police. In the aftermath, large numbers of people dispersed into neighbouring ghetto areas or returned to the rural districts they'd originally come from, whilst some of the Rastafarians like Prince Emmanuel and his followers sought shelter in the hills overlooking Bull Bay.

Singer Desmond Dekker hadn't witnessed any of this in person – he'd only seen it reported on local television – but the song that he wrote about it, '007 (Shanty Town),' left people in no doubt about what had happened, or his own feelings towards it. Within weeks of Prince Buster breaking into the UK Top 20 with his reissue of 'Al Capone', Desmond went four places better with '007 (Shanty Town).' This was no novelty hit tailored for commercial success, but a show of support for people who'd been cast aside by scheming politicians like Seaga, who'd been renamed 'the minister for warfare and devilment' by PNP followers. '007 (Shanty Town)' was a record that reeked of authenticity, yet the majority of overseas fans who bought the single and sent into the UK charts during the Summer of Love knew nothing of this. They just found it catchy and different and loved the new, slowed down rocksteady beat behind it – a stylistic evolution that would inspire countless singers and vocal groups as the sixties drew to a close.

Desmond was born in Kingston but had spent most of his early years near Seaforth in St Thomas, where some of Jamaica's bloodiest slave uprisings had taken place. By the age of 15 he was working as a welder in west Kingston and dreaming of becoming a singer like his idols Nat King Cole and Sam Cooke. Coxsone and Duke Reid both turned him down, and he had to audition for Beverley's several times before getting the nod from Leslie Kong, whose faith was rewarded when Desmond's debut, 'Honour Your Mother And Father', topped the local charts in 1962. Kong hadn't cared much for Desmond's actual surname of Dacres, rebranding him 'Desmond Dekker.' At Desmond's prompting, he also auditioned a young Bob Marley, who worked at the same welding shop. Kong recorded a handful of tracks with him, including the country music covers 'Judge Not' and 'One Cup Of Coffee.' He even tried renaming him 'Bobby Martell', but nothing came of it.

Dekker's career flourished, though. He and guitarist/arranger Lynn Taitt struck up a good partnership and the hits kept coming – especially after he'd teamed up with a vocal group called the Four Aces, who sealed their alliance with 'Problems.' The rude boy era was in full swing by then and Dekker and the Aces joined in with rocksteady classics such as 'Rude Boy Train', 'Keep A Cool Head' and 'Rudie Got Soul.' In common with other local singers, Desmond had also been inspired by Emperor Haile Selassie I's state visit to Jamaica the previous year, as heard in a growing number of songs devoted to spiritual and cultural themes, including 'Wise Man', 'Mount Zion' and 'Pretty Africa.' Around the same time '007 (Shanty Town)' was heading for the UK charts, Desmond and the Aces were voted runners-up in the Jamaican Song Festival with 'Unity', and won it the following year with 'Music Like Dirt', aka 'Intensified '68.'

The group's next hit was a song written about Jamaica's sufferers called 'Israelites' that opened with a description of having to rise every morning and slave for a living. It took a year for 'Israelites' to capitalise on its popularity in reggae dances and top the charts in West Germany, Sweden, Holland, Canada and South Africa as well as the UK, where it became the first-ever reggae song to reach number one – even Millie hadn't managed that. But Desmond's new-found celebrity came at a cost, requiring him to spend increasing amounts of time away from Jamaica. Somewhat surprisingly, the lure of fame and money didn't turn his head and he remained loyal to Leslie Kong, rejecting the advances of every other producer who approached him.

Derrick Morgan's career path worked out rather differently. He'd started out with Duke Reid, then voiced his breakthrough hit 'Fat Man' for Simeon Smith's Hi Lite label before joining Prince Buster on Blue Beat. His defining hits, however, were all produced by Leslie Kong for the Beverley's label. 'Blazing Fire' and 'House Wife Choice' the latter shared with Patsy, came out in 1961, and then 'Forward March' became a veritable anthem as Jamaica celebrated its independence. The following year, Beverley's released a debut album, also called *Forward March*, that helped establish the dapper, pork pie hat-wearing 23-year-old as one of Jamaica's biggest stars. After their musical clash, Prince Buster invited Derrick to sign with Emil Shalit and leave for London. Leslie Kong advised him against it and offered to pay him more money, but Derrick had dreams of making it big in the UK and signed anyway. As it turned out, Derrick only spent six months in London and then on his return he discovered that his partner Patsy had defected to Treasure Isle.

'Patsy left and I say that I was gonna try and go back with Leslie Kong, but when I go to see him now, Leslie didn't want to know. He said that I can't work for him when I'm under contract with Shalit so I form a group called Derrick Morgan and the Blues Blenders and went to Coxsone...'

It was Edward Seaga who stepped in and got Morgan released from his contract with Shalit, and the first thing Derrick did after hearing the news was to go and see Beverley's.

'All I wanted was to go back to Leslie Kong, and that's how he get 'Tougher Than Tough', because this rude guy come to me and said that he wanted me to make a song off him. His name was Busby and I was afraid he would come and cut me, so I tell Leslie that he was threatening me and I must make a song for him and bring it to the dance on Friday. Desmond Dekker did the harmony for me, and we recorded it on the Thursday. Then the following night Busby had a box of beer and when that record play and he hear me sing "strong like lion, we are like iron", he get all excited, blow out the beer and crush it against the wall so that it wet up some girls who were there. They were wearing these red and white outfits because they were with a gang called Spanglers or something like that…'

Busby became yet another victim of Kingston's gang wars soon afterwards, but 'Tougher Than Tough' did well for Beverley's and that wasn't the only thing that Leslie Kong had to thank Derrick Morgan for. Few people knew of Jimmy Cliff – then known as James Chambers – when he'd first visited Derrick back in 1962. The young singer from Somerton, near Montego Bay, had voiced a couple of songs for Count Boysie and Sir Cavalier that had gone nowhere, and was attending night classes in radio and television engineering at Kingston Technical College when he had the idea of approaching Derrick with a song he'd written with Leslie Kong in mind called 'Dearest Beverley.' Kong had agreed to give Jimmy a try, renamed him 'Jimmy Cliff' and then, at Derrick's instigation, recruited Prince Buster's backing band to play on the session. That's what had sparked off the feud between him and Buster, but it ended up working wonders for Kong and Jimmy himself, who followed 'Dearest Beverley' with singles such as 'Miss Jamaica', 'King Of Kings' and 'Trust No Man', some of which appeared on Island Records in the UK. A cameo appearance in the film *This Is Ska* – shot in black and white at the Sombrero Club in Kingston, with backing by Byron Lee and the Dragonaires – then led to him being invited to perform at the World Fair in New York. Confident as ever, Jimmy seized the opportunity with both hands and got the best write ups when the Jamaican artists' performances were reviewed in *Cash Box*, *Billboard* and *Record World*.

'United Artists wanted to sign me but this guy Byron Lee wanted to jump on the bandwagon and I said, "no, no, no. I am Jimmy Cliff and I am here as the guest with your band. I'm not a part of your Dragonaires", and he was fuming and bitter. He said some nasty, racist things but I didn't care, and in the end I didn't sign with United Artists.'

It was in New York that Jimmy met Island Records' Chris Blackwell, who was there with Millie. 'He approached me and said, "come to England" but I said no. I wanted to stay in America instead, but then he said something that made me change my mind. He said, "there are plenty of singers like you in America, but there is maybe just one like you in England." I heard that and left for England about three months later, but when I first came over and looked out the window, I wanted to get back on the plane! I thought, "oh man, is this London? I want to go back home!" I didn't like it one bit. But then I met up with some other Jamaicans and things got better. To be truthful, I had to adapt and I found that difficult at first because I was a star in Jamaica. I had three or four hit records in the charts and I'd toured every nook and crevice on the island, but then I thought, "I need to do something different now", and that's why I decided to take up Island Records on their offer. I came here with the intention of doing my own music, which was ska, but it didn't work out that way. The audiences there weren't ready, and so I had to sing R&B, soul and rock'n'roll and mix it all up, and by doing that it made my music even richer...'

Jimmy describes London as being 'a Mecca for new creativity.'

'There were some great bass players, drummers and horn players there, and I played with a lot of them,' he said, during one of several conversations with me. 'The way the music business was in Jamaica at that time, producers like Coxsone, Duke Reid and Beverley's all had their own little families, where the members worked on each other's music, just like at Motown. That was the same kind of set up that Island had in the early days as well, because Chris Blackwell had artists like the Spencer Davis Group and if you listen to their records, you can hear me singing in the background. You can hear this voice going, "hey, hey, hey" and that was me! When Island Records bought that church on Basing Street and turned it into a studio, it became like a blues party, y' know? That's where I recorded my album, *Hard Road To Travel*, and it's where that picture on the cover was taken.'

You could hear the rock, pop and Motown influences coursing through that 1967 debut album. The title track, produced by Jimmy Miller, was straight soul, although Cliff would later rework it into a characteristically resilient reggae number.

'I would say that my songwriting became extended rather than changed when I was in England, because I recorded a first cut of 'Hard Road To Travel' there before going back to Jamaica and doing that other version. I also wrote songs like 'Sitting In Limbo' in England, which was very much like a blues progression and if I'd have been in Jamaica, I don't think that I would've written a song like that or 'Keep Your Eyes On The Sparrow', which was kind of rock-based. I was open to all different kinds of music at that time, because when I was in the UK, that's when I started hearing music from different parts of Africa as well, and I loved that. It broadened my scope and my mind to a great extent. When I'm writing a song, it has to fit in any mode of music you want to put it in. It can't just belong to one category and that's it. That's how it was it for me, and so I was considered a soul singer in the UK, even more than a ska or a reggae singer until I made a reggae song that was a hit.'

Someone once said that it's not where a song comes from that counts, but where it takes you. Jimmy would base his career on writing songs that were universal and defied all attempts to be categorised, although the inspiration behind them was often more clear-cut. Brazil had a profound impact on him when Jimmy first went there in the late sixties, and he ended up staying there far longer than he'd expected.

'Brazil was a very interesting place. The military ruled the country at that time, but I got the invitation to go there to sing in a song festival, and I went with this song 'Waterfall' by a group called Nirvana that was signed to Island Records. They were the original Nirvana and it was like a little pop song, y' know? I didn't like it, to tell you the truth, but it gave me a chance to leave Britain, because I really wanted to get out by then. This was in 1968 and I went and sang this song and it turned the stadium upside down! There were all these great people on the show, like Paul Anka, and there I was representing Jamaica, but my life changed after that. I won the Festival and I was only supposed to be there for just a short time – maybe for like a month – but I stayed in Brazil for about half a year! That's where I discovered that different places had a particular energy that can have a profound effect upon us as individuals. Brazil had that for me, and that's where I started writing a number of songs, including 'Wonderful World, Beautiful People.' But it was a love and hate situation, because I loved the country and I loved the people, but I really couldn't take the system they had there. It was too hypocritical for me. But overall, that was a very good experience, and Brazil has always been a very special place for me. After I left there I went to Argentina, Chile, Uruguay, Panama and Puerto Rico, and when I finally arrived in Miami I had all of these songs half-written, including 'Many Rivers To Cross' and 'Vietnam', so I checked into a hotel room and finished them before I left for Jamaica. I was ready!'

Island followed his *Hard Road To Travel* album with *Jimmy Cliff In Brazil*, which featured some of the same tracks. But it was Trojan's 1969 set, *Jimmy Cliff*, that made him a star. This was the album, co-produced with Leslie Kong in Jamaica, that contained the revamped 'Hard Road To Travel', 'Many Rivers To Cross', 'Vietnam' and 'Wonderful World, Beautiful People', which peaked at number six in the UK national charts during late October and gave Jimmy his first international hit. Thanks to his willingness to search out fresh experiences and sources of inspiration he'd been reborn as a singer with purpose—one with lyrics and melodies to die for, who pulled no punches in getting his message across. 'Many Rivers To Cross' is surely one of the greatest songs ever written by a Jamaican artist – Bob Marley included – but everything about Jimmy Cliff had changed since he'd left Jamaica, even his appearance. For instance, the tie-dyed, collarless shirt and fringed jacket he wore on the sleeve of *Jimmy Cliff* wasn't typically Jamaican but was more like something a rock star would wear. Also, he was looking directly into the camera on the front cover, with no hint of showbiz whatsoever. It was the gaze of someone who knows what they're about and is determined to fulfil their destiny come what may. Witness, too, the artwork on the back cover, because that slogan painted in red on the wall behind him, whilst incomplete, spelt FIGHT, and made a statement that couldn't be ignored.

CHAPTER ONE

1970: SHOCKS OF MIGHTY!

'A year ago they were a minority, a violent curiosity in an age of hippie benevolence,' began a British article from early 1970, reprinted in the *Gleaner* and retitled *The Skinheads, Greasers And Rudys – England's New, Violent Teen Style.* 'Since then, however, they've been breeding like fleas, spreading and taking root throughout the country until their numbers are now estimated at anything up to a million.' It told of youths from working class backgrounds wearing trousers above their ankles, T-shirts, braces and 'bovver' boots," their hair shorn to within a fraction of an inch and who feel antipathy towards hippies and gay and Asian people. The author goes on to describe them as being 'dumb, ugly and boorish,' yet their appreciation of Jamaican music and artists like Desmond Dekker was beyond question.

Desmond Dekker's role in introducing ska and rocksteady to audiences overseas cannot be underestimated, and he reinforced his record-breaking chart success with dynamic stage perform-ances. A little after the New Year he, Jimmy Cliff and Jackie Edwards played in north London, where he received 'tumultuous support from the many skinheads present,' according to one reviewer, who wrote that 'the English youths have taken him to their hearts. Desmond has that rare gift of direct communication with his audience and he teased, taunted, titillated and courted their attention.'

He'd been quick to adopt the same dress code as the skinheads, and regularly wore Ben Sherman shirts and trousers hitched several inches above his ankles, although his songs remained resolutely Jamaican in character. The follow-up to 'Israelites' was 'It Mek', which again raced into the UK Top 10. Dekker and the Aces toured non-stop thereafter as his popularity continued to soar, although the pressures of being on the road so much took their toll and a different line-up of Aces had backed Desmond on his latest single, 'Pickney Gal.' The level of success he'd experienced to date was unbelievable, especially when you consider the extent to which reggae was being derided by the UK music establishment. The BBC had initially refused to play 'Israelites', whilst Radio 1 DJ Tony Blackburn denounced reggae records live on air in front of millions of listeners – a situation that compelled representatives from Trojan and Pama to seek urgent peace talks with BBC officials.

Unusually, Desmond Dekker had stayed with just the one producer – Leslie Kong – throughout his rise to fame, and he continued to make music that was free of artifice or pretension. He wrote about what he saw around him, and his lyrics were invariably rooted in traditional values.

'I never looked to complicate my music,' he admitted. 'That's not how it goes in reggae. You're supposed to keep it straightforward, so that all manner of people can relate to it, and you can sing about anything within that same basic structure. It's a simple music, and it has a message everyone can relate to. Admittedly, my style of writing and pronunciation would make it a little bit unusual at times, but that's how it was. Everyone would try and come up with something different, and that's one of the things that made the music of that period so interesting.

'Ultimately I tried to be myself and just talk the way I do normally, using my own accent. I didn't try to put on anything, but just sing the way I felt. The idea was to give you food for your feet as well as your brains, and that same combination is always there in my music.'

Beverley's was by now the most successful record label in the island's history, despite having released fewer tracks than more established competitors such as Studio One and Treasure Isle. The Kong family owned a real estate business as well as a pharmacy, an ice cream parlour and Beverley's Record Den 'for the latest in local and foreign hits.' The latter aside, there was little in Leslie's background to suggest that he was going to have a career in music, since he couldn't sing or play an instrument, write a song, engineer a session or even dance too well. He didn't have a sound system like his rivals, or an entourage of heavies to intimidate the opposition. All he had going for him was an uncanny ability to recognise a hit when he heard one, astute business sense and a determination to treat the people who worked for him with a measure of respect.

Both his parents were born in mainland China before traveling to Jamaica and starting a family. They had four boys – Cecil, Lloyd (who was also known as 'Fats'), Leslie and Kenneth – and two girls, Gladys and Mavis. These weren't typical Chinese names, and such choices speak volumes about their parents' desire to integrate. Leslie attended Wolmer's High School for Boys in Kingston, and clearly took the school motto, '*Age Quod Agis*' – 'whatever you do, do it well' – to heart. But then, the entire family were driven in making something of their lives.

Kong's Real Estate had opened in 1961 and quickly gained a share of the market for selling and renting commercial and residential properties. Their offices were at 135a Orange Street in downtown Kingston, just round the corner from Drummond Street. Kenneth was an ordained Roman Catholic priest, Cecil ran the business with his father and Lloyd managed the label and record store with Leslie.

Beverley's stable of artists certainly punched well above their weight. By the end of the sixties Toots and the Maytals had joined them, although they'd failed to impress Derrick Morgan when auditioning for Beverley's back in 1963, and so had gone to Studio One instead. They'd also recorded for Prince Buster and Byron Lee before Kong took them in the studio for 'Do The Reggay', now widely regarded as being the first song to mention the word 'reggae' in its title. It was a hit, naturally, although Byron Lee hated the fact they'd left him for one of his competitors. Toots claimed that the Maytals were deliberately sabotaged because of this, and that some police were bribed to have him arrested for something he didn't do. He described how he and the Maytals were Jamaica Song Festival winners but still couldn't afford a car, and so would travel up and down the island for shows on two motorbikes, with Toots riding one and his backing vocalists – Henry 'Raleigh' Gordon and Nathaniel 'Jerry' Mathias – sharing the other.

'I was riding my bike and Jerry was riding his going to Ocho Rios to do a show and that's where the grudge came in, because this policeman stopped Jerry, saying he wasn't licensed to carry Raleigh on his pillion,' said Toots. 'The policeman tell us to go to the police station, so I leave my overnight bag with the police and ride back to Kingston to get our manager. They wait until I come back, then this policeman open my bag and say he find ganja in it. It was like a joke because I never even smoked weed at that time!'

Marijuana – also known as 'herb' and 'ganja' – was illegal in Jamaica, and the government had recently announced that anyone found with it in their possession should be jailed. Toots was declared guilty and spent the next eight months on a prison farm, although in truth it sounded more like house arrest...

'They just hold me there for no good reason, and they know it. They give me my guitar and my own clothes, and I had a nice room to sit in and play my guitar. I had my own meals as well that my wife bring me. That's where I write this song, '54-46 Was My Number', but that wasn't really my prison number, because I didn't have one. I just added that later, but I come out of jail and get to number one again right away, just like that – boom!'

Toots decided to stay with Beverley's because, unlike Byron Lee,

Leslie Kong had taken the trouble to visit him in prison. On the same day he was freed, he heard that a Beverley's session was happening at Dynamic and went straight there. Half an hour later, '54-46 Was My Number' was ready to rival Elvis Presley's 'Jailhouse Rock' as the greatest prison song of all time. A flurry of other hits quickly followed, including 'Monkey Man' (written about Leslie's brother Lloyd), 'Sweet And Dandy' (another Song Festival-winning entry, this time inspired by his niece Etta's wedding) and 'Pressure Drop', which Toots penned in disgust after being told that Byron Lee wasn't going to pay him money the group was owed now that they'd gone over to Beverley's.

On 12 February, Prince Buster was shot at four times by a number of men in the vicinity of Princess Street. Buster told the police that he'd been continuously threatened since December, although they already knew this because another man – who'd since been arrested – had fired a shot at him in front of his shop on Orange Street three weeks earlier. The reasons for this are unknown, although Buster had gained a reputation as a troublemaker. Not only was he a Black Muslim, but he'd led protests against Ian Smith's separatist regime in Rhodesia and also against the government's treatment of Guyanese lecturer and Black Power activist Dr Walter Rodney, who'd been refused re-entry into Jamaica just eighteen months before, despite being employed by the university in Kingston and his wife and children living on the island with him.

The anger and resentment at Dr Rodney's treatment by Shearer's government led to riots breaking out in parts of Kingston, yet the administration's overly authoritarian stance showed no sign of abating. One JLP politician even called on Shearer to ban hippies, especially those from the US and Canada, as he claimed their presence 'affected other aspects of the tourist industry' and that they spent their time 'smoking ganja with Rastas in the hills.'

When the JLP issued a list of twenty 'undesirables' barred from entering the country, Walter Rodney's name was on it, alongside other radicals like Stokeley Carmichael, Roosevelt Brown, Clive

Nunez and Bobby Clarke. Rodney responded with a largely derisory open letter accusing the rulers of Jamaica, who were predominately black, of being 'white-hearted' and more concerned with serving the interests of foreign capitalists than members of their own constituencies, many of whom remain culturally and economically oppressed. He pointed out that it was fear which motivated them to take 'such stupid and panic-stricken measures', and that the question of colour is something that terrified them. In that same letter, Rodney laid bare to the myth of Jamaica being a harmonious, multi-racial country as promised by the national motto of 'out of many one people.' He noted how Shearer's government had banned a programme that Rodney made for the JBC on Black Power, and prevented several other leading black activists from entering the country, including Stokeley Carmichael, Elijah Muhammad and Malcolm X.

Rodney went on to discuss how he used to take his Black Power message directly to the people, even if it meant venturing into the most deprived areas of the city.

'It wasn't just the talking that was important,' he said. 'I was trying to contribute my analysis, my experiences in travelling and reading, and I was also gaining from them.'

The Rastafarians were slowly gaining acceptance in certain areas, because it was the participation of Rasta artists at the Institute of Jamaica's annual National Exhibition of Paintings that caught the eye of one reviewer who declared that they added 'exciting colour and a new dimension to this most important group exhibition of the island's artists. Not only do they liven the walls of the Institute with their bright imagination, but the artists themselves, by their colourful garb and easy manner, have been bringing a special excitement to the Institute Gallery and especially on opening day.'

Ras Everald was one of the exhibitors. His first work was a religious painting for the Ethiopian church where he was a minister, and a year before he'd had his first exhibition at UWI's Creative Arts Centre.

'The true Rasta is a man of peace,' Everald said. 'Many of the brethren have a gift to do artistic things, and there are many more artists besides me who put pictures in the Institute. I find it is mostly foreigners who appreciate what we do. They know it is something new and they appreciate it. Some people might tell you that Rastas should have nothing to do with foreigners, white people, but that is not so. Rastafari knows that good people can be white, black, pink, brown or any colour.'

Cedric Brooks, 'a young tenor player, fresh from the musical pastures of America', would surely agree. In February, he appeared at Jazz On A Sunday Afternoon, held in the lounge of the Hotel Kingston, as a guest of pianist Cecil Lloyd. Dermot Hussey reviewed the show in *The Daily Gleaner* under the heading 'A Sunday Miracle' and, after dismissing Carol McLaughlin's set as 'potted plant music hustled as content', credited Cedric with having taken charge of the session 'in a quite hypnotic way. He is attempting, as Sonny Rollins did earlier, a synthesis of West Indian rhythms with jazz.'

Hussey went on to describe Brooks' sound as having 'the muscularity of Rollins, with overtones of Archie Shepp in his avant-garde moments. It was pure poetry. Each time he would indicate a certain rhythmic pattern to the drummer, he would then lead the horns through improvisatory passages. His musicality and spontaneous energy spurred each man on to play above himself. It was an unbelievable Sunday.'

Brooks was from Denham Town and had learnt music theory and piano at the Alpha School, where his fellow students included Don Drummond and Johnny 'Dizzy' Moore. He'd then played clarinet in the Jamaica Military band whilst learning to play tenor sax and flute. After leaving Alpha, he played with the Vagabonds, Sonny Bradshaw, Kes Chin's Souvenirs and the Granville Williams' Orchestra, spent a year in the house band at Club 35 in Montego Bay and then left for the Bahamas, where he joined Carlos Malcolm's group. He wasn't there long before migrating to the US in 1968 and enrolling at Combs College of Music in Philadelphia, where he met (and was influenced by) Rollins, Leon Thomas and members of Sun Ra's Arkestra.

His arrival back in Jamaica in 1970 caused considerable excitement among Jamaica's jazz fraternity, but in the aftermath of his homecoming, Brooks also forged a musical rapport with Count Ossie and became a session musician for Coxsone Dodd, who was a keen jazz fan himself. Brooks' own reggae sides still had jazz overtones, but most of the tracks he played on at Studio One were for artists like Burning Spear, whose debut single 'Door Peep Shall Not Enter' was released in March.

Coxsone sponsored two weekly radio shows to promote his own releases. *Sounds Of Jamaica* was broadcast on JBC at half past midnight on Saturday nights, whilst *Muzik City Presents* went on air every Saturday afternoon on RJR. The Heptones' 'Message From A Black Man', the Ethiopians' 'You'll Want To Come Back' and the Freedom Singers' cover of John Lennon's 'Give Peace A Chance' jostled for position in the Muzik City Top 20, but it was Burning Spear's 'We Are Free', featuring Winston Rodney's earthy, chanted lead vocals, that stood out. He'd appropriated the name 'Burning Spear' from Kenyan president Jomo Kenyatta, and been recommended to go and audition for Coxsone by Bob Marley after they'd met by accident in the St Ann hills one day while Marley, who had been doing some planting, was out walking with his donkey.

'You see Bob Marley?' asked Rodney. 'He and I were messengers together, and he was singing songs with a message long before I was. That's why I ask him for advice. He start out in his own way and sing in such a way where people could reasonably understand what he was saying. He was looking to express divine will in his music, and then I and I came after as another singer who was intent on delivering a message through their music.'

Spear, together with his backing singers Rupert Wellington and Delroy Hines, duly journeyed to Kingston one Sunday afternoon for an audition and cut the aforesaid 'Door Peep Shall Not Enter', a sombre invocation that was quite unlike anything else in the charts at that time. It's very much to Coxsone Dodd's credit that he took a chance on them, given that their songs had little obvious commercial appeal. It's highly doubtful, for instance, that Spear would have been welcomed over at Treasure Isle, and that an act so raw and unpolished would have stirred Leslie Kong into recording them. Also, lead vocalist Winston Rodney wasn't exactly a great singer, at least not in the technical sense. His music worked because of its depth of feeling, and the righteous sincerity that poured from every note. If there were comparisons to be made with any other Jamaican group of that era it was with the Abyssinians, whose hymn-like 'Satta Massagana' was attracting attention among musicians and the Rasta faithful, but had yet to circulate any further.

Drummer Leroy 'Horsemouth' Wallace and bassist Leroy Sibbles, lead singer with the Heptones, were the rhythm section on those early Burning Spear records, although they hardly saw Spear outside of the actual sessions as he continued to live in St Ann, only coming into town when needed. The Heptones themselves were in unbelievable form. Apart from 'Message From A Black Man', they'd been busy working on songs like 'Be A Man', 'Young Generation' and 'Choice Of Colour.' They also had another album ready, called *Black Is Black*, that included more songs reflecting Sibbles' growing interest in Black Nationalism. He and the other members, Earl Morgan and Barry Llewellyn, all came from Trench Town, and the latter two had a group called the Mighty Squirrels before joining up with Leroy in the Hep Ones, as they were first known. Former Skatalites' road manager Ken Lack got them off the mark with their debut single 'Gunmen Coming To Town', but it was Coxsone who produced their breakthrough hit 'Fatty Fatty', which was banned on its release in 1967 because the lyrics were said to be too suggestive. News travels fast, and 'Fatty Fatty' was soon blaring out of every jukebox and sound system on the island, together with Jackie Mittoo's instrumental cut 'Ram Jam.'

Jackie was Coxsone's resident arranger and keyboard player, who'd begun playing with bands like the Rivals and Sheiks whilst still at school. When Coxsone opened his new studio on Brentford Road in 1963, he'd asked Jackie to run the sessions. In addition to playing piano with the Skatalites, he's thought to have come up with chords and basslines for other musicians, as well as his own piano and organ parts.

'A lot of our hit records from that period were done with Jackie Mittoo,' says Marcia Griffiths, who joined Studio One in 1964. 'Jackie was everything. Everything! Jackie Mittoo *was* Studio One, and the place would never be the same without him. He was a genius, and once you walked into that studio then everything was in his hands because he not only arranged everything, but would come up with all the ideas as well.'

Marcia was from Hannah Town in central Kingston and first sang with her two sisters in church. She'd met Keith Anderson – later known as Bob Andy – at a Paragons' rehearsal and, after they became romantically involved, became his muse. Andy had been partially raised in Maxfield Park children's home, where he learnt the piano. After leaving the Paragons – and inspired by Marcia – he wrote the majority of her biggest hits at Studio One, including 'Feel Like Jumping', 'Truly', 'Tell Me Now' and 'Mark My Word.' Their parting shot for Coxsone was the duet 'Really Together', by which time they'd left Studio One and had begun recording for Harry J, aka former insurance salesman Harry Johnson, who asked Bob Andy to cover Nina Simone's 'Young, Gifted And Black.' Andy thought it might work better as a duet with Marcia, so they recorded it and then returned to their own solo projects. Marcia had recently travelled to Germany with the Cooper brothers' group the Fabulous Five, where they'd done shows and recorded an album as The Reggaes.

Marcia had also recorded two solo tracks in German backed by a thirty-piece orchestra and signed a contract to return there in early 1970, but all this was forgotten when 'Young, Gifted And Black' – with added orchestration – entered the UK charts in March, peaking at number five during its three-month residency in the charts. Bob and Marcia had immediately left for London and embarked on a hectic schedule of shows and media engagements both in the UK and Europe. It was during a trip to Amsterdam that the German agent who'd signed Marcia for the tour with the Reggaes appeared in their dressing room, demanding that Marcia leave with him for Munich and honour their contract. Bob Andy's mood veered between anger and bewilderment at hearing this and Marcia was so embarrassed she longed for the ground to swallow her up. In the end a compromise was reached after she and Bob agreed to squeeze a few German shows into their already busy itinerary.

On 26 April they headlined the Caribbean Music Festival at London's Wembley Stadium which also starred the Pioneers, Maytals, John Holt, Desmond Dekker and Millie Small, among others. Pioneering black filmmaker Horace Ove's footage of these artists (along with the concertgoers) later appeared in his 1971 film *Reggae*. The MC at the festival was Count Prince Miller – a big man with an outsize personality, best-known for his novelty hit 'Mule Train.' He'd left Jamaica in 1964 after touring with Byron Lee and the Dragonaires and his own band, the Vagabonds. He used to perform 'Mule Train' on stage, but it had become his signature tune ever since he'd returned to Jamaica two years previously, the musicians at Federal Recording Studio launching into the song by way of a greeting as he entered the room. He'd joined in and, unbeknown to all of them, the session was taped. Producer Bunny Lee turned up later, liked what he heard and pressed it on a 7-inch. The first thing Miller knew about all this was when Derrick Harriott phoned him to say that 'Mule Train' was the No. 1 hit in Jamaica. Surprise!

The backing band at Wembley was London-based group the Pyramids. Originally called the Bees, they'd played rhythm and blues but later switched to blue beat after being admonished by front man Roy Ellis, who told them, 'what are you guys doing singing '(I Can't Get No) Satisfaction'? You're all black men, and you're not supposed to be doing that. You should start playing Jamaican music instead!'

Various changes of personnel took place before they met ska legend Laurel Aitken, who produced their debut single 'Jesse James' and got them dates backing Prince Buster, the Maytals and Ethiopians. That was in 1967, the same year that Guyanese singer/musician/producer Eddy Grant renamed them the Pyramids, and wrote and produced most of the songs on their debut album for President Records.

'Eddy played a lot of instruments on it, too, like guitar, bass and drums, because the musicians in the Bees still weren't very good at that time,' admitted Kingston-born Roy. 'He was very talented. When we met him, he was still with the Equals, y 'know? He said he wanted to do a reggae session, so we went along with it and we became the first Jamaican band living in England to have a Top 40 hit on the national charts.'

That was 'Train Tour To Rainbow City', released in November 1967. They'd been in danger of becoming one-hit wonders thereafter, but the Pyramids went on to play lots of shows off the back of that song, both in the UK and Europe.

'We'd been touring in Europe,' Roy told me, 'and when we came back we met producer Graeme Goodall who said, "you guys have so many Mod friends. Why don't you write some skinhead songs?" They weren't really skinheads. They were like Mods, dressed up in suits and with short hair, but he said that Derrick Morgan had this song named 'Moon Hop' and we should use the rhythm and come up with some lyrics about skinheads. It was a good idea and so that's what we did. We licked over the rhythm, I did some rapping on it and we called it 'Skinhead Moonstomp', but those opening lines came from Sam & Dave, because they had this song called 'I Thank You.' That's where it came from, but I changed it to fit the story we had – one take and that was it!'

The title track remains an all-time early reggae classic and has an intro – created impromptu by Roy – that grabs you within seconds.

Whilst it was an immediate club hit, the original 'Skinhead Moonstomp' – released as a 7-inch single on Goodall's label – failed to chart as the BBC refused to play it. But, luckily, the pirate stations knew a hit song when they heard one, despite skinheads having a bad reputation. Unfortunately for the Pyramids, any hopes they'd had of capitalising on their latest hit were soon dashed after Eddy Grant's manager reminded them that the band was still signed to Pyramid Records and they couldn't use the name 'Pyramids.' So they spelt it backwards instead – Symarip. Then Goodall had the idea of putting a photo of some white skinheads on the album cover and the real band members were relegated to the back, without being credited at all.

'That's why people bought it, because it was all white guys on the cover!' Roy exclaimed. 'Some people knew it was us because they recognised my voice, but the majority of them didn't, even though no white guy could sound like that. It was a black voice they were hearing, but we took the ska, the reggae and rocksteady and combined them so that white kids could dance to it. We did it so that everybody could shake a leg – even those people in the pubs who weren't part of the Jamaican scene. Like I said, it was a novelty, and it really took off.'

Goodall soon ran into financial difficulties and sold his company to Trojan Records, who carried on using the same cover, thereby compounding the problem. That left the band struggling to capitalise on their chart success on two counts – firstly, because everyone thought they were white, and secondly, because skinheads had a reputation for violence, which meant promoters were reluctant to risk having to pay out money for damages caused at their shows.

'We had to leave England because of 'Skinhead Moonstomp',' said Roy. 'We couldn't get any gigs because we had such a big skinhead following and everywhere we played, they'd come and smash the place up! All the promoters said, "we can't use you guys because the money we get, we have to double it since we have to pay for the damage!" They had to replace chairs and windows, and if anyone with long hair came to our gigs, then the skinheads would beat them up. We went to Germany after that, because nobody in England wanted to book us…'

Dave Barker's 'Shocks Of Mighty' came out in March 1970 and was another skinhead favourite. Again, it wasn't so much a vocal record as a rap – something to get a crowd of people on their feet and dancing. It very nearly didn't happen. One evening Barker and Glen Adams were walking along North Parade when Lee 'Scratch' Perry pulled up outside Randy's [record store] in the green Jaguar he'd bought in London a few months earlier. Scratch was living the life, cruising round Kingston with an entourage and wearing green velvet trousers with black, high heeled boots. He and his friends had hired Randy's Studio 17 for a session and Dave and Glen followed them up the stairs and watched as Perry played the 'Slip Away' rhythm and told Busty Brown to sing on it. Try as he might, Busty, who was soon to replace Scotty in the group the Chosen Few, couldn't manage it and Scratch became increasingly frustrated. It was Glen Adams who advised him to try Dave instead, which he did. By his own admission Dave was very nervous but when the rhythm filled his headphones, words and phrases came tumbling out of him and Scratch, whom he'd never met before, was ecstatic.

'Scratch then said he needed something for the flipside like a deejay thing, a rap thing,' Barker remembered. 'He asked me if I could do a talking thing on there. I say, "Scratch, just run the track, man," and I came up with 'Shocks Of Mighty.' He said, "wonderful, but before that, I want you to say 'This is upsetting'." I say okay and so before the rhythm starts I say, "Shocks of mighty. Hit me back", and Scratch the Upsetter takes off his hat and throws it up in the air with joy. That night we jump in his car and go to a few clubs, because that's how they would do it back then. They'd give it to the DJs in the clubs to play and then watch the crowd's response. And believe me, the people got up from their seats and danced!

'We did an album after that called *Prisoner Of Love* and every time I went into the recording studio I wasn't thinking of money. I just wanted to sing for the whole world to hear, and I genuinely trusted these people. As a child growing up, my childhood wasn't too nice. My grandmother used to do night work at the Alpha Boys School and when she came home early the next morning I used to get some beatings... I used to get some blows, and some punches and kicks... I grew up in a tenement yard where people were always moving in and out, and sometimes when I got a beating I used to cry so hard... I'd find some empty house and just go in there and sing, because I found that the more I sang, the more the pain would ease. So every time I went in the recording studio I felt joy, because there were times when I wouldn't have anywhere to sleep. I remember sleeping one night outside this store on King Street, on the pavement amongst the homeless people, and the next morning all I could feel was this policeman's boots kicking me as he told me to move and get up. Even when I did *Prisoner Of Love* and those songs, I used to sleep in old cars and trucks, so every time I go in the studio it was a relief. A joy would come over me because can you believe that this same child is still with me—that same innocent child who trusted people? As a child I thought the world was a beautiful place. It *is* a beautiful place! But as I got older, I met people who were just dark and terrible and that broke my heart.'

Desmond Dekker returned to Jamaica on 12 April and he too found that placing your trust in people can prove expensive. It was during this visit back home he discovered that Leslie Kong was credited with the authorship of a number of compositions that Desmond claimed he alone had written, including 'Israelites.' On the plus side, he was informed that later in the year he would be awarded a bronze Musgrave medal, issued by the Institute of Jamaica in recognition of his 'outstanding achievement in pop music', and that the ceremony was to be televised for the first time.

The same day Dekker arrived, Clancy Eccles was headed the

other way. He was looking to arrange a promotional tour for King Stitt and Cynthia Richards, and also license an album he'd produced featuring both artists as well as the Coolers, Barry and the Affections and himself. Trojan duly obliged – they called it *Herbsman Reggae* – and it did well for them, but then the musicians who played on it were the cream of Jamaican session men. Eccles named them the Dynamites, since they'd played on virtually every hit to come out of Dynamic Sound, including all those Beverley's UK chartbusters. With faultless taste in sidemen and material, Clancy was a veteran in the business already, despite not yet reaching 30. After leaving his native St Mary for Kingston as a teenager he'd voiced songs like 'Freedom' and 'River Jordan', backed by the Skatalites. A stint with Lindon Pottinger's SEP label proved less than satisfactory; he became a tailor for a while, but the lure of music proved too strong, and by 1968 he'd launched his own New Beat label and made a comeback with songs such as 'Africa', 'Black Power' and 'Credit Squeeze.' By then he was taking note of what Michael Manley, the newly elected leader of the People's National Party, was saying, in addition to producing early deejay records with King Stitt such as 'Fire Corner', 'Lee Van Cleef' and 'Vigorton 2.'

Carl Dawkins also recorded for Clancy Eccles. He was from Spanish Town, but had grown up in Allman Town and been introduced to the music business when he was young, as his father was the drummer with Sonny Bradshaw's group. Carl started out with J. J. Records in 1966 and his two biggest hits to date, 'Get Together' and 'Satisfaction', were both recorded for that label. He'd written 'Satisfaction' after being released from prison. Like Toots, he'd been jailed on a ganja charge – indeed, they'd worked together in the same prison bakery. Two of his songs were banned from the airwaves because of their Black Power-related content: 'Walter Rodney', which he'd voiced for Eccles, and 'This Land.'

Despite their initial spurt of success at Studio One, by 1970 The Wailers still hadn't tasted commercial success. It couldn't have helped their self-esteem to go cap in hand to Beverley's, searching for hits, especially as releases on their own Wail 'N Soul 'M label had largely failed to make an impression. They weren't opposed to singing love songs, but they had fire in their bellies after soaking up influences from America where James Brown, Aretha Franklin, the Temptations and Curtis Mayfield were in the vanguard of Black Power-inspired soul and funk. Indeed, the Wailers had recently adapted James Brown's 'Say It Loud – I'm Black And I'm Proud', which Randy's had retitled 'Black Progress.'

Hux Brown played on their Beverley's album and said the Wailers didn't arrange any of the material that came from those sessions, nor did they assist with the production in any way, but he admired their harmonies and appreciated how they were so well-rehearsed. This made the recording process so much easier, and the songs were good too, even if none of them charted locally – not even 'Soul Shakedown Party', which was the most obvious candidate. The three Wailers – Bob Marley, Peter Tosh and Bunny Livingston – had delivered an accomplished set of songs, but there wasn't anything there that would make people spring to their feet with joy nor greatly admire. There was no soul-baring, no dazzling display of invention or a song so edgy that listeners would return to it again and again, searching for hidden meanings. The closest they came to any of this was on 'Caution', thanks to Marley's warning that black people need to do better than that.' Peter, who'd penned the group's first-ever Rasta song (1966's 'Rasta Shook Them Up'), was in a hootenanny mood on 'Go Tell It On The Mountain' and 'Stop That Train', whilst 'Soon Come' was written by the Coasters' Jimmy Norman, who'd visited Jamaica with Johnny Nash and his manager Danny Sims a couple of years back. Marley and Tosh had been hired to write material for Nash in the wake of his success with 'Hold Me Tight', but nothing of note had come from this arrangement as yet. Bob's wife Rita was doing okay, though. Her group the Soulettes had recently appeared at the House Of Chen in New Kingston where, according to a local advertisement, they were 'thrilling from the word go. Fantastic versatility and dynamic entertainment.'

45

In the meantime, another of the Wailers' former Studio One stablemates, Ken Boothe, was sitting pretty at number one on the island's album charts with an LP for Beverley's. The title track, *Freedom Street*, had all the ingredients that the Wailers' songs lacked – the emotionally charged vocals leapt out at you, as did the message. The harmonies were punchy and Ken sang as if he was addressing the listener personally, whether singing of love, Biblical themes ('In The Beginning') or everyday struggle, as on 'Drums Of Freedom.' Like the Wailers, Boothe was from Trench Town, although he'd also spent time in Denham Town as a schoolboy. In those days he would dive for pennies in Kingston harbour and sell newspapers by the roadside to raise a little extra money. He and one of his sisters then performed dance routines before Boothe entered local talent shows and accompanied Stranger Cole on a string of ska hits, including 'Artibella' and 'World Fair.' Soon after embarking on a solo career with Coxsone he toured the UK with Alton Ellis and the Soul Vendors, then returned to Brentford Road for hits like 'When I Fall In Love', 'Puppet On A String' and the Bob Andy-penned 'I Don't Want To See You Cry.' It was disappointments over money that drove him into the clutches of rival producers such as Phil Pratt and Sonia Pottinger, and compelled him to join the artists' collective Links, together with the Melodians, Gaylads, 'Bumps' Oakley and Delroy Wilson. Their ambition was to free themselves from unscrupulous middlemen and take control of their own affairs, but distributors were warned against handling their releases and radio DJs paid not to play their records, leaving these artists feeling even more dispirited. Recording for Beverley's was the least painful compromise both for Boothe and the Gaylads' B. B. Seaton, who wrote several of the songs on his friend's album, including 'Freedom Street' itself.

Though the old guard became disenchanted with Coxsone and left Studio One, his premises on Brentford Road continued to act as a magnet for talented unknowns and especially Rasta artists, who knew they wouldn't be discriminated against, because Burning

Spear was there. One such hopeful was the 20-year-old Lincoln Thompson, who lived in Jones Town before moving to Cockburn Pen. Inspired by Alton Ellis, he started out as a member of rock-steady vocal group the Tartans, sharing harmonies and occasional lead with Devon Russell, Cedric Myton and Lindberg 'Preps' Lewis.

'We call 'im "Red Socks" at that time,' recalls Devon 'cause 'im wear the wickedest socks in the world, believe me!' A year later, the Tartans made their debut for Merritone with smash hit 'Dance All Night', recorded at Federal. After notching up further hits for Ken Lack and Duke Reid, the group disbanded in 1969. Prince Lincoln left Cockburn Pen at this point and went to live in a Rasta community in Hunts Bay just outside Kingston, where he began writing songs and meditating upon Rastafari. Hitching his guitar on his shoulder, he walked miles under the burning sun on his frequent visits to Studio One, where he sought to establish himself as a solo act. Most of the well-known names had left by then, but Carlton Manning was still there and Thompson befriended Freddie McGregor, who could play drums as well as sing. Lincoln talked of being in the company of 'hopefuls, up-and-coming stars and wannabe stars', but the first track he recorded for Coxsone, 'Daughters Of Zion', placed him firmly in the middle category. He then followed it with two other songs of haunting beauty and integrity, 'Live Up To His Name' and 'True Experience.'

By the middle of August 1970, U-Roy had the top three records on both Jamaican charts. This was something that had never been done before, and definitely not with a deejay or 'toaster' as the featured artist. The canny Duke had seen which way the wind was blowing and, acting on John Holt's recommendation, had got King Tubby's mic man to deejay over some rocksteady hits he already had on tape, all of them by the Paragons, and with snatches of the original vocals left in the mix. That's how 'Wear You To The Ball', 'Rule The Nation' and 'Wake The Town' were made, and nothing would ever be the same again.

U-Roy wasn't quite the originator – Sir Lord Comic, King Stitt and Count Machuki all preceded him. But these earlier artists' main function had been to keep the crowd entertained in-between records and, lyrically, they had little to offer beyond stringing together simple rhymes and exhorting people to dance and have a good time. They were cheerleaders, essentially, but U-Roy had assimilated what they were doing and turned their rhyming jive talk into an artform – one that took on a life of its own as he skipped effortlessly from line to line, keeping his delivery steady but always remembering to make it entertaining as well. By 1970, his performances on King Tubby's sound system had already made him the talk of Jamaica and, once immortalised on vinyl, his catchy, uplifting rhymes could be heard on radios and jukeboxes throughout the island. 'Wake the town' became a clarion call and the floodgates opened as producers rushed to record other deejays such as Dennis Alcapone, Lizzy and I-Roy.

Real name Ewart Beckford, U-Roy was born to deejay. From an early age he'd sneak out of the family home near Olympic Way to attend local dances, although he didn't get behind the decks until the age of 19, when he began spinning records for Doctor Dickie's, or Dickie's Dynamic as it was also known. Dickie's was owned by the same Dickie Wong who ran the Tit For Tat nightclub on Red Hills Road. A spell with Sir George The Atomic followed, and then U-Roy joined Coxsone's sound system, where he came under the influence of Count Machuki, who U-Roy credited with having been 'the baddest deejay who ever talked on sound system.'

Those aforementioned hits for Treasure Isle weren't U-Roy's first recordings – Keith Hudson, Lloyd Daley and Lee 'Scratch' Perry had all taken him in the studio at least a year earlier. The latter had teamed him with Peter Tosh for 'Earth's Rightful Ruler', whilst 'Dynamic Fashioned Way' was a version of Ken Boothe's 'Old Fashioned Way', produced by Hudson.

'They were powerful songs, but they didn't get nowhere really,' U-Roy told me. 'There were lots of people who really didn't like the Rastafari faith at that time, and we were talking about Jah and stuff like that in 'Earth's Rightful Ruler', so these people didn't appreciate that. But for me, we were doing the work that the Most High wanted us to do, so some day or other, they were going to have to come around to it, y' know?'

U-Roy was man of the hour at Independence shows held in August at the Carib and State Theatres, which were jam-packed. One reviewer called him 'Mr Sensation' and reported that he 'almost literally tore down the houses of both theatres' – this despite fierce competition from Festival Song winner Hopeton Lewis, Derrick Harriott and the Chosen Few, who were praised for their 'exceptionally good harmonising, clowning and dancing.' Harriott also hosted nights at the VIP Club by Half Way Tree – a venue once called the Glass Bucket, and known for its 'casual elegance.' His show featured singers like himself, popular radio DJs, a sound system (the Musical Chariot Disco) and Ramon The Mexican, of 'Golden Chickens' fame.

Tinga Stewart and Ramon grew up in the same neighbourhood. The pair were at Dynamic one day, fooling around and imitating Clint Eastwood, when Derrick said, 'hey, let's record this!' 'Spaghetti westerns' were very popular at the time, as Harriott remembers.

'Oh, Jamaicans loved those movies! They'd go crazy over them! That was a real inspiration to us – when the western thing come around, Lee Perry had 'Return Of Django', I had 'A Fistful Of Dollars' and 'The Undertaker', and Clancy Eccles was slipping in with one or two as well. I used to close my store early on a Wednesday and head straight for the Carib Theatre for the matinee at five and everybody would be there watching these westerns – it was a real knockout! They inspired us a lot, and look what came out of it, eh? Ramon happened because there were always Mexicans in those films, whilst 'The Undertaker' was actually taken from *A Fistful Of Dollars*, where someone says "what can I do for you Mister? I'm the undertaker." That's when Clint Eastwood said, "build me three coffins", and then comes back and says, "my mistake, make that four".'

The Upsetters' 'Return Of Django' had charted in the UK late the previous year, around the same time as Harry J All Stars' 'Liquidator.' The success of these tracks was just the tip of the iceberg – gimmicky instrumentals were all the rage, especially when allied to a theme like spaghetti westerns, doctors or horror movies. Derrick Harriott's 'Undertaker' was his biggest-selling single in that style, although being a consummate singer himself, he was still a keen fan of vocals and had been championing the Chosen Few since the group's formation. Several of the members had previously sung with the Federals, whose biggest hit was 'Penny For Your Song.' David Scott sang with both groups, but Derrick renamed him Scotty, turned him into a deejay and produced his breakthrough hits 'Riddle I This' and 'Sesame Street.' Noel Brown's brother Busty, of the Messengers, took his place in the Chosen Few, whilst another of the Brown brothers, Errol, replaced Richie McDonald. The group's fanbase grew rapidly from that point onwards. 'Psychedelic Train' was a number one hit in Jamaica and was followed by 'Time Is Getting Harder', a sufferers' lament featuring a moving lead falsetto in the style of Slim Smith. Their manager Derrick Harriott – who was voted *Swing Magazine's* Producer Of The Year – had his finger on the pulse for sure, and promoted the Chosen Few as Jamaica's answer to the Chi-Lites or Stylistics – smooth American soul groups with a polished sound and taste for garish, matching outfits. Honeyed, harmony vocals were their stock-in-trade and they added some of those to 1970's Jamaica Song Festival winning entry, Hopeton Lewis' 'Boom Shack A Lack.' Lewis was 23, and had learnt to sing at the Burnt Savannah Wesleyan Holiness Church in Westmoreland.

'My mother died when I was very young,' he said. 'I was about 2 months old, so they took me to the country where my aunt raised me and then after a certain age I went back to Kingston and attended school in Trench Town for a few months, before my grandparents took me in and I moved to Mountain View Avenue. From there I went to Camperdown High School, but the whole transition wasn't that bad because I'm very adjustable to life, really.'

He needed to be, because both his grandparents died when he was 15, and from there he was on his own. A sense of ambition, his zest for life and love for music inspired him to form his first group, The Regals, who recorded their debut for Coxsone in 1965.

'That didn't work out too well to be honest. Lee 'Scratch' Perry auditioned us, but a lot of people were there at that time. Ken Boothe was there, the Heptones, John Holt and Delroy Wilson... Freddie McGregor was there with the Clarendonians. That was the place to be if you were a singer or a musician. You'd see all these people in the yard, singing and making up songs, and then someone would call your name and you'd go in and do your thing. I went on to Federal after that, which was owned by Ken Kouri, but the two guys who worked at the pressing plant, Sam Mitchell and Keith Scott, were in charge of the sessions.'

Hopeton had difficulty with his timing when voicing 'Music Got Soul' and so asked the musicians to slow down the beat on his next recording. That was the session that resulted in 'Take It Easy', which Hopeton and many others insist was the first rocksteady tune. It got called that because when they'd finished recording the song, pianist Gladdy Anderson said, 'boy, that one a rocksteady man!' 'Take It Easy' was released in late 1966 and became the title track of Hopeton's debut album two years later, but the young singer wasn't exactly enamoured with the financial arrangements at Federal.

'The Khouris, they were business people, but to me they were very selfish people, too. Yeah, they weren't all that warm and I never felt too close to them. I was supposed to get royalties and this is why we had a falling out, because when I questioned what I was getting, they said I had to find an accountant and if they were right, I had to pay for it, but if they were wrong, they'd pay. It got too complicated and so I went to Duke Reid to speak to him about my situation. He got me a lawyer and found out that I was under age when I'd signed my contract with them.'

He wrote songs for other artists at Treasure Isle at first. They included the Techniques' 'There Comes A Time', 'I Can't Stand It' by Alton Ellis and 'Right Track' for Phyllis Dillon. He also wrote 'Tom Drunk', which he recorded with U-Roy, whose name is spelt 'Hugh Roy' on the actual record.

'At Treasure Isle, I was working there from nine in the morning until nine in the evening, right? And if there was no session happening, then I was there with Mr Smith as he was mixing songs. I'd sit with the artists as they were trying to write songs. That studio was beautiful, man, trust me. It was a beautiful place to work. It had a relaxed atmosphere... well, at least until Duke got tight and bust a shot or two! Everything was nice apart from that. He had a speaker downstairs so he could listen to what was happening up there and if the music wasn't coming through right he'd come up there, let off two shots and everything start happening proper after that! Duke was alright, though. He was a fun guy and, to be honest with you, he'd make sure that your rent was paid and you have food on the table. He brought this young lady out of America called Joya Landis and we did quite a bit of work with her. Phyllis Dillon, too, because I wrote that song she did called 'Take My Heart' as well.'

While all this was happening, the Wailers ended their brief partnership with Leslie Kong and had been turned down by Bunny Lee. He already had quite a large stable of artists at the time and so he recommended they hook up with Lee 'Scratch' Perry instead. The Wailers knew Scratch already from their time at Studio One and had dismissed him as being a bit of a clown. The Hippy Boys/Upsetters weren't keen on Scratch either after they'd toured the UK with him as the Upsetters late the previous year and he'd left them stranded in London with no money. Keyboard player Glen Adams, writing in his as-yet-unpublished autobiography, confirms that Lee Perry had treated them badly and kept the receipts from that tour for himself.

'Scratch would come and get me at nights and we would go to almost every bar or club that had a one-arm bandit. People played those games with the intention of winning money, but Scratch already had some and was just throwing it away instead of paying us what we were supposed to get. It wasn't easy working with a man who thinks he was above the rules, because he'd break them at his leisure, and not paying his musicians was one such example. The only way that you could get any money was to take some records and sell them to shops, except most people had already bought them by then. This kind of behaviour became so obnoxious that I wanted to leave the group and also the country. Scratch felt my vibes so he came to me and said, "Bob, Peter and Bunny want to start a project with the Upsetters." He touched my weak spot, knowing that if we had a vocal group on tour with us it would be great. So I thought about it and decided to change my plans because there was new blood in the stable, and I had respect for that trio. I thought that things would be handled differently and more business-like – that the vibes would be stronger once the Wailers became our personal focus. They'd returned to the scene with new life and it was a ray of hope, imagining them being backed by our group the Upsetters, who also worked under different names and were leading hitmakers. Suddenly there was magic in the air, but things started to go wrong after Lee Perry began losing money in slot machines and making cash gifts to bartenders and barmaids. He also tried going around us by using another group called the Soul Syndicate, that I was the musical instructor for, because he was hoping to use them as our replacements.

'He called a session recording a track that was supposed to be for 'Duppy Conqueror' but Bob and the other two Wailers weren't pleased with it, so Lee Perry came back asking us to re-record it and that was fun, knowing that we were about to show off our skills! The Wailers were tense, especially Bob, knowing that he'd gone against the band. We therefore had something to prove, because if 'Duppy Conqueror' wasn't a hit we would be out in the cold. So we did what we were asked to do – make a number one hit with Bob Marley and the Wailers! That's how I came up with a style called 'the Creep' and with Family Man [bassist Aston Barrett] locked in with his brother Carly [drummer Carlton Barrett].'

'Duppy Conqueror' fulfilled all expectations when released on 45 in Jamaica. It entered the local charts in late August and less than a month later was at number one, having edged out Dave and Ansel Collins's 'Double Barrel' and Alton Ellis's latest single, 'You Make Me So Very Happy.' It was a triumph for both Lee Perry and the Wailers, who sounded rejuvenated after a spell when little had gone in their favour. 'Duppy' is the name given to ghosts or bad spirits, and so for a Jamaican to claim they're a 'duppy conqueror' in a country where fear of the supernatural is rife took courage. Bob Marley certainly had that, yet the melody line was joyous, and the harmonies just right. The Wailers were still clearly influenced by what was happening in American soul music – and by James Brown in particular – but throughout those five months spent with Perry they forged a completely new sound for Jamaica – one that was rooted in something far greater than just melodies and chords. There was a spiritual dimension to what they were doing, and that was evident on songs like 'Put It On', 'Fussing And Fighting', the Biblically inspired 'Corner Stone', Peter Tosh's 'No Sympathy' and '400 Years', and the Wailers' first-ever herb song, 'Kaya.' These tracks were very different from the ones they'd recorded for Beverley's. They were more organic and sounded as if they were part of a long-term journey, rather than anything more contrived. Leslie Kong specialised in making crossover hits, whereas the songs the Wailers had recorded with Perry seemed to resonate with people on a deeper level. Marley spoke of how the Wailers had found themselves musically and finally got the sound they'd wanted. When asked about this, Glen Adams remembers Bob calling the Upsetters 'the most bumbaclaat creative musicians in the world!'

Randy's had upgraded their studio to four tracks by the time those Wailers sessions took place. The same night they cut

'Dreamland' – a song the Wailers had first voiced for Coxsone, and that Bunny Wailer had adapted from the El Tempos' doo wop classic 'My Dream Island' – Little Roy had recorded 'Don't Cross The Nation' featuring Bunny on kette drum and Peter Tosh on guitar. The latter wasn't seen hanging out so much as the other two Wailers. He'd just turn up at the Green Door or Randy's when needed, but otherwise kept a low profile—difficult to achieve when you're six foot four and wearing a Black Power pendant round your neck! Although still living in Trench Town, Peter would go back to Westmoreland to visit his mother and old friends quite regularly but the rebel streak in him was always there, and made him fearless when it came to dealing with authority.

Joel Gibson, aka 'Joe Gibbs', would discover this to his cost. The 25-year-old producer hailed from Montego Bay and had trained as an electronics engineer in the US before opening a television repair shop at 32 Beeston Street in Kingston. He sold records from there too, and experimented with a two-track tape recorder in a back room. Lee Perry produced Roy Shirley's 'Hold Them' for him, and Gibbs learnt fast, because he was soon licensing tracks to Trojan Records for the UK market. After Perry left, he took aim at Gibbs on 'People Funny Boy'; Gibbs countered with the equally scathing 'People Grudgeful', under the name Sir Gibbs. By then, Gibbs had moved his retail operation to 11 South Parade and set up a small studio at his home in Duhaney Park, where he prepared to welcome a new era of reggae music, the laidback, soulful strains of rocksteady having run its course. Peter Tosh and the Pioneers recorded for him, and so too Nicky Thomas, whose nickname was 'Nigel'. In-between pursuing a singing career, Thomas scraped a living doing construction and gardening work, and so it surprised a lot of people when 'Love Of The Common People' became a UK Top 10 hit in June 1970. Neither he nor Joe Gibbs had even placed a Top 10 record on the local charts before, let alone overseas. It didn't seem all that long ago that Nicky was singing at school dances back in Portland. He'd been encouraged to keep singing by Derrick Harriott, but his delivery was so over-the-top and his expression so tortured, few imagined that he would make it.

Over in the UK, Johnny Beering, producer of the BBC's *Radio 1 Club*, had just pronounced reggae music as 'a fad', whilst DJ Tony Blackburn suggested they split reggae into two categories – good and bad.

'The good reggae we will play, meaning properly produced songs that we believe the public will like,' he said. "Young, Gifted And Black' is just great, and if Jamaican producers continue producing songs like this one, I think reggae will last.' Record sales in Britain overwhelmingly depended on national airplay, as only a fraction of white record buyers were likely to hear Jamaican music played on sound systems or in shebeens. Exposure on BBC radio and television was therefore vital, as Horace Faith discovered when scaling the UK pop charts with a cover of Sonny Charles' 'Black Pearl.' When that song was played on *Top Of The Pops*, it was introduced by a smug-looking Tony Blackburn, arbiter of reggae taste, who, however implausibly, would soon be welcoming Nicky Thomas to British shores.

Joe Gibbs hosted a farewell show for his surprise hitmaker at the Sombrero at which U-Roy, the Wailers, Ken Boothe, John Holt and the Fabulous Five all performed. The Wailers played songs from their new album *Soul Rebels* and that was 'the talk of the town', according to the *Gleaner*. Despite the poor sound quality, they got 'an encore and a great show of appreciation from the very together audience' whilst U-Roy, 'resplendent in a red, gold and green pullover', had the five hundred-strong crowd singing along to his three current hits. When Derrick Harriott then ended the show with 'Psychedelic Train' and 'Close To Me' 'he was received with ecstatic screams from many of the young women who were present, reminiscent of the passionate Beatles' concerts.'

A month later, Derrick Harriott hosted another unforgettable evening at the VIP Club in the company of Alton Ellis, Rastafarian drummers Bongo Herman and Bongo Les and the Wailers, who were introduced by RJR radio presenter Don Topping 'amidst screaming, hopping and stomping of feet.'

'From the first note of the first song 'Soul Rebel' everyone went into a sing-along,' reported the *Gleaner*. 'Even some known radio and entertainment personalities climbed on to chairs to get a good look at Jamaica's number one singing group. 'Sun Is Shining' – a rooted, moaning sound which featured Peter Tosh on the recorder – followed 'Soul Rebel' and the crowd kept up their sing-along right into the number one song in Jamaica today, 'Duppy Conqueror.' Again the Wailers, like Alton Ellis, have not yet displayed the fulness of their talent on stage but I suspect that day is near and Jamaicans are going to have a lot to talk about.'

In late August, Bob & Marcia returned to Jamaica after a successful tour of the UK and Europe. Their first appearance since coming back was at the House Of Chen on Knutsford Boulevard, where they performed their latest single, 'We've Got To Get Ourselves Together.' The rest of their set included 'If I Had A Hammer', 'You're All I Need To Get By' and 'Michael Row The Boat Ashore', which suggests that it was a cabaret-style affair. Their debut album *Young, Gifted And Black*, produced by Harry J, had recently been released by Trojan, who chose to fill it with cover versions. In fact 'Peace Of Mind', which Bob wrote and sang on his own, was the only original song on it. It seems strange that one of Jamaica's most highly rated songwriters should be underused in this way, but he gave the tracks a distinctly Jamaican sound – even the Bob Dylan ones, which is something.

Fellow Trojan artist Desmond Dekker wasn't known for singing other people's songs either, although his new single, a cover of Jimmy Cliff's 'You Can Get It If You Really Want It', had just roared to number two in the UK charts, so he wasn't complaining.

'It was Leslie Kong's choice to do it,' he said. 'I love that song, but I had this reputation for never having recorded a cover version. All of my songs I'd written myself and all of my hits were my own compositions, and that was quite an achievement, because the competition in Jamaica was very strong. Everyone was writing very good songs and recording good music, so if you weren't in the race then you would be left behind…'

As September dawned, Bobby Bloom had a Top 10 hit in both the UK and America with 'Montego Bay.' He was a white guy from Brooklyn whose claim to fame before 'Montego Bay' was recording jingles for Pepsi, and writing songs for the Monkees and fictitious pop band the Archies.

'It's the kind of place that makes you write about it,' he explained, when asked about Montego Bay. The song itself isn't half bad for a pop tribute, and the Jamaica Tourist Board no doubt loved it, even though the girls shown in the video are all white. Bloom will quickly fade from view, but if you were searching for a potential Jamaican superstar, there was a 13-year-old known as 'the Boy Wonder', heading for the local charts with his debut hit 'No Man Is An Island', who fitted the bill perfectly.

Dennis Brown had been making public appearances for several years already, either at school concerts or shows promoted by Byron Lee. His father was Jamaican scriptwriter and journalist Arthur Brown, but his mother had died when he was nine and he went to live with an aunt in a large tenement block at the corner of Orange Street and North Street, known locally as 'Big Yard.' As a child he was often seen outside J. J. Johnson's record store on Orange Street, singing popular songs for pennies. When he was 11, his older brother Basil, a comedian, called him up on stage at the Tit For Tat, where he was backed by the Fabulous Falcons. Dennis regularly appeared on stage with them after that, and would share lead vocals with a revolving cast of singers, including Cynthia Richards, Pat Satchmo and the Chosen Few's Noel Brown. He then made his first recording for Derrick Harriott, who took his time releasing 'Lips Of Wine', so Dennis went to see Coxsone instead. 'No Man Is An Island' wasn't his first recording for Studio One, but was easily his best to date. Everyone agreed that he was a precocious talent, and other producers were already licking their lips like hungry wolves.

'I never had no family behind me at all,' Dennis told Rich Lowe. 'It was just me. I grew up literally on my own, like from about 15. While I was recording at the studio, I went along with the other guys who were recording there at the same time. After school, you then go down to the studio and meet up with these guys. My family didn't have any knowledge about the business, so I had to "man up." I had to do things for myself. You might be thinking I must've been robbed then because I was very young. Everyone goes through various changes working with Downbeat, but I wouldn't see it as being robbed because that was my first opportunity to be exposed to the outside world. I just wanted to record...'

During the first week of October, Jimmy Cliff returned to Jamaica to start work on a locally produced full-length film, tentatively entitled *A Hard Road To Travel*, scripted by Perry Henzell and Trevor Rhone. The crew were using Super 16 cameras, which was a first for the Caribbean, and whilst cameraman David McDonald was English, the cast was made up entirely of Jamaicans. Filming had started in mid-September in Confidence View Lane near Standpipe, and was expected to last until the end of December. Prince Buster wasn't happy about any of this and claimed that he, not Jimmy Cliff, was the first to be offered the lead role.

'I took my things to Perry Henzell and auditioned, spent time rehearsing this and that, but I still didn't get to star in no film,' he lamented. 'Perry Henzell came in my shop one day, saying I can't star in this film. I asked him why not, and he say the man who was supposed to put up the money had decided he wasn't going to finance it, because he thought it wouldn't appeal to regular society. That left Perry Henzell having to search for help in getting the film made. I was disappointed but tried not to show it because he seemed determined to find the money, and then somebody told him to speak with Chris Blackwell, to see if he could get the money from him. I heard that he went there and Chris decided he would put up the money on condition that Perry use Jimmy Cliff, because Jimmy was Chris' artist. At the same time, Perry was saying the film can't go nowhere because he didn't have enough money, and so I agreed that he can let Jimmy make the film and in return he'll save a part for me in his next film. I like Jimmy you understand, but I never saw him as Rhygin...'

By Rhygin, Buster means the Jamaican cop killer on whom the lead role is based. Whilst it's true that Jimmy Cliff isn't the gangster type, it would be unwise to underestimate his drive, talent and determination to make a success of anything he was involved with. His latest hit was a cover of Cat Stevens' 'Wild World' and Chris Blackwell – who was also a director of the film's backers, International Film – was indeed his manager, and a good one too, as it happened. Jimmy had recently spent time in the US, where he'd recorded an album that was 'quite different' from what he'd done to date. He wasn't lying, either, because he'd voiced it at Muscle Shoals studio in Alabama, where Aretha Franklin and Wilson Pickett recorded some of their classic hits.

By 28 October, U-Roy's 'You'll Never Get Away' had replaced the Wailers' 'Duppy Conqueror' at number one on the local charts. Other entries included two songs by Alton Ellis – 'Sunday Coming' and 'You Make Me So Very Happy' – and the Melodians' 'Rivers Of Babylon', but something very strange occurred that day, with the *Gleaner* reporting how 'hundreds of curious persons chased through the streets of downtown Kingston.'

'For the majority the object of their chase was both elusive and invisible,' the paper wrote. 'With pedal cyclists setting a hot pace, higglers, office clerks and schoolchildren rampaged along King Street, Orange Street and Beckford Street, invaded Tivoli Gardens and then doubled back on the route, all the while searching for a glimpse of the object. The chase was provided with additional fuel by a spate of fanciful and weird rumours. A policeman shot at it in Spanish Town, a rumour stated. He was immediately stricken and taken to the Spanish Town hospital in an unconscious condition.

The Spanish Town police denied that any member of the force was so incapacitated, however several persons claim they had seen the object. They described it as a coffin with three wheels – two at the back and the other at the front, and with a John Crow perched on top. The witnesses professed seeing the unguided coffin at various points in the corporate area. Some claim that it only appeared to the eye at infrequent intervals.'

The reports varied in truth. One of the witnesses said there were three John Crows perched on top of the coffin – two big sized ones and a little one – and she described the John Crows as being dressed in clothes. 'The little one in the middle had on a red coat and the two big ones at either end had on black coats.' She said the little red-coated John Crow asked one of the teachers at St Peter Claver Primary school if she knew John Brown. The teacher fainted and then when one of the coffin's wheels ran over a little boy's foot, he too fainted. This witness also claimed that the apparition 'appeared and disappeared.' There were reports that Spanish Town Road in the vicinity of the May Pen cemetery was blocked by thousands of people. Large numbers of people also turned up at Maxfield Park Primary School whilst chasing the phantom-like coffin with its three vultures, which was said to have travelled from Mandeville through Porus, May Pen Old Harbour and Spanish Town before appearing in the Corporate area.'

There was no evidence to suggest it had been anything else but a hoax or case of mass hypnosis. Bunny Livingston claimed that it was a publicity stunt dreamt up by Brown's Funeral Parlour, but Scratch lost no time in reaching for the Soul Syndicate's discarded cut of 'Duppy Conqueror' and getting Bob Marley to revoice it as 'Mr Brown.' Niney the Observer rushed to cash in on the story as well, but his 'Mr Brown's Coffin' arrived too late, and sold badly.

December was always a busy time for artists and concertgoers in Jamaica, and two days after a Skateland fundraiser, the annual Nuggets Gala Show took place at the Carib Theatre under the patronage of Prime Minister Hugh Shearer and the Governor

General. Billed as 'The Biggest Show Of Them All', it was an occasion designed to raise aid for the poor, hence the slogan 'Nuggets For The Needy.' 1970's edition starred American female vocal group the Three Degrees (led by Sheila Ferguson), U-Roy ('Jamaica's New Sensation'), the Blues Busters, Melodians, Inner Circle, comedians Bim & Bam and Byron Lee and the Dragonaires. Both of these shows were broadcast live on JBC radio and television.

On 11 December, The Biggest Show Of Them All was superseded by The Greatest Show Ever To Hit Jamaica, when Stevie Wonder, backed by the fifteen-piece Motown Show Band, played three shows at the Carib Theatre. Alton Ellis opened for the newly married 20-year-old, described as being 'Blind, Black and Beyond Soul!' That same weekend, Alton performed at the Island Inn Hotel in St Mary as did Hopeton Lewis, Winston Francis, the Soulettes, the Heptones and Clancy Eccles. This three-day event was advertised as 'The Million Dollar Weekend', but the entertainers merely served as window dressing for a Record Industry Exhibition and its attendant seminars, stalls and networking opportunities. The advertising men and copywriters had been in overdrive, and then another big show was held on 12 December at the National Arena. This was the 'Grand Christmas Charity Ball', headlined by 'the world famous' Desmond Dekker (who'd been presented with his Musgrave Medal the day before) and Calypso Queen, backed by the ubiquitous Byron Lee and the Dragonaires. This event was held annually to raise funds and treats for the children of West Kingston and the patron of the 1970 show was Edward Seaga, minister of finance and planning. Prime Minister Hugh Shearer also attended.

In contrast to such extravagant productions, fewer than twenty people attended the Sombrero Club, where Count Ossie, the Mystics and saxophonist Kenny Terroade performed in late December.

'The truth is that this new sound demands keen listening to be fully appreciated,' wrote Julian Jingles. 'What I'm afraid of is that this sound will be allowed to bounce around without proper administration until we hear something similar coming from America, then it will be praised as being a very original and authentic sound and the true source will be forgotten. I would very much like to see Count Ossie's group, the Mystics and Kenny Terroade combine and begin administering their own affairs. Real jazz has long been assassinated in Jamaica.'

The sound to which he's referring was a fusion of jazz, reggae and Rastafarian drumming that was unique to the group of musicians assembled at the Sombrero that night. The Mystics were formed by Cedric Brooks and trumpeter Dave Madden, whilst Terroade had only recently returned to Jamaica after playing with Archie Shepp and travelling to Algiers for the Pan-African Festival with Sunny Murray's band. The synthesis between revolutionary jazz and Jamaican music wasn't so unusual when you consider that these musicians were searching for roots both ancestral and musical, and how that journey had directed their thoughts towards Africa.

Count 'Ossie' Williams was the elder of this group as he was in his early forties. He had practised on upturned paint cans before playing drums and fife in the Boy's Brigade and joining Saint Saviour Call Troop's marching band. He then witnessed nyahbinghi drumming evolve through the intermingling of Rastafarians and the Burru people, many of whom lived in the Kingston shanty towns. Salt Lane especially was considered a dangerous area when Ossie was young, but he was a regular visitor to the Rasta camp there and would sit under a tree and reason with brethren like Brother Job, who schooled him in the art of Rasta drumming. Three kinds of drums are used to play nyahbinghi (the bass or 'thunder' drum), the mid-pitched funde (which Ossie started with) and the higher pitched repeater or kette drum that Brother Job played. It was Brother Job's teacher Watto King, then living in Trench Town, who made Ossie's first proper drum. In those days Ossie and his mother lived in Rennock Lodge, although he'd spent his childhood in the village of Bito, above Bull Bay. The Wareika hills weren't too far away and Brother Issie Boat's Rasta camp became another of his favourite hangouts. The first-ever Rasta convention had been held there in December 1949, and ten years later Rasta preacher Brother Love would read from the Bible as the drums and chanting carried over the hills and visiting musicians like Rico Rodriguez, Don Drummond and the Gaynair brothers jammed along with them.

Some of the dreadlocks who hid out in the hills were criminals and gave law-abiding Rastafarians a bad name. As a result, many innocent Rasta people were persecuted by the police: beaten, their locks cut off (often with broken bottles or rusty knives) and forced to look on helplessly as their huts were set alight. Many were locked up for days without food or water, despite having broken no law. Prince Buster wasn't the only one to take Count Ossie's drummers into the studio – Harry Mudie, the producer from Spanish Town, did the same thing back in 1961. But it was Coxsone who continued with that tradition as the seventies began.

Count Ossie was scheduled to perform with the Wailers and other local groups at the Balle d'Harambee at Curphey Place on Christmas night. Young, conscious artists like the Wailers didn't view what Count Ossie and his Rasta drummers were doing as an anachronism but as a living tradition they could embrace for themselves. The knowledge and sense of belonging that they were searching for was boundless and everlasting, and they would continue to incorporate elements of it into their songs.

Max Romeo was best-known for the controversial 'Wet Dream', but that was hardly representative of what he'd since become. He originally came from St D'Acre in St Ann, and his mother had left for the UK when he was 10. Life with his preacher father proved too restrictive and he left home at 14 to stay with relatives who shared his love of Fats Domino and other rhythm and blues singers. Four years later he won a talent competition and moved to Kingston. After starting out with Smokey and the Heroes, he then sang in the Emotions with Kenneth Knight and Robbie Shakespeare's brother Lloyd, before changing his surname from Smith to Romeo and fronting the Hippy Boys. It was Bunny Lee who produced 'Wet

Dream' and other early solo singles, but 'Maccabee Version', which he'd recorded on his return to Jamaica in the summer, was the hit that confirmed his change of musical direction.

Legend has it that Max saw Robbie Shakespeare with his head buried in a book one day and questioned him about it. He was reading the book of Maccabees, which had been left out of most bibles but not the one issued by the Ethiopian Orthodox Church. In May 1970, Abba Mandefro had arrived in Kingston with a view to officially establish a branch of the Ethiopian Orthodox Church in Jamaica. He'd been greeted by hundreds of Rastafarians singing hymns and waving Ethiopian flags and would have certainly brought some of the Church's religious texts with him.

'The book of Maccabees was the same age as the Bible,' Max explained, 'and it was silenced universally, together with a few other books that spoke of the evils of religion and politics of the self. These were the books that we were keen to read. Not only because they were banned, but since we were searching for more knowledge, outside of what the church had taught us. A great example of that is King James, who was in control at the time. In the course of our studies, we discovered that when the guy who read from the scrolls told him what was in these other books, King James ordered them to be left out.'

Max claims that 'Maccabee Version' was his own production, but Niney the Observer said it was his and that Max sold the stamper to Derrick Harriott without permission. Niney wasn't best pleased, and so took the Soul Syndicate to Randy's Studio 17 and cut 'Blood And Fire' in response. He didn't have any money to pay the musicians – they played for free – and couldn't afford to press many copies, and so had to make do with just a single acetate. Glen Adams heard it and told Bob Marley that Niney had used elements of the Wailers' 'Let The Sun Shine On Me' in it. He hadn't – 'Blood And Fire' is quite different – but a drunken Lee Perry seized on the story with glee and urged Bob and the Wailers to go looking for Niney in retribution. Marley had already voiced 'Mr Chatterbox' about Niney, on a remake of the Wailers' ska hit 'Mr Talkative.' It was a scathing put-down produced by Bunny Lee, but this time the threat was physical and Niney suffered a beating when the Wailers finally caught up with him.

It was Christmas Eve by the time he finally managed to get a stamper of 'Blood And Fire', taking it to Mr Wong's pressing plant in Chancery Lane. When he was there a fight broke out and a man covered in blood staggered through the door, looking for somewhere to hide. Mr Wong panicked and ordered the plant to close immediately, even though they were still pressing copies of Niney's record. He ended up with just a hundred or so copies, and none of the shops and distributors wanted any – not Randy's, Joe Gibbs, KGs or Aquarius. It was Clancy Eccles who took it on, pressing up more copies and making sure that all the stores stocked it. The man with three names – he was known variously as Niney, Winston Holness and George Boswell – had a hit of his own at last, and his lyrics spoke of finality, as he repeatedly urged 'Let it burn.'

CHAPTER TWO

1971: ANOTHER CYCLE

On New Year's Day 1971, the Equals' lead singer Eddy Grant, just 23 years old, suffered a heart attack and a collapsed lung. If lifestyle had played a part, it wasn't because of alcohol abuse, drugs or a bad diet, but Grant's only vice – a hectic schedule. The timing of it was cruel as well, since the Equals' latest single, 'Black Skin Blue Eyed Boys', had only crashed into the UK Top 10 four days earlier. It was the Equals' most political song yet, and for once it wasn't just Eddy's bleached blond hair or the group's multi-racial line-up that was getting attention, but what they were actually saying. In the lyrics he pointed out that mixed race people have no country or creed to call their own but are denizens of a brand new nation, 'with brand new people.'

Eddy was born in Plaisance, British Guyana and grew up listening to calypso and 'tan singing', an Indo-Caribbean vocal style with roots in south Asia. His father played dance band music – mainly calypso and jazz – but he was a multi-instrumentalist and, inspired by Harry James, liked playing trumpet most of all. In 1960 the family moved to London, and five years later a 17-year-old Eddy formed the Equals, Britain's first multiracial band. Their best-known songs, all released on the President label, included the number one hit 'Baby Come Back', 'I Get So Excited', 'Laurel And

Hardy' and 'Viva Joe.' 'Black Skin Blue Eyed Boys', meanwhile, became an anthem for British youth, many of whom could relate to the lyrics.

By 1971 Eddy had also written and produced hits for Prince Buster ('Rough Rider'), the Pyramids and several other mainly UK-based artists for his own Torpedo label, which issued an unbelievable number of singles in 1970, including a few for UK soundman Lambert Briscoe. It's little wonder that the pressure had become too much for the Equals' frontman.

The day after Grant collapsed, Desmond Dekker's cover of Jimmy Cliff's 'The Song We Used To Sing' was released. A reviewer in the *Gleaner* hailed it as Dekker's 'greatest recording', and forecast that it would join some of his previous singles 'in the top ranks of international bestselling records.' It didn't, and Desmond's phenomenal run of hits in the UK charts ended just as suddenly as it had begun. Two weeks later, Harry Johnson announced that he was building a recording studio – to be called 'Harry J's' – on Roosevelt Avenue, near the National Stadium. He felt that a better sound was needed to compete with the American market, and had a vision of turning it into another Hitsville USA. To this end he appointed Bob Andy as one of the in-house producers and promised that it would be available to hire as well. This was unusual since in Jamaica, only Dynamic and Randy's hired out studio time on a regular, commercial basis.

Jackie Mittoo had a vision, too, and it no longer involved Studio One, despite Coxsone having released the *Macka Fat* album, which contained highly rated instrumental cuts to songs by Burning Spear, the Heptones and Dawn Penn. Jackie himself was more interested in *Wishbone*, which Carl DeHaney produced for a new Canadian label called Summus Records. Those recordings took place at Eastman Sound in Toronto, where the keyboard maestro had been busily reinventing himself as an avatar of lightweight, string-drenched, funky reggae. It's a development Jackie described as being like 'sunshine from the islands – a kind of exciting, mixed rhythm that makes you want to keep time by nodding your head instead of tapping your feet.

'Actually, reggae is a cross between calypso and jazz,' he continued. 'As you know, in Jamaica this particular form of calypso rhythm was first called ska, later to become very popular in England and on the continent. Picking up elements of American soul, it evolved into what was called soul rock steady. The style further developed into what is now known as reggae.'

It sounded far removed from the hits that Larry Marshall had continued to make at Studio One – 'True Believer', 'It Makes Me Feel' and a cover of Peter Tosh's 'Maga Dog' among them – and nothing whatsoever like Burning Spear's latest releases, but then 'Ethiopians Live It Out' and 'Zion Higher' were designed to express something altogether more profound.

'When I first felt the inspiration and the spirituality of Rastafari, it was on Key Largo beach,' says Rodney. 'That was the place we hung out. As a matter of fact, everything that became Burning Spear was based upon that beach — music, my way of life, everything. People would sit down and share knowledge with each other. People like myself who came up with a lack of knowledge, we used to sit down and we would be listening to people talking to us and telling us things. That is how we ended up learning a lot of things and know about a lot of things.'

The group most comparable with Burning Spear was the Abyssinians. They were another vocal trio who sang of spiritual and cultural themes, where one person sings lead and the other two harmonise. Bernard Collins was their front man. He was raised between St Catherine and Kingston before forming the Abyssinians in 1969 with brothers Donald and Linford Manning. Bernard and Donald had already written 'Satta Massagana' before Linford joined. He previously sang with another Manning brother, Carlton, in the Shoes, whose best known hit was 'Love Me Forever.' That's Linford singing harmonies on 'Satta Massagana', but it was the other two who contributed the most.

'Donald never did any recording,' Collins told David Katz. 'He wasn't recognised as a singer, even among his brothers, but he give me the vibes to go onto a cultural level. In those days we used to be closely involved with the Ethiopian Orthodox Church, 'cause Donald was a foundation man there. He used to actually get books from Ethiopia with Amharic language and interpretation back into English. We used to have a school there where we used to teach news. People used to just come in during the days, to the church school, and we teach them from the books we get. Learning ourselves, we shared it with the people in the community, so the whole concept is from the Ethiopian Orthodox Church coming up in caves, climbing up on rocks, to go there and worship and pray.'

It was Donald Manning's liking for minor chords that helped shape the Abyssinians' distinctive sound, together with Bernard's yearning vocals. The latter claims that the words to 'Satta Massagana' just came to him as if in a dream, yet Donald Manning disagrees, and told *The Beat*'s Michael Turner that the song originated with himself.

"Satta Massagana' was the first song I do. Because at that time I was the only Rasta man in the Abyssinians and in that song I was talking about God, the King of Kings and Lord of Lords because I was reading about those things. It come out of me. That was my inspiration, but Bernard sing the first line and I sing the second line, and when I do that I run up to my house to get a pen and we start writing in the dark. My brother Carlton, he sang a song named 'Happy Land' before that which also tells of a faraway land where there is no darkness, but only day.'

'That's the song my brother sings. 'Satta Massagana' say the same thing, just put in a different way, y' understand? I never know that we were cheating on my brother and so we have one hell in the yard! Because Bernard come there and want to steal my brother's songs all the time, and Linford and me, we have to stop my bigger brother from fighting him. After that now, Bernard stopped coming to our house and we have to go to his house so we can keep on singing as Abyssinians.'

The Abyssinians produced 'Satta Massagana' themselves, although they recorded it at Studio One using members of Coxsone's house band. This arrangement cost them £90 and was made possible by Carlton, who was a session guitarist for Coxsone at the time. When the session had finished, engineer Sylvan Morris asked what the song was called and Donald said "'Satta Massagana'", and Bernard said "'Far, Far Away'." Morris clearly preferred the latter, and when the song came out it had 'Far, Far Away' printed on the label. It didn't sell too well at first. It wasn't until the Abyssinians launched their own Clinch label (which they named after a clenched fist, denoting togetherness) that it began to gather momentum, along with other singles such as 'Yim Mas Gan', 'Declaration Of Rights' (for Studio One) and an alternative version of 'Satta' called 'Mabrak.' They re-recorded 'Satta' because on the initial cut they were giving praise to God whilst using a phrase that Ethiopians would greet an equal with, and they wanted to correct this. Also, they weren't best pleased when Joe Gibbs cut a version of the same rhythm for Peter Tosh's 'Here Comes The Judge', and they wanted to reclaim it as an Abyssinians' original.

By the end of February, Dr Walter Rodney's book, *The Groundings With My Brothers*, went on sale in good bookstores everywhere except Jamaica, since the banning of revolutionary persons and materials was still in force. Rodney wrote the book whilst he was living in Jamaica and in it, among other things, he discusses slavery and its deleterious effects on black people throughout the Diaspora.

'We have gone through a historical experience through which, by all accounts, we should have been wiped out,' he wrote, referring to slavery – a system he says was designed to kill people. He then marvelled how so many black Jamaicans, born into poverty 'are performing a miracle every day. They live and they are physically fit. They have a vitality of mind. They have a tremendous sense of humour. They live in depth.'

When Rodney was barred from re-entering Jamaica, none of those who'd assisted him in promoting Black Power were arrested or charged, yet, by the same reckoning, they too would have fallen foul of laws prohibiting sedition, treason or subversive acts. One prominent member of the island's General Legal Council recognised this and was moved to announce that, 'we in Jamaica think we are educated, and fail to realise there are numbers of restricted literature that we are not allowed to read.' He also warned that if this erosion of people's human rights were not addressed, then Jamaica could become a dictatorship state.

'Walter Rodney was a much admired, popular and beloved Black Power advocate,' Bob Andy recalled. 'He spent a lot of time in the communities, learning what was going on and passing on wisdom and knowledge of things. He was an essential figure back then and most of us would have had dealings with Walter Rodney. At that time we had *Abeng* magazine, which was taking the news of Black Power and Africa to interested people. The government before Hugh Shearer's was headed by Norman Manley, who was an intellectual, and I like to see him as the father of the nation. He would have been more tolerant if Rodney had been lecturing under his administration, but Shearer was antagonistic towards any kind of movement like that, because he banned certain books and people from coming into Jamaica and he made a mistake by telling the police not to preach any Beatitudes, and to shoot and ask questions later. Shearer was president of Bustamante's trade union and wasn't qualified to be prime minister. He was Bustamante's favourite and he'd got in because Donald Sangster died after only being in government three months, but he was antagonistic towards intellectuals and Rodney from the get-go.'

Muhammad Ali was also banned from entering Jamaica. He and Joe Frasier fought for the heavyweight crown at New York's Madison Square Garden on 8 March, and expectations were running high. Ali predicted that the fight would go the distance and last fifteen rounds, which it did, although Frasier was the victor after sending

Ali crashing to the canvas with a thunderous left hook that ballooned his right cheek into a grotesque shape, causing an uproar among the frenzied crowd of twenty thousand, along with the millions watching it on television. Ali's remarkable comeback bid had ended with the first defeat of his professional career, and he spent the following day rather ungraciously claiming that he was robbed, and challenging Frazier to a rematch.

Less than a week later, Marcia Griffiths performed at the grand re-opening of the VIP Club, backed by the Mighty Vikings. The place was under new management, who promised patrons go-go dancers and a psychedelic light show, but it was the Wednesday night talent shows that would prove most popular. The auditions took place between the VIP Club and New Dimension studios on Eastwood Park Road, where Inner Circle, Now Gen and musicians from other leading bands were hired to put the entrants through their paces. Marcia was quite the celebrity by then. Her photo even appeared in Silver Top Gin adverts, but music was the focus of her career, and that was how she came to sing harmonies on some of Lloyd Charmers' productions, including the album *Censored!*, credited to Lloydie and the Lowbites. Charmers felt no shame about making such risqué records – as far as he was concerned, he was just showing his versatility. He'd been in a duo with Roy Willis called the Charmers whilst still a school boy living in Trench Town. Prince Buster produced their biggest hit of the ska era, 'Time After Time', although the Charmers also recorded for many other producers before the pair went their separate ways. Alton Ellis was a neighbour of Lloyd's in Trench Town and taught him about harmonies. One night he and Lloyd broke into a local school so that Alton could show him one or two chords on the piano; soon afterwards, local DJ Jeff Barnes recommended Lloyd get lessons from a man living in Greenwich Farm called 'Fish Head.'

Soon he was proficient enough to play on sessions for Bunny Lee, although he continued singing, too, both as a solo act and as a member of the Uniques with Slim Smith. Lloyd produced the

Uniques' 'Watch This Sound', and then led the Hippy Boys – featuring the Barrett brothers – on catchy instrumentals like 'Five To Five', 'Zylon' and 'Dr No Go', which became a number one hit in Jamaica. By this time he'd launched his own Splash label, played on Andy Capp's seminal 'Pop A Top' and began issuing albums under his own name for Trojan, beginning with *Reggae Is Tight*.

There was a sticker on *Censored!* declaring that the contents were 'Not Recommended For Air-Play – Adults Only.' Tracks with titles like 'Open Up', 'Free Grind Ticket', 'Bang Bang Lulu' and 'Pussy To Kill You' left nothing to the imagination, although Charmers was a natural comedian and much of what he did with the Lowbites was tongue in cheek.

Making sexually explicit records wasn't a crime, unlike armed robbery. On the afternoon of 15 March, a man with his hand covered by a newspaper strolled into the Franklyn Town Post Office and shouted, 'this is a hold up!' A special constable on duty was ordered to lie on the floor; everyone else was told to stay still. The man then signalled for three others, all brandishing guns, to enter the post office, whereupon they demanded keys to the strong room and stole several hundred dollars. The first robber, whose name was Orlando Wong, was just 19. He was arrested after a clerk from the post office picked him out of an identity parade at the Central Police station. Wong was then charged with robbery with aggravation and transferred to the lock-up at Spanish Town Police station, in readiness for his trial the following day. By the following morning he'd escaped, leaving his cell door open and the padlock wrenched off.

A troubled soul whose father had died when he was young, Wong had lived in Brown's Town before relocating to Rollington Town, north of the Windward Road. His mother, Ruby Myers, was a factory worker, and she and his grandmother apparently spoiled him as a child. He was bright, too, and attended Camperdown High School whilst at the same time becoming acutely aware of the social divide between rich and poor. Soon, he was smoking herb and learning about Pan Africanism from a Rastaman named Negus, who Wong credits with being his main inspiration.

'He actually started a group of us and was very influential at that time in Dunkirk,' Wong told me, although he was better known as the dub poet Oku Onoura by the time I interviewed him. 'There was a ghetto school and community centre there called Tafari that I was a part of from an early age, and which [Negus] started to help the local youths. Negus was a radical who knew Walter Rodney very well. He was one of the Rastamen in that time who was very instrumental in terms of the movement and what was taking place. People like him, they were motivated to act against police brutality and police killings. We'd also get young doctors to come where we were to examine people and especially the children. That was the only way medical assistance could become available to them, because if something happened and they were rushed to the public hospital, they might have to spend all day there because conditions were so bad.'

Wong's rebellious nature initially led him to take part in demonstrations and to paint slogans on walls, but when Tafari ran into financial difficulties he began engaging in guerrilla activities from a base in the hills around Kingston, and this was how he came to be involved in the post office robbery.

'We had a school and were providing alternative education, and we had a feeding programme. Every evening after classes the children would be fed. It could be some lemonade, sugar and crackers... maybe even a pudding, because Negus was a great baker, and the children loved it as a snack. After all that finished I went to war! I wrote poems and painted slogans; I attended meetings at a place called Kennington in Rollington Town and I distributed *Abeng*, because in those times the police would hold you if they saw you with a copy of *Abeng*. You'd get beaten and all the copies would be confiscated, but then after a while I just got fed up, because despite all the demonstrations and everything, we didn't see any changes taking place...'

The magistrate officiating at his trial didn't know about the circumstances that had driven Wong to commit the robbery and probably wouldn't have taken them into account even if he had. In the accused's absence he was sentenced to fifteen years' imprisonment and twelve lashes, an island-wide manhunt having already got away.

By the end of March, Dave and Ansel Collins' 'Double Barrel' was at number one on the UK charts, after gradually building momentum for six months. Dave Barker's send-off coincided with the opening of Skateland in Half Way Tree, where they and the other artists were backed by the Upsetters, although the drummer on that track was Sly Dunbar, still a teenager when it was recorded.

'When I was young and we went to parties, we'd listen to funk, so when Ansel called me to listen to this piano track, I came up with the bass-line,' remembers Sly. 'If you listen to 'Double Barrel' and then listen to the Isley Brothers' 'It's Your Thing', you can hear the similarities. 'It's Your Thing' was a big smash at the time and we knew from when the intro came in that people were going to get into it, because the bass-line was so funky. But 'Double Barrel' was a reggae song. It was a one-drop, and whilst it also had an element of funk in it, it wasn't total funk… it's just that we took one percent of funk and put it in the reggae. The reggae was still there, and everything we did on that song, we did in Jamaica.'

Ansel Collins was born on Maxfield Avenue, and his father had a barbershop. He was encouraged to play piano by his mother, but started out as a singer with Bobby Aitken and the Carib Beats before teaching himself to play drums and mentoring Sly, who played with him in the Rainbow Healing Temple Bakery Invincibles band. Ansel's first sessions were for Bunny Lee and included Slim Smith's 'Never Let Go' and Val Bennett's 'The Russians Are Coming', whilst Sly made his debut on 'Night Doctor', a funky instrumental that Ansel had produced, but Lee Perry got the credit for. 'Double Barrel' was Ansel's production as well. Lynford Anderson had engineered it at Dynamic, and told Winston Riley about it. He then got the tape off Ansel and overdubbed Dave Barker's part. Ansel didn't know Dave at the time, and wasn't there when his verses were added to the backing track.

'I had a bit of difficulty getting a vibe for that track,' said Barker, 'but it was me, Winston and his brother Buster who were there and the track was being played over and over again… I was trying to create a vibe to it, but it takes time and Buster Riley said to me, "why don't you imagine you're on the highest mountain in the world and you feel strong. You feel gigantic like Superman and you feel like James Bond." Immediately he said that, I went up to the microphone and came out with, "I am the magnificent…" We are all blessed with special gifts, but it's how you use them… sometimes when you go into yourself, these wonderful inspirations come to you just like that and sometimes they come when you least expect them. You can't just call them up any time you want to, because they're from some higher source. We are instruments for them to channel through, but you have to maintain that connection. When you're younger they just pour through you, but as you get older you have to work harder at it. You take on all the problems of the world and all these harmful and destructive things serve to block the channels… We become lost in total darkness, but the light is still there, waiting for us.'

When he first visited the UK in 1971, Barker was surprised at the reaction to his music. 'That was the first time Ansel and I had ever been on a plane. When the plane started to take off, Ansel held onto the plane seat so tightly! I didn't even have time to go home and put on some decent shoes and clothes – when we land, I didn't have any socks on and the shoes I had on were lean because the heel was all worn. We were rushed on the plane, but I'd just started a family back home and I didn't even have time to tell them goodbye. Coming from the tropics, we found it cold, y' know? We just landed at Heathrow and from the minute we first walked into Trojan we were told that we had to leave immediately to go on *Top Of The Pops*, so we were rushed over there and to us it was a brand new world, I tell you. We'd never seen anything like that before. We had our own dressing room and then we went into the green room where we met Rod Stewart, Cliff Richard and Lulu. We thought, "wow! This is different!" I was both nervous and excited rolled into one, and I stumbled a bit because our own musicians hadn't arrived from Jamaica yet, and they put these guys dressed in grass skirts with us who didn't have anything to do with Dave and Ansel Collins!

'At that time you had this sound system called People's Sound. I became friends with these guys and they took me to some of the dances and I was surprised by how many of my songs were being played – especially songs like 'On Broadway' and 'Just My Imagination.' At that time I hardly spoke. I just sat in my quiet space and observed everything, and people treated me with kindness. Then when we started touring these Top Rank clubs, and after we came off stage I was surprised to be mobbed! We had to run to the car with people hanging off our clothes. We were doing maybe three shows a night, driving from one to another and with the fans screaming and shouting... it was crazy but fun! We made appearances with the Pioneers and I remember we went to Bournemouth that first year and met this guy Phil Lynott from Thin Lizzy – he was great, and I loved his music...'

Dave Barker's own music at this point was divided into excitable deejay tracks like 'Shocks '71' and 'Only The Strong Survive', primarily aimed at club-goers, and other tracks, such as 'Out Of Love' and 'What A Confusion', on which he rivalled Slim Smith.

It was the talking records that won out, though – something effortlessly underlined after he and Charlie Ace combined on the Wailers' 'Small Axe.' Bob Marley and Lee Perry had written the lyrics as a thinly veiled threat to 'the big t'ree' of the Jamaica record industry, namely Federal, Dynamic and Studio One because whilst those companies dominated, there was a younger generation sharp as an axe, ready to cut them down.

Max Romeo's 'Let The Power Fall On I' was at number one back home, and there were several other classics among the also-rans, not least Delroy Wilson's 'Better Must Come', Phyllis Dillon's 'One Life To Live' and two songs by the Ethiopians, 'Selah' and 'Love Bug.' Derrick Morgan was the producer for 'Let The Power Fall On I' – in fact, he voiced a cut of it for himself called 'Give Thanks' – but Derrick himself was slipping from favour, despite his own best efforts and those of his brother-in-law Bunny Lee, who renamed him Rob Walker for a cover of British pop singer Sandie Shaw's 'Puppet On A String' that unfortunately sounded more like a throwback than a fresh start.

Glen Adams, one of Jamaica's most in-demand keyboard players, left for New York in April. He, Max Romeo, Family Man Barrett and Niney The Observer had been living in the same guesthouse in Pembroke Hall, not far from Washington Gardens. He'd played on the chart-topping 'Let The Power Fall On I' and also 'Maccabee Version', but in such a rough and tumble environment, musicians didn't always get the credit they deserved.

'The last tracks I played on with those guys before coming up to New York were for Bunny Lee, because we did John Holt's 'Stick By Me', Delroy Wilson's 'Better Must Come' and 'Jordan River' by Max Romeo. It was me who wrote that tune with Max and I was credited as one of the two artists on it until it became a hit. Then I hear that someone – presumably Max – changed the label and my name disappeared! That was soon after I played on some tunes for Herman Chin Loy under the name Augustus Pablo, like 'Aquarius One', although I didn't play on the original rhythm track, which was called 'Old Kent Road'. I played on 'East Of The River Nile' as well though, y' know?

'Then, in early 1971, Danny Sims came to Jamaica to seek out Bob and the Wailers, who had done some recordings for him previously. Bob asked us, as the Upsetters, to take part in a new project. We rehearsed at Johnny Nash's house in Russell Heights while Mr Sims waited for funds to arrive from the US. When they came through, we went to Randy's studio at 17 North Parade to do a number of songs, although I don't remember the titles of most of them. I was so upset with Scratch at the time that all I wanted to do was to leave Jamaica, which finally I did. Bob was taken to Sweden to do some work with Johnny Nash and the rest of the group stayed in Jamaica. I arrived in New York on 5 April and began to make a new life for myself. But my heart was still in my hometown, which one man ruined.'

The new project that Marley had alluded to resulted in early versions of 'Concrete Jungle' and 'Stir It Up.' The Wailers had ended their relationship with Scratch by then, partially as a result of his dealings with Trojan, and partially because other funds had gone missing that couldn't be accounted for. Bunny Livingston attacked Perry at the Sombrero one night, sending tables and chairs flying; on another occasion, the Wailers called a meeting with him and things got ugly after Peter Tosh discovered that Perry had a vial of acid at the ready.

'Bunny Livingston was never too keen on Scratch, because he was using up the money,' confirms Niney The Observer. 'Scratch was never too clever with all that, because I think it was Bunny Lee who get him the money for his house as well. The guys, they find out that Scratch wasn't dealing with them straight and that cause an argument between them. But Scratch give them a few ideas, it's true. Lee Perry, he couldn't sing, but he'd have an idea and pass on these little off-key things to Bob, who'd make something out of it. Ah, so it go with them.'

Bunny Lee used to tell a story about the time John Holt pulled up to the studio in a brand-new car that he'd bought with the proceeds from 'Stick By Me', saw the Wailers looking on enviously and mocked them. 'Duppy Conqueror' had been a big hit by then, but they had nothing to show for it. That incident resulted in yet another beating for Perry. Bunny, meanwhile, was fast becoming Jamaica's most prolific producer. He and his posse could often be seen travelling through Kingston in a convoy of three or four cars. It was like something from a movie, and the affable Lee revelled in such grand gestures. Unlike the majority of his competitors, he embraced all forms of Jamaican music – from light, Nat King Cole-style balladry as practised by Jackie Edwards to rampaging rude boy songs like 'Mr Chatterbox.'

Several of the artists in his stable had defected from Studio One and weren't at all shy about re-recording some of their best-known hits for him. His two most successful acts to date were John Holt and Delroy Wilson, and neither could claim to be singing exclusive music since the irrepressible producer often used the same backing track for any number of singers, deejays and instrumentalists. What he'd do was voice half a dozen of them on the same rhythm, then cut certain ones on dub plate and give them to U-Roy, who would then play them on King Tubby's sound system and let Bunny know which ones got the most reaction. Those were the ones he released on 7-inch, but dancehall fans got used to hearing different cuts of the same rhythm, and that's how 'version' came about. It also saved the wily producer money, because the musicians only got paid once but his artists benefited from featuring on a hit rhythm and, of course, it kept his circle of studio engineers, dub cutters and sound men busy at the same time. Just one man generated all this activity – someone who didn't have his own studio or sound system, and was unafraid to go up against the likes of Coxsone with impunity.

Bunny Lee was a rogue, for sure, but it was impossible not to like or admire him. His other hits during the summer of 1971 included Delroy Wilson's 'Who Cares' and 'Cool Operator', and also tracks by the Soulettes, Dennis Alcapone – whose first tune for him was a cut to 'Better Must Come' – Carl Dawkins, Ernest Wilson, Max Romeo and Slim Smith. Smith was rarely out of the studio during that period, leaving record buyers torn between singles like the mournful 'Send Me Some Loving', 'Love I Bring' (a collaboration with U-Roy), Slim's cut of Jimmy Cliff's 'Keep Walking' or an upbeat cover of the Temptations' 'My Girl' – the list was a lengthy one.

Bunny mainly recorded at Studio 17, which, like Randy's record store downstairs, was owned by Vincent Chin and wife Pat, who everyone called 'Miss Pat.' Born into poverty, Miss Pat grew up amidst twin cultures – Indian on her father's side, and Chinese on her mother's. Her journey brought Jamaica's national motto, 'Out of many, one people', into sharp focus and offered insight into why several of the most successful early Jamaican producers were Chinese.

'A lot of Chinese started their own little business just like my grandfather did, and that's how it developed,' said Miss Pat. 'The Chinese shop is where the community would come, buy their groceries and talk about what's going on in the neighbourhood. It became a spot where the politicians and the church people would come and congregate, and then the music would be playing right there. That's where it all started, and then often the Chinese people had the money to buy equipment, so the Chinese shop played a very important role in the development of the music. It serviced everybody and became a hub. That's how many Chinese children got involved with it, either as producers or musicians.'

Her father suggested that she work in a bank, but Pat's life was turned upside down one summer in the late fifties, just as rock'n'roll swept America. Miss Pat, who lived in Greenwich Town, was studying to be a nurse when the herb-smoking, music-loving Vincent Chin stole her heart and whisked her around the island on the back of his motorbike as he replaced the hit 45s in jukeboxes from Kingston to Montego Bay. That's what gave them the idea of selling the used records, renting their first retail outlet inside someone else's store on the corner of East and Tower Street in downtown Kingston. Business was good, and they weren't there long before opening Randy's Record Mart at 17 North Parade, just a few blocks from the Kingston waterfront and within a minute's walk of Orange Street, or 'Beat Street,' as it's also known.

The young couple had named their shop after a radio station in Tennessee called Randy's that played mainly country, jazz and rhythm and blues. Vincent was a keen fan of the station and loved jazz especially, as did the majority of Jamaican musicians back then. Producing their own records seemed to make sense and Vincent enjoyed a run of hits during the ska era, beginning with Lord Creator's 'Independent Jamaica' in 1962. Work on the studio was finally completed by the end of the decade, much to Vincent's son Clive's delight. He and Randy's engineer Errol Thompson had been friends at school, and whilst everyone else called Errol 'E. T.', Clive often referred to him as his brother – 'not in blood, but in spirit.'

Lee Perry and Bunny Lee regularly hired the studio, as we've heard already. The Lyrics and Ethiopians had also visited recently, whilst Jimmy London had been working on tracks like 'A Little Love', 'Shake A Hand', 'It's Now Or Never' and current hit 'Bridge Over Troubled Water', but it was an aborted session with Dennis Wright that proved most auspicious. Wright's vocals didn't make the grade and so Clive and E. T. wiped them, got their friend Horace Swaby to blow melodica on the rhythm and then added a vocal hook by Chosen Few. The result was 'Java', and this was the track that put Augustus Pablo on the map.

Swaby had already played on a few tunes under that name. The daughter of one of his friends had a melodica, but treated it as a toy; Swaby, however, was intrigued and asked to borrow it. He had it with him when visiting the Aquarius record store by Half Way Tree one day, and owner Herman Chin Loy asked the young musician if he could play it. Swaby duly played a few phrases and Herman quickly arranged a session that resulted in his debut single, 'Iggy Iggy' Rather than put Horace Swaby on the label, Herman credited it to Augustus Pablo. This was a fictitious name that he'd used for instrumentals played by Glen Adams, but once the quietly spoken Swaby had recorded 'Java', it became his alone.

Herman Chin Loy was still in his early twenties, and another musically inclined Chinese Jamaican. He was born in Trelawny on Jamaica's north coast, but spent part of his childhood in Clarendon before making his way to Kingston, where he DJ'd at clubs like the Lotus A Go Go and Spinning Wheel, and worked as a record salesman for KGs. He and Neville Foo-Loy ran the One Stop record store on King Street until 1969, when Herman and his half-brother Lloyd opened their own store and launched a record label, which they named Aquarius. Their first hits on the Aquarius label were with the Hippy Boys, but in early '71 Herman sent the tapes of Bruce Ruffin's 'Rain' to England, where Tony King added strings to Geoffrey Chung's arrangement. Trojan Records had been looking for another hit to follow 'Young, Gifted And Black' and got one, since Ruffin's song just scraped into the UK Top 20 in May. Herman had ambitions of becoming an artist himself and released 'To The Fields' on a single, along with songs by Ken Boothe, Alton Ellis ('Arise Black Man'), Busty Brown, Dennis Alcapone, the Eternals and Jimmy James, who recorded the provocative 'If I Wasn't Black Would I Be Black?'

After a brief absence, Max Romeo's 'Let The Power Fall On I' had gone back to number one on the Jamaican charts at the end of April. It was around this time that the Wailers released 'Kaya' – a herb tune that Bob Marley had written with Lee Perry during a trip to Hanover. It was the first release on the Wailers' own Tuff Gong label, and unashamedly pro-ganja, although that wasn't the reason Trojan unexpectedly turned down the group's *Soul Revolution Part II* album. This was more likely to do with Lee Perry, who issued it on his own Maroon label regardless and with a photo on the cover of the three Wailers cavorting in his garden, brandishing toy guns.

Soul Revolution Part II was a more coherent collection than its predecessor, and tracks like 'Duppy Conqueror', 'Sun Is Shining' (featuring Peter's melodica), 'Kaya', 'Don't Rock My Boat', 'Fussing And Fighting' and a revamped 'Put It On' were outstanding. Despite the group's lack of crossover success, their preference for sticky, one-drop rhythms and meaningful lyrics would prove highly influential. The era of fast-paced quirky instrumentals and novelty records was over, and British reggae's lowly status was also slowly beginning to change. This was helped in part by BBC Radio 1 presenter John Peel, who'd broadcast his first live reggae session featuring British band the Rudies back in late December. Fast forward to 12 May and the Rudies were invited to play at Mick Jagger's wedding in St Tropez. It was a rushed affair, since the Rolling Stones' frontman and his Nicaraguan girlfriend, Bianca Perez Mora Macias, had only informed the guests (and musicians) of their plans the day before. The seventy-five-person guest list included members of the Beatles and Rolling Stones, Julie Christie and Brigitte Bardot, with the reception being held at the Café des Arts, where the Rudies – or Greyhound, as they now called themselves – opened for Terry Reid.

The band had a new lead singer, too, with Freddie Notes having given way to Glenroy Oakley. He was born in Jamaica, where he lived with his grandfather for a while before relocating to England in 1960, aged 11. After finishing school he trained as a tailor, although he soon got bored of that. Music was his passion and he joined the nightclub circuit singing blues, soul and country music. It was Admiral Ken, manager of the Equals, who booked Glenroy's band the Oracles into clubs throughout the UK and occasionally in Europe, but he then got a call inviting him to audition for a rock band.

'The auditions were at Island studios in Basing Street, but as soon as I got there I was told that the Rudies would like me to join them! I became the singer with them, but then everywhere we went Freddie Notes would be there trying to steal the show. He tried that for a while, but the reason he wasn't with them anymore was because he'd wanted 50 per cent of the money for himself. After that, we started to do studio work and then we got called to do Mick Jagger's wedding, which was a bit of a disaster, really. I was told that Mick used to go down to the Roaring Twenties a lot and listen to reggae. I didn't know him, but he rang Trojan and said that he wanted a reggae band, and so they sent us. We only just got on the plane in time, but we were well looked after, and everyone got treated the same, actually. We all had our own rooms, and after they got back from the registry office they came to the reception, which was within walking distance, and that's when the party began. It was a good experience, and it was right when the Beatles were breaking up, because just Paul and Ringo came. Rico Rodriguez played as well...'

Two weeks later, Delroy Wilson's 'Better Must Come' had taken over the number one slot in Jamaica, thanks in part to its anti-establishment lyrics. People had tired of Shearer's government and wanted a change. There was growing dissatisfaction with the way the country was being run and a distinct lack of political will in tackling the island's social problems, unless it was to issue ever more draconian directives. Soon, the government would declare that anyone caught in possession of a ratchet knife with intent to commit a criminal act would be sent to prison for up to twelve months, but such knives were still on sale, so if somebody had one in their pocket, how could the police or anyone else determine what their intentions were? Young people in particular were searching for alternatives, and the impact of Rastafarian culture was being felt more and more – especially in music, theatre, poetry and the visual arts. Alton Ellis, who had been crowned 'Mr Soul of Jamaica' during his rocksteady heyday, embraced the tide of Black Nationalism with real fervour during 1971. He was still a master of romance – his latest single for Randy's, 'A Little Loving', was proof of that – but his lyrics in songs like 'Black Man's Pride', 'Arise Black Man', 'Back To Africa' and 'Blackish White' went straight to the heart of the struggle.

''Black Man's Pride' was really a love song and I just said, "no, switch the vibes now – no more of this love song thing",' said Alton. 'We were living in Trench Town then, and [Rastafari elder] Mortimo Planno, he was always the one who was into the cultural side of things, and what was happening in Jamaica, in Rastafari, and he was close to Bob Marley, as we know. Well, being as we lived three or four doors apart, it was time to switch to some of them culture things instead of just the love songs.'

Ellis said this change in tone did not come as a surprise to his audience. 'It was just the times, really. The Rasta thing was gradually spreading through, so it came from seeing and hearing the culture spoken every day on the street, and things like that. Hearing it on record now was just a next step in that direction, an extension of the culture and the sound, so to speak. In America, Marvin Gaye and James Brown were singing about those black things, too y'know? It was just the timing, really.'

Ellis was already producing his own tracks and spending a fair amount of time in London, although he still visited Jamaica regularly. He would occasionally voice tunes for Coxsone in exchange for free studio time, and that's how he got to produce two songs with Dennis Brown, recorded at Studio One whilst Coxsone was away on business. Alton gave the 14-year-old Brown a song he'd written called 'If I Follow My Heart', although Brown couldn't manage the bridge and so ad-libbed his way through it. Both knew it would be a smash hit regardless, but then Coxsone returned and things got a little tricky from there…

'Coxsone heard the tape and immediately the studio time went sky-high, financially, and everything gone up to the ceiling!' Ellis recalled. 'He didn't want to give it to me, so we fall out for maybe a month or two. I didn't go to the studio during that time. Then one day, I'm there in the ghetto, I get broke and want money so I go to him and say, "Mr Dodd hear what you do. Just pay me for the tune and keep that." And that is what he wanted to hear, I guess.'

Alton voiced 'Lord Deliver Us' and 'Back To Africa' for Lloyd Daley first, but then sang them over at Studio One, after Coxsone demanded a piece of the action. This angered Daley no end, and especially when Pama pressed them up in England and told him that Ellis had given them permission to do so – something the singer bitterly denied. It was a mess, but the songs themselves were rather special.

Lloyd Daley called himself and his sound system 'the Matador', but heroism didn't really suit him. He was a staid, responsible type who worked for the Times Store in Kingston, repairing electrical equipment, before opening a shop on James Street and building valve amplifiers for early sound systems like Jackie's Hi Fi, Count Muncy and El Toro. He was innovative, though, and Lloyd The Matador was one of the first sound systems to use 18-inch speaker cabinets. By the summer of '71 he'd spent two years building premises on Waltham Park Road that housed his own electronics business, a record store and his wife's beauty salon. That's where he rehearsed his artists before taking them to Federal and sometimes Dynamic for sessions. Little Roy's 'Bongo Nyah' and 'Hard Fighter' were two of his biggest hits to date, although he'd also produced tracks by the likes of Audley Rollen ('Repatriation'), Lloyd Robinson, the Ethiopians, the Uniques ('Secretly') and U-Roy, whose 'Scandal' was one of his bestsellers. Dennis Brown and Alton Ellis had been alerted to Daley by hearing his releases on RJR's *Sound Of The Wise*, hosted by Charlie Babcock. Brown's two songs, 'Baby Don't Do It' and 'Things In Life', were among his best tracks to date, whilst Ellis's original 'Lord Deliver Us' was imbued with spiritual longing, and it's sad that Daley wasn't allowed to enjoy it before Coxsone interfered.

By early June, Skin, Flesh & Bones were the resident band at the Tit For Tat on Red Hills Road. They were a new band, featuring bassist Lloyd Parks, organist Errol 'Tarzan' Nelson, guitarist Ranchie McLean and drummer Sly Dunbar, who played with Ranchie during the Volcanoes' brief residency at the Calypso Colony hotel in Runaway Bay, backing American singer Dee Dee Warwick. That's when Sly's nickname (his real name is Lowell) well and truly stuck, because of his passion for Sly and the Family Stone's music. Now Generation, Tommy McCook and the Supersonics and the Dynamic All-Stars were among the island's top bands, although a shift was occurring as younger bands like Inner Circle, Soul Syndicate and the Upsetters continued to make their presence felt.

Aston 'Family Man' Barrett, bassist with the Hippy Boys and Upsetters, wouldn't be around for a while however, since he'd gone to play for tourists on the cruise ship MS Starward. Just over a year earlier, customs officials had seized 250 kilos of ganja from the MS Starward that had been packed in plywood boxes and readied for shipment to Georgia. Family Man must have heard about this beforehand. It would have definitely raised a chuckle or two, but he'd taken the gig because Bob Marley had recently left for Sweden to join Johnny Nash. In his absence, Family Man was taking the opportunity to step back from the hustle and bustle of the Kingston studios and earn some regular money for a change. Bob Marley's departure coincided with Johnny Nash's 1959 film *Take A Giant Step* being re-shown at local cinemas, while Nash himself was shooting his latest film – co-starring Christina Schollin – in Stockholm, in between working on songs with Texan keyboard player John Bundrick, who everyone called 'Rabbit' because of his protruding front teeth.

Marley arrived in Sweden during the summer of 1971. He'd been invited to stay at the rented house Nash shared with his manager Danny Sims and Rabbit, and to write songs with and for Johnny Nash, including some intended for the film's soundtrack. Rabbit had never heard any reggae before, or heard of Bob Marley who he described as being shy, and a bit of a loner. The latter presented Nash with songs like 'Stir It Up' and 'Comma Comma' during their stay in Sweden which then ended suddenly when everyone was issued a formal notice, in writing, that all their salaries were cancelled forthwith.

'We were working for free,' Rabbit wrote in his journal. 'The whole she-bang had gone bankrupt. Danny and Johnny had lost all their money in a poker game, and I really don't know what happened to Bob. All I do know is that his air ticket, Johnny's guitar and Johnny's tape recorder all disappeared, along with Bob. Johnny never forgave him for taking his guitar, but Bob disappeared as magically as he had arrived.'

Peter Tosh, meanwhile, was recording for Joe Gibbs. 'Maga Dog', with harmonies by the Soulettes, and 'Leave My Business' were the pick of them. The latter featured a harmonica and had a country and western feel to it; 'Black Dignity' found him chanting in Amharic, just like he'd done on 'Earth's Rightful Ruler', whilst the lyrics to 'Arise Blackman' were both insistent and steeped in apocalyptic imagery, as the moon turns to blood, the sun stops shining and floods cover the earth…

Niney was the one who took Tosh to see Joe Gibbs and would later state that 'Gibbs never know anything about 'Maga Dog.'

All he did was pay for the session. Him never know anything about music. When Joe Gibbs call a session, everyone look towards me, because he didn't know where to start. He could only suggest covering someone else's song or to say, "I want it to sound like Lee Perry's song." Most of the songs he did with singers like Nicky Thomas, they are my productions. He financed them, but they're mine really. We have no agreement other than me hand them over, and he give me some money. At the same time, me never understand publishing yet, and so he claim that for himself as well.'

Beverley's put out an album with the Maytals called *Greatest Hits*, although '54-46 Was My Number' was the only major hit on it, and some of the tracks hadn't even been released. Toots had every reason to feel miffed, just like the Wailers when Kong had released their album and called it *The Best Of*. Bunny Livingston is alleged to have told Leslie Kong that if he really thought their album for Beverley's was the Wailers' best, then he didn't have long to live. All things considered, it was hard to understand why Kong began to oversell his output all of a sudden. Maybe he felt that his dominance had begun to slip a little, and especially after checking the UK national charts, where Greyhound's 'Black And White' was at number six and Dave and Ansel Collins' 'Monkey Spanner' was at number seven.

It was Trojan producer Dave Bloxham who'd suggested Greyhound cover 'Black And White', which was written in 1954 after a US Supreme Court decision banned segregation in state schools. The original lyrics reflect this with talk of judges in their robes, whereas

Greyhound's described black and white children learning to read and write together. They'd changed the context completely and lightened the mood, turning the song into a pop hit. Trojan's liking for strings was still very evident, but Oakley's soulful lead vocals saved 'Black And White' from becoming too saccharine. The band embarked on a UK tour in support, but their next single, 'Follow The Leader', failed to make an impression. They also recorded an album for Trojan, again produced by Dave Bloxham, that married Stax-influenced instrumentals to the strings-drenched pop/reggae classics for which they were best known. That didn't sell either – maybe because tastes had changed, and mainstream audiences begun to tire of reggae somewhat. The Maytones' version of 'Black And White', recorded in Jamaica, was far more down to earth and rootsy, making Greyhound's chart hit sound overly elaborate by comparison.

In late June '71, Jimmy Cliff had been performing in Georgetown, Guyana accompanied by Count Prince Miller. He'd recently taken to wearing one of the same gun belts that had previously got Eddy Grant into trouble with the Guyanese police, but Jimmy had no such trouble there. His belt held blank cartridges that had been used to shoot at him when he was in Jamaica filming the movie with Perry Henzell. He wore it with such pride and sense of style, but on arriving in Trinidad the police confiscated it immediately, telling him that it was illegal to wear a belt like that. Even though he protested that it was part of his stage costume, it was to no avail and he only got it back as he was leaving.

Jimmy's latest album, *Another Cycle,* had been co-produced by Guillermo Bright, who also co-wrote the majority of songs. This was the album he'd recorded at Muscle Shoals Sound Studios in Sheffield, Alabama with the Swampers – a crack US session band who'd backed a wealth of top American acts. There was more blues, rock and soul in those ten tracks than heard in any of his Beverley's recordings, and yet it was unmistakably a Jimmy Cliff record. It's hard to think of another Jamaican artist who would have dared try something like that without losing themselves in the process. There was serious risk involved, and yet with Jimmy it was his muse who called the shots, not the fickle dictates of market forces.

'After I had finished the album that had 'Vietnam' and 'Wonderful World, Beautiful People' on it, I took a turn,' Cliff admitted. 'Instead of continuing on that same track with those kinds of songs, I went to Muscle Shoals and recorded *Another Cycle*. It was a different form of music, but in the back of my mind I always knew that that I had to go and complete that chapter, because fans and friends were saying, "why don't you just continue on the same track? Why did you have to go over there and do something different?" But as an artist I cannot allow myself to be trapped. I just have to express how I really feel.'

His trip to America's Deep South yielded 'Sitting In Limbo', which Island released on 7-inch with 'The Harder They Come' on the flipside. Meanwhile, Jimmy was approached by EMI, who wished to sign him. Chris Blackwell told him that Perry Henzell's film would be out soon and so he should stay with Island. There was no enmity between them, only the sense that Jimmy had outgrown the role of a Jamaican reggae star, and wanted something more. Maybe he imagined something similar to what Harry Belafonte had achieved after becoming an all-round entertainer, hosting television shows and enjoying credible acting roles. Cliff certainly possessed sufficient talent, but following such a path required enhanced levels of support, and he probably considered EMI to have more clout than Island.

On 30 June, the Jamaica Festival Song results were announced and Eric Donaldson won with 'Cherry Oh Baby.' Tommy Cowan and Claudie Massop took him to Dynamic and Bunny Lee produced the studio version, using the same Inner Circle band that had backed him throughout the competition.

''Cherry Oh Baby' was the first time I ever see my father order five thousand records at one time,' remembers Clive Chin. 'The radio stations played that song there until them sick! Sir Lord Comic was the salesman for Dynamic Sounds and I see him trade in his motorbike for a Ford Capri on the strength of that tune. When he drive down Chancery Lane, every man have to stand aside because he bought himself a brand new red Capri. He was the number one salesman for Dynamic, and Count Machuki was the salesman for Federal, but he was more low-key. He never rushed for the limelight like Comic, but they were some of the very first toasters, before King Stitt and all those other men who pick up a mic.'

Freddie McKay, who was at number one in Jamaica's national chart with 'Picture On The Wall', came third with another of his Studio One recordings, 'Sweet You Sour You.' The 24-year-old singer from St Catherine had until recently been a virtual unknown, despite having voiced a handful of early tunes for Prince Buster, Beverley's and Duke Reid. After a brief spell with Harry Mudie, he joined Linstead band the Soul Defenders as their lead singer and accompanied them to Studio One, where he'd since recorded an album's worth of songs, including 'Father Will Cut You Off', 'You'll Be Sorry', 'High School Dance', a remake of 'Love Is A Treasure' (which he originally cut for Duke Reid) and, of course, 'Picture On The Wall', which was also the title of that debut album.

According to drummer Vin Morgan, Freddie voiced 'Picture On The Wall' in just one take. Carl Dawkins, who recorded his own version of 'Picture On The Wall', claims that he and Freddie wrote the song together in Canada after Freddie had got all emotional about losing his girl, whose picture was indeed on the wall. Carl told Freddie that the girl was bad for him but he wouldn't listen and the song developed from there. From what Vin says, Freddie could have been overcome with guilt, and not grief, since he insists that Freddie persistently mistreated this same girl, who then finally walked out on him. When they were together, Freddie was always cheating on her, and he'd even throw stones at her when she complained. A security man who worked at Caymanas Park then stole her away and got her pregnant, leaving Freddie heartbroken.

It's no wonder that Vin recalls Freddie as being a passionate performer who 'cries when him sing.' He'd been singing with the Soul Defenders from long before they went to see Coxsone, and was well experienced as a result.

'We were the resident band in a hotel, and you learn a lot by doing that,' said Vin. 'We also played at a few clubs like Club Jamaica and the Lions Club in Bog Walk, which was just a few miles away. Linstead was the central area, but we went all about and even up to St Mary, but a lot of the Studio One artists used to come to Linstead, like Burning Spear, Horace Andy, the Heptones and Dennis Brown, who was about 15 years old. Mr Dodd came to all of our shows in the area, and he'd sometimes come and spend the night with us, because everyone loves the country. We had this little spot we call Africa... it was a place where most of the artists who performed at the Theatre Royal would come afterwards to smoke herb and all that. Toots never used to smoke, but he lived nearby so he would come and hang around there all day, playing his guitar, and we had a friend called Lloyd Jones who did a song named 'Rome'.'

Vin had played with the Vulcans before teaming up with Festus Walker and Ronald 'Privy' Campbell. That band was called the Ewartonians at first, because they were based in Ewarton, which is just a few miles from Linstead. Val Whittaker, who later migrated to the US, joined on guitar, and that's when they became the Soul Defenders. The lead singers were Claudette 'Nana' McLean, who was Vin's girlfriend, and Freddie McKay.

'Freddie joined us because we'd all grown up together and that's where Joseph Hill, who formed Culture, got his start as well. He was a wonderful percussion player. He could take up two bottles and the sound he made could blow you away! He used to live in my neighbourhood in Linstead and I took him to Studio One where we recorded his first two songs, as the Neptunes. When the Soul Defenders first went to Studio One we did seven songs that we'd been playing on the bandstand. We'd never done any recording before then and we got four number one hits from that first session.

Four! That same week I left my job, because I decided that I wasn't going back to the 9-to-5 anymore.'

Dennis Alcapone had recently celebrated his first official UK release with a cut to 'Cherry Oh Baby.' Two years earlier he'd been the number one deejay on El Paso sound system, which the owner had named after a Marty Robbins hit. Lizzy and Dillinger were the other MCs on El Paso, but it was the Clarendon-born Alcapone, real name Dennis Smith, who was the boss deejay. When U-Roy was having great success with Duke Reid, Alcapone was matching him hit-for-hit for Coxsone, who released his debut album *Forever Version* in 1971. Dennis' simple rhymes were easy to understand and sing along with, and they won him many fans in Jamaica. That gangster name was a misnomer in truth, although he'd recently voiced an album for Bunny Lee called *Guns Don't Argue* which suggested otherwise. Gun crime was now a serious matter and had prompted the Jamaica Chamber Of Commerce to send a telegram to the prime minister, warning that it had reached unacceptable levels. They'd asked that a joint police and military operation be despatched to the Wareika hills, as the situation was becoming more than alarming, with people fearing for their lives when walking the streets day or night, and 'fire must be met with fire.'

In late July, Prince Emmanuel Edwards and eighteen of his followers, all dressed in flowing white robes and ceremonial garb, called on the minister for external affairs, Dr Neville Gallimore, to request assistance with their proposed emigration to Ethiopia.

'For all captives to be set free, we must go back home to Ethiopia,' said Edwards. The Rasta delegation were told that the Jamaican government could not help subsidise their trip, but would not hinder their emigration, provided that the brethren obtained the appropriate visas from the Ethiopian Embassy in Washington DC and were accepted by the Ethiopian government.

Prince Emmanuel's base camp was originally in Ackee Walk, but it was ransacked by police in 1959 and his followers thrown in jail. A lawyer who had previously defended the Mau Mau helped free them. Since then, Prince Emmanuel had established another encampment in the hills overlooking Bull Bay. All the buildings, including the Prince's longhouse, were decorated in red, gold and green, and visitors weren't generally welcome. The Emmanuelites, or 'Bobo dreads' as they were known, wore their locks wrapped in turbans and observed the Sabbath each Saturday. Adherents made brooms, straw mats or sandals to raise money and followed a strict set of codes governing their diet, dress and prayer rituals. They also produced a pamphlet called *Black Supremacy*, distributed among members of the sect. It wasn't surprising that they took positive action in seeking repatriation. Prince Emmanuel and his followers were serious people who'd been battle-hardened by adversity and persecution, and it didn't look as if they were about to back down any time soon.

Bob Andy had spent time in the Rasta camps up in the Wareika hills a few years earlier and became totally immersed in the lifestyle and teachings he discovered there. For a period of time, he and his friend Flippins walked barefoot, didn't wash, and eschewed the ways of Babylon. He surrendered completely to the will of Jah, and his erratic behaviour undoubtedly made life very difficult for those around him, both in the personal and professional sense. It wasn't until he came out of this phase that he returned to Studio One and began writing songs once more. His and Marcia Griffiths' success was therefore a celebration in more ways than one, although their follow-up to 'Young, Gifted And Black', a cover of Crispian St. Peters' 1966 pop hit, 'Pied Piper', stalled at number eleven on the UK charts in June. Arranger Tony King had again followed Trojan's instructions and smothered it in strings, but the duo's second album – also named *Pied Piper* – thankfully had a lot more input from Bob Andy himself this time. He was credited with having produced it, in fact, after spending several weeks in London working at Chalk Farm studios and striving to get the best possible results. It has been said that Bob Andy was in his element during that period, whilst collaborating with top-rate musicians, and having access to better facilities. That's because he was only too aware of the limitations imposed upon him back in Jamaica, and he enjoyed working in an environment where he could explore and test his capabilities to greater effect. It was all part of his ultimate ambition, to be rated alongside major American artists like Marvin Gaye and Sam Cooke.

The pair were touring constantly by then, and had invested in a van and equipment of their own to cut down costs and give them greater autonomy. This is something that the Pioneers had yet to do, but when you have a UK Top 5 hit, your live shows are being compared to those of the Temptations or Four Tops and girls are screaming for you everywhere you go, you can be forgiven for skipping on more mundane details like having your own transportation. The group had just returned from a tour of the Middle East when someone at Trojan played them an unreleased song by Jimmy Cliff called 'Let Your Yeah Be Yeah.' All three members loved it and after a swift visit to Chalk Farm, it was soon winging its way up the national charts. A recent review had hailed the Pioneers as 'the most celebrated Jamaican group in Europe', who were 'singing and dancing their way into the hearts of overseas' reggae fans.' They were still mixing soul covers in with reggae originals, and the influence of black America was writ large in Jackie Robinson's dynamic lead vocals, their close harmonies, immaculate dress sense and synchronised dance moves. Trojan wasted no time in putting out another album with them (called *Yeah!*), and as they posed in matching bright yellow suits with big lapels, the photo on the cover spoke volumes about both their influences and direction of travel.

Trojan's insistence on appealing to mainstream tastes – and that of BBC DJs like Tony Blackburn – was now wearing thin. Whilst compilations such as *Club Reggae* and the *Tighten Up* series were still popular – so popular, in fact, that Pama had recently launched a rival series called *Straighten Up* – there was a nagging suspicion that Trojan would be left behind unless they embraced the shift towards roots and culture songs as Max Romeo had done on his recent hit, 'Let The Power Fall On I.' This was a Christian song originally, but in Romeo's hands it become the utterance of a Rastaman, despite all the religious connotations surrounding a word like 'power' – which is firmly associated with the Holy Ghost – having been left intact.

'A song like that comes from a search into oneself for true identity, so I was actually going through the process of that,' he explained. 'I was trying to determine a trend, and deciding how long I wanted to be around in this business. And if I wanted to do that, then I had to change the trend because otherwise it's just gimmickry, and doesn't stay for long. It's the more serious stuff that lasts, so I get well into the conscious and start to find the right kind of religious climate. After going through various religions like Christianity, Islam and so on, I find them too cultist and restricted. Then I started reading up on Rastafari, ancient Africa and the prophecies of Marcus Garvey, and I figure that is more of what I want. It's a lifestyle more than a religion because when I, as an individual, test religion, I find that it's an enslavement of the mind.'

Bob Marley booked some studio time when he got back from Sweden, and that's when the Wailers recorded 'Screwface', 'Guava Jelly', 'Trench Town Rock' and 'Redder Than Red', which Bunny Lee licensed to Trojan. Their rocky adventures with Lee Perry were now safely behind them and Marley was clearly happy to be back in Kingston and among family and friends. He wrote 'Trench Town Rock' in a yard on First Street, where the Wailers used to store items of equipment until they were 'confiscated' in a police raid. Never before had reggae music – or the Kingston ghetto that spawned it – been so joyously celebrated, and that hook proclaiming that when music hits, 'you feel no pain' was a work of genius. Other songs followed at a furious pace, including 'Lick Samba', 'Satisfy My Soul Jah Jah' and its secular companion 'Satisfy My Soul Babe', 'Craven Choke Puppy' and 'Lively Up Yourself', another anthem-in-the-making.

In August, Bob Marley was invited to crown Miss Musical Chariot at the Sombrero Club in Molynes Road. This was shortly before the news broke that Leslie Kong had died of a heart attack at his home on Northbrook Acres Drive in Kingston. There had been no obvious signs that the 38-year-old record producer was ill or undergoing more stress than usual. A hush descended upon the local music industry, and hundreds of mourners attended his funeral on 15 August, despite the heavy rains. Leslie's brother Kenneth conducted the service, whilst Lloyd and Cecil were among the pallbearers. Many personalities from the entertainment and advertising fields were at the graveside, including Jimmy Cliff, Desmond Dekker, Toots and the Maytals, Warwick Lyn, Island's Dave Betteridge, Ranny Williams, Clancy Eccles, Byron and Neville Lee, Tommy Cowan, Herman Chin Loy and Richard Khouri. Jamaica's most successful international hitmaker was no more, and any words on his passing from Bunny Wailer, who was now thought to have mystical powers, having allegedly cursed Kong shortly before his death for releasing Wailers tracks against their wishes, alas went unrecorded.

Artists like the Melodians, Gaylads and even Desmond Dekker would never surpass the albums they recorded for Beverley's, which folded soon afterwards. There was no one else among the Kong family with Leslie's patience, business acumen and instinct for picking sure-fit hits, and whilst Trojan would endlessly recycle material from his back catalogue, his absence would be keenly felt. It's a matter of conjecture as to whether he would have made the transition from early reggae to roots songs, dub or deejay records. There had been a surfeit of the latter since U-Roy's breakthrough, and whilst people were quick to note the similarities between him and I-Roy, U-Roy refused to be drawn on any possible rivalry.

'Trust me, I have no time for cursing and fussing,' he insisted. 'We are all in this business, we all have to eat and we all have to live and survive, but this brother called I-Roy imitated my voice, my words and everything. I didn't make it a problem, though, because guess what? If you know what you're doing and you originate stuff, you just don't worry about other people.'

U-Roy ruled, but I-Roy – whose current hits were for Spanish

Town producer Harry Mudie – was a serious contender. Mudie was relatively new to production, but confident enough to tell I-Roy what topics he wanted him to deejay about after taking him into the studio for cuts to the Ebony Sisters' 'Let Me Tell You Boy' and Dennis Walks' 'The Drifter.' The 27-year-old Roy Reid originally came from St Thomas, but then earned a scholarship to Dinthill Technical College in Linstead. He worked as an accountant for a while, before trying his hand at deejaying on Soul Bunnies sound, which played down by the Kingston waterfront every Wednesday. He was also the MC on Son's Junior and a Spanish Town sound called Stereo, before joining 'Ruddy' Redwood's Supreme Ruler of Sound (SRS). He was quick-witted, articulate, and a definite force to be reckoned with.

There was a brief flurry of excitement in early September at the prospect of Gladys Knight, Junior Walker, King Floyd and Clarence Carter headlining a two-day Rock-Soul Festival at the National Stadium, with special guest Muhammad Ali. Ali then went on RJR to state that he wasn't coming to Jamaica after all, because Elijah Muhammad, leader of the Nation of Islam, was barred from visiting the country. This wasn't recent news, since the Nation of Islam's leader had been denied entry almost a year previously. But once Ali pulled out, the whole event was cancelled, despite lots of tickets already having been sold...

Richard Roundtree was starring in *Shaft*, then showing at cinemas throughout the island. PNP supporters however, had another hero in their sights. Their current slogan read 'A Change Is Coming With The PNP. Power For The People.' But first there had to be an election, and when Shearer finally announced that one would take place on 29 February the following year, Manley began campaigning in earnest. Now known as 'Joshua', Manley cast Shearer, who was actually his cousin, as a Biblical Pharaoh. In his autobiography, Edward Seaga talks about how music was indispensable to political campaigns in Jamaica and was used to convey a message, as well as encourage crowd participation. He mentions two songs in particular as being especially effective – 'Better Must Come' by Delroy Wilson and 'Let The Power Fall On I' by Max Romeo. In his own words, the latter 'emphasised the prominence of the Rasta duality of the physical I and the mystical I and associated Manley further with a Black Power slogan of power, which the PNP had already adopted as a campaign slogan.'

Manley's campaign had all the best tunes (just like the devil, or so it's said), and the latest was Junior Byles' 'Beat Down Babylon.' The lyrics to this powerful blast of anti-colonial sentiment were written by Junior, his friend Harold Meikle and producer Lee Perry, who added the sound of whip lashes to enhance the song's dramatic impact. The JLP could summon nothing like it. Shearer's party was still haunted by the Ethiopians' 'Everything Crash', recounting the waves of strikes that brought the Jamaican economy to its knees two years earlier, and the JLP's current slogans were appeals, basically. 'One Good Term Deserves Another' and 'The Change Has Happened Already' were two examples, but only committed JLP followers took any notice of them.

Manley, meanwhile, launched his election campaign at a PNP rally in Montego Bay, and in the very same place where Sam Sharpe – organiser of Jamaica's most famous slave rebellion – was hanged. The crowds stretched as far as the eyes could see, and later that same month a revue of singers and political speakers called the PNP Musical Bandwagon accompanied Manley on an island-wide tour. Ken Boothe, Max Romeo, Delroy Wilson, the Chosen Few, the Wailers, Dennis Brown, Alton Ellis and Judy Mowatt were among those who took part, and all were backed by the Inner Circle band. The tour was not without incident– Manley was shot at when they arrived at Black River. Fortunately, no one was hurt, but by endorsing Manley's campaign, everyone who performed as part of the PNP Bandwagon also put themselves in harm's way. They had participated because they agreed with his socialist vision for the country – Manley made no secret of the fact that he respected the Rastafarians after all, and was prepared to listen to their concerns.

101

This was something new, and to underline the point Manley had taken to brandishing a sceptre that Emperor Haile Selassie I had given him, which promptly became known as 'the Rod Of Correction.'

It's a shame that Manley didn't take it to the UK and wield it there, because there was a record by the Piglets called 'Johnny Reggae' at number three in the national charts which was the brainchild, if we can call it that, of record producer Jonathan King, whose approach reflected the disdain for reggae shared by more than a few music industry types in Britain. For instance, the vocalists were session singers who, in his own words, he'd 'coached to sound like teenage scrubbers.' Did this kind of attitude stem from having heard one too many novelty songs or cover versions? Or was it down to racism and thinking that all Jamaicans were backward?

By late November, Joe Gibbs was advertising Peter Tosh's latest release, 'Them Have Fe Get A Beatin'', a thinly veiled attack on Shearer's government that was immediately co-opted by the PNP. This follow-up to Tosh's number one hit 'Maga Dog' arrived just in time for the JLP party conference at the National Arena. 'Keep Jamaica Ahead With The JLP', announced one of the banners draped behind the stage. Even those who'd been led to think of Jamaica as a sun-kissed, tropical paradise with white sand beaches and happy, smiling locals, like in the travel brochures, might have scoffed at that. The most illustrious tourists of 1971 were former Beatle Paul McCartney, his wife Linda and their children, who visited Jamaica in early December. According to the *The Paul McCartney Project* website, this was when the McCartneys discovered and fell in love with reggae music, which inspired Linda to write her first song, 'Seaside Woman.'

'We both loved the music, and going to Jamaica became our big ambition,' recalled Paul. 'When we did, we really fell in love with it: the country, the people, the music, the lifestyle, the weather... we spent weeks there, soaking up a lot of reggae – it was the start of rap, but they used to call it toasting. We always used to say that if all the money went, if we became broke, then we'd go to Jamaica and live in a little shack.

'Some of my happiest memories of buying 7-inch singles come from the Jamaican record shop that we used to go to when we were on holiday in Montego Bay. In the town there was this place called Tony's Records on Fustic Road. It was great. There were records there and you didn't know what they were, because they weren't by established artists, so it was kind of a great adventure, just asking the guy behind the counter, "what's this like? Is it any good?" There would be songs with titles like 'Lick I Pipe', and another was called 'Poison Pressure' by Byron Lee and the Dragonaires, written by Lennon and McCartney. I had to buy that one. Had they just recorded one of our songs? No. It was something completely different, and we all presumed it might be a couple of guys called Tony Lennon and Bill McCartney. Either that, or it was a total scam! Something else we noted on those 7-inch singles in Jamaica is that they did the same thing as the early 1960s vocal groups: the B-side would be the A-side's instrumental, because they would just take the vocal off. On these Jamaican records, they would call it 'version.' I remember being in a club and some guy who was a little bit of a hustler was showing us around. This song came on and I said, "Oh, I love this. Did you just take the vocal off?" And he would not accept that they'd just taken the vocal off. He saw it as a completely blank canvas...'

CHAPTER THREE

1972: EVERY TONGUE SHALL TELL

Greyhound returned in January 1972. The group had been in danger of being written-off as one-hit-wonders, but their bouncy, orchestral cover of Henry Mancini's 'Moon River' hovered just outside the UK Top 10 and played right into the hands of critics who'd been quick to dismiss all reggae as absolute dross. This was the conclusion all those worthy tastemakers at the BBC had reached after refusing to playlist any reggae tracks that couldn't easily be mistaken for vapid pop fare made by black – or preferably white – people with goofy grins and nothing to say for themselves except for inanities.

It really didn't have to be like that. Back in Jamaica, Now Generation had been busy demonstrating that it was possible to make quality, radio-friendly reggae music without sacrificing any integrity in the process. Peter Tosh's militant 'Them Have Fe Get A Beatin'' is as fair an example as any, since it was one of the island's best-selling singles, despite its uncompromising message. Now Generation – or 'Now Gen', for short – had also played on Tosh's last hit 'Maga Dog', as well as Lorna Bennett's 'Breakfast In Bed', the Chosen Few's covers of 'Shaft' and 'Do Your Thing', Derrick Harriott's 'Have You Seen Her' and 'Let Me Down Easy' and several recent Dennis Brown hits, including 'Silhouettes',

'Musical Heatwave', 'Things In Life' and 'The Song My Mother Used To Sing.'

'I'm not putting down other bands, but the ethics that we had were different from theirs,' guitarist Mikey Chung told Angus Taylor. 'People used to label us as an "uptown band", because when we went into the studio we spent time on the music. If we cut a song and then were doing another one, we didn't want it to sound like the other one, so we tried to improvise and get a good sound. We spent so much time on sessions, because we were listening to everything, y' know? We started using more than just major and minor chords. We started using unusual ones and pushing arrangements. People like Derrick Harriott and the Chosen Few liked that, because we paid more attention to the music.'

'Everything was meticulous with that band,' confirms keyboard player Robbie Lyn. 'Dougie and Mikey Chung, and also his brother Geoffrey to some extent, would sit down and work out the lines, because, if you notice, the bass and guitar often plays the exact same thing from beginning to end. If you listen to songs like 'Silhouettes', you can hear the pick guitar playing exactly what the bass-line is doing. It's not just repetition of a simple little three note bass-line, but was worked out properly.

'We did three days a week at Federal as Now Gen and every day we were there, we'd maybe take two hours off and drive up to New Kingston or go eat just up the road, to Hagley Park Road. But then there were other days when we'd just go to this record shop that used to import music that no other store would have. We had limited legal pressings on the island at that time. Certain places would press up limited numbers of Atlantic or Columbia releases, but otherwise a lot of those things had to be imported. We developed a liking for a lot of rock music and so we'd go to the stores and say, "hey Junior, do you have this new album by so and so yet?" He'd say it was coming next week or something like that, but that's how we cultivated a liking for a whole lot of different music. I don't think many people apart from us – meaning myself,

Mikey and Geoffrey – would have even known about rock groups like Yes, Deep Purple, Jethro Tull and Blood, Sweat & Tears... we listened to a lot of that, and also people like Rick Wakeman, who was combining classical music with rock, and of course we had the influence of American rhythm and blues as well. We liked a lot of Stevie Wonder and that kind of thing, because he was probably the biggest influence on everybody at the time.'

At the end of January, the Wailers arrived back in Jamaica after completing their first-ever US dates. During their two-week tour, they played venues in the Bronx, Manhattan, Pennsylvania, Queens and Delaware, and, according to one reviewer, 'all the shows were attended by capacity crowds who responded to the Wailers' music with tremendous enthusiasm.'

Glen Adams went to see them perform in New York, and writes about his experience in his autobiography.

'I didn't attend the Bronx show, knowing they were coming to Brooklyn's President Chateau on President Street. I arrived at the show and saw Bob, Bunny and Peter standing by the front door. That's when I found out they didn't want to work, as that gig hadn't been arranged like the others. The manager who brought them to New York was a friend of the owner's and things started to get dismal. Rude boys wanted to hear the Wailers sing, and when they found out that there was not going to be a show everybody start to get worried, knowing that a lot of hot steppers were present. One disciple of that steppers group came and asked Bob to go and sing, which he and the group did. The Wailers went through a couple of songs, and as I was standing in the audience, Bob kept looking at me, giving me signal to enter the stage and take over the organ as he was getting ready to do 'Soul Rebel', so I did just that. The Wailers hadn't come with a band, so I was the first of the Upsetters to play with the Wailers outside of Jamaica! The show then went on, but as the group got ready to do their current hit song, 'Screw Face', Bob was approached by one of the rudies saying, "don't sing that song. It offends us and we will fire some shots." Suddenly the place became full of police and everyone started to run. I stood firm with my friends and then Mikey Jarrett loaded us all up in the back of his van and took us to Papa Roy's home in an area in Brooklyn called Bushwick. Papa Roy was Rita Marley's father, and that's where I left them.'

Michael Manley was still on the campaign trail as the election was just a month away. On 30 January he hosted Bandwagon '72 at Kingston's National Arena, where the Wailers, Max Romeo, Eric Donaldson, the Chosen Few, Scotty, Dennis Alcapone, Delroy Wilson, Clancy Eccles, Ken Boothe, The Jamaicans, Junior Byles, Judy Mowatt and B. B. Seaton all performed. There was a palpable sense of victory in the air, but then Manley was a powerful orator. It had been a long time since Jamaica had come within touching distance of a leader with charisma, who could stir the hearts of people who'd grown accustomed to feeling defeated.

In early February, Tracy Nicholas interviewed Amy Jacques, widow of Marcus Garvey, who told her, 'white people have always given us hand-picked leaders, for instance W. E. B. Du Bois. He taught at Fisk University, but never rallied the sharecroppers and poor people there. He was a brilliant scholar, but not a leader of the black masses, and he never tried to be. Black people want a revolution for change, like it took the Russians and the Chinese years to achieve. You can have cadres of activists, but running out in the streets with a gun is not a revolution, it's damned silliness. You've got to have everyone organised like soldiers, to do the right thing at the right time. This is how America will be brought to its feet, and to recognise that it was black people who built their bridges, cities and nursed their babies...'

Jamaicans reading her words could be forgiven for hoping that the kind of change she described was imminent. On 21 February, Manley addressed a meeting at the corner of Rum Lane and Laws Street in downtown Kingston and told the gathering that earlier in the day his entourage had been attacked and nine bullets had been fired at him. He said that he survived thanks to the women of central Kingston 'who, when the bullets started to fly, gathered around me like a wall of love.

'No way did God let a bullet touch me,' he declared, 'because my mission is love. I have watched men teach people to hate each other, to teach the black man to hate blackness and poor to hate the poor. When my people need unity to break the bond of oppression, they are taught to hate.'

He said that most gang members didn't know why they were shooting each other, and that he wanted to engineer a truce between the Skulls and Spanglers.

'I'll tell them, "turn in your guns and let me put you to work",' he said. 'But if I make the offer and they don't turn in the guns, then I will stamp out gunmanship. I will let loose the wrath of God upon them, because there will be no place to hide.'

A few days later, the JLP took out a full page ad in the *Gleaner*, asking, 'which rod?' alongside a photo of Manley holding an ordinary walking stick that had clearly been doctored. 'Everyone knows that he has been touring the country with two rods – a Rod Of Discovery and a Rod of Correction,' it proclaimed. 'Look at this. Behold the rod. Where is the Rod of Correction?' And in large capitals underneath it said. 'Who Trusts The PNP? Not You, Not Me! Vote JLP.'

Seaga, writing in his autobiography, reiterated how Manley used his Rod of Correction to embellish his position and his platform. He'd returned from a trip to Africa with it, and claimed that he would use it to destroy all corrupt officials.

'Amazingly, the rod acquired magical properties in the view of the people, many of whom simply wanted to touch it,' Seaga wrote. 'At a meeting one night in Coronation Market, the principal meeting spot in West Kingston, there was a very loud explosion in a nearby lane. Soon after Manley arrived, the lights at the meeting went out. It was not an attack. No one was hurt, but the audience screamed and scampered away. Manley was on the platform with his rod, he was hustled away and the meeting ended abruptly. The next day people were saying that Manley had lost his rod in the confusion and that a little boy had found it. That story gave me an idea, and a facsimile rod was quickly carved and given to me. I used it to great effect by claiming in the melee that Manley had run away and dropped the rod, which had been recovered by a little boy and given to me. Once I had the rod, I proclaimed that Manley was a shepherd without a staff, a Joshua without a rod, a leader without power. "I have the rod", I said, and I waved it to great cheering by the crowd.'

Manley quickly responded in a full page ad of his own, stating, "Seaga's stick is a childish trick, Jamaicans will not be fooled." The controversy raged over who had the right rod, but the JLP had reduced some of the magical power in the PNP campaign. This incident demonstrated two things about Edward Seaga – one, that he was a cunning, if not ingenious politician, and secondly that he was prepared to lie and cheat in order to get what he wanted. Whilst he did succeed in casting doubt about the rod momentarily, Manley won the election by a landslide and immediately set about initiating a series of socio-economic reforms. It was the first time that Black Nationalism had been introduced as a platform issue by one of the two major parties, and a Jamaican politician had drawn upon the struggles of black people as part of their election campaign.

'Hallelujah Free At Last,' sang Clancy Eccles on his latest single, but Jamaica's current number one was Errol Dunkley's 'Black Cinderella.' Writer and producer Jimmy 'One Foot' Radway had funded its release, thanks to a loan from businessman Lloyd Gentles, who lived on the same street as him in Jones Town. Radway's actual name was Ivan Lloyd Rodway, but a friend had persuaded him that 'Jimmy' sounded better. He was an upholsterer by trade, although he'd studied at the Jamaica School of Art when he was younger and had always had a creative streak. It's possible that he would have become a singer or even a musician but for his disability, sustained in Jamaica's worst-ever rail crash, when a train carrying an estimated 1,600 passengers was derailed as it approached the quiet town of Kendal in Hanover. Close to two hundred people lost their lives and several hundreds more were badly injured – many of them belonging to the Holy Name Society of the St Anne's Roman Catholic church, who were returning to Kingston after a day out in Montego Bay. The twelve coaches were all wooden, and the splinters from them caused serious injuries. The 4-year-old Radway lost one of his legs that fateful night in September 1957, but as he got older he always appreciated the fact that he'd survived, unlike so many of his fellow travellers.

When he was 15, he would hang around Coxsone in the early days of Studio One and watch the Skatalites rehearse. A few years later he teamed up with Tony McKinley, but this partnership ended in acrimony after they'd produced Teddy Charmers's 'I Want It Girl.' It wasn't until early in 1972 that he tried his hand at production once more and launched the Fe Me Time label with 'Black Cinderella' and matching cuts by Big Youth and Augustus Pablo.

Aston 'Family Man' Barrett, who'd decamped from MS Starward as soon as Bob Marley returned from Sweden, played on 'Black Cinderella', and also produced Errol Dunkley's album *Darling Oh*, which ended up in Sonia Pottinger's hands. Family Man had a band called the Youth Professionals, and it was they who played on the *Darling Oh* sessions. He'd been teaching Robbie Shakespeare to play bass, and the youngster made his debut on Dunkley's 'You'll Never Know', which was a cover of the Beatles' 'I'll Be Back.'

'Everyone hear about me, this little bass player that play like Family Man', Robbie said, proudly. Marley had again left for London, where he rejoined Johnny Nash, whose latest single was a cover of 'Stir It Up.' He and Nash played a few low-key acoustic gigs together, including one at a secondary school in Peckham. Members of the Cimarons backed them on the occasions they needed a band, as guitarist Locksley Gichie recalled only too well.

'Bob was a soul rebel in those days. He had this massive Afro, and his manager Danny Sims talked to us about doing a couple of gigs in London, so we started to rehearse with Bob and Johnny Nash. We did a couple of gigs with them, and it was good, because Bob Marley was quite big in Jamaica by then. Not in England, but he was a nice brother. We used to move with him a lot at that time. Him and Johnny Nash were staying in Bayswater, sharing this big flat. We did a gig at the Bouncing Ball in Peckham and then one in Bristol. We also did a couple of shows with them at the Apollo in Willesden High Road, but it was just Bob staying in London, because this was before he'd met Chris Blackwell.'

In March 1972, American singer Paul Simon's 'Mother And Child Reunion' entered the UK Top 10. It was his first solo hit since quitting Simon & Garfunkel, and had been recorded during a brief visit to Jamaica in 1971. Dynamic's resident band, the All-Stars, played on it, and that wasn't the only song they recorded with him during that session; guitarist Hux Brown says there were at least three or four others.

'But he didn't know anything about reggae, and so we were the ones who found the rhythm,' says Hux. 'He just played guitar and sang the song; we ran it down about three times, found the groove and then put everything together. It wasn't no big deal to us, because we didn't know who he was! It was just an opportunity to play a session and get paid in American dollars, and it was no big production either. We didn't have written music to work from or anything like that, but he was well satisfied, I tell you!'

The song title, 'Mother And Child Reunion', was inspired by a restaurant menu that listed a dish combining chicken and eggs, although you'd never know it from the lyrics, which paint an emotional response to Jimmy Cliff's song 'Vietnam.' It's a very moving tribute, written with great sensitivity and, according to Simon, was the first reggae hit by a non-Jamaican white guy outside of Jamaica.

'Paul Simon and I met in New York,' Cliff recalls, 'and he was like, "wow! It's great to meet you!" He said that he and Bob Dylan had sat up for the whole night listening to my album *Jimmy Cliff*, the one with 'Many Rivers To Cross' and 'Vietnam' on it. That's when I was told that Dylan had said 'Vietnam' was the best protest song ever written. Paul Simon told me that. He said that after he himself listened to 'Vietnam', he wanted to go to the same studio and use the same musicians, and that's what he did. He booked the same studio and musicians, came down to Jamaica with 'Mother And Child Reunion' and recorded it.'

Paul Simon was signed to Columbia, and there were rumours going round that Bob and Marcia were either about to join him, or had already signed a deal with them too. Coxsone Dodd was an old hand at stealing his former artists' thunder by now, so issued Bob Andy's *Songbook* album right on cue. It's an absolute classic, showcasing a master singer/songwriter who had yet to receive due recognition outside of Jamaica, despite those two crossover hits with Marcia. All the key tracks are there – 'My Time', 'Desperate Lover', 'Life Could Be A Symphony', 'Too Experienced', 'I've Got To Go Back Home', 'Let Them Say', 'Unchained' and 'Feeling Soul'– but its arrival proved a bittersweet experience for Bob Andy himself.

'I was just a bright kid who was happy to have an outlet when recording for Studio One. I never thought of how much dollars I was going to get, I swear to God. Never, ever! I just had a ball having an idea, transmitting it to musicians and hearing the eventual poetry in the mix. Being a part of all of that and seeing it come to light was my joy! That's what those people didn't like about me in those days. They all viewed me as an upstart, but I was a guy who was just reflecting on life as it happened, and I was so happy to know this thing that was coming out of me was so true.

'People ask, "but what about Coxsone and royalties?", and I say there's no room for bitterness or disappointment, regrets or envy and all of that, because they will poison us, and if I go through the confusion and the madness still holding onto those things, then I will not have been redeemed because, you know something? They broke my spirit, but that is what God loves. He loves to remodel a broken vessel.'

Coxsone was actually on a hot streak, releasing a lot of music during 1972. Burning Spear's debut album, *Studio One Presents*, had tracks like 'Ethiopians Live It Out', 'We Are Free', 'Door Peep Shall Not Enter', 'He Prayed' and recent single 'Creation Rebel.' Larry Marshall's 'Run Babylon' would be played in dances for decades to come, and so too Freddie McKay's original 'I Am A Free Man.' But it was Horace Andy's 'Skylarking', written about the youths seen on every street corner, that would resonate most with many reggae fans.

Horace Hinds, as he was first known, was raised in Allman Town, near National Heroes Park. That's where he used to practise his guitar at night. His father was a carpenter, his mother did domestic work, and as he had siblings, he did a fair amount of babysitting! He voiced his debut, 'This Is A Black Man's Country', in 1966 for Phil Pratt and attended Ethiopian World Federation meetings, where he learnt about African history and studied the Bible, especially Psalms, Genesis and the Book of Revelations. Delroy Wilson, Alton Ellis and Ken Boothe were his favourite singers, and after some dedicated practise, he and a friend called Frank Melody auditioned for Coxsone in 1970 as a duo. They were turned down, but Horace went back on his own and got accepted. A few days later he recorded 'You've Got To Be Sure', 'Something On My Mind' and 'See A Man's Face', but some of the musicians were disparaging about his tremulous vocal style. He had left Studio One the previous August, and only returned in January of 1972. He then revoiced some of the tracks that he'd recorded previously, which Coxsone had since included on Horace's debut album *Skylarking*.

Studio One recordings have such a distinctive sound, and especially tracks recorded by the Soul Defenders band. They're densely mixed, and seem to reverberate within your entire body. There's nothing quite like hearing a Studio One selection on a decent sound system, and when time travel is available to all, we could do a lot worse than set the dial to New Year's Eve 1970 and visit the sound clash between Killer Whip and Ruddy's Hi-Fi in Spanish Town, with I-Roy on the mic for Ruddy's and a virtual unknown called Prince Jazzbo in Killer Whip's corner. Coxsone was in the crowd that night, and watched as Jazzbo won round after round by deejaying over Studio One rhythms. He invited Jazzbo to come to Brentford Road to record and Jazzbo was there at 5 a.m. the next morning! That first session for Studio One had taken place in January 1971, when he recorded 'Imperial I.' He was just 21 and couldn't manage to voice it at his first attempt. He pestered Coxsone for another chance though, and as a cut of Burning Spear's 'Door Peep Shall Not Enter' filled the room, he smashed it in one take. That debut track, 'Imperial I', would stay in the vaults for quite some time, but Prince Jazzbo singles were now coming thick and fast. Best of all was 'Crab Walking', voiced on the same rhythm as Horace Andy's 'Skylarking.'

After a rousing introduction, Jazzbo then scats with such a confident swagger, you'd swear that he'd been recording for years. Yet tracks like this were voiced right there on the spot, one after the other, without him having written anything down first. They were delivered in real time, just as the tape rolled.

'You have to make a good composition right away,' he told *Jamaica Way*, 'but when you listen to the singer and the lyrics, then you know exactly what you need to put everything together. All I needed was a punchline and as soon as I get that, I know exactly what to do. Doing that every night on sound system, it becomes very easy to come up with a composition and not make a mistake, and it was the same thing in the studio.'

Dennis Alcapone remembers walking into Studio One around that time and being met by the Heptones, who warned him there was a new deejay in town come to snatch his crown. The MC they were referring to was a gangly 22-year-old known as Big Youth who'd been deejaying on Tippertone sound for just over a year. Prior to that he would ask I-Roy – then filling in for U-Roy on King Tubby's Hi Fi – for a talk on the mic and, in Big Youth's own words, 'mash him up every time.'

By his own account, Youth grew up 'in chaos and poverty.' He was one of five children raised by their mother, a preacher. Real name Manley Buchanan, he left school at 14 and worked as a labourer and an auto mechanic. The Sheraton Hotel was under construction at the time, and that's where he practised deejaying, in the empty elevator shaft. It was Gregory Isaacs who took him in the studio for the first time. 'Movie Man' wasn't an immediate success, but his cut to 'Black Cinderella' was – and then 'S90 Skank' happened.

The S90 was a lightweight Honda motorbike that was perfect for whizzing around Kingston. It had a top speed of 64 mph and was cheap to run. Everyone wanted one, and when producer Keith Hudson wheeled one into Dynamic and revved it up on the intro to Big Youth's 'S90 Skank', it caused a sensation. No one had done anything like that before, and it would become one of the biggest songs of the year. Interestingly, the only reference to motorbikes in that song came when Big Youth warned that ride one like lightning, then 'you'll crash like thunder.'

Hudson was among the vanguard of Jamaican producers issuing different cuts of the same rhythm. He recorded Augustus Pablo and Dave Madden's new group Zap Pow on the same rhythm as 'S90 Skank', but his other bestsellers at that time were Dennis Alcapone's 'The Hudson Affair' and a vibrant cover of Hugh Masekela's 'Riot', played by Soul Syndicate and featuring Johnny 'Dizzy' Moore on trumpet. 1972 was also the year that Hudson released his debut album *Furnace* and promoted himself as a singer – 'True True To My Heart' being the standout. Dave Henley once defined Keith Hudson's own music as 'desolate introspection.' 'Satan Side', an eerie cut of War's 'Slipping Into Darkness', certainly matched that description, but then his office at 127 King Street (above the Wailers' record store) only had the one dim light and if it wasn't for the caretaker at the nearby Marcus Garvey Liberty Hall 'liberating' electricity, Keith's place wouldn't have had any power at all.

It's often the gifted innovators who suffer, and this was true of Vivian 'Yabby You' Jackson, another singer/producer with his own distinct vision. He first sang with the Ralph Brothers, and listening to their debut single 'Conquering Lion' was to be led into the presence of something strangely and deeply spiritual. It's a chant in praise of Emperor Haile Selassie I and is utterly compelling, yet Jackson had issues with most Rastafarians and remained largely faithful to the Christian beliefs instilled in him by his mother back in Clarendon, where he grew up. Ever the wanderer, he left school at 15 and started work at a foundry in Waterhouse. There were no health and safety regulations and he suffered from the effects of inhaling the scalding, dry heat thrown out by the flames.

'When Yabby got ill, he was around 20,' recalled his friend, Mitch Graylan. 'At the foundry they'd make alluvium pots, and the temperature in there was hot! It was molten copper they used and Yabby collapsed in there. It had nothing to do with lack of nutrition at that time.'

Even as his lungs shrivelled and his health rapidly deteriorated, he pursued his interest in spirituality and would often reason with the Rastafarians he met in places like Ackee Walk.

'When I was younger I wasn't really Rasta,' Yabby told me, 'but I adopt the Rasta style because I eat no flesh and wear no form of leather shoes, things like that. Me also grow locks and travel with my own pot, and then when night time catch me, I lie down wherever I am before walking on again. And I never talk to people, so all they see is this little man who keep silent and walk with his little crocus bag all around Jamaica...'

After drifting from place to place and effectively being homeless for long periods, Yabby suffered from the combined effects of malnutrition, pneumonia, an ulcerated stomach and what he euphemistically described as 'brain fever.' However unlikely it seems, his only income during this period came from being a tipster. Jackson's religious beliefs wouldn't allow him to gamble personally, but he'd predict winners at the local racecourse, then others would place the bets and give him a share of the winnings. It had taken him three years to raise the money needed to record 'Conquering Lion', which developed from ad-hoc rehearsals on the gully bank near where he lived. Once heard, the insistent chorus he and the Ralph Brothers came up with – revolving around the same phrase, 'Be you, yabby, yabby you' repeated over and over – can never be forgotten. That's where Jackson got the name 'Yabby You' from, although others called him 'Jesus Dread.'

'In Jamaica, all of the dreadlocks were against me because they say I disrespect His Majesty,' he explained. 'But I say that I worship the creator of man, and not man himself. If you notice when you hear my music, even those tracks where I'm not singing, you can still feel the message in it, and that's real reggae music to the bone, because it will put you in the right frame of mind for the things that are conscious and belonging to the truth. This is the real meaning of it, and it's nothing to do with any church or religion, and especially Rastafari!

'Instead, I use music to teach black history, and to remind the world of what it takes to be a human being. That's what I try to do; I try to highlight black history as I see it, and to show my people that we are all one nation, coming from ancient Africa. Because we stem from such a strong root, and by immersing ourselves in that we can emerge as peaceful people and with love in our hearts, unlike most of these so-called Rastas.'

In May 1971, after David Madden and Danny MacFarlane left the Mystics and formed Zap Pow, Cedric ''Im' Brooks and Count Ossie decided to pool their vision, talent and resources in a collective called the Mystic Revelations of Rastafari, which they premiered with a performance at the Creative Arts Centre on the University of West Indies' campus.

'Mystic Revelations is a soul expression,' they had declared. 'Drums are the foundation of the music, expressing its basic philosophy through rhythm. The horns then complete the drums, from which melodies emerge only as a result of constant repetition, and this makes the music more jubilant.'

One of their first actions was to outline plans for a new cultural organisation in association with the Harambee Theatre Group at Seven Miles, which they felt should include a basic school for children living in the immediate area. They also embarked on a series of ground-breaking recordings at the New Dimension studios in Kingston with producer Arnold Wedderburn. These sessions resulted in the triple LP set, *Grounation*, a project that was well-named since it was the closest thing to actually being at a grounation – a meeting where Rastafarians discuss religious, social and political topics – yet committed to vinyl. The combination of chanting, drumming, poetry readings and inspired jazz-inflected improvising by Cedric Brooks and other members of the ensemble was spellbinding, especially on band favourites like 'Bongo Man', 'Lumumba', 'Ethiopian Serenade', 'Oh Carolina' and the Crusaders' 'Way Back Home.'

'Count Ossie and the Mystic Revelations of Rastafari are the latest examples of the Rastafari as folk hero,' commented musicologist and broadcaster Dermot Hussey. 'The Count and his men, the embodiment of Rastafari sensitivity, have sought to return the drum to a focal point in our culture in place of the violin, the instrument of our cultural synthesis. Besides forging an African consciousness and an African-derived lifestyle, the gypsies have influenced ska and reggae, inspired poets, writers, painters and choreographers. Now they stand outside the walls of a broad public acceptance.'

The launch party was held at the Harambee Theatre and was a crowded affair, according to the *Gleaner*. Guests included Joe Higgs, who sang 'World Upside Down' accompanied by conga drummer Larry McDonald, but it was the Mystic Revelations Of Rastafari themselves who lit up the occasion and most enthused Hussey.

'They are at their most dread when two things occur – the presence of a 'live' audience and the presence of Kenny Terroade, who acts as a catalyst,' he wrote. 'During 'Maiden Voyage', Herbie Hancock's composition became something different – an excursion into unbelievable free blowing and interplay between horns and drums. Kenny Terroade, fresh from a tour with Sunny Murray and the Mystic Revelations, more together since their Trinidad trip, were in full cry. 'Ethiopian Serenade', with its eastern sound, was stretched to the limit, taking on a wailing, dervish quality, while Terroade's soprano on top of clarinet took on wings, and those of us who loved John Coltrane knew how grateful we were and had to be.'

One of the poetry readings at the launch was given by someone called 'Oku.' It was a name that Post Office robber Orlando Wong was using, and less than a month later, the *Gleaner* reported that he'd been admitted to Spanish Town hospital suffering from gunshot wounds after a clash with the police. 'Wong allegedly attacked the policemen with a machete and was shot in the left leg and abdomen,' it said. 'His condition is regarded as serious and he is under heavy police guard.'

The New Dimension studio, where *Grounation* was recorded, was on Eastwood Park Road. An inspiring young singer named Beres Hammond was walking past there one evening when he heard Winston Blake rehearsing a band in readiness for a talent show that he was organising. Hammond put his name down, and when the big night came, Blake was left open-mouthed as the youngster from Annotto Bay sang a couple of Sam Cooke and Arthur Pryce tunes. Beres stayed in Kingston with Winston for the next few days, learning new songs and preparing for a Merritone show at the VIP Club in Halfway Tree. He was just 17, new to city ways; it was also his first time performing in front of a Kingston audience. When the moment arrived, he walked on stage wearing a blue turtleneck top and the crowd howled with laughter.

'Back in my community, that would have been regarded as sharp dressing,' said Beres, with a wry grin. 'I didn't realise they were so fashion-conscious in Kingston, and my shirt was kind of backwards. The truth is I'd never done anything like that before. I usually sang at community concerts and church events, but there I was, making them all laugh at my first big appearance! I was hurting a little bit, but I kept smiling because I realised I had to get through it the best way I could. It was all part of going through the growing pains, y' know? It was a lovely top I had on, too...'

In late April, Michael Manley announced that his government would be launching a massive island-wide literacy programme, recognising that 'illiteracy among a large section of the population is affecting the social and economic development of the country.' Within a short time, the National Literary Project began placing ads in the local media declaring that 'Half A Million Jamaicans Cannot Read And Write. Jamaica Is At War With Illiteracy. Fill out a registration card at your local Post Office.'

Less than a week later, Manley was at Excelsior High School, answering questions from the students there. One asked about reports that Rastafarians had begun squatting on crown land because 'it was power time now.' The prime minister said that the capturing of lands was not a Rastafarian phenomenon – it was a poverty phenomenon, but the Rastas got the blame because they stood out more than others. He paid tribute to how Rastafarians 'very often had a greater sense of self-confidence and a greater sense of peace in their identity', and insisted that he did 'not accept the middle-class intention to cut them off from society.'

The Mystic Revelations Of Rastafari, the Morant Bay Ecumenical Singers and Jamaica Folk Singers were among the acts who performed at Manley's official residence on 23 May, where he hosted an event in honour of the Workers Movement In Jamaica. Thousands attended despite a power cut and sporadic rainfall, and Manley greeted them by saying 'my brothers and sisters, truly the word is love. I welcome you to Jamaica House and want you to know that Jamaica House is not my house, it is the people's house.'

Two weeks later, on 5 June, Perry Henzell hosted the world

premiere of his film *The Harder They Come* at the 'too small for the occasion' Carib Theatre in Kingston.

'Result – all hell broke loose,' announced a reporter in the *Gleaner*. 'The fence around the theatre was torn flat to the ground. Doors were ripped open, water pipes from the toilet at the back were torn away. Nothing, it seems, could stop that mob. Everyone wanted to see their own Jamaican movie. Dignitaries were stranded outside. No way could they get in. Every entrance and exit was surrounded by the crowd. And why was there this great mad rush to see this movie? I found that most of the people thought that after the Monday night showing, the film would leave the island for its overseas run. Many said the advertisements had given them this impression. Inside the theatre it was unbelievable chaos. I got in with a mob, rushing in through a broken exit door. Half the people inside were without shirts, it was so hot that most of the men had to take them off. Some were seen wringing the sweat out of their shirts and airing them. Others danced in the aisle during the musical interlude which preceded the film. In a short time the theatre was so crammed there wasn't even room for standing. People sat two to a seat, others sat on top of the backs and handles of seats. The Carib was jam-packed with squeezing room only. It was a very good film – indeed very enjoyable, mainly because one saw oneself being portrayed on film. It was a complete Jamaican situation with Jamaican people... The film was very enjoyable and no one should miss it.'

The Harder They Come was the first feature film written and directed by a Jamaican and shot on location using an all-native cast. It provided Jamaican audiences with the opportunity to see their own culture projected onto a big screen for the first time – hence the ecstatic reaction at the premiere. Perry Henzell's wife Sally was the art director and played a little-heralded role in ensuring that the film's visual impact was so arresting. Released in the days before relatively cheap package holidays to Jamaica, *The Harder They Come* was a revelation to most foreign cinemagoers, who got their first taste of ghetto life in Jamaica and the island's criminal underbelly. It changed people's perceptions, even in places like England where Jamaican music was a part of the everyday pop milieu, and the population were no strangers to Caribbean influences.

Jimmy Cliff played the role of Ivan Martin, a budding singer from the Jamaican countryside who gets caught up in the renegade world of drugs and violence in the slums of Kingston.

'All of that was going on in Jamaica and the rest of the world didn't know about it, so Perry's film was really the vehicle that exposed what was happening there,' Cliff said. 'It carried those things to all these other places, and that's why it had such a major impact on so many people from around the world. It showed people where the music was coming from, how the music was created, how it came about and all of that. I'm grateful at having been in the right place at the right time to be a part of that. Reggae was a completely new music form that was coming out of the small island of Jamaica, and so it had a big impact on the world.'

Less than a week after the Kingston premiere, Michael Manley married the broadcaster and former model Beverley Anderson in a private ceremony. The fact that he'd chosen to wed a black woman rather than someone who was white or of a similar light complexion to himself resonated strongly with many among Jamaica's predominately black population. If they'd wanted a wedding song they would surely have chosen a Jamaican record, yet the Staples Singers' 'I'll Take You There' – currently climbing both pop and R&B charts in America – would have fit the bill perfectly. It's worth noting that the song was written by Stax Records' Al Bell, who penned it after one of his brothers was murdered. After returning home from the funeral, he sat on the hood of an old bus in his father's back yard and wrote the lyrics, giving them to the Staple Singers, who recorded it at Muscle Shoals. The bassline, as any reggae fan could have told them, was taken from Harry J All Stars' 1969 hit 'Liquidator.' Guitarist Jimmy Johnson had recently been on holiday in Jamaica and bought 'Liquidator', but neither the All Stars or their bass player Aston 'Family Man' Barrett got a mention, let alone a share of the royalties.

Family Man had already left Jamaica by this time, flying with his brother Carlton and the three Wailers to London, where Johnny Nash was waiting to put a tour together.

'As far as I understand it, Johnny Nash had a tour of the UK and they were labelling him "The King Of Reggae",' noted British-born singer/actor Brinsley Forde, who befriended the group during their visit. 'The Wailers were supposed to be the support act, but whether it was done purposefully or whatever, their visas ended up at the Jamaican Embassy and they only managed to do two shows in the time they were there. They sat and they waited and waited to go on this tour, but it never materialised.

'I don't think people really noticed them. They went completely unnoticed, and no one was the wiser as to who they were. We played football sometimes, over at the Welsh Harp. I was round at the house quite a bit and each of them had their rooms. I would be there jamming with Family Man, and he and I really locked. He wanted me to play bass, but I wanted to sing and I could never sing and play bass at the same time.'

Brinsley was best known for his role in the schoolboy series *Here Come the Double Deckers.* He had an old Cortina and would take the band members to places like the Four Aces in Dalston, Mr B's in Peckham and the Roaring Twenties in Carnaby Street. They were staying in a house by the Circle in Neasden by this time, and travelling to Rondor Music studios in Kingston-upon-Thames most days, where they would rehearse. They had to go by train because they didn't have their own transport, but this didn't seem to worry them.

The Cimarons' guitarist, Locksley Gichie, was present at some of those sessions and played lead on early versions of 'No More Trouble' and 'Concrete Jungle.' He says that few if any Jamaican guitarists played the kind of sound that Bob Marley wanted, which was closer to blues and rock than reggae. Soul bands like Funkadelic and the Isley Brothers were headed in the same direction. There was a coming together of styles happening, although the Wailers couldn't quite get to it just yet.

Johnny Nash had already recorded 'Stir It Up' and released it as a single. He'd included three more Bob Marley songs – 'Guava Jelly', 'Comma Comma' and 'You Poured Sugar On Me' – on his new album, *I Can See Clearly Now*, and the title track was an immediate hit in the UK, where it stayed on the charts for nearly four months, peaking at number five. The story of what happens next is well-known. 'I Can See Clearly Now' became a big hit in America and Johnny Nash promptly went over there to promote it, leaving the Wailers stranded in London. A meeting was arranged with Chris Blackwell, who'd recently lost Jimmy Cliff to EMI. He signed the Wailers on the strength of the demos they'd just recorded and agreed to finance a debut album for Island Records once they'd returned to Jamaica.

In the meantime, the UK premiere of *The Harder They Come* had taken place in September at the Classic cinema in Brixton, home to one of Britain's most well-established Caribbean communities. Jazz musician and critic George Melly called it 'a remarkable film on any level. Entertaining and serious, funny and tragic, political in the widest sense,' whilst Ray Connolly, writing in the *Evening Standard*, called it 'an interesting new film which has unfortunately been much officially overlooked. This is the first truly Jamaican film, a piece so uncompromising in its attempts to depict a certain section of West Indian society that subtitles are necessary to translate the dialect, and where no attempts have been made to gloss over the shanty town poverty. When shown in the heavily West Indian-populated Brixton area, the whole cinema was jumping with excitement, and after seeing *The Harder They Come* you can forget about the pretty images of the lazy life in sun and sea created by all those Harry Belafonte pictures. It is in many ways a remarkable film, not least because of the way it takes the old cliché of "country boy comes to city to make a record and finds stardom" and stands it completely on its head in a story that runs through murder, beatings, the Rasta sect, police corruption and, finally, the lonely death of a man in love with a fantasy.'

Chris Blackwell was one of the film's backers, and Island Records released the soundtrack. It was a brilliant (if dated) collection, featuring hits by Toots and the Maytals (who are seen voicing 'Sweet And Dandy' in the film), Scotty, Desmond Dekker, the Slickers and Melodians as well as Jimmy Cliff himself, whose contributions include 'You Can Get If You Really Want', 'Many Rivers To Cross' and the title track.

'They originally wanted me to write music for the soundtrack,' Jimmy explained, 'but when they said they had to stop filming and try and get some more money, that's when I went off to Muscle Shoals to complete *Another Cycle*, but they only used one song from it, which was 'Sitting In Limbo.' The rest of the music was made up of songs that were already established and they were chosen by Perry Henzell and Chris Blackwell, who took them from different labels.'

Toots and the Maytals had won the Jamaica Festival Song competition for the third time with 'Pomp And Pride' in late June. There was disruption at the finals held at the Minerva Club in Mandeville after Derrick Morgan's 'Festival 10' lost out, despite having enjoyed a slight lead prior to the count. When Toots was announced as the winner, cries of 'robbery' were heard, led by Bunny Lee, who said the count was unfair and that some voters had been intimidated by gunmen who forced them to vote against their choice. Toots had returned to recording for Byron Lee after Leslie Kong's death, whereas not much was happening for Derrick. Were these gunmen acting on behalf of Byron Lee? We'll never know, because no one from Dynamic dared say anything.

Toots and the Maytals headlined a big Independence show at the Carib on 7 August, where they shared a bill with Horace Andy, Junior Byles, Ernie Smith (who was riding high with 'Pitta Pitta'),

Dennis Brown, John Holt, Derrick Harriott and blind gospel singer Adina Edwards. Lloyd Parks, bassist with Skin, Flesh & Bones, also performed that day, singing his recent number one hit, 'Officially.'

Junior Byles had entered the Jamaica Song Festival with a song called 'Da Da', produced by Lee 'Scratch' Perry, who included it on Junior's new album *Beat Down Babylon* along with other favourites such as 'A Place Called Africa', 'Joshua's Desire' and the title track. 'Demonstration' was a rewrite of his song 'What's The World Coming To?', but thankfully without the strings this time and with minor changes to one verse.

The majority of songs were recorded at Dynamic, although Scratch was building a studio at his family home in Cardiff Crescent and had an album of his own out, credited to the Upsetters. He'd been telling people that he found working with singers too much trouble. This may explain why *Cloak And Dagger* was an instrumental album, but Junior Byles had never sounded better and Neville Grant's 'Blackman's Time' was another gem, commenting on Jamaica's worsening inequality.

King Tubby had also been busy creating his own studio facilities at home. When Dynamic decided to make changes to Studio B, Tubby bought their MCI console and installed it in a back room of his mother's house in Drumlie Avenue. That board had been used to mix some of the biggest hits of the early reggae era, although it wasn't the standard issue because someone at the American studio where Byron Lee got it from added a high pass filter, which was generally used to eliminate 'parasitic frequencies.' It would take a genius like Tubby to unleash its true potential, and an opportunist like Bunny Lee to exploit every advantage the situation had to offer once things were up and running. No sooner had 'Tubbs' got everything working than Bunny Lee turned up with Delroy Wilson, who christened the place by voicing 'Cheer Up' and 'Here Come The Heartaches.' The floodgates opened after that. Bunny's stable had now grown to include Horace Andy, Freddie McGregor, Big Joe and Cornel Campbell, who Bunny had first seen perform with the Eternals and a band called Big Relation featuring Robbie Shakespeare. Cornel had been earning decent money as a printer, but was persuaded to take up music full-time by Alton Ellis, who considered him the finished article. His recent singles for Bunny included 'The Minstrel', 'Dearest Darling' (a cut to Slim Smith's 'Just A Dream') and 'Girl Of My Dreams.'

Slim Smith was a key member of Bunny Lee's entourage, along with Delroy Wilson – whose latest album was *Greatest Hits* – and John Holt, the master of laidback lovers rock. His *Pledging My Love* album found him covering several Johnny Ace tunes, including 'The Clock', 'Anymore' and the title track. It also had a version of the Tams' 'Riding For A Fall' with the most delicious flute, presumably played by Tommy McCook. Bunny Lee may have been extraordinarily prolific, but his productions had style, and he knew only too well that reggae audiences encompassed a far greater demographic than just pop fans or rebellious youths searching for identity.

Talking of pop fans, they really missed out on Shorty The President's 'President Mash Up The Resident', toasted over a cut of the Uniques' 'My Conversation' that Rupie Edwards bought from Jimmy Riley. It worked brilliantly as both a dancehall and novelty tune, but the man from rural Trelawny who made his name on the Conquering Lion sound system didn't get the crossover success he deserved. It was left to Judge Dread, the one-time bouncer, professional wrestler and debt collector, to take reggae to the masses in the UK with the risqué 'Big Six' and 'Big Seven' during the last few months of 1972. He was the first white artist to record for Trojan after voicing a slack ditty inspired by Prince Buster, and playing it to label manager Joe Sinclair.

'When Dread brought in his demo, we didn't exactly think it was a national hit but we reckoned we could pick up something around the region of 70,000 sales with the help of a change of title,' Sinclair explained. 'Judge called it 'Little Boy Blue', whereas I thought 'Big Six' would create interest by making the association with Prince Buster's 'Big Five' more obvious. It sold 300,000 copies and spent twenty-seven weeks in the British charts!'

The BBC banned 'Big Six' and follow-up 'Big Seven', which he'd written with Rupie Edwards, because of their lewd content, but this didn't dent Judge Dread's appeal in the slightest. Lloyd Charmers took full advantage and rushed out Lloydie and the Lowbites' *Censored! Vol. 2*, featuring instantly forgettable tracks like 'Shitting On The Dock Of The Bay', 'Yum Yum Pussy', 'My Baby Keeps Farting' and 'Spermy Night In Kingston.' 'When we go into the studio, we don't know what is going to happen or what we're going to record,' Charmers told me. 'We just group together and see what happens. A man might say, "Charmers, what are we going to do now?" and I'd say, "follow me." I'll just start playing something, and then the band will fall in behind me, argument finished!'

The Lowbites raised a few giggles but failed to chart. The next UK reggae crossover hit belonged to Dandy Livingstone, whose 'Suzanne Beware Of The Devil' went to number fourteen in September.

'I went to Jamaica in January 1972,' Livingstone told me. 'I did that song and a few more things but it wasn't voiced or anything. Lee Gopthal at Trojan wanted a B-side for some other song called 'What Do You Want To Make Those Eyes At Me For?' He wanted to rush this thing out and didn't have a B-side, then I remembered that I had this song 'Suzanne Beware Of The Devil' and I asked Vic Keary to open up Chalk Farm studio at six o'clock in the morning. I got there at quarter to six and Vic was very annoyed. He was saying, "what kind of time is this?" I reminded him that I'd made the arrangement to be there but he'd probably been drinking heavily the night before and wanted to sleep off the booze. Anyway, he came down in his pyjamas, put on his jacket and we did the song just like that. We knew right then we had our B-side. Lee put the record out, and then DJ Emperor Rosko phoned Trojan one afternoon and said, "you people have a hit record!" The person who answered said, "which one?" Rosco said, "the B-side of Dandy Livingstone's song", but the person at Trojan didn't know which song he was talking about. 'Suzanne Beware Of The Devil,' Rosko told him, and that was that, but guess what? Nicky Thomas had just come out with a follow-up to 'Love Of The Common People.' I can't remember what it was called, but it flopped, so Lee said to me, "why not give Nicky your song, 'Suzanne Beware Of The Devil'?" So they put seventy-six trombones on it, and nothing happened. Two weeks later, they released my version and bam! It went straight to the charts, simple as that.'

Remember Eddy Grant? He'd gone back to Guyana whilst recovering from his heart attack. He returned to London earlier in the year and set up the first black-owned recording studio in Europe, Coach House, and began recording music for his own Ice Records label. Coach House was situated in Stamford Hill in NE London, and a local group called 90 Per Cent Inclusive was among the first acts to record there.

'90 Per Cent Inclusive weren't intent on just following a Jamaican feel, because at that time I was heavily into guitarists like Steve Cropper, Albert King and Big Jim Sullivan,' remembered guitarist Hugh Francis. 'I was desperate to get a taste of what they had, but there wasn't a manual for a bunch of guys living in Tottenham. There was nothing happening for us. But then along came Eddie, who said he understood where we wanted to go, even though we were combining reggae with a lead guitar sound that came straight from rock music. People would say to us, "Why are you guys messing with lead guitars and fuzz boxes? What are you trying to do? That's not reggae." They didn't understand there was a new movement going on – that guys like Jimi Hendrix had changed things round and I wanted to be a part of whatever was developing out of that.

'Eddie signed us and introduced us to Phonogram, so we recorded a few songs for them. The Coach House only turned into a studio once Eddie had bought some equipment from Manfred Mann, who had a place in the Old Kent Road. The studio just evolved around us, and at the same time we were playing at all the universities. We weren't doing the reggae clubs, and those students loved the Fender guitar, the fuzz box and our whole approach. That's where we belonged. After a lot of our gigs, we'd thank the audience and invite Eddie on stage with us as an encore. I think that's where he got the buzz from to get back into the whole thing, because he was a guitar man, too.'

Back in Jamaica, the Wailers were kept busy throughout September recording tracks at Dynamic, Harry J and Randy's. They'd been rehearsing the tracks in London and so the recordings came together relatively quickly. Blackwell had advanced them £4,000 to make the album and wasn't too concerned that Bob Marley's solo 'Reggae On Broadway' single had flopped. That's because Island was home to rock and folk acts like Traffic, Cat Stevens, John Martyn and Nick Drake, who sold albums, rather than singles. The audience for reggae had expanded since *The Harder They Come*, and in Blackwell's opinion the Wailers were well-placed to capitalise on the cultural shift taking place. In addition to the Barrett brothers, they used musicians like Robbie Shakespeare, Gladdy Anderson, Reggie 'Alva' Lewis, Winston Wright, drummer 'Sparrow' Martin and the Lewis brothers from Inner Circle. Bunny played bass on 'Midnight Ravers', and Marcia Griffiths and Bob's wife, Rita, sang backing vocals on one or two tracks, including 'Rock It Baby.' There were other tracks recorded at the same sessions that didn't make the final cut – 'All Day And All Night' and 'High Tide Or Low Tide', for example. Both are love songs, written with half an eye on future chart success, which may well have swayed Chris Blackwell's decision to omit them.

Robbie Shakespeare was asked to play bass on 'Concrete Jungle' and 'Stir It Up', but had a hard time convincing people that it was him and not Family Man playing on those songs.

'I used to play like Family Man,' he admitted, 'and then when I play on 'Concrete Jungle', it took us a whole day to figure out which one of us would be better playing on that song! That's when

I decided to change my style a little, but a lot of people never liked it at first. They said it was too jazzy, which was probably true, but I liked it that way. I never knew it then, but it's my sound. It has melody like Family Man, but then after a while I start playing melody lines along with the singer, and I also take into consideration whether it's drum and bass or just rhythm alone. That means if you take out the vocal you can still have a wicked rhythm to dance to, and you don't miss the vocal. I start more thinking on those lines.'

The sound had changed at Randy's since the Wailers recorded there with Lee Perry. Vincent Chin had taken the console to record a concert by Bishop Gibson and the K. C. choir, and it was never the same again.

'It was one Rassclaat mission to get back that sound,' said Clive Chin. 'You can imagine them just taking the equipment there as a good deed, except when they brought it back to the studio they couldn't find that deep bass sound. That's what had inspired Lee Perry to move on and build the Black Ark and then, right after that, we upgraded it to sixteen-track and get the 1-inch tape.'

'Randy's was the focal point of Jamaica's music scene at that point, because if we produced our little records individually, we could always sell Miss Pat a couple of boxes,' recalls Junior Dan, who played bass, guitar, melodica, percussion and even drums on sessions at Randy's. 'People from England would come there looking for new products, so all the musicians, the singers, the soundmen and producers would be hanging in that area. Being there was a real experience. You'd leave your house to go down there and there wasn't much money, so sometimes you'd walk into the market to buy a slice of pudding or something. You had to live a real life. You had to live with the people and not like you were some big star.'

Junior's band Generation Gap played on Jimmy London's *Bridge Over Troubled Water* album at Randy's Studio 17, and that's also where Dennis Brown recorded 'Cheater' and 'Meet Me At The Corner.' Alton Ellis passed through also, and voiced a hit version of the Cornelius Brothers' 'Too Late To Turn Back Now' that he remembered as being fun.

'It was a side session. Randy asked me to do two tracks and I played keyboards on that one. Leroy Sibbles played the bass and a Heptones played guitar. We got a drummer, I think it was Horsemouth, but the rhythm guitar on 'Too Late' was a cheese grater and that make the record sound so exciting, I tell you! Those were the creative days of reggae, because we used to have to mic up everything back then.'

Clive Chin was there for that session, and admits that the attention-grabbing surge of reverb heard in Ellis's song wasn't intentional.

'It was a mistake I made! When we were doing the final mix of that, it was a Sunday evening and Errol Thompson and myself were there. 'Too Late' was running from the multi-track down to the two-track quarter inch tape, and I'd been burning a spliff. I was leaning on the board, feeling nice, and I just pull on some blood-claat level through being fidgety and give it full reverb! The reverb was already set, but I just push it up more on account of this spliff, then just pull it back down really quick. I was listening to it on a big monitor and get the fright of my life!'

Niney the Observer's latest single was 'Beard Man Feast', and whilst it was unlikely to challenge Lorna Bennett's 'Breakfast In Bed' or Scotty's answer version 'Skanking In Bed' on the charts, it was a topic that gave rise to some heated discussion, as Bunny Lee explained.

'When Michael Manley started his campaign and the PNP came to power, that's when the Rastas came forward and Tony Spaulding and some other men show how rootsy them is. That's the way they got more votes, so he could build up them garrison. You have some very decent Rastafarians, whereas there were others we'd call "beard man." If you call some man a dread him might get vexed with you, because he sees that as a dreadful thing. Some murderers grow beards to hide from the police, but more time it was decent Rastafarians who get the blame. For instance, Woppy King was a

Rastaman but he used to go out at night time and kill people, y'understand? That's why the real Rastamen, they would call him a beard man.'

U-Roy was still in London at this point, and was the headline act at the Grand Rastafarian Ball, hosted by the Ethiopian World Federation, in Woodland Hall, Acton, late in September. Rico's band Undivided backed him, and the stage was memorably draped with green, gold and red. It was the first-ever public event presented by a Rastafarian organisation in the UK, and certainly wouldn't be the last.

In early October, Michael and Beverley Manley attended the seventh Heads of Government Conference of Commonwealth Caribbean Countries in Trinidad, where Beverley created a stir with her Afro, and her husband cajoled Barbados, Guyana and Trinidad into siding with Jamaica by agreeing to establish diplomatic relations with Cuba. This was in direct opposition to American foreign policy, which sought to isolate Communist Cuba from the rest of the Caribbean and the world. There would be repercussions, of course, but Manley's new government was still enjoying its honeymoon phase, and his followers were no doubt delighted.

The same day all that took place, Slim Smith was battling his demons, imbibing too much alcohol and smoking herb. When he got back to his parents' home later that evening, they were out, and he couldn't find the key. In his frustration he broke a window, badly lacerating his arm. He then slumped to the ground where he tragically slowly bled to death. The 24-year-old singer had a history of mental illness, and had previously spent time in Bellevue sanatorium. At his passing, a chill seemed to pass through the reggae fraternity. Both radio stations played tributes to him all the next day, and there wasn't a sound system on the island that didn't play a Slim Smith selection in his memory. His absence cast a shadow over the Grand Musical Spectacular at the Ward Theatre a few days later, where Delroy Wilson, Ken Boothe, Dennis Brown and Horace Andy all performed, backed by the band The In Crowd.

Trojan had only recently released Smith's latest album, *Just A Dream* – a collection of Bunny Lee productions that included 'Blinded By Love', 'Never Let Go', 'Closer Together', the title track, 'I Need Your Loving' and a cut of Jimmy Holiday's 'Turning Point' that was guaranteed to send shivers down the spine.

Lloyd Charmers had known Slim Smith since the latter was singing with the Uniques, and when he wasn't playing for laughs with the Lowbites, he was demonstrating his qualities as a producer of high class reggae music, as demonstrated on Ken Boothe's latest album, *Boothe Unlimited*, and the singles 'Ain't No Sunshine' and 'Is It Because I'm Black' both of which were outstanding. Ken was no songwriter, but his interpretations of those Bill Withers and Syl Johnson hits were first rate. Meanwhile, Johnny Nash's 'I Can See Clearly Now' was at number one in America, having ousted Chuck Berry's 'My Ding A Ling' from the top slot. It was the first ever reggae record to reach number one in the US and there were already rumours going around that Bob Marley and not Johnny Nash – the credited author – wrote it. In Nash's defence, it's strange to think that Marley could write a song like 'I Can See Clearly Now' without any references to it or demo recordings having emerged. We should therefore give Nash the benefit of the doubt and trust that he was visited by angels on that one occasion, as it's difficult to find another hit song that he's written.

On 1 November, Larry McDonald's group played a show in Kingston and their special guest was Jamaican poet Allan Hope, otherwise known as Mutabaruka.

'That was the first time Muta appeared live with a band reciting his poetry,' Larry says. 'The poem he recites on my album was one of the poems he read back then. In 1972 I had a band called Truth. There were four drummers in that group, and I got him, and two of the guys from the Mystic Revelations of Rastafari, Bongo Herman and Marjorie Wylie, who was the director for the National Dance Theatre in Jamaica. I had two drum sets – one for Carl McCloud, who is probably one of the finest jazz drummers to have ever come out of Jamaica. He was the drummer on the Don Drummond hit 'Don Cosmic', and the other drummer was Sly Dunbar, who everybody knows. That was the line-up in the studio on the first day.'

Mutabaruka means 'he who is always victorious' in Rwandan. He grew up in Rae Town, Kingston and was raised as a Roman Catholic, but was writing poems containing social commentary even before studying electronics at Kingston Technical High School and then working for the Jamaica Telephone Company. It was shortly afterwards that the former Allan Hope became Mutabaruka, changing his diet, ceasing the combing of his hair and embracing Rastafari. He was one of a group of radical poets championed by university lecturer Mervyn Morris, whom Muta has credited with legitimising their work, which was written and delivered in the raw Jamaican patois heard in the streets. Larry couldn't remember which poems Mutabaruka recited that day, but in 1972 his most recent included 'Retrieve', which contains a wonderful description of kumina dancing.

When the movie *Screaming Target*, starring Oliver Reed and Jill St John, was shown at the Carib and Harbour View cinemas in late 1972, the accompanying advertising stated that, 'killing was a very old fashioned word for what Harry had in mind.' *Screaming Target* was also the title of Big Youth's debut album, produced by Gussie Clarke – an orphan who'd had to fend for himself from early, and was just 18 years old.

'Gussie grew up in the neighbourhood where I come from,' Big Youth told Steve Milne. 'He was a youth from school. Remember that I say, "Wednesday gone I went to the Carib and I saw this movie?" Well, when *Screaming Target* came about it was all about Clint Eastwood, but if you notice I was telling you that this guy's ranker than Dirty Harry. This one's called *Screaming Target*. It was a whole gun show thing, and this guy was firing shots wickeder than Eastwood, man. It was just hyping and then within the song now, through poverty, a lot of people don't have no education so I was telling people that they're not supposed to be illiterate. They must go to literate places and get civilised. That song, it wasn't all

135

about the movie. It was about civilisation and people fe learn education and have sense and be sensible and don't be a fool.'

There had been a glut of Big Youth singles for other producers released throughout the year – 'Tell It Black', 'Phil Pratt Thing', 'S90 Skank' and 'Chi Chi Run' among them – but Gussie Clarke wouldn't be denied. Three of the album tracks had already appeared on 7-inch, including 'The Killer' and the title track. Most popular of all was 'Tippertone Rocking', which was a tribute to the inner city sound system where Big Youth learnt his craft and first earned his unassailable reputation.

Gussie has claimed that Big Youth's debut was unique in that it was recorded, mixed and manufactured in record time.

'Big Youth was just coming on the scene at that point,' he told me, 'and his album *Screaming Target* should be in the *Guinness Book Of Records* because it was recorded and manufactured within twenty-four hours! We recorded all of the tracks at Dynamic Sounds. It was edited by Sid Bucknor, we mastered it that same night, printed the sleeves and then it went straight into the UK because I left for England the very next day. It was phenomenal.'

Whilst on the subject of world-beaters, heavyweight champion boxer Joe Frazier and challenger George Foreman were in Jamaica to sign the contracts for their 15-round bout, due to take place at the National Stadium in January 1973. The signing ceremony was held at the House Of Chen on Knutsford Boulevard, and the owners couldn't have been more proud. 'The House Of Chen – superlative Chinese and Oriental cuisine, luncheons and dinners. It only looks expensive!' bragged the publicity material. It's not often that world heavyweight title fights were staged outside of the US, principally because Americans have dominated the division. In fact, there hadn't been a world heavyweight title fight held outside of the USA since 1966. Foreman wasn't happy with the decision to bring the fight to Jamaica; it was also scheduled to take place on 22 January, which was the very same day that his pregnant wife was expecting to give birth.

American guitarist Eric Gale first visited Jamaica in 1966 with Johnny Nash. His parents were from Barbados and he trained as a chemist before becoming a musician – guitar was always his speciality, but he could also play bass, trombone and tenor sax. By the time he landed in Montego Bay and paid Jamaica a return visit towards the end of 1972, he had an unbelievable CV as a session guitarist, having played with the likes of Aretha Franklin, Nina Simone, Marvin Gaye and Quincy Jones.

'You must be a good reader of music and people,' he said, when Dermot Hussey asked what it takes to mix in such exalted company. 'You must be a good diplomat, and you must keep your mouth shut.'

Eric had recently left his role as Roberta Flack's musical director, having signed an album deal with CTI, and was looking forward to working on solo material.

'My next album is going to surprise a lot of people,' he promised. 'They won't know what to do with it. They won't be able to categorise it. I'll use reggae on some of the tracks and it will wipe them out. Man, you should hear the sounds I have in my head.'

Scenes from the forthcoming James Bond film *Live And Let Die* were being filmed in Ocho Rios and Montego Bay as he'd arrived. The locations were stunning, of course, but Jamaica had also become world-famous for its music, and there was no genre so fresh and exciting as reggae right then. Ernie Smith had just won the Yamaha Music Festival in Tokyo with 'Life Is Just For Livin'', and when Joe Higgs won the Jamaica Tourist Board's Tourism Song Competition with 'Invitation To Jamaica' at the Regal Theatre, he was paraded around the packed auditorium amidst wild applause. It took some time before he could be returned to the stage, where Prime Minister Michael Manley handed him a cheque for JA$1,000 and gave him a congratulatory kiss on the cheek, to roars of delight from the audience. Joe also received the promise of an all-expenses-paid trip to New York, and an invitation to audition for the world famous William Morris Talent Agency.

All of that was happening when members of the The Rolling Stones arrived in Jamaica in late November. Keith Richards had first visited the island in 1969, holidaying at Frenchman's Cove. This time he and the Stones were in Jamaica to record a new album and, he said, 'the place was blooming.'

'The Wailers were signed to Island Records, Marley was just sprouting his locks and Jimmy Cliff was in the cinemas with *The Harder They Come*,' Keith wrote in his 2010 autobiography, *Life*. 'There were plenty of gunmen in Kingston and the town was rife with an exotic form of energy; a very hot feeling, much of which was coming from the infamous Byron Lee's Dynamic Sounds. It was built like a fortress, with a white picket fence outside as it appears in the film.'

The Stones were said to be at a low ebb after their 1972 album *Exile On Main St*, but Keith especially enjoyed the experience.

'Our way of doing things changed while we were recording, and slowly I became more and more Jamaican to the point where I didn't leave. Dynamic Sound was an amazing place: the drum kits and amps were nailed to the floor. The album itself didn't take that long, but we recorded an awful lot of tracks. There were not only Jamaicans involved, but also percussion players who came from places like Guyana; a travelling pool of guys who worked in the studios there. It was interesting to be playing in this totally different atmosphere. Geoffrey Chung, the engineer at Dynamic for example, was a Chinese man. You realise how much Jamaica is a multi-racial environment.'

Dynamic's 16-track board was the first of its kind in Jamaica, whilst the Yamaha piano, limiters, microphones and echo units were of a high standard. Jimmy Miller – one of two engineers the Stones brought with them – said the sessions went really well, and were 'probably the easiest I remember with the Stones. The studio in Jamaica was just right, and the sound in the room was perfect.'

Nicky Hopkins, the Stones' piano player, disagreed. He didn't like Jamaica, and called Kingston 'one of the dirtiest, poorest places in the world. It really depressed me. We worked at Dynamic right through every night and it wasn't brilliant, but it was all right, considering. We were there two and a half weeks and I was really glad to get out. They stayed on for another week and Billy Preston went down to work with them.'

By the time Billy Preston joined them in mid-December, Mick Jagger had flown to Europe for damage limitation talks after French police had issued arrest warrants for Keith and his partner Anita Pallenberg. The other Stones had been wrongly implicated in the drug-related charges and there was much to discuss. Meanwhile, Mick's wife Bianca was back home in London with the flu, although the couple were hoping to return to Jamaica in the New Year.

When asked how the Stones had managed to slip into Jamaica virtually unnoticed, Jagger said they'd worn wigs and used false names. He was joking, of course – whilst most Jamaicans would have heard of them, news of their arrival hadn't caused that much interest, not like when Nina Simone had visited back in the summer. Jagger was also asked if the Stones were thinking of performing in Jamaica, and he expressed doubts that their music would be accepted there, although he did say that the whole group loved reggae, and it was the only music in England that he could really enjoy dancing to.

'Reggae is very interesting,' Keith told a Jamaican news outlet, 'but we won't be playing it. We love it, and we like dancing to it, but we believe that you Jamaicans play it a lot better than we do, and really there is nothing that we have to offer to reggae.'

This may explain why fans would search in vain for reggae influences on the album that resulted from their time at Dynamic, named after a local delicacy, *Goat's Head Soup*. The only hit from it was 'Angie' – a ballad, no less – but the rest of the album proved largely forgettable, even for Stones' aficionados. The one real positive to come out of their trip was Keith Richards falling in love with the country. He and Anita had brought their children Angie and Marlon with them and after the album was finished they all headed for Mammee Bay, on the north coast midway between Ocho Rios and St Ann's Bay. Anita was allegedly rude to some of their neighbours and the local police, and so was thrown in jail for a short time 'as punishment for ignoring their warnings', according to Keith. She and Keith had been renting a house, Casa Joya, from local entrepreneur Ernie Smatt, who then showed them round Tommy Steele's home Point Of View which was situated on a small cliff overlooking the bay, and had been designed by Italian architect Giuseppe 'Pino' Maffessanti.

'During the day you get the breeze off the sea from the front, which overlooks the harbour,' writes Keith. ' At six o'clock in the evening the breeze changes and comes down from the mountain. He had it shaped so the cool breeze comes down past the kitchen from the land. It's a brilliant piece of architecture and I got it for eighty grand.'

In authentic rock star fashion he paid cash for it too. Allegedly.

CHAPTER FOUR

1973: THE HIGHER THE MOUNTAIN

1972 had been a good year for Jamaican entertainment. Ernie Smith had won an international Song Festival in Japan; reggae had topped the American charts for four successive weeks; there'd been endorsement from the likes of Paul Simon, The Rolling Stones and Staples Singers; Jamaica had celebrated its first locally made full-length film and there'd been three mammoth shows held on the lawns of Jamaica House since Michael Manley had been elected prime minister. Big Youth was hailed as the greatest sensation since U-Roy, whilst Dennis Brown was the island's most popular singer, and was now gaining fans overseas after his recent shows in Canada. He'd had three awards in '72 from the *Record Retailer*, *El Suzie A Go Go* and *Swing Magazine*; sung on the same bill as Nina Simone at the National Arena and had girls screaming for him everywhere he went. In September he had five singles on the local charts and virtually everything he released was a hit, including 'Cheater', 'Black Magic Woman', 'Concentration', 'Lips Of Wine', 'Let Love In', 'What About The Half' and the Studio One singles 'Make It Easy On Yourself', 'Easy Take It Easy' and 'If I Follow My Heart.' It's hard to remember sometimes that 'the Boy Wonder' was only 15 and still at school.

But all anybody was talking about in January was the 'Sunshine

Showdown' between heavyweight champion Joe Frazier and George Foreman, booked for the 22nd. Both boxers arrived in Jamaica at the beginning of the month, and the media attention was intense. Foreman arrived later than expected after he'd discovered that he wouldn't be able to bring his dog with him, then the day after he landed his wife Adrienne gave birth to their daughter. He and his entourage were staying at the Skyline Hotel, whereas Frazier stayed at the Sheraton, where the pre-fight weigh-in happened on 15 January. Frazier was the favourite for the fight, but Foreman won a lot of local support from those who'd seen him train that week. People had been questioning whether Frazier had sufficiently recovered from his fight with Ali ten months earlier and how Foreman, who had a 10lb weight advantage, possessed a sledgehammer left jab and could in all probability hit Frazier harder than anyone he had faced in any of his previous fights. Foreman was slower and would definitely be easier to hit than Frazier, who had a vicious left hook. He'd been throwing them several at a time in training with near perfection – and I dare say with relentless fury.

The Staples Singers had finished their trio of shows at the Regal Theatre the night before the fight. There were lengthy queues outside the National Stadium as the 36,000 capacity crowd took their seats, and over a million closed-circuit television viewers tuned in. Ernie Smith, Judy Mowatt, the Chosen Few and Clancy Eccles entertained the crowd beforehand, backed by Inner Circle, and the fight began at 10 p.m. Anyone expecting another fifteen-round marathon would have been disappointed, as the referee stopped the fight just over a minute into the second round. Foreman had floored Frazier six times by then – three times in each round – in a display of near brutal savagery. It was an annihilation, and at no time did Frazier look able to withstand the thunderous rights and lefts of his younger challenger, who attacked him mercilessly from the start. There was no stopping his fury and he destroyed Frazier, who had won all his previous fights – twenty-five of them by knockout. Before leaving for home the next day, Foreman told the press that 'the cheers of the Jamaican people went through my veins and I couldn't let them down.' He also promised to return with his family for a vacation, whereas Frazier said very little, as you might expect.

Big Youth had spent time with Frazier and his entourage – including sparring partner Ken Norton – during their stay in Jamaica. He had praised Joe Frazier on his 1972 single 'The Big Fight', but then had to recant on the follow-up, 'Foreman Vs Frazier', after Foreman had won the heavyweight title. Both were produced by Joe Gibbs, and voiced on the same cut of Burning Spear's 'He Prayed.' Big Youth couldn't put a foot wrong at the time, but there were few lyrics in either of those songs. His attempt to imitate the action – 'biff 'n baff 'n boof' – stood out, but little else did, in truth.

We don't know if any of the Rolling Stones attended the fight, but the band was still in Jamaica and had been joined by other rock stars, including Elton John, then celebrating his first US number one hit, 'Crocodile Rock.' Paul Rodgers, vocalist with Free, went there on holiday and recorded a song called 'I Just Want To See You Smile', and whilst Cat Stevens didn't stay long after he arrived in late January, he was expected back on the island within the next few weeks.

'Reggae, Reggae, Reggae' was the headline on the cover of the *Sunday Times Magazine* in the UK on 4 February. Inside was a report on sound systems, reggae and the culture of West Indians in London by Colin McGlashan, who wrote how 'a top sound system is thirty to 100 times as powerful as a domestic hi-fi.

'The point isn't volume, but the amplification of the bass until it sounds like the world's biggest drum... until it becomes music you can *feel*. You feel it in your feet, in the vibrations of a Coke tin with an unlicensed shot of scotch inside, you feel it through your partner's body. The first time you hear it it's unbelievable, unbearable... oh my God! But you get used to it. You grow numb through that and there's a cool, cool joy, a sedative high. Ice in the spine. No pain.'

On 8 February, *The Harder They Come* opened in New York at two cinemas simultaneously, the New Embassy in Times Square and the 86th Street Playhouse, between Second and Third Avenues, with Jimmy Cliff himself in attendance. Perry Henzell's film had already won a major prize at the Cork Film Festival. After *The Harder They Come* was shown in Los Angeles, the *LA Times* lauded Jimmy Cliff's performance as 'magnetic' and said that he was 'clearly a major talent.' The film was described as 'nothing short of amazing', whilst the *Hollywood Reporter* referred to it as 'a major cinematic event not to be overlooked.'

Bob Marley was in New York while all this was happening. He'd spent time in London first, where he put finishing touches to the Wailers' new album. John 'Rabbit' Bundrick had added keyboards, and since Marley was still enamoured with the idea of adding rock guitar to a couple of tracks, Chris Blackwell obliged by introducing him to American guitarist Wayne Perkins. Once the album was complete he then left for New York and a meeting with Danny Sims, whereupon Marley demanded to be released from his contractual demands with JAD. A deal was struck, and when Traffic played at the New York Academy of Music – supported by Free and John Martyn – during the second week of February, Marley watched from the wings. It was at an after-party that the Wailers' de facto manager, Dickie Jobson, introduced Marley to American artist and filmmaker Lee Jaffe and Jamaican actor Esther Anderson, who'd recently starred in *A Warm December* with Sidney Poitier.

'*The Harder They Come* had come out in New York by then and in my world it was like an underground hit,' says Lee Jaffe. 'It was playing at the Elgin Theatre at midnight and whilst Bob wasn't in that movie, he personified what it was about. But I just wanted everyone to hear that cassette. Also, Bob was so amazingly charismatic in such a humble sort of way that you just wanted to be around him. You just felt like this guy was so special, but without the ego, and that was part of his attraction.

'I immediately bonded with him and took him to meet some of

my friends in New York, including some of the biggest art dealers in New York. I played harmonica and he played guitar, I brought him to jam with some of my friends, including Dickie Landry, who was a brilliant musician and part of the original Philip Glass ensemble. I introduced him to all of these musicians and took him around so he could jam with people and smoke herb. Then, after a while, Chris wanted to take him back to Jamaica so that he could start rehearsing, because he needed to tour in support of *Catch A Fire*. I took him to 48th Street, where there were all these music stores. It was incredible, because you saw people who were buying their first instrument, rubbing shoulders with musicians like Carlos Santana. That's when I helped Bob pick out that Les Paul. I thought that was the perfect guitar for him, because it had this great tone, and it was thin enough and light enough so he could move around on stage with it. It was definitely his guitar.'

Lee and Esther ended up returning to Jamaica with Bob and Chris Blackwell, and were invited to stay at Island House on Hope Road. If he hadn't done so already, Blackwell would soon add Lorna Bennett, Joe Higgs and Toots and the Maytals to the Island Records' roster. Toots' latest hit was the foot stomping 'Funky Kingston', which was also the title track of his latest album for Dynamic.

'It was Chris Blackwell who gave me the idea to write that one,' said Toots. 'He said, "Toots, there is this this song called 'Funky Nassau', so can you write a song about Kingston?" I go away and write 'Funky Kingston', which became another of my number one songs.'

Island, meanwhile, released Jimmy Cliff's album, *Struggling Man*. Songs like 'Let's Seize The Time', 'Come On People', 'Better Days Are Coming' and 'Struggling Man' itself left us in no doubt of his social conscience. He had been outlining such concerns, as well as playing music, during his two week stint on RJR's *GMM Show* which aired early every weekday morning in late February. RJR advertised his appearances by using a quote taken from the liner notes of *The Harder They Come* soundtrack album.

145

'Every day hundreds of kids flock into the slums of Kingston from the hillsides of Jamaica, drawn by the promise of the transistor, and sure that they can get it if they really want. Jimmy Cliff was one of those kids and that dream is still at the roots of his music. Nevertheless, in Jimmy's case it can be further stated that his dream came true.'

American journalist Maureen Orth quoted from Jimmy's song 'The Harder They Come' in an article for *Newsweek*: 'Jamaican Rock – big sound on US Pop Scene.' After tracing the music's origins and subsequent development, she noted how reggae was still being frowned upon by many upper- and middle-class Jamaicans.

'These people, who are English-orientated in their speech, dress and manners, find the music uncouth in its use of patois and a dangerous influence on the increasing social unrest and tension between the islands poor and affluent,' she wrote. 'They worry because their children listen to the popular disc jockeys who talk about freedom and play reggae songs like the one by Jimmy Cliff.'

On 21 February, P. J. Patterson, the minister of industry and tourism, welcomed Miriam Makeba to Jamaica and paid tribute to her struggle for the recognition and dignity of her South African people, as well as the excellence of her art. He pointed out that Manley's government had made contributions to the African Freedom Fighters Fund, and revoked an order dating from 1967 that prohibited Makeba's husband, Stokeley Carmichael, from entering Jamaica. At a press conference the following day, Makeba was asked whether she was sympathetic to her husband's work. She replied saying that she was not on her husband's staff and only a fool married someone whose ideas were not similar to their own. She was booked to do four shows – one at the Palladium Theatre in Montego Bay, followed by two shows at the Regal Theatre and then another in the Sheraton Hotel's Independence Ballroom.

'Miriam Makeba, in her forty-five minute performance, captivated the audience with her touching explanations, a demonstration of Xosa clicking pronunciations and a number of songs done in her controlled, yet very pleasant style,' reported the *Gleaner*. 'She sang 'I Shall Sing' and 'The Click Song', told the story of the South African miners "working for just $18 a month", and did an original composition by her bassist Bill Soltar, who'd started writing it in the Congo and then finished it in Jamaica during his and Miriam's first visit there in 1967. At the end of her performance, she received ear-splitting applause for nearly five minutes. She thrilled the large audience with a multi-talented display rarely ever seen on a stage in Jamaica.'

Unfortunately, the love and respect shown to 'the Empress of African Song' would not extend beyond Jamaican shores, as she recounts in her autobiography *Makeba – My Story*.

'When I arrive on the island of Jamaica for a concert, at first I am glad to find an airport where there are no FBI agents to trail me, and the concerts go very well. In the audience is Dudley Thompson, a Cabinet minister in the government of Prime Minister Manley who knew me from a time when we were in Kenya together. But when my musicians and I go to the airport to return to the US, I am not permitted to board. I am shocked. Why? What has happened? The agent is very cool. You do not have a visa. For many years I have travelled on a Tanzanian passport, and because I am not a citizen of the US, I obtain the necessary visas to go into and out of the country. But things have changed and I tell them, "but I am married to a US citizen." This does no good. I send my musicians on their way, and I go to Dudley Thompson's house. He agrees to put me up, and after I drop off my bags I go to see the American ambassador. I sit and sit, but the ambassador will not see me. When I do not go away, he comes out of his office at last, but he will not talk to me. He will not even look at me. Instead, he says to his secretary in a very nasty voice, "tell her I'm not giving her a visa." The ambassador goes back into his office and slams the door. I go to Mr Thompson's house and called Stokely. He is furious. He says he's coming down right away. The first thing he does is contact the people he knows in the Congressional Black Caucus in Washington. They are also made angry by my treatment. He checks to see if Prime Minister Manley has lifted the ban that kept him from entering Jamaica, which is a British Commonwealth country. This has been done, so Stokely takes the plane down and meets me. By this time the American newspapers have gotten wind of my problem. The stories say, "Miriam Makeba blocked in Jamaica." The press stories are making an embarrassment, and the Congressional Black Caucus is putting on pressure but the American ambassador tells Stokely, "I'm still not giving her a visa." My husband just smiles. He is so cool. "Fine. I'm going to spend the whole weekend here, in Jamaica." We leave. Stokely being on the island makes the ambassador nervous. Many officials in America are very paranoid about him. In Maryland, where Stokely was speaking just before Dr King was shot, the governor there, a man named Spiro Agnew, is blaming Stokely for inciting the black people to riot in the city of Baltimore. It is as if the assassination of Dr King had nothing to do with what the people did. We get a call at Mr Thompson's house. The American embassy is closed, but the ambassador wants us to come over right away. He looks uncomfortable when he speaks to Stokely. "Well, you know, your wife can have a visa, and you can leave anytime you want." Stokely just sits back and laughs. "I'm glad to hear that my wife can go back but you see, I've decided I want to stay. I have a lot of meetings here with the people, and a lot of folks I want to see." The ambassador looks wretched when we leave, because Stokely won't go, and I get to enjoy the island for a few days until my husband is ready to go home.'

At the beginning of March, Chris Blackwell and a few friends – Bob Marley and Esther Anderson included – decided to visit Trinidad for the Carnival and go island hopping. During the return trip they were all placed under house arrest in Haiti by gun-wielding Tonton Macoute, as they'd landed there without permission. Bob and Esther became separated from the others, and when they finally got back on the plane, the aggrieved pair began writing a song urging listeners to action called 'Get Up Stand Up.' Bob also wrote 'I Shot The Sheriff' soon after returning from Trinidad and with a line about planting and then killing a seed said to have been a reference to Esther's insistence on taking birth control pills, since she and Bob had started a relationship by this time.

Catch A Fire wouldn't be released for another few weeks, but the Wailers were already writing songs for their next album, which had the working title of *Reincarnated Souls*. They also needed to find a keyboard player, since Winston Wright couldn't be prised from the Dynamic All Stars and the two keyboard players that the band sometimes used – Bernard 'Touter' Harvey and Tyrone Downie – weren't considered old enough yet to accompany them on tour.

They chose Now Generation's Earl Lindo instead. Also known as 'Wya', he'd played on lots of notable studio sessions at Treasure Isle and Federal, and studied theory and composition at the Jamaica School Of Music. Wya had flourished under the guiding hand of Now Generation's Geoffrey Chung, and been expanding his musical horizons by listening to rock groups like Yes, who incorporated symphonic grandeur and sweeping, jazz-like improvisations into their music.

'Geoffrey was a strong leader,' said Wya. 'He was someone I looked up to and he knew some big chords, I tell you! Geoffrey played like Fifth Dimension, who I would say were the ultimate back then because of their time signatures and all the chord changes. Very few musicians could play like that, but we got over-exposed after a while. We became *exhausted*, but there were good things happening, too, because Dennis Brown was our lead singer and we played on a lot of his hits from that era.'

Wya had been a fan of the Wailers ever since hearing Bob Marley's voice wafting out of King Tubby's speaker boxes singing 'Rock My Boat.' He especially liked the songs they made with Lee 'Scratch'

Perry, and already knew Peter Tosh from sessions they'd played on together at Treasure Isle.

'I used to see Bob at a distance, after he came to one of our shows. He was like a soul rebel and he'd make these signs to me, showing me that he liked what I was doing. He was a big star to me, but I could see that Peter was different from the other two, right from the beginning. He was the breakaway Wailer who always wanted to have his own style from a long time back. Bunny and Bob, they were more into soul music, whereas the stuff that Peter played, you never heard it anywhere else.

'The other two Wailers wouldn't talk or smile a lot, and when they were in a crowd, you couldn't make them out. They'd be sat round a chalice and you can't even see one face! But those kinds of things impressed me, because Now Generation weren't like that. I saw the Wailers as hippies, and that's what attracted me to them really.'

Marcia Griffiths, meanwhile, was operating at the other end of the scale, wearing sophisticated outfits and performing as a cabaret artist in Kingston's upmarket clubs and hotels. Her favourite singers at that time included Aretha Franklin, Nancy Wilson, Carla Thomas and Patti Labelle, whose song 'Down The Aisle' had become her calling card when first meeting Bob Andy and the Paragons back in 1964. Showcasing her talents in a cabaret setting gave her the opportunity to not only look glamorous, but also to sing the same kind of material as those artists who'd originally inspired her.

Her latest single was 'Sweet Bitter Love', a Van McCoy song earlier recorded by Aretha Franklin on her album *Take A Look*. Lloyd Charmers was the producer, but Bob Andy's jealousy and his mounting frustrations regarding his own solo ambitions proved to be something of a hindrance at first.

'Marcia Griffiths was his woman at the time, and he was having a go at me, saying to her, 'yuh nuh sing nah bloodclaat tune fi 'im', said Charmers. He was laughing as he related that story, because the relationship between the three of them greatly improved thereafter, and they became the best of friends.

Charmers had a licensing deal with Trojan and he'd also been working with Ken Boothe, whose latest album was *Black, Gold And Green*. Bob Andy wrote the liner notes and, as you'd expect, they were very articulate.

'As I followed Ken's career, I began to consider his singing as being in the same kind of soul groove as the late, great Otis Redding. Ken's tradition though, is based in the powerful religious messages reflected in the native Jamaican religion of Pocomania, and these roots have grown to produce the greatest Jamaican pop singer of our day – an opinion I hold along with many others. I had written a song called 'I Don't Want To See You Cry', and one day Ken approached me about recording it. It seemed the perfect song for him and I was delighted when it became so very successful.'

Several of the tracks were repeated from previous albums, but 'Black, Gold And Green' itself, written by Ken, was something of a departure as it was a song of hope and nationhood, and referenced the colours of the Jamaican flag. The land of wood and water is also the land of Rastafari, and the presence of nyahbinghi drumming on 'Inna Di Yard' was therefore only fitting. But then, Ken had always been a conscious person, even if he didn't have dreadlocks.

'The hair is like a symbol, but what about the mind?' Boothe said. 'I don't follow the bandwagon, because it's the kind of person you are that's the key, really. There are so many people who wear dreadlocks like a fashion, and yet if you ask them about His Imperial Majesty, they don't know nothing about that! When they keep a nyahbinghi in Denham Town where I was born and raised, I always used to pass by there as a little youth and listen to the Rastaman's celebrations. Even the word "Babylon"... At one time, Rastaman would "fire bu'n the Queen" and "bu'n this and that", but to me that is stupidity. To me, Babylon is people who are not treating you good – someone who's trying to exploit you for their own benefit, because I don't fight people, I fight systems...'

Whilst it wasn't on the new album, Ken's latest single for Niney The Observer, 'Silver Words', was superb, and so too his cover of Syl Johnson's 'Is It Because I'm Black', which merited comparison to works by some of America's greatest soul singers. He, Delroy Wilson and B. B. Seaton had by then formed a group, the Messengers, with Busty Brown of the Chosen Few. This four-man team had agreed to record on one another's tracks and in different combinations, and to split the proceeds equally. With the exception of Brown, this was the same group of singers that had formed the Links collective a few years earlier – a bid for autonomy that major players within the local record industry, opposed to the idea of artists gaining control over their own destinies, had cruelly sabotaged.

Aside from his recordings with the Messengers, B. B. Seaton was concentrating on his solo career after the break-up of the Gaylads and had just released his debut solo album, *Thin Line Between Love And Hate*, named after the Persuaders' song. It was both too soon and unwise to denigrate such classy productions when there was a musical uprising taking place in Jamaica. The Wailers' *Catch A Fire* came out in mid-April and 'that one album changed everything, because all of a sudden there was a whole new audience for this music', David Rodigan remarked.

'It was a watershed, and I was absolutely delighted. I no longer cared what other people said, and I never shared the criticisms regarding the overdubs and slide guitar, because that's called production. Chris Blackwell realised what had to happen with the music, and he did it. He got some stick from the diehards, but he'd signed this band and wanted to promote them, so that's what he did. He believed in them, and made their music accessible to as big an audience as possible.'

The music was brilliant, of course, but the Zippo lighter cover design was also inspired and the marketing extremely effective. Island promoted the Wailers' debut album like they would a rock release, with advertising in the influential, mainstream music press and support from BBC radio and even television. The band's UK tour began towards the end of April, but it was their appearance on BBC2's *The Old Grey Whistle Test* that tipped the scales and introduced the Wailers to the rock audience.

'It would be very hard to exaggerate the extent to which reggae was despised among rock fans, so a job of conversion had to be done,' said Island A&R man Richard Williams. David Cavanagh, writing in *Good Night And Good Riddance: How Thirty-Five Years Of John Peel Helped To Shape Modern Life,* elaborated on this, stating, 'Reggae, to a rock fan in 1973, is music from another planet. It's a radically different way of approaching the bassline, the backbeat, the song format and the English language. To many rock fans, all reggae sounds the same. But to some reggae fans, and Chris Blackwell at Island is one of them, rock is the first frontier that needs to be crossed if reggae is to go international. At his insistence, the Wailers' first album for Island, *Catch A Fire,* has had extra keyboards and guitars added by white American session musicians. The hope is that audiences weaned on guitar solos and rock arrangements will find this conciliatory form of reggae agreeable to the palate, and they will then dive in and go searching for the harder stuff. Blackwell is under no illusions that the struggle to turn rock fans onto reggae will be an uphill one. Radio 1 refuses point blank to playlist the Wailers' new single 'Stir It Up', even though it playlisted Johnny Nash's pop version of it last year and Bob Marley wrote the song in the first place.'

Blues And Soul was the first music publication in the UK to feature Jamaican music on a regular basis. This was due almost entirely to the enthusiasm of Chris Lane, who pioneered reggae writing at a time when the music was either ridiculed or ignored by the white rock press. Chris reviewed one of the Wailers' shows during their four-day residency at London's Speakeasy between 15-18 May.

'It was at 1.50 a.m when the lights of the stage at London's Speakeasy club shone on the Wailers, who had just walked onto the stage. They started off with a Rastafarian chant entitled 'Rasta Man.' Bob Marley was singing the lead vocals and playing bongos, and the other guitarist/singer, Peter MacIntosh, was playing a very large, home-made Rasta drum with his maracas. Bunny Livingston, the other singer, was also playing bongos and the bass and drums of Aston and Carlton Barrett combined nicely, as always, with the organ of Earl Lindo.'

When Lane asked the band about Lee Perry, who he rated as 'Jamaica's best and most entertaining' producer, Bunny exclaimed that the island's producers were, 'all parasites who live off the artists they cheat.' This was why the artists were becoming their own promoters, because they were being used. The youths of Jamaica had now realised what was going on and they were going against these people. 'There is a wave of consciousness in Jamaica and reggae is part of it.'

If there was any further proof needed that the reggae genre wasn't just limited to one style but was, in fact, richly diverse, then Judge Dread provided it with his latest UK chart hit 'Big Eight', which was promptly banned because of a line suggesting that one of the characters in it had been playing 'with little boys.' It still made the Top 20 though, and Trojan also released his album *Dreadmania – It's All In The Mind*. As tracks like 'Ding A Ling', 'Donkey Dick' and 'The Biggest Bean You've Ever Seen' demonstrated, Judge Dread's whole schtick had more to do with British music hall and northern working men's club culture than anything else, yet he was well on his way to becoming one of the biggest-selling artists of the year in the UK, and without any airplay!

More discerning reggae fans would have been listening to the Royals' 'Pick Up The Pieces', produced by lead singer Roy Cousins, or Gregory Isaacs' 'All I Have Is Love', which was making girls swoon, and was the lanky 22-year-old's biggest hit to date. His delivery was quite mournful, and the way he expressed vulnerability in his songs was what set him apart. It lent his music a seductive

Rita Marley at 56 Hope Road © Lee Jaffe

Big Youth and admirers © Lee Jaffe

Robbie Shakespeare with spliff © Lee Jaffe

Aston "Family Man" Barrett © Lee Jaffe

David Hinds of Steel Pulse © Robert Landau

Peter Tosh the Bush Doctor © Lee Jaffe

Dennis Brown, former Boy Wonder © Werner Otto

Bob Marley on stage © Alamy

The Specials take a break © Trinity Mirror

Desmond Dekker © Pictorial Press

Bob Andy © Dave Hendley

The charismatic Bim Sherman © Dave Hendley

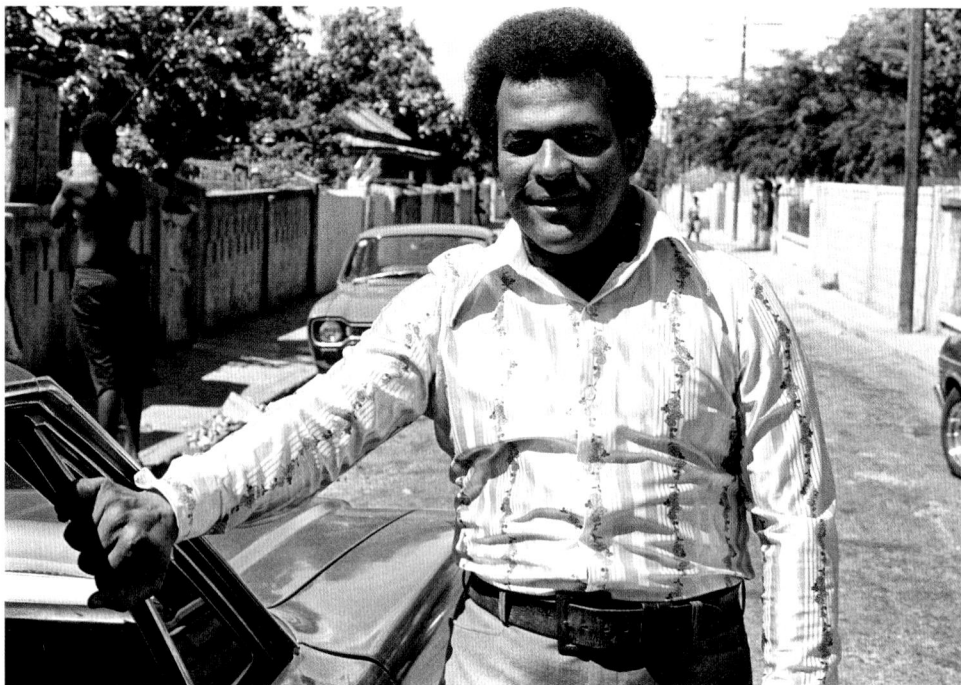

Bunny "Striker" Lee © Dave Hendley

Aswad at play © Mike Loveridge

quality that many women found irresistible, as heard on other recent singles like 'Loving Pauper' and 'Lonely Soldier.'

Isaacs grew up in West Kingston and was raised by his mother, whose singing around the house fostered his love of music, together with songs played on local radio.

'In those early days, I used to listen to a lot of rhythm and blues by singers like Sam Cooke, Otis Redding, the Drifters and the Platters – also Jamaican groups like the Paragons,' he told me. 'I'd just listen to any kind of music, from jazz and funk to the Mighty Sparrow. We'd listen to it mainly on the radio, and then we'd go and hear music in the dancehalls as well.'

During his teenage years, Isaacs trained as an electrician and cabinetmaker, in between practising the guitar and exploring the vibrant music scene happening all around him. Gregory lived in Denham Town, a ghetto community adjoining Trench Town where some of the island's best-known artists – including Marley, Peter Tosh and Delroy Wilson – still lived. After winning a talent show at the Queen's Theatre, he made his recording debut with 'Another Heartache', then joined the Concords, who voiced a handful of sides for Rupie Edwards. This arrangement proved short-lived, as Gregory had always thought of himself as a solo artist. He also ventured into production early on, after launching the African Museum label with Errol Dunkley. Gregory's 'My Only Lover' was a yearning tale of young love that quickly established his reputation for romantic heartbreak, whilst Errol's first for African Museum was 'Movie Star.'

'Me and Gregory Isaacs were the first two artists to really go out and produce ourselves,' Errol said. 'We used to use studios like Dynamics, which at that time was WIRL, and then Randy's when it was ran by Randy's brother Keith. Clive Chin and Errol Thompson were there too, 'cause Gregory and I used to put our money together, rent the studio and do a song or two. We used to pay the musicians and everyt'ing – ah so we used to work.'

Errol gave a cut of his 'Baby I Love You' rhythm to Gussie Clarke, who voiced U-Roy on it. That single was called 'The Higher The Mountain', and it was the first on the young producer's Gussie label.

'I've always been a creative person, coming up with ideas and looking for human resources that can assist me in delivering them,' Gussie said. 'I would save my lunch money to buy electrical parts because I had a technical bent and I made an amplifier, which I swapped with Errol Dunkley for a cut of that 'Baby I Love You' rhythm. From there I began importing foreign records into Jamaica, which I sold to all the top sound-systems, and I bought a dub machine from Duke Reid at Treasure Isle and cut dubs upstairs at the house where I was in Church Street. We were doing so good that nearly every record producer in Jamaica took their two-track tapes and gave them to me so that I could sell them to the sound-systems as dub-plates. It was like I became the promotional arm of the music in Jamaica at that time, and even abroad, because that's when I also started exporting records to shops in England and New York.'

Dub plates were in demand, and not just among sound system owners, because members of the public would call into the Aquarius record shop at Half Way Tree and ask Herman Chin Loy for them. He recognised that there was a market for dub, as opposed to instrumental music, and so he got together with his engineer and a group of musicians and cut some tracks which he pressed up on an album called *Aquarius Dub*. When he went to cut the stamper someone at Federal asked, 'what kind of foolishness is this?' It soon caught on, though, but Clive Chin swears that Randy's got there first. It's just that their dub album wasn't commercially available initially, but had been put together for the sound system guys.

'People say that *Blackboard Jungle* is the first dub album, but Scratch didn't even have a studio at that time, and for him to experiment with breaking down rhythm tracks he needed to have had a studio for that purpose,' Clive explains. 'Scratch could barely pay for his studio time, and the same is true of Herman Chin Loy.

That's why I keep telling people that *Java Java Java Java* was the first. It was so plain and so dry that you could tell we were doing it before Tubby modified it by putting in special delays and stuff like that. Dub was what you'd call a version, by taking out the vocal and just letting the rhythm run. We had a spring reverb, which we put into it, and we would sometimes even rewind a two-track tape backwards and then fast forward it, before putting it on the drum and bass track to get that whirring sound. You couldn't get those sounds on a sound effects album. Those things came out of just experimenting, and Errol came up with the idea of taking good selling tracks and modifying them.'

Clive also produced Augustus Pablo's debut album, *This Is Augustus Pablo*, which was mainly built from scratch, rather than using existing rhythm tracks – although they did borrow a couple from Lee Perry and Leonard 'Santic' Chin. Pablo and Clive were both teenagers at the time, and eager to make their mark in the music business by incorporating new and exciting developments such as dub and deejay in their quest for a new 'rebel rock sound.'

Pablo and his brother had launched their own Rockers label in '72 and were releasing singles by artists like Paul Whiteman and Dillinger. There was a growing trend in Jamaica for artists having their own labels and becoming more self-reliant. For instance, Big Youth's first release on his Negusa Nagast imprint was 'African Daughter.' He then followed it with a reggae version of War's 'The World Is A Ghetto.' Dennis Brown and the Heptones sung backing vocals on that one, but Big Youth now fancied himself as a singer too, thanks to encouragement from Prince Buster.

'We put seven songs in the two charts, and if you saw my house down the street it was nowhere for a human being to live,' he told Angus Taylor. 'And with all that I created and having all of these guys driving nice vehicles now? Come on! So I took a song named 'World Is A Ghetto' and I just turn around and call it 'Streets in Africa.' When I did that they said I can't sing, you know? They fight us within the business and to be honest with all of this fame and things I create, that's the only time I saw a change that meant I could move out of that dilapidated building. And people were even vexed, because they still wanted me to stay there to uplift them, while they want to carry you down. Cho! It was then I realised and say "alright, I'm not going to sing a song for no producer. When it comes to singing vocal I sing for Negusa Nagast – Big Youth".'

The Wailers were well-practised at producing themselves and other artists but when they returned from their UK tour, Bunny Livingston announced that he wouldn't be touring with them anymore. This was a serious development – not only because his harmonies were integral to the Wailers' sound, but also since bands that depend on selling albums rather than hit singles had no choice but to tour if they wanted to grow their audience. One of the last gigs they played in England – at the Edmonton Sundown in north London, with Desmond Dekker – was an Ethiopian Famine Relief concert organised with help from Judge Dread, who performed on the same bill. British reggae band Matumbi were also part of the line-up that day. Their most recent singles, produced by bandleader/guitarist Dennis Bovell and distributed by Trojan Records, included 'Can't Get Enough Of That Reggae Stuff', 'Wipe Them Out' and a cover of Hot Chocolate's 'Brother Louie.' However, musical differences between Matumbi and their record label wouldn't take long to surface.

'We had an entirely different idea in mind,' explained Dennis, 'so we just pressed up some white labels, gave them to sound systems and then waited for them to put the record out, but they released something else instead, like that cover of 'Brother Louie.' That was me singing on it, but we only did it as a joke at the end of a session. It was like a muck-about, because there was a Mellotron in the studio that had belonged to Brian Jones of the Rolling Stones. Hot Chocolate had used a Mellotron on that song and we were like, "oh, there's a Mellotron. That's what they used on that song 'Brother Louie', so let's do a reggae version." And we did, not realising that the record company would like it enough to actually put it out. We thought, "oh no! We don't want our first record out to be a cover version", but they said that was the deal. All of the reggae labels were doing reggae versions of pop songs, but we didn't want to do that. We felt that we had something to say, but unfortunately the tide was against us, and all any of these companies could think about was cover versions. So after that, they said, "will you do a cover of 'Law Of The Land', the Temptations' song?" Then it was, "will you do a cover of this Kool and the Gang track?" Eventually we said, "no, we don't want to do any more", so halfway through recording all that lot, we were vying with them. We said that we'd do certain things for them if they would let us do our own stuff as well, but we ended up spending more time on their cover versions than our own creative efforts, so there were serious disagreements. Then one day we went into the studio and, lo and behold, they couldn't find the tapes of our original music. What a coincidence...'

Trojan knew what they wanted, because their biggest selling album of the year was John Holt's *1,000 Volts Of Holt*, which was well-stocked with covers of middle-of-road songs like 'Baby I'm A Want You', 'Help Me Make It Through The Night', 'Mr Bojangles', 'Killing Me Softly' and 'The Girl From Ipanema.' Holt's album featured orchestrated tracks and a style of ballad singing that resonated with older black and white audiences in the UK, but did little for younger or more conscious listeners, despite Holt wearing a psychedelic shirt on the cover and making the sign of Emperor Haile Selassie I by pressing his thumbs and fingertips together. The strings were arranged and conducted by Brian Rogers, although Tony Ashfield originally produced it for Chaguaramas Records in Wembley Park, using rhythms he'd recorded at Dynamic. He then repeated the process on another John Holt album that year, called *The Further You Look*.

'The first time I come to London I met Tony Ashfield, who said that he wanted to do an album with me and that he liked John

Holt,' says Jimmy Riley. 'I say, "well, come to Jamaica and let's do it." So I get John Holt, and he do that album called *The Further You Look*. They release the John Holt and even though I do my album as well, him just push John Holt alone. Trojan release just one single from my album, called 'Lord Pity Us All', then they claim they fall into bankruptcy, so my album didn't come out. That's the story on that, but Tony Ashfield was the first white man who say 'im like the dreadlocks image on an album. He was the first individual in the world who come with an album like that, but he didn't get permission to use that artwork on the jacket. He just saw Ras Daniel Heartman's drawings and took one to use on the album, to try and make John Holt look like him Rasta! But John Holt was no Rass them times there. John was still cabaret-style in his career at that point, but that made him big in Europe, with all them strings and that shit. That was the beginning of things for him, and every time him see me, he give me a laugh.'

'Memories By The Score' was the hit from *The Further You Look*, and two more John Holt albums followed in quick succession – one for Treasure Isle and the other produced by Harry Mudie, who hired John Bell to arrange the strings on the majority of tracks on *Time Is The Master*, except 'It May Sound Silly', which Tony King did. John Holt's departure for pastures new and Slim Smith's death meant that Bunny Lee had lost two of his main artists in less than a year, although he still had Cornel Campbell, Delroy Wilson and Horace Andy. Cornel's first album should have been a Studio One set by rights, but Coxsone had been in no hurry to issue some of the singer's earliest recordings. Highlights on his debut album for Bunny Lee include 'My Confession', 'Didn't I' and 'Queen Of The Minstrels' – a song adapted from Curtis Mayfield's 'Minstrel And Queen', and that Cornel made his own.

Horace Andy's 'You Are My Angel' was a soaring tour-de-force and Trojan made it the title track of his new album, which also included an impressive cover of Bill Withers' 'Ain't No Sunshine.' Horace had now left Coxsone and just to annoy him further, covered a handful of songs that were synonymous with Studio One such as 'Can I Change My Mind', 'Don't Break Your Promise', 'Riding For A Fall' and 'Rain From The Skies.' Bunny regularly got artists in his stable to cover the same songs, and especially those by Delroy Wilson, whose forthcoming album *Captivity* he produced. Highlights included covers of Delano Stewart's 'Don't Believe In Him' and Junior Byles' 'Beat Down Babylon' – also a reworking of 'Here Come The Heartaches', which Delroy had originally recorded for Coxsone in the ska era.

The liberties that Bunny Lee took with Studio One material were staggering, really. Delroy had also covered Tyrone Davis' 'Can I Change My Mind' for Coxsone, and when the Hoo Kim brothers opened their new Channel One studio on Maxfield Avenue, Bunny took Delroy there to revoice it. Dennis Alcapone voiced 'Cassius Clay' on a cut of 'Drum Song' the same day, and whilst Muhammad Ali would have been mightily pissed off at hearing Dennis use that name, he would have surely appreciated the lyrics, which made him favourite to beat George Foreman in a title fight. Jo Jo and Ernest Hoo Kim were Chinese Jamaicans, and they rented out jukeboxes and one-armed bandits until the latter were outlawed by the government. That's when they decided to get into the record business. Jo Jo bought equipment from the US, including label-printing gear, and after a spell with Sid Bucknor as their engineer, Ernest then took over at the eight-track console, learning the ropes as he went along.

The next tune Delroy voiced there was 'Living In The Footsteps Of Another Man.' The rhythm for it was built at Harry J's, and Gregory Isaacs had voiced it first but got the words wrong, so his attempt never got released. 'Trying To Wreck Up My Life' was another sizeable hit and the irony of that song wasn't lost on Bunny, as Trojan were already in financial trouble and closing down their subsidiary labels. Pama Records had all but ceased trading too, and their place would be taken by other UK based labels like Cactus, DIP, Count Shelly and Lord Koos. By late July '73, Bunny was in

London making alternative arrangements and watching I-Roy make his first appearance in England at Battersea Town Hall, backed by Matumbi. Lee Perry and his partner Pauline Morrison were also there, and Pauline was asked to announce I-Roy, so she went on stage and said something to the effect of, 'ladies and gentlemen, introducing to you – U-Roy!' It was both embarrassing for her and I-Roy, who already had one album out – *Presenting I-Roy* – and another on the way, called *Hell And Sorrow*, both for Trojan. Gussie Clarke produced the former, although he got some of the rhythms from other producers. I-Roy was the most literate of all the Jamaican deejays, U-Roy and Big Youth included. His vocabulary was more extensive and his lyrics more insightful, intelligent and humorous than anything heard to date. He deejayed about roots and culture ('Red, Gold And Green', 'Black And Proud' and 'African Descendant'), social commentary ('Pusher Man', 'Screw Face', 'Jah Lion Jungle' and 'Black Man Time'), sound systems ('Coxsone Affair') and even tourism. You'd think a track with lyrics like 'Sugar Candy' would be lightweight, but no, as he was urging the girl in the song to reach for the sky. On 'Buck And The Preacher', he boosts the Sidney Poitier film starring Harry Belafonte with an all-black cast – I-Roy was clearly a film buff, because his first track for Gussie Clarke was 'Magnificent Seven' whilst 'Dr Phibes' – voiced on a majestic cut to 'Sidewalk Doctor', decorated with flute – is a reference to the character Vincent Price plays in Robert Fuest's movie *The Abominable Dr Phibes*. There was no subject that I-Roy wouldn't turn into verse, as he also voiced lyrics comforting Joe Frazier after he was beaten by Foreman, and with the Melodians' Tony Brevett crooning 'Don't Get Weary' behind him.

When interviewed by Carl Gayle during his London visit, I-Roy insisted that he considered deejaying as a serious art form.

'Right now, I'm trying to project my thoughts to a more mature crowd,' he said. 'You see the lyrics come and go, but reality lives for ever – it's like practical history, it never fades out. I'm catering for the kids, but at the same time I'm trying to get the mature crowd to listen because it's a message, whether I sing it or talk it. I'm trying to reach out and touch the people who are so far away and who live in a world of fantasy. They can't even take the time off to see what they're made of, y' know?'

Lee Perry didn't stay in London all that long, and he licensed his *Rhythm Shower* album to Trojan at precisely the wrong time, since it would only appear as a very limited edition, and even then with a blank label. In a lengthy interview with Chris Lane for *Blues And Soul* he talked about the various ingenious sound effects he used, from crying babies, motorbikes, whiplashes, breaking glass and ringing phones to running water, clocks and backward tapes, as well as his (illegal) sampling of soul records. He also announced that his studio would be finished in December and that he was about to launch a new label, called Black Art.

'I want to change the beat,' he said. 'The people are getting tired of hearing the same thing over and over again, and the musicians are getting bored with playing the same rhythms all the time, At the moment I'm thinking of ways to make the beat more demanding, more powerful and new...'

I-Roy's 'High Fashion' appeared on the Upsetters album *Double Seven*, which was mainly comprised of instrumentals. The cover photo showed Lee Perry voicing in the studio, making it look as if Scratch himself was the featured artist. That's fair enough, you might say, but he didn't sing or deejay on that album and it was unprecedented for a producer or engineer to receive star billing in that way. He and King Tubby were now firm friends. The latter now regularly received visitors who wanted him to either cut dubs, mix existing tapes or voice tracks. He couldn't record actual rhythms at his studio, as it was only the size of a small kitchen. Nevertheless, he'd developed more of his own style when mixing dub versions, and producers like Perry, Glen Brown and Bunny Lee loved hearing the rhythm tracks fall away, leaving the vocals hanging in the air a cappella style, or simply vanishing completely under an onrushing battery of drum and bass. The album *Upsetters 14 Dub Black Board*

Jungle, which he and Scratch worked on together, was truly ground-breaking, and featured instrumental versions of songs that Perry had produced by artists like the Wailers and Junior Byles.

The latter was still in Scratch's camp, and he'd had two recent singles on *The Upsetter*. 'Rasta Pick Pocket' made further pronouncements on the idea that not everyone with dreadlocks lived by a righteous code. It's not someone's hairstyle that makes them a dread, Byles had chided, but the heart within and their behaviour, or livity. The other was 'When Will Better Come.' This was a cut of Delroy Wilson's 'Better Must Come' but with a completely different message as it was an eviscerating assessment of Manley's first year in office. Scratch always did have a gift for identifying new talent, and the latest debutant to have searched him out was Dillinger, or Young Dellinger, as Pablo called him. The 20-year-old deejay started out shadowing Dennis Alcapone on local sound systems and was in a tearing hurry to start his recording career.

'Dillinger used to be with me back home,' Alcapone told Ray Hurford. 'When we used to play the sound system El Paso, Dillinger used to come along and I used to give him the mic. People used to curse me, saying, "how can you give this little boy the mic?" They'd say that they'd come to see me. That was before I did a record, and then Dillinger went to record for the *The Upsetter*. I can remember the first day because I was there. Dillinger wanted to get inside the business, so Scratch said, "go on then, go inside the studio" and he was there working, working, one tape after the other. I think he did about twenty tune that night, and not one hit come out of it.'

Alcapone performed with other reggae artists at the Edinburgh Festival in August '73, backed by the Cimarons. The host, Judge Dread, introduced him as Jamaica's 'King of the Talk Over', and there were cheers as he launched into 'Cassius Clay' and his latest single, 'Wake Up Jamaica', on a cut of 'Moonlight Lover.' It was an assured performance. UK vocal trio the Marvels were on next, and then Nicky Thomas, who sung 'Is It Because I'm Black?' with his face screwed up in pain, his body jerking as if shot through with electricity as sweat literally poured from him. The crowd loved him and then warmly greeted the Pioneers as they took the stage dressed in matching black silk suits and launched into Jackie Wilson and Temptations' numbers whilst giving a slickly rehearsed performance, complete with synchronised dance steps. To all intents and purpose, the Pioneers were a soul act, which is funny because Eddie Kendricks, who had split from the Temptations two years earlier, was in Jamaica looking to do the opposite.

Kendricks' manager Frank Wilson told the *Gleaner* that they were looking to record an album of reggae, backed by some of the island's top musicians, and hoped to soon start recording at Dynamic.

'Reggae doesn't sell in our country' Wilson opined, 'but what we are trying to do is put it on a scale that will make it sell.' Somewhat surprisingly, he said that 'soul music in the US doesn't have much soul' and that reggae actually had more of it than many American acts. 'Reggae is much freer music,' he continued, 'and after this album, other musicians are going to come here to get something going and to get the feeling.'

It sounded like he'd been listening to Dennis Brown, whose new album *Super Reggae And Soul Hits* was produced by Derrick Harriott and recorded with Now Generation at Federal and Harry J's. It was very accomplished, and every track was either a potential single, or had already been released on 7-inch. 'Silhouettes', 'Wichita Linesman', 'He Can't Spell', 'Musical Heatwave', 'How Could I Let You Get Away', 'Lips Of Wine' and 'Let Me Down Easy'… It was a faultless collection. But Dennis was like a butterfly and flitted here and there, wherever there was some good music happening.

He would often stop by the Packing House, for instance, a place in Kingston where Munchie Jackson and Little Roy had set up a two-track studio for use by themselves and their friends. Dennis voiced 'Set Your Heart Free' on the same rhythm as Little Roy's

'Mr T' there, whilst 'Foot Of The Mountain' was produced by Eddie Wong, who'd recently started his own Down Town label.

'He used to run a Chinese restaurant in Jamaica,' Dennis told Ian McCann. 'I was introduced to him through Busty Brown of the Chosen Few. He knew who I was, we worked out something and decided to record. I had two songs for him, because there was one called 'Bitter Tasting Day To Come', and when I told Alton Ellis the title, he was horrified. He said, "Dennis, it's not good for us to sing certain songs because it might fulfil." When he told me that I got scared, so I scrapped that one and just finished 'Foot Of The Mountain.' I didn't bother with 'Bitter Tasting Day To Come'.'

The Heptones also liked the vibes at the Packing House, although their latest album *Book Of Rules* was recorded at Harry J's, where former Studio One engineer Sylvan Morris ran the sessions. The combination of Leroy Sibbles' lead and Barry and Earl's close harmonies was mouth-watering, whilst the title track was one of the best songs they'd ever written.

'That tune was unique,' Morris told Angus Taylor. 'As a matter of fact, the Heptones said they came there for me to do the tune, and when I heard the beginning it sounded so beautiful, man. But when I started to mix the tune, it was like the sound changed. What I had to do was take back all the equalisation and just bring up the levels, the faders, until I heard it sound the way it sounded to me, and then just tweak – just barely tweak.'

Harry J had an eight-track Helios board, which Morris said was 'totally advanced from Coxsone.' Some people claimed that Chris Blackwell had invested some money into the business, because Harry J's became the studio of choice for all of Island's acts, including the Wailers. Their first proper US tour had got underway in mid-July at Paul's Mall in Boston, where they performed five nights before supporting Bruce Springsteen at Max's Kansas City in Manhattan. They'd replaced Bunny Livingston with their former mentor Joe Higgs and all but completed their next album when Peter Tosh overdubbed vocals to 'Get Up Stand Up' whilst they were in New York. His contributions had the kind of bite that only he could provide, and added the final flourish to a song that would quickly become a mainstay of the Wailers' repertoire. The band then opened for Sly and the Family Stone a few times before being unceremoniously dumped from the tour in Las Vegas – not because they blew Sly off the stage, as reported in some quarters, but since they'd failed to impress the Family Stone's audiences, who struggled to appreciate the unfamiliar sounds of reggae. San Francisco DJ and promoter Tom Donahue came to their rescue and booked them to play the Matrix on 19 and 20 October. The first show coincided with Peter's birthday and the release of the Wailers' new album, *Burnin'*. Bunny, who was still missed, had three songs on it, including 'Reincarnated Souls', which was initially touted as the title. 'Rastaman Chant' was the nyahbinghi song they'd been opening their shows with; 'Burnin' And Lootin'' bristled with revolutionary ardour, and there were re-recordings of 'Put It On', 'Duppy Conqueror' and 'Small Axe.' The centrepiece, however, was 'Get Up Stand Up', urging people to abandon the lies told to them by church and state and take matters into their own hands.

Lee Jaffe, who'd befriended the band during his stay in Jamaica, was the Wailers' tour manager. He was there at the Matrix and would never forget what he saw.

'I stood at the mixing board, urging the engineer to pull up the bass, and as the place began to throb, the crowd grew more and more ecstatic,' he said. 'Bob was dancing, almost athletically. He made an unforgettable move, bending backward so far as to almost touch the floor. I couldn't believe he didn't fall, but somehow, miraculously, he pulled himself up, and with his right arm swinging, his hand came down on a chord with perfect timing as he sang "slave driver, you're gonna get burned..."'

Donahue booked them into the Matrix for two further shows, but first they travelled to Los Angeles and played a closed-door concert at the Capitol Records Tower in West Hollywood that Shelter Records' Denny Cordell filmed; the footage wouldn't see the light of day for decades. Joe Higgs left the band shortly after-wards and wouldn't perform with the Wailers again. His departure would bring an end to the group openly promoting nyahbinghi as part of their stage act.

As the veteran Higgs had returned to Jamaica, the Mystic Revelations of Rastafari were preparing to open a community centre in a two-storey building on the outskirts of Glasspole Avenue, overlooking the lower section of Rockfort. It was built with help from members of the local community and had eight rooms. Along the concrete wall was a mural painted by students from the Jamaica School Of Art, depicting 'the togetherness of the venture and the spirit of brotherhood and peace.' There were plans to incorporate a basic school, a medical service station, a music study, a library, an art and craft department, a language and cultural area, an indus-trial training centre and a space for indoor sports. Count Ossie and his people were appealing for part-time teachers to work there on a voluntary basis, but they wanted the school to be affiliated to the Ministry for Education and therefore eligible for grants, and at least one qualified full-time teacher. Three thousand books were prom-ised for the library from various universities, 'because without reading there can be no sound background for worthwhile educa-tion', proclaimed the Count. He and his group had already started to give music lessons, and doctors from the UWI and other hospi-tals had promised to donate their services at the medical centre. Amharic and Swahili were to be taught in the cultural centre, and this was reflected in the name of the centre, Makfacha Ambasa Bet, which is Amharic for 'Key Lion House.' Stokeley Carmichael had already paid a visit to the centre and pledged financial support, and the Mystic Revelations were also involved in negotiations with the Ministry of Housing to provide land for a self-help housing project in the Wareika hills. Their spokesperson, Brother Sam Clayton, said this pilot scheme would not only provide houses, but also help train local youths in construction skills.

In addition, Cedric Brooks had recently been giving a series of workshops on Jamaican music in collaboration with the Institute of Jamaica and this had resulted in an album, credited to Cedric 'Im' Brooks and the Divine Light, called *From Mento To Reggae To Third World Music*, a collection of Jamaican music that according to the liner notes penned by Verena Reckord, was not only highly entertaining, but also chronicled the history of a colourful indigenous music.

'Take some heavy African drumming patterns, add a blob of spicy Cuban rhythms, a pinch of Haitian merengue and a little Latin American beat,' he writes. 'Mix in such a way that the polyrhythmic weave makes beautiful music even without a melody line and you're on your way to discovering the background of reggae.'

Guest vocalists included Lynford Miles ('Put It On' and 'Satta Massa Gana'), Brother Lloyd Brown ('Carry Go Bring Come'), Liz Campbell and Sharon Miles ('Nobody's Business') and Nambo ('Let's Do Rock Steady'), whilst saxophonist Barrington Sadler played penny whistle on 'Merry Hop', an exciting take on mento music. Brooks, a talented multi-instrumentalist, wanted his music to reflect 'the total Jamaican experience – African, Euro Western and Jamaican.' He was more interested in acquiring (and passing on) knowledge than chart hits, and this same sentiment was also shared by Jimmy Cliff, who, by his own admission, had entered what he called 'a heavy spiritual and cultural thing.'

His most recent LP, *Unlimited,* was released through Total Sounds in Jamaica and EMI elsewhere. Jimmy produced it, and it's clear from songs like 'I See The Light', 'Poor Slave' and 'Under The Sun, Moon And Stars' that he had been exploring truths relating to the past and present subjugation of black people. He accused slave traders of stealing his history and destroying his culture in the lyrics of 'The Price Of Peace' whilst 'Born To Win' was triumphant in the same way that 'The Harder They Come' was, informing us that his fore-parents worked from 'sun up to sun down' without reward, and he's determined to break the cycle. There was talk of 'disaffection from rejection' in 'Oh Jamaica', and 'World Of Peace' was a sufferers' lament, making *Unlimited* his most outspoken set of songs yet.

Jimmy Cliff was a superstar, yet Dennis Brown had continued his incredible rise to fame, and in September '73, he performed at Madison Square Garden in New York on the same bill as Big Youth, Lorna Bennett and the Heptones. He then returned to Jamaica and enrolled at St Stephens College in Cross Roads, although there were those who expressed surprise at this, given the scale and intensity of his musical activities. All came crashing down the following month, when he was hospitalised and told that he must rest. Fatigue had caught up with him and caused him to experience chest pains amidst rumours that he had tuberculosis, and even worse.

'They say I've only got one lung, and say that I've got no lungs,' Dennis told Trevor Williams of the *Reggae Directory*. 'They said all sorts of things, and if I wasn't strong, I would've given up the business a long time ago, but I have a work to do and I know nothing else. I've only done music. When you're in the spotlight, people always have all sorts of derogatory things to say. It's not everyone that's going to like you. Some of the guys who think that you shouldn't be going where you are going have their ways of saying things to try and hurt you, but if you're a good guy then it won't hurt you. It's like going through fire and surviving, but this is my weapon here,' he said, pulling out a worn Bible. 'God is my shield and when man's hopes and aspirations have all crumbled, his only alternative is to resort to the Bible. Just love God and live.'

Niney the Observer didn't believe the rumours for a minute, because he went to the hospital and smuggled Dennis out for a recording session.

'In those days the music was fun,' he recalled. 'I even remember making that record without no drum, 'cause Santa the drummer was going on with something and I say, "you don't want to play? OK, forget it, we're going in." I just take up one of Randy's broomsticks, break it in two and say to Sticky the percussionist, "here, sit down 'pon this." All we use is a foot drum, a piece of stick and one hand. That's how we make Dennis Brown's 'Cassandra', and it turn out to be a big hit, I tell you!'

Trojan had released Dennis Brown's last album, but by November the company was finding it difficult to get their records pressed, and facing the prospect of going out of business unless they could attract either new owners or additional investment. The Jamaican recording industry also had its problems, and several leading studios had closed since the Jamaican Federation of Musicians decreed that musicians must be paid $60 each per session, and each session should not extend beyond four hours. Such a raise would mean that Jamaican producers had to pay musicians the same rates their counterparts in places like the US and Britain received, which had much bigger markets.

The Studio Operators and Manufacturers Association, in a letter to the media, claimed that the proposed fees were too excessive and to conform with the union's request 'would result in total financial disaster.' They accused the JFM of using dictatorial attitudes in handling the decision, leaving them with no alternative but to retaliate by closing all studios to session musicians and session producers. As Christmas approached, producers and musicians alike would usually be looking forward to their busiest time of the year, yet Dynamic had been shut for nearly a month and Federal for even longer. Byron Lee, Dynamic's CEO, was in the unusual position of having been barred from his own studio, since he was also leader of the Dragonaires and a member of the JFM. Most thought the dispute would soon be over, but there would be far fewer new releases over the holiday period, and many disgruntled producers and musicians feeling the pinch.

This is what 18-year-old deejay Tapper Zukie came home to after leaving the UK in late 1973. He'd been sent to London by his mother some months previously, after the Kingston police wanted to arrest him. He got to record an album whilst he was away but was told that it hadn't sold, so was feeling dejected when he stepped off the plane into the strong Jamaican sunshine.

According to most people, including himself, he was 'a little rude boy', and that wasn't the half of it. Real name David Sinclair, he grew up between Greenwich Town and Trench Town and became feral, in a sense, after his parents separated. Music called to him from early on, and at first he'd wanted to play drums. It would be an exaggeration to say that he was taught by Leroy 'Horsemouth' Wallace, since all he did was mess about and get in the way. Horsemouth found him an irritation and sent him packing, although he did play drums for a little band called the Supremes at one stage. (Not the Motown group, I hasten to add.) It was his mother who called him 'Tapper' during his drumming days, whilst the name Zukie came from the gang he moved around with at school, called the Zukies. By the age of 12 he started going to dances in his neighbourhood and imitating his favourite deejays, King Stitt and U-Roy, on the local sounds Maccabees and I-Oses Discotech. He was too small to be seen behind the amplifier, so they'd have to stand him on a box, but he loved being the centre of attention and knew no fear.

'Tapper Zukie's talent arise from politics,' he told David Katz. 'When I used to run away from home, I used to go and sleep over by the PNP headquarters. They used to advertise the PNP at the meetings, like, "this is the master PNP, blah blah!" Me start take the mic and start chat, so every day, them would carry me down and give me the mic. Political rally all over them put me on, and I was the little boy who was riding the donkey that was leading the political meetings.'

PNP activists soon introduced him to the sound system. 'Them start give me the mic and me start to mash up the place, so people start send for me everywhere. I was on I-Oses Discotheque, down Greenwich Town, and some of the other sounds, me never did even know the name.'

He was the first little boy deejay and thrived in the spotlight, but all that changed once he reached his teens. Trench Town had become a political battleground as people in Wilton Gardens (known locally as Rema) warred with those in Arnett Gardens, or Concrete Jungle, and Tapper soon found himself in trouble.

'I used to play sound and everybody rate me, but they say that I was a hyped youth. I'd do crazy things so Bunny Lee, my brother and my mother decide to send me to England when I was 17 to escape these crazy things that I do.'

Bunny Lee was a friend of Tapper's brother, who they called Blackbeard. Magnanimous as ever, Bunny had recruited Tapper as his bodyguard, but the youth was unmanageable, and the police determined to teach him a lesson. For any ghetto youth this could spell death – literally – and so that's when his mother packed him off to the UK.

'I had never recorded, never appeared on a show, and Bunny Lee introduced me on this show U-Roy had in Ladbroke Grove,' he said. 'They played the rhythm for Slim Smith's 'The Time Has Come' and I toast over it. At the time, everybody had me as a warrior. People were scared of me, for what, I don't know! I'm just a guy who stand up for my rights and don't let nobody push me around, so that's when I made that album *Man Ah Warrior*.'

Ethnic Fight's Larry Lawrence was at the U-Roy show and took Tapper in the studio for 'Jump And Twist', although Tapper's *Man Ah Warrior* album was released first.

'I was in no doubt when I heard Zukie on the microphone of a sound system and immediately I went to him and told him that I would like to do some work with him,' wrote producer Clem Bushay in the liner notes. 'I made a booking for a studio session and Zukie came along. He recorded 'Man Ah Warrior', his first song, which is a great hit. Well dig some more good music on this album and you will have to watch out for TOPPER ZUKIE in the near future.'

'Actually, that album with Clement Bushay, *Man Ah Warrior*, it wasn't produced by Clem Bushay alone,' Tapper told Peter I. 'About five tracks on it is by Clement Bushay. The other five tracks was my production, because people used to say I follow bad company.

You can call it that I was a rudie, a lickle rude bwoy, but I just had to do something for myself.'

Delroy Washington knew the young deejay and Tapper's 'Message To Pork Eaters' was voiced the same night as Delroy's 'Jahman A Come', since the singer was recording for Count Shelly at the time. He says that when Tapper and his friend Sal came to London they caused a whole heap of trouble – that there were reports of people getting stabbed and Tapper smashing a Coke bottle over Junior English's head. Such acts of mayhem soon escalated to the point where certain Harlesden bad men were out to get him, but musically at least, he'd made rapid progress. Although it wasn't as well received as Tapper hoped, *Man Ah Warrior* had its moments. He was a lively and entertaining performer, with a touch of Dennis Alcapone in his delivery, and spirited with it. The choice of rhythms was good too. 'When Zukie Day Yah' is a cut to Lloyd Parks' 'Slaving', whilst the sparse backing behind the title track and 'Cally Dolly' borrows from the Temptations' 'Papa Was A Rolling Stone.' This is something Tapper acknowledged further down the playlist. 'I'm not a rolling stone you know,' he admitted. 'I'm just a warrior.' His nerve is infectious, as Greil Marcus once observed, and his lyrics surprisingly cultural, given his antics outside the studio.

The Wailers' second UK tour was supposed to start on 19 November, but the first four shows had to be cancelled after Peter Tosh contracted bronchitis. His presence was vital, since Bunny remained adamant that he wasn't going to tour and Joe Higgs had declined to make the trip. There was nothing for it but to wait until Peter was well enough to travel. He'd become increasingly unhappy with the situation the Wailers found themselves in, as he didn't care much for Chris Blackwell, and objected to Bob being treated like he was the focal point of the band. Only one of Peter's songs had been included on *Burnin'*, and the message of togetherness that he'd voiced in 'One Foundation' was already wearing thin. A few days after a memorable night at Leeds Polytechnic on

27 November, this depleted line-up of the Wailers would head back to Jamaica, where the group would finally unravel.

'Peter and Bunny, they could see that favouritism with Bob from they get the approach from Island, and that's what caused them to react in the way they did,' said Israel Vibration's Apple Gabriel. 'We heard all this talk, of how Peter was arrogant and Bunny Wailer was scared of planes and didn't like to fly, but people went and created that story to hide what was really going on. Peter and Bunny could see how Bob was being singled out instead of the focus being put on the three of them, and this is what caused the problem from the beginning.'

Wya Lindo agreed, and said that it broke his heart when Peter and Bunny left the Wailers.

'The Wailers were always so tight before that, but something broke that special bond that kept us all together. It must have been some divine power – I think so, but Island seemed keen to promote Bob on his own, and we didn't all talk together like we did before. Bob kept more to himself, and the standard of music wasn't like before. It was like we were just jamming, and I still can't understand what went down. The break-up actually shattered my mind. I wasn't mentally insane or anything, but just emotionally drained and disillusioned. Bob kept coming to my house and looking for me, trying to talk to me. He recognised what I was feeling because I think he felt it too really, but I just couldn't deal with it. After that, everybody just fell away to follow their own tangent and go out on their own.'

CHAPTER FIVE

1974: THE TIME HAS COME

In December 1973, Chris Lane went to Jamaica and stayed with Lee Perry at his new studio, the Black Ark, for nearly a month. He was there in Kingston when Big Youth performed at the Carib Theatre with dance group Scorch and the Generation Gap, and wrote about what he'd witnessed in *Blues And Soul*.

'Big Youth entered to wild screams from his many fans in the audience while Scorch continued skanking in the background. He was dressed in platform boots, gold-coloured trousers, a maroon velvet coat with a white fur collar and a hat with his dreadlocks hanging out of it. His hat, by the way, is an important part of his act, at a certain point in his performance he would take it off and shake his head at the audience who just go wild at the sight of his locks flying about.'

He would soon have red, gold, and green gems set into his front teeth and, according to the *Encyclopaedia of Rock*, earn the nickname 'Human Gleaner,' because 'it was from his records that many young Jamaicans learnt what was going on in society around them.'

'The thing about Jamaican music is that it wasn't ever just about the music,' Lane told Angus Taylor. 'It was about the attitude of it and about the people who made it. Look at Bunny Lee. To me Bunny Lee is the epitome of what I always call the 'personality

176

producer', because once you got beyond just buying a few records, you very quickly realised that you liked the Upsetters, and you liked the Crystalites, but they were different, and then you liked the Clancy Eccles and Dynamite stuff, but they were different again, as was the Studio One stuff. You realised that a lot of the time the producers are the ones who are actually talking on the records and making the intros, and giving them that particular stamp.'

The Institute of Jamaica, mindful of the cultural renaissance then taking place, began collecting reggae 45s 'for the purposes of historical record' in 1974. They were especially interested in Rasta songs, and had recently published their wanted list. Larry & Alvin's 'Press Along Nyah' was on it, and so too the Conscious Minds' 'Suffering Through The Nation', the Ethiopians' 'Starvation', Joe Higgs' 'Know Yourself Black Man', Prince Buster's 'Police Trick Rasta' and Junior Byles' 'Beat Down Babylon.' The Institute's interest in these records was an indication of how successfully Rastafari was being assimilated into Jamaican society. As the title of their 1979 book *Rastafari – A Way Of Life* suggested, author Tracy Nicholas believed that Rastafari, above all else, is a way of life.

'It offers approaches and answers to real problems black people face in daily living: it promotes spiritual resilience in the face of oppressive poverty and underdevelopment. It produces art, music and cultural forms which can be universally recognised and appreciated. More importantly, Rastafari provides a positive self-image, an alternative, to people who need and cannot find or accept one elsewhere. Even with its black foundation and orientation, Rastafari is open to anyone, of any race, who chooses to discover and is able to accept it.'

Beverley Manley wasn't a Rasta, but she had begun to look for something more meaningful to do in her second year as the prime minister's wife, and made child education one of her major priorities. To begin with, she observed teacher training techniques and visited most of the basic schools in Jamaica. These buildings were often shabby, and the circumstances in which children had to learn were inadequate. The more she toured these schools, the more determined she became to ensure that every child was able to receive a good early education. She was impressed by the often untrained, dedicated women who generally taught these children and her husband immediately made arrangements for more government help in this area. As a result, these schools were able to subsidise salaries and make training available for teachers. She also opened a basic school – supervised by the Ministry of Education – in the grounds of Jamaica House, in the hope that it would set an example for the rest of Jamaican society to follow.

She was also involved with revising the laws governing illegitimate children, of which there were many. This revision would ensure they were given equal status in law, the same as children born within marriage. There were also plans to introduce a bauxite production levy, programmes to create jobs and a home guard, and plans to nationalise the energy and bus companies. The governments of Jamaica and Cuba were also working together in establishing direct air links. The people of Jamaica had wanted change and were getting it, although Manley could play tough when he needed to. On 1 April of all days – who's fooling who? – he announced the opening of a 'Gun Court' where anyone caught with an unlicensed firearm would be tried and then sentenced to indefinite detention, plus hard labour. Not for nothing was 'Heavy Manners' being spray painted on walls in Kingston ghettos controlled by the PNP.

The Interns' 'Gun Court' told the reggae fanbase all about it, using the same formula as Prince Buster's 'Judge Dread.' 'Nothing Is Impossible' was even better, as they resisted attempts to deny them hopes of a better future. Somewhat confusingly, the Interns were also known as the Viceroys. Their three founder members were all born in the countryside, before their families moved to Kingston. Daniel Bernard was from Westmoreland, whilst Linval

Williams, aka Bunny Gayle, hailed from St Mary. Tinglin, who lived in Denham Town and attended Jamaica's School of Art, had led the group when they'd hit with 'Ya Ho' in 1968, for Studio One. They recorded an album's worth of tracks for Coxsone, but only a few were released so they did the rounds until Winston Riley suggested they change their name to the Interns for a fresh start. It had worked so far.

Meanwhile, Al Brown's cover of Al Green's 'Here I Am Baby' was already being hailed as one of top tunes of 1974, and it was only March! Al's real name was Irving Brown and he was a welder by day, and the lead singer with Skin, Flesh & Bones by night. He'd recorded a couple of tunes with Cynthia Richards before Dickie Wong suggested he cover 'Here I Am Baby', which stayed at number one on the local charts for three weeks. Shortly afterwards he won Best New Vocalist at the Red Stripe El Suzie Awards, held on 31 March at the St Andrew's Club in Cross Roads. Cynthia Richards won Top Female Singer for 1973, Niney was voted Top Producer and Big Youth Top Performer. The Heptones won Top Vocal Group whilst In Crowd was voted Top Band. The only real surprise was Horace Andy beating Dennis Brown to the title of Top Male Vocalist, and Brent Dowe's 'Build Me Up' winning Best Song, although it was a rather lavish production.

People had been asking what had happened to the documentary on reggae that Calvin Lockhart had been filming in Jamaica several months previously, as Boris Gardner's theme song was already getting a fair amount of local airplay. Eddie Knight, owner of the Bronco nightclub, had told him that a film company was looking for someone to write music for a forthcoming film called *Every Nigger Is A Star*. Boris had met with Lockhart, then he and his brother Barrington wrote the theme tune, and also a fair amount of the music that eventually appeared in the film. Inner Circle and the Mystic Revelations of Rastafari contributed to the soundtrack too, whilst Big Youth did his own version of 'Every Nigger Is A Star', shared with the I Three.

179

'That song was written by me, Calvin Lockhart and Boris Gardner,' he told Steve Milne. 'The movie was a flop, but the critics say I was the best thing in it. That song was made in a ballad kind of way and we put that group with Rita, Marcia and Judy together, the I Three. It's like Big Youth was so dynamic and magnificent... I was just the thing and they were my friends. I call them sisters, y' know? Because I really used to admire Bob Marley a lot and we were always moving as a family. Some people's star shines and some heading for stardom. We was a one family thing.'

Big Youth voiced 'Craven Version' for the Wailers' Tuff Gong label, but the I Three – it's a singular term, and not plural – had first come together at the House Of Chen in early March, when Marcia Griffiths shared the bill with comedian The Fantastic Hezekiah. At the end of her set she invited Rita Marley and Judy Mowatt on stage, whereupon they sang a Sweet Inspirations medley. Rita and Marcia had already sung harmonies on the Wailers' 'Rock It Baby' together, and had then gone to Studio One and done the same thing for Coxsone who, unbeknown to them, had also invited Judy Mowatt to the session. That was actually the birth of the I Three – but it was their performance at the House Of Chen that had got people talking about them, and had fired Bob Marley's imagination ahead of recording his first album without the other two Wailers. It was on 13 April that the I Three made their official stage debut, at the opening of a new club in Seven Miles called I Land In The Sun, where they shared the bill with Dennis Brown, Horace Andy and Cedric Brooks' new band, Divine Light. Their first single was a studio version of the same Sweet Inspirations medley they'd sung at House Of Chen, produced by Bob Marley no less.

He and Lee Perry had remained friends, and members of the Wailers' circle often visited the Black Ark in Cardiff Crescent, not far from Washington Boulevard. It's hard to believe that this suburban setting was home to Jamaica's most daring sound laboratory, from where innovative songs began to issue forth on a regular basis. It's also scarcely credible that all that hullabaloo took place in the same space where Scratch and his partner Pauline Morrison were raising a young family, and various musicians would occasionally stay, including Junior Byles and Derrick 'Watty' Burnett from Port Antonio, who'd rarely miss a session.

'I start with Scratch from 1968,' Burnett remembered. 'I did my first 45 with him and stayed with him from there, singing 'Rainy Night In Portland' and a few more singles. Scratch's studio was a very small place and he only had this little four-track recorder, so he'd have to keep backing up tracks, like doubling them up. It had a sound, though.

'I remember one day Bunny Lee came and he was just laughing at Scratch. Bunny used to do a lot of work at Channel One, and that was the most advanced studio in Jamaica at the time, so when Bunny told Ernest Hoo Kim about Black Ark, they just crack up! Everybody came to see, and it was like a joke. The place was a little box and had no windows. It was hot like hell and everything went down on this little Teac reel-to-reel. The piano was out by at least two octaves, and everything there was like a toy. Even the percussion instruments were like kids' toys, and there was no fixed time for anything. Scratch would just come out and say, "okay, call Ernest Ranglin or call Brubeck [keyboard player Winston Wright]." It wouldn't matter what time it was, it was just Scratch's vibes. He'd just call people at midnight or whenever. He never had no special time, because when he got the vibes he'd just say, "okay man, let's do something", but we were always there. We lived there and all we thought about was music, and so we were always writing and putting together something. There was no set programme and even up until this day I could never sit down and say, "okay, I'm going to write a song." That could never happen, because there's no set time to write a song – you just get a vibes and the song comes. It just has to come naturally.

'Sometimes you'd do something pretty and extra nice, but he wouldn't want that. He'd want something on the rough side, depending on how he was feeling, but it was everyone there who put in the work, and it wasn't him alone. Everyone there put in 100 per cent and everyone was excited to hear the work trim up like that. That's what really happened. It all happened as the result of so much love, really.'

The first sign that something extraordinary was happening at Black Ark came with the release of Junior Byles' 'Curly Locks.' The rhythm was played by Lefthand Bassie (aka Junior Dan), Pablove Black and Benbow from the Solid Foundation band. They were the resident band at Black Ark for a while, and Perry wanted them to tour the UK, but they refused to go as Scratch insisted they cut their hair first. We don't know the reason, but can probably file it under the heading of general craziness.

Susan (actually Anne) Cadogan was the daughter of theologian Claude Cadogan and singer Lola Cadogan, who released several 78s of devotional music in the fifties. JBC radio DJ Jerry Lewis had written a song he wanted his girlfriend Teresa, to sing, but Teresa suggested he ask her best friend Anne instead, and so the three of them went to the studio.

'I was always singing, but I never thought of singing professionally,' she says. 'But when I went to that studio, put on those headphones and heard the voice in my head, it was so clear that I could hear my saliva… I couldn't believe it. I thought it was fabulous! Jerry said, "let's try it as a duet", but my friend froze and so she came out. He said, "sing it again", so I sang it again and when I came out Lee Perry met me on the step and was so excited. He said, "hey Jerry, lend me your singer", then turned to me and said, "do you know this tune?" and played me 'Hurt So Good.' Well, I did know it, because I loved Millie Jackson and that's all I used to listen to – soul music. I wasn't into reggae, y' know? That was the first reggae song I did and I don't know if it had a voice on there already but I sang the song right through and he was so happy. When I came out he said, "what's your name?" I said, "Anne Cadogan" and he pulled a face. He said that I have a sexy voice and Anne wasn't sexy, so I have to be Sus-Anne! Apparently he'd recorded another girl singing it before me and she was annoyed when he took her voice off the tape and put mine on there instead. She went and recorded it somewhere else and the producer paid off the radio station to play her version. Lee Perry was so vexed that they wouldn't play his.'

'Hurt So Good' appeared on the Perries label in Jamaica, credited to Suzan Cadogan and the Diamonds. Perry then licensed it to Dennis Harris, who issued it on DIP in the UK. Ken Boothe's 'Everything I Own' was the current number one in Jamaica, closely followed by Gregory Isaacs' 'Love Is Overdue', Ernie Smith's 'Duppy Gunman' and Delroy Wilson's 'It's A Shame.'

'I did my own rendition of 'Everything I Own', even though it was not my song,' says Lloyd Charmers. 'It was my chord construction and not Bread's, because the guy who wrote the song, David Gates, he did it differently. I took it and I did it my way.'

'Everything I Own' was originally intended for Marcia Griffiths, who'd picked out the song from an Olivia Newton John LP that Charmers had lent her. Marcia had already scored a hit with 'Sweet Bitter Love' for him but she didn't get round to voicing 'Everything I Own' for quite some time.

'Then one day Ken Boothe walked in the studio and said, "boy Lloydie, me love that song, y'know?" So me just change it round from how I was going to do it with Marcia to suit Ken, and I didn't even know that song properly, which is why I gave Ken some different lyrics to sing, because some of them weren't in the David Gates song. I put my lyrics in it and it sounded okay but when I went back and did it again with Marcia, nothing happened.'

He had better luck with Bob Andy, who later recorded 'Fire Burning' and 'Games People Play' with Charmers at Federal Records.

Charmers had got to know the Khouri family who owned Federal when he was working as a salesman for Byron Lee. After Richard Khouri had invited him to work with them and handed over keys to the studio, that was it. They launched the Wildflower label and Federal had hits galore with singers like Ken Boothe, Pluto Shervington ('Ram Goat Liver'), Derrick Harriott and Ernie Smith, whose *Life Is Just For Living* set was recorded there. Federal became known as 'the sophisticated reggae studio' and people compared it to Gamble and Huff's Philly sound, which pleased Charmers greatly.

'At one time, we had numbers one, two, three, four and five on the charts,' he said. 'We did Dobby Dobson's 'Sweet Dreams' and that mash up Jamaica, Trinidad, Barbados and the whole of the Caribbean. Wildflower started to take life, and everybody loved that label in England as well.'

There's no record of Marvin Gaye having put in an appearance at the Turntable Club on Red Hills Road on 19 May, but his name did feature in all the advertising. 'Appearing as special guest of honour, Marvin Gaye', it proclaimed, whilst the event itself was billed as 'Marvin Gaye's Welcome To Jamaica' and with a supporting line-up recruited entirely from Bunny Lee's stable. There must have been a lot of people left disappointed that night, despite John Holt, Delroy Wilson, Johnny Clarke and Cornel Campbell all performing.

Two days later, Marvin headlined 'The Biggest Benefit Show Of All Time' at the Carib Theatre. 'Come and enjoy the thrilling music, the artistry and showmanship of "Mr Trouble Man", supported by a Big 20 Piece Band', invited the posters seen around town.

That occasion was a fundraiser for a new Sports Complex in Trench Town and was followed on 23 May by the Mammoth Labour Day Musical Spectacular at the National Stadium. Bob Marley and the Wailers, Cedric Brooks and Divine Light, Ernie Smith, Zap Pow and Skin, Flesh & Bones were among the other support acts. Marvin was said to have come out swinging, with a full band roaring behind him. The musicians wore matching uniforms, the orchestrated arrangements were well drilled, whilst Gaye himself was in fine voice amidst all the screams and adulation. Lines like 'this ain't living, bills going sky high' resonated with many of those present, as he alternated between love and reality songs. It was a masterly performance by an artist who'd incorporated message songs into his repertoire, and yet still realised that an element of show business was necessary to keep his audience on board. That show was a highlight of the Jamaican musical calendar, and the Wailers' performance that night – with Peter and Bunny having briefly rejoined – earned them many new admirers. Keyboard player Bernard 'Touter' Harvey even called it 'an awakening', because a lot more middle class Jamaicans became Bob Marley fans after that show.

'Bob Marley was always a rebel, but he was also Rastafari and that frightened a lot of people, because they didn't like what Rastafari stood for in Jamaica, or what they *thought* Rastafari stood for. They saw it as a threat, but then when he became popular outside of Jamaica and their friends in London, Miami, New York or wherever said, "hey, have you heard of this guy Bob Marley? He's so great!" all of a sudden these same people decided they wanted to identify with him.'

US blues singer Taj Mahal decided to cover 'Slave Driver' on his next album and invited Marley and Family Man to the studio in San Francisco, where the recording was taking place. Alan 'Skill' Cole and Lee Jaffe went with them, and afterwards they all visited Shelter Records in Los Angeles. Denny Cordell's label had been the first to release 'Duppy Conqueror' in the US and he also arranged the filming of that Wailers' session at the Capitol Records Tower last October. During their most recent trip, Lee and Family Man had also gone to Tulsa and met members of Eric Clapton's band, fresh from their recording of 'I Shot The Sheriff.' Clapton had been jamming on some blues and rock tracks before second guitarist George Terry introduced him to the Wailers' *Burnin'* album.

'I was just presenting him with different things to noodle with, y' know? I was like, "have some fun. You might enjoy playing to this." He was at the Thunderbird Hotel and took the record, listened to it for a day or two then came back and said, "this stuff is incredible. I've never played stuff like this before, so let's go for it." I kept pushing 'I Shot The Sheriff', and Eric liked it, but he was hesitant. He wasn't sure that he could do it justice, and so the decision came down to Tommy Dowd really liking the song, and he pushed for it. He said, "I know that you like the song and I know that you want to do it, so let's just roll some tape, we'll play it back and if you really like it, we'll run with it." After we'd done it, Robert Stigwood [Clapton's manager] was going, "oh that's fantastic. That's wonderful. Eric has never done something like this. It's wonderful".'

We've already mentioned Ernie Smith's 'Duppy Gunman.' That song told the story of when Ernie was approached by an unseen gunman, and the singer took off faster than top Jamaican sprinter Donald Quarrie. It topped the Jamaican charts just as quickly, but it was the new entry from Bob Andy that attracted most attention, on account of its uncompromising lyrics. 'Fire Burning' was banned by both radio stations, and when Bob Andy let his objections be known, Michael Manley met him face to face so they could try and resolve the situation. Is there any other country except Jamaica where that kind of thing would happen? Because there was another line in it which said, 'We'd like to ask you leaders, "what have you got in mind?", and Manley obviously took him seriously enough to respond.

'Michael Manley was really quite radical,' said Andy. 'He was very much pro-Black Power and Rastafari, because he really walked through the grassroots to get to power, and got love and admiration from the people for the fact that he'd married a black Jamaican who was a radio and television personality. You see, Manley was quite erudite and articulate. I'd say that Michael Manley played a key role in opening up the political consciousness of Jamaican people and apart from that he was quite Hollywood, with his looks and his charm. I liked him, although I had one meeting with him which I didn't like too much, but that was just a personal thing, after he'd taken issue with 'Fire Burning.' He and myself, we had a chat at Jamaica House and he told me he was the biggest poet in Jamaica and I should tell my friends that!'

Other notable new releases included Bob Marley's 'Road Block' – the debut single from his forthcoming album for Island – and Johnny Clarke's 'None Shall Escape The Judgement', an early example of 'flyers.' Skin, Flesh & Bones' drummer Sly Dunbar was a keen fan of Gamble & Huff's Philadelphia label, and had already adapted their distinctive hi-hat sound on Al Brown's 'Here I Am Baby.' Astute as ever, Bunny Lee got his band of Aggrovators to follow suit, then saturated the market with it. Some say that 'flyers' refers to the actual sound, whereas others say it came from Lee's liking for Kentucky Fried Chicken, because he called the wings 'flyers'. He was now so prolific they called him 'Striker', because every time he went in the studio he came out with a hit – so many in fact that he spread his releases over several different labels, including Jackpot, Lickpot and Justice.

Johnny Clarke's 'Every Day You're Wondering' had been a minor hit for Rupie Edwards, and when Bunny saw him perform it at the Turntable Club one night, he was impressed. Shortly after that, Earl Zero wrote a song that he couldn't quite manage and so Bunny offered it to Johnny Clarke instead, who didn't waste a second making it his. That was 'None Shall Escape The Judgement', and the combination of the 19-year-old's fresh vocal style and the track's distinctive sound worked wonders.

'The flying cymbal brought about a difference in reggae as far as the arrangement of the drum pattern was concerned,' Clarke explains. 'The drum pattern had changed to a form of calypso, where it was running at a faster tempo. Me being a newcomer, and at the same time linking up with a new sound, that just made we different and exceptional, y'know? It's like the massive just accept that with open arms, and bwoy it just run away, 'cause after that everybody start using the flying cymbal. Even bigger artists than me, 'cause that's the only way they could get some form of sales back then. In those times we were 100 per cent original, both in the background and the lyrics, because as a new artist you couldn't introduce yourself with a cover song. You'd have to find time to meditate and be creative and then make some original lyrics, which is the reason why those songs come in with a certain lasting vibes.'

His first album for Bunny, also named *None Shall Escape The Judgment*, was a mix of romance, reality and religiosity. Some of the love songs – 'True Believer In Love', for example – had already been hits for other singers on Lee's payroll. It was therefore originals like 'Joshua's Word About The Gun Court' and 'Enter Into His Gates With Praise' – also the single 'Move Out Of Babylon' – that registered most.

Incidentally, Cornel Campbell had been offered 'None Shall Escape The Judgement' first, but Bunny owed him some money, so he'd let the opportunity pass him by. When Clarke's song became a hit, Cornel sang 'Gun Court Law' on the same rhythm, but it arrived too late to make a difference. The older youth was left in need of a hit until he visited Bunny in Greenwich Farm one night, and inspiration came to him as the music played and people were dancing and having fun. His next single would be 'Natty Dread In A Greenwich Town', and it let the listeners experience just what it was like to be at a reggae dance in Jamaica. That song was the closest we could get to the real thing, audio-wise, until 'sound-tapes' became more popular. Rumour has it – there's that phrase again – that Mick Jagger was the first to tape a live Jamaican dancehall session during the Stones' visit in 1971. That could well be, but the first recorded instance – and which most of us heard retrospectively – was of a King Tubby's Home Town Hi Fi dance in Kingston somewhere, from 1974. Cassettes were new on the market, and the audio quality wasn't great, but there it was, with the bass-lines rumbling like thunder, and U-Roy making spontaneous interjections as the stylus bit into dub-plate versions of the latest Horace Andy tunes.

King Tubby's studio never really got going until 1974. He'd

bought a dub cutting machine and spring reverb and, more importantly, mastered that MCI console that he'd got from Dynamic. His famed high pass filter's eleven frequency steps allowed extreme sweeps to be performed with ease, and created a unique sound that would become Tubby's trademark. Errol T was doing something similar at Randy's, when cutting dubs 'live' to acetate using a parametric equaliser. The differences between his dubs and those of Tubby's were slight at this point. Generally, Errol T used switches for bringing sounds in and out of the mix, whereas Tubby had slide faders which made for a smoother sound. But those two – together with Lee 'Scratch' Perry – were definitely pushing back the boundaries, both technically and otherwise.

Dub From The Roots was the first King Tubby album produced by Bunny Lee, and the music on it sounded as if it had been beamed down from outer space, as disembodied voices appeared and disappeared in the mix, like those of phantoms. Tubbs had a gift for stretching and contracting time in such devastating fashion, you'd never believe such wizardry came from relatively basic equipment. For proof, compare his dub versions of well-worn rhythms such as 'Please Be True', 'Declaration Of Rights' or his favourite, 'Ali Baba', to the originals. The release of that album, which was better distributed than its predecessors, prompted Winston Edwards to compile *King Tubby Meets The Upsetter At The Grass Roots Of Dub*, which outsold many a vocal set and helped pave the way for a flood of other dub albums in its wake.

Herman Chin Loy had been busy in the meantime completing Jamaica's first twenty-four-track studio at his premises on Constant Spring Road, near Half Way Tree. Rosser Electronics of Wales designed it, including the console that housed the Studer tape machine. Dynamic was still the studio of choice, however, and Jimmy Cliff returned there to record his latest album *House Of Exile* with the All Stars – a collection of songs brimming with love, universal truths, wise counsel and protest that found him rejuvenated after his adventures in London and Alabama.

He was back on RJR each weekday morning with the show *Good Morning Man*, and appeared as a guest on Dermot Hussey's radio programme *Progressions* over at rival station JBC a short time after. He and Rex Nettleford, Artistic Director of Jamaica's National Dance and Theatre Company, also appeared on the API television show *Expression* hosted by Neville Willoughby, who quizzed them about the NDTC's latest production, *A Tribute To Jimmy Cliff*, hailed as 'their most satisfying performance to date.'

Jimmy may have had enough of rock and roll, but Eric Clapton and his entourage, who arrived in Jamaica during August, were still enamoured of reggae. Clapton spent the first three weeks of his visit at Dynamic, recording tracks for his album *There's One In Every Crowd*, although these sessions produced little of note. Peter Tosh, who'd recently been arrested for possession of ganja, sang harmonies on Eric's cut of 'What You Gonna Do' – a song that he'd already written and released on his own Intel Diplo label. The magic wasn't there, and he and Clapton's wildly different lifestyles meant there was little spark between the two of them, not like when Peter and Ras Michael got together. The latter had learnt the art of hand drumming in various Rasta communities scattered throughout downtown Kingston and had formed his group of drummers and singers, the Sons of Negus, in the early sixties. He was the first Rastafarian to host a reggae radio programme in Jamaica (*The Lion of Judah Radio*, which aired in 1967) and 'Lion Of Judah' also became the title of his debut single, issued on his own Zion Disc label. 'Ethiopian National Anthem', which served as the basis for Peter Tosh and U-Roy's 'Earth Rightful Ruler', was another of his early, self-produced singles. To finance his label, Ras Michael played on sessions at Studio One, where he contributed to Jackie Mittoo's 'Drum Song.' He also drummed on the Wailers' 'Midnight Ravers', but he and Peter Tosh were near neighbours, as the Sons of Negus was based in Hunt's Bay, whilst Peter and his girlfriend Yvonne Whittingham (who'd accompanied the Wailers on their US tour) lived on Solitude Road. Ras Michael and the Sons of Negus' debut album *Nyahbinghi*, which Peter played on, was produced by Tommy Cowan, who'd learnt the business whilst working as a salesman for Dynamic. He licensed that LP to Trojan during a visit to the UK in August, but Starapple was the label he used for Jamaican releases, such as a previous Inner Circle album, *Dread Reggay Hits*, which Trojan later renamed *Rock The Boat*. Only their cut of 'None Shall The Escape The Judgment' merited putting a picture of the Gun Court on the sleeve, with its watchtower, razor wire fence and sign above the gate saying GUN COURT in big letters. With the exception of 'Westbound Train', the remaining choices are unremarkable, although their lead singer Jacob Miller brought verve and enthusiasm to the band's covers of soul and reggae hits, and had several excellent singles of his own out – including 'Forward Jah Jah Children' and two produced by Augustus Pablo, 'Keep On Knocking' and 'Baby I Love You So', with the majestic 'King Tubby Meets Rockers Uptown' on the flipside.

Pablo had been prolific by his standards, and especially when producing tracks for his own Rockers and Pablo International labels. He'd recorded albums for Randy's (*This Is Augustus Pablo*) and Tommy Cowan, who released *Ital Dub* on Starapple. This set recycled many of the same Inner Circle rhythm tracks the band had used for their own recordings. It was astonishing how Pablo invested his humble melodica with such an aura of spirituality, but then he'd fully embraced Rastafari by then, later telling me the story of how this had come about.

'The time when I and I come was like revolutionary times, coming out of the sixties and into the seventies,' he explained. 'People in America and Jamaica were working towards freedom. It was all about Black Power or black this and that, and we didn't really put up with what our parents had been through. We couldn't accept it, and even though the authorities sent force against us, after a while they had to leave us alone and realise that no matter how they burn or shoot we, we weren't going to change. It ended up a calling, but a whole heap of youths joined Rastafari at that

191

time. Some died, and others end up falling by the wayside. It was a hard trod, but I was into music and loved it with all of my heart and so eventually I learn that I have to do more than just be in the music, y' know? I have to look towards the inner part of my being and find out what's really going on in certain directions and discover more about the Almighty, 'cause it may look simple, but He rule the music in every aspect.'

Pablo didn't join any Rastafarian organisation like the Twelve Tribes of Israel. 'I'm not really into those things,' he explained, 'because I had more of a calling from within myself, y' know? Except you have to deal with people out there, like elders and all that. I used to go around to the herb camp and see a brethren there called Bongo Pat, who do some songs for me as well. I'd go there, draw fi the chalice and sit as a youth listening to the elders talking, and that's how I learnt about the spiritual path. I never talk at all, I just listen and smoke herb. Anyone who love Rasta would come there and see what a gwan with the elder Rastamen and as time went by we just learn more and more.'

'Herb camps were the seats of knowledge at that time, because there were always elder Rastafarians there, or herb smokers who were very knowledgeable about Africa and the system so to speak,' agreed Bob Andy, who'd recently started his own Jamrock label and was producing songs with Delroy Wilson, Leroy Smart and Richard Ace. 'I learnt about Ethiopia before I ever read anything about Ethiopia. I learnt about Ethiopia in a ganja camp out by Rockfort called Poco Flat, where you had elders like Elder Roy and Scaramouche. There was this gully and right on the other side was the Church Of God, and the pastor would prevent the police from raiding the ganja camp. He would say to them, "you don't trouble me. I won't trouble you. You do what you do, and I do what I do." Mortimo Planno, who was one of the most eloquent and exposed Rastafarians, had gone to Ethiopia. Bob Marley spent a lot of time with Planno, who toughened him up in the ways of Rastafari and the world. He guided him somewhat, and 'Natty Dread' is a song

I think might have been inspired by Mortimo Planno, but yes, some of us would seek out elders like that, and certainly to the extent where you'd start forming your own opinion.

'Don't forget that Marcus Garvey preceded Rastafari, and as a matter of fact he was like John The Baptist to the emergence of Rastafari in Jamaica. It all happened within a relatively short period of time – Jamaica's Independence, Marcus Garvey, Rastafari and Black Power consciousness.'

Burning Spear's latest single was 'Marcus Garvey', which producer Jack Ruby released on the Fox label. Real name Lawrence Lindo, he'd grown up in Greenwich Town before heading for the north coast and working as a hotel waiter. His first sound system was Laurie's, and when he went to live in Ocho Rios he renamed it Jack Ruby's Disco. Like Winston Rodney, he was a regular visitor to Key Largo Beach, where musicians would hang out and discuss the latest sounds. Jack met an early line-up of Burning Spear there around the same time they first went to Coxsone and recorded 'Door Peep Shall Not Enter.' When that relationship ended, Spear approached Jack at a local cricket match and told them the group had two new songs they wanted to record. After makeshift rehearsals at the Jamaica Hilton with Tyrone Downie, Jack Ruby took Spear to Randy's, where they recorded 'Marcus Garvey' and 'Tradition' on the same day. The engineer was George Philpott, although he was only there for a short period.

'He came from Dynamic,' says Clive Chin, 'but hear the joke now. Errol T started the session for Burning Spear's *Marcus Garvey* album, and then left during the early stages. I couldn't believe it when that happened and I almost fell out with my old man over it because my thinking was that if Errol wanted more money, then pay the man! Errol worked hard, and he told me that the reason he left was all to do with money, because the family wasn't treating him properly where that was concerned. But to me, he was a family member and he wasn't just an engineer either, but somebody who helped to create the sound as well.'

'I was the first one to sing about Marcus Garvey,' says Winston Rodney. 'We are from the same town, St Ann's Bay. In fact, we are from the same street, but the first time I really heard the name 'Marcus Garvey', it was right at the corner of Main Street and Market Street in St Ann's Bay. Three men were standing there talking and I had no understanding of what they were saying, but I sure remembered the name 'Marcus Garvey.' After that I start to ask questions and realise that Marcus Garvey is a black hero. He was one of those men from an earlier time who stood for something. I started digging in a bid to learn more and at some point I saw that Marcus Garvey was framed, and especially in America, but I didn't want to be too political, or to be mistaken for a politician.

'As a matter of fact, when I first start singing about Marcus Garvey there was a tailor's shop back in my home town where they did some recording. Well I went in there and they said I should sing what I had and when I sang, "do you remember the days of slavery?" they said, "no, no, no. that can't work. Slavery days was many hundreds of years ago." They said I should sing another song, and when I sing, "Marcus Garvey's words come to pass", they said, "no, no, no. Marcus Garvey died years ago! We don't want anything like that." They turned me down. They didn't take any of my songs. They acted like those songs were dangerous! They didn't want nothing like that but you see, nothing ever happen before the time and that's where Jack Ruby came in, because 'Slavery Days' was on the album we did together, along with 'Marcus Garvey', and things start happening after that.'

Spear had already left Studio One but Coxsone, couldn't resist blunting the impact of the group's resurgence with the album *Rocking Time*, which included classic sides like 'Swell Headed' and 'Foggy Road', as well as the title track. The man who'd recommended that he go to see Coxsone, Bob Marley, was in London with the Barrett brothers, working on Marley's forthcoming solo album. A number of tracks were finished already, including 'Lively

Up Yourself', 'Bend Down Low' and recent single 'Rebel Music (3 O'Clock Road Block)', featuring Lee Jaffe on harmonica, and that Bob had written after being stopped at police checkpoints. Marley didn't actually have a band at this juncture, as Bunny, Peter and Joe Higgs had all departed, and Wya had left to join Larry McDonald in Taj Mahal's band. He still liked the idea of incorporating rock guitar into reggae, and Al Anderson – an American from New Jersey who'd come to the UK with the Detroit Emeralds – fitted the bill perfectly. He was already well versed in soul, African and rock, and the solo he played on 'No Woman No Cry' got him recruited on the spot. Replacing Peter and Bunny's harmonies wasn't so straightforward, but rather than try and emulate them, Bob opted for something quite different and, acting on Delroy Washington's recommendation, used Candi McKenzie and a couple of girls from Wolverhampton on a couple of tracks (who weren't credited).

Notting Hill Carnival took place during his visit, and in between sessions at Basing Street, Marley and the Barretts wandered round, taking in the sights and sounds of Europe's largest street festival. London sound system Sir Coxsone had set up by the flyover under a big banner emblazoned with Rasta colours. Bob had given owner Lloyd Coxsone exclusive mixes of tracks they'd been working on, and reggae fans who were there talked about these dub-plates for months afterwards. Mind you, they were spoilt for choice that week, as the Jamaica Showcase came to Britain, featuring Dennis Brown, Toots and the Maytals and Dennis Alcapone, backed by Skin, Flesh & Bones, whose residency at the Tit For Tat on Red Hills Road had been attracting sell-out crowds all summer. In July they'd recorded lead singer Al Brown's debut album at Dynamic, named after the hit version of Al Green's 'Here I Am Baby' that had fuelled so much of the attention they'd been getting. The band had recorded a couple of other Al Green tracks on the album (including 'Love And Happiness'), as well as soul hits by the Van Dykes and New York City. The Philly influence was unmistakable, but still couldn't overshadow Skin, Flesh & Bones' own exciting Jamaican sound. Their UK tour opened at the Top Rank in Reading, and then the Rainbow Theatre in Finsbury Park. The following night Dennis Brown joined Dennis Alcapone and Desmond Dekker at the Empire Ballroom in Leicester Square and got a great reception, as did Bob Marley when he was invited on stage, but it was memories of the *Jamaica Showcase's* free concert in London's Hyde Park on 31 August that stayed with drummer Sly Dunbar the longest.

'That was the first time reggae appeared at some big festival in the UK,' he said with pride, 'and from there I started thinking totally different, because we didn't have enough energy inside of reggae, and that was something we learnt from doing that concert. We had to find a way of dealing with it, because our music wasn't fast and we couldn't go back to ska, even though it had the energy we needed. That's when I start looking around and experimenting, trying to get the drum sound up as far as possible...'

Toots, who wore a bright red jumpsuit that day, gave a typically enthused performance. The Maytals had tied with the Wailers for Best Group at the *Swing Magazine* Awards the previous month, whilst his latest LP, *Roots Reggae* – also issued with a rearranged running order as *In The Dark* – made Album Of The Week in Jamaica. Produced by Warwick Lyn at Dynamic, it had master blasters like 'Time Tough', 'Fever' and their cover of John Denver's 'Country Roads' on it. Those songs sent audiences crazy, and Toots and the Maytals earned their role as headliners, as none of the other acts could have followed them. The tour ended with a rousing farewell at London's Hammersmith Palais, but Dennis Brown decided to stay in the UK for a while longer. In the weeks ahead he would tour clubs up and down the country, backed by the Cimarons, whose new lead singer Winston Reedy featured on their debut album, appropriately titled *In Time*. It started promisingly enough, with a cover of the O'Jays' 'Ship Ahoy', but their original songs sounded lightweight by comparison, despite Carl Gayle hailing the group as 'the backbone of English reggae.' Anyone listening to Winston Groovy's latest single 'Please Don't Make Me Cry' would no doubt agree, but their most impressive release during this period wasn't on their album or even planned, yet 'Talking Blues' made the whole reggae world sit up and take notice.

The band had met up with Bob Marley at the Empire Ballroom, where he complained that the Cimarons were always doing covers, but they hadn't done one of his songs yet. Not long afterwards they were at Chalk Farm waiting on the Pioneers, who didn't show. Rather than waste time, the Cimarons recorded the backing track for 'Talking Blues' in just one take and then forgot about it. It wasn't until weeks later that engineer Sid Bucknor played it back to them. They liked what they heard and voiced it straightaway. Trojan's Webster Shrowder then played it to Tommy Cowan who took it back to Jamaica with him, where it joined a long queue of tracks waiting to be released.

There had been upsetting news from Ethiopia by then, claiming that Emperor Haile Selassie I was under house arrest, and that he'd been stripped of the autocratic powers he'd held for over forty years. His personal advisors had been jailed, his Crown Council abolished, his personal court of justice disbanded and his military advisory committee scrapped. In addition, a coterie of rebel officers called the Dergue, led by Mengistu Haile Mariam, had announced the nationalisation of the Emperor's fifteen palaces and all his private enterprises, including the country's bus service. They'd also seized incriminating documents detailing where all the country's wealth had gone, and demanded that the Emperor return money deposited in overseas bank accounts totalling half a billion dollars. Cries of 'Hang the Emperor! Hang the Emperor!' were heard in the streets outside the palace where he was being held and the people's anger towards him hardened yet further two weeks later when Jonathan Dimbleby's Thames TV feature *Ethiopia: The Unknown Famine* was shown on national television. This report had been filmed in April, by which time over 100,000 of Ethiopia's inhabitants had died of starvation. It showed desolate, heart-breaking footage of human suffering, including children so ill and malnourished that they were beyond help. Typhus, cholera, pneumonia, dysentery, fever, malaria, tuberculosis or gastroenteritis were rife as there was no sanitation in the camps where the destitute gathered in the hope of receiving food. What the programme didn't show was how Emperor Haile Selassie I lived, nor his exotic pets, including lions, leopards, a black panther, an anteater and flock of flamingos that were fed each morning as he strolled through the park adjoining the New Palace in Addis Ababa. He also owned a fleet of twenty-seven luxury cars including Rolls Royce limousines, Mercedes-Benzes and Lincoln Continentals. Crucially, since there were no public schools or universities in Ethiopia, he'd begun the process of sending young people from favoured families overseas to Europe or America so they could obtain a good education. This backfired, however, since many of those who returned looked around them and agitated for radical change.

The day after the film was shown, as reported in Ryszard Kapuściński's book *The Emperor*, military trucks pulled up in front of the Palace. Three officials in combat uniform made their way to the chamber where the Emperor had been since dawn. After a preliminary bow, one of them read the act of dethronement. The text, published later in the press and read over the radio, accused the Emperor of having taken advantage of his authority, and misusing it for his own personal ends. It also claimed that the 82-year-old monarch was incapable of meeting his responsibilities because of his advanced age. On 12 September, such claims resulted in His Imperial Majesty being deposed and the Provisional Military Committee assuming power in his stead. He was then taken to the Menelik Palace in the hills overlooking Addis Ababa, whilst most of the Imperial family were sent to Kerchele prison, known locally as Alem Bekagne or 'I've Had Enough Of This World.'

Two days later, Eric Clapton's single 'I Shot The Sheriff' topped the Billboard Hot 100 in the US and introduced many thousands of American music-lovers to the songwriter – Jamaican reggae artist Bob Marley. It was a prestigious event for both him and the reggae genre, yet his own album wasn't out as yet, no tour dates were planned and Island Records hadn't even announced the break-up of the Wailers, which had happened nine months earlier. Clapton himself was still in Jamaica when the news broke, although he'd finished recording and was holidaying on the North coast. Despite his initial reservations about its authenticity, the single's success not only confirmed Clapton's return from the wilderness, it also gifted the reggae genre additional credibility with rock audiences. The British guitarist wasn't pretending to be Jamaican and had sung 'I Shot The Sheriff' in his own voice. It was also properly credited and made Marley more money than he'd ever seen before, both from sales of the single and its inclusion on Clapton's album *461 Ocean Boulevard*, which went to number one in the US and number three in the UK.

No sooner had Clapton left Jamaica than Andy Fairweather-Low had a UK Top 10 with 'Reggae Tune', and then Ken Boothe's 'Everything I Own' went to Number one. Even veteran US flautist Herbie Mann had been getting in on the act. His new album for Atlantic, *Reggae*, had been recorded at Dynamic with the All Stars, but attracted criticism from both jazz and reggae fans. In response, Mann told Jim Newsom that for a musician to limit themselves to just one style or approach 'is like saying you can only have one dish on the smorgasbord table, especially for a flute player where there is no jazz tradition. Every civilisation, every musical tradition, has flute and drum music so I thought, "why shouldn't you enjoy yourself and why should you limit yourself to any one diet?" So I went to Brazil, Africa and Jamaica, and all these things had validity for me.'

Mann wasn't keen on many of America's jazz critics, and during an interview with the *New York Times'* Robert Palmer, he accused the likes of Dan Morgenstern and Nat Hentoff of always wanting to put jazz on an intellectual level and 'to take it away from the basics, from the sensuality of African and Afro-Cuban music.

'The audience I had developed wasn't listening intellectually,' he complained. 'They were listening emotionally, yet so many of the writers were afflicted with what I call the 18-year-old syndrome. When I was 18, I only wanted purity – an 18-year-old's idea of purity, and everything else was selling out. But I think it's a much bigger lie to only try and satisfy somebody else. Life is too short for somebody else to set a standard for me and decide what my tastes in music should be.'

Reggae aficionados wanting something more authentic were best advised to check out what was happening at Channel One, where the Hoo Kim brothers were making good progress.

'Channel One had such a good sound,' says the Wailing Souls' lead singer Winston 'Pipe' Matthews. 'From the day I went there and to Studio One, I knew that those were the two best studios in Jamaica, and do you know the reason why? It's not like anybody could just go ahead and build a studio. The building was there and they built the studio inside of it. It's more compact that way, and the recording room was so tight, but everything that came from Channel One was a hit. People talk about how they feel, but the main thing is to know...'

Channel One's musicians recut the rhythm of the Wailing Souls' Studio One hit 'Back Out', then Jo Jo Hoo Kim called the group to come and voice it. Pipe refused, and said that he'd write a different song for it. The result was 'Things And Time', which was a big hit. Dillinger's cut 'Natty BSc' caught on fast, and so, too, Ernest 'Fitzroy' Wilson's 'I Know Myself.' Ernest was a member of the Clarendonians when they had several number one hits in the ska and rocksteady eras. He then went solo in 1967 and recorded a string of hits for Coxsone, including 'Money Worries', 'Storybook Children', 'Undying Love' and 'If I Were A Carpenter', but 'I Know Myself' – recorded at Channel One and issued on the Hoo Kims' own Hitbound label – did wonders for his popularity in 1974, and especially with sound system crowds.

We should also mention Leroy Smart, who would tell people that the only thing his parents left him was his name. That's because he was orphaned from the age of 2 and attended Maxfield Park Children's Home until the age of 12, when he transferred to the Alpha Boys School. Delroy Wilson was the singer he most admired, whilst recording his first records for Mr Caribbean, Joe Gibbs ('Ethiopia') and Gussie Clarke, who produced the first cut of 'Pride And Ambition', which he recently re-recorded for Channel One and was all set to become his biggest hit since the previous year's 'Mother Lisa.'

Ansel Cridland also had an unhappy childhood. When his father left for England, Ansel was placed in the care of a stepmother who mistreated him. A neighbour offered to put him on a bus and send him back to an uncle, who then passed him on to his grandmother who lived in Kingston, near a yard where singers like the Tartans rehearsed. Ansel would climb up a breadfruit tree and sit and watch them sing from high in the branches before forming a group of his own called the Linkers, who recorded a handful of songs for La Fud Del – a label owned by a shoemaker on the Spanish Town Road – between 1971-73. Ansel was living in Majestic Gardens by then, a place whose name couldn't be more inappropriate, as it was one of the most deprived areas in Kingston. Locally it was known as 'Baktu', and it epitomised what someone once said of ghettos, that they were places 'where human souls are ground into dust by the same self-serving iniquity that invented slavery.'

It was around this time that Ansel met up with Danny Clarke, who'd voiced a couple of tunes at Studio One whilst a member of the Righteous Flames. He was from Jungle and played melodica on Ansel's solo tune, 'Sitting On The Sidewalk.' When they heard that Channel One were holding auditions, they went along with Winston Watson and sang Ansel's song 'Woman Is Like A Shadow.' Ossie Hibbert was there and got them to record it straight away, but Jo Jo didn't like the lyrics, and wanted them to change it. Luckily for the Linkers, as they were known then, Ernest Hoo Kim disagreed, but the song was left on tape, and wouldn't be released for quite some time.

On 29 September, the *Gleaner* published an article referring to recent events in Ethiopia, entitled 'What will the Rastafarians do?'

'For a number of years, the members of the Rastafarians have hailed Haile Selassie as a God or God incarnate,' it began. 'However, these Rastafarians are quite unrealistic. They are overlooking the unfavourable conditions existing in Ethiopia. Our black brothers and sisters are suffering and experiencing the pangs of death. All of these conditions are attributed to Haile Selassie's rule, while the Emperor, his family and close associates lived in extravagant luxury. Behold, the writing was on the wall. Haile Selassie had been ruling unjustly and now we know what had been happening over these forty-four years... for too long this man has been held in high esteem without us knowing what he was really doing to help his country.'

It was too soon to know how Rasta artists like Bob Marley would respond, and especially since Island planned on releasing *Natty Dread* on 25 October, credited to Bob Marley and the Wailers. This choice of name proved controversial, since the backing band was now called the Wailers, and Peter and Bunny's contributions would be consigned to history. Bunny was so upset by this betrayal that he vowed to call himself 'Bunny Wailer' from then on, so that people wouldn't forget who the name really belonged to. *Natty Dread* was a great album regardless, despite having been put together without a regular band or harmony singers. Marley even used a drum machine on tracks like 'No Woman No Cry' and 'So Jah Seh', but it was social commentaries like 'Them Belly Full (But We Hungry)', 'Rebel Music (3 O Clock Roadblock)' and 'Revolution' that would set this album apart. Oh, and the title track, of course, which took listeners on a triumphant and unforgettable trip round the streets of Trench Town, as seen through the eyes of a Rasta sufferer.

Island had finally announced the break-up of the original Wailers just prior to the release of *Natty Dread* and, according to Family

Man, 'Talking Blues' was written about the other two, especially the line about their feet being too big for their shoes. Despite his defiance over the name change, Bunny patched up his differences with Bob, whereas Peter continued to keep his distance.

Within a few days of Muhammad Ali regaining his world heavyweight title against all odds after an emotional fight in Zaire – the so-called 'Rumble In The Jungle' – with reigning champion George Foreman, the Mighty Dells and Aretha Franklin's sister Erma performed at the National Arena, supported by Bob Andy, Judy Mowatt and Junior Byles, backed by 'Jamaica's number one band Zap Pow.' Junior's 'Curly Locks' was already well on the way towards becoming one of the biggest selling songs of the year. The lyrics told of a girl's father getting upset because she's dating a dreadlocks man – a scenario that had become increasingly common in Jamaican society. Junior's career had faded after the initial promise of 'Beat Down Babylon.' In fact he'd given up and become a bus driver for a while, but was now back on top with help from his original producer, Lee 'Scratch' Perry.

Prince Jazzbo recorded 'Penny Reel' for Perry's Upsetters label, and after announcing that he was 'a Youth In Service', began producing himself. The resulting tracks included 'Step Forward Youth' and 'Kick Boy Face', on which he echoed the sentiments heard on Big Youth's 'Every Nigger Is A Star.' He actually voiced that rhythm twice, with 'Rough Time' offering the reminder that poor people were still suffering, even as the rich got richer.

Jazzbo's voice carried authority, but there was another talented deejay with ambition who'd come to stake a place among Kingston's elite. It was Scratch who first gave Dr Alimantado a break, after inviting him to chant a few lines on the flipside of Junior Byles' 'Beat Down Babylon' and 'A Place Called Africa.' Like so many other aspiring Kingston youths, he'd grown up amongst poverty and violence, and sought refuge in Rastafari. After his parents forcibly cut off his dreadlocks he ran away from home and, inspired by U-Roy, had taken up deejaying. After discarding his real name of Winston Thompson, he was known variously as Winston Prince, Winston Cool and then Ital Winston for the magnificently funky 'Ride On' and its companion, 'I Am The Greatest Says Muhammad Ali', which he produced for his own Vital Food label. He'd launched that label with 'Just The Other Day', on which he pointed out that everybody wants money or status, but few want to be farmers, whose work is most important of all. After yet another name change – to Dr Alimantado – he launched another label called Ital and paid tribute to President Julius Nyerere for having all but eliminated illiteracy in Tanzania, and significantly improving healthcare. Nyerere's wide-ranging reforms weren't entirely successful – he banned all foreign music from the country, for example – but Dr Alimantado's lyrics demonstrated a keen intelligence and liking for offbeat topics that would serve him well in future.

Alimantado was an outlier, but then so was Keith Hudson, whose singing voice was so wounded and worn, you'd swear that it had cracked round the edges. It wasn't as mannered as that of Tom Waits, and lacked Dr John's musicality, yet it was somehow compelling, even though – or perhaps even because of – there being something dark and unsettling about it. The former dental apprentice had enjoyed a run of success as a producer, but he had recently begun concentrating on his own career as a singer, as heard on the album *Entering The Dragon* – a collection of vocal and instrumental tracks that varied from wild versions of 'Rockfort Rock' and 'Riot' ('Man From Shooter's Hill'), to warped and occasionally corny love songs.

In September '74 he left for London with tapes of the rhythm tracks that would underpin his next album, the dark masterpiece that was *The Black Breast Has Produced Her Best, Flesh Of My Skin, Blood Of My Blood*. Hudson had been introduced to the writings of Franz Fanon during an earlier trip to London and his lyrics would reflect this, since they related to black liberation and other themes such as matriarchy and motherhood. Those who claim that *Flesh Of My Skin* was reggae's first true concept album certainly have a point. When it was released on Hudson's own Mamba label in November, *Black Music's* Carl Gayle described it as being 'disturbing, truly evocative' and 'the best album of the year without a doubt.' It was unlike anything else heard by a Jamaican producer up until then, and the sound of it was as revolutionary as the subject matter.

'Keith was always ahead of his time, and especially with some of the mixes he'd do,' says Junia Walker, who was part of Hudson's team in Jamaica. 'There were certain sound effects that Keith would try that were really off the wall, and never applied to what was going on at the time. It was only years later that people heard what he was trying to do, and see that it fit in with whatever else was happening. In the days when *Flesh Of My Skin* was recorded, that wasn't the kind of reggae coming out of Jamaica. Nobody had ever taken it to that level, y'know? The arrangements, they were almost orchestral, but the track of his that really grabbed me was this instrumental where they recorded a brook, leaves, and birds... It was a Rasta rhythm, played on the drums and it has all these sound effects, like you can hear someone walking through leaves and all of that. I was like, "is this reggae?" That blew me away, and I was looking forward to meeting him when I heard that!'

Junia is referring to the original cut of 'Hunting', which Hudson had recorded back in Jamaica, featuring the Barrett brothers on drums and bass, and nyahbinghi drumming by Count Ossie and members of the Mystic Revelations Of Rastafari. It was Carlton Barrett who'd suggested they crumple up dried leaves to imitate the sounds of a hunter walking through a forest, which was similar to the rice grains and paper experiments they used whilst finishing the Wailers' *Burnin'* album at Basing Street. Remember, this happened in an era long before sampling was invented, when creativity and imagination, rather than technical innovation alone, made all the difference.

The Barretts' rhythm section could also be heard on Hudson's *Pick A Dub*, which is generally considered to be the first dub album to have been planned and mixed as such, rather than having been compiled as an afterthought. It featured some of the producer's hardest rhythms like cuts to 'Satta Massagana' and 'Don't Think About Me', and there were no gimmicks on it whatsoever – just powerful, stripped down drums and bass, mixed with fragments of melodica, guitar, voice and keyboards. After a short run on Mamba, Brent Clarke issued *Pick A Dub* on his Atra label, which was also home to a compilation cheekily entitled *Jah Guide, Jamaica's Greatest Hits*, since the majority of tracks on it hadn't sold, despite the inclusion of Horace Andy's 'Problems', some early Augustus Pablo sides and Freddie McKay's 'I'm A Free Man.'

The UK was reggae music's first major outpost and, as well as London, sound systems had sprung up in cities like Birmingham, Bristol, Nottingham and Leeds. Apart from hosting Carnival every August Bank Holiday, Notting Hill was home to a large and well-established black community that had weathered race riots and persistent police harassment over the years. Sufferer sound system played at the Metro in Ladbroke Grove every Friday night, but the premises were only licensed until 11 p.m., so at closing time, owner/selector Dennis Bovell would pack up his gear and drive along Shoot-Up Hill to the Carib Club on Cricklewood Broadway, where he'd play from midnight until six in the morning. On the night of Friday 13 November, Sufferer was booked to clash with rival sound Lord Koos, who had Bunny Lee in their corner.

'Next to me was Lee Perry, and it felt like he and Striker were re-enacting the old Jamaican-style sound clashes they were famous for,' said Bovell. 'Lee Perry had arrived from Jamaica earlier that day, and Larry Lawrence had gone to the airport to meet him and bring him to the Sufferers camp. We knew then that the dub plates he had for sale were not going to go any further than our record box. There was this one dub plate featuring trombonist Vin Gordon – it was a version of 'Real Rock' that started like it was a ragtime tune, and when I put that on the crowd was jubilant! Lord Koos got battered, then all of a sudden there was all this fighting happening on the dance floor between the police and people. Lee Perry looked at me, pulled up his collar, said "I am the Upsetter" and walked out!

'It turns out that some people I didn't know had decided that they were going to free a man who was being taken outside by the police. A fight ensued, but I didn't know anything about this until the next day when someone said to me, "you'd better hide because last night in the police station, all they asked us was, 'who was the Sufferers' DJ?'" I was like, "what? That's me!" So I went to the police station and said, "I've heard that you're looking for the Sufferers' DJ, and that's me." They accused me of taking the mic and stirring up the crowd against the police, and yet nothing was further from the truth. The crowd had been going crazy because I'd played that record! It's just that whoever was there when the police were arresting the man, seized that moment to snatch him away from them, right? And that's when the fight had started. Two police officers lied and said they saw me on the stage with a microphone, but I was never on the stage at any time. Then other police officers who'd come into the dance after the fight started said they heard someone on the microphone saying it, but it could've been a talking record by I-Roy, U-Roy, Big Youth or Prince Jazzbo... any of them. When I told the judge this he said to me, "do you expect me to believe that people talk on records?"'

Dennis was arrested and charged with affray. He was initially sentenced to three years for being the 'ringleader', but served only six months before the decision was overturned.

'The police excuse for having gone into that dancehall in the first place was because the driver of a car had been acting suspiciously. When the police followed him, the driver had jumped out and run into the club. Back-up was called, and hundreds of police arrived at the club. Everyone who was there that night got a slap in the face, a thump in the belly or were bitten by a dog. Castro Brown was arrested that night, and during the trial I didn't even have the presence of mind to call him or Bunny Lee as witnesses.

At the end of it, the judge said I would go to prison for three years, and I was relieved because that meant I didn't have to get up and go to court the next day. Because I'd had to do that every day for nine months up until then, between 10 a.m. and 4 p.m. That meant I couldn't work, and the only way I could make money was by going into the studio at night and making dubplates. Sound system people would come to the court, I'd give them the tapes, then they would cut the dubs and bring them back by 4 p.m... I was selling dub plates to survive...'

Less than a week after Dennis Bovell was arrested in London, Peter Tosh reluctantly appeared at the Half Way Tree courthouse in Kingston after being charged with possession of ganja back in July. He wrote and recorded a scathing protest about the raid, called 'Mark Of The Beast', in which he questioned what he'd done to be incriminated and also humiliated. Naturally, no answer had been forthcoming. Instead, he was fined $75 and told that failure to pay would result in him being jailed for three months.

It was ironic that Manley's government had recently unveiled their latest slogan 'Socialism Is Love'; that love clearly didn't extend to herb smokers.

'Democratic socialism is first an ideal, a goal and an attitude of mind that requires people to care for each other's welfare,' he explained at a public meeting in North Parade, whilst standing by a statue of his father. 'Socialism is a way of life. A socialist society cannot simply come into existence, but has to be built by people who believe in it, and practise its principles.'

Hugh Shearer resigned the day before the JLP's annual conference on the 24 November, when Edward Seaga was elected party leader whilst standing under a banner proclaiming that, 'The Time Has Come. Free up the country and make money flow again.' The former deputy got a rousing reception when deriding socialism as 'a philosophy of something for nothing' and explaining that it couldn't possibly mean equality when half of Jamaica was victimised and denied housing and work by the present government. Nor could it be mistaken for love when socialists could shoot up a church holding a memorial service for a 90-year-old woman, as had occurred recently. Manley later admitted that gunmen were terrorising Kingston at night and the threat of rape was striking fear into women's hearts. The situation was grim, and yet the police and government were fighting back with every means at their disposal.

I-Roy sang about the need for a change of approach on 'Guns At Large,' and made no secret of who he thought responsible – namely the politicians. That track had been lifted off his latest album, *Many Moods Of I-Roy*, again for Trojan. It wasn't his best, and his attempts at singing were risible, in truth. With the exception of 'Thinking Cap' and 'Deck Of Love' – cuts to 'Can I Change My Mind' and 'Stars', respectively – the remaining tracks are largely forgettable, unlike recent singles 'Forward I Back A Yard' (on the 'Step Forward Youth' rhythm), the Glen Brown-produced 'Rasta On A Sunday' and 'Sufferers Psalm' which was an adaptation of *Psalm 23*, and decried how capitalists scheme to keep the sufferers poor.

Gregory Isaacs' first song for May Pen producer Alvin 'GG' Ranglin's Hit Records was 'Innocent People Cry', with lyrics warning gunmen to change their ways, otherwise they will 'surely go to jail.' He was less specific when voicing 'Way Of Life' for the Royals' Roy Cousins, which was addressed to all of mankind. 'We should be loving and kind to one another,' he advised. 'You must try and understand each other, instead of fighting your brother every day, or you'll never reach nowhere.' Gregory was capable of real poetry no matter the subject, but never more so than when he turned his attention to affairs of the heart. He was heard begging for a second chance on recent single 'Don't Go', pleading to be told why his girl's leaving him on 'Ba Da' (produced by Lloyd Campbell), and admitting to being a prisoner of loneliness on 'Love Is Overdue', which was number one for weeks. He then flipped the script on 'I'll Be Around' for Leonard Chin, when assuring the girl that he would be there for her. He was the master of seduction and his debut album – again produced by GG's, and showing him sitting at the wheel of a new red Ford Capri, the car of the moment – sent his popularity with female listeners sky high.

He, like Johnny Clarke, had started out recording with Rupie Edwards, who made history when issuing the first-ever one-rhythm album in late 1974. Rupie used the same cut of 'My Conversation' for all twelve tracks, which included Slim Smith and the Uniques' original. Shorty The President's 'President A Mash Up The Resident' was the standout deejay cut, and there were also instrumentals led by organ, melodica, guitar and drums. It was a radical development – one that most music fans probably wouldn't have seen the point of, though reggae heads were already used to hearing versions played in the dance, and so accepted it without question.

Rupie Edwards had visions of becoming an artist himself and had a Top 10 UK hit with 'Ire Feelings (Skanga)' in late November. When Radio 1 DJ Johnny Walker played it for the first time he called it 'a most unusual record', which is hardly surprising. It was a cut to the same rhythm Rupie had used for Johnny Clarke's 'Everyday Wondering' and, apart from dubbed up snatches of the original song, there were few vocals to speak of – only repetitive bursts of words and sounds and a spate of singing, with Rupie letting us all know that he's feeling high, 'so high…'

Rupie included Johnny Clarke's original version on the compilation *Rupie's Gems*, along with tracks by Dobby Dobson, Errol Dunkley, the Heptones, the Ethiopians and the Rupie Edwards All Stars. He also produced the debut LP by Jamaican deejay Jah Woosh, who sang in a duo with Reggae George before joining Prince Lloyd's sound system in Tivoli Gardens. He then made his solo debut in 1972 for a producer named Blue who took him to Channel One, ran a piece of Little Roy's 'Prophesy' rhythm and told him to deejay something about Angela Davis, which he did. 'Try A Thing' for Blacker Morwell came next, and then Jah Woosh began recording for Rupie. His three singles for the producer – 'The Wanderer', 'Crooked Man' and 'Judy Drowned' – were among the best tracks on the album, which Rupie licensed to Cactus, whose offices were on Harlesden's High Street, London NW10.

It should be apparent by now that mainstream British radio DJs tended to promote reggae singles that were comical, ribald or gimmicky in some way. Either they thought that UK pop audiences were too dumb to appreciate other, more authentic styles of reggae, or they were trying to give the impression that Jamaica produces novelty records and not much else. They hadn't caught onto Pluto Shervington's latest hit, 'Dat', yet, which was his follow-up to 'Ram Goat Liver' and told the story of a Rastaman who found it hard not to eat pork, which was forbidden, and so had to change the wording when buying it from a butcher by calling it 'dat t'ing' instead.

Paul Khouri had produced it for Federal's Wild Flower label, which Lloyd Charmers helped get off the ground. The latter had kept faith with Marcia Griffiths after she missed out on 'Everything I Own', and produced her Wild Flower album *Sweet And Nice*, which was perfectly tailored for her cabaret routine, thanks to songs like 'Everything I Own', former single 'Sweet Bitter Love', the Manhattans' 'There's No Me Without You' and a flawless rendition of Roberta Flack's 'The First Time Ever I Saw Your Face.'

Ken Boothe had followed his own chart-topping 'Everything I Own' with an original song, 'Crying Over You', which he opened with a corny spoken intro, telling of how he'd been left alone. Thankfully, it was saved by a vocal delivery that ached with soul. Two weeks before Christmas – around the same time that Columbia Records issued Barbara Streisand's cover of Bob Marley's 'Guava Jelly' – 'Crying Over You' peaked at number eleven in the UK, although it spent nearly three months on the charts in total. Ken had three albums in the shops by then – *Let's Get It On*, which included covers of 'Is It Because I'm Black?', 'Comma Comma', 'That's The Way Nature Planned It' and 'Down By The River', and two called *Everything I Own* with different track-listings (the one on Wild Flower was better).

211

The same week that 'Crying Over You' just failed to make the UK Top 10, John Holt was at number six with a full-blown cover of Kris Kristofferson's 'Help Me Make It Through The Night', produced by Tony Ashfield. There was nothing about this record that could connect it to Jamaica – not even in the vocals, because there was not a trace of an accent anywhere to be heard. Was this a trend? Because Sharon Forrester's debut LP *Sharon*, released on Geoffrey Chung's Ashanti label, was similarly stripped of local character. She was a complete unknown before embarking on that album with Now Generation, and, inspired by what they heard Roberta Flack and Minnie Riperton doing, they pulled out all the stops aiming for the international market.

'That's what we saw and we heard and we visualised,' confirmed Mikey Chung, 'and with French horns, strings and full orchestration. We wanted to show what was possible. It was symphonic reggae, and played to a very high standard. Believe or not, that's where Wya Lindo was headed. We started an album with him as Now Generation that just folded, but Wya had some wicked ideas, man. What he was coming with was out of this world. It was something brand-new, played with electric piano and melodica... That's where he was headed. He was forever coming round to my house in Vineyard Town, and we used to sit on the veranda and work out songs together. We were always writing songs and talking about what we were going to do.'

By the time Sharon Forrester's album was released, Lindo was living in the basement of Taj Mahal's house in San Francisco, working on songs in-between touring the US and performing in venues like Carnegie Hall. He'd created a new life for himself after leaving Jamaica, whereas Muhammad Ali, world heavyweight champion boxer, was headed in the opposite direction, and on 29 December was presented with the key to the city of Kingston at a mass rally in the National Stadium attended by 20,000 people.

'With you behind me there's not a man in the world that can whip me,' he told them. He then announced that he was planning to buy a home in Jamaica, and that prime minister Michael Manley was helping him find somewhere suitable.

Manley described Ali as 'a symbol of courage – a man who has climbed to the mountaintop and stretched out a helping hand to help the suffering people of this earth,' whilst Kingston Town Clerk Basil Daniels reminded the gathering that as a young man, Ali had 'set an admirable example to the youth of today as regards strength of character in moral and social issues, and the ability to face up to adversity with unswerving courage.'

Amen to that. Now, bring on the noise...

CHAPTER SIX

1975: HAVE YOU HEARD THE NEWS?

Edward Seaga gave his first major speech as JLP leader in January, before a crowd of 25,000 in Montego Bay. After pointing out that tourism was down 10 per cent, he warned that 'the famine is coming. The cost of living is a crisis situation for people and it is driving people out of the country and out of their minds. Never have we seen so many mad people walking on the streets. These are the harsh facts of life, and in order to distract you from these factors, the government is campaigning in the country on the basis of something called socialism is love, but socialism is not love in the way they are practising it. They strive to sell it to you only as milk and honey and without the bitter and the gall. It is a system which does not believe in ownership by private individuals. The PNP claims that it is a form of socialism made in Jamaica, but if one looks at it carefully, one would see the stamp reading "made in Cuba".'

In recent months, the Garrison Gang, a pro-PNP faction from Concrete Jungle, had kept JLP areas under a constant barrage of attacks. The gang moved around on motorbikes, attacked JLP rallies and meetings, and terrorised, shot at and killed JLP supporters. They were said to operate under the protection of a certain PNP politician, and when the notorious PNP enforcer Winston 'Burry

Boy' Blake was killed in March, Michael Manley attended his funeral, despite Blake having been tried and acquitted of murder at least twice. Manley later explained his presence by claiming that his former chauffeur-cum-bodyguard was a reformed character, but was met with howls of derision. Blake's coffin was draped with a PNP flag and he was sent on his way with a tumultuous graveside gun salute, but less than an hour earlier, eight mourners were injured when the procession came under fire from snipers as it passed by Tivoli Gardens. Edward Seaga didn't deny that his supporters did the shooting, but blamed those in the funeral cortege for passing so close to his constituency, even though they were on a public thoroughfare. He called for an immediate meeting between himself, Manley and the heads of the security forces, 'in order that we may effectively join hands in the fight against crime and violence.'

The *Gleaner* newspaper set the daily agenda in Jamaica by the way it portrayed certain individuals and events, and 1975 would be the year it declared war on Manley and his policies by unleashing what was described as 'a strident cacophony of abuse.' The *Gleaner*, long-established as the bastion of conservatism, was originally the voice of the island's plantocracy and had rejoiced in the hanging of Bogle and Gordon, before hounding Marcus Garvey, who, on his return to Jamaica in 1924, was met with a *Gleaner* editorial that said, 'it is with more than profound regret that we picture any leader of thought and culture on this island associating himself with a welcome given to him.'

Few reggae fans had heard of Garvey before Burning Spear sang about him in 'Marcus Garvey' and 'Old Marcus Garvey', yet the Jamaican-born activist and Pan-African leader once headed the world's largest black self-help organisation and founded important trade links between Africa and the black Diaspora.

'Marcus was speaking about and against the people who would prevent black people from really living the life they should be living, and getting the things they should get,' said Spear's Winston

215

Rodney. 'His aim was to unite the black population, because Africans living at home and abroad must be free. This was the kind of direction he was heading in. He wasn't involved with violence, or trying to overthrow the United States. Marcus Garvey was a man who stood up for equal rights and justice, and who did a lot of important things for African-Americans. He showed them how to open their mouths and talk and ask for certain things. He showed them to stand up for themselves and how to think. He showed them how to be brave, to pray for guidance, and to create an aura of self-confidence. He showed them how to help themselves, and gave African-Americans a lot of important information, even if they were scattered around the world. They had no one else to speak for them at the time, so you can see the importance of Marcus Garvey, because he is the man who came to straighten out black folks and set the pace for Dr Martin Luther King, Malcolm X and all the others, so that they could go out there and let others hear their voice and create continuance for black folks.'

On Easter Monday, Neville Willoughby hosted a half-hour film called *Burning Spear* on Jamaican television. The programme examined Spear's philosophy and featured a number of his hit songs, including 'Marcus Garvey', but we're getting ahead of ourselves. Many Jamaicans were still under the spell of American culture, and especially where music was concerned. Early in 1975, Stevie Wonder won four Grammy Awards, including Best R&B Song for 'Boogie On Reggae Woman', but it was the Jacksons' concert at the National Stadium on 15 February that had caused most excitement and delighted the 15,000 strong audience. The group, led by younger brother Michael, had starred in their own TV series, as well as recording a string of hits for Motown including recent US number one, 'Dancing Machine.' Since the majority of their fans were teenagers, the Jacksons performed first, and only two thousand people were left by the time Bob Marley and the Wailers took the stage. The show had been stopped twice by then because of seating problems, but ended with people dancing in the aisles and clamouring for more. Peter and Bunny rejoined for the occasion, as they had for the Marvin Gaye concerts, and Tosh threatened to grab the headlines by previewing his forthcoming single 'Legalise It', which had a defiantly pro-marijuana message.

Lee Jaffe took photos of the Jacksons when they visited Marley at Island House, as 56 Hope Road was still called, where 20-year-old Cindy Breakspeare now lived in a small apartment. Born in Toronto to a Jamaican father and Canadian mother, Breakspeare had been raised in Jamaica from the age of four and had previously lived at Island House between 1971-73, whilst working as a clerk at the Sheraton Hotel. After returning to Hope Road, she managed the Dizzi Disco in New Kingston and was also a physical fitness instructor at the Spartan Health Club on Lady Musgrave Road. Bob Marley, who would soon to become her landlord, immediately became enchanted with her.

'He would go by the door and glance sideways to see if anybody was around and attempt to engage me in conversation,' she told Roger Steffens, 'and of course it would always be philosophy and talking about how you see yourself, how you present yourself as a woman and all the things you should and shouldn't do, because of course doctrine was everything then. And he would sit on the steps out the back of my apartment there with a guitar and sing. I remember hearing 'Turn Your Lights Down Low' like that. His gestures were very innocent and very boyish. He would offer a mango as a gift or simple little things like that, which I thought were very charming, especially since I had been involved with people whose style was quite different. I found it very disarming.'

In April, Marley and his new manager Don Taylor went to New York where they met with Puerto Rican singer Martha Velez at Sire Records' offices. They'd signed her after she turned up there one day clutching a copy of Johnny Nash's 'Stir It Up' and announced that she wanted to make a reggae album with Bob Marley. They admired her chutzpah, flew her to Jamaica and booked her into the Sheraton for three weeks. After recording two songs with Bob and Lee Perry, including 'Disco Night', she returned to New York for a while then went back to Kingston and recorded the rest of the *Escape From Babylon* album at Harry J's.

Lee Perry meanwhile, had been working on an album with Susan Cadogan. He'd given her a cassette with some songs on it and told her to learn them before the sessions commenced at Black Ark.

"In The Ghetto' wasn't on it, or 'Fever',' she recalls. 'I told him that I knew 'Fever' but the words I knew didn't fit the rhythm. I didn't know that Junior Byles had sung a version of it, but Lee Perry played that for me. He said "just sing it, man!" but I had to leave out the bridge as there was no space for it. Glen Adams was back in Jamaica and Lee Perry used to send him to come and get me. Glen was so handsome. He wore a cowboy hat, platform shoes and some tight shirts... he and myself, we started to go out, and Perry was mad as hell. He told me that if I got involved with Glen it would interfere with my career and he didn't want that for me, so whenever I went to the studio, it was only me and him, because he locked the door and shut them out! I was so shy at the time. I told him that I didn't like him to see me singing, and so he would turn off the lights. I would just see his little head through the glass, with all this smoke curling up, and he'd say, "you ready fi me? Rolling!" He was very eccentric. He'd wear all these rings and chains. He always had on this merino vest and he had strange ways, but that little man treated me nice.'

They hadn't quite finished her album when 'Hurt So Good' became a surprise hit in England. Everything changed after that, and at considerable speed.

'When I heard that 'Hurt So Good' was on the charts in England, I couldn't believe it! It spent three months on the charts altogether, so I came up to England and there was all this excitement around me. I remember when I went to Magnet, they inspected me like I was an object. They walked round me saying, "oh, she's quite a pretty girl." They had to fancy me up to go on TV, but they couldn't get me any contact lens in time, and of course I couldn't wear glasses, so the first time I went on *Top Of The Pops* I couldn't see a thing – I was blind as a bat! When I went there I'd just cut my hair and I had this low Afro so they made me wear this wig which was like something that the guards at Buckingham Palace would have on. It was in the style of Angela Davis and they made me wear these big earrings with it that were so uncomfortable, plus I couldn't see, and of course I was miming.

'It was Magnet who'd promoted 'Hurt So Good' and put it on the BBC chart, but then Trojan came and said, "excuse me, but that's our song." Lee Perry must have known that he was a Trojan artist, and yet he'd sold out the song to Magnet as well! They said I had to sign a contract with them, because they owned the rights to 'Hurt So Good' and they were looking after me, but when Lee Perry came to London he was furious. He was in a real temper and he grabbed me by the wrist, held me tight and said, "if you ever sign that contract I'll make sure that you never get a cent from this record!" He then stormed out of the room and banged the door and guess what? I signed it and never got a cent...'

The row over 'Hurt So Good' meant that Susan never finished the album. Perry got his wife Pauline to fill in the gaps on tracks like 'Feeling Is Right' and 'Fever' instead, whilst Susan stayed in London for a while longer. Scratch hadn't exactly wasted his time there, because Dennis Harris, proprietor of DIP Records, licensed the LP *Kung Fu Meets The Dragon* from him for release in the UK. He described it as 'the Upsetters' finest dub album' and predicted that it would become more popular than *Return Of Wax* or *Musical Bones*. The title and front cover reflected the current kung fu craze, because cinemas everywhere – including Jamaica – were screening martial arts films at the time, especially those starring Bruce Lee.

Upon his return to Jamaica, Scratch worked on tracks with Max Romeo, Junior Murvin and members of the Congos and Meditations at the Black Ark. Boris Gardner and Keith Sterling had now joined the Upsetters and Dr Alimantado was another occasional visitor. He was at Randy's when he first had the idea of playing around with different voices on a cut of Horace Andy's 'Ain't No Sunshine,' but it was Scratch who helped bring it to life after the deejay started frequenting the Black Ark. Together they created musical mayhem – a crazed relative of Rupie Edwards' 'Ire Feeling' inspired by a local fried chicken commercial, and with the Doctor's multi-layered vocals doused in echo and reverb and even speeded up in places. It's little wonder that people were already calling Scratch a genius although his methods – whilst inspired – were also erratic, according to Adrian Sherwood.

"He's never short of ideas and if you push him when you're in the studio with him, he'll develop an idea and take it even further. He's a great person to work with and he's such good fun as well. He's got this naïve madness about him, and I think that's why so many people gravitate towards him. He's like a mischievous child but he's also got this innocence about him, and a kind of charm that's missing in so much of the music we hear today."

Scratch commissioned the Gladiators to play some rhythms for him, but then he and Albert Griffiths had a falling out, so bassist Clinton Fearon ended up going there alone for six months or so. He played bass on tracks by Max Romeo, Junior Byles, Jah Lloyd and the duo Bunny and Ricky, who voiced 'Bush Weed Corn Trash' and 'Freedom Fighter' at Black Ark. Ricky was Leslie Kong's nephew. His real name was Errol, but he would become better-known as I Kong. When he was growing up it was unthinkable that a Chinese person would become a singer, but he loved singing and was a founder member of the Jamaicans before working as a bartender on a cruise ship for two years. After his return to the mainland, he called himself Ricky Storm and recorded 'The Way It Is' for Tommy Cowan's Top Cat label, backed by Inner Circle. Tommy was working at Dynamic, and that was his first production. Ricky, as he was then, also recorded for Warwick Lyn, but then he and Bunny became fast friends after the latter had returned from New York in 1973 and the pair voiced 'Freedom Fighters' on a cut of Junior Byles' 'Beat Down Babylon.' Lee Perry renamed them

Bush Weed and Corn Trash after they'd discovered that the best way to avoid being stopped by the police when smoking herb was to act mad. They were so convincing that it had worked every time, but Bunny especially was very talented.

He voiced his debut solo album, *To Love Somebody,* at Black Ark. It was credited to Bunny Scott, although everyone knew him as 'Bunny Rugs.' Just to confuse matters further, his given name was William Clarke. Like many others, he'd started singing in church. His father was an Anglican preacher, but his grandmother attended the Church Of God, which Bunny himself preferred.

'I always loved going there,' he said. 'The energy released in a church is incredible, and especially in the Church Of God, where they clap, play tambourines and sing. They'd get everybody on their feet, and it was a hell of an experience, because you would come out of there feeling as if you'd been cleansed. You'd see people talking in unknown tongues and all that, and when grandma came back home from a church service she was a completely different person from when she'd gone there! She'd been in there sweating and singing, dancing and all that, whereas at the other churches you'd just have to sit there listening to rhetoric.'

It was his grandmother who called him Bunny, because he was always jumping from place to place as a child growing up in downtown Kingston, just a few blocks below South Parade. He loved making up songs and entertaining the other kids at school, but he had his heart set on becoming a visual artist, and attended Jamaica School of Art for a while, before joining Charlie Hackett and the Souvenirs. He then left for New York in 1971, where he became lead singer with Hugh Hendricks and the Buccaneers. Scraping together a living from music wasn't easy, and this led to problems in his marriage. After his first wife got him a job in a mailroom, he'd pretend to go to work in the mornings, but would head for Central Park instead, where he'd hire a rowing boat, go out in the middle of the lake and sing and play guitar all day. After a few months doing that he decided to pursue a career in music no matter what, and after returning to Jamaica under the guise of Bunny Clarke, had a hit with a cover of Neil Diamond's 'Sweet Caroline.'

'That song was on the Jamaican charts for about eighteen weeks, but singing live and in the studio are two entirely different things, and I wanted to learn more about recording, so I went to all the studios in Kingston... I went to Federal, Dynamic and Harry J's, but I loved what Lee 'Scratch' Perry was doing at Black Ark, so I went there to study and ended up staying there for two years! He was the only person who was doing anything different at that time, even if it was in a simple, silly little way, y' know? There were some amazing things going on at Black Ark, but the LP they released with me wasn't supposed to be an album. I was just there doing tracks every now and then, and then one day I had one of the greatest experiences ever when, Bob Marley came there and spent the entire day recording 'Natural Mystic' and this other song, 'Rainbow Country.' Watching the communication and the vibes between him and Scratch was fascinating. Bob sat on a stool with his guitar for about six hours singing those two songs. It was a great learning process being there with him, and I'll always be grateful to Lee 'Scratch' Perry.'

It was at Black Ark where Junior Delgado established himself as a solo artist. After the group he was in – Time Unlimited – had begun to unravel, guitarist Earl 'Chinna' Smith produced 'Tichion' and 'Disarm The World' with him, although it would take time for them to be released. 'Tichion' was ghetto slang for politician, and that song would carry Delgado's throaty roar far beyond the confines of the local recording industry. In the meantime, he and Scratch were busy working on a tune described by the *Independent*'s Phil Johnson as 'one of the very greatest of reggae records; as apocalyptic a mix of social commentary and millennial dread as you could imagine.' Inflamed by righteous sufferation, 'Sons Of Slaves' was the epitome of word, sound and power, which is astonishing considering that Delgado was only 16 years old when he recorded it.

Around the same time, Perry produced Michael Rose's 'Observe

Life', which came out on Dickie Wong's Tit For Tat label, backed by Skin, Flesh & Bones. Michael was the former lead singer with Happiness Unlimited, who were well-known on the hotel circuit. After the manager discovered someone in the band had been smoking marijuana, Michael was asked to say who it was but refused, and was fired. He entered a talent show at the Bohemia in Half Way Tree after returning to Kingston, and that's where Niney the Observer first saw him. Michael was heavily influenced by Dennis Brown at the time, as heard on his first two songs for Niney, 'Freedom Over' and 'Love Between Us.'

Dennis himself had two albums out. *The Best Of Dennis Brown*, produced by Joe Gibbs, failed to live up to its title, despite the inclusion of 'Westbound Train', 'Silver Words', 'Poorer Side Of Town' and the original cut of 'Money In My Pocket.' *Just Dennis*, released on Trojan, was much better, but then Niney was the producer for that one. 'Show Us The Way' had been popular on dubplate for months and several of the other tracks were former singles, including 'I Am The Conqueror,' 'Cassandra' and 'No More Will I Roam', and Dennis's latest 7-inch, a cover of the Gaylads' 'Africa.'

Trojan had also licensed *Live At The Turntable* and *Dubbing With The Observer*, mixed by King Tubby, from Niney when he and Dennis had paid another visit to the UK earlier in the year. The extrovert producer was calling himself 'Sir Niney' by this stage and everything was going well, although that would change once Trojan were bought out by Marcel Rodd's Saga Records in the summer. Trojan had used Saga's pressing plant when Ken Boothe's 'Everything I Own' was a hit, but then had trouble paying the bills, so Rodd made a deal to buy Trojan whilst avoiding any responsibility for its debts. This meant that when artists and producers who were owed money by Trojan went to Rodd for payment, he told them he wasn't liable.

John Holt was one of those artists and, unfortunately for him, manager Tony Ashfield's production company Chaguaramas filed for bankruptcy two weeks later. The fallout from Trojan's demise would prove messy, and Judge Dread was another of their artists with cause for compliant. His latest UK Top 10 hit was characteristically non-PC. 'Je t'aime (Moi Non Plus)' told the story of a judge and a man who dressed in women's clothes in a case of mistaken identity and sold like hot cakes, but the cheque for £386,000 that Trojan sent him allegedly bounced, and recent changes that had been made within the UK music industry would affect him greatly. Basically, the powers-that-be decreed that only certain high street shops like Woolworths and W. H. Smiths would be able to file UK chart returns in future. The thing was, retailers like them didn't generally stock reggae releases, and especially not banned ones like Judge Dread's, and his prospects severely suffered as a result.

Back in Jamaica, there was disappointment of a different kind after director Calvin Lockhart's film *Every Nigger Is A Star* finally opened at cinemas in May. The response was underwhelming to say the least, and even Big Youth's presence wasn't enough to save it from quickly being forgotten. A week later, on 8 May, almost a hundred shotguns went missing from a freighter that lay anchored a mile off Port Royal. The guns were part of a consignment headed for Peru, and the *Gleaner* reported that investigations into the theft were being carried out 'under a shroud of secrecy.' Within just a day or so, gangs of armed men describing themselves as 'agents of the Ministry of Housing' began terrorising citizens living on the Spanish Town Road by invading houses, destroying furniture, ransacking, robbing and shooting residents, one of whom was shot the night before he was due to appear in court and give evidence against one of the Garrison gang. Members of the gang also went on a rampage in Payne Avenue after seven houses belonging to JLP supporters were invaded and smashed, and a car was torched. Another known JLP supporter was beaten, thrown into the trunk of the car and taken to a nearby gully where gasoline was poured on him and set alight. In the aftermath of such terrible events people understandably looked for signs of leadership, but how could that be forthcoming when Jamaica's two main parties were actively engaged in perpetuating the violence?

Right on cue, the Nation of Islam held its first ever rally in Jamaica at the National Arena that same month, and Minister Louis Farrakhan told the large crowd that 'if Jamaica is going to lead the world it must take the lead in morality as well as in other endeavours. Therefore you have to stop indecency, corruption and all other vices to build a strong nation. The right thing to do is not to run to America to make a pile of money and come back here. Stay right here and build a strong Jamaica for all Jamaicans.'

Tommy Cowan's Talent Corporation was already doing just that, and their headquarters at 1C Oxford Road in New Kingston was a major hub for artists and musicians at the time.

'Now that was the place!' enthused Bunny Rugs. 'It was amazing. You'd see Bob Marley stop by and buy half a dozen fish from Kiddus I, and see Ras Michael and the Sons Of Negus sat in the corner. It was the place where everyone used to meet – Gregory Isaacs included – and there was always a football game going on with people like Bob Marley, Bunny Wailer, Jacob Miller and Tommy Cowan. Those were great times. The community was hot, hot, hot, and everything was buzzing. Everything was still brewing and those artists were still searching for direction. Things had started to happen and everything was different from before. The earlier songs used to have that American kind of vibe, because they would be following what the radio stations were playing, but by the time of 1C Oxford Road everything had started to change and the roots rock reggae was really coming into play.'

'There was something magical about that place, because in the evenings, everyone would come around there,' agreed Beres Hammond, who'd recently joined Zap Pow as their lead singer. The band rehearsed in the same premises as Talent Corporation and their latest hit, 'Sweet Reggae Music', was already on its way to becoming an anthem. In-between working on Zap Pow's own tracks, the group's horn section played on a lot of sessions at Harry J's. That unit was comprised of trumpeter David Madden, sax player Glen DaCosta and trombonist Vin Gordon, and other band-members were also involved in side-projects. For example, bandleader Mikey Williams, who shared lead vocals with Beres, launched the Sho-Jam promotions company and signed Zap Pow to Island Records, who released their debut album *Zap Pow Now*, but then swiftly withdrew it for some reason. Beres had sung with Tomorrow's Children and Tuesday's Children, covering soul numbers by the likes of the O'Jays and Manhattan Transfer at the New Top Hat Club before joining Zap Pow. His predecessors included Jacob Miller, who was now firmly established as Inner Circle's frontman. The ebullient 'Jakes' as he was known, had paid some dues before being hailed as 'The Man With The Bionic Voice' and impressing all and sundry with his outstanding debut album, *Tenement Yard*, containing tracks like 'Suzie Wong', 'Tired Fi Lick Weed', 'All Night Till Daylight', 'Forward Jah Jah Children' and 'Roman Soldiers Of Babylon.' It was all killer, no filler, and the Lewis brothers' produc-tion was first class. A dub companion called *EE Saw Dub* and credited to the Fat Man Riddim Section was great, too, just like Jacob's latest single for Augustus Pablo's Rockers International label, 'Who Say Jah No Dread.' The 23-year-old singer warned against the commercialisation of Rastafari on that tune whilst deliv-ering the lyrics in a halting, stuttering voice that would become his trademark.

Contrary to certain opinion, Jacob wasn't born with the prover-bial gold spoon in his mouth, as he never knew his father and his mother worked as a bus conductor. Although born in Mandeville, he was schooled in Kingston and sang with several bands, including Paul Naughton and the Night People. Naughton wrote 'Nanny Goat', a 1968 hit for Larry and Alvin. Jacob was supposed to sing it for Coxsone but couldn't manage it. He then joined the Jamaicans (a group including Tommy Cowan) and the Schoolboys, before auditioning for Duke Reid, who Jacob told the *Gleaner* 'dressed like Two Gun Kid or Jesse James with two loaded revolvers worn in holsters on both sides of his hip, and sometimes he carried a double-barrelled sawn off shotgun – loaded, of course.'

Jacob went to work as a draughtsman for a firm of architects for a while, before joining the RHT Invincibles – a band led by baker Father Gooden, who paid the members with bread, saying they shouldn't love money. He then returned to Night People briefly before singing with the Rotations, Spell and Now Generation, although the Chung brothers and Earl 'Wya' Lindo had left by then.

'I stayed for about a year with them, then did nothing much for a time except kick stones. My mother had already migrated and I was living in the ghetto by then, so life was hard. I did some work with In Crowd and Augustus Pablo, writing 'Keep On Knocking', 'Each One Teach One' and nuff, nuff tunes. I also jammed with Tomorrow's Children, then I saw Inner Circle at Jamaica College one night and afterwards spoke to Ibo Cooper about me singing with them. Ibo was a baldhead guy at the time and didn't seem too keen, but Cat Coore took out his guitar and told me to sing, which I did. Ian Lewis came up and said I sounded like Dennis Brown who, incidentally, grew up with me in the same neighbourhood. I heard nothing further from Inner Circle until several months later when the oppression had got really hard and I was hanging out on Red Hills Road. Ian came up and asked me to join the group, because Prilly Hamilton, Cat, Ibo, Willy Stewart and Funky Brown had all left by then, leaving Roger and Ian and the novices behind. We went to San Francisco on our first overseas tour backing Dennis Brown and Toots and the Maytals. We cut two LPs, *Heavy Reggae* and *Dread Reggae*, and I also had a hit single with 'Forward Jah Jah Children.' Then, when Tommy Cowan left Dynamic Sounds, he and his wife Valerie, along with Warwick Lyn, Gayman Alberga, Roger and Ian Lewis and myself, formed Talent Corporation.'

Third World had formed in 1974, after keyboard player Ibo Cooper and guitarist Cat Coore tired of playing Top 40 hits with Inner Circle.

An earlier line-up of the band recorded an album's worth of unreleased demo tapes called *Sleepless Nights In Macka Bush* before Third World journeyed to London, just to see what was happening. Chris Blackwell saw them perform at a night club in the capital and signed them to Island, who released their debut single, 'Don't Cry On The Railroad Track.' The label's reggae roster was growing, but their main act was still Bob Marley and the Wailers, who embarked on the US leg of their *Natty Dread* tour in June. The Barrett brothers had been joined by guitarist Al Anderson, keyboardist Tyrone Downie and Bob's friend and mentor, percussionist Alvin 'Seeco' Patterson, whilst Rita Marley and Judy Mowatt sang harmonies. Ten thousand people saw them perform at the Schaeffer Music Festival in Central Park – all of them having witnessed a style of reggae they'd probably never encountered before. Marley's songs and delivery offered little room for compromise, yet neither did they cling to the narrow confines of the Jamaican scene.

In article published in *The Daily Gleaner* titled 'Reggae: What of the Future?' Fitzroy Nation railed against the misguided notion that reggae had to be watered-down to gain wider acceptance and lamented the fact that it remained 'shunned by detractors as being boring, monotonous music lacking in imagination and hard to understand.' He attributed such criticism to the unconventional nature of the Jamaican sound which had 'no scales, no quavers, no crotchets. No fancy strings and no bars.' He then quoted from Ralston Kallynder and Henderson Dalrymple's book *Reggae – A People's Music.*

'The most bitter attack on reggae today comes from the fact that most of the music is not composed in the traditional manner,' they argued. 'But some of our greatest musicians have never been able to read or write one line of music in the conventional sense. Their musical talent derives from their terrific sense of hearing, and feeling for rhythm. They have played by ear all their lives.'

This was true, of course. Reggae music, like blues was largely about feeling and, to a growing extent, the desire to communicate a message. Kallynder and Henderson's book also warned that in their haste to recoup large profits, the big companies could attempt to whitewash the music even further.

'We feel that the strong revolutionary essence of the music with its real blackness and powerful emotive significance will be lost to the whitewash – cheap wishy washy music. On one hand there is the argument that reggae in its raw state will never make it. On the other hand comes a view tempered with a mixture of patriotic fervour and sound reasoning, that whitewashed reggae is not truly Jamaican in flavour and would lead to a monopoly of the sound by foreigners. The choice our music leaders take will determine the success or failure of the sound.'

Bob Marley had made his choice already, and other artists and musicians were following his example, including Bunny Wailer and Peter Tosh, both of whom had been busily writing and recording songs for forthcoming solo albums. Those that Bunny had completed already – at Aquarius' newly opened 24-track studio – included 'Rasta Man', 'Fig Tree', 'Armageddon' and a revamped 'Reincarnated Souls.' Peter played guitar and sang harmonies on several of them, and finally released 'Legalise It' with help from Talent Corporation. 'Peter Tosh. Contribution to Festival '75. Legalise It. Available at all leading record shops' stated the adverts. What a joke! Because there was no way that a song as controversial as 'Legalise It' would have been accepted for the annual Jamaica Song Festival. A short time later, Tommy Cowan took out a much large advert quoting the lyrics in full after the song was banned from the airwaves. Peter Tosh approached Prime Minister Manley demanding that he reverse the ban, to no avail.

He and Bunny were still following Bob Marley's example and playing laidback 'one drop' reggae, yet 'flyers' or 'flying cymbals' had been all the rage for a year already, ever since Al Brown hit with 'Here I Am Baby.'

'Bunny Lee then started using it on a lot of songs, which was a good idea,' said Sly Dunbar. 'That created a kind of fusion between reggae and the disco music, but then I decided to take it back and slow it down on the Mighty Diamonds' 'The Right Time', and after that the flying cymbals was dead! I was playing with Skin, Flesh & Bones at night in those days and used to play sessions at Channel One every Saturday. We had a variety of songs that we were listening to, and that's when I realised that R&B and reggae had the same tempo. Philadelphia International was a popular soul label at that time, and that was the drum sound I was trying to get, but we were always experimenting. In those days if you played a rhythm you could cut it straight onto a dubplate and take it to a dance that same night. Channel One was the busiest studio in Kingston because it was going 24/7, and sometimes we'd be in there playing all through the night until the next morning, but we were just a group of musicians based around myself and Ansel Collins. We would go down there and record sessions sometimes and Ranchie McLean, who was a guitarist really, he played bass with us and Rad Bryan, aka Dougie, played guitar.'

It was Jo Jo Hoo Kim who renamed them the Revolutionaries, and the first tracks they played on at Channel One were Delroy Wilson's 'Call On I' and 'It's A Shame.'

'What Sly did, he brought the Studio One sound into the youth era,' said General Lee. 'That was when the rockers come in, and everyone wanted it after that. If Sly was licking over 'Real Rock', for example, the first thing he'd do would be to match the tempo. After you capture that you can come up with a different bassline and different horns, but if the tempo is there, then people will be grooving to the track as if it was the original. That's what made Sly famous – he created a whole new way of using drums to take hit Studio One rhythms to another level, but Coxsone Dodd couldn't take the pressure of watching that happen and so he came and thumped down Jo Jo one morning. He knocked him out cold! They had to throw water over him to bring him round, and then Leroy Smart start some argument as well, because in those days he had this little one-pop gun that he'd run up and down with…'

It was the Mighty Diamonds' debut hit 'Shame And Pride', produced by Jah Lloyd, that had alerted the Hoo Kims to the group's potential. Lead singer Donald 'Tabby' Shaw and harmony singers Lloyd 'Judge' Ferguson and Fitzroy 'Bunny' Simpson were known as the Limelights at first, before Tabby's mother suggested the Diamonds. It wasn't until they'd won every talent competition going that the 'Mighty' was added, just in time for their earliest recording sessions. 'Shame And Pride' came out in 1974, but within a short time of them first setting foot in Channel One a flood of hits followed and by the summer of 1975 they were being hailed as Jamaica's latest sensation – the combination of the Diamonds' sweet vocals and the Revolutionaries' lively rockers rhythms having proved irresistible on songs like 'The Right Time', 'I Need A Roof', 'Have Mercy', 'Back Weh (You No Mafia)' and 'Country Living.'

In mid-July, Bunny Lee and his stable of artists, including Johnny Clarke, Cornel Campbell, Derrick Morgan, Joy White and Delroy Wilson, left for Canada where they planned to stay for several months. Striker lived up to his name by releasing two albums apiece by Delroy Wilson (*Sings For I & I* and *Mash It Up*) and Cornel Campbell, whose biggest hits of the year were 'Natty Dread In A Greenwich Farm' (the follow-up to 'Dance In A Greenwich Farm'), a cover of Gene Chandler's 'Duke Of Earl' and 'The Gorgon' – a battle cry of sorts that he'd originally cut as a dub plate for King Tubby's sound system. 'The Gorgon Speaks', with a Mexican style intro from Tapper Zukie, was Campbell's next hit. 'Conquering Gorgon', bearing a heavy gospel influence, then brought the 'Gorgon' series to an end, as well as spawning an alternative Rasta version called 'Lion Of Judah.'

Love songs had long been Cornel's stock-in-trade, except many singers like himself were now embracing Rastafari, growing dread-locks and voicing cultural lyrics. His two albums for Bunny, *Dance In A Greenwich Farm* and *Natty Dread In A Greenwich Farm*, contained many of the same tracks, including 'Natural Facts', 'Girl Of My Dreams', 'Lost In A Dream' and an alternative cut of 'Stars' called 'The Sun.' It was an impressive body of work – one fuelled by the competition between him and Johnny Clarke as they vied for supremacy within the same stable.

Bunny's band of musicians, the Aggrovators revolved around Chinna Smith and Santa Davis from Soul Syndicate, along with bassist Robbie Shakespeare and Bernard Touter' Harvey on organ. They were tight and heavy – deadly when playing in a flyers style, and prolific, too, since they played on all four Johnny Clarke albums that Striker released in 1975, as well as sides by Leroy Smart, Jah Stitch ('Bury The Barber') and Linval Thompson, who was introduced to Bunny by Johnny Clarke and had an instant hit with 'Don't Cut Off Your Dreadlocks.' He followed that with 'Long, Long Dread Locks', 'Jah Jah The Conqueror' and 'Cool Down Your Temper' – songs that had been playing in blues parties and reggae dances all summer, just like Johnny Clarke's 'Move Out Of Babylon.' Tracks like those hadn't impacted on mainstream radio or national charts outside Jamaica at all, and yet they were thrilling examples of what was new and vibrant at grassroots' level.

How did Bunny keep all his artists happy? 'You have to put yourself in a next man's place,' he said. 'When you have so many artists around you, you can't be treating one as a favourite or putting one above another, otherwise that will cause problems. You have to treat it as a wheel, because if a spoke gets loose and you don't tune it back up, then next thing you know the whole thing is out of synch and the wheel mash up. That's how I used to run my organisation – like a wheel, so if one artist come and they want preferential treatment then it's better them go see a different producer because I couldn't just pay John Holt and not Delroy, Cornel Campbell or Johnny Clarke. I wasn't like that, because everybody had to go home at the weekend with the same money as a next man, and that's how I used to keep my thing together. You can't give one twenty pounds and the other thirty. That would cause a problem, and that's why everything run smooth...'

In late June, Jimmy Cliff adopted the Muslim name Naim Bashir, meaning 'Blessings Of The Divine' and 'Bearer Of Good Things.' Prior to this, Jimmy was known as James X within the Muslim community. He had been a student of Islam for several years already and regularly worshipped at the Wildman Street mosque. Writing in *Sounds*, Mike Flood was full of praise for Jimmy's latest album, *Brave Warrior*.

'Despite an erratic recording career (which comes, I suspect, from his willingness to take risks) Jimmy Cliff remains one of the key figures in contemporary reggae and this is one of his best ever albums. His voice has rarely been put to better use and the range of his talent – though only hinted at sometimes, comes over more effectively because of that feeling of strength in reserve. Compared to *Natty Dread* it has its weaker moments, but then Jimmy Cliff has something different to say and that of course, is what counts.'

Jimmy had recently made his first trip to Africa, but the experience proved bittersweet, because he spent some of it in jail. The only good thing to result from that situation was the song he wrote about it, called 'Have You Heard The News?'

'I was in Nigeria and touring all over, starting in Lagos. By the time I reached Kaduna, the cops knocked on the door and said, "we have a warrant for you." I said, "for what?" And they said, "it's because of a civil offence that somebody took out against you. You were supposed to come to Nigeria in the past and didn't come and so we don't have a choice and we have to take you." So the show was cancelled that night and they took me to the jail, and the next morning they flew three of us on a 747 to Lagos and put me into another cell with a lot of other people. It was at a stage of my life when I was studying Islam, so I prayed and all that sort of thing in the prison, then I went to court on the Monday morning and the judge threw it out. What a relief!

'I was shocked by it, because the tour had started so differently, and I got the kind of welcome I thought was reserved for the Beatles and Rolling Stones! From I arrived at the airport there were thousands of people there, and then on the way from the airport to the hotel there were thousands more lining the streets. People gathered outside the hotel all night singing songs and I'd thought to myself, 'Jimmy Cliff, you have arrived!'"

Bob Marley and the Wailers' arrival in London and the two nights they played at London's Lyceum on 17 and 18 July weren't quite on the same scale, but British music journalist David Hepworth, writing in his book *Uncommon People*, hailed the second night as being the best show he'd ever seen.

'The crowd included curious rock fans, volatile rude boys, London scene makers and middle-aged Africans, all in unaccustomed proximity. Although the music being played spoke of unity and transcendence the experience of being in the audience was spiced with danger, as gig-going so often was in those days, when things could go off at a moment's notice. There was certainly more at stake in this music than we were used to. It was there in the titles of songs like 'Burnin' And Lootin'', 'Them Belly Full (But We Hungry)' and 'Get Up Stand Up.' It was there in the words – stern, unbending schoolroom words like "hypocrites", "tribulation" , "curfew" , "brutalisation" and "sufferation." It was there in the way the music of the rhythm section seemed to be redistributing massive columns of hot summer air around the Lyceum. It was there in the figure of Marley, high-stepping on the spot like the leader of his own guerrilla infantry, his dreadlocks rolling back and forth, as he seemed to sway suspended in the strobe's light's glare. This was the night when Chris Blackwell's plan came to pass. The boss of Island Records wished to reposition a form of music previously regarded by smart opinion as good only for novelty hits and skinhead dance parties into the stuff of serious rebellion – and at the same time anoint Bob Marley as the first rock star of the Third World.'

News travelled fast, even in the pre-internet era, and a *Gleaner* article wasted no time in informing the Jamaican public that 'entertainment writers in North America, Britain, and other countries have been reaching into their store of superlatives to describe the fantastic talent of Jamaica's reigning King of Reggae — Bob Marley.

'On his tours of Britain, and more recently of Canada and New York, every reviewer has extolled the dynamism and talent of this young man who has set the world of popular music aflame with his searing rhythms and lyrics, backed up by the compelling beat of Jamaican reggae.'

There was a separation developing between Marley and the rest, and it wasn't entirely because of musical reasons or Island Records' marketing skills. Rock fans could relate to him because he had long-hair, rebelled against authority, smoked herb, played guitar, wore denim and liked women. He was also good-looking and wrote songs that people could believe in, but there was something else that was already luring people into its orbit. It was the same, elusive quality that Dylan had, and to label it charisma just wouldn't do, since any number of other reggae artists had that. Marley – no matter how grounded he appeared to be in interviews – had an aura of greatness about him, and which had the power to transform earthly events into mythology. Every genre needs stars to help define them, but whatever Bob Marley had was special, and there were a growing number of people in the media who recognised this.

It was ironic that whilst Marley and the Wailers were taking London by storm, Johnny Nash was sitting pretty at number one in the UK with 'Tears On My Pillow', which one reviewer called 'a classic example of a good singer rescuing a mediocre song.' The song in question wasn't the Little Anthony and the Imperials' hit but a cover of Ernie Smith's 'I Can't Take It.' Nash changed the title and as a result, Smith experienced difficulties in claiming his rightful share of the publishing revenue. Meanwhile, John Peel had predicted that Louisa Marks' 'Caught You In A Lie' could 'do a Susan Cadogan' and break into the national charts. The 15-year-old had won the talent competitions hosted by Sir Coxsone on Wednesday nights at the Four Aces in Dalston three weeks running with her version of Robert Parker's 'Caught You In A Lie', which happened to be Coxsone's signature tune. Lloydie Coxsone commissioned Dennis Bovell – who already knew Louisa – to produce the song for him, and the recording took place at Gooseberry studios on Gerrard Street. Junior Byles' 'Curly Locks' was still very popular, and so Dennis thought that he'd start 'Caught You In A Lie' with a similar intro, thus ensuring that reggae heads would pay attention from the start.

'I decided not to include the saxophone, though. I thought that was pretty lame, so I used a Moog synthesiser instead. Bunny Lee, Johnny Clarke and Robbie Shakespeare were in the studio with us and I remember pointing at the Moog and saying to Robbie, "you haven't got one of these in Jamaica!" The thing is, it was a mono Moog synthesiser and you couldn't play two notes on it, so in order to get it to sound like a polyphonic Moog synthesiser I had to overdub it two or three times. That was the first time I used it as well.'

Lloydie Coxsone took 'Caught You In A Lie' to Trojan and Webster Schroeder offered him £300 for it. Coxsone turned him down, which is just as well because Trojan would soon go into administration. In the end he licensed the song to Safari Records, which owner Reg McLean had launched less than a year previously. The Chiswick-based Safari released Coxsone's *King Of The Dub Rock* album as well, and assigned pressing and distribution of 'Caught You In A Lie' to EMI. According to their own press release, Louisa Marks' debut sold ten thousand copies in its first week of release and went to number one on the Capital Radio reggae chart. It was almost unbelievable that a British reggae release, made on a shoestring and featuring an unknown artist, should do so well, but Louisa Marks was the embodiment of every teenage girl with dreams of becoming a singer, and the song itself – telling of heartbreak and deceit – was tailormade for a young black UK audience that had stayed under the radar until then. British lovers rock is said to have started when Louisa sang of forbidden love between cousins, as she did on 'Caught You In A Lie.' Its success opened the doors for other budding UK singers like Jean Adebambo, Janet Kay and Carroll Thompson, but the financial arrangements involved caused nothing but trouble. Lloydie Coxsone heard from EMI that the song had generated over £60,000, and Louisa Marks had already been paid a quarter of that, but he himself still hadn't received anything, so one day he angrily cornered Reg McLean and in the scuffle that followed, broke the Safari boss's jaw.

'I never make a penny out of that record,' Coxsone complained. 'I get a prison sentence, that's what I get, and that's one of the biggest tunes ever made in this country.'

Things couldn't have been more different within Bob Marley's circle, who were celebrating the release of Judy Mowatt's debut solo album *Mellow Mood* on the Wailers' Tuff Gong label. The title track was her biggest hit to date, and she also covered Marley's 'You Poured Sugar On Me', despite being a talented songwriter in her own right, as demonstrated on 'I'm Alone', 'What An Experience' and 'Rasta Woman Chant.' She and producer Alan 'Skill' Cole were also romantically involved by then and had recently launched their own Ashandan label – named after they'd combined their respective Twelve Tribe names, Asher and Dan.

To commemorate Emperor Haile Selassie I's birthday, the Twelve Tribes held a dance at 56 Hope Road on 23 July. Junior Dan had recently left the Generation Gap, but the band came with their equipment and backed all the artists who performed that day, including Fred Locks and Little Roy. No sooner had the latter launched into 'Columbus Ship' and sung the line 'bring Babylon on' than police burst into the front yard and a burly sergeant demanded that they stop the music. After a few words with Bob Marley – who we're told joined the Twelve Tribes that very same day – he backed down and the celebrations continued.

Little Roy's 'Columbus Ship' was one of several singles – together with 'Mr T,' 'Jah Can Count On I,' 'Ticket To Zion' and 'Prophesy' – released on Munchie Jackson's Tafari label. He'd recently moved to New York and issued Little Roy's debut album *Tribal War*, which the singer himself described as being 'unofficial.'

'That's because I didn't even write a word of 'God Is Good' beforehand, and 'Cup Is Overflowing' and 'Hail Brother Nyah Hail' weren't even made in a proper studio but that same packing house round Coolieville Avenue. Scratch usually come along there also, because some of the other tracks were made at Black Ark. Scratch is the only one who could work on a quarter-inch tape and make it sound good, and he got all his sounds from just four tracks! I voiced 'Jah Can Count On I' with him and I make 'Tribal War' and 'Blackbird' on the same day, voiced and mixed, y' know? Not even a day, more like within a couple of hours! We were there working on 'Tribal War' and Dennis Brown walked in, took up the bass and just played so I voiced it and that was it.'

Little Roy and Fred Locks were close friends and Fred had an even longer history in the music. Real name Stafford Elliot, he grew up in a strict Catholic home in Franklin Town along with eleven brothers and sisters, although the family moved out to East Kingston near Bull Bay when he was 10. He sang with a group called the Flames from schooldays and wrote his first song when he was 12. Four years later he joined the Lyrics, who started their career at Studio One in 1967 and also recorded for Lee Perry and Randy's before one of the members migrated to Canada. Disillusioned by the hardships he faced whilst trying to make it as a singer, Fred embraced Rastafari and became known as Fred Locks, since he was said to have the longest dreadlocks on the island. His father had thrown him out of the house by that time and he was living on the beach, but a friend taped him singing 'Black Star Liner' – a song that he'd written about Marcus Garvey's shipping line – and played it to Twelve Tribes member Hugh Boothe, who persuaded him to record it. The majority of musicians on that session were Twelve Tribes members and formed the core of what came be known as the Twelve Tribes band. Boothe released it backed with 'Last Days' on Jahmikmuzik in Jamaica and Grounation in the UK. Whilst hard to find, it was well-received by roots fans, as was Burning Spear's *Marcus Garvey* album.

Jack Ruby finally released *Marcus Garvey* in early August and it sold two thousand copies on the first day. Spear had left for a six-week tour of the US just days beforehand, and by the time they returned to Jamaica the group had become the latest addition to Chris Blackwell's roster. Island would issue their own pressing of *Marcus Garvey* in December, with an arresting black and white illustration of tribal warriors on the cover. It was a stunning work, led by the singles 'Slavery Days' and the title track, together with other haunting and powerful roots and culture songs of similar calibre – not least their debut Island single 'Old Marcus Garvey.' Whilst the album was immediately hailed as a classic, opinions were divided as to the finished mix, since certain tracks had been speeded up – presumably in a bid to appease white rock fans. Nor did Island escape criticism with the release of *Garvey's Ghost* – a dub companion to the album which curiously failed to convey the dread power of *Marcus Garvey* itself, yet served to introduce many overseas' reggae fans to the world of dub.

Clive Chin couldn't get over how Errol Thompson had been allowed to leave Randy's for Joe Gibbs, and that Jack Ruby and Burning Spear had then chosen to follow suit rather than finish the *Marcus Garvey* album where they'd started it i.e. Randy's Studio 17.

'When Errol left, quite a few of our clients took their work over to Joe Gibbs,' Clive said. 'He duplicated everything that was at Randy's – he got the same sound board, the same speakers and outboard equipment... the truth is, I didn't like the way Joe Gibbs brainwashed Errol to go with him, and so Joe Gibbs became my worst enemy. Technically speaking, he wasn't really a producer. He was more of a businessman, because when you say you're a producer and yet you're not on the session but then just add your name after everything is done... I don't rate people like that, and then he had his name on every damn record as Mighty Two or whatever. In the early days he got Lee Perry and Niney to do all the work for him, just like Alvin Ranglin, who used to pay musicians like Winston Wright to do everything at GGs. Producers like them didn't come into the business with any creativity. They didn't give any directions or ask to change the sound in any way, nothing like that.'

By way of consolation, Carl Malcolm's 'Fattie Bum Bum' – a Randy's production – became a UK Top 10 hit during September, but then sales drastically fell away after the singer's debut on British television.

'He didn't have a strong voice,' Clive admitted. 'He had nice lyrics and good songs but his voice was very weak, which is why we had to double-track his voice on those three hits we had with him – 'No Jestering', 'Miss Wire Waist' and 'Fattie Bum Bum.' After the latter became a hit they wanted him to tour, but I knew that Carl couldn't do it, and sure enough when he was invited on *Top Of The Pops* he demonstrated no capability at all! He had a one-month tour booked, but everything just collapsed after that.'

The first releases credited to the Mighty Two – Joe Gibbs and Errol T – appeared shortly after Gibbs had relocated to 24 Retirement Crescent, where he installed a sixteen-track board and pressing plant. Whilst Errol continued to release music on his own Errol T label, his technical expertise and imaginative sound explorations soon made a difference to Joe Gibbs' productions and also to those of every other producer who hired his services. Jimmy Radway had recently been offered a distribution deal by Micron Music and together they launched the Capricorn Rising label. One of their first releases was a new arrangement of Leroy Smart's 'Happiness Is My Desire' entitled 'Mr Smart.' Desmond Young's 'Warning' soon followed and Jimmy then used the same rhythm for Big Youth's 'Wolf In Sheep's Clothing.' It was Micron's Pete Weston who persuaded Radway to issue a dub album from the rhythm tracks used on Fe Me Time and Capricorn Rising releases, and who also recommended that Radway get Errol T to mix it at

Joe Gibbs. Unfortunately, the deal with Micron didn't work out and the resulting album *Dub I*, credited to the Fe Me Time All Stars, quickly disappeared once the initial pressing sold out.

Errol also mixed *Africa Dub – All Mighty*, but the rhythms weren't all that recent and nor did they feature Gibbs' new house band, the Professionals. Their line-up, like that of the Revolutionaries, wasn't immutable. Such groups just came together for recording sessions and Sly Dunbar's drums anchored both of them. He, Robbie Shakespeare and Lloyd Parks were key members of the Professionals, and so too Franklyn 'Bubbler' Waul and guitarist Winston 'Bo Pee' Bowen. Lloyd Parks had formed another band called We The People for stage shows, but he also maintained a singing career. He didn't just sing about romance, either, because his latest album, *Girl In The Morning*, contained topical songs such as 'Strike', 'Famine' and 'Stop The War Now.'

At some point in 1975 the reformed Skatalites gathered at Joe Gibbs to record tracks for an album tentatively entitled *Reunion*, produced by Glen Darby. Guitarist Jah Jerry was the only surviving original member missing from the session, but otherwise they were all there, and augmented further by the likes of Ernest Ranglin, Augustus Pablo and Ras Michael. It was the first time the Skatalites had played together for a decade – not that you'd notice from the quality of what they recorded during those sessions. *Reunion* never did appear, but certain tracks eventually found their way onto *Herb Dub – Collie Dub* and *Heroes Of Reggae In Dub*, mixed by King Tubby, who was in dazzling form as he launched Tommy McCook and Lester Sterling's tenor saxes into orbit via his adroit use of echo, or transformed Don D. Junior's trombone into shuddering death throes.

Gregory Isaacs also passed by Gibbs' new studio when recording 'Babylon Too Rough', which borrowed from the chorus of Slickers' 'Johnny Too Bad' as he described police who bend the rules. Gregory exuded star quality, was adored by women fans for his love songs and respected by male ones for his bad boy reputation and sheer talent. When in Kingston he could often be found at his African Museum record store in Chancery Lane, home of Idlers' Rest. This was a place in downtown Kingston where singers and musicians would hang out in between sessions, since there were several studios nearby. Gregory was familiar with most, if not all of them since his work rate was phenomenal. In addition to writing and producing his own hits – something few other Jamaican singers could manage to any notable degree – he continued to record for an ever increasing number of outside producers. Recent gems included a winsome cover of Bob Andy's 'Sunshine For Me' for Channel One and 'Rock On' for either Lloyd Campbell or Niney The Observer, according to which label copy you believed. Whilst Gregory's popularity owed a great deal to songs about romance, he applied similarly insightful writing skills to other subjects too – most notably when commenting on ghetto runnings. 'Babylon Too Rough' we've mentioned already, but 'Thief A Man', for example, was a condemnation of those who steal from the poor, and even Rastas who he sneeringly accused of being part of Babylon's plan.

By his own admission, Gregory wrote the majority of his songs in the studio, although he once told me that he always kept a dictionary, Bible and pen and paper by his bedside. Asked whether he wrote songs from real life experience, he replied that whilst this was true in certain cases, he mostly wrote from putting himself in the mind of other people.

'A man might be upset about something or experiencing problems and so I'll look at that, then write about it from my own point of view. I write songs as if I'm in the presence of other people. That's how I do it, so it can come from everywhere, and I can write about anything. I also read a lot, and that helps me compose in all kinds of different styles. From as long as a man can talk about a thing, then he can write about it, because my favourite subject at school was composition. I was always down with that, 100 per cent, but I just make songs come to me when I'm ready. I hear the rhythm, and then everything happens from there.'

Bob Andy had wholeheartedly approved of what Gregory did with 'Sun Shines For Me', and was working on an album with Geoffrey Chung called *The Music Inside Me* at Treasure Isle, where Sonia Pottinger was busy producing songs with Marcia Griffiths. She and Bob Andy had parted some time previously but remained friends. Marcia hadn't accompanied the other I Three on the recent Bob Marley and the Wailers' tour because she was pregnant with her first child, Kemar. His father was DJ Errol Thompson – another 'ET' who was MC of choice on all the big shows in Jamaica.

'Miss Pottinger was the only female producer in the business,' Marcia recalled. 'It was a totally different experience working with her and I guess that's why we ended up doing so many hits together. Judy Mowatt was recording for her at the same time and for the first time I felt free; I had a much better feeling than when I was recording for other producers. We could relate to each other woman-to-woman, and from just talking to her she gave you that comfort...'

Marcia's favourite song from those early sessions with Pottinger was 'Survival', which Brent Dowe wrote in support of women abused by their partners. He and the Melodians celebrated their recent reunion with 'Dry Up Your Tears', again produced by Sonia Pottinger, who also recorded hits with Ken Boothe – most notably 'Say You' and 'Lady With The Starlight', written by B. B. Seaton. The latter said it was the acoustics at Treasure Isle that set it apart from other studios, and he and Errol Brown issued the album *Gun Court Dub* during this same period. Errol was Duke Reid's nephew and had been given license to experiment whilst developing his skills at the mixing-board, although this didn't mean to say that he could take liberties.

'I remember one time I mixed this song and it sounded good to me, but my uncle heard it and said, "listen man, this song don't mix yet." I get upset and complain. I say, "uncle Arthur, what are you talking about?" I make a frown and go back upstairs and by the time I sit down, the door to the control room had burst open.

It was my uncle and he was upset that I'd talked to him like that. He'd come from downstairs with a gun on his side, like a cowboy and he had a shotgun over his shoulder, which he then took up and fired into the wall, y 'know? The control room was no bigger than about eight by ten feet and so can you imagine what that sounded like in there! It was like a storm hit, and everything fly all over the place! He was trying to frighten me and show me I should do what he wants. I went through some things with him, y 'know? But when I study it he was right. He knew the sound that he wanted and it was the same whenever we were in there recording. He couldn't sing or nothing, but he always insisted upon getting the very best quality out of everyone whether it was guitar, bass, piano or whatever. Everybody respected him and listened to what he would say, and that's what really help to change the sound, y 'know?'

Errol used to cut dubs for King Tubby at Treasure Isle, before the latter built his own studio and began mixing vocal and dub records for producers like Bunny Lee, who did more to establish Tubby's reputation than anyone after elevating him to star status on the albums *The Roots Of Dub* and *Shalom Dub*.

'We then put out another LP named *Brass Rockers* with Tommy McCook playing over some of Johnny Clarke's flying cymbal rhythms,' said Bunny. 'After that now from a man just get any old dub they say King Tubby mix it, and so we began to see a lot of fraudulent Tubby albums out on the streets...'

King Tubby Meets The Aggrovators At Dub Station was genuine, and so too *Dubbing With The Observer*. The sleeve of *Presents The Roots Of Dub* showed Tubby sat in his studio wearing a crown whilst the text described him as 'The Dub Master' and 'The Dub Inventor' – titles that few could argue with as he was a genius at it. Give him a rhythm track he would transmute cymbals into scything whirlwinds of razor-sharp sound – bass-lines would plummet like depth charges and vocals disintegrate into vaporous trails of echo and reverb.

Another key sonic explorer, Keith Hudson was in New York where he was promoting his latest album *Torch Of Freedom*. When sound systems had played tracks from *Flesh Of My Skin*, it was as if a door had opened into some parallel universe. Hudson's music often spoke of liberation, yet it also carried an air of menace and was anchored by rhythms so heavy and uncompromising they were the epitome of 'dread.' The Barrett brothers again played on two of the tracks from *Torch Of Freedom*, namely 'Five More Minutes Of Your Time' and 'Lost All Sense Of Direction.' Hearing him croon the latter and then scatting on the second verse as if he'd already ran out of lyrics didn't endear him to everyone, but then recording love songs did tend to highlight his deficiencies as a singer, at least in the accepted sense. Whereas *Flesh Of My Skin* had told the story of a spiritual journey, the main theme of *Torch Of Freedom* would be cries from the heart. Following on from terrain charted in 'Lost All Sense Of Direction', he reused the 'Don't Think About Me' rhythm for the soul baring 'Like I'm Dying.'

'You leave me crying,' he lamented, while asking his girl to think about the future he'd mapped out for them both. Other rhythms were laid at Dynamic, with the Soul Syndicate then taken to London for overdubs at Morgan studios in Willesden by the same musicians he'd used on *Flesh Of My Skin*, including a synthesiser player. This was typical of Keith Hudson. He was unafraid to experiment, as demonstrated by the fuzz and wah wah guitar on tracks like 'Don't Look At Me So', 'Turn The Heater On' and 'Don't Let The Teardrops Fool You', on which he warned the listener not to be fooled by a woman's crying. The lyrics on that track weren't fully formed. They were more like a chant or invocation, as if he was still deciding what to say during the actual recording. Even the vocals on 'Torch Of Freedom' itself were semi-indistinct. Such unconventional techniques allied, to dense mixes and unfamiliar instrumentation, made his music quite inaccessible at times. There was talk of him having entered negotiations with Stax Records in the autumn of 1975, but nothing came of this, if it had even been true in the first place.

Back in Jamaica, the Carib Theatre was jam-packed on 4 August for yet another Independence Day showcase, this time featuring Jamaica Festival Song winner Roman Stewart ('Hooray Festival') and Jacob Miller and Inner Circle, who'd recently returned from West Coast dates with Toots and the Maytals. There were screams and cheers throughout Dennis Brown's performance as he sang 'Some Like It Hot', 'Tribulation', 'No More Will I Roam' and a closing 'So Long Rastafari Call You.' He was the showstopper, but one of the opening acts, Pablo Moses, also attracted attention after making his breakthrough earlier in the year with four singles that were revolutionary in both form and content.

'The first song I did was 'I Man A Grasshopper' and the people at the radio station banned it because it was about ganja,' he said. 'At that time they were strictly against ganja or marijuana, but I was showing them the reality of that because they were persecuting us for something that is natural. We Rastafarians were outcasts because of it, and that's because most of the Jamaican people were too Christianised and brainwashed to accept it.'

'Give I Fi I Name' was another powerful message song although not every black Jamaican welcomed being reminded that they were descended from slaves.

'A lot of them would say things like, "why aren't you using the name that your mother and father gave you?" I would say, "but that is not our name – our original names would have been African." Fortunately some people grasped onto it and appreciated it, but they were in a minority.'

In the lyrics of 'Blood Money', he mourned how some people kill and injure others for material gain, whilst 'We Should Be In Angola' made reference to how the MPLA, led by poet Agostinho Neto, were fighting for Angola's freedom against US and South African-backed militia. Fidel Castro – who the Manleys had visited earlier in 1975 – had already sent medical supplies and construction workers to the former Portuguese colony. Geoffrey Chung produced those Pablo Moses songs, and also the singer's debut album, *Revolutionary Dream*. 'I Man A Grasshopper' was recorded at Black Ark, but the remaining tracks – including the nine-minute opus 'Come Mek We Run' – were recorded at Joe Gibbs, and to a very high standard.

'Geoffrey Chung was the talk of Jamaica at that time,' Pablo confirmed. 'He made some very good music, and I have never known any other producer as strong and as talented as him. Maybe Clive Hunt, who was one of his protégés, but nobody else. I would say that he had a musical vision that very few other musicians and producers had, and he always tried to use instruments to their maximum benefits.'

Geoffrey was Soundtracs' in-house producer, but the Abyssinians requested that Clive Hunt produce their album instead. He and the group had already collaborated on 'Yim Mas Gan' and work on the album had been going well before the director of the company encountered some (politically related) difficulties and left Jamaica before it was finished. Clive didn't name the person in question, but this could refer to Soundtracs' Pat Cooper, who ran an advertising company and bravely stood as a PNP candidate in Tivoli Gardens against Edward Seaga. After announcing that he would build two thousand homes, he called a first public meeting in Regent Street and, according to Max Romeo, 'never stopped running till he reached the United States!'

Rather than abandon the Abyssinians' project, Clive completed the tracks at Joe Gibbs' studio and paid for the sessions out of his own pocket. Once Chris Blackwell heard the album he offered a substantial sum for the rights to release it, but Clive says the Abyssinians wanted cash up front and so the deal with Island never happened. It was at this point that someone from Soundtracs contacted him, requesting that he make a stamper of the album and send a test pressing to an address in Miami. The pressing plant took two weeks to return the stamper and by then there were pirated copies of the album on sale all over London and New York. Clive told Angus Taylor that Jacob Miller came to see him and said, 'Clive, the man them want to kill you.' When asked who he was referring to, Jacob mentioned the name of one of Jamaica's most notorious gangsters. Clive was already on the run from the Jamaica Defence Force and so he and his wife bought tickets for New York and fled immediately. Meanwhile the Abyssinians' album – called *Satta Massagana* – had been rapturously received, and hailed as an outstanding example of spiritual reggae, thanks to its devout lyrical themes, divine harmonies and soaring melodies. Highlights included reworkings of the title track and 'Declaration Of Rights', 'Forward Onto Zion' and former single 'Yim Mas Gan.'

Yabby You once told me that he tried to 'invoke the presence of angels' on his records, and as was the case with the Abyssinians' best work it often sounded as if he'd succeeded, since rarely has music expressed the awe and grandeur of Biblical prophecy with such yearning conviction. It was amazing how this nervous and insecure man, haunted by religion and the effects of poverty and ill health, could make such celestial music, but somehow he did, proving that miracles can and do happen. He released a number of hard-to-find but essential singles on his own Prophets label in 1975, including 'Beware', 'Run Come Rally', 'Jah Love' and 'Jah Vengeance.' He also produced songs by Big Youth and teenage singer Wayne Wade, whose early singles 'Black Is Our Colour' and 'Man Of The Living' had already signalled that he was a name to watch. Roy Cousins' group the Royals backed Yabby You and the Prophets on 'Carnal Mind' and 'Run Come Rally', both recorded at Perry's Black Ark, and their revamp of the former Coxsone single 'Pick Up The Pieces' is another fine example of what joys a stirring song and lead vocal, backed by close harmony singing, can bring.

George Lamming, writing in *Rasta and Resistance*, put recent developments into perspective with the observation that 'Rastafari has extended from a small and formerly undesirable cult into a dominant force which influences all levels of national life and it has done so against formidable odds, political harassment and general condemnation.'

Within a comparatively short time, Rasta music had emerged from the confines of nyahbinghis and cultural events like those held by Count Ossie and the Mystic Revelations Of Rastafari, infiltrating Jamaican popular music to a degree that would have been unthinkable three or four years prior. Unlikely as it seems, the connection with Jamaican middle class mores was still there. In August, Bob Marley had received a standing ovation at the Little Theatre in Kingston when artistic director Rex Nettleford and the National Dance Theatre premiered a new work entitled *Court Of Jah*, inspired by three songs taken from *Natty Dread*. Two days later, Horace Ove's film *Reggae* opened the Jamaica Film Festival at the State Theatre. Shot at the Caribbean Music Festival held at London's Wembley Stadium in 1970, this was a valuable snapshot of the early reggae era, but hardly typical of what was happening presently, as the influence of Rastafari could be seen and heard everywhere.

Big Youth's latest LP, *Dreadlocks Dread*, released on Klik in the UK, was already being hailed as 'Best Album Of The Year', although *Sounds'* Mister Brown wasn't so sure. In his opinion, Big Youth was 'a very colourful man who doesn't actually sing too good', but whose 'image and significance' made up for any lack of original musical talent. He went on to write that without 'the inimitable Skin, Flesh & Bones, the album would not be worth listening to' and described the 'predominance of bass and drums, spacey phasing, big black gaps in the music, inspired repetition, synthesised silences and excess of religious-political armchair power ravings', before concluding that it was 'a very fine record.' He got there eventually.

The album starts with Jamaica's number one deejay calling for unity and outlining his ghetto credentials. 'Lightning Flash (Weak Heart Drop)' is Big Youth's cut of Yabby You's 'Conquering Lion', while 'Marcus Garvey Dread' is an apocalyptic companion to the Burning Spear song. Various producers contributed tracks, and

Prince Tony Robinson filled out the album with sparkling instrumentals – a couple of them featuring harmonica, which was unusual. He was also the driving force behind U-Roy's *Dread In A Babylon* set, which used some of the same rhythms, put a fresh spin on some old rocksteady tunes and reinstated U-Roy in the minds of the Jamaican people after his lengthy absences whilst touring overseas. 'Runaway Girl' made for a bright opener, 'Natty Don't Fear' rides the 'You Don't Care' rhythm and 'Chalice In The Palace' was a rollicking celebration of Rastafari's rise. Prince Tony licensed this album to Virgin in the UK, and they again used Eric Tullo's photos of U-Roy with chalice in hand, disappearing into a cloud of ganja smoke. Police from St Catherine had recently spent two days burning over twenty acres of ganja plants in the Sligoville hills before the photo was taken. No arrests were made, but then the officers on duty that day probably couldn't stand up once they'd finished.

U-Roy denied that it was dangerous to be shown smoking a chalice like on the album sleeve. 'You didn't see me physically do it,' he said with a smile. 'I'm in the picture, yes, but it doesn't mean I was doing it in my yard so I didn't have no fear or anything like that. To me it was real fun and anyway, what could they do about it?'

He would later describe Prince Tony as 'one of these fast-talking, crook-ish kind of persons, who was always thinking he could outsmart you', but was grateful for Virgin's support. Richard Branson even visited U-Roy at his home in Kingston once, aiming to emulate Chris Blackwell and sign more reggae acts. U-Roy's closest rival, I-Roy, wasn't part of Branson's thinking at this point, since the deejay had recently signed to Micron, whose offices were on Retirement Road in Kingston.

'I-Roy is a superstar,' wrote Micron's Pete Weston. 'There is no doubt in my mind about that. He is the number one DJ for King Tubby's Hi Fi and has made such an impression on the people of Jamaica, the US, Canada and England during the past two years that I am expecting an international hit for him anytime now. He rarely DJs a tune that sells under five thousand – a remarkable feat for any Jamaican artist.'

Truths And Rights was his latest album, and it opened with a scathing riposte to Sonny Bradshaw, who'd publicly rubbished the deejay art. 'Natty Down Deh' took no prisoners, and that was true of several other tracks as well. I-Roy complained about the rising crime rate on 'Double Warning' – voiced over Desi Young's 'Warning' – then defended Manley's vision of democratic socialism on 'Every Mouth Must Be Fed.' He was in cantankerous mood, as Prince Jazzbo discovered to his cost. Micron also reissued I-Roy's single 'Straight To Prince Jazzbo's Head', on which he famously told his fellow deejay that if he – Jazzbo – was a jukebox, he wouldn't put a dime in his slot. Jazzbo counteracted with 'Straight To I-Roy's Head', calling I-Roy a poor imitation of U-Roy.

Another of Jazzbo's recent singles, 'Donkey Concubine', prompted Big Youth to voice 'African Daughter' in reply, but his friend Leggo Beast went one step further and chased Jazzbo out of Randy's record store whilst threatening him with a broken bottle. Jazzbo ran out into North Parade and was knocked over by a van, but fortunately wasn't too badly hurt. I-Roy gleefully seized on this and recorded 'Jazzbo Have Fe Run', which mockingly suggested the deejay couldn't get first aid. The lyrical battle had now got personal. Jazzbo accused his rival of being a cross-dresser on 'Gal Boy I-Roy', then back came I-Roy with 'Padlock', telling the story of how 'Princess Jazzbo' was chased by a duppy and lost her teeth in a boxing match before sneezing 'with a mouth full of cheese.' It was funny, ruthless and highly inventive, but because Jazzbo never replied, their feud fizzled out thereafter. It won't surprise you to learn that Bunny Lee, the grand wizard of marketing, produced all those tracks whilst creating a situation that was the talk of Jamaica, and caused a great deal of excitement at the time.

Micron also signed Joe Higgs and Tyrone Taylor in 1975. The latter was a highly-strung 18-year-old singer from Westmoreland who recorded his debut tune 'Delilah', a cover of the Tom Jones hit, when he was just 12. It was songs like 'Rastafari Ruler', 'Don't Call Me Nigga' (inspired by Sly Stone) and 'I Want To Go To Zion' that had heralded a change of direction and resulted in his recent hits 'Fight It Blackman' and 'Move Up Blackman.' Micron's other signing was well proven by comparison. Joe Higgs' latest single was 'Wages Of Crime' and Micron also released his album *Life Of Contradiction*, which he'd originally recorded for Island. Joe claimed that Chris Blackwell signed him and placed him on a retainer whilst he was working on the album, but then refused to release it once it was finished as Island didn't know where to place it. They said it was too different from everything else coming out of Jamaica at that time, but Joe wasn't convinced and thought it was a ruse to hold him back so that Island could promote Bob Marley in his place.

American guitarist Eric Gale played on *Life Of Contradiction*, in addition to recording an instrumental album of his own for Micron called *Negril.* In the late 1960s Gale was one of several American musicians, together with Richard Tee and Cornell Dupree, that Danny Sims had brought to Jamaica to record with Johnny Nash. Peter Tosh and Family Man Barrett knew him from those times, which is how they got to play on *Negril*, named after the hippy haven on Jamaica's west coast. It was an easy listening, jazz/reggae fusion that enhanced the island's reputation among musicians overseas, and included a timely version of Bob Marley's 'I Shot The Sheriff.'

Whilst Bob Marley's own *Natty Dread* album hadn't proved a big seller by rock or pop standards, it had conclusively assuaged any doubts about his ability to go it alone. He and the Wailers had been working on tracks intended for a follow-up album when news of Emperor Haile Selassie I's death was announced on 28 August. A report from Addis Ababa claimed that the Emperor had been found dead in his bed the day before, although he'd been under house arrest for nearly a year by then and had only recovered from a prostate operation two months earlier, which is why his son Crown Prince Asfa Wossen Haile Selassie, then living in London, demanded an independent autopsy.

To say that Rastafarians were shocked is an understatement. To them, Emperor Haile Selassie I was (and still is) the messiah. His reign was the second coming as prophesied in the bible, and his earthly passing, if true, understandably rocked the foundations of their entire belief system. If His Imperial Majesty was the living god, then He couldn't die and so many Rastas didn't know what to think, or how to respond. They were left feeling bereft of direction and confused, and that's what inspired Bob Marley to write 'Jah Live', which he sang with such resolute assurance. By doing so he turned the whole situation around, and he chose Lee Perry, of all people, to produce it with him.

The Wailers had already laid the rhythm before Marley and the backing singers went to Harry J's and voiced 'Jah Live.' Island weren't keen on it, and did hardly anything by way of promotion, but the song meant a great deal to the Rasta community, and gave them something to hold onto in a time of great uncertainty. A few days later Judy Mowatt appeared on a show called Reggae Exemplified at the Sheraton Ballroom and had the crowd eating out of her hand when singing 'Rasta Woman Chant.' Jacob Miller and Inner Circle were also well received, but it was Toots and the Maytals who closed the show and gave a super star performance.

'Toots proved that he is a master entertainer as well as singer as he tore into hits such as 'Country Roads' and '54-46 That's My Number',' wrote a *Gleaner* reporter. 'He then treated us to another facet of his multi-talented self as he played both the conga drums and the regular drums as well as the guitar without flaw. The show came to an end, much to the regret of the audience as they clearly were enjoying themselves.'

Toots' latest hit was 'Reggae Got Soul', and the group were about to leave Jamaica for a four-week European tour, which was scheduled to include Germany and Holland, as well as the UK. On their last visit to London, a British journalist, as quoted by the *Gleaner's* Bob West, wrote that 'Toots Hibbert, the group's lead singer and songwriter, is without doubt the outstanding male soul vocalist to emerge since the death of Otis Redding – Al Green notwithstanding. Dressed in bright orange pants and jacket with black lapels, Hibbert exhorted, cajoled, kidded and charmed the audience into his act. His melodies come straight from American gospel, and what vocals! He had the crowd singing loudly.'

He and the Maytals seemed to have found an extra gear after signing with Island, who quickly issued an album for the US called *Funky Kingston*. This was not a reissue of he and the Maytals' 1973 LP, but instead a compilation of tracks that Toots had recorded for Dynamic. It was nothing new, in other words, but 'Reggae Got Soul' was a thrilling indication of what might lie ahead, and when Toots and the Maytals headlined the third Jamaica Festival at Madison Square Garden's Felt Forum in November, New York journalist Michael Goodwin called them 'the greatest reggae group in the world.'

The live version of 'No Woman No Cry' Bob Marley had recorded at London's Lyceum had entered the UK Top 30 by then – just days after Brazilian footballer Pele had visited Jamaica and played against Skill Cole's team Santos. After more than ten years of trying, an original Wailer had finally managed to come up with an international hit. On 4 October, Bob and the Wailers supported Stevie Wonder at the National Stadium, titled the Dream Concert. Wonder was a major star – a multiple Grammy winner and flagbearer for the contemporary brand of soul pioneered by himself and Marvin Gaye. Peter and Bunny had finished their respective solo albums by then, and both rejoined the Wailers' line-up once more. Bunny sang 'Dreamland' and 'Battering Down Sentence', whilst Peter launched into 'Mark Of The Beast', 'Can't Blame the Youth' and then won tumultuous applause for 'Legalise It', which he performed whilst waving his spliff in the air right near where police officers were standing.

Such breath-taking defiance would help define Peter Tosh's solo career, but his and Bunny's cameo appearances at the Dream Concert marked the three founder Wailers' last-ever performance together.

Less than a week after that epochal show, the Nation Of Islam formally opened their Temple Number Two in Charles Street. Jimmy Cliff was one of the speakers, and four days later he left Jamaica for yet another US tour, accompanied this time by a different set of musicians that included Skin, Flesh & Bones' Ranchie McLean and Sly Dunbar. Jimmy had taken to calling himself 'The Thumb', because whilst he was part of the same hand as the four fingers (that made up the rest of reggae music), he wasn't the same as them. The fact that he chose Islam rather than Rastafari reinforced such claims, and there were also musical differences, highlighted on his latest album *Follow My Mind*, which the *New York Times* said 'failed to keep coherent for all its many virtues. Apparently the problem with Cliff is that, unlike Marley and Toots and the Maytals, he did not stick to the riddims of Jamaica, but sought to twist some of the British and American strings and horns into the beat.'

Whilst Jimmy was away, Nanny of the Maroons and Sam Sharpe, leader of the Baptist War slave rebellion, were inducted into Jamaica's canopy of National Heroes. There was movement on the musical front, too. New chart entries included Junior Byles' 'Fade Away', Burning Spear's 'Travelling', the Mighty Diamonds' 'I Need A Roof' and Big Youth's 'Wolf In Sheep's Clothing', which reviewer John Ingram enthused over, noting how, 'apart from rigid bass and drums, the music is an almost random assemblage of horns, piano and guitar, interweaving almost subliminally. It possesses every quality that made white rock singles vital a few years ago, and will never get played on the radio, but it should be your duty to hear it.'

Elsewhere, he dismissed Derrick Harriott's 'Eighteen With A Bullet' and Justin Hinds' 'Carry Go Bring Come' as being 'useful as ashtrays.' Not too long ago, overseas critics had been touting reggae drenched in strings as being the only kind worthy of their attention, but the criteria had clearly changed. It was now all about 'authenticity', which meant that artists had to be Rastas, and singing about life in the ghetto. Harriott's sophisticated brand of Jamaican soul was no longer relevant it seemed, whilst Justin Hinds' status as a cultural pioneer meant nothing to voyeurs who couldn't see past his lack of dreadlocks.

When reviewing Max Romeo's *Revelation Time* album, Bob West referred to the music and lyrics as being more advanced than in the past. 'This brother has completely restructured his music, both in lyrics and arrangements,' he wrote. 'Max now bases his recordings on the depressed conditions in which some people are forced to live. Roots music is now the order of the day ... since the start of this year Max has turned over a new leaf and also, since he migrated to his new St Thomas residence, his ideas have started to flow in the right direction.'

The new album was produced by Clive Hunt and Geoffrey Chung for Soundtracs and recorded between Black Ark, Randy's and Dynamics. Carl Gayle noted that anger and revenge provided some of its central themes, and mentioned how 'titles like 'Warning' and 'Blood Of The Prophet' reeked of conflict, death and destruction', whilst 'Three Blind Mice' described the 'blind terror of Saturday night partygoers whose scene was suddenly invaded by baton-swinging police.'

Max, being an intelligent and perceptive person, took great interest in world and local affairs, and especially those concerning black people. He would have been monitoring what was happening on 19 October, when the first Cuban army unit arrived in Luanda, Angola. Four days after that and South Africa sent a further two thousand troops from Namibia into southern Angola to support UNITA and the FNLA. Namibia was already occupied by South Africa, and regular units of the South African army had crossed the border into Angola from there. Jamaican prime minister Michael

Manley felt compelled to announce his support for the Cuban intervention, despite the US having asked him to remain neutral on the subject. As expected, retribution was swift and in no time at all *The New York Times* published a vicious and largely inaccurate article about Jamaica, talking about the alleged presence of Cuban troops and secret agents on the island which gave the impression of an imminent Cuban takeover. Meanwhile, all aid to Jamaica slowed to a virtual halt and shadowy additions were made to the US embassy staff in Kingston.

Trade deals continued as usual – at least for the time being. In November 1975, Jamaican company Record Specialists signed a deal with A&M Records for the manufacture, distribution and promotion of their releases in Jamaica and several other Caribbean territories. As part of this deal, A&M arranged for Joe Cocker to record his next album in Jamaica at Dynamic Sounds. He duly arrived at the beginning of November, but slipped over to Randy's one night and recorded a cover of Bob Dylan's 'Man In Me' on the fly, as it were. Peter Tosh played on that session, but was then involved in a near-fatal car crash on the night of 11 November that left his girlfriend Yvonne in a coma from which she never recovered. He'd inadvertently driven down a one way street and was left both physically and mentally scarred by the incident. Friends claimed Peter never fully recovered from it, especially regarding his mental well-being. Bob Marley and Bunny Wailer had visited the hospital to see them as soon as they'd heard the news, but were turned away by police who shouted at Bob that he was 'a dirty little Rasta boy.'

Marley's album *Live! At The Lyceum* was released on 5 December and succeeded in capturing all the excitement and fervour of those two concerts in July. The tracks were mainly taken from the second show and included hits like 'Trench Town Rock' and 'Lively Up Yourself', as well as selections from *Burnin'* and *Natty Dread*. Marcia Griffiths wasn't on that tour, but she and the other two members of the I Three performed on The Love Show at the

National Arena that same night, dressed in matching cultural robes and swaying in unison as they sang hits by the Three Degrees, Natalie Cole and the Sweet Inspirations. American soul favourites the Stylistics were the headliners but, according to the *Gleaner*, it was the Mighty Diamonds who stole the show.

'This group of three very young men sang their hearts out,' crowed the reviewer. 'The Mighty Diamonds are bound to be the reggae stars of 1976. Their brilliant performance on the Love Show proved that not only are they a first-class reggae group, but they are going to be something else when it comes to putting down R&B music. Their performance of the Manhattans' 'There's No Me Without You' was so stimulating one young man in the audience ran up to the stage and handed lead singer Donald Shaw a $10 bill. Their hit songs 'When The Right Time Come,' 'Back Weh (Mafia)' and 'I Need A Roof' were definitely among the three biggest reggae hits from 1975 and the audience's familiarity with the songs turned their performances into a singalong dance routine.'

As Christmas approached, most people agreed that 1975 had been a great year for Jamaican music. Apart from the records covered in this chapter, my own favourites included the Bim Sherman singles 'Tribulation', 'Love Forever' and 'Danger' – also Winston Francis's 'Let's Go To Zion', which would remain buried in Coxsone's vault for a decade, Ronnie Davis' 'Won't You Come Home' and the Itals' 'In A Dis A Ya Time' (both produced by Lloyd Campbell), Pluto Shervington's 'I Man Born Ya', the In Crowd's 'Milk And Honey', Prince Jazzbo's 'Dreadlocks Corner', Sugar Minott's 'Have No Fear' and 'Roof Over My Head' and Earl Zero's 'Please Officer', which Lloydie Coxsone would play every time the police raided one of his dances – a relatively regular occurrence…

Christmas doesn't mean much to Rastas, but Bob Marley had cause for celebration when becoming the official owner of 56 Hope Road on 18 December, buying Island House from Chris Blackwell.

This wasn't a gift, as has been widely reported elsewhere, and the deeds are there to prove it. British reggae band the Cimarons also had some good cheer after receiving a call from Trojan whilst they were touring Japan with the Pioneers, informing them that 'Talking Blues' was at number one on the Jamaican charts. They arrived on the island just in time to perform at the Carib Theatre on Christmas morning, and then at the People's Ball at the National Arena, where they shared a crowded bill with Ras Michael and the Sons Of Negus, the reformed Skatalites and many more, including Johnny Clarke, who won Top Male Singer at the Red Stripe Swing Awards.

However, Niney the Observer would enjoy no such luck in his own dealings with Trojan. He and Dennis Brown had returned to the UK earlier in December because Trojan still owed them a large amount of money and the five cheques they'd received from the company so far had all bounced. We've already heard how Trojan were bought out by Saga, who refused to assume responsibility for Trojan's debts. Niney wasn't having any of that, and the police were called after he'd got involved in an altercation at Saga's offices in Kensal Rise, although no charges were made. It was incidents like this that prompted Dennis to start his own label, DEB, an acronym for Dennis Emmanuel Brown. He and Niney had met up with Castro Brown, who owned a record shop and label called Morpheus, based in Thornton Heath. He agreed to press and distribute DEB records in the UK, beginning with Brown's own 'Life's Worth Living' and titles by Junior Delgado and Vin Gordon. After the deal was struck, Castro would tell people that he and Dennis Brown were brothers, although they weren't actually related. They did become close, though, and especially after Castro had booked Dennis for five nights straight at the Georgian club in Croydon in late December, supported by Sir Coxsone. Those who were there talked of those shows for months with undisguised reverence. Everyone except Niney, that is, who soon found himself sidelined.

'Dennis Brown and I, we come to England and Trojan mash up by then so I say to Castro, "let's form a company." That's when we come up with this DEB business and I was never allowed be a part of it, neither. You help to create something and then you're out, so you just have to leave it alone..."

CHAPTER SEVEN

1976: HEAVY MANNERS

1976 was an election year, and it began ominously with an editorial in the *Gleaner* warning that Michael Manley, aided by Cuba, was preparing for a Communist takeover of the country. It was a blatant attempt to create division within the PNP and discredit him personally, providing a platform for what his wife Beverley once described as 'anti-Communist hysteria.'

'The intention was to strike fear in the hearts of Jamaicans, particularly those in the middle and upper classes – many of whom were already leaving in droves,' she said. 'The battle lines were decidedly drawn.'

Three days later, on 5 January, Jamaica hosted a three-day convention for the IMF and World Bank, attended by finance ministers, officials and media people from well over a hundred countries. Shortly before they arrived, fierce gun battles broke out between heavily armed JLP and PNP gangs near the city centre, carrying on through the night. The following day, a large group of PNP supporters protested outside the Pegasus Hotel on Knutsford Boulevard, where many of the delegates were staying. They were demonstrating against the organisers' decision to invite a delegate from apartheid South Africa, but chanting and placard-waving regressed into violence after JLP thugs began throwing stones. As the conflict escalated, shops were looted and set alight, many people were injured and four policemen were killed, including two who were guarding the American consulate. Manley had to visit the police barracks and give personal assurances to officers who'd threatened to strike because of the mounting violence, even as the minister for national security announced the arrest of nineteen gunmen who were allegedly being trained for operations against the government by representatives of the JLP and CIA.

On 7 January, the *Gleaner* headline read: 'Fires Rage In Rema Area.' 'Firemen retreat under attack by armed gangs', added the standfirst.

'Fires raged unchecked, five persons were shot – one fatally – and several hundred people fled their homes last night as politically motivated violence escalated in the Jones Town, Trench Town area of Kingston,' the story continued. 'The fires blazed out of control after firemen rushing to the scene in the heart of the troubled area were forced to retreat by armed gangs who attacked them with stones and bottles and threaten them with firearms. Several of the streets were also blocked with blazing tyres, large stones, trees and oil drums, hampering the movement of police and soldiers going into the area to restore order.'

Police and soldiers worked through the night in an attempt to clear the roads so that firemen could reach the fires, despite the mayhem happening around them. War had broken out between Rema and Arnett Gardens. Meanwhile, several hundred desperate people gathered outside neighbouring police stations seeking refuge. Many had lost their homes while others had fled the area because they feared for their lives. Eye witnesses later reported that the conflagration had started after an angry mob had set a shop on fire at the corner of Seventh Street and Collie South Drive, and the blaze quickly spread to adjoining properties.

A shocked and embarrassed Manley announced that anyone found guilty of possessing an illegal firearm would receive a mandatory life sentence and that all marches and demonstrations were banned until further notice. He talked about how 'cold blooded political forces were trying to damage the government in any way it could' and this was behind his party's decision to form community self-defence groups drawn from members of both parties. Anyone joining these Home Guard units would be offered basic training in the use of small firearms and patrol duties, and their activities would be restricted to their own neighbourhoods. True to form, the JLP accused Manley of forming a private army. The arguments were still going back and forth when a section of Trench Town again went up in flames. People living in houses adjoining Rema had come under increasing pressure to evacuate their homes. Then, in the early hours of 18 January, those who hadn't already left were woken by arsonists yelling death threats and wielding Molotov cocktails. All the houses went up in flames, and when the fires had been put out, all that remained of the area stretching from Collie Smith Drive to West Road and Sixth Street was a charred wasteland.

Less than a week later, two people died in St Thomas after eating flour contaminated by the pesticide parathion. Thirteen people, including a 3-year-old child, had died from eating poisoned flour and the minister of health responded by imposing an island-wide ban on the sale and use of counter flour, which was an essential part of many Jamaicans' staple diet. Manley's troubles were increasing by the day, and not all of them were self-inflicted.

It was into this febrile atmosphere that British folk-rock singer John Martyn and his family arrived in Jamaica. Signed to Island, Martyn's last UK tour – the one that yielded his album *Live At Leeds*, which he'd self-released amid disputes with Island – hadn't gone well, and he was still grieving the loss of his friend, folksinger Nick Drake. Chris Blackwell had suggested that Martyn bring his wife Beverley and their three children to Jamaica and stay at Strawberry Hill, up in the hills overlooking Kingston.

'Blackwell's house was amazing,' Beverley wrote in her autobiography, *Sweet Honesty*. 'It lay about 15 miles from Kingston, up this dirt track of a mountain road. It was originally a plantation house with lots of land and outbuildings where the staff lived. You couldn't help but feel better in such a glorious place, but unfortunately even in Jamaica, John would have his usual episodes and everyone around us was careful not to mention my tell-tale bruises. But it was a holiday and John loved it. He would terrorise the local population by going into town and drinking white rum then sounding off in his broad accent.'

Martyn was already using a tape delay on his recordings, which fused folk with slurred vocals and atmospheric, jazzy improvisations. As Lee Perry was also experimenting along similar lines, Blackwell suggested they meet, and that's when the Martyns' family holiday took a different turn.

'Both Scratch and John loved the Echoplex,' wrote Beverley. 'John had taken his to Jamaica with him, so he and Scratch sat and played together happily. Scratch was an amazing man, but somewhat strange. He was a genius in the studio, but he also smoked a lot of ganja. Whatever the reason, he was given to making bizarre pronouncements when you least expected them, but every musician on the island came out of the woodwork. When we went to the Black Ark there were hundreds of them sitting on the walls outside, some with goats tethered by them, some conducting ganja deals while they waited as women walked along with bales of bananas on their heads. It was crazy and fascinating... the atmosphere was incredible and we were so lucky to be witnesses to a moment in musical history.'

Martyn told his biographer Graeme Thomson that he played on 'tons of stuff' at Black Ark, including tracks by Max Romeo. He also joined the sessions for Burning Spear's album *Man In The Hills*, but these were impromptu affairs, to say the least.

'He was paid in fistfuls of fake American dollars, pornographic videos and bottles of coffee liqueur,' wrote Thomson. 'It wasn't always a smooth blend of cultures. A large, loud, inebriated Scotsman in a suit pitching up uninvited to a session armed with a phase shift pedal and an echo box was not to everybody's taste.'

'In certain Jamaican recording studios, the very mention of John Martyn's name would scare staff and locals,' affirmed Blackwell. 'No mean feat. His interaction with Perry too, could be erratic. I think I made a huge mistake by introducing them, because they were the worst influence on each other.'

John Martyn wasn't the only British musician to visit Jamaica during the early months of 1976. David Bowie spent January in Ocho Rios, rehearsing for his forthcoming US tour at the home of Rolling Stone Keith Richards, and the Cimarons were still on the island after recording tracks at Channel One and Black Ark for their forthcoming album *On The Rock*. They went to see Bob Marley during their stay, although he wasn't best pleased to see them, apparently, since he was upset about them covering 'Talking Blues.' When Gichie said, 'but Bob, you suggested it' he scowled and retorted, 'yes, but I didn't say to take it to number one!'

The Cimarons played a five-day residence at the Chela Bay Hotel in Boscobel, just 9 miles from Ocho Rios, between 21-26 January. Joe Higgs, who'd just completed a US tour with Jimmy Cliff, had opened the regular Roots Club sessions there soon after New Year. Legend has it that the thirty-room hotel – which was situated next door to Playboy Club – was owned by wealthy ganja smugglers from Atlanta but that didn't matter to Michael Epstein, who ran My Father's Place in Long Island and would soon organise all-inclusive trips to the Chela Bay Hotel for fellow reggae fans from New York.

'Boscobel was the kind of place where people would go to cock fights after church on Sundays,' he said. 'You could see Cuba from there. One of Bob Marley's cooks, a tall Rastaman called Fuck Up, lived there. He was so dread in appearance that few questioned how he'd got his name.'

Over the coming months, a succession of reggae artists would appear there, including the Mighty Diamonds, Third World, Ras Michael, Peter Tosh, Burning Spear and Freddie McGregor, who'd come into his own recently with the singles 'I Man A Rasta' and

'Rastaman Camp' for Coxsone, following his decision to join Bob Marley and Dennis Brown in the Twelve Tribes Of Israel. Freddie and Dennis had known each other for a while, but it wasn't until they were both members of the Twelve Tribes that their friendship developed into what Freddie describes as brotherly love. Rasta songs would form an important part of their repertoire from thereon, although both continued to voice love songs. Fred Locks took a more direct approach as heard on his debut album *Black Star Liner* and songs like 'True Rastaman', 'Vision Of Redemption' and 'Time To Change.' One of the tracks, 'Don't Let Babylon Use You', was addressed to the gunmen terrorising communities in Jamaica, as well as those who supplied them with weapons, whom he accused of living off blood money. He had strong words for fake Rastas, too, on 'Wolf Wolf' – pretenders who dress in sheep's clothing, but 'deal with nothing.' The musicians on that album were all Twelve Tribes members and included Sangie Davis, who handled most of the arrangements whilst making a meagre living selling juice and ital food from his house in the Hermitage, near August Town.

'I was always cooking at my yard,' he says. 'I was a man who made juice, and so Bob Marley used to come there almost every night time to eat an' t'ing. He usually came with eight, nine, ten people, but this particular night at around one o'clock he came alone and I was there practising some of my music. I was getting up from that to make him some juice when he said, "Sangie, me nah going to drink juice tonight. I want to hear some of your songs them. People say that you've written some big songs and I'd like to hear them." So I sat down and played Bob the songs. When Bob hear them he said, "so long you've known me and you make me wait so long to hear them? Hear what me want you to do. Tomorrow morning I want you to come to Hope Road, then you and I can make some music." From he tell me that, the next morning me wash out the pot, turn off the blender and just walk down to Hope Road and when him see me, he call me over and we start to smoke, and that's how the songs them start to come…'

Marley was already incorporating Twelve Tribes references in certain songs. That line in 'Positive Vibration' where he asked if they're picking up now was a quote from Prophet Gad, leader of the Twelve Tribes. Not everyone at Tuff Gong approved of the organisation's growing influence on Marley, but there were various reasons why he allowed that to happen. There was strength in unity for one, and to choose godliness instead of the gun or politics sent out a positive message to all who took note of what was taking place at 56 Hope Road.

The Mystic Revelations Of Rastafari were another group who continued to project an image of Rastafarians that was far removed from the perception of them as 'blackheart men.' In February '76 they were planning to commission a life-size statue of Marcus Garvey to be placed on the Harbour View roundabout, where it would greet everyone who arrived at the nearby airport. This group of forward-thinking Rastafarians were still in the process of building a self-help housing project and community centre at Rennock Lodge, but the response to their latest LP *Tales Of Mozambique* proved rather muted. They were clearly missing ex-members such as Cedric Brooks and trombonist Nambo, who'd formed a new band called The Light Of Saba. In the liner notes, Verena Reckord described their debut album as having created 'a richly textured weave, highly coloured by instrumentation hitherto unknown to Jamaican popular music,' whilst Ras Michael and the Sons Of Negus' recent album *Tribute To The Emperor Rastafari* had been timed to coincide with the group's residency at the Chela Bay Hotel. Following them were Burning Spear and the Jack Ruby Disco. Ruby had recently been the subject of a *Gleaner* article that described him as 'probably the leading record producer at the moment.' He was said to have the Midas touch after producing hits for Burning Spear and Tyrone Taylor, whose new album *Move Up Blackman* was partially recorded at Muscle Shoals. Ruby had accompanied him there and then headed for London where he spent two weeks working on *Garvey's Ghost* (the dub companion to Burning Spear's *Marcus Garvey* album) and attempting to book Spear on a show at Wembley Stadium on the same bill as Isaac Hayes or Marvin Gaye. Third World – who T Boots Harris has called 'one of the most unique and mind-blowing musical aggregations around' – also spent time in London during early '76, where they completed their first album for Island. They were brave to include covers of the Abyssinians' 'Satta Massagana' and Burning Spear's 'Slavery Days', but these worked out beautifully whilst 'Kumina' – named after an Afro-Jamaican religion – was a drummer's delight.

Having promised to represent DEB in the UK, Castro Brown entered an agreement with Oval Records, who recently had a UK Top 10 hit with Pluto Shervington's 'Dat.' Oval was owned by *Radio London* presenter Charlie Gillett and he in turn had a distribution deal with Virgin Records, but then everything fell apart after Castro was found to be pressing up the same tracks on 7-inch singles and supplying them to shops independently, in breach of his contract. The deal was quickly scrapped and Gillett got so angry and disillusioned he even stopped playing reggae on his highly influential radio show. As a result, DEB releases featuring Dennis Brown, Junior Delgado and others didn't get the level of promotion that Castro had promised, and the artists themselves had hoped for. We don't know if Niney the Observer ever whispered 'I told you' to Dennis, but if he did, no one could say it wasn't justified. It was Niney's know-how that provided Dennis' *Deep Down* album with highlights such as 'Travelling Man', 'Open The Gate' and the hymn to resilience that is 'Tribulation', but DEB was still in its infancy and lessons were there to be learnt.

Remember Tapper Zukie? After he'd returned to Jamaica he briefly deejayed on Ray Symbolic and befriended Ranking Dread, who became his apprentice on sound system and no doubt in other areas as well. Tapper also fell out with a prominent politician and switched his allegiance from PNP to the JLP, which was highly unusual. He was volatile and Bunny Lee – who knew him well

– was reluctant to voice him at first, but relented and cut 'Jah Is I Guiding Star' and a version of Johnny Clarke's 'No Woman No Cry' with him. Bunny also gave him the use of some rhythm tracks, and this led to Tapper forming the Stars label and recording an album – named *MPLA,* and dedicated to 'the movement' – that he licensed to Klik Records in the UK. Klik let off some singles from it, including the title track, 'Ten Against One' and 'Pick Up The Rockers', but the album itself didn't gain wider traction until Virgin later reissued it with fresh artwork and better promotion. It remains one of the all-time greatest Jamaican deejay albums, and features outstanding music and lyrics from start to finish. Tapper issued an accompanying dub album, mixed by King Tubby, on Stars, and also found time to produce other artists like Prince Allah, whose 'Bosrah' was inspired by the Biblical account of the Lord returning from there 'on the day of vengeance', and wearing 'a robe dipped in blood.'

Klik also issued U Brown's *Satta Dread* album; like Zukie, he was a dancehall man through and through. Whilst growing up, Huford Brown moved between Denham Town and Tower Hill, where he listened keenly to tunes on local jukeboxes, and studied U-Roy first-hand whenever King Tubby's Home Town Hi-Fi played in his neighbourhood. As his confidence – and skills – increased, he became U Brown and was then asked to take over U-Roy's slot on King Tubby's, a dream come true for the teenager.

'It happened accidentally, because U-Roy was going to a dance one weekend on his bicycle and a goat run out into the road, tripping him up and fracturing his leg,' U Brown recalled. 'I-Roy was the other big deejay at the time and he was Tubby's friend, so him play the sound for a while until he start to travel. Then Dillinger take over as the deejay, carrying the swing, but his style didn't fit with Tubby's, so this guy who would help string up the sound tell Tubby that he should come find me instead. After I get the break I was always there when Tubby's play out, and from then on we just go from strength to strength until this guy called Scorcher and his police friends mash up Tubby's sound one night. The police had been doing that to his sound for many years, but this was the worse one, because it make Tubby decide that he wasn't gonna mess around with sound system anymore. After that now you have this guy named Rupert Brown, who come in with a sound called Soul Attorney. U-Roy, he was playing that sound as well, 'cause him and Tubby had fallen out by then, but then U-Roy leave Soul Attorney after they changed their name to King Attorney, and me and Ranking Trevor start to deejay on it instead, sharing U-Roy's fee between us as the two new apprentices.

'We stay with them a while, then King Attorney change into Socialist Roots and the politics come in after that. One night they shoot up a dance in Barbican and one of the guys who operate the sound got shot in his mouth real bad. The owner got a contract to work for the Government and people start to brand it as being a politics sound, y'know? So I leave after that, 'cause Jack Ruby invite me to work on his sound in Ocho Rios instead. When I was there he was recording Burning Spear's *Marcus Garvey* album, and doing songs with Justin Hinds, Ken Boothe, Delroy Wilson and Tyrone Taylor... he was working with so many great artists.'

U Brown recorded a couple of tracks for Jack Ruby, although it was Bunny Lee who produced the tracks on *Satta Dread*. U Brown wasn't thinking about money, but just wanted to hear his songs play on the radio and on the local sound systems. It was all about achieving recognition, but then he cut 'Train To Zion' with Linval Thompson for Socialist Roots producer Tony Welch and his fame spread quickly after that. That song was a response to the worsening violence in places like Rema and Jungle – an unprecedented level of social unrest that compelled Thomas Wright, in a letter to the *Gleaner*, to declare that he'd never known Jamaica to be so confused and upset and in such a state of anarchy.

'People are in a panic,' he wrote. 'They fear for the security of their property, those who have property. They fear for their lives, and the safety of their loved ones. They fear revolution. They fear anarchy. The possessing classes have been scared out of their wits by the rhetoric of suffering and socialism that has come to dominate speech patterns in government circles. People who used to be reassured by the sober language of moderation and gradualism extolling the virtues of free enterprise have been shocked by the flaming revolutionary utterances of men dressed in tams who've suddenly appeared in the most exalted offices in the land...'

U-Roy had been renowned for playing Linval Thompson dubplates on King Tubby's sound system, and we can only imagine the atmosphere at those dances as the singer's voice drifted through the still night air. After he and U Brown hit with 'Train To Zion', Linval started his own label called Thompson Sound, which he gradually built up by voicing songs for producers like Bunny Lee and Winston Riley, and asking to use some of their rhythm tracks in return. The ubiquitous Bunny produced Linval's *Don't Cut Off Your Dreadlocks* album and then released it via Count Shelly's Third World label in the UK, along with Jah Stitch's *No Dread Can't Dead*.

The title of the latter makes reference to Jah Stitch having survived an attempt on his life and being left disfigured in a dispute between rival sound systems, but then life had always been hard for the one-time Melbourne James. His mother was too poor to look after him when he was little and so an aunt in St Mary raised him before he rejoined his mother in Papine. When he then fell out with his mother's boyfriend, he joined the Spanglers, a street gang based in downtown Kingston affiliated to the PNP. This put paid to his schooling after the age of 11 or 12, but luckily he was subsequently drawn to music and, like Big Youth and Dr Alimantado, learnt his skills as a deejay on Tippertone. It was some girls among the sound's following who named him 'Stitch' because of his smart dress sense. The 'Jah' came later, once he'd embraced Rastafari and made his first trips to the studio, circa 1975. Bunny Lee produced his breakthrough hit 'The Killer', by which time Stitch had left Tippertone – after accusing them of financial irregularities – and joined Black Harmony sound, based in Fletcher's Land. They had links to the JLP, and this is what led to Stitch being threatened by a Spanglers hitman, who wanted him to rejoin Tippertone. Stitch refused and so the man tried to stab him. When that failed, he left to get his gun, came back, found Stitch sheltering in a nearby bar and shot him in the face. The deejay spent four months in hospital and came out with his mouth all twisted, but his lyrical ability and gruff delivery proved sufficient to get his career back on track, despite his injuries.

As Jah Stitch lay recovering in hospital, the biggest tune out on the street was Leroy Smart's 'Ballistic Affair' for the Hoo Kim brothers' Well Charge label. Leroy had written it with fellow singer Frankie Jones in Greenwich Farm one night as they talked about the island's spiralling crime rate and how everyone was living in fear 'through this ballistic affair.' It's a song imploring the youths to throw away their weapons and unite. 'We used to lick chalice, cook ital stew together,' he reminded them. 'Play football and cricket as one brother. Nuh true? You rest a Jungle and you might block a Rema...'

He was backed on that track by the Revolutionaries, whose *Revolutionary Sounds* LP had a drawing of Che Guevara on the cover. It was more of an instrumental than dub set, showcasing the actual rhythms rather than feats of engineering wizardry as heard on more conventional dub albums, and led by 'MPLA', which was a cut to Little Richard's 'Freedom Blues'. All the tracks were given revolutionary titles like 'Angola', 'Che', 'Leftist', 'Victory', 'ANC' and 'PLA', and Errol Brown followed suit with *Revolutionary Dub*, which was later pirated and reissued as *Orthodox Dub*. Brown had mixed that album at Treasure Isle using rhythms supplied by B. B. Seaton, who was attracting interest from Virgin Records at the time.

'Sid Bucknor came in with a B. B. Seaton record and Simon Draper liked it so we put it out,' said Jumbo Vanrenen. 'An ill-fated deal with Brent and Sebastian Clarke's Atra label then bought us

Keith Hudson. He came into the office one day to complain that he hadn't received any royalties and didn't want to work with them anymore. We, being green, believed him and as he was a fine producer we gave him lots of space to make a rather bad record at Chalk Farm, called *Too Expensive*. It was not an expensive record, despite its title, but Keith had some strange idea that this was his crossover record. Brent Clarke then tried to kidnap Richard Branson after some argument over stock.'

Brent Clarke had worked for Danny Sims and Chris Blackwell, and Keith Hudson's *Pick A Dub* was among Atra's earliest releases. Virgin agreed to release their product in the UK, but their contract would be terminated just months later, in March 1976, after Richard Branson woke up one morning to find three men standing by his bed. They knocked him around for a bit and dragged him downstairs whilst demanding £5,000 in cash by way of compensation for Virgin having allegedly pressed and sold more records than they'd accounted for. The case didn't reach court until eighteen months later, when Sebastian and Brent Clarke, together with Dennis Bartholomew, were charged with blackmail and assault with intent to rob. Those charges were later dropped as Branson couldn't positively identify the men who'd entered his house, and little was heard from Brent Clarke thereafter.

The majority of tracks on *Too Expensive* were recorded at Randy's, and sounded as if they'd been targeted at black American audiences rather than Caribbean or European ones. It was a strategy rooted in either folly or genius, but then Hudson moved to New York in 1976, so maybe it had been intended as a calling card. 'Introduce Me', which probably should have opened the album rather than 'Smoking', featuring lyrics about an overflowing ashtray and unfulfilled hopes and dreams. 'Civilisation' and the title track were certainly funky enough to win over R&B fans with their choppy guitar licks and synths, but it was his idiosyncratic vocals, as always, that divided opinion. Around the same time Virgin Records unveiled *Too Expensive*, they announced deals for the debut albums by Peter

Tosh and the Mighty Diamonds. Branson's label was now well and truly enmeshed in the reggae business and providing competition for Island Records, who'd recently signed Bunny Wailer.

Virgin used one of Lee Jaffe's photos of Tosh sat in a ganja field with pipe in hand for the front cover of *Legalise It* – a decision that was only fitting, since the title track was reggae's most controversial herb tune. He'd recorded 'No Sympathy' and 'Brand New Second-hand' before and there was a country feel to 'Whatcha Gonna Do' and 'Til Your Well Runs Dry', but then members of Eric Clapton's backing band – who were from Tulsa – had played on the album, as well as assorted Jamaican A-listers. Lee Jaffe was Tosh's manager, and had helped to arrange those sessions and also the ones held at Miami's Criteria studio with Albhy Galuten that lifted 'Igziabeher (Let Jah Be Praised)' out of the ordinary. Peter's latest single – a swipe at the British monarchy called 'Babylon Queendom' – wasn't included, and nor was 'Mark Of The Beast.'

Tosh had been courted by Denny Cordell's Shelter Records, but former Island lawyer Charles Levinson used his influence to sign *Legalise It* to Virgin for the rest of the world, excluding the US. Jon Savage, author of *England's Dreaming*, commented that the reggae world 'carried with it a volatile business subculture which Branson didn't know how to deal with.' Increasingly, he didn't need to, since his cousin Simon Draper and Jumbo – who was one of London's first world music DJs – were always on the lookout for new music and contacts. When asked what impressed him most about the music coming out of Jamaica at that time, Jumbo replied that it was 'the militancy and ever-evolving riddim. The lyrics are still truthful today in a Third World strugglers' scenario, and us hippies found in dub a perfect stoners' music.'

That was all too evident in the marketing of *Vital Dub* – a collection of dub mixes from the Mighty Diamonds' *Right Time* album, and with a seriously stoned individual (a friend of Don Letts' called Horace) on the front cover. Art director John Varnom, who lived in Brixton – home to the notorious Railton Road 'frontline' – had already played a key role in establishing Virgin's reputation for challenging graphics. Trevor Key did the actual artwork, but it was Varnom who came up with the title of *The Front Line* for Virgin's first reggae sampler, a ten-track collection rounding up songs by various artists on their roster, and that sold for the price of a 7-inch single – just 69p. On the cover of *The Front Line* was a black fist against a white background, clenched over barbed wire with red blood seeping from it. It was an unforgettable image – one that quickly registered with reggae's core audience of Caribbean migrants and disaffected hippies. The latter had tired of rock music's increasingly extravagant excesses and readily identified with reggae's utopian, anti-establishment message.

The Mighty Diamonds offered all of that and more. Tabby's lead vocals had just as much soul as that of many an American superstar, and the group's harmonies were to die for. The Hoo Kims had already issued the Diamonds' debut album *When The Right Time Come* on Weed Beat. The three of them were stripped to the waist on the cover and barefoot. Judge was sharpening a machete, and none of them had dreadlocks as yet. It was a sleeve design that spelt 'pure ghetto', but Virgin substituted it for a head and shoulder group shot and included a lyrics sheet that left fans in no doubt of the potency – and also poetry – in songs like 'Why Me Black Brother Why?', 'Them Never Love Poor Marcus', 'Go Seek Your Rights' and 'Africa', as well as the hits 'I Need A Roof', 'Have Mercy' and 'Right Time' itself.

Arrangements had already been made for them to perform a series of shows in New York promoted by radio DJ Ken Williams, and they also received a great reception when appearing on the same bill as Jacob Miller at the Sheraton Ballroom and then the Carib Theatre over the Easter holidays. Virgin booked a UK tour for them in the summer, to be shared with U-Roy, whose follow-up album for Branson's label was *Natty Rebel*, again produced by Tony Robinson. Dennis Morris' cover shots show U-Roy wearing an African tribesman outfit and holding a staff painted in Rasta colours.

It was images like those that reinforced the Afrocentric messages in the music, although U-Roy approached his craft with a lighter touch than many of his rivals. Curiously, 'Fire In A Trench Town' a track written by Owen Gray about the devastation unleashed in Kingston earlier in the year that might have found U-Roy challenging Big Youth's role as the 'Human *Gleaner*' – doesn't feature him at all. Ultimately it was the cuts to the Diamonds' 'Have Mercy' and Marley's 'Soul Rebel' that stayed in the memory longest, while Virgin's two albums with I-Roy were more impressive lyrically.

The first of those, *Musical Shark Attack*, was produced by Jo Jo Hoo Kim at Channel One and voiced over a set of rhythms by the Revolutionaries. It opened with 'Semi Classical Natty Dread' – storytelling in excelsis – whilst 'Tribute To Michael Holding' offered praise of the West Indies' cricketer (nicknamed 'Whispering Death') who'd recently made his debut in the World Cup victory over Australia. I-Roy was a natural at that kind of thing, but it was hard-driving tracks like 'Love I Deal With', 'Social Development' and 'Tribute To Marcus Garvey' that highlighted his interest in more cultural concerns.

Prince Tony was able to forge a productive relationship with Jumbo Vanrenen, and after playing him the Gladiators' 'Know Yourself Mankind' he was quickly commissioned to produce an album with them. Gallimore Sutherland had recently joined the group and accompanied them to Joe Gibbs' studio, where the Professionals and members of the Gladiators themselves laid the rhythms for *Trenchtown Mix Up*. The band's own songs – 'Hearsay', for example – bristled with gritty realism, although 'Hello Carol' was a remake of their former Studio One hit, whilst Marley references abounded on the opening 'Mix Up' and covers of the Wailers' 'Soul Rebel' and 'Rude Boy Ska.' Lead singer Albert Griffiths even sounded like Marley, who was no doubt embarrassed when *Playboy* magazine ran a piece on him under the heading of 'Bob Marley The Prophet.'

'Let's say this right up front and underline it twice,' it began. 'Bob Marley and the Wailers seem to have finally emerged as the finest rock and roll band of the seventies and what's more, they're as heavy a group as we've heard in the twenty-two year history of the music. They're right up there with any of the giants you care to name, from Chuck Berry, through to Sly Stone. And that includes the Beatles, Otis Redding, and the Stones, all of them. That's how good they are.'

The writer went on to liken Marley to Dylan and Jagger and claim that his music 'speaks of real and present dangers, of righteous, religious faith, of not giving up the fight. It has the power to play upon an audience's emotions as no music has in years.'

Island released Bob Marley and the Wailers' latest album *Rastaman Vibration* on 30 April, a week after gang wars had resumed in central Kingston. This time it was the Skulls and Tel Aviv posse – supporters of the JLP and PNP, respectively – who came to blows and left a trail of violence in their wake. Attempts were made to set houses alight in Rosemary Lane, and four people lost their lives in the conflict. Two days later, four more people were killed in Olympic Way. A spokesman explained that the sudden flare-up of violence in the area was the result of a gun slaying on the West Bay Farm Road, but then two other men were shot dead and homes burnt to the ground by armed marauders in Jones Town and Craig Town.

The crime rates – and death toll – had been continuing on an upward trajectory all year and in the face of so much unrest, it was hardly surprising that *Rastaman Vibration* contained a great deal of social commentary. Marley had a gift for extracting universal truths from what he saw happening around him, and when he sang of the mother mourning the death of her son from a stray bullet in 'Johnny Was', he could have been describing a woman in any war torn country through the ages, whilst he famously adapted the lyrics of 'War' from Emperor Haile Selassie I's 1963 address to the United Nations.

A struggle for power was tearing Jamaica apart, and whilst race also came into it (since black people suffered the most), it wasn't just about that. The haves were not prepared to concede anything to the have-nots, and therefore Manley's socialist government constituted a threat to the status quo. There were people who felt that he must be stopped at all costs, and if that meant sacrificing the lives and well-being of countless ordinary people who were just looking to survive and make something of their lives, then so be it. They are the reason why peace remains so elusive, and when Bob Marley referenced how political violence was filling the city in 'Rat Race' and then declared that no Rasta would work for the CIA, everyone knew who and what he was referring to. The Americans – allegedly with help from Seaga and his JLP insurgents – were trying to destabilise the government, and when Henry Kissinger left the island in January after being told that Manley wasn't going to row back his support for the MPLA, the die was surely cast. Songs like those and also 'Crazy Baldhead', 'Who The Cap Fit' and 'Want More' were from the soundtrack of a country teetering on the brink of civil war, and Marley's call for peace in 'Positive Vibration' was but a candle in the windy darkness.

In April, Marley and the Wailers left for Pennsylvania, where they began their latest US tour – one that would include two dates at New York's Beacon Theatre and a celebrity date at the Roxy in Los Angeles. His songs were now all over the radio back home, though not all of them were actually sung by him. Marley had written the plaintive 'I'm Still Waiting' in the ska era, and Delroy Wilson's cover was now on its way to becoming his biggest hit in at least two years. The producer was Lloyd Charmers, who got excited at the very mention of it.

'That's my creation!' he said gleefully. 'Bob Marley's own song never sounded as good as that! People had begun to realise that Bob Marley's songs could sound so and it was a monster! When it came out in Jamaica it exploded, but that's the joy of being in the studio sometimes, because whatever mood you're in, the microphone picks it up. The studio vibe is like a ghost, y'know? It's a spirit, and whatever vibe you feel when you go in the studio, that's what's going to come out in the music. You have to believe that, because it's coming from within you so if you go in there with a good vibes, then you'll get a good sound. Such things are beyond us, because we can't understand them. That's God's work and that's how I feel it, because when I go into the studio, I have no idea what I'm going to do. I just depend on my inner spirit to bring out my innovation, so that whatever's inside me can come out.'

Lloyd also had a hit with the Mexicano's 'Move Up Starsky' on the same rhythm, then got Ken Boothe to sing two further Bob Marley covers on the album *Blood Brothers*, which was full of great singing but poorly packaged. That's because of the four emaciated young boys – suffererers one and all – staring balefully from the cover. It's a haunting image, but had little to do with the highly polished music within the sleeve. This was an indication of how far the dial had moved, although there was still a sizeable market for supreme stylists like Boothe and John Holt, especially in the UK, where the latter's *2000 Volts Of Holt* was selling briskly. This wasn't a compilation but a genuine follow-up to *1000 Volts Of Holt*, again produced by Tony Ashfield and the singer himself, with Brian Rogers having arranged most of the orchestration. It was middle-of-the-road, certainly, as shown by the choice of songs, including 'Touch Me In The Morning', 'Alfie' and 'On A Clear Day You Can See Forever.' That album even included a cut of Marley's 'Keep On Moving' – possibly as a reminder to fans that Holt was a Jamaican, but music like that was fast becoming an anachronism. It was for 'big people', meaning older listeners, and the tide of roots reggae was turning into an unstoppable flood.

Dennis Brown idolised singers like Holt and Delroy Wilson but was working on new tracks with Niney at Lee Perry's Black Ark. 'Take A Trip To Zion' was a righteous take on the Drifters' 'On Broadway', but it was 'Wolf And Leopards' that would shake up everything and be met with a cacophony of yells, whistles and pounding on walls and doors at reggae dances in the coming months. He was telling the faithful that they were at a crossroads and it was a time for decision – that the wolves were to be separated from the sheep. A few weeks later 'My Time' appeared – a Rasta victory chant that was a cue for yet more pandemonium in the dancehalls, except few noticed that when Castro Brown released it on Morpheus, he was credited as the producer and not Niney. Dennis had already introduced his namesake to Gregory Isaacs, whose first UK shows included some at the Georgian in Croydon, where Dennis had starred several months earlier. The two singers were already close friends. Both were no strangers to hardship, and whilst Gregory was more business-minded, they shared the same concerns. Increasingly, Gregory had been supplementing tales of romance with songs illuminated by insight and steeped in conviction. He addressed 'My Religion' to those who took Rastafari too lightly and thought that wearing their hair in dreadlocks automatically made them Rastas. We can feel the dismay in his voice on 'Black A Kill Black' as he warned that the system not only oppresses black people, but plays them off against one another, whilst he cast himself in the role of a fugitive in 'The Philistines', someone who'd been wrongly accused of a crime so forced to go on the run knowing that the police would find it easier to jail a Rasta like himself, rather than determine the truth. Injustice was the driving force behind several of his newer songs. In 'Set The Captives Free' he criticised the use of indefinite detention whilst observing that when governments come under pressure, they start taking away the very rights they're supposed to defend, almost as a reflex action. This didn't apply to everyone, of course, since 'the wicked are walking free.'

Micron were now distributing his *All I Have Is Love* album, produced by Sidney Crooks, and would soon be exercising their marketing skills behind 'Mr Cop', produced by Lee Perry. Gussie Clarke also included one of Gregory's tracks on his compilation *The Right Tracks*, along with others by Dennis Brown ('In Their Own Way'), Horace Andy, Leroy Sibbles and Delroy Wilson.

'If you look at that album sleeve you can see me standing along-side the dub cutting machine which I had upstairs in Church Street,' Gussie pointed out. 'That was probably the best part of my life back there. Everything was just so spontaneous and there was so much love in the music. We weren't thinking of money. We just loved what we were doing and felt good when a song was out and everybody in England was coming to buy it and export it back there. It was passion time.'

As we know, reggae sound systems earned their reputation by playing exclusive music on dub plate, and that music could remain unavailable to the buying public for months or even years in some cases. That's how the Meditations' 'Woman Is Like A Shadow' became popular and why Coxsone was able to capitalise on it, thanks to Sugar Minott.

'That song was on tape for so long, and at the same time Jo Jo was licking over Coxsone's songs,' explained the Meditations' Ansel Cridland. 'Coxsone heard that Jo Jo had an original tune that mash up dancehall and so he sent one of his confederates to buy a dubplate of it. He make the Gladiators play over the riddim because Albert Griffiths wanted to sing the song. I don't know whether he couldn't follow the words or what but Sugar Minott was there and they make him sing it instead.'

Sugar Minott sparked a trend by singing new songs over old Studio One rhythms during that period and making hits from them, 'Live Loving' being the perfect example. He'd been singing over those same rhythms on the sound system near where he lived since childhood, and already had original lyrics for them. Coxsone was mightily upset that the Hoo Kims kept versioning his rhythm tracks and it must have pleased him greatly to see Sugar hit with a song that Channel One owned, but had so far failed to release. It was Sugar's success with 'Woman Shadow' (he'd shortened the title) that compelled Jo Jo to release the original, credited to the Meditations – a single that reportedly sold 40,000 copies in the first month. The Meditations were on the map at last, and the follow-up, 'Tricked', was again produced by Dobby Dobson, who knew talent when he heard it.

'That song come after I see two brothers shoot one another – one Labourite, and the other PNP,' reflects Ansel. 'I was still living in Majestic Garden at the time and it was really heart-breaking to see how the brothers and sisters were living, and how the people in the neighbourhood were acting among each other over the thing named politricks. So I write in the song, "can't you see we've been tricked?" And then they banned it.'

'Tricked' had lyrics deploring black-on-black violence, whilst another of the Meditations' songs, 'Running From Jamaica', was recorded at Black Ark. Ansel wrote it after the news broke that many middle class Jamaicans were fleeing Jamaica and taking their money with them. 'When the gate is closed, we don't want no knocking,' he sang—in other words, 'don't bother coming back…'

All these tracks appeared on the Meditations' debut album *Message From The Meditations*, released on Dobson's Double D label. Each of the three members contributed songs and shared lead vocals. They were like the original Wailers in this respect, and Ansel's phrasing even sounded a little like Bob Marley's at times. The Meditations would have made a fine addition to Island's roster, but they signed Dillinger instead. Chris Blackwell's label released two of the deejay's albums in quick succession, gifting him immediate exposure and establishing him as Jamaica's Super Fly, since he was quick witted, stylish and had lyrics in abundance. Let loose on rhythms from the Channel One dub box, including cuts to recent hits by Mighty Diamonds, Leroy Smart, Gregory Isaacs and the Wailing Souls, he came out with a slew of entertaining tales of everyday life as a natty dread. It was a lyrical journey that took us all over the island, introducing listeners to characters like Ragnampiza the dub organiser, Miss Lou in Harbour View with her ital stew and Old Mother Wallace who was there when, chalice in hand, he headed for Buckingham Palace. That's not forgetting the Chineyman at Caymanas Park, where Dillinger had a flutter on the horses (as told on 'Race Day'), or the Uncle Rufus who pops up in 'Plantation Heights', which, like 'The General', promoted a Rasta lifestyle that invested dreadlocks people with superpowers, including the ability to become invisible. 'Bionic Dread' and 'King Of The Road' continued along that same crazed path, whilst on 'Natty BS' he reminded us that most dreadlocks couldn't even afford a bicycle in the past, and yet some of them now had flash cars and motorbikes, including Dillinger himself on his brand-new 'CB200.'

Island named an album after that track, and there was a song on it called 'Cokane In My Brain' – which they released as a single – that brought his much vaunted Rasta credentials into question. It took the form of a two-way conversation between Dillinger and a less worldly friend who, when asked to spell New York, has the regular spelling rejected. Instead, Dillinger steps forward with a catchy line of doggerel and the admission that he's got cocaine, and a surfeit of it, running around his brain...

This was the same Dillinger who'd recently voiced 'Freshly' for Yabby You, on which he declared 'this is 1976 and I'm well strict.' Hmm, maybe... Yabby You himself was in overdrive, releasing two albums under his own name – *Walls Of Jerusalem* and *Ram A Dam* – an electrifying dub set (*King Tubby's Prophesy Of Dub*), several singles by the deejay Trinity and Wayne Wade's debut LP *Black Is Our Colour*. In addition to the title track, the latter included Rasta hymns like 'Run Come Rally' and 'Man Of the Living', but it was 'Gang War', 'Poverty In The Ghetto' and 'Politics, Politics' that most closely addressed the realities of life in Jamaica for the sufferers. Yabby's own output included the occasional social commentary, the most harrowing example being 'Fire In Kingston', each verse of which lamented the dire conditions endured by sufferers living in ghetto neighbourhoods such as Mathews ('Matches') Lane, Jones Town, Tivoli Gardens and Trench Town.

On 19 May, approximately fifty armed thugs affiliated to the JLP surrounded an overcrowded, ramshackle tenement yard in a PNP area and firebombed it. As frightened residents tried frantically to escape, they were shot at, forcing them to risk death by fire or the bullet. Eyewitnesses reported seeing small children being thrown back into the inferno and gunmen firing at rescue workers. It was a miracle that only three adults and eight small children perished that night, but it's estimated that over 500 people were left homeless, having lost everything except what they were wearing when fleeing to safety.

Carl Rattray, the minister of justice, called what had happened 'an act of lunacy on the part of persons completely depraved and inhuman.' More than forty other people were said to have died as a result of tribal infighting that same month, including members of the PNP's youth organisation. There was also wholesale destruction of houses and shops, leaving gaping holes in many poorer areas of Kingston. On 6 June, Dudley Thompson, Jamaica's foreign minister, told a news conference in Santiago that recent events may have been deliberate attempts to destabilise Manley's government, although he made it clear there was no proof that the US government was involved. He also complained that recent reports about Jamaica in the US and world press gave a totally distorted picture of the Manley government, and cited an article by Jack Anderson in the *Washington Post* that compared Rastafarians with certain left-wing terrorist groups. 'The Rastafari are like hippies,' said Thompson in their defence. 'They preach the Bible and walk around smoking marijuana, and as a lawyer I believe in evidence.'

Bob Marley, Jamaica's leading advocate of Rastafari, was touring in Europe throughout June. He and the Wailers were supported by Toots and the Maytals and also the Heptones on certain UK dates, but Leroy Sibbles quit the Heptones and took off to Canada before the tour had ended. The four nights Marley and the Wailers played at London's Hammersmith Odeon proved most memorable, and not just because of the poor sound quality on some nights, or crowd unrest caused by inadequate security measures. 'Rastamania hits Britain', screamed the headline of a review in the *Gleaner* that attributed Marley's success to 'hard work, perseverance and blessed talent.' That same article revealed how *Time Magazine* had been among a phalanx of well-known publications – including *Playboy*, *Crawdaddy*, *Cashbox* and *Oui* – 'lining up at the famous Hope Road house to get an interview and capture the man who is now generating the kind of musical excitement America only experiences when The Rolling Stones start a tour. When they performed at the Roxy Theatre in Los Angeles the audience included Jack Nicholson, Warren Beaty, Neil Diamond, Carole King, Joni Mitchell, members of Led Zeppelin, John Lennon, Ringo Starr and Harry Nilsson.'

On 19 June – the same day that Marley and the Wailers played at Cardiff's Ninian Park in Wales – Michael Manley gave a televised address to the Jamaican people, saying 'over the past several months, we have witnessed a type and scale of violence unique to our history. Since the start of the year, Jamaica has been beset by urban terrorism, confrontation with the security forces and other agents of the state, and widespread arson. We cannot and will not stand by and allow the sabotage of our country to continue.' Then came the bombshell, when Manley announced that he'd requested permission from the Governor General to declare an indefinite State of Emergency, and that under its wide-ranging provisions 'the security forces will be authorised to arrest and detain all persons whose activities are likely to endanger the public safety.'

According to Manley, much of the violence had been stage-managed by forces hellbent on rendering his elected government incapable of leadership. In his mind, he'd been the subject of repeated attempts to unseat him, yet Edward Seaga called the State of Emergency 'a blatant attempt to stifle mounting political op-position to its objectionable government.' This was disingenuous, since the JLP had themselves called for a State of Emergency a year earlier and the situation had worsened since then. What really concerned the JLP's leadership was the PNP's recent lurch leftwards towards Democratic Socialism, and what Manley's detractors insisted on calling 'Communism.'

Two days later, nine people – including top-ranking JLP officials – were detained under the Emergency Powers and taken to the heavily guarded detention centre at Up Park Camp. This was the subject of much debate, but then came news that one of the delegates at a JLP convention in Montego Bay was found to have certain documents in their possession that constituted a terrorist threat. One of these documents listed supplies such as rifles, submachine guns and explosives, whilst another told of a paramilitary exercise called 'Operation Werewolf' that declared its willingness to 'take up arms against the Communist regime and purge them from our shores' – and also to destroy Manley and his government 'at all costs.'

It went on to say that 'Operation Werewolf' was to be 'directed by high command, which would liaise with sympathetic local or foreign forces.' Was this a reference to the JLP and CIA? And who exactly headed the high command? Intrigue and supposition were rife, but here at last was vindication of Manley's warnings about terrorism and plots to overthrow his government.

Dennis Brown's 'Whip Them Jah' was another victory chant by the 19-year-old Rasta singer, and it soared into the Jamaican charts on crisp drums, a dancing bass-line and little else. Ossie Hibbert, who oversaw auditions at Channel One and played keyboards when needed, was the producer, but Dennis was now spending most of his time at Joe Gibbs' studio, where Gibbs and his regular house band the Professionals were issuing hit after hit on a profusion of different labels – Belmont, Joe Gibbs, Town & Country, Reflections and Crazy Joe included. Driven by the militant drumming of Sly Dunbar, their sound would come to epitomise the rockers era, together with that of the Revolutionaries. The fact that Sly and Robbie were now integral to both groups shouldn't be underestimated, because they were the most exciting reggae drums and bass pairing since the Barrett brothers. Also, the blend of swashbuckling bass and melodic mid-range and treble that gave Gibbs' productions such vibrancy was largely down to Errol Thompson, who was busily exploiting every advantage offered by the 12-inch format, with its wider grooves and enhanced playback performance. Hearing a deejay seamlessly take over from a singer on one side of a six- or seven-minute 12-inch was thrilling, and the closest record buyers could get to the sound system experience without being in an actual dance or listening to a sound tape. Club DJs loved them, and the impact of these disco 45s was of vital importance in helping to popularise reggae outside of its own constituency.

Errol still had his own label, which he used for songs by artists like Bobby Melody, who'd been with Joe Gibbs ever since the studio had opened. 'Let It Be' and 'Jah Bring I Joy' (a Gaylads' cover) both did well locally, and the latter also got to number two on the *Black Music* chart in the UK. Bobby – real name George Vincent Hanson – was originally from Trelawny. He sang with the Ralph Brothers, who'd backed Yabby You on 'Conquering Lion', then morphed into the Divine Brothers when recording songs like 'Best Dress' and 'Warrior' for Lee Perry. After they'd had a falling out over money, Scratch gave them the stampers and original tapes and told them he wanted nothing more to do with them. That's when Bobby started his own label, Hi-Rock Records and met up with Errol, who'd introduced him to Joe Gibbs in 1975.

'I'd voiced that song 'Jah Bring I Joy In The Morning' two times already, but Joe Gibbs kept saying to voice it again,' Bobby told me. 'They liked my vibe but decided that the harmonies were unprofessional, so they said, "voice back the lead and then we'll get harmonies done by some proper harmonisers." My brethren, they didn't feel away still because certain parts, it's like them nah carry it right, so Joe Gibbs and Errol T draw for the Heptones and Lloyd Parks, and I think Enos McLeod might have sung harmonies on it, too. He was the gateman there, y'know? Then you had Glen Washington, with this little song 'Rockers Nu Crackers...''

Glen Washington was better known as a drummer than a singer, and there were a few surprised faces when 'Rockers Nu Crackers' hit – not because of anything to do with the song, which was a celebration of the new rockers beat, but since no one had expected it of him.

'I used to live in May Pen, 32 miles away, but every morning I'd be on a bus going to Kingston. It was as if I lived there, because I started going to Joe Gibbs' studio religiously every day. I used to go there and when I got tired, I'd lay down under the mixing board. I'd sleep under there, wake up and go look for some food then come back again, but I was there for all the recording that went on at Joe Gibbs during that time. I used to listen to Sly Dunbar because when he was in the studio playing, I was always stood there right behind him!

'My first band was DC35 Incorporated, with Joseph Hill as the drummer. I took instruction from Joseph at a very important time, because it was him who showed me how to feel the beat and develop my own style. After that I sang with a band called Stepping Stones in Spanish Town, then I started playing drums with Sons Of Jah, backing Culture...'

Joseph Hill had recorded for Coxsone, with and without the Soul Defenders, before returning to Linstead and fronting a vocal trio called the African Disciples with his cousins Albert Walker and Kenneth Paley. It was Jah Lloyd who recommended they audition for Joe Gibbs, where Blacker Morwell renamed them Culture and they recorded their debut single 'This Time.'

'Yes, and that is a song that got no justice, governmental-wise,' Joseph said. 'As the song was released, that same week both Jamaican radio stations yelled "ban it! Ban it!" because they were convinced it would cause a riot. The fires were burning and everybody's still blind! That was our first recording for Joe Gibbs. I started chanting from early, early times though. Ancient times! I grew up with the chanting and can't do without it. I have to chant. 'Behold' was my first-ever song. I recorded that for Coxsone when I was just 13 years old. We were all from St Catherine and I was born in the district of Rencomb, near where the rivers flow and the land is so fertile. You can always hear sounds coming from nature, and that will always bring you a song if you listen keenly...'

Joseph brought the songs that he'd written in the Jamaican countryside to Joe Gibbs' studio, where the Professionals built rhythms for them. The latter were augmented by horn players on their instrumental LP *State Of Emergency*, which conveyed little of the drama and urgency caused by Manley's special measures. It was the dub album *African Dub All Mighty Chapter Two*, with its striking black and white cover (depicting a crowned minotaur), that generated more of such qualities, hence the ads declaring it to be 'Hotter Than Hot – Greater Than Number One!' The Professionals didn't exist when those tracks were recorded. It was the Soul Syndicate who played on that album's selection of familiar Studio One and Treasure Isle rhythms, which were all renamed to reflect the times. Their remake of the rhythm for Alton Ellis' 'I'm Still In Love' hence became 'Angola', which Trinity then immortalised on 'Three Piece Suit.' He'd also been voicing for Channel One and Yabby You, but the first man to record him was singer Enos McLeod, who financed the session with money he'd earned selling salt fish on street corners. Like Blacker Morwell, Enos worked for Joe Gibbs in various capacities in-between recording the hit single 'I've Made Up My Mind.' Trinity, who was raised in Two Mile, was still known as Wade Brammer when Enos first met him. It was Winston Edwards who renamed him Prince Glen, by which time he'd graduated from Sir Percy The Welterweight, Veejay The Dubmaster and Simmit The Weapon, and was sparring with Prince Jazzbo on a sound called Soul Hombre. Bearing in mind that Jamaica was still reeling under the spell of spaghetti western fever and his own brother had called himself Clint Eastwood, you'd be forgiven for thinking that his next name, Trinity, was inspired by the Trinity brothers, comedic fraternal cowboys played by Terence Hill and Bud Spencer in a pair of early seventies Italian western movies, but this wasn't the case. According to the older Brammer, it came from the Holy

Trinity, after Jo Jo Hoo Kim, who'd teamed him with Dillinger on 'Crank Face', saw it in the Bible.

Yabby You had been championing Trinity for a while and issued a glut of singles by him. They included 'Tradition', 'Jamal Foundation', 'Consumption Tax' and 'Words Of The Prophet', but the *Uptown Thing A Swing* EP, shared with the Heptones, was Trinity's cheekiest release. Why? Because producer Prince Tony Robinson pressed it up in Jamaica and co-opted the same artwork Virgin had used for the *Front Line* sampler, with the clenched fist gripping barbed wire. It's said that imitation is the best form of flattery, but thanks to Bunny Lee, Johnny Clarke had a genuine connection with Virgin. He'd become the definitive 'rockers' singer, and no grassroots session was complete without his cool, relaxed vocals floating from the speakers over some serious reggae drums and bass. Prolific as always, he voiced two albums for Virgin – one backed by the Revolutionaries (*Authorised Version*) and the other featuring the Aggrovators (*Rockers Time Now*). Both were dominated by roots and culture songs, and *Authorised Version* even included some obligatory Bob Marley covers – his 'Crazy Baldhead' was outstanding – although Marley wasn't best pleased with them, and especially since Bunny had recruited Family Man Barrett for the sessions. Clarke's covers of classic Abyssinians and Burning Spear tracks were the pick of *Rockers Time Now*, along with 'They Never Love Poor Marcus', whilst 'African Roots' was a rallying call for African descendants, just like 'Roots Natty Roots Natty Congo.' I-Roy versioned some of these tracks on his album *Crisis Time*, which Virgin issued on their Caroline Records subsidiary. Bunny Lee had presumably lent him the rhythms and then licensed another Johnny Clarke album to Total Sounds, named after Marley's 'No Woman No Cry.' The wily producer had no doubt wanted to offload tracks in a hurry because those flying cymbals were already sounding dated...

At the beginning of the year, Lloyd James, who'd recently arrived from Canada, had taken over from Pat Kelly as King Tubby's assistant engineer. His first session was for Bunny Lee, who'd immediately christened him 'Prince Jammy.' Once he and his family had moved to a house on nearby St Lucia Road, Jammy began producing tracks for himself. Yabby You got him started with a cut of 'Shank I Sheck' that Jammy mixed and released as *Zambia*. He then booked some time at Joe Gibbs and recorded Michael Rose's original cut of 'Born Free', which Jammy's friend, London soundman Ken 'Fat Man' Gordon, released in the UK. While not a big-seller, 'Born Free' got played in dances and brought Rose to the attention of Black Uhuru's Ducky Simpson who, like Jammy, was living in Waterhouse at the time.

King Tubby was busy working on the first instalment of Harry Mudie's *In Dub Conference* series whilst all that was taking place. The centrepiece of that album was a pair of orchestral tracks, 'String Dub In Rema' and a version of the Heptones' 'Love Without Feeling' called 'Dub With A Difference', both of which provided a fresh benchmark for the dub idiom. King Tubby's other album release was *Surrounded By The Dreads At The National Arena*. This was a selection of dubs compiled by Winston Edwards that Tubby was supposed to have played at the National Arena in September 1975 whilst supporting the Wailers and keeping the crowd entertained for twelve hours straight, from 6 p.m. This version of events is open to question, and whilst live recordings of Jamaican sound systems from 1975 do exist, they're very few in number.

Marley's musicians, The Wailers, were there when the Heptones were recording tracks for their debut Island LP *Night Food*, but the tracks they and the Heptones did together at Black Ark sadly weren't included. Produced by journalist Danny Holloway, the songs on *Night Food* were recorded at Harry J's, and most of them found the group revisiting former hits such as 'Book Of Rules', 'Country Boy', 'Sweet Talkin'', 'Fatty Fatty', 'I've Got The Handle' and 'Love Won't Come Easy.' Trojan's *Cool Rasta* set was again recorded at Harry J's, but shared several of the tracks also found on their *Book Of Rules* LP. As hinted at earlier, the Heptones were on the brink of self-destructing just as Island Records were affording them some decent promotion at last, and at a time when other Island reggae acts such as Marley, Burning Spear, Third World and Toots and the Maytals were doing so well.

Toots had been touring America's east coast and promoting his group's latest album, *Reggae Got Soul*, which contained its share of re-recordings but still sounded like a coherent collection of songs, rather than a collection of singles. The opening 'Rastaman' was a Biblically infused portrait that exuded love and good vibes; the same was also true of 'I Shall Sing', 'Everybody Needs Lovin'' and 'True Love Is Hard To Find.' Toots was the original Jamaican 'Mr Feelgood', and his live shows were so exciting they bordered on frenzied – reggae got soul, indeed. The front cover photo showed him leaning back in the crucifixion pose with arms outstretched, a mic in his right hand and eyes closed as he let rip with one of his trademark screams. It's little wonder that he was being compared to Otis Redding, but he was being pushed hard by Jacob Miller, who had the whole of Jamaica talking after his performance at Carifesta 76. The *Gleaner* had recently published an account of how 'Jacob Miller shot like a bolt from the rung of the ordinary and emerged as the new reggae star of the land.'

'There was no stopping Jacob on any of the shows,' the paper continued. 'Saturday night he gave a dazzling display of superb footwork and voice range and control using the echo most people now referred to as his bionic voice. He floats around the stage as if his weighty body had wings. He hit at the politicians, the police and the rent man with equal vigour and the crowd liked that. He set such a dazzling pace that it was extremely hard for the others to keep up.'

The crowd were said to have 'clapped until their palms were sore' and yet Jacob didn't win the 1976 Jamaica Festival Song competition as expected.

'Although my entry, 'All Night Till Daylight', was a hit, I was given second place because the panel of judges didn't wish to have a dread represent Jamaica in Carifesta,' he said in an interview.

'All Night Till Daylight' wasn't his only triumph however, because his distinctive lead vocals and obvious charisma were very much in evidence on Inner Circle's *Reggae Thing*, which was the group's debut LP for Capitol Records. A year or so previously, Inner Circle had played shows in San Francisco backing Toots and Dennis Brown. There they met Journey's manager Lou Bramy, who got them their deal with Capitol. There was no leader in the band as such, but Roger Lewis handled some of their business affairs and he, his brother Ian and keyboard-player Touter Harvey did most of the writing and arrangements. Jacob wrote songs as well, so it was a family affair, since most of the band lived together at a big house in Kingston's Beverley Hills. *Reggae Thing* was the first Inner Circle album to showcase Jacob as lead singer throughout, and his contributions gave the band fresh impetus, since it meant they were no longer so reliant upon covers of popular soul and reggae hits. New songs '80,000 Careless Ethiopians', 'Roman Soldiers Of Babylon', 'Tired Fi Lick Weed In A Bush' and 'Forward Jah Jah Children' were proof of that.

Jimmy Cliff gave his first home performance in many years at Carifesta, backed by the Jamaican Experience featuring Ernest Ranglin and Joe Higgs. He also got rave reviews. 'Jimmy was terrific for his 45 minutes,' stated one. 'He swung into 'You Can Get It If You Really Want', his arms flailing, his feet stomping and his body gyrating. A bundle of energy backed by a dynamic aggregation, the ten-year wait for Cliff to make his first appearance in Kingston since becoming a star was worth it.'

Another reviewer in the *Gleaner* wrote how Cliff had 'the mesmeric quality of a true star, combining deep sincerity with a conscious sense of mass manipulation, which is at the heart of stage charisma. He held the audience in the palm of his hand and myself among them.'

Michael Manley, who'd recently survived an assassination

attempt after his Jeep was stopped at a roadblock, was sat in the VIP section along with several Cabinet members during Jimmy Cliff's performance. Midway through 'Sons Of Garvey', written by and co-starring Joe Higgs, Manley was asked why politicians were so well-paid while poor people starved, which must have been somewhat embarrassing. A week later, Cliff appeared on JBC TV's *Where It's At*, singing his latest single, 'Turn The Tables.' This was a song that urged unity and collective effort in order to turn Jamaica's fortunes around, but too few heeded the advice.

US author Stephen Davis had recently written an article in *The New York Times* titled 'Fear In Paradise', in which he'd described Jamaica as 'an angry, insecure Third World state with an almost bankrupt economy that barely supports its two million citizens.' Words like those offered a distinct contrast to what half a million tourists a year experienced – namely 'an archetypal paradise spangled with crystal beaches, flowered with bougainvillea and oleander and washed by a tropic sea so aquamarine that on a bright day the eye is blinded by the diamonds of sunshine glistening on the water.' That was Jamaica in a nutshell – heaven and hell combined. This same duality could be found everywhere – in the people, the music, the religion and also the local politics. Davis painted an apocalyptic picture of each party's 'goon squads, most of whose members are in their teens, mounted on Honda CB200 motorbikes and armed with ratchet knives, pistols and sawed-off shotguns.' He alleged there were private armies camped in the Blue Mountains, waiting to either thwart or instigate a coup against the government, and suggested that Jamaica's most prominent business families were liquidating their holdings and fleeing the so-called Socialist regime for Florida and Canada. To quote one businessman, 'the rich and the middle class have been protected in Jamaica for literally hundreds of years. They always have been able to buy or influence their way around inconveniences, customs regulations and tax laws. But now Manley is closing up their loopholes. All my friends are in panic. Everybody wants to run.'

It was no surprise that photographer Adrian Boot and writer Michael Thomas had called their recent book *Babylon On A Thin Wire*. There was now so much tension and uncertainty in the atmosphere that you couldn't blame wealthy Jamaicans for leaving. We should spare a thought, however, for the majority who were too poor to do anything other than endure what was happening all around them. They were the sufferers that many of the Rasta artists were singing and deejaying about, and their options were minimal. They were people who'd grown up with some of the artists currently making hit records, and they were also the ones who looked to the music for solace and guidance in their everyday lives.

Burning Spear toured the US in August to promote their latest album *Man In The Hills*, and when they returned to Jamaica, Winston Rodney announced that he'd jettisoned his two backing singers.

'It's wise that we part because it doesn't make sense if I'm interested in this idea and they're just interested in themselves, that can't work,' he told Dave Hendley. 'They wanted the opportunity, the access, the money and the fame – those were the things they wanted, but when it came to the work it's like you have to go and lift a man up to get things done and them things no right, so now I deal with myself and it's better.'

The new album seamlessly carried on from where *Marcus Garvey* had left off. 'It is good for a man to think for himself,' he sang on 'It's Good', in-between calling for 'No More War' and revisiting his debut single 'Door Peep' for another spine-chilling, magisterial chant. Hearing him exult in his ethnicity on 'Black Soul' or imploring his race to such compelling effect on songs like 'Lion' and 'People Get Ready' was to bear witness to a preacher tugging at the heartstrings of his people and urging them forwards. Though hardly blessed in terms of technique, Rodney's lead vocals were wonderfully expressive, especially when he would break down into fits of sobbing or emit strangled cries. Jack Ruby was still credited with production, but Rodney had recently launched his own Spear label and was clearly more inspired than ever by Garvey's doctrine of self-reliance.

This was something he shared with Augustus Pablo, who played organ, piano, clavinet and melodica on his latest album *King Tubby Meets Rockers Uptown*, issued on Yard Music. The majority of tracks were recorded at Randy's with musicians like the Barrett brothers, Robbie Shakespeare and Earl 'Chinna' Smith, before King Tubby attended to the final mix. It was music of the spheres, Jamaica-style, and imbued with a spiritual majesty that cut through all attempts to categorise it as belonging to either downtown or uptown. 'Keep On Dubbing' and Pablo's cut of 'Satta Massagana' were among the highlights, whilst the title track, a dub version of Jacob Miller's 'Baby I Love You So', possessed a terrifying strength all of its own. It remains one of the most essential rockers dub albums, together with Lee 'Scratch' Perry's *Super Ape*.

Although credited to Scratch and the Upsetters, *Super Ape* wasn't a vocal set exactly, but rather a kaleidoscope of dread rhythms, deejaying and male and female vocal harmonies that was instantly recognisable as a Perry creation. There was a painting by Tony Wright on the cover of a huge gorilla ripping up trees with a giant spliff in one hand, but it was the caption reading 'Dub It Up, Blacker Than Dread' that served as a mission statement of sorts. Scratch continued to experiment at every opportunity. Anything that made a sound and could then be transformed into something else was fair game. But whilst his creativity was of the insatiable, demented type, Perry rarely lost focus and still delivered hit songs and albums capable of competing in the fast-growing reggae market. It was this idiosyncratic, yet pragmatic approach that influenced Chris Blackwell to sign him to Island Records and license ground-breaking releases by him and the Upsetters, George Faith, Max Romeo and Junior Marvin over the coming months.

Island either passed on (or weren't offered) Prince Jazzbo's *Ital Corner*, recorded around the same time. Jazzbo put in a cameo appearance on *Super Ape*. That's him chatting on 'Croaking Lizard'

– a track named after a real life lizard that lived at Black Ark. There had been a lime tree out in the yard that offered shade as well as fruit. Most days the musicians would sit under it during their break whilst eating their lunch, smoking a spliff and just reasoning or working on songs. For some reason (and despite the protests of Black Ark regulars), Scratch decided to cut down the tree and build a urinal in its place. No sooner had he finished than a big lizard set up residence there.

'First the tree came, then the lizard came – that's how it happened,' Scratch later confirmed. 'We were just there amusing ourselves with the new building, and then he come. It was the biggest we'd ever seen. It was a God, and then he said I must leave forever or he was going to eat me, and that if anyone wants to test him, he will teach them a lesson...'

Watty Burnett agreed, saying 'that lizard never run from *no one*. It was a croaking lizard, and it was like a pet. You could actually feed it. It wouldn't leave so that lizard was special as far as I'm concerned...'

Vivien Goldman, who visited the Black Ark in October 1976, made no mention of the lizard – only the studio walls being covered in Bruce Lee posters, and the nightly screenings of kung fu movies and pornographic films.

Island may have missed out on Jazzbo, but lost no time releasing Max Romeo's *War In A Babylon*. Songs like 'One Step Forward' and the title track – together with Perry's trademark, multi-layered mixing style – made this album an instant classic. Another track, 'Uptown Babies Don't Cry', drew an indelible line between Jamaica's middle classes and those who lived in the ghetto. On the very next track Romeo was strapping on his iron shirt and chasing the Devil 'out of earth.' He and Scratch had been among the first reggae artists to take fake Rastas to task, but on 'Stealing In The Name Of Jah' it was Christian preachers who came under attack.

'That's a real serious song!' Max exclaimed, 'and it was actually talking about the role that the church plays in today's world. It's a church and state situation, where the church keeps you docile so that the state can dig out every penny from your pocket 'til you become humble. The humblest calf suck out the most milk, except that particular calf sucks out blood and you find all the milk has disappeared! I've never seen a poor preacher unless he's just entering the arena, but as soon as them open their mouths, poverty disappears, y'know? And yet your reward is in heaven – an unknown, unseen place, so you must be out of your mind to think that way! Because they are getting their reward now, and yet you're not supposed to get anything but promises. Also, they bring in a word called "blaspheming" to defend their plan, where lightning will strike and all that. It's a fear and a scare type of tactic.'

He and Scratch fell out after Max discovered that Perry had pocketed most of the money that Island had paid to license *War In A Babylon*, despite Max claiming to have written and performed all the songs. The irascible Perry then became annoyed in turn and wrote a song about Max called 'White Belly Rat' which he released with 'Judas, De White Belly Rat' on the flipside. Max had already left Black Ark by then, and been commissioned to compose a song for the Jamaica Tourist Board's Motivation Project. 'Ah Fi Wi Country' was the result, which they released on the Jamaica label. This all happened around the same time that Junior Murvin turned up at Black Ark to visit Watty and wrote 'Police And Thieves.'

After recording for Derrick Harriott as Junior Soul, Murvin had returned to Port Antonio and joined Young Experience – a band that became fairly well-known on the hotel circuit. They split up in 1975 with just the one single, 'Wise Rasta Man', to their name. It was in May 1976 that Junior auditioned for Perry and recorded 'Police And Thieves.' Three weeks later, Chris Blackwell heard it and licensed it for Island, together with Jah Lion's cut 'Soldier And Police War.' Jah Lion, who was also known as Jah Lloyd, would later complain that Island had released his album *Colombia Colly* with a photo of Perry on the sleeve and not him. Yet it was the producer's distinctive rhythms that made the album stand out, and

298

whilst that's also true of Junior Murvin's recordings for Scratch, it was more of an equal partnership in his case, given the quality of his songwriting and also that memorable falsetto of his, as heard on 'Roots Train' and an alternative cut to 'Police And Thieves' called 'Philistines On The Land.'

John Martyn had returned to the UK upon hearing that his friend Paul Kossoff, the guitarist with Free, had died from a drug-induced heart attack on a flight to Los Angeles. He'd left Jamaica with half-written songs like 'Dealer', 'Smiling Stranger', 'One World' and 'Black Man At Your Shoulder', and by late summer was busy recording them at Woolwich Green Farm near Reading when Scratch arrived. One morning at breakfast, the diminutive producer began playing with a set of china animals, putting them in sexual positions whilst mumbling nonsensical phrases like 'big muff and powder puff.' Such off-the-wall spontaneity resulted in the track 'Big Muff', once Perry had joined Martyn in the studio and plugged in phasers, reverb and the rest. He didn't stick around to mix it, but did show up sometime later at the Martyns' house in Heathfield, Sussex where, according to John's wife Beverley, he spent most of his time watching wrestling on TV and eating nothing but ice cream.

Toots and the Maytals and the Mighty Diamonds had played at the Shaefer Music Festival in Central Park during early August, performing to a crowd of over six thousand delighted reggae fans. They'd also sold out the Bottom Line within just a few hours, which prompted Island's vice president of sales Herb Cusack to declare 'it's all happening now! In the wake of the Wailers gold album, the success of the Maytals tour and the sudden surge of interest in the music, this is the time to strike.'

Virgin thought so too, which is why they flew in the Mighty Diamonds and U-Roy, backed by the Revolutionaries, for some UK dates. The tour began at London's Lyceum on 25 August; Sly Dunbar remembers that show like it was yesterday.

'That was a time when the sound of the drum was changing,

because before I came with the Channel One sound, everyone was playing like Carly Barrett,' he recalled. 'On the night of the show, I saw people jumping up and down and couldn't believe it! It was like the drum was the lead singer, and everybody love it. I didn't mean to steal the show, because all I did was the same thing that they'd been hearing on the records. It's just that it was the first time people in London got to see it played live and the Lyceum was packed. It was at full capacity and the place just rocked. It was fun, man...'

Two days later they played at the Reading Festival on the same night as Gong, Supercharge and Mallard. A section of the crowd grew impatient during U-Roy and the Mighty Diamonds' performances and tour manager Copeland Forbes wrote in his autobiography that 'punks in the crowd threw tomatoes and enough eggs to make a giant omelette at the Diamonds.' Reggae illustrator Jerry Neville remembers it rather differently. He reminds us that there were no punks as yet, and the dissenters were simply rock fans who'd been turned against reggae by UK influencers dismissing it as novelty music and worse.

'Reggae was something that most of the people just weren't used to,' Jerry said. 'The Diamonds and U-Roy were the only reggae acts there, and they were playing a different kind of reggae to what people would have been accustomed to, which were chart hits and reggae cover versions. When U-Roy came on, he only lasted about twenty minutes. He looked bewildered by the whole thing, because there were cans being thrown at the stage at that point. They were being thrown from quite far back so none were hitting him, but he was up there on his own and just deejaying rather than singing... hip-hop and rapping hadn't gone mainstream by then and these people's point of reference would have been nil, but the Diamonds must have played for at least an hour. There was a small and enthusiastic group down by the front enjoying it but then you had these other idiots running down to the front trying to get close to the stage so they could throw their cans more accurately. It was really bad, so some of us had to try and stop them – we had to turn round and physically prevent them from coming any further. I remember this one moment when someone threw a can and Tabby just caught it in his hand whilst he was singing. He didn't throw it back or miss a beat – he just smiled and let it drop onto the stage. That night was cited as one of the events that started *Rock Against Racism*, but in no sense was it a riot. It's just that most of the crowd probably hadn't heard much reggae and were thinking, "what the hell is this?"'

That same weekend, London's Notting Hill Carnival descended into chaos after the police tried to arrest some of the revellers. Rioters fought back with stones and other missiles, and more than 160 people ended up in hospital. Police harassment intensified after the rioting, leading to even greater unease. Radio London had hosted the first live broadcasts of Carnival in 1973, followed by Capital Radio. Such exposure helped to make Europe's largest street party even more popular, and over 250,000 had attended the 1975 event. The police presence intensified in 1976, despite relations between black youths and the authorities having worsened since the widespread use of stop and search tactics. Confrontations were inevitable, especially given the sweltering heat that summer. Tensions erupted on the second day of Carnival, resulting in what the BBC described as 'rioting rarely seen on the streets of an English city', and 'fearful and bloody battles between black teenagers and the police in which over three hundred police were injured, and more than 30 hospitalised.' Amidst newspaper headlines screaming 'Rampage At The Carnival' and 'No Surrender To The Thugs', Carnival organiser Selwyn Baptiste claimed that heavy-handed policing 'to great effect, was responsible for the breakdown of the situation. Carnival is a happy, fun-loving affair. It is not a war.'

'Black youths were feeling marginalised and disenfranchised because of the SUS law,' said Ishmahil Blagrove, author of *Carnival*. '1976 was a coming-of-age for the first-generation black youths born in this country expressing themselves and forging an identity separate from that of their parents; letting the state know that these weren't the same type of naive, Christian, immigrant visitors they were dealing with before. The state began to realise the fear of the black male – it made the state aware of the forces of black anger.'

Such attitudes were reflected in the music of bands like Aswad, Misty In Roots and Black Slate, as well as the songs thundering from reggae sound systems across the capital. John Peel's listeners were introduced to Aswad when he played their debut single 'Back To Africa' just days before Carnival. The lyrics were designed to resonate with black British-born youths reeling under a vicious cocktail of police harassment, racism and lack of equal opportunities, but feeling empowered by the Rasta music coming from Jamaica. The members of Aswad weren't trying to sound Jamaican; they'd grown up between two different cultures, and didn't feel like they truly belonged to either of them. They were searching for their own identity, but their lyrics were firmly rooted in the same tradition as bands like the Wailers, Abyssinians and Burning Spear. 'Back To Africa' was an immediate hit on the *Black Echoes* charts and was in the same class as Bunny Wailer's 'Dream Land', except that Aswad wrote all their own lyrics. In the early days, Aswad used to rehearse above the Gangsterville record shop on Harrow Road. They recorded some demo tracks there and a short time later an ad-hoc group of young black musicians armed with just a name, a cassette and bags of confidence marched into Island's Hammersmith office and set up camp there, in hope of a record deal.

'We just walked into Island Records and said that we wanted to speak to someone about signing us up,' said drummer Angus 'Drummie Zeb' Gaye, marvelling in retrospect at their nerve. 'The receptionist told us to go away, but we just sat there for about four hours until she said someone would see us.'

That someone was A&R man Richard Williams.

'There we were in his office, smoking weed and thinking we were rude boys, but he put on the cassette and after he'd finished listening to it he said, "Okay. I'd like to offer you a deal." It was just an arrangement for us to get some studio time so we could record more demos, but that's how we came to make 'Back To Africa'.'

After Williams recommended they slim down to a five-piece, keyboard-player Tony 'Gad' Robinson was ousted, but remained close to the band as a new line-up took shape, with Brinsley Forde, aka 'Chaka B' or 'Brinsley Dan', on vocals and rhythm guitar, Drummie on drums, bassist George Oban, guitarist Donald Griffiths and keyboard-player Courtney Hemmings, also known as 'Khaki.' When their debut album – called simply *Aswad*, which means black in Arabic – came out earlier that summer, the *NME* crowned them 'kings of the concrete jungle' whilst Penny Reel, writing in the new UK music weekly *Black Echoes*, coined the phrase 'Young Lions of British reggae.' Their follow-up single 'Three Babylon', produced by Karl Pitterson, was written after police tailed Drummie, Tony and Donald as they cruised the streets of west London late one night. Their music was hypnotic, but it was their chronicling of the black British experience that got them noticed and spoke directly to the Rasta youths hanging out on the street corners.

Bunny McKenzie played harmonica on that first album, while his sister Candi sang backing vocals with Delroy Washington, whose own involvement with Island proved short-lived. He ended up signing with Virgin instead, who released his debut album *I Sus*, featuring members of Aswad and Wailers' guitarist Al Anderson. Delroy's manager was Mikey 'Reuben' Campbell – 'the man with the longest dreadlocks in Ladbroke Grove', according to one news report. He wanted Aswad to be Delroy's backing band, but they had ambitions of their own, and so Mikey became their manager as well.

Dennis Bovell had only just come out of jail in autumn 1976 when Castro Brown approached him to produce 'Black Skin Boy' by London-based teenaged all-girl vocal trio 15-16-17. Jah Bunny played drums and Dennis found the chords and played the rest of the instruments. That track became Castro's first production for the Morpheus label, which he'd previously used for songs licensed from other parties. Dennis Harris of DIP Records then recruited Dennis to be the engineer at a new studio – named after his wife Eve – he'd built in the basement of the couple's record shop in Upper Brockley Road, South London. Guitarist John Kpiaye, who'd previously played in the Cats and In-Bracket and had backed Dandy Livingstone, contributed to a lot of the sessions there.

'It was all a bit chaotic,' he recalls, 'although the studio was fairly big and laid out quite professionally, with proper sound-proofing and a separate control room. He had an organ and a piano there too, which was useful. It was the mic situation that wasn't so good, and also the actual desk itself, which had been put together from a multi-track recorder that Steve Wayley from the group Los Bravos had built as some kind of prototype. The equipment was very basic in fact, and so those recordings were understandably lo-fi.'

'You could hear the difference in quality compared to the stuff recorded elsewhere but those DIP productions had a kind of rough, Jamaican edge to them, and that's what drew people in,' adds Dennis Bovell. 'Funnily enough, because the equipment was so bad, the tracks recorded on it sounded great on sound system, and especially since everything from there was mastered in mono as well.'

DIP had been largely dependent on cover versions until then, and so Harris must have been delighted by how quickly the two musicians were able to forge an original sound of their own. John recalls him bringing records into the sessions and then pointing out a particular guitar sound or arrangement in order to get his views across. 'He was aware of how music was actually put together,' he says, 'but would happily just let everyone get on with what they were doing if he thought you were working on something distinctive.'

Bovell produced two albums by the 4th Street Orchestra at DIP; both *Ah Who Seh Go Deh* and *Leggo Ah Fe We Dis* were released on Rama, which was another of Dennis Harris' labels. In doing so, Bovell rewrote the form book, and exploded the popular myth that serious dub, roots and vocal reggae couldn't be created anywhere outside of the Caribbean.

'That's down to the original Dub Band which I put together for sessions, so we could maintain a particular quality by using the same musicians all the time,' he explains. 'The nucleus of the band was Drummie Zeb and Tony Gad from Aswad, John Kpiaye and myself. We cut endless records in the studio, and for all kinds of different producers during the late seventies. In fact, one time we looked at the *Black Echoes* chart and saw that we'd played on about fifteen records out of the Top 20. It was unbelievable!'

As in Jamaica, aspiring singers and bands got noticed by entering talent competitions in their local music venues and youth clubs. That's how Louisa Marks got her break with 'Caught You In A Lie', if you remember. A group of young roots reggae musicians who'd named themselves after a racehorse – Irish Derby winner Steel Pulse – won one such event held at the Santa Rosa in Birmingham during early 1976. First prize was a session with Dennis Bovell at a studio in Handsworth, where they recorded an early version of 'Handsworth Revolution.' Their first release, however, was the moody 'Kibudu, Mansatta, Abuku' – a song about three slaves from West Africa that came out another of DIP's subsidiary labels, Concrete Jungle.

Black Slate had made their debut four years earlier whilst Anthony Brightly was still at school. He'd played organ with the house band at Phebes in Stoke Newington from the age of 11 before recruiting Keith Douglas and a couple of other friends for a band called the Young Ones.

'We had that name until I was about 14, and then we changed it to Black Slate,' says Brightly. 'We used "slate" because we'd seen the writing on the wall, whereas "black" referred to us as a people. We always said that we'd make music that carried a message, because Desmond and I had seen the Wailers play at the Sundown Theatre and that show changed our lives.'

In addition to backing visiting artists from Jamaica with Black Slate, Anthony took over his father's Sir George sound system and began making exclusive tracks to use as dubplates. He released a couple of them on the Black Slate label but kept 'Sticks Man' back because in his own words 'it was carrying the sound.' Elroy Bailey, who'd already left school by this time, wanted to buy it. Anthony refused, but then someone stole all his records and dubs. He lost everything, and that's when he agreed to release 'Sticks Man' under the name Black Slate, with Elroy singing lead vocals.

Early pressings of the single soon sold out and 'Sticks Man' became Black Slate's breakthrough hit. It was at number one on the *Black Echoes* reggae charts for weeks during 1976, which is when Prince Far I's album *Psalms For I* first caused a stir, with lyrics derived almost completely from the *Book of Psalms*. The former King Cry Cry, who'd started his career at Studio One before recording for Joe Gibbs, had conceived the album on behalf of the illiterate who couldn't read the Bible for themselves. His gravelly voice was thick as tar, and made him sound like Moses reading from tablets of stone, prompting whoever wrote the liner notes to claim that 'this album sends the most powerful message ever issued musically.' *Psalms For I* was Prince Far I's first full album, and after Micron's Pete Weston played the tape to Chips Richard and his junior partner Adrian Sherwood, it was issued on the pair's Carib Gems label based in Harlesden. Carib Gems also released U-Roy's *The Originator* LP in 1976, with tracks produced by Bunny Lee and mixed by King Tubby. It was a tough album and began with U-Roy boasting that, 'I originate, so you must appreciate whilst the others got to imitate, y' know?'

U-Roy already seemed like a veteran, although he'd only made his breakthrough five years earlier. Times change, and his status as Jamaica's number one deejay had been under threat for some time. The latest contender was Jah Woosh, who had three records in the *Black Echoes* Top 10 when he visited the UK in May. At last count, there were four albums bearing his name in the shops, including Trojan's *Dreadlocks Affair*. Jah Woosh's ascent had been spectacular, but the deejay crown still belonged to Big Youth, who had not one, but two new albums for Trojan – *Natty Cultural Dread* and *Hit The Road Jack*. Make no mistake, the 27-year-old was a ghetto superstar – his off the wall sing-jaying and dread Rastafarian chants had captured the hearts of his audience like no other deejay before or since. On the front cover of *Natty Cultural Dread* he was facing the camera with his locks out, a big spliff in his mouth and wearing bright orange sunglasses. Turn it over and there he was, flashing teeth with red, gold and green gemstones set in them (although it was a black and white photo so most of us didn't know what colour they were at the time). The choice of tracks was exceptional, too, and included former singles 'Wolf In Sheep's Clothing' and 'Every Nigger Is A Star.' 'Hell Is For Heroes' was a manifesto, and he invoked John Coltrane and the Last Poets on 'Jim Squashey.' A cut of Ansel Collins' 'Stalag 17' underpinned that one, whilst 'Keep Your Dread' was revelatory, and opened with the declaration that black people had been beaten and stripped of their name, language, religion and culture. It was somehow typical of Big Youth that in the midst of such unvarnished truth-telling he then launched into three soul covers with such gusto you'd be forgiven for thinking that he was joking, rather than simply enjoying himself. Anything could happen on a Big Youth record and often did, but covering Diana Ross's 'Touch Me In The Morning' was risky, as was his opening *Hit The Road Jack* with a warbling medley of Marvin Gaye, Ray Charles and Harold Melvin and the Blue Notes hits. There was a cut of the Wailers' 'Get Up Stand Up' on *Hit The Road Jack*, but sadly not the superior cut produced by Glen Adams and shared with Dennis Brown. The sounds of sirens, thunder and lightning embellished 'Hotter Fire', which wasn't voiced about the Orange Street disaster but the hellfire he wanted to see visited upon the wicked, whilst 'The Way Of The Light' was a companion to 'Wolf In Sheep's Clothing' and shared the same rhythm. By this time Big Youth was driving around Kingston in a green Mustang and only Bob Marley and Dennis Brown could rival him for popularity in Jamaica. He'd also successfully kept away from politics, which took some doing in such a volatile atmosphere.

Jah Love Muzik, which formed when two sounds belonging to the Twelve Tribes joined forces, managed the same difficult feat, as their resident mic man Brigadier Jerry explained to the *I Never Knew TV* YouTube channel.

'Jah Love was the only sound that could play anywhere. All the other sounds get brand as either a Labourite sound or a PNP sound. Well, Jah Love was a Rastaman sound and they couldn't mix Jah Love with politics, so any little peace dance like the one they held in Tivoli Gardens in 1976, Jah Love play there and everyone – PNP and JLP – mix up and come into Tivoli Gardens. When we drive in there, two dead bodies were there. It was a funeral and they were keeping the service in the Community Centre, but as soon as the two hearses drive out of the place – pure rain! There was a shower for maybe fifteen minutes, and then it stop. I deejay for more than twelve hours in that dance. U-Roy and Ranking Trevor were there, and that was the night when U-Roy say that I am the greatest deejay he ever see.'

Tivoli Garden was packed that night, but then three weeks later the violence started up again. In mid-September, former CIA operative Philip Agee, author of the bestselling book *Inside The Company*, embarked on a series of public meetings sponsored by the Jamaica Council For Human Rights. He was on a one-man crusade to expose the CIA's clandestine practices around the globe, and Agee's revelations concerning the use of destabilisation techniques such as inciting strikes, organising arson attacks and murders and the funding, arming and advising of opposition groups amounted to a carbon copy of what had been happening in Jamaica. He went so far as to name eleven CIA agents then based in Kingston – three of whom left on the first available flight back to the US. He also cited the CIA's ability to inspire articles in the US press that were designed to undermine and ultimately destroy the reputation of

Manley's government in the minds of the US public. Tourism had already been badly affected by the many articles in *The Washington Post* and *The New York Times* in particular, even though murders in tourist areas were rare.

Two days before Agee's talks had begun, Island released Bunny Wailer's debut album, *Blackheart Man*, which was widely acclaimed and established him as a serious artist in his own right. It's one of those landmark releases that defined their genre and is deserving of a place alongside other classic seventies' albums by the likes of Marley, Stevie Wonder, Marvin Gaye and Curtis Mayfield.

'It was a blessing for me to have been inspired in making that album,' Wailer said. 'The messages that come from it are like a summing up of the journey of I and I, coming up to this present time. It's something that I always have to be reminiscing on, or using as a guiding force in my life, because I don't think I will do an album that is better than *Blackheart Man*. Some people tell me that it changed their lives, and that listening to it made them better people. Along with some other stuff, I think that it was responsible for keeping people on the right track as far as making them feel proud of themselves was concerned, and treating each other as if we're all part of the same human family.'

The album informed the way some people viewed the world around them, and at a time when relatively little was known of the Rastafari faith. 'Rastafarians had been ridiculed,' Wailer said. 'They'd been abused and accused of doing all kinds of religious misdeeds after saying that His Imperial Majesty is the supreme power of all creation, and that was something a lot of people had yet to come to terms with.'

When Stephen Davis asked Michael Manley if he still maintained contact with Rasta culture, Manley replied, 'look around you, and see what colonialism has done to the displaced people. Man has a deep need for religious conviction, and Rasta resolves the contradictions of a white man's God in a colonial society. Sometimes I think that the only Jamaican who truly knows who he is has to be the Rastaman. They're very beautiful and remarkable people.'

Bunny Wailer says exactly the same thing throughout *Blackheart Man*, especially on songs like 'Rasta Man' and the title track, a reminder of how children in Jamaica were cautioned against going anywhere near Rastas, who have 'no friend, no home, no family.' In 'Fighting Against Conviction', he told the story of a sufferer born into poverty, with five kids and a pregnant woman to care for who is then trapped and imprisoned by the authorities. 'The Oppressed Song' and 'Reincarnated Souls' were originally earmarked for the Wailers' *Burnin'* set, 'Dreamland' was adapted from an R&B song by the El Tempos, whilst 'Armagideon' warned of wars and "rumours of wars," and was voiced over a loping rhythm masterminded by Family Man Barrett. Bunny produced Marcia Griffiths' 'Tribulation' in-between the *Blackheart Man* sessions. She and Bunny had known each other since attending kindergarten in Hannah Town, but when Bob Marley heard 'Tribulation' he warned her against singing anything that she wasn't actually experiencing, otherwise it might manifest. Peter Tosh, meanwhile, was on the cover of *Black Music* accompanied by a strapline that asked if he was 'Reggae's Next Giant?' The fairest answer was probably, 'not yet', but the band he put together for his forthcoming US tour showed that he meant business, because it included two former Wailers – Earl 'Wya' Lindo and Al Anderson – and the unbeatable reggae drums and bass pairing of Sly Dunbar and Robbie Shakespeare.

Veteran trombonist Rico Rodriguez returned to Jamaica in September for sessions at Randy's and Joe Gibbs, where he recorded his best album, *Man From Wareika*. Chris Blackwell had signed him after hearing him play over a rhythm recorded back in May for Ijahman Levi, whose two recent Concrete Jungle singles – 'Jah Heavy Load' and 'I Am A Levi' – had also been interesting staff at Island. They were being kept busy because Jack Ruby finally delivered the Justin Hinds' album that Blackwell had commissioned two years earlier, featuring the same musicians – the Black

Disciples – who usually played with Burning Spear. Carl Gayle's liner notes made the point that Hinds and the Dominos had 'never recorded a song that did not make a worthwhile comment on some aspect of the strife of life. From the start, their music stood out because of their predominant use of traditional everyday sayings, the righteous themes of their songs, and because of Hinds' own country/gospel vocal style. Their music, like that of the early Maytals, seemed church-like in spirit, flavour and atmosphere. Hinds had that Baptist church feeling, and he quoted from the Bible quite naturally.'

The album was called *Jezebel* and marked the group's comeback after 'four years in limbo.' Hinds spent most of that time farming and had more or less retired from the music business until teaming up with Jack Ruby. Prior to that he'd remained loyal to Duke Reid, who'd produced all the Dominos' ska and rocksteady hits for Treasure Isle – the original 'Carry Go Bring Come' included. When the Duke took ill and appointed Sonia Pottinger to run the studio, Justin became disillusioned and chose to stay away. It must have grieved him to hear that Reid had finally lost his battle with cancer on 26 September, at St Joseph's Hospital in Kingston. Three weeks later on 19 October, Count Ossie was killed driving home after a show at the National Arena. It was National Heroes Day and a drunken bus driver had crashed into the master drummer's truck on the road to Bull Bay, killing the Count, two band members and his infant son. Thousands of people, including the prime minister and Edward Seaga, attended Count Ossie's funeral a week later, when numerous tributes were paid to this 'plain and simple man' whose drumming was 'a source of joy and a spiritual source of strength.'

It seems almost sacrilegious to mention that Patti Smith played two nights at London's Hammersmith Odeon whilst Count Ossie's body was lying in state at the Mystic Revelation Of Rastafari's HQ in Glasspole Avenue. She'd been hailed as America's 'punk poet laureate' after the release of her breakthrough album *Horses* in late 1975, but ticket sales for her shows at the 3,000-capacity Odeon were slow, possibly because it was her second visit to London in just five months. When a journalist questioned her about this during a press conference she yelled, 'fuck you!' and pelted the assembled media people with food. The shows went well, however, and halfway through one of them reggae fans were treated to the sight of Tapper Zukie strolling onstage, bold as you like, and duetting with Patti on a burning rendition of 'Ain't It Strange.' That cameo appearance helped to raise Tapper's profile whilst adding to Smith's credibility. It was another visible expression of rock music's affinity with reggae, and there would be more to come – especially in the wake of a letter published in the *NME*, announcing the launch of a campaign called *Rock Against Racism*, inspired by Eric Clapton's racist outburst whilst performing in Birmingham, when he endorsed Enoch Powell's view that England had too many immigrants. 'Come on Eric, own up,' the letter-writer goaded. 'Half your music's black. You are rock music's biggest colonialist.' As a parting shot, the author then asked, 'who shot the sheriff Eric? It sure as hell wasn't you.'

By then, Lee Perry had returned to Jamaica after his adventures with John Martyn and he and Bob Marley recorded a new song called 'Smile Jamaica', to coincide with a free concert planned for 5 December in Kingston's National Heroes Park. Permission for the event was granted by the Cultural Section of the prime minister's office, and Wailers' guitarist Al Anderson tried to warn Marley that JLP supporters felt very unhappy about this. Bob took no notice other than to say he was 'turning the other cheek.' This lackadaisical response alarmed Al greatly, and was the main reason why he left the Wailers and joined Peter Tosh's band instead.

To be fair, Bob may have been distracted, since he'd recently began dating Cindy Breakespeare, who was still living at 56 Hope Road and had recently won Miss Universe Bikini in London. When she then accepted an invitation to compete for Miss World, critics in Jamaica urged her to stand down as South Africa – then ruled by an apartheid regime – had said it would be sending two contestants, one black and one white. Cindy refused, citing the £2 million raised during the previous Miss World contest that had gone to charities acting on behalf of handicapped and underprivileged children. It was a proud moment for Jamaica on 19 November when she was crowned Miss World in front of twenty-five million television viewers, but her involvement with Bob Marley would soon prove problematic and attract unwelcome attention from the British press, and also over-righteous Rastafarians.

'The Rastafarian influence was so heavy,' Cindy told me. 'It was a very oppressive kind of influence. You had to dress in a certain kind of way and you weren't allowed to be overtly sexual. You had to very much be a reflection of your man, and to shadow everything he was saying. I remember when I would go off to do promotional things and be dressed up to the eyeballs with make-up and everything and I'd be in the car or on the plane scrubbing it all off before I got back home. That's because I knew there'd be so many Rastafarians hanging around Hope Road or wherever Bob was, and I had to prove myself before I could walk into that type of environment. Rastafari had undergone such a complete evolution in Jamaica at that time, and permeated every echelon of society. You would have been hard-pressed to find a Jamaican female entertainer looking sexy on stage back then. It just was never like that. There were women who could sing, yes, but they had to be wearing lots of fabric.'

Forty-eight hours later and Michael Manley was at a PNP rally in Montego Bay, addressing a crowd at least 120,000 strong. It was said to be the largest gathering ever recorded in Sam Sharpe Square, where the leader of Jamaica's most famous slave rebellion had uttered his final words of defiance before being hung. Manley had launched his successful 1972 election campaign there, and after speaking for an hour, announced that the country's next general election would take place on 15 December. Bob Marley, unwittingly, found himself in the midst of an election campaign, especially after the prime minister's office had ensured that its name was prominently displayed on the posters.

It now looked as if the Smile Jamaica concert was a joint promotion by him and the PNP, yet this simply wasn't true. Marley had wanted to give a free concert out of love for the people and wasn't doing it to take sides with any political party. While he himself refused to show concern, other members of the Wailers' inner circle were understandably worried.

'I left that day of the shooting', recalls Marcia Griffiths, 'and because of that, they were saying that I knew about the plans and what have you, but all I was going by was the inspiration from God – vision, and things like that. And it's not like I didn't pass it onto Bob, because I said to him, 'Bob, please don't do that concert, otherwise something terrible is going to happen', plus Judy dreamt about throwing a stone at a fowl, but the stone she threw missed the big fowl and hit three little chickens instead. When she told me that, I said the big fowl was Bob, and those three little chickens is we. I'd been at the rehearsals every night, and all the time I was in there, I was just nervous, 'cause I was expecting something. I could feel it in the air, and I was just so tense. Oh Lord, it was just like God had shown me something, so I just tell Bob I have a show to do in New York, and from I land in my sister's house that night, Ms Pottinger call me and say, 'Marcia, they've shot Bob', and I couldn't move from my chair for hours'.

The Wailers were rehearsing in a room at the back of 56 Hope Road on the night of 3 December. It was around nine in the evening when seven gunmen entered the grounds – Marley's security guards having inexplicitly vanished from their posts. Bob was in the kitchen adjoining the rehearsal room, talking to Don Taylor, who had his back to the door. Rather than targeting their intended victims, the gunmen pointed their weapons round the doors and fired indiscriminately into both rooms. They then shot at Rita Marley's car, which was parked nearby, before exiting the premises the same way that they'd come. The entire incident lasted just a few minutes, and miraculously no one died, although Don Taylor was shot three times – once in each thigh and once in his side. Tuff Gong helper Louis Griffiths was shot in the back, a bullet grazed Rita's skull, and another had passed clean through Bob's left arm and skimmed his chest just below his heart. All were taken to the university hospital and, Taylor almost died through loss of blood, as one of the bullets had severed a main artery. He would spend the next six weeks in hospital, but Bob and Rita were released the same night and Chris Blackwell, who'd been at Black Ark with Lee Perry when the shooting took place, immediately had them taken to his house up on Strawberry Hill.

'There's no need to ask who shot him,' said one insider, who wishes to remain anonymous. 'They were from the party whose name wasn't on the posters.'

Marley still performed at the Smile Jamaica concert, despite his injuries and the absence of various Wailers, including Family Man, who'd sought refuge at a Rasta camp in Bull Bay. Members of Third World filled in where necessary, and during Bob's set the stage was crowded with musicians who'd bravely put themselves in possible harm's way, just in case the gunmen chose to finish what they'd started. A day or so after the concert, Marley left for Nassau in the Bahamas, where he spent the next two weeks with Cindy and various band members, writing songs like 'Time Will Tell.' He then flew to London and wouldn't return to Jamaica for almost eighteen months. This was just as well, since tribal violence would continue right up until election day. During the final run-in, two of Seaga's party faithful were sleeping in a car outside their burnt-out party office one night when PNP insurgents approached the vehicle and shot them in the head at point-blank range. Soon afterwards, a PNP candidate was gunned down in broad daylight and Manley – who'd already been shot at during his election campaign – had to dodge yet another attempt to kill him. In the end, he won the election by a landslide. The turnout had been high, too, although there were reports that gunmen had held up polling stations and taken away ballot boxes that were then stuffed full of PNP votes and returned. Numerous cases of multiple voting were also recorded and a team of forty men were said to have been going from one polling station to another, voting at each until the police intervened.

Whilst all this had been happening, reggae crooner Barry Biggs' cover of Blue Magic's 'Side Show' had entered the UK Top 10, peaking at number three. There was clearly still an appetite for showbiz-style reggae in Britain, but *Gleaner* writer Dan Hedges advised against rashly dismissing such music in his review of Bob Andy's latest album, *The Music Inside Me*.

'The songs are so unusually tasteful and tuneful for today's reggae sounds that a casual listener might be tempted to dismiss Bob Andy as being middle-of-the-road, but they'd be making the biggest mistake of their listening careers,' he counselled. 'Messages as heavy as any currently issuing from JA are transmitted via songs infectiously irresistible as the pinkest, fluffiest bubble-gum music. The meaning is the nut inside the pink sugar coat.'

The lyrics of his recent single 'War In The City' found Andy lamenting how the violence had got out of hand and led to so much burning, looting, shooting and fighting. With no respite forthcoming, he imagined that only divine intervention could break the cycle by Jah sending down blood, fire, 'lightning and some thunder...'

1975 had been Dr Alimantado's breakthrough year, thanks mainly to 'Best Dressed Chicken.' He'd followed up that flurry of success with 'Poison Flour' and 'The Barber Feel It', but still hadn't appeared on a stage show. His debut was scheduled to take place at the Carib Theatre on Boxing Day. Feeling nervous, he went to meet a friend at the beach that morning, but the Doctor couldn't swim too well and took in so much water that he almost drowned. His friend said for him not to worry because he was going to give the best show of his life that evening, so he went home, showered and then headed for the tailors, who had his suit ready. As the deejay strolled along Orange Street, a bus suddenly mounted the pavement, knocked him over and dragged him along the street. It wasn't until some passers-by saw what had happened and flagged down the bus that it stopped. Dr Alimantado was adamant that the bus had deliberately swerved to hit him because his locks were out, and the driver hated to see a Rastaman looking so happy and carefree.

Needless to say, he didn't make it to the Carib Theatre that night, and the Boxing Day celebrations continued without him. Zap Pow played at the Epiphany Club in New Kingston that evening. Island had recently reissued the band's 1973 hit 'This Is Reggae Music' whilst Vulcan released their new album *Now*, despite Trojan confusing matters by having repackaged Zap Pow's *Revolutionary* album for Harry J as *Revolution*. Their new singer, Beresford Hammond, hardly featured on it, but then he'd been working hard on his debut album *Soul Reggae* with Harold Butler and Willie Lindo at Aquarius – the same studio where Bunny Wailer had recorded *Blackheart Man*. Owner Herman Chin Loy had said for them to just go in there and make some songs, and he must have been delighted with the results because *Soul Reggae* was capable of standing alongside most major label American soul releases, and every track was an original. It's easy to imagine Al Green or Marvin Gaye singing 'You Didn't Have To Lie', 'Oh Take Me Girl' or 'Don't Wait Too Long', whilst the bright and breezy 'Your Love Won't Shine' would have suited Zap Pow. Beres would inherit the mantle of 'Mr Soul of Jamaica' from Alton Ellis on the strength of this album, which wasn't intentionally aimed at the American market as you might think, but had evolved from the belief that once all the right ingredients were in place, then an artist like Beres could really shine. He and Willie even recorded live strings on certain tracks, and they used quite a few horns as well. The rhythms and arrangements raised the bar, as did the lyrics, since Beres showed great empathy, and was already writing songs with highly charged emotion content like 'Got To Get Away', 'Oh I Miss You' and the broken-hearted 'Somebody Lied.'

The 21-year-old singer was living in Rollington Town at the time of those Aquarius sessions, and couldn't always afford the bus fare home, meaning he often had to walk home at night from Half Way Tree to Crossroads, then all the way down South Camp Road. There were few streetlights and he was twice hit by cars – once outside the Gun Court when he was thrown against the fence, and another time after a driver had fallen asleep at the wheel and veered off the road. It was Herman Chin Loy's brother Lloyd that provided him with the biggest challenge, however. He was hoping to manage Beresford, as he was known then, and made several attempts to change his name. First he suggested 'J. D. Stone.' Then, after inviting Beres to his office one day, he pointed to a bowl of fruit and said, 'welcome to your new name – Blueberry!' In the end, he was persuaded that 'Beres' would do just fine, but it was touch and go for a while…

CHAPTER EIGHT

1977: WHEN TWO SEVENS CLASH

In the New Year, Count Shelly challenged Brixton sound D Unis Hi Fi to a clash at the Four Aces in Dalston, and reggae fans travelled from all parts of London to be there. Shelly had ruled the Four Aces before concentrating on his Third World label and distribution business. He no longer played out so often, but Castro Brown was in his corner for this clash and, late in the evening, he handed Shelly a Dennis Brown dubplate. Everyone present knew of Castro's closeness with Dennis, and so expectations were running high. After a slow chanted intro that cast a spell over the gathering and lasted almost a minute, Dennis delivered his opening lines, which took the form of a prayer. Pandemonium broke out, and the crowd's wild reaction let everyone know that Shelly had won the clash. Then, in the midst of the uproar, Castro took the mic and declared triumphantly, 'one cut! The original tape was burnt in a fire.' As what he said sank in, people realised that they'd witnessed something very special, or so they thought. They'd just heard the only surviving copy of a Dennis Brown track sung with such reverence, it had given them goosebumps. It was all those dancehall fans could talk about afterwards and then, a few weeks later, 'Immanuel God Is With Us' appeared on a 7-inch single and sold briskly over the counters of every specialist record store in the land.

Castro would press up Dennis' 'Children Of Israel', Junior Delgado's 'Devil's Throne' and Gregory Isaacs' 'Set The Captives Free' on DEB Music in the coming weeks, but it was the sightings of Bob Marley and various Wailers in the UK capital that generated most interest. Marley and his entourage had arrived in London during early January. The band members were staying at an apartment in Harrington Gardens, whilst Marley had his own place in Oakley Street, in the fashionable borough of Chelsea. Cindy Breakspeare, the reigning Miss World, would spend time with him in London whenever her busy schedule allowed.

'Whilst we were staying here in London he had to have two flats,' she recalled. 'One where when you went to open the door, the smoke would knock you over, and then there was another one on the next floor up, where he'd try and get some shut-eye. He was always surrounded by people anyway, and I think a lot of the things he wrote about came from what he saw, because he never had a moment's peace, that's for sure. By the time he got around to sitting down for dinner, someone had eaten it and people would disturb us all the time, even when we were in bed! He had no peace, no matter where in the world he was. No peace at all. It was as if he would have had to leave earth to get any peace. Also, he never turned people away. Never! Even when he was exhausted, miserable and wrecked, he just felt like it was his responsibility to see to them and that he had to do it. I certainly learned a lot from him, because his life was all about discipline and commitment. Single-mindedness and a sense of purpose are always the phrases that come to mind.'

Cindy was Bob's muse, and songs like 'Turn Your Lights Down Low', 'Is This Love' and 'Waiting In Vain' would reflect his infatuation with her. The two of them were now very close, and we can only imagine the hurt that this must have caused Rita, who shared an apartment nearby with Marcia Griffiths and their friend Inez, who cared for Marcia's infant son Kemar and cooked for them all. Judy Mowatt hadn't travelled with them as she was heavily pregnant, and it was Marcia who sung most of the harmonies on the new songs that Bob and the Wailers were recording at Island's studio in Hammersmith.

Back in Jamaica, Sonia Pottinger had been putting finishing touches to Marcia's *Naturally* album, which featured mainly old songs re-recorded in a reggae style. Seven of them were written by Bob Andy and there wasn't one ballad among them, which was unusual given that she had been a successful cabaret artist until joining Marley's retinue. It was seeing Bunny Wailer sing 'Dreamland' on one of the Wailers' reunion shows that had inspired her to cover it for Ms Pottinger, who'd assumed control of Treasure Isle since Duke Reid's death and used the Revolutionaries on most of her sessions. Bob Andy had also been working at Treasure Isle, although he'd taken his own tapes with him, and the *Lots Of Love And I* album he recorded there was his production and not hers.

'That came about because of the relationship between Marcia and myself,' he told Ray Hurford, 'because she was working with Pottinger. At the time, I was a bit frustrated and she sent a message via Marcia that said, "you're a very good artist. Why don't we pool efforts and see what can happen?" We did that, and the result was *Lots Of Love And I*, but I was disappointed that it didn't get much attention. The Jamaican music public didn't really have any time for me, because Marley was swinging, Tosh was and also Culture… I mean, who was this guy Bob Andy? I felt cheated, because 'Ghetto Stays In The Mind' was never played on Jamaican radio.'

You can hear the despair in his voice on that track as he expressed the hopelessness caused by poverty, whilst 'Stepping Free' was a call for unity and an end to the 'crab in a barrel' mentality that compels many people to help themselves at the expense of others. Bob Andy wasn't the only rocksteady star to work at Treasure Isle and write social commentary – it's also where Alton Ellis recorded 'Confusion', another song voiced over a Revolutionaries' rhythm, which later appeared on Alton's album *Still In Love*. In the lyrics he mourns how black people were left suffering from worry, starvation and disillusionment after being robbed of their land, gold and cultural heritage. It was a powerful statement from an artist best-known for love songs, and yet who refused to be pigeon-holed or left feeling irrelevant.

In the New Year, Jamaican TV audiences were treated to a one-hour edition of *Where It's At*, featuring the Abyssinians, Leroy Smart, TIME and the Rockers dance group. Later that same evening there was an hour-long special showcasing Lloyd Parks' band We The People and guests Cynthia Richards and Barbara Jones. Harry J was recording albums with the Melodians and Cables, who had been recommended by Earl Morgan. His sister was in a relationship with Cables' lead singer Keble Drummond, who'd previously sung with Earl and Barry Llewelyn in the Sylastians. The Heptones themselves had by now transferred their allegiance to Lee Perry, who produced their latest album, *Party Time*. 'Mystery Babylon' and a reworking of 'Pure Sorrow' that Perry had also produced weren't included, but *Party Time* was another impressive outing from the group, despite several of the songs having been recorded before. Their renewed attempt at Dylan's 'I Shall Be Released' was superb and well-suited to an album that was ablaze with social commentary. For proof, listen to 'Sufferers' Time', 'Road Of Life', 'Serious Time' and 'Mr President', penned with Gerald Ford in mind, not Jimmy Carter, who'd only recently been inaugurated as US president when Island released the album.

The new album was well received, but the divisions in the group still hadn't fully healed. Leroy had spent time away from the others in Canada after tiring of Earl's poor technique. The harmonies had to be restructured in order to accommodate him and, ironically, the Heptones were said to have created a new style as a result, but Leroy found such restrictions frustrating and it was inevitable that he would eventually go solo.

The Mighty Diamonds had no such problems, and after giving a memorable performance at the Kingston nightclub Epiphany on 19 January, which was filmed, they headed for the US and an appearance at the Reggae Spectacular with Burning Spear in New York's Felt Forum. By the end of the month they'd finished recording an album in New Orleans at Allen Toussaint's Sea-Saint studios. It was the first time that the legendary producer had worked with a reggae act and he contributed three songs to the project, which found the Diamonds' music being rebranded as 'cajun rockers.'

'Atlantic had distributed *Right Time* in the US, Allen Toussaint heard it and asked to work with them,' explained Jumbo Vanrenen. 'Both Simon Draper and I were impressed by his interest, but the *Ice On Fire* album was a real turkey – if only they'd taken Sly and Lloyd Parks along! It was much unloved by all and nearly destroyed the Mighty Diamonds' career, but luckily Jamaica ignored it...'

Toussaint's leaden rhythm tracks dragged the Diamonds down, whilst his arrangements sounded clumsy. Not only that, his band's attempts to play reggae, as heard on 'Get Out Of My Life Woman' and 'Back Weh Mafia', were risible. And why re-record 'Country Living' when the first cut for Channel One had been so successful?

'The change was too drastic, too sudden and too much, so it never really worked,' Judge admitted to *Black Echoes'* Pete Johnson. 'At the time we never really wanted to do it, but they said we should experiment, so we did.'

They stayed at the Holiday Inn in New Orleans. Tour manager Copeland Forbes had hired a car for his personal use, as he was the only one in the Diamonds' entourage with a US driving license. Tabby took the keys one day, thinking he would go for a drive, and ended up crashing into two other cars, including a brand new Mustang, even before leaving the parking lot. Forbes had to take the rap, and Virgin presumably paid the bill. The label placed full-page ads for the *Ice On Fire* album in all the leading UK music publications, and also window and in-store displays in the high street stores. It still didn't sell though, and when they returned to Channel One for their next single, 'Stand Up To Your Judgement', there must have been sighs of relief all round.

Violence had again flared up in Rema whilst they were away. Two truckloads of gunmen posing as rent officers had gone there and begun to evict people from their homes, threatening to shoot them if they resisted. Over a thousand residents were made home-less, acid was thrown on personal belongings and an old woman's house set on fire after she was dragged into the street. Yet many residents maintained they weren't in arrears, whilst others had been protesting for months that they hadn't dared go to the Housing Office to pay their rent as it was situated in Concrete Jungle, where they would have faced grave hostility.

Bob Marley was following such events from afar, even as he worked on new songs like 'Guiltiness' and 'Heathen.' Donald Kinsey, the guitarist who'd played on 'Rastaman Vibration', had left the Wailers after the Hope Road shooting. His place was taken by Junior Marvin – a journeyman musician born in Kingston who'd lived in London from the age of 9, when he'd started auditioning for parts in TV commercials and stage productions. He performed in the West End musicals *King Kong* and *Hair*, starring Marsha Hunt. After a stint in White Rabbit, featuring Linda Lewis, he signed to ELP's Manticore label and fronted a three piece band called Hanson that played Hendrix-inspired rock music. After they spilt up, he became part of the Island family and guested on numerous sessions by the likes of Sandy Denny, Stevie Winwood, Toots and the Maytals (*Reggae Got Soul*), Rico Rodriguez and Delroy Washington. Chris Blackwell recommended him to Marley and he became a Wailer on Valentine's Day 1977. He played the guitar solos on 'Waiting In Vain' and 'Heathen' and his style of playing fit perfectly with Marley's vision of an international reggae music that could appeal across the board. Soon after he joined the Wailers, Junior introduced Bob to electronics genius Roger Mayer, who'd previously worked with Jimi Hendrix.

'When I first met Bob I asked him what he wanted me to do and he said they wanted to sound international. He said it with a smile, but I said okay, because that's what I'd been doing with

Stevie Wonder and the Isley Brothers when they changed from a mainly black sound into something more international. Had the Wailers' sound remained the same before Junior came aboard for *Exodus*, the band would have sounded too Jamaican, and therefore couldn't have been marketed internationally. The music can travel after that, but if you haven't got the quality in the recording and it doesn't sound perfect, then it's not going to happen, is it?'

Early in March, Bob and Family Man were stopped while driving in Notting Hill and a small amount of marijuana was found in the car. When Bob was asked where he was staying, he gave them Rita and Marcia Griffiths' address, knowing that they wouldn't have anything like the same amount of herb there. Some of his clothes were there too, because he would spend the night with Rita sometimes and couldn't resist Inez's home cooking, although the police didn't believe he was staying there at first. It was only when Marcia's little son Kemar woke up, came into the room and climbed into Bob's lap that they grudgingly conceded that maybe he was telling the truth, and left him in peace.

Lloyd Coxsone was still part of the Wailers' inner circle and had recently been working with singer Jimmy Lindsay, who'd also come to England at the age of 9. He was a Hendrix fan too, whose debut single had been a tribute record to the deceased rock star. Jimmy had spent five months in Ghana before meeting Lloyd, who played him a rhythm and booked some studio time so they could record a cover of the Commodores' hit 'Easy.' Jimmy got there first, and voiced the tune as Dennis Brown watched from the control booth.

'By the time Lloyd arrived we had my vocals recorded and I decided to do the backing vocals and invited Dennis to join me,' Jimmy wrote on his website. 'After two or three takes we had nailed it so we mixed the track. My version of 'Easy' was recorded and I went home with happy vibes. Some days later I received a call from Lloyd telling me that Chris Blackwell loved the track and wanted to release it. In February 1977, 'Easy' was released and it took off like a rocket. Island Records contacted me about setting up photo shoots and press interviews and I was receiving regular updates on sales. It was selling over five thousand copies a day and was number one in the reggae charts…'

Sadly, things didn't turn out as Jimmy hoped and all he got from 'Easy' was £700, despite its success on the *Black Echoes* charts, being voted Best Reggae Single and selling 73,000 copies on Lloyd Coxsone's Tribesman label. It was Chris Blackwell's idea to put Faybiene Miranda's 'Prophesy' on the flipside – a track that Coxsone says he got from Jack Ruby in exchange for studio equipment. She was born in Panama to an American father and Panamanian mother, but left for America with her family aged 4 and had moved around a fair bit before settling in California. As a teenager she was inspired by the Civil Rights movement and Native American issues, before relocating to Jamaica in March 1974, where she worked at the Playboy Club in Ocho Rios. She was primarily a writer and a poet at that time and co-authored a book with Mutabaruka before hitching a ride into Kingston one day with Jack Ruby, who was the personification of a socialist in her eyes, since he had a sound system, a football team and took care of so many people. Miranda showed him her book of poems and he encouraged her to think about singing some of them, especially 'Prophesy', which she'd written in tribute to Marcus Garvey.

It wasn't until late 1976 that he took her to Randy's with the Black Disciples band and she'd voiced the song in just two takes. On its release, 'Prophesy' was banned by both JBC and RJR according to Section 15 of the Emergency Act, which implies that it was considered politically dangerous. She followed 'Prophesy' with a song called 'Destiny' – again for Jack Ruby – on which she asked 'what is our destiny? Where is our place in the society? When did we lose our identity? Why did we lose it and why did we choose this?' By then she was managing and performing with the Keith Foote Group, a theatre troupe that was briefly popular on the hotel circuit. Miranda then left for Canada and later told *Reggae Vibes'* Peter I that the only money she ever received for 'Prophecy' came from Island, who paid her £150 after including it on a compilation. Lloyd Coxsone paid her nothing, although he'd repress it enough times. He released a dub LP (*Presenting The Coxsone Affair*) and several other singles on Tribesman in 1977, including Delroy Wilson's 'What Is Man' (another Jack Ruby production), Fred Locks and Creation Steppers' 'Life' and Jerry Baxter and Joy White's cover of the Bob & Marcia hit 'Always Together.' His alliance with Island ended as quickly as it started, for reasons that weren't stated but were apparent to anyone reading between the lines.

Blackwell's label had issued Leroy Smart's all-conquering 'Ballistic Affair' on 7-inch, and it was therefore surprising that they hadn't followed through by releasing the album. Conflict issued it instead, in a gatefold sleeve with an accompanying 12-inch. Leroy's cover of Ken Boothe's 'Without Love' had been a big hit in Jamaica by then, together with John Holt's 'Up Park Camp', the Wailing Souls' 'Things And Time', the Meditations' 'Woman Is Like A Shadow' and Jacob Miller's 'Forward Ever', taken from his *Jacob 'Killer' Miller* album. This was a roots set, produced by Tommy Cowan and aimed at a very different market than the one Inner Circle had courted on their *Ready For The World* LP for Capitol. Robert Margouleff, who programmed the synthesisers on Stevie Wonder's *Innervisions*, co-produced *Ready For The World* with Roger Lewis as they shed all semblance to a Jamaican band and channelled their inner Earth, Wind & Fire. The only real highlight came when Jacob Miller adapted Marley's 'Soul Rebel' for 'I'm A Rastaman', which closed the album. He and Inner Circle had recently filled the 4,000-capacity Student's Union Hall on a night promoted by Talent Corporation, who were now distributing the Abyssinians' album *Satta Massagana*, described as being 'a cut above anything else released this year' and 'deeply religious.' In addition to producing Ras Michael's latest release *New Name*, Tommy Cowan had also been promoting a series of shows at the Epiphany – most recently featuring artists signed to Virgin including the Mighty Diamonds, U-Roy and Johnny Clarke.

A bootlegger once proudly informed U-Roy that he'd pressed over a million copies of the deejay's *Rasta Ambassador* album in West Africa, which gives some indication of U-Roy's popularity at the time. Prince Tony Robinson was again the producer, although the tracks were recorded at Harry J's and not Joe Gibbs. It was the same old U-Roy, though – his rhymes kept simple yet cultural, and were interspersed with off-the-cuff adlibs and homilies that were comfortable as a pair of favourite slippers, even on tracks like 'Mr Slave Driver', 'Evil Doers' and 'No More War', and especially when revisiting past hits 'Wear You To The Ball' and 'Tide Is High.' His latest was a cover of Marley's 'Small Axe', but it was another album, *Dubbing To The King In A Higher Rank*, recorded at Channel One and released on King Attorney's label, that captured U-Roy at his most unfiltered, chatting over dub-wise cuts of rhythms made popular by the Mighty Diamonds, Leroy Smart and others. 'Truthful Dub' was a brutal piece of Alexander Henry's 'Please Be True', on which U-Roy announced that Attorney don't play any soul music, 'just strictly rockers.' Fragments of vocals add atmosphere along with splashes of cymbals and heavily echoed guitar and organ, but U-Roy's namechecks for various members of the sound crew soon became tiresome, especially since there were more exciting deejays doing the rounds.

Dillinger, for example. By the time 1977 drew to a close he had six albums out and nearly two dozen singles. Bunny Lee either produced or co-produced five of them, one of which – *Top Ranking Dillinger* – had a picture on the sleeve of him wearing the same red, green and gold striped suit that he wore at Dingwall's in London's Camden Lock. The lighting wasn't great that night, and it was only those of us near the front who realised that the colours had been painted on (and clearly without the aid of a ruler). That album had cuts of Marley's 'Waiting In Vain' and 'War' on it – sung by different artists – and also 'Cry Tough', a tribute to top ranking badmen like Zackie The High Priest, Woppy King, Busby and Rhygin. Revisionism ruled on 'King Pharoah Is A Baldhead' and he licked out against domestic violence on 'Don't Watch Your Wife', but it was his *Talkin' Blues* set, released on Magnum, that had the strongest rhythms, some of them made popular by Johnny Clarke and Leroy Smart. Robbie Shakespeare merged a little disco with the rockers when playing bass on 'Jah Love' and Bunny Lee said that Prince Jammy was at the mixing-board during that session, as he, Trinity and Jah Stitch all looked on.

Some of the same tracks appeared on *Super Star*, but *Answer Me Question* was either made up of scraps or Dillinger had rushed in the studio with Bunny, fearful that the hype surrounding him would soon melt. 'Natty Dread A The Ruler' and 'Leggo Violence' are reality songs, as is 'Liar Linda' after a fashion, but the girl singing the hook on 'Three Piece Suit And Thing' was so off-key that listening to her made your teeth hurt. The deejay's *Marijuana In My Brain* LP was the preferred option, not because of the title track (which he performed on Dutch television), but the versions to hits by the Abyssinians, Burning Spear and others. Dillinger was managed by Lawrence Evette at that time, whose idea it was to book Chalk Farm studios and have Dillinger and Trinity share an album. *Dillinger Versus Trinity* was decidedly threadbare, but then both deejays had struggled to cope with the cultural differences between Jamaica and the UK.

'When you're there in Jamaica, you can get vibes off a certain things,' Trinity explained, 'but when you're in London it's a different living. In England your mind had to really open wide to catch onto what's happening, and that means you can't find lyrics like you can in Jamaica. That's why you find that Jamaican deejays and the singers can click more when they're back home, where recording is concerned. The vibes is different and you can find ideas more easily because if go out on the road and hear a slang, you can put that in a recording. In England now you don't hear slang more than "innit" and them things there, and you can't put them on a record because everybody in England was saying it. It come like A, B, C to them already. When we make our own slang now, people in England were more supportive of that, and they want to hear new lyrics everyday, too.'

There was slang, and then word, sound and power – utterances that could cut like a knife and force people to look at themselves and tremble. Back in January, Orlando Wong gave a poetry reading at the Parish Library on Tom Redcam Drive, accompanied by an armed prison guard. Wong was a 25-year-old inmate of the Fort Augusta prison – he'd been jailed for armed robbery after holding up a post office, if you remember – but the authorities had given permission for him to do the reading on the grounds that he'd showed exceptional talent. The previous year he'd won a bronze medal and certificates of merit for poetry in the Literary competition of the 1976 Jamaica Festival. His poems had appeared in the *Daily News* and *Arts Review* and in November his radio play *Confrontation* was broadcast on JBC radio and then repeated by popular demand. Minister of justice Carl Rattray was at the Parish Library and said that Wong's poems were 'a true reflection of the society and of Jamaican life.' Also present were journalist Barbara Gloudon, university lecturer Mervyn Morris and Rasta drummer Mackie Burnett, who played at intervals throughout Wong's two-and-a-half hour performance. When he recited the line, 'fi di yout' a de ghetto there's a t'in line between freedom an' jail', all anyone needed to do when searching for confirmation was to look in his direction. *The New York Times* described 'Beat The Drums Rastaman', dedicated to Count Ossie, as 'one of the rawest bits of dub poetry yet recorded', whilst a *Gleaner* writer noted that Wong 'saw the ghetto experience itself as a kind of imprisonment, a concept which might suggest a new approach to the imprisonment theme found in so many poets.'

Wong himself denied that he was a poet. He said that all he did was 'to amplify the voice of the people', and hopefully influence them to do something to clear up 'the garbage heap in which we are living.' There had been a couple more readings since that first one in January, and justice minister Carl Rattray had attended all of them whilst noting that despite being held in captivity 'Wong holds up a mirror to what we are in Jamaica, and refuse to move it until we see what we are and try to improve.'

The minister was again present at a fundraiser for the Prison Rehabilitation Fund held at the UWI Students Union on 5 March that featured Wong and fellow poet George Fraser. 'At a time like this, we cannot afford to turn our backs on our brothers and sisters who, because of some unfortunate situation, find themselves cut off from society,' Rattray told the gathering. 'We need a fusion, a welding together of our people of our nation.'

Just four days earlier, twelve residents of Harbour View had appeared in court after being detained during a demonstration where they protested against the killing by police of 20-year-old Errol Edwards. The poet Michael Smith was among them. It wasn't just singers and deejays on the front line, although some of the older, classically trained musicians still favoured a more traditional approach. They wanted to raise the people's consciousness towards a shared African heritage, and Cedric ''Im' Brooks was still working tirelessly towards this. His United Africa big band performed at the Epiphany in March with special guest Leslie Butler. He also released an album called *One Essence*, recorded at Treasure Isle, but Brooks' powerful synthesis of soul, funk, jazz and reggae had barely time to sink in before Coxsone Dodd reached into his vaults and pressed up a collection of tracks that the saxophonist had recorded at Studio One several years previously. The Sound Dimension had been given free rein on the majestic 'Give Rasta Glory' and 'Glory To Sound', whilst the cuts to 'Satta Massagana', 'Skylarking' and 'College Rock' were a real treat, and not just for sax aficionados. It was good to know that there were still a few quality reggae instrumental (as opposed to dub) albums around, most notably by horn players like Tommy McCook and Bobby Ellis, guitarist Earl 'Chinna' Smith (*Sticky Fingers*) and the keyboard wizards Harold Butler (*Meditation Heights*) and Jackie Mittoo, whose *Hot Blood* and *Showcase Volume*

3 was produced by the ubiquitous Bunny Lee. By the end of '77 he had released albums by John Holt (including *World Of Love*, which mischievously got repackaged as *3000 Volts Of Holt*), Jah Stitch, Leroy Smart, Cornel Campbell, I-Roy, Derrick Morgan, Delroy Wilson (*Mr Cool Operator*), Ronnie Davis, Big Joe (*Keep Rocking And Swinging*), Johnny Clarke (who added at least four more Bunny Lee produced titles to his extraordinary tally), Hortense Ellis (*Jamaica's First Lady Of Songs*) and U Brown, whose first three LPs were for Striker. The latter's output was simply phenomenal, yet, apart from the albums he licensed to Virgin – and there weren't all that many of them – most of his releases were never stocked by high street stores outside of Jamaica and could only be purchased in specialist shops or by mail order. They weren't reviewed in mainstream publications all that often either, and national airplay in the UK for Bunny's vast catalogue of vocal, deejay, dub and instrumental reggae was virtually non-existent.

Joe Gibbs' productions fared much better and got more exposure. His oeuvre encompassed something of everything, whether Rastafari, popular love songs or topical dancehall ditties – all mixed perfectly for sound system and general airplay and featuring the island's leading talent. Dennis Brown was his flagship artist, and within days of its release in early March, a *Gleaner* reviewer hailed his new album *Visions Of Dennis Brown* as 'the best album ever produced by Joe Gibbs, and also the best effort ever by Dennis. I would like to stick my neck out and say this is the best cultural album of the year so far.'

Readers of *Black Echoes* and *Melody Maker* agreed as they voted it Reggae Album Of The Year, although *Visions* was only available on import for what seemed like an eternity until Lightning finally released it in the UK. Unusually, it only had one Dennis Brown composition, despite the title, but every song suited him. Although still only 21, Dennis had already mastered the art of presenting Rasta songs as high art, with well-written, coherent lyrics and clear diction on songs like 'Deliverance Will Come', 'Jah Can Do It' or the sufferers' lament 'Concrete Castle King.'

Clive Hunt, who played in Dennis' band the Falcons, had written 'Milk And Honey' with the singer in mind, but then went ahead and recorded it himself after Dennis didn't show up for the session. Clive was on the run from the army at the time, which is why his name hadn't appeared on the label. Dennis's version used the same backing track, and there was also a story behind 'Malcolm X', written by Winston McAnuff, who tried singing it for Gibbs but was told that he couldn't manage it. Winston had gone to the audition straight from school and must have been crushed, but went and fetched his friend Earl Sixteen, who sung it in his place. That version was accepted, but when the youngsters heard 'Malcolm X' playing on the radio, Dennis Brown was singing it and not Earl! It was at that point they took the song to Derrick Harriott, who produced Earl's second cut and also Winston's debut single, 'Ugly Days.'

Dennis also covered Eric 'Monty' Morris's 'Say What You Say' and Carlton and the Shoes' 'Love Me Always' on *Visions*, whilst 'Repatriation' and its explosive companion, 'Jubilation Dub', would terrorise reggae dances in the months that followed. Sir Coxsone still had their residency in London's Carnaby Street and hearing it there as the bass, dramatic sound effects and disembodied vocals ricocheted off the walls was an experience never to be forgotten. The dub version was taken from *African Dub All-Mighty Chapter 3*, which took Gibbs' *African Dub* series to a whole other level and secured Errol Thompson's place alongside King Tubby and Lee 'Scratch' Perry in the ranks of Jamaica's greatest dub mixers. Dennis Brown's other big tune in the spring of 1977 was 'Here I Come', which Castro Brown issued on Morpheus, but had been written and produced by Niney, who also sang harmonies on it.

'I tell Dennis that 'Here I Come' will last him until he's an old man walking with a stick but it's the Father's works, not Dennis or mine,' Niney said. 'It's a blessing, because listen to the words...

"My head is anointed, and my cup runneth over. Surely goodness and mercy shall follow I, all the days of my life." That song is a prayer, man, and Dennis never stopped singing it from there...'

The Cimarons had laid the rhythm at Chalk Farm but there was no mistaking the fact that it had been voiced and mixed at Black Ark, under Lee Perry's supervision. There was still animosity between Perry and Joe Gibbs, but Gibbs was smart enough to realise that Dennis Brown was a free spirit and a more possessive approach wouldn't have worked. He also had plenty of other artists in his camp to look after, like Marcia Aitken, who was invited to join Gibbs' stable after Lloyd Parks had seen her sing at a concert featuring pupils of Excelsior High School. At the tail end of 1976 she'd recorded 'Narrow Minded Man' – an answer version to the Meditations' 'Woman Is Like A Shadow' – and followed it with 'When I Need Love' and a cut of Alton Ellis' 'I'm Still In Love With You' sung from a female perspective, which got everyone excited. Ruddy Thomas, who shared engineering duties with Errol T, was also a fine singer and 'Let's Make A Baby' did well, but it was Culture, led by Joseph Hill, who were Gibbs' biggest stars after Dennis Brown. They got a tremendous reception after headlining A Night Of Rockers at the Epiphany, where they performed their two current hits, 'Jah Jah See Them A Come' and 'Two Sevens Clash.' The latter became the title track of their debut album for Joe Gibbs, who also wrote the liner notes.

'Culture – a name that stirs the imagination. Culture – a name that defies the insidious pranks of the Creator of the rat race and cold, ruthless jabs of the powers that be, and has emerged undoubtedly victorious. Their message? The unforgotten suffering of their ancestors as they toiled in blood, sweat and tears only to perish. Their jubilation? The realisation that for this inhuman act, someday Babylon will pay.'

The front cover showed the three members in silhouette by the sea, one standing apart from the others in profile with his arms folded, beard jutting from his chin and dreads sticking up and out from his head, looking like an elf or magical being. The album itself contained ten tracks of unadulterated, righteous joy, set to irresistible reggae beats. *Two Sevens Clash* generated so much excitement on its arrival that import copies were soon exchanging hands for silly money. *Rolling Stone* later described it as 'one of the coolest records ever made', although Joseph's lyrics were soaked in Rastafari and Garveyism and spoke of black people's struggles, with no concessions to commercialism, unless you count catchy, uplifting melodies and an abundance of feel-good bonhomie.

It was Marcus Garvey who prophesised that divine revelation would come 'when the two sevens clashed', and the title track duly became an anthem, but since virtually every song was delivered with such uninhibited relish, it wasn't easy to choose between them. 'Black Starliner Must Come', 'Calling Rasta For I', 'I'm Alone In The Wilderness', 'I'm Not Ashamed', 'Get Ready To Ride The Lion To Zion', 'See Them A Come' and 'Natty Dread Taking Over'... the titles were self-evident, whilst the rhythms – played by Joe Gibbs' Professionals – were quintessential 'rockers' and sounded remarkably fresh and inventive.

Joseph himself toasted on 'Informer', a cut to 'See Them A Come', although George Nooks – under the name Prince Mohammed – would soon take over that role as Culture's deejay of choice. He'd started out singing in his local choir before entering talent shows at the Bohemia and Tropic, which is where he met Joe Gibbs. He was already proficient as a deejay, and heavily influenced by Dennis Brown when singing. His first recording for Gibbs was a cut to Culture's 'Zion Gate' called 'Forty Leg Dread.' The lyrics were inspired by talk of a Rastaman who'd been found dead and when police moved the body, a lot of bugs – probably millipedes – had come out from under his dreadlocks. George knew that some people would take any opportunity to denigrate Rastas and so he refuted the rumour in that song. What he didn't know until the record actually came out and he saw the label was that Joe Gibbs had changed his name to Prince Mohammed! He was credited as George

Nooks for his cover of John Holt's 'Tribal War' though, which was a sizeable hit around the same time.

The last time we'd heard about Trinity, he was voicing for Channel One, although that alliance proved relatively short-lived. His popularity then exploded in the wake of 'Three Piece Suit' – a song that revelled in the latest fashion to hit Jamaica, and which he voiced over Marcia Aitken's cut of Alton Ellis' 'I'm Still In Love With You.' Joe Gibbs quickly released an album named after that breakthrough hit and Trinity was unstoppable on bright, up-tempo numbers like 'Queen Majesty' and 'John Saw Them Coming' (a cut to the Heptones' 'Hypocrites'), whilst the cartoonish backing vocals on 'Mohammed Ali' were straight out of *Looney Tunes*. Trinity was a deejay with lyrics for everyone and every occasion, although his humorous, semi-ribald tale of paying a visit to his 'big fat thing' in Constant Spring, dressed in his three-piece suit, would remain the defining hit of his career. Some people swore that Trinity's younger brother Robert, aka Clint Eastwood, wrote those lyrics, in which case it was a truly generous act of brotherly love, although after listening to 'Badder Than You', which Eastwood voiced for Gibbs on the same rhythm, I somehow doubt it. It was Trinity's time, however – an impression confirmed by his *Shanty Town Determination* album, produced by Prince Tony Robinson and arranged by Yabby You.

Trinity eased up on the humour when he voiced for Yabby, as you might expect. He was outstanding on tracks like 'Rasta Determination', 'Fire Down A Town', 'Tribal War' and 'Samson The Strongest Man', which was another version to 'Conquering Lion.'

'The fairest producer me work for never give me no money at all, but me see mileage from it,' Trinity said when reminded of this album. 'Because them other guys, they will give you a little money as an advance or for food, but Yabby You gave me riddims and after me work with him, I could inherit something more, 'cause me know we will be sharing it fifty-fifty, y'see me? Those next producers want it all but me appreciate t'ings, and even the ones who a rob me teach me more about who I am now. Me go inna them t'iefing school but me wise up now and they can't touch nothing again, y'know what I mean? Because once I was blind, but now I can see...'

Visitors to Joe Gibbs' studio on Retirement Road – which he advertised as 'The Golden Sound of the West Indies' – would have encountered Prince Far I – a large, formidable looking individual who combined chanting over rhythms with his duties as one of Gibbs' security men. Far I was friends with JLP enforcer Claudie Massop, but generally avoided politics, despite his album *Heavy Manners* being named after a slogan inspired by last year's State of Emergency. Lyrically, he was more concerned about keeping the peace, self-discipline and Rastafari. His 'Big Fight' wasn't another 'Frazier Versus Foreman', but described a bout between Babylon and Dreadlocks – a champion 'with a lot of love in his heart' – whilst 'Deck Of Cards' was a cut to 'Satta Massagana' and 'Young Generation' a matching version to 'Ghetto Girl.' He had his own Cry Tuff label by this time and issued a heap of singles in 1977, including 'Message From The King', 'Jah Never Fail I' and 'Blackman Land', voiced over a majestic slice of the 'Drum Song' rhythm.

Jacob Miller was a regular visitor to Joe Gibbs' studio, despite being Inner Circle's lead singer. In between issuing two albums by Ras Michael and the Sons of Negus – one of which, *Kibir Am Lak Glory To God*, included the single 'New Name' – Tommy Cowan also found time to promote two shows called Reggae Ting, one at the Turtle Beach Theatre in Ocho Rios, and the other at Fort Clarence on Easter Monday, where Inner Circle, the Mighty Diamonds, Dillinger, Leroy Smart and Lloyd Parks performed for a crowd of six thousand or more.

'The star was Inner Circle's lead vocalist, Jacob "Killer" Miller,' reported the *Gleaner*. 'He, believe it or not, was demanded on stage twice for encores by the huge audience, and when he ran out of energy on the third call and could not make it back on stage, the crowd appeared to be getting out of order. However, Tommy Cowan and his crew soothed things a bit by allowing Ras Michael to do a stint, but the crowd could not get enough of Miller. They roared appreciation with every tune he did, and when he left the stage the first time a tremendous roar, demanding his immediate return, sent the promoters scuttling to his dressing room to find him. Jacob came back on stage and did several more tunes, including his latest single 'Forward Ever.' The crowd roared for more, but the very energetic Jacob called it a day. This show, as well as that held at the Turtle Beach on Saturday night featuring the same array of artists, has tremendously enhanced the reputation of Talent as the leading promotion agency currently operating in the island, and Jacob Miller as the number one reggae attraction onstage.'

Earlier that morning, the Carib Theatre in Kingston had been full to overflowing for the Channel One Review, featuring Earth & Stone, Jah Thomas, Wailing Souls, John Holt, Joy White, Gregory Isaacs, I-Roy and Dillinger, backed by the Revolutionaries. The star of the show was Leroy Smart, who'd almost come to blows with promoter Clancy Eccles after the singer had marched onstage – uninvited – at the previous year's Jamaica Arts Award show, again promoted by Eccles, asking "what happened to Leroy Smart?" just as the awards were being handed out. Clancy was understandably upset, but as a result people realised that Leroy was an artist who wouldn't hesitate to speak up if he was feeling hard-done-by. His recent *Super Star* set, produced by Bunny Lee, had been recorded before *Ballistic Affair*, and was therefore his debut. But Smart clearly lived up to his name and had learnt from the experience, because his next two albums – *Dread Hot In Africa* and *Impressions Of Leroy Smart* – were self-produced. This was something that rivals such as Johnny Clarke and Cornel Campbell hadn't managed yet, because both had new albums out produced by Bunny. Cornel's was called *Turn Back The Hands Of Time*, although the hits 'Investigator' and 'The Stal-A-Watt' weren't on it and he'd recorded another single, 'No Man's Land' during a visit to Joe Gibbs. Johnny Clarke wasn't going anywhere though, and would end the year with a quartet of albums for his brother-in-law – none of which involved Virgin, who had most likely dropped him. All included roots and lovers rock songs, but this 'throw everything at the wall and let's see what sticks' approach had probably run its course, and it would be wrong to assume that fans of 'Blood Dunza', 'Dread Natty Congo' or 'Love Up Your Brothers And Sisters' would equally appreciate covers of old rocksteady tunes. No one's saying that the albums *Sweet Conversation, Don't Stay Out Late* and *Girl I Love You* didn't have merit, but *Super Star Roots Disco Dub* won out because, as with other releases in Lee's *Super Star* series, every vocal was accompanied by a matching dub. This was catnip for the growing army of reggae DJs and sound systems making its presence felt in clubs and blues parties throughout Europe and America. Striker released a further showcase album by I-Roy (*Can't Conquer Rasta*), but the producer's stable of artists had started to look a little threadbare by previous standards as John Holt and Dillinger had left for pastures new, Delroy Wilson was attracting attention elsewhere with albums produced by Bob Andy (*Last Thing On My Mind*), Lloyd Charmers (*Sarge*) and Tapper Zukie's brother Blackbeard (*Unedited*), Horace Andy was in America, Linval Thompson was producing himself as well as other artists and U-Roy was on a roll with Prince Tony Robinson. Bunny did have Barry Brown, though – a youth who'd been running errands for him in Greenwich Farm, but had recently scored a debut hit with 'Mr Money Man', on which he implored the wealthy to give the little man a helping hand.

It wasn't just the rocketing popularity of sound systems that changed reggae music. The impact of Island and Virgin's investments in the genre was a major factor, too – not only in boosting record sales and exposure overseas, but also in altering perceptions of what the music represents, and introducing different criteria by which artists and records were judged. Just five years previously, it would have been inconceivable for any Jamaican artist wearing a suit and covering soul tunes to be derided for being a sell-out, and likewise any group decked out in matching outfits and performing synchronised dance steps as part of their stage act. That style of presentation now smacked of Uncle Tom, and audiences in 1977 wanted to feel that they were hearing and witnessing *lived* experiences, and nothing contrived. They wanted to share the artists' search for identity and their struggles against poverty and adversity – not as cultural tourists or voyeurs, necessarily, but because many reggae fans were able to relate to what was being said in certain songs, irrespective of any cultural differences. Babylon didn't discriminate on the grounds of race alone but also according to power, class, money and education – gender too, because women still faced an uphill battle for equality, and not least in the home and workplace. I remember speaking to Jamaicans who had no idea that white people could be destitute and homeless in wealthy countries like Britain and America, and yet the saying 'who feels it, knows it' just as surely applied to them as well as their fellow sufferers in the Caribbean. It was the extent of the deprivation and the amount of welfare available to such people that varied, but there was still a lot of want, despair, anger and resent-ment among disenfranchised whites and people of other nationalities, who felt neglected and abandoned by the society they supposedly represented. These were some of the driving forces behind the emergence of punk, which was a youth movement rooted in feelings of alienation, deprivation, anger and despair, and pointed the finger of blame at a rapacious, capitalist system that cared for nothing and no one in its quest for profit. We were all just collat-eral damage in the race for dominion and aside from punk, there was no other genre that expressed all of this as forcibly, and with so much righteous bravado, as reggae music. It was in reggae – and Rasta music in particular – where we discovered the poets and seers who steered us in the direction of a world founded on love and hope, rather than greed and fear. 1977 was the year when all of that came to the fore and the three original Wailers – Bob Marley, Bunny Wailer and Peter Tosh – were in the vanguard of a musical uprising that had its roots in Jamaica, but was rapidly spreading around the globe.

Peter Tosh had taken his road band Word, Sound & Power into the studio soon after completing his US tour. They'd wanted to give him a defining sound of his own, separate from that of Bob Marley and the Wailers and to a large extent they succeeded. Led by Sly and Robbie, they recorded new versions of 'Downpressor Man', '400 Years', 'Stepping Razor' and 'Get Up Stand Up' at Randy's, and the latter – which now belonged to him, just as surely as Bob Marley – became the opening track on his second album *Equal Rights*, released in April. The title track was an object lesson in how to deliver a profound message in as simplistic a form as possible since Tosh is saying that he's not asking for peace, but equal rights and justice. The inference behind such words was that if fairness and equality were granted to all, then peace would result of its own accord. He didn't mention South Africa in the lyrics of 'Apartheid', although since only whites could vote there and the UN had issued resolutions referring to how the regime had resorted to 'massive violence against and wanton killings of the African people, including schoolchildren and students and others opposing racial discrimination', there was little doubt as to which country he had in mind. 'African', too, was significant, a unifying message that allowed no room for doubt or misinterpretation since regardless of what nationality they were, all black people were automatically Africans to his way of thinking.

Just days after the release of *Equal Rights*, Clive Chin left Jamaica for New York to join his father, who was preparing to set up a branch of Randy's in Queens. Peter Tosh was on the same plane and so the two of them sat together. Half an hour into the flight Peter took out his pipe, packed it with ganja and lit it. Much to the cabin crew's dismay, Peter refused to stop, the smoke went everywhere and when they landed at JFK, the police arrested both of them.

'I'd never had such a drama in my life,' says Clive, who spent the night in jail for simply having sat next to his friend. 'Oh man, they made sure we were put away!'

It was Clive's first trip to America, and when the pair appeared in court, Peter told the judge that he was the minister for ganja and that he'd come to legalise marijuana. He was freed eventually, but Tosh would continue to court controversy on a regular basis. On 27 May – African Liberation Day – he turned up at Howard University in Washington DC and was asked during an interview about the liberation struggles taking place in South Africa and Rhodesia. Ras Karbi didn't properly hear the question, but he sure heard the answer. 'I'm going to arm the South African freedom-fighters,' Tosh had replied. It was bluster, of course, but the intent was real enough.

Bunny Wailer also released a second solo album in 1977. His was called *Protest*, but the fireworks promised by the title failed to materialise, despite the profusion of newspaper clippings about Idi Amin on the sleeve and the inclusion of Bunny's own version of 'Get Up Stand Up', which fell short compared to Peter's version and the Wailers' original. Another cover, that of the Slickers' 'Johnny Too Bad', fared better, but songs like 'Moses Children', 'Scheme Of Things' and 'Who Feels It' lacked lustre, even if they did articulate similar themes to those on *Blackheart Man*. The magical aura that had distinguished his debut – and also a companion set, *Dub Disco Vol. 1* – was missing, whilst the singles 'Love Fire' and 'Bright Soul' were presumably recorded too late for inclusion.

Bob Marley and the Wailers had begun their comeback tour in Paris, where Bob hurt his foot playing football. In the wake of this setback – which Marley had more or less dismissed – they did shows in Belgium, the Netherlands, Germany and Scandinavia before playing four nights at London's Rainbow Theatre in early

June, when Island released their new album *Exodus*. Those dates in May and early June were guitarist Junior Marvin's first with the band, and his onstage antics drew a mixed reaction.

'My first show with Bob Marley was in Paris, where Bianca Jagger and a whole heap of celebrities came,' he reflected. 'My second show was at the Rainbow Theatre in London, and I'd grown up in the area, so all my school friends, my family and my teachers came, and they couldn't believe that this kid they'd known since I was little was up there playing with Bob Marley. Everybody thought it was my show, because there were all these people calling out my name, and my cousins were all laughing at me from the front of the stage. Growing up in the theatres and all that I was used to dancing on stage, and so when I play, I dance. The thing was, no one else in the Wailers would dance with Bob, because the rest of them would just stand still like Family Man. Tyrone might do a little bop now and then, but I was up and down the stage and I remember the first reviews tried to put me to shame. They said I was a disgrace by playing rock style guitar, and then, on top of that, I was dancing and doing all these Jimi Hendrix licks. They slagged me off big-time, plus Bob had people around him saying I was trying to upstage him. But after the show he came up to me and said, "I love what you're doing, because it gives me chance to take a break".'

The Rainbow shows had sold out weeks beforehand, and the single of the title track and the album itself both charted. Bob Marley was finally crossing over – and with a rousing repatriation song, no less. But the man who wrote *Exodus* had nearly lost his life in a hail of bullets just six months earlier, and this was only too apparent in places, as the lyrics traced a journey from reflection ('Natural Mystic' and 'So Much Things To Say') to resistance ('The Heathen') and then exultation ('Jamming'), before dissolving into expressions of love both personal ('Turn Your Lights Down Low' and 'Waiting In Vain') and universal ('One Love / People Get Ready'). The release of *Exodus* was the moment when roots reggae music truly came of age and provided the genre with an album worthy of comparison with anything by the Beatles, Bob Dylan or any other internationally famous rock act. It had great songs, written and sung by an artist with real charisma, whilst the musical backing, arrangements and production were exemplary. Yet *Exodus* still managed to retain enough authenticity to keep grassroots' reggae fans onboard.

'"Turn Your Lights Down Low" is a lovely song and it portrays a side of Bob I liked because very few people saw him like that,' said Cindy Breakspeare. 'Everybody saw him as being really angry, so it's nice when you can see another side of someone. There's such a range of different material in his catalogue, but a lot of it wasn't exposed back then.'

Cindy – the reigning Miss World, remember – was in a loving relationship with Marley throughout those recording sessions, and the songs that he wrote at the time reflected this. Meanwhile, back in Jamaica, Greek filmmaker Theo Bafaloukos had begun shooting a feature film financed by producer Patrick Hulsey and starring reggae drummer Leroy 'Horsemouth' Wallace, who he'd met when Burning Spear had played New York's Central Park. His inspiration for the film had started with seeing *The Harder They Come*. Theo's appreciation of the music and culture of Jamaica had deepened after he'd witnessed Augustus Pablo and Bob Marley in concert, and he began avidly listening to all the new music coming from Jamaica. That's why he decided to call his film *Rockers*. But filming on the island during a time of such turmoil would test his resolve in ways that he'd never imagined.

'It was quite obvious from the get-go that something quite extraordinary was taking place in Jamaica at that time,' he told me. 'It was a very scary enterprise, because it really wasn't a good time to be in Jamaica. The first time I went there I realised how volatile it was, but that just made it all the more fascinating, and the movie made itself, in a way. It was purely motivated by the music and the culture of Jamaica, and I had the privilege to see all that with my own eyes.'

344

The actors were all local people with no formal training, yet they brought such character to their roles.

'It's a shame more movies aren't made that way,' Bafaloukos said. 'We made up things, and that was the backbone of the movie. The characters were playing themselves and the same guys who acted in it play on the songs that we use in the film as well. We did a lot of filming in Maxfield Avenue where Horsemouth lived, and that was a tough neighbourhood because even the cops didn't go there! A lot of crazy things happened and I had to explain myself a million times, but it really couldn't have worked any other way, and it was nothing scary in truth. There was a lot of yelling and screaming and fighting, but nothing physical... It never got to that, and I never tried to involve the police or the government either, because that would have been a mistake I'm sure so anything that went down, we managed to resolve it amongst ourselves.'

Bafaloukos hadn't originally intended Horsemouth to be the film's central character. '*Rockers* started life as a documentary,' the film-maker explained, 'but halfway through writing the script I decided on having him as the star. After that concert by Burning Spear we hung out a little bit, and then in January or February he came back to New York and we spent more time together. What I wanted was a vehicle that could take you through this simple linear story, and after a while I realised that he could actually pull it off. And he did! Horsemouth was fantastic. He's an unbelievably bright guy. He learnt very fast and has amazingly good hearing. He expresses himself very well, and most of the time he says interesting things. He has this way about him that's very real and yet he also accommodates others. For instance, he'd never acted before, and yet he knew how to project himself. He was leading when he had to, and he was holding back when he had to. He was aware of the scene in general, and wasn't just interested in projecting himself. That helped a lot, but you have to remember that Horsemouth had nothing to lose. You're talking about a kid that came out of nowhere, who was kicked out of Alpha School and had an incredibly hard

345

life. Music for him is a religion. He said that when he was a kid, he'd sometimes listen to music and pretend that it was food and try to fill his belly with sound. He wasn't bullshitting, either. That was for real.'

Max Romeo and Dillinger both appeared on NBC television in the US during late June. Max was in New York working on the musical *Reggae*, which was scheduled to open on Broadway in November. It was about a young Jamaican woman who'd been a rock star in America, who returned to Jamaica to explore her Rastafarian roots. Melvin Van Peebles co-wrote the script, the director was Leon Gluckman and the credits for music and lyrics were shared between Max, Randy Bishop and Ras Karbi.

'I wrote the lyrical content for it,' said Max. 'I actually wrote the songs and worked alongside the choreographer to make sure he get the Jamaican feel, y'know? This guy from *Miami Vice* called Michael Thomas was involved, but *Reggae* only ran for seven weeks because the critics claimed that the moral content was too politically motivated, and the message too strong, so it received some bad press and that helped to close it down.'

Like Joe Higgs, Max suspected that Island Records were too focused on making Bob Marley a success to help the other artists on their roster get anywhere, and Carl Dawkins, whose album *Bumpity Road* had been recorded at the same time as *War Ina Babylon*, agreed with him. Artists like them didn't appreciate being in a position where they were reliant upon a record company's largesse, and so began looking at alternatives. *Reconstruction*, which Island released on their Mango subsidiary, was Max Romeo's own production and it started with a wake-up call, and him urging black people to reverse the destruction of their heritage, and embark on a reconstruction programme. That same message was echoed in the upbeat 'Take A Hold', and also on unity songs like 'Let's Live Together' and 'Where Is The Love', whilst 'Martin Luther King' served a similar purpose as Burning Spear's 'Marcus Garvey', high-lighting a fallen warrior whose teachings were still relevant. There was a lot of idealism on the album, though Max was also mindful of the obstacles faced by those seeking a better life and talked about them in 'Poor Man's Life', addressing the worsening inequality seen in countries the world over. 'Melt Away' was the track heard most often in reggae dances, where audiences cheered its description of Jah battering the wicked to pieces and seeing them melt away, screaming, just like ice cream.

More reggae stars were now living in London, Toronto and the US than ever before. Many had fled Jamaica's poverty and violence, only to discover that the music sounded different to that recorded at home. This wasn't necessarily a bad thing, but each studio had its own individual sound and a lot rested on whoever mixed the record, which is why Horace Andy took the master tapes of his album *In The Light* back to Jamaica and got Prince Jammy to mix it at King Tubby's. That project was funded by Everton Da Silva, a New York gangster with a fearsome reputation who liked the idea of being a record producer but was dependent on artists like Horace Andy and Augustus Pablo taking care of the actual work involved.

Horace had moved to Hartford, Connecticut in early 1977, and life there would prove anything but idyllic. He was shot in the arm in a skirmish and then had to prevent his two children from being kidnapped as his first marriage floundered. He still wrote songs, though, and whilst Everton Da Silva was a dangerous and volatile choice of partner, his involvement meant that Horace could continue with his career. The basic rhythms for *In The Light* had been recorded in Kingston, but then overdubs were added at A&R Studios in New York. Lead guitarist Andy Bassford, who lived in Hartford, remembered that session well.

'I was 22 and just played in bars, really. I'd got into this little reggae band in Hartford that played at the local West Indian club on the weekends. They didn't pay us much and there were a lot of us, but one day Horace came to our rehearsal and I'd never seen anyone with such an entourage before. I saw that and thought, "he must be famous", but he came and sat quietly in the corner watching us and the other band members were all very anxious about it. At the break he came up to me and said, "I like how you play. Are you from Jamaica?" I said, "no, I've never been south of Philadelphia", and he said, "well, I'm making a record and I was going to use the band, but you're the only one that I want, so what are you doing Wednesday?" I told him I was going to be home so he said, "we'll come and pick you up at one o'clock and take you to the studio." He seemed like a nice guy, so Wednesday came and I was sitting in my apartment and no one came. I thought that he'd been bullshitting me, but around three-thirty this van pulls up, the bell rings and I go downstairs with my guitar and wah wah pedal, they open the van door and a big cloud of smoke poured out. Horace and Wayne Jarrett were sat in the van with three or four other people. They said that the studio where we were going was in New York and so I figured they meant Brooklyn or the Bronx. My idea of New York geography was extremely vague at the time, but we passed through the Bronx and into Manhattan, so I was thinking, "oh, it must be in Harlem. That makes sense." Except we carried on all the way to Eighth Avenue and 55th, where A&R studios were. I met the rest of the band, and in retrospect they could have been a lot more unfriendly towards me than they actually were. I got the feeling that they had no idea I was coming, and it must have seemed very unusual to them, because there weren't too many white people playing reggae at that time.

'Roland Alphonso's son Noel was there, there was a guy named Myrie playing bass and the keyboard-player was Touter, who'd played on Bob Marley's 'No Woman No Cry.' It was very intimidating knowing that, but I'll never forget that session, because 'Do You Love My Music' was the first song I ever recorded in my life! I'd never been in a studio before, and if you listen to my solo you can hear this incredibly loud note at the beginning of it. I didn't realise that you don't have to turn up the volume for a guitar solo when you're in a studio, because the engineer does that. It was my first time playing on a record and I didn't know anyone there but

Horace. I was completely terrified, because if you were a musician living in Hartford, no one ever went in a studio and made records. Also, the guy who set up the session was Major Little, who worked on a lot of James Brown's records for Polydor, and then Dennis Thompson turned up at one point and started mixing. Luckily I had no idea who he was, but he was Marley's soundman and so I would have completely wet my pants if I'd known!

'When we'd finished I said to Horace, "how do I get paid?" and he said, "well, that's up to Everton, but you get paid when the record comes out." I wasn't used to patois and so I didn't understand everything that was being said, but when the record came out I bought a copy then called Horace and said, "the record's out, so I'm thinking that I should get paid." He agreed and so he and I ended up driving my mother's car to Corona, Queens, which was a very dubious area of the city at that time. We go in this building and all these kids in the lobby start saying, "you're going to buy weed, aren't you?" I was so naïve. It turns out that it's a weed camp, because there were these huge locks on the door and whoever was inside didn't want to open it, but finally they recognised Horace and let us in. There was nothing in the room but an unfriendly looking girl, a Doberman and a guy with a sub-machine gun with the safety catch off. On the back of the door there was this enormous sack full of nickel bags, and then on the floor there were four or five shopping bags stuffed with bills – fives, tens and twenties. I'd never seen so much weed or money in my life, and at the same time I had a guy pointing his gun at me and a dog growling, then this other guy asks Horace what he wants. He points to me and says, "this man here is a musician who needs to get paid." The two of them had a heated argument in patois – both the girl and the dog were snarling at me, and finally the other guy, which is Everton, kisses his teeth and asks me, "okay, how many songs did you play on?" I said, "seven and it's $30 a song", so he slaps down $210, which was more money than I'd ever held in my life. He says, "here, take this and don't ask me for any more." Then Horace said to me, "I think we should go now", and that was it. When we got out of there my mum's car was still parked where we'd left it, which was a relief, but I was very grateful to Horace because there aren't many singers who would have stepped in to help me like he did.'

Horace also sang for Lloyd Barnes' Wackies label, based at premises on the White Plains Road in New York's North Bronx. Although inspired by the likes of Studio One and Lee Perry, Barnes, who was Jamaican, wasn't trying to copy the music from back home but forge his own distinctive sound through imaginative use of echo, reverb and equalisation. The results were as immediate and individual as reggae music recorded elsewhere, but few radio DJs or sound systems outside of New York supported them in the early days.

'I guess we were a little ahead of our time, because I couldn't give our records away!' Barnes recalled. 'The encouragement wasn't there, and it's only now that I'm beginning to understand how ahead we were. For instance, Ras Menelik and I would sometimes overdub live drums straight onto tape, because there was no room for them otherwise. They were some original vibes happening, and no two mixes were the same because of us doing it that way. There was actual art going on, and that's what people still respond to, I guess. It's like there was a master behind it, driving that inspiration, and with the energy coming from the love of all the people gathered around, so we'd just mess around. Then, when the good Father said "go that way", we'd apply it. We got some real nice things that way.'

In 1977, Barnes released two albums by the Bullwackies All-Stars – *Creation Dub* and *African Roots Act 1* – Augustus Pablo's *Pablo Nuh Jester* and two volumes of their *Reggae Goodies* series. New York was already well on its way to becoming a major stronghold of reggae music outside of Jamaica, as were certain cities across the border in Canada.

'Toronto may seem an unlikely place to hear reggae,' wrote

producer David Clayton Thomas in the liner notes of an album by local band Ishan People. 'For decades, southern Ontario has been a second home to thousands of migrant West Indian workers who brought their families, their culture and their music with them. The beer halls that once stomped out rockabilly every Saturday night began to sway to the infectious, lopsided rhythm of rocksteady and reggae, the blues turned inside out.'

Ishan People's line-up featured 'Bumpy, a Trench Town survivor and street singer who can dance all day and all night.' Bumpy was another name for Johnny Osbourne, who'd hit with songs like 'Warrior' and 'Come Back Darling' before leaving Jamaica in 1970. Resilient as ever, he'd continued his musical career the best that he could in Canada.

'To survive musically, I had to sing with a band and just do whatever they were doing,' he said. 'I'd be singing on the nightclub circuit and covering soul and chart material just to make a living for myself. I did that for a while and then once I'd joined Ishan People, we played on the university circuit as well. That's when David Clayton Thomas got to hear us and decided to produce that album. He was the singer for Blood, Sweat And Tears, and Ishan People used to open for them sometimes. David loved reggae, and we would go to his house and hang out with him. We were like family, but I still missed Jamaica.'

The two (or rather four) sevens clashed on 7 July, and there was a full day's programme of events held in Morant Bay, beginning with a revival service in Stony Gut, birthplace of Jamaican national hero Paul Bogle. After lectures and discussions on topics such as the Morant Bay rebellion, there was a march from there to Morant Bay Square, retracing the steps taken in October 1865 by Bogle and the hundred others who'd joined him in protesting against injustice and widespread poverty. Vigilantes fired upon the marchers, who then burned down the courthouse and nearby buildings. Twenty-five people died, which led to Bogle being charged with inciting a riot and the governor declaring martial law. Troops were ordered to hunt down the rebels, and three hundred people were arrested, including Bogle and House Of Assembly representative George William Gordon. He and Bogle were executed, and it was estimated that four hundred other people also lost their lives during the rebellion. At 7 p.m. precisely, Michael Manley addressed the gathering and promised that 'Jamaica will be a republic by 1981.'

Many Rastas and church folks alike had prophesised cosmic upheavals on that day. In the end they had to settle for record levels of absenteeism throughout the island and Linstead Town Hall being struck by lightning, before Culture's Joseph Hill's very eyes.

'Things were happening, man!' he exclaimed. 'The spirit of victory was all around that day and I felt victorious, I tell you!'

A week later, the JLP called for the government to conduct a public investigation into the rising levels of violent crime, including recent attacks on two police stations. A senior ranking Army officer then resigned in mysterious circumstances, and it was revealed that four gunmen who'd attacked the Runaway Bay police station were ex-soldiers. Incidents like this heightened people's fears – and also suspicions – that secretive forces were at work, and that the glue holding Jamaican society together was quickly becoming unstuck.

Lee 'Scratch' Perry was now more driven than ever. One day he'd be making Rasta music with the Meditations or Junior Delgado ('Sons Of Slaves' was especially potent) and the next he'd be in the studio with a balladeer like George Faith, whose versions of soul and pop tunes – most notably 'To Be A Lover' and 'I've Got The Groove' – coincided with the rise of lovers rock in Britain. Island Records were getting ready to release Faith's album *To Be A Lover*, together with Junior Murvin's *Police And Thieves*, named after his big hit from the previous year. The combination of Murvin's high-pitched vocals, his socially minded songs and that churning Black Ark sound proved irresistible, and whilst 'Roots Train' and 'Tedious' were chosen as singles, any of the other tracks would have worked just as well. There were rumours going round that

Junior had signed a three album deal with Island, but *Police And Thieves* would be the first and last of them – probably due to Perry's shenanigans, although nothing was said publicly. Scratch must have had a liking for falsetto voices though, because the Congos' Cedric Myton also sang in that style. Their album *Heart Of The Congos* would prove a landmark release, and Scratch was at his creative peak when it was recorded. He was multi-tracking on a four-track Teac machine and whilst the density of the overall sound owed a little to tape degeneration, the feel and complexity of it all was thrilling. Apart from a little delay, reverb and whatever else he could coax from his trusty Mutron phaser, Scratch used no other effects except those sampled from natural sources.

'Anything that moved, whether it was birds or whatever, we'd tape it and work it into the tracks,' explained Watty Burnett. 'When you hear strange sounds in some of Scratch's records from those times, most of them were coming from what we'd taped like that. We had so much freedom back then. We loved to create and put different things into the music, like rain and thunder.'

Watty would become the Congos' third member, and was there at Black Ark the day that Cedric and Roydel 'Ashanti Roy' Johnson arrived. The latter was an old friend of Perry's from back in Hanover, whilst Cedric was from Old Harbour originally and started out singing in the Tartans alongside Devon Russell and Prince Lincoln. He'd remained on good terms with the others after the Tartans' break-up, but after giving his all to the Royal Rasses, had been left empty-handed. It was at this point he became friendly with Roy, who'd recently left the Peace Corps. The pair had met at a Rasta grounation, and both sang with Ras Michael for a time. The two friends not only sang together but sold Rasta knitwear to stalls and shops all over the island. In early 1977 they went to see Scratch at the Black Ark, who helped out with lyrics and arrangements, and then invited Watty to sing with them after the group's earliest efforts left the producer feeling dissatisfied.

After Island turned it down, Scratch had released an earlier mix of *Heart Of The Congos* on Black Art, but this little-heard artifact doesn't sound as bright or richly textured as the later remixed version, and was also missing certain overdubs. The addition of Watty's baritone – and those famous cow noises – lent depth to the Congos' sound and served to counterbalance Cedric's flights in a higher register. The effect was spellbinding, and set the Congos apart from other Jamaican vocal trios, although the Meditations also sang harmonies on some of the tracks. 'Fisherman', written in tribute to the Rastafarian lifestyle, was their debut for Scratch, whilst 'Congoman' was a hypnotic chant driven by insistent drumming and a vertiginous bassline. That song gave them their name, but Rasta themes informed every track and the lyrics were awash with Biblical references, as heard on 'Sodom And Gomorrah', 'Ark Of The Covenant', 'Solid Foundation' and 'Can't Come In', which underlined the need for righteousness. 'Open Up The Gate' was about repatriation and, on 'Children Crying', they prayed for 'another prophet to lead the nation', thus reinforcing the continuing relevance of their message. Some of Jamaica's top musicians – including Sly Dunbar, Ernest Ranglin and bassist Boris Gardner – played on the sessions, and the tapestry of sound created by their rhythms, added to Perry's unique skills at the mixing-board and the Congos' evocative vocals, would secure the album's reputation as being among reggae music's crowning achievements. Work on *Heart Of The Congos* ended in mid-summer, and in July, soon after putting finishing touches to Keith Rowe's 'Groovy Situation', Scratch travelled to London, where he stayed in the flat above Island's Basing Street studio.

Don Letts' four month stint as a DJ at punk hangout the Roxy in London's Covent Garden had ended in April. Letts was the person nominally credited with turning the punks onto reggae – if you were to draw lines between the two genres, he would be standing at the main intersection. He also was a reactionary. In 1971, sporting an Afro, he'd attended a UK Black Panther meeting, stoned out of his gourd and in no fit state to learn anything. Several years later he'd taken Ari Up, the Slits' resident wild child, to a Twelve Tribes gathering. The pair hadn't been there long before being asked to leave after he'd invited her to smoke from a chalice that was being passed around. Letts the Upsetter saw no reason for her to be excluded just because she was a woman, and he was right of course.

Letts had taken an interest in Rasta after being caught up in the rapture of Bob Marley's performance at London's Lyceum in late 1975. After growing dreadlocks, he'd continued to break with tradition by wearing earrings and unusual clothes – hence the bondage trousers that Bob Marley famously quizzed him about. Not too many dreadlocked black men would confess to having attended gay discos at that time, but Letts made his living working in trendy clothes shops on the Kings Road such as Acme Attractions and Boy, where customers – including future punk icons – could buy vintage clothes and bondage gear, or just hang out, listening to the heavy reggae and dub he played incessantly. He was 20 years old in 1976, but Don was never a punk, just like he was never a Rasta. He was just there soaking up the energy and the vibes, searching for ways to express what was inside of him. Luck and determination, rather than skills – since he'd never DJed before – led him to the Roxy in Neal Street, where he played reggae mixed with tracks by the Stooges, Ramones and New York Dolls. It was around this same time that someone gave him a Super 8 camera, which he used to make *The Punk Movie* – a film of admittedly poor quality, but that possessed a surfeit of cultural significance. The UK media quickly turned punks into folk devils after highlighting their anti-social behaviour, but whilst they and the Rastas were anti-establishment, there were important differences. Punks didn't have a Messiah, mythical homeland or proud cultural heritage. Like the Rastas, they wanted to tear down the system, or Babylon, but unlike the Rastas, they didn't have any idea of what to do with the remains. Their vision – if we can call it that –was nihilistic, despite punk's impact on fashion and its crazed entrepreneurial spirit. It was an era of extreme hairstyles, ripped T-shirts, frenzied pogo-dancing, safety pin jewellery and fishnet stockings, which is why Don has described punk as 'the last complete subculture in the UK – complete in that it produced not only music, but also writers, photographers, poets, journalists, fashion designers and film makers. It remains a blueprint for how a youth-based movement can effect real change in music and art.

'I often get asked what reggae got out of punk, and the answer's always the same – all it got was exposure and that's all it needed. The music itself did the rest, because from that time up until today, it's never gone anywhere. It's the same thing that *The Harder They Come* did for reggae, because reggae wasn't being played on the radio and so people didn't get to hear it. But once they did, the music did the rest. That's all reggae got out of punk rock, but it was enough. I mean, thank God the reggae musicians didn't try and play punk rock! It was just American bands like Bad Brains who went down that path, and Jamaicans wouldn't have liked that, either. Jamaicans didn't give a fuck about punk music – come on, give me a break! They'd be far more likely to listen to the Beatles or Rolling Stones. But they did like the attitude.'

Back in April, John Peel had played the Clash's 'White Riot' – a song described as 'a battle cry to the youth of Britain.' Peel and the band would soon fall out – he even called them 'unbearably pretentious' – but the Clash briefly usurped the Sex Pistols as frontrunners of the punk movement after signing with CBS. I say briefly, because the Sex Pistols, who'd signed and been dropped by A&M in short order, then came roaring back with 'God Save The Queen' just in time for the Queen's Silver Jubilee. CBS had released the Clash's debut LP by then, which included a cover of Junior Murvin's 'Police And Thieves.' They'd included that track as an afterthought, but it alerted a lot of non-reggae fans to the original, despite generating its share of criticism. When he first heard it, Murvin himself is said to have retorted 'they've destroyed Jah's work!' Apparently Lee Perry wasn't too keen on it either, but agreed to work with them regardless. Allegedly, it was the Clash's version of 'Police And Thieves' that inspired him to write 'Punky Reggae Party', and then rush Bob Marley into Island's Basing Street studio to record it. None of the Wailers played on that initial session – just a couple of musicians from Third World and Aswad's Drummie Zeb, who thought the invitation to take part was a wind-up at first.

'I nearly didn't go, but I took my drum set to the studio and I was shaking,' he remembered. 'I walked in there and saw Bob Marley sitting on this speaker box, smoking a big spliff and surrounded by all these dreads. I was thinking to myself, "it's true!" Those times were wicked, man...'

Scratch would later restyle the rhythm to 'Punky Reggae Party' after returning to Jamaica, but Island didn't exactly get behind it even then, thanks to Chris Blackwell's low opinion of punk.

'I was never that keen on it,' Blackwell admitted. 'I didn't consider it as music and I didn't care for the musicianship, or rather the lack of it. I mean, the attitude behind it was good, in a sense, but there wasn't much music to it, or at least music that I felt was any good. For instance, I hate that record 'Punky Reggae Party', and I'm always angry when people say that they like it. I just didn't see the charm in it at all.'

His view of punk was shared by many other reggae insiders. I've lost count of all those I've heard praise the punks' anti-authoritarian stance, only to clarify their assessment by making disparaging remarks about the actual music and production. They forget that early reggae suffered in similar ways, but it was the spitting, the uncouth behaviour and couldn't-care-less attitude towards other people that really seemed to stick in their craw. Rasta music was rooted in peace and love, just like the hippy movement, but reggae's push/pull relationship with punk was no fleeting attraction, at least in the UK, because where they did connect – apart from wanting to tear down the status quo – was in the struggle to get their records pressed, distributed and promoted. There weren't enough major labels to go round, and artists and producers from both genres weren't all that convinced they were needed in any case. The gap was filled by a profusion of indie labels, many of them short-lived. Greensleeves Records, owned by Chris Sedgwick and Chris Cracknell, were an exception. The duo had started out with a small record shop in West Ealing, but had recently moved to new premises in Shepherd's Bush, where they specialised in soul and reggae imports, most of which couldn't be ordered again once they'd sold out.

'The business was very haphazard, and we had a lot of people requesting items that we simply couldn't supply,' said Cracknell. 'I remember thinking that there was all this great music coming out of Jamaica and such a demand for it, but nobody was really catering for it. Someone might stop by with a few boxes of records and say, "I live here but my cousin or whosoever is in Jamaica making music and I've got these singles, so would you like to buy some?" It was very much like that. There was no organisation, and few people were looking at it like a business, so we often couldn't get the tracks again. It was just chaos, but the music coming out of Jamaica was so vibrant and alive, and that's really what made us think about starting a label. We didn't know how the music business worked at first, so we took professional advice and then thought, "well, if we are going to do this, then we've got to do everything properly", and that's how we started. I suppose we were lucky in a way, because punk was just starting to happen, and the whole indie scene was beginning to come together.'

The first batch of Greensleeves 7-inch singles included 'Where Is Jah' by London band Reggae Regular and Dr Alimantado's 'Born For A Purpose', written after the deejay's near-death experience on Orange Street. He'd spent weeks in hospital recovering from his injuries and still couldn't move too well, even after being allowed to go home. One day, as told to David Katz, he was lying in bed when the idea for a song came to him.

'I started to sing it and I needed to get some kind of paper or pen to write it down but wasn't able to move, and there was nobody else in the house, right? I didn't want to forget the idea, so I use my hands to pull myself off the bed, which was very painful, and start to pull my whole body along. You don't know the beauty of your foot until you're in that stage. To get from there took me nearly half an hour, and when I reach there I was just feeling for a pen and some paper...'

He was still on crutches when he went to Channel One and explained that he had a tune he wanted to record, but didn't have the money to pay for studio time or musicians. Jo Jo Hoo Kim told him not to worry, and that's when he recorded 'Born For A Purpose', telling the story of when he was almost killed for walking along the sidewalk, flashing his dreads. He called it 'Reason For Living' at first, but then Jo Jo suggested they rename it 'Born For A Purpose' prior to it being released on Hitbound. Dr Alimantado would later reissue it on his own Ital Sounds label, before Greensleeves licensed it for distribution in the UK.

On 16 July, Capital Radio DJ Tommy Vance invited the Sex Pistols' John Lydon to play some of his favourite records on a programme titled *The Johnny Rotten Show: The Punk And His Music*. Any listeners expecting to hear wall-to-wall punk were in for a surprise, since his eclectic selection included plenty of reggae, which he said he'd been listening to 'from the early skinhead days.' He demonstrated impeccable taste by playing songs like Peter Tosh's 'Legalise It', Culture's 'I'm Not Ashamed', Augustus Pablo's 'King Tubby Meets Rockers Uptown' and Yabby You's 'Fire In Kingston'. But it was Dr Alimantado's 'Born For A Purpose' that held special meaning for the Sex Pistols' frontman.

'Just after I got my brains kicked out I went home and I played it and there's a verse which goes "if you have no reason for living, don't determine my life",' he told Vance, 'because the same thing happened to him. He got run over because he was a dread. Very true.'

Rotten's championing of Jamaican music would have a persuasive effect upon members of London's rock press, some of whom had derided reggae for years before he made it fashionable.

'Reggae was the only other radical music that was completely underground and not played on the radio,' he later wrote in his autobiography. 'It wasn't played on air until I did that appearance on the Tommy Vance show on Capital.'

That's not strictly true, of course, but admittedly national airplay was notoriously hard to come by for reggae releases in 1977. Don Letts would accompany Lydon to black clubs like the Four Aces in Dalston, where he says that 'everybody left him alone. He could walk into places white people could never go with total immunity. It was amazing that Johnny Rotten was so acceptable to the Rastas. They might not have liked his music, but it was like outlaws banding together. We all felt like society's outlaws.'

Again, this is hyperbole really, since there were more than a few white people who frequented black clubs and blues dances in those days, myself included. Just up the road from the Four Aces in Roseberry Place was Cubies, where Jah Tubby often held court. All Nations in London Fields was just a stone's throw from there, whilst Vincent White owned Phebes on Amhurst Road, where White's son Glen DJ'd upstairs in-between sets by bands like Black Slate. Friday nights in the basement belonged to sounds like Jah Shaka and Fat Man, and the latter also played at the Nightingale in Wood Green. Club Noreik on the Seven Sisters Road in Tottenham was another popular spot, as was the 77 Club on Holloway Road. Sir Jessus controlled Shepherd's Bush in those days, until Diamonds crossed the river from Battersea, whilst Lord David was based at the Swan in Stockwell, and we've already heard about the Metro Club in Notting Hill and the Apollo in Willesden, owned by the Palmer brothers. And let's not forget the Shepherd's Youth Club on Railton Road in Brixton, where many a future recording star practised their mic skills. Ravers south of the river could also choose between the 200 Club on Balham High Road, the St Mary's Centre in Lewisham and the Crypt in Deptford, which someone once described as a 'damp, mildewy, rundown place with dirty walls, a dirty floor and a dodgy loo without doors.'

That sounds about right, but once the vibes and the music were good, little else mattered. It was the more militant reggae style known as rockers that got the most reaction in clubs like those, but most of the UK sounds already played a little soul and found that homegrown lovers rock sweetened the dance just as well. In 1977, Dennis Harris introduced producer/guitarist John Kpiaye to three young girls – Caron Wheeler, Pauline Catlin and Carol 'Kofi' Simms – whose group he'd named Brown Sugar.

'I had this typical rub-a-dub tune for them with lines like "I'm in love with you baby", but when I sat down with them I soon realised they were into roots music, especially Caron, who was listening to a lot of Burning Spear at the time,' John explained. 'This meant I had to go back to the tune and have a rethink, because a year or so earlier, Dennis Harris had released this big seller called 'Curly Locks' by Junior Byles and so very cynically, I changed my tune round to 'I'm In Love With A Dreadlocks' as an answer version, written from a woman's perspective. That's when Dennis Harris became aware that we'd stumbled onto a different kind of sound. That's what made him think about putting it out on a different label, which he called Lovers Rock.'

Dennis Bovell recalls how Harris loved to play around with different names, and credits him with drawing the heart and arrow design that became the Lovers Rock logo.

'Lovers rock started to get recognised after that, because we were calling it lovers rock or lovers, as opposed to rockers, on sound system way before that. That's how it started really, 'cause on Sufferers we'd call out a line like, "This is lovers rock, so come rub-a-dub a daughter", or something to that effect.'

'I'm In Love With A Dreadlocks' went to number one on the *Black Echoes* reggae charts, as did Brown Sugar's second single, 'Hello Stranger', which had previously been a hit for Barbara Lewis.

'It was Dennis Harris's idea to cover that song,' said John. 'I wanted them to sing strictly originals, because whilst 'I'm In Love With A Dreadlocks' was strictly lovers rock, the lyrics had a slight roots connection and I wanted to keep going in that direction. But Dennis Harris insisted otherwise. He said to do 'Hello Stranger.' I told him that I didn't like it and then the next thing I knew it went straight to number one on the *Black Echoes* chart!'

The group's third single, 'Black Pride' was a return to John's original idea – a message song, albeit one reflecting their own reality, rather than one borrowed from their parents' Caribbean background. If Castro Brown felt jealous that Brown Sugar had eclipsed 15-16-17's popularity, he didn't say anything publicly. He and DEB Music were then riding the crest of a wave with yet another new Dennis Brown album, *Wolf And Leopards*. No less than eight of its ten songs were former singles, but nothing could stop it from flying to number one on the *Black Echoes* chart. 'Whip Them Jah Jah' was on there, and so too 'Emmanuel (God Is With Us)', 'Created By The Father', 'Here I Come' and the title track. If 'Lately Girl' sounded familiar, it was because DEB called it 'Promise Land' when issuing it on 7-inch, whilst 'Rolling Down' and 'Party Time' were covers of past Studio One hits by Delroy Wilson ('Rain From The Skies') and the Heptones.

Dennis Brown was now semi-resident in London, and he and Castro had opened a record shop at 79 Battersea Rise, not far from Clapham Junction. This was DEB's London headquarters, but the situation was far from straightforward, with Joe Gibbs, Castro and Niney all claiming to represent Dennis' business interests. Niney had visited London again earlier in the summer and licensed a number of tracks to Count Shelly's Third World label, including Dillinger's 'Flat Foot Hustling' Big Youth's 'Six Dead Nineteen Gone A Jail' and I-Roy's ribald 'Maggie's Breast', all of them versions to popular Dennis Brown rhythms. Despite his disagreements with Dennis and Castro, Niney had kept busy doing what he did best – producing hit reggae songs. His recent output included two songs by Tyrone Taylor ('Sufferation' and the jaunty 'I Got A

Feeling') and Ken Boothe's 'Silver Words', which was arguably the singers' most radio-friendly hit since 'Everything I Own.' Niney also produced the Ethiopians' *Slave Call*, although this was really a solo album by Leonard Dillon – Stephen Taylor having been killed two years earlier by a passing car as while working at a gas station on Washington Boulevard.

'I took sick after Stephen died,' Dillon said. 'I was suffering from shock for nearly two years, and so went home to Port Antonio, plus I wasn't singing. A lot of people used to ask, "what happen man? How you just rest so?" Then, when I sit down in my yard with my guitar and make my noise, people would say, "oh, that sounds like a record. Yuh nah record them songs there?" Them see how me live and I keep on writing, but I wasn't recording for nobody.'

It was Niney who enticed him back in the studio for the *Slave Call* sessions. The arrangement they had was that Leonard came up with the songs, whilst Niney booked studio time at Treasure Isle and paid the Soul Syndicate to back him on the sessions. The pair were then supposed to split the proceeds, but Leonard insists that he never got 'a penny' from the album, which Niney again licensed to Count Shelly. It was a fine outing nevertheless – one that opened with the 'Ethiopian National Anthem' and featured nyahbinghi drums throughout, even on his recut of 'Train To Skaville' and a righteous reading of the Beatles' 'Let It Be.' The emphasis on Rastafari provided a contrast with some of the Ethiopians' earlier hits, but Dillon laughed at the suggestion that his embrace of Rasta was something recent.

'I am a natural Ethiopian from the Ashanti tribe, y' know? Yeah man, and a leopard cannot change his spots because my mother and my grandmother used to teach me a lot about Africa when I was little and that's how I know that my African name is Tal, and I originate from Ghana. My grandparents told me that from even before I left Port Antonio for Kingston and start singing. A lot of elder Rastamen with knowledge give me some guidance and that help me too, y'know? The spirit of Jah inspired I even from those early times, because you cannot look upon a person and say them a Rasta. You can't say that – only by their works shall you know them, because Rasta is righteousness and cleanliness, and the man that you see wear the wool on his head is under the highest power because we are all kings, priests and prophets. And woe to those who disrespect it, because it will turn round and bite them.'

Max Edwards had rejoined Soul Syndicate by the time those sessions took place, as Santa Davis had left to go on tour with Jimmy Cliff. A guy called Easy Money then took the band to the US, where they met promoter Warren Smith. He had a friend called Richie who lived in a big house in Marin County overlooking the Golden Gate Strait. The band members stayed there for two months, which is when Warren became their manager. After they returned to Jamaica, he booked them into a rundown hotel in Ocho Rios where they rehearsed for about a month before going into Harry J's studio to make their debut album, *Harvest Uptown/Famine Downtown* – a set which, according to the liner notes, reached 'beyond the traditions of reggae through rhythm and blues, and into African roots to create a sound uniquely their own.'

Freddie McGregor went on a US tour with Soul Syndicate in 1977 and they recorded several songs together, including 'Revolutionist.' Freddie had the vocal finesse of a soul artist, something Niney the Observer was quick to recognise when taking him into the studio for a cover of Carole King's 'Oh No Not My Baby', although when the single came out it had Freddie's cut of 'Satta Massagana' on the B-side, 'Rasta Have Faith.' 'Do Good' and the understated yet heartfelt 'Run Come Rally' also came from those same sessions and helped introduce the former Studio One protégé to a wider audience. He and Chinna Smith often worked together and the guitarist's instrumental LP, *Sticky Fingers*, arrived during that same period courtesy of Bunny Lee, who'd licensed it to Third World. It differed from those by fellow Jamaican guitarists Ernest Ranglin and Willie Lindo because Chinna used a wah-wah pedal – not excessively, since he was no Hendrix, but in such a way that it gave his music a little extra colouring. After playing with Marley, Bunny Wailer and other major reggae stars, Chinna was Jamaica's guitarist of choice, except he still found time for his old friend from Greenwich Farm, singer Earl Zero. He was recording for Bertram Brown's Freedom Sounds and sang of what's 'never been told' on 'Shackles And Chains.' Brown had launched his label two years previously from premises on East Avenue and had also released the more up-tempo 'Vision Of Love', as well as singles by Phillip Fraser ('Come Ethiopians') and Prince Allah, whose current songs for Freedom Sounds included 'Black Rose', shared with Fraser, and 'Mama No Fight.'

UK music journalist Dave Hendley interviewed Earl Zero and other artists in Greenwich Town and called Earl one of the most sincere and gentle people that he'd met in Jamaica. 'He practices his Rasta beliefs in his everyday life, which is not always an easy thing to do in a place like Kingston.' Hendley reported how the local Rastas 'spend most days at the Cornerstone, a large yard where they meet to meditate, lick chalice, reason or just get on with daily chores like building chicken-wire fishing traps, the sea being a major source of food.'

Prince Allah had lived in Trench Town before embracing Rasta, growing locks, and his father banished him from the family home. After that he'd headed for the beach at Greenwich Farm and joined up with Milton Henry and Roy 'Soft' Palmer in the Leaders. Disillusioned by the lack of opportunity, he then retired from music and spent several years at Prince Emmanuel's Rasta camp over-looking Bull Bay. He became one of the priests there and when he ventured back into secular life, his songs were steeped in Biblical lore. It was Chinna Smith who took him to meet Bertram Brown, but Tapper Zukie needed no such introduction. He overheard Allah singing when walking past the artist's house one day, and a short while later the pair were at Lee Perry's Black Ark, recording 'Man From Bosrah.' Tapper released this song and Allah's follow-up, 'Daniel (In The Lion's Den)', on his own Stars label. Their friendship surprised a lot of people given that Prince Allah was a Rastaman, and Tapper had a reputation that was completely at odds with the pursuit of righteousness. Yet in addition to Allah, the deejay was producing songs with Junior Ross and the Spear, and he'd also taken an interest in a Rasta vocal group from Rema called Knowledge.

Meanwhile, Patti Smith was in an American hospital writing a lengthy, free form poem called *Tapper The Extractor* about 'the thread of return.' Back in January, at a show in Tampa, Florida, she'd seriously injured herself, falling off stage and fracturing two of her vertebrae on the concrete floor fifteen feet below. Tapper had visited her and Lenny Kaye in New York and even cooked them a roast fish dinner, as they'd discussed the possibility of Patti reissuing his *Man Ah Warrior* album on her own Mer label. She was a big fan of the album, as we've already heard, and had invited Tapper onstage at the Hammersmith Odeon the last time she'd been in London. When the reissue of Tapper's debut finally appeared, it featured a photo by Robert Mapplethorpe on the cover and liner notes by Penny Reel. It also included two extra tracks – 'Viego' and 'A Message To Pork Eaters' – whilst omitting the three non-Zukie related titles. It was a much improved package and, unlike his album *Dub Master*, didn't quietly slip into obscurity almost as soon as it appeared.

Deejay newcomers were coming thick and fast. Although not a novice as such, Jah Woosh had two albums out, *Marijuana World Tour* (produced by UK reggae band Creation Rebel) and *Lick Him With The Dustbin*, the last of which which showed him on the cover, dustbin at the ready and poised to rout the wicked. Like Big Youth, Jah Woosh sang as well as deejayed, but not nearly so often. Creole Records had released his debut LP *Jah Woosh* in 1974.

'After that I went on tour to Nassau and whilst I was there I got in some trouble and was put away. They cut off my natty dread, but I am strictly a Rasta man who stick to his culture and now I am on the right track there will be no turning back,' he promised in the liner notes. 'Because after all those troubles I came back strong on the scene with a sure fire hit called 'Love Jah And Live' and many more since, e.g., 'African Music', 'Challis Blaze', 'Religion Dread' and 'I'm Alright'.'

Welton Irie was still a teenager, although he'd been deejaying on sounds like Echo Tone Hi Fi, Gemini and Virgo for some time. He'd also been recording for Glen Brown, who put out 'Lamb's Bread Callie Man', but Welton's biggest hit of 1977 was 'Chase Them Crazy', produced by Coxsone Dodd at Studio One and shared with his friend Anthony Waldron, aka Lone Ranger. Waldron was only 19 and had spent much of his childhood in Tottenham, London, before his family returned to Jamaica in 1971. Once back on the island and throughout school he would buy records with his lunch money. U-Roy and Big Youth were his favourite artists, and after writing lyrics in an exercise book, he'd practise deejaying to the versions on the B-sides. Waldron sang, too, and was in a vocal trio called I-fenders, before chatting on sounds such as Soul Express and Arrows International. Ranger, Carlton Livingston and Welton Irie were among a group of friends who used to go to Tony Walcott's house and practise. When they were ready, he'd take them to Studio One and introduce them to Coxsone. In addition to 'Chase Them Crazy', the veteran producer recorded an album with Lone Ranger called *On The Other Side Of Dub* that was a riot of storytelling and verbal flourishes spread across five tracks, and voiced over a succession of hit rhythms. Sugar Minott was rightly credited with resurrecting Studio One in the rockers era (his recent debut LP, *Live Loving*, was a classic example), but Lone Ranger played a crucial role in this too, with tracks from his album and singles like 'Screw Gone A North Coast' and 'The Answer.'

First they were the Viceroys, and then the Interns. Lee Perry even renamed them Truth Fact & Correct for 1976's 'Babylon Deh Pon Fire', but their fortunes didn't improve after that either, so they returned to Studio One and recorded new songs such as 'Slogan On The Wall', 'The Struggle' and 'Jollification', which described life in a tenement yard. Coxsone had a surfeit of material with them, both old and new, and chose to release a remixed version of 'Yah Ho.'

'A pirate has no friends and to see the pirate's gold, you know it is the end,' chuckled lead singer Wesley Tinglin. 'I vision the whole thing, but how that song started, I had a book called *Caribbean Reader*, and at the same time I was interested in the history of Jamaica and all the things that happened in the past. I was reading about the pirates and how they controlled Port Royal, and that's how I came up with those lines. I wrote it in Kingston, but it could have easily been written in Port Royal!'

Another of Jamaica's well-respected vocal trios, the Tamlins, went on tour with Peter Tosh. Their first show with him was at the Maurice Gusman Concert Hall in Miami, but their hopes of gaining additional exposure as a result of this never materialised, and travelling overseas led to some unpleasant surprises – like when they discovered copies of their album *Black Beauty* selling in London shops after Byron Lee had craftily licensed it to State Records without having told them. Needless to say, they didn't see any money from the deal – not from State Records or Lee himself.

An early edition of the Royals had split up by the end of 1975. Some of the members left to form The Jayes, and by the time the Royals' debut album *Pick Up The Pieces* was released in 1977, the group consisted of Roy Cousins, Errol Davis and Carl Green. The songs on this album have been described as 'some of the most musically sublime expressions of Rastafarian faith and the hardships of ghetto living Jamaica has produced.' Several of them, including 'Peace And Love', 'Only For A Time' and 'When You Are Wrong', were former singles, whilst the title track was a recut of a hit they'd recorded for Studio One back in 1973, which they delivered in a new, improved and more mature fashion. Roy had launched his own Tamoki label as far back as 1972. He'd also produced Gregory Isaacs' haunting 'Way Of Life', but five years later he was still working for the Post Office as he knew that was the only way the Royals could keep going and stay independent.

The Royals' situation was one the newly crowned 'Mighty' Maytones may well have related to. Vernon Buckley and Gladstone Grant recorded their debut LP *Madness* for producer Alvin 'GG' Ranglin in 1976, and 'Money Trouble', shared with I-Roy, was their biggest hit to date. We should also mention the Travellers, a quartet from Waterhouse who had recently been recording for Prince Jammy. When Bunny Lee had struck a licensing deal with Third World in early 1977, Jammy had been with him, and gave them albums by the Travellers and U Black, in addition to the dub set *Jammies In Lion Dub Style*. Comprised of just nine tracks, the latter had cuts of rhythms he knew might interest sound systems – 'Death In The Arena', for example – along with tracks that he'd been working on with another local Waterhouse group called Black Uhuru. Lead singer Michael Rose had previously voiced 'Born Free' for Jammy and was Black Uhuru's main songwriter, although founder member Derrick 'Ducky' Simpson was their spokesperson. Jammy produced their debut album *Love Crisis*, credited to 'Black Sounds Uhro' and later reissued by Greensleeves as *Black Sounds Of Freedom*.

'The majority of those tracks were recorded at Channel One, but some of them were recorded at Harry J's and Joe Gibbs also,' Jammy recounted. 'We all came from the same area and grew up locally, but it wasn't just Sly and Robbie playing on that Black Uhuru album, as some people think. I only did about two tracks with them, because the majority were played by the High Times band.'

The musicians listed on the sleeve differed from those mentioned by Jammy, but it was still a majestic effort. Distinguished by Rose's yearning vocals and deeply conscious lyrics, strong harmonies and tough roots rhythms, the first Uhuru album didn't generate a lot of sales or media attention, yet created great excitement among soundmen who wasted no time championing tracks like 'I Love King

Selassie', 'Hard Ground', 'Sorry For The Man', 'Time To Unite' and the group's mesmerising cover of Marley's 'Natural Mystic.' It wasn't until the LP arrived that facts emerged about their history. Duckie was born in Jones Town, but then moved with his family to the countryside. He was just 11 when his mother died and he was sent to live with his aunt in Waterhouse. Two years after that, she threw him out the house because of his growing interest in Rastafari. We've been hearing that story a lot, and once again it was music that provided him with much needed focus and purpose. He, Garth Dennis and Don Carlos had formed the original line-up of Black Uhuru in 1974, when all three were living in Waterhouse. Ducky was known as Uhuru (which means 'freedom' in Swahili) even before forming the band. Their debut single, a cover of Curtis Mayfield's 'Romancing The Folk Song', was met with limited success, so the group split up. Garth left to join the Wailing Souls and Don embarked on a solo career. Errol Nelson from the Jayes was invited to replace Garth, and it was this second line-up – with Michael Rose on lead vocals – that recorded for Prince Jammy. They were a new group competing for attention in an already over-populated field, and with no recognisable faces in their line-up. They were also less melodic than other roots trios like Culture or the Mighty Diamonds, because Uhuru had a militant air about them. The group assumed the mantle of ghetto revolutionaries and chanted black liberation with dignified assurance.

As mentioned previously, Prince Jammy had started his label with a rhythm that Yabby You had given him. Unlike Jammy, Yabby continued to experience difficulties getting his records distributed, yet his musical and spiritual objectives remained resolute as ever. It's said that you can hear the church in the best soul music, and the heartbeat of ancient Africa in some classic Jamaican roots reggae, but rarely has music expressed the awe and grandeur of Biblical prophecy so completely as that of Yabby You's, especially tracks mixed by King Tubby, whose wild flights of sonic invention provided the perfect foil for Yabby's productions.

'If you notice when you hear my music, even those tracks where I'm not singing, you can still feel the message inna it, and that's real reggae music to the bone,' says Yabby. 'It will put you in the right frame of mind for the things that are conscious and belonging to the truth, and it will draw your attention to whatever can be described as oppression. But it's nothing to do with any church or religion. Instead, I use music to teach black history, and to remind the world of what it takes to be a human being, so anyone hearing it will get the opportunity to see those things. That's what I try to do – I highlight black history as I see it, and to show my people that we are all one nation, coming from ancient Africa.'

He'd reissued the albums *Conquering Lion* and *Walls Of Jerusalem* on his own Prophet label, but it was *Deliver Me From My Enemies*, released on Grove Music and with liner notes by Linton Kwesi Johnson, that did most to attract attention in the UK. This wasn't just because of the strong material on it – although it was arguably his most cohesive set yet – but because Grove Music was a new label based in Notting Hill that had recently turned heads with a flurry of 7-inch singles by the likes of Yabby ('Chant Down Babylon Kingdom' included), King Sounds, Ras Ibuna ('Diverse Doctrine'), Glen Roy and Cynthia Richards. There was also Trevor Bow's group Sons Of Jah, and Tommy McCook and Bobby Ellis, whose *Blazing Horns* album was a recent addition to the label's roster.

Deliver Me From My Enemies was the jewel in Grove's crown, but the real Jamaican roots heavyweights were on Island, who released Burning Spear's third album for the label in August. *Dry & Heavy* was his first self-produced set, and Jack Ruby was conspicuous by his absence, as were Winston Rodney's two backing singers. It was to Spear's credit that none of those people were missed, although key members of his usual backing band the Black Disciples were still there – Robbie Shakespeare, Horsemouth and Chinna included. Spear had switched from recording at Randy's to Harry J's, in search of a more rounded sound, although the lyrical content was little different as he was still preoccupied with Black Nationalism, Biblical tradition, the wonders of creation and fundamental human values based around the family and respect for others – topics that he'd remained faithful to on each of his albums to date. Whilst it was hard to separate any of his Island releases – since all three were essential – *Dry & Heavy* was a truly remarkable set, and indicative of his growing powers as a singer, producer and songwriter. There was a trance-like quality to so many of the tracks, and each of them was remarkably consistent. Spear used repetition like a great blues singer would and extended his vocals with cries and adlibs that said more than any words could. At his best he made hypnotic, soulful reggae music that put us in a spell, as heard on the title track, 'The Sun' and two songs – 'It's A Long Way Around' and 'Black Disciples' – that were serious upgrades on the Studio One tracks 'Creation Rebel' and 'Swell Headed.'

Bunny Rugs had joined Third World by the time the band recorded their second album for Island, *96 Degrees In The Shade*. His lead vocals were as soulful as those of any R&B singer, the harmonies and melodies heard on every track were joyous, whilst the rhythms crackled with energy and a percussive drive that owed much to drummer Willie Stewart. There was a billboard on the road by the Hermitage Dam in Kingston that read in large gold letters: 'Third World. Red Hot. 96 Degrees In The Shade.' Island Records were presumably responsible, although there was no logo on it. Chris Blackwell's label had picked another winner, regardless, and Third World were now primed for international success in much the same way that Inner Circle were, by making music that was tailored for mainstream airplay and capable of crossing over to pop and soul fans. Despite their music's commercial veneer, Third World had never lacked for meaningful subject matter. For proof, listen to 'Tribal War', 'Third World Man' or 'Human Market Place', whilst they wrote '1865 (96 Degrees In The Shade)' about the same slave uprising that Michael Manley referenced in his speech on 7 July.

Bunny Rugs sings on the title track, although the narrative belonged to Paul Bogle himself. 'Some may suffer and some may burn, but I know that one day my people will learn, as sure as the sun shines way up in the sky. Today I stand here a victim, but the truth is I'll never die.'

On 6 August, Independence Day, former Prime Minister Sir Alexander Bustamante was buried in Kingston's National Heroes Park. Hundreds of mourners followed the procession in the rain, and the interment took place as ninety-three gunshots were fired, one for every year of his life. 'It was the end of an era,' according to Edward Seaga, who claimed that his mentor's 'heroic life made Jamaica's independence possible.' The opposition leader, watched by Manley standing nearby, also spoke of Bustamante having championed the workers' cause. 'He demanded a better life for them,' he told the large gathering, 'and this led to the creation of the first truly island-wide trade union to represent them with a powerful voice. He changed the course of Jamaica's history by creating a future for underprivileged Jamaicans against all odds. His was not a revolution of guns and nor of constitutional battle. He used his strength of character to demand the rights the people never had, and he succeeded.'

Seaga's friend Byron Lee, owner of Dynamic Sound, generally steered clear of anything to do with Rastas or rants against the system. Instead, he'd kept faith with Barry Biggs, singer with the Dragonnaires, whose last single 'Three Ring Circus' had only just failed to enter the UK Top 20 in July. It was the lead track on his new, middle-of-the-road album *Sincerely!* and he looked pleased with himself as he posed cigar in hand on the cover wearing a patterned shirt with outsize collars that was unbuttoned halfway down to his navel. Just as he had done on various Trojan albums, Tony King arranged the strings, which were recorded at Morgan studios in London. The word 'anachronistic' springs to mind, because Trojan themselves had moved on since John Holt's *1,000 Volts Of Holt* was hailed as the epitome of Jamaican musical excellence.

Their latest release was Big Youth's *Reggae Phenomenon*, which the deejay produced himself and first issued on the Agustus Buchanan label. Its arrival on Trojan – repackaged as a double album with ten other tracks – represented a real triumph for the label, considering that it had nearly gone out of business a year or so ago. *Pop Matters* music critic Maurice Bottomley called Big Youth's lyrics 'urban poetry at its most sublime, and over as fine a set of rhythms as anyone has ever heard', then singled out the track 'Riverton City' for special praise, describing it 'a tour through the poorest of the poor, and that is done with warmth, dignity and love.' It was all true of course, and only Big Youth would have dared start such a song with the nursery rhyme 'Old King Cole.' He sang rather than deejayed on that track and also most of the others, including 'Papa Was A Rolling Stone', which asked questions of Papa's other half – i.e. the narrator's mother. That was clever, whilst 'Hip-Ki-Do' was an off-the-wall bubbler, and educational with it. But following *Screaming Target*, *Natty Cultural Dread* and *Hit The Road Jack* was never going to be easy.

As August came to a close, there was talk that Bob Marley had been taken ill after three dates in New York were cancelled at short notice. People were wondering if the US leg of his *Exodus* tour was now in doubt, but the staff at Island were tight-lipped. What we now know is that Marley went to see a doctor about the injury to his toe, which hadn't healed properly, and that he'd been diagnosed as having melanoma cancer. He was told to choose between 'toe or tour', and since Marley didn't want them to amputate his toe, he wasn't going to be touring any time soon – despite having just delivered the best album of his career. Also – and to far minor extent – it probably didn't make him feel any better knowing that Leroy Smart and Johnny Clarke were having hits with their covers of 'Waiting In Vain', whilst his own cut still hadn't been made available on single.

Johnny Clarke performed at London's Hammersmith Odeon in early September, supported by Jah Stitch. Producer Bunny Lee was there, dressed in his finery and wearing the white yachting cap he'd become synonymous with. Johnny had recently covered John Holt's 'Up Park Camp', which told the story of a youth in jail who regretted not having listened to the good people around him, who'd urged him not to go wild. Up Park Camp was the name of a military barracks in Kingston and home to the Jamaican Defence Force, as well as a prison. Holt's song became the title track of his new album for Channel One and received a warm welcome. After all those orchestrated songs for Tony Ashfield, he was back on the reggae beat and just like Marley and Burning Spear, he'd been upgrading some of his old hits – hence new versions of songs like 'A Love I Can Feel', 'Only A Smile' and 'Have You Ever Been In Love.' It was quite difficult for someone like him to reinvent himself, but recent photos indicated that he was now growing dreadlocks, and how radical was that?

John Holt had visited Britain many times, but the news that Big Youth would soon be arriving for his first ever UK dates, backed by a Jamaican band and on the same bill as Dennis Brown, was a definite cause for celebration. The promoter was Tony Bullimore, who sound engineer Chris David has described as 'an unbelievable character, and with boundless energy.'

'He'd been a mercenary in the Congo before becoming a South African citizen and wrestling in the Olympics,' adds Martin Disney, who also worked on that tour. 'He then had to leave South Africa because he wanted to marry a black woman, but when we went to his house to discuss the tour he greeted us wearing just a small towel, and insisted on us all watching a cowboy film on this huge television set whilst we talked to him.'

The 5 ft 2 Bullimore was owner of the Bamboo Club in Bristol, where many reggae artists had played over the years. However, he'd never promoted a tour before, as David and Disney discovered during their meeting. He'd already booked three nights at London's Rainbow Theatre, and further shows were planned for Bristol, Birmingham and Manchester, but Bullimore had insisted on only booking Friday and Saturday nights, which meant that the sound truck, lighting gear and crew would be tied up with nothing to do the rest of the time. This was bad enough, but then the musicians were delayed in New York and this greatly affected the team's ability to promote the London dates properly. Also, Bullimore hadn't wanted to pay for any rehearsal time, and then David and Disney found out that he hadn't booked any hotels for the band in London either, planning to have them stay in Bristol and ferry them back and forth to London in hired limos.

'When we were trying to get him to rationalise all this,' said Martin Disney, 'he kept saying, "you don't understand black people. I'm going to show Harvey Goldsmith how to do it. Mick Jagger's going to be there. They're all going to be there. And when Big Youth takes that tam off and shakes those dreads, they're going to go crazy!" Well they didn't, because they didn't come. On the first night at the Rainbow there was hardly an audience at all. It was about a quarter-full, and even the other two shows were only about half-full. That's because there had been no upfront publicity, and then we learnt that posters for the Birmingham show had been put up in Manchester, and posters for the Manchester show had been put up in Bristol... In the end they had to hire a van with a speaker on top and drive around the streets advertising the gigs like that. The Bristol show was actually fairly well-attended and Birmingham was certainly better attended than the shows at the Rainbow, but the Manchester date was mercifully cancelled...'

Disney and David were very grateful of the artists and musicians' good-natured acceptance of the circumstances they found themselves in, and whilst David nearly didn't get paid, he at least had the advantage of living in the same town as Bullimore.

'We'd asked him for our money a number of times before going down to the Bamboo Club and being shown to his office, where he was sitting with his brother, who was a *Peaky Blinders* type of a guy,' David recalled. 'There was more than enough cash to pay us on his desk, alongside a gun and some other stuff, but Tony

said, "I'd really love to pay you, except I really don't have a penny."
I was looking at this pile of cash, but the gun persuaded me that
I really shouldn't be arguing about this, so we left and shortly
afterwards he came to see us and said "guys, you need to sue me,
and you need to do it today because otherwise there won't be any
money." We went straight to our lawyer and got paid in full,
whereas other people sadly wouldn't have got a cent. Afterwards,
we heard that Tony's brother had deviously drawn up an agreement
dated 30 February which everybody seemed happy with at the
time.

Despite such disappointments, Big Youth and his contemporaries
continued to build on their following among black and non-
Caribbean audiences alike. Keith Levene, who played with both
the Clash and John Lydon's Public Image Ltd, spoke to *3AM
Magazine*'s Greg Whitfield about this, describing the feeling he got
from listening to Jamaican rockers to 'being high without any ganja.'

'It was incredible. We all loved those huge, stepping bass-lines
and mic chanters – people like Big Youth, who was so hip at the
time. Dub music and versions on those Jamaican dub plates fascin-
ated me, because they had nothing to do with accepted structures
and formats at that time. Nothing to do with 12 bar structures!
Nothing to do with the blues or rock music. Those dubs sounded
so strange, like music from another planet – they sounded like
rhythms from an African settlement on Mars! I fucking loved them,
and they influenced me a lot. John was influenced by them a lot,
too, but we never imitated them. That was always very important
to me, and still is. Like I said, dub had nothing to do with rock'n'roll
vocabulary, but was dealing with frequencies and sounds that had
never even been invented before that time.'

Levene didn't mention Keith Hudson in that interview, although
we can be sure that Levene and Lydon were both aware of Hudson's
latest album, *Brand*. The album served up dubs of tracks that would
feature on the maverick vocalist/producer's forthcoming vocal LP
Rasta Communication before the album-proper itself – an unusual

step, as artists usually waited until after a vocal album's release to put out the dub version.

'*Brand* is a hot iron burnt into flesh', went the promotional blurb. 'Encouraged by the critics and perhaps through his musical and physical dislocation from Jamaica, Hudson concentrates on his own music rather than producing others. His vocals, variously described as "eerie", "awkward" and "discordant", sit perfectly in a dub setting.'

They did indeed. *Harry Mudie Meets King Tubby In Dub Conference Vol. 2* wasn't as edgy as *Brand*, but was even more impressive in certain ways, especially when the strings came in on 'Planet Dub.' In lesser hands such a thing might have ended up sounding MOR, but not with Tubby sat at the mixing board. His handiwork was all over Augustus Pablo's first self-produced album, the classic *King Tubby Meets The Rockers Uptown*. The original pressing had appeared a year earlier, but copies had been difficult to find and expensive. The price and distribution had improved since then, and it was sitting pretty at number one on the *Black Echoes* chart by late autumn 1977. There was a mystique about Pablo, who rarely gave interviews and didn't often play live, unless it was to make the occasional guest appearance on his brother's sound system. His music was unlike anyone else's, and it was intriguing how he managed to invest it with so much spirituality by playing the humble melodica.

'This instrument now, everyone is portraying it as nothing,' he admitted to Ray Hurford, 'but it's just like a keyboard, with the same scales and notes. The only thing is that it plays at a higher frequency. An ordinary piano wouldn't carry that frequency, but it's the same notes there. It's just that it's a blowing instrument, and so the music travels within the wind and no one can hold it or catch it. It's just like the breeze, because can anyone catch the breeze or touch the sun? These things come from within and any instrument I touch, it's the same song I'm going to get.'

Recent Pablo singles like 'East Of The River Nile' and 'Vibrate

On' – which couldn't have been made anywhere else but Black Ark – were selling briskly in the shops, and he'd also been producing the 15 year old singer Hugh Mundell, who came from a middle class family and attended Ardenne High School. Already and somewhat predictably, the teenager's involvement with Rastafari was causing difficulties between him and his family. You could hear how young he was on the single 'Let's All Unite', yet there was a maturity to the lyrics that belied his age, whilst 'Book Of Life' – a cut to Pablo's 'Keep On Dubbing' – was remarkably assured for someone with such little experience.

Junior Delgado, who was only a teenager himself, was another of the youths in Pablo's circle. He'd been voicing songs for Scratch and Niney but was also one of Dennis Brown's closest friends, which explained why he had two singles out on DEB Music – one a cover of the Heptones' 'Love Won't Come Easy', and the other, 'Tiction', a brooding attack on perpetrators of gun violence produced by Chinna Smith and voiced on the same rhythm as Alton Ellis' 'Mr Ska Beana.' 'Tiction' has been spelt in several different ways but is generally understood to mean 'politician.' Brown, meanwhile, was so smitten by 15-16-17's latest DEB release 'Girls Imagination' that he announced plans to record an album with them in Jamaica. The rhythm on that track was played by the same musicians who had backed him and Big Youth on their ill-fated UK tour, because when musicians of that calibre were in town – Sly Dunbar and Lloyd Parks included – it was an opportunity that couldn't be missed (and especially not by Castro Brown).

DEB Music was doing well. Castro was quite the man about town, and DEB's profile was boosted considerably when Gregory Isaacs gave them an album to release that the singer had produced himself at Channel One with the Revolutionaries. Gregory was best-known for aching love songs, but he'd been exploring roots and reality themes of late, and rather than losing him fans, singles like 'Thief A Man', 'Black A Kill Black', 'Mister Cop' and 'Set The Captive Free' had increasingly earned him respect among the reggae fraternity. *Mr Isaacs* would mark the first time he recorded an entire album of songs like that, but it would prove exceptional in more ways than one. Only Gregory could sing about pent-up rage and resentment in such laidback fashion as demonstrated on 'Slave Master', 'Set The Captive Free' and 'Handcuff', which he'd written after being stopped by police during the State of Emergency. He sang of inner peace on 'Storm', and there was a Biblical slant to 'Sacrifice' as he contrasted the black man's hell with a white man's paradise. Few Jamaican artists had expressed the human – or indeed, a black man's – condition with such pathos. Isaacs had often cast himself as an outsider in certain songs, and 'The Winner' was yet another example of that. Only his cover of the Temptations' 'Get Ready' disappointed, mostly because he'd held back, rather than joined in the excitement as the Revolutionaries flashed their disco chops.

An album like *Mr Isaacs* deserved all the advantages that being signed to a major label could provide, but DEB was still growing and Gregory obviously felt they were worth supporting. He was being actively courted by members of The Rolling Stones at the time, who were looking for artists to sign to their own record label. One day in late 1977, Keith Richards' manager phoned Michael Epstein – aka 'Eppy' manager of My Father's Place on Long Island – to ask if he could arrange for Keith and Ronnie Wood to meet Gregory Isaacs.

'There was more and more reggae coming out on different record labels,' Eppy explained. 'Marley had just released *Exodus* and he and Peter Tosh were touring... It was right at that time when Jane Rose phoned me and said she had a problem. She said Keith and Ronnie Wood wanted to come out to Long Island and see Gregory Isaacs, and she was worried about sending them out there. I told her it was no big deal, but she yelled back, "you don't understand. They're Rolling Stones!" I didn't give a shit about The Rolling Stones. I was a reggae fan. But she started talking about how she wanted proper security and all that. I knew Jane Rose because she'd been an assistant to a promoter who did shows downtown. Anyhow, Keith and Ronnie came, and we had these guys sat round the table with them who looked distinctly Gestapo-like. They were horrible. They created this negative zone that was so fucking sad. Keith came up to me and said, "can't you get rid of these guys?" I said, "thank God, but make sure Jane doesn't find out about this." He told me not to worry and started chuckling to himself. But like I said, Gregory was the first artist they wanted to sign to their label and they wanted to sit with him so they could discuss it with him. I was surprised about it, because Gregory wasn't really pop. If they were looking for commercial success then there were other reggae acts who they should have asked first.

'Gregory met Keith and Woody at the club and he knew who they were but couldn't make a decision. They were getting ready to make a record with him, but Gregory only had one thing in his mind, which was that fucking white powder. That's when Woody told me their second choice was Peter Tosh, and could I introduce them to him? I called Peter and I remember the conversation. "Peter. The Rolling Stones want to produce a record with you." He said, "I man don't need no Rolling Stone. I don't play rock'n' roll. I'm a reggae artist." I couldn't believe that he hadn't known who The Rolling Stones were. How could you *not* know who the Rolling Stones are? The details are kind of hazy, but Keith and Ron did fly down there to sit with him and discuss what they had in mind, in terms of a record deal.'

In truth, there were more important matters to think about. In a September article for *Rolling Stone*, Carl Bernstein, the reporter who had helped expose the Watergate scandal, claimed that 'more than four hundred American journalists, including senior news executives, columnists and reporters, had secretly carried out assignments for the CIA during the last twenty-five years.' Bernstein said CIA records showed that officials at numerous key media outlets had co-operated with them by hiring agency operatives as journalists and that the agency's most valuable assets included *The New York Times, The*

Washington Post, *Associated Press* and *Reuters*, all of whom denied the allegations. Michael Manley certainly wouldn't have been surprised to read such claims, since virtually every media outlet that was listed had been complicit in spreading scare stories about his government throughout his time as Jamaican prime minister.

There was also shocking news from South Africa regarding the death of anti-apartheid activist Steve Biko, co-founder of the South African Students Organisation and Black People's Convention. He was arrested in mid-August for having violated a banning order imposed upon him four years earlier for being a 'subversive threat', and having urged fellow black people to rid themselves of any sense of racial inferiority. After being arrested he was taken to a police station in Port Elizabeth where he was handcuffed, shackled, chained to a grille and interrogated for twenty-two hours. Two weeks later, he suffered a massive brain haemorrhage after being beaten by several officers, but was chained to a wall and forced to remain standing. The first doctor who examined him reported there were no signs of injury, but when his condition then rapidly deteriorated he was loaded into the back of a Land Rover, naked and manacled, and driven over 700 miles to a hospital, where he died the following day, alone and in a cell. An autopsy revealed that in addition to extensive brain injuries, he had died of internal bleeding and acute kidney failure. It would be a mistake to assume that such news didn't impact upon people in Jamaica, and it certainly didn't escape reggae artists such as Peter Tosh and Tapper Zukie, nor some of the island's revolutionary poets who'd started to make their voices heard.

Early in 1977, prison guards had escorted Jamaican poet Orlando Wong to a reading in Kingston whilst he was still serving a lengthy jail sentence for having taken part in an armed robbery. Thanks to Justice minister Carl Rattray, he was then pardoned by government decree, but his rebel instincts remained undimmed because two weeks after being freed, he informed the *Gleaner* that he wrote poems that might influence people to 'do something to clear up the garbage heap in which we live.'

Upon his release, Wong enrolled at the Jamaica School of Drama in central Kingston, which Linton Kwesi Johnson described as 'the cradle of dub poetry in Jamaica.' He joined a band of performance poets who shared a similarly revolutionary mindset, and on 28 September, he and Michael Smith gave a reading at an evening of Jamaican culture presented by the Jamaica Development Bank. Smith told the *Gleaner* that 'artists in general get their inspiration from the people, and so they have a duty to reflect this life.' Both read works based on their own experiences in Kingston's ghettos – experiences that many people chose to ignore, and that gave members of the audience a lot of things to think about.

Wong's first poetry collection, *ECHO*, had soon followed. The launch was held at the Kingston Library on 2 October where he was accompanied by drummers from the Light Of Saba. The reading room was packed that day. Barbara Gloudon, who'd helped champion his release, spoke first, whilst the minister of justice warned that 'Wong's is a voice saying very important things to us, and we can't survive if we don't listen.' *ECHO* started with 'I Want To Write A Poem' – a mission statement designed to wake the senses, and 'kindle a burning desire in man to destroy exploitation.' Further themes of destitution and despair were explored in poems like 'A Slum Dweller Declares', 'How Long', 'Dread Times' and 'Pressure Drop', whilst strident images haunt 'Reflection', 'Sketches' and 'Unity.' Ghetto living is precarious, and 'Echo' and 'Tin Line' offered vivid testament to this. One minute some youth could be stood on the corner with his friends, enjoying life, and then within minutes of the police arriving he might be face down on the ground getting kicked and beaten, or being forced into a police van. Such youths walked a razor's edge, yet Wong, who had intimate knowledge of their situation, addressed them with a mix of hope, strength and pride in 'Change Yes Change.' Because yes, they had to change, 'but not into a zombie, puppet, jumping to the snap of the establishment.'

The I Three's Judy Mowatt gave a copy of Wong's book to Bob Marley. Her latest single, 'Black Woman', was the finest tribute to black womanhood yet recorded, with lyrics telling them to pray for strength, and acknowledging how their journey began on the auction blocks when they were chained and sold, 'handled merchandise.'

Back in London, anticipation ran high in advance of Burning Spear's two nights at the Rainbow Theatre in early October. He'd taken his Jamaican musicians with him to the US, but was backed by Aswad on those UK dates.

'When I first met Burning Spear in the rehearsal room, it was like meeting Moses come down from the mountain,' recalled Drummie. 'I just looked at him in awe. He had one pant leg rolled up, and I'd never seen anything like that before. You could feel the power coming from him, and I had the same feeling when we worked in the studio with Bob Marley. It was overpowering, because we were just youths from over here, and we were around all these legends from Jamaica.'

Aswad weren't really a backing band as such. They didn't have the same level of experience as the Cimarons, for example, and were only offered the gig after Steel Pulse, who were the support act, had turned it down. West London's finest had been thrown in at the deep end, although two of Spear's regular backing musicians – trumpeter Bobby Ellis and conga player Phillip Fulwood – were there to ensure things ran smoothly. Or at least that was the general idea.

'I remember the first time I played the Rainbow,' Spear told me. 'That was a really exciting concert. The first night it was so loud, and then the second night there was a lot of police. Far more people turned up than they'd expected, and I remember being asked not to sing certain songs in case they stirred up the atmosphere. That's because on the first night, when I was singing songs like 'Slavery Days', people were getting out of control. A lot of stuff was taking place, and then all of a sudden we saw all these additional police with dogs and the fire brigade… they treated the crowd like they were in control, but people were getting wild!

'That's why, on the second night, they told me that if I'm going to be singing 'Slavery Days', then the show can't take place. Because they were hiding a lot of things from people. Nobody was telling them about the true history of Africa, about slavery and how the people had been treated. Nobody was saying anything about that. And so when I came and started to sing songs like those, everybody was astonished! That's when the authorities say, "who is this guy?" Because that wasn't going to take place again.'

His statement about nobody having told black people in Britain about their African ancestry wasn't entirely true, as Alex Haley's six-part TV series *Roots* – which traced his family's history, from the time his distant relative Kunta Kinte was abducted from an African village and sold into slavery – had been screened on British television back in January, and was of the zeitgeist even before Spear's Rainbow performances. Steel Pulse's live show was also striking, albeit for different reasons.

'Michael Riley got the idea for our costumes and was big on presentation,' wrote singer/guitarist Basil Gabbidon on his website. 'When we appeared on stage at the Rainbow, the whole place went crazy. I wore African robes, Ronnie dressed up as a sultan, David wore a convict costume with arrows and Michael looked like a preacher with a wide-rimmed Quaker hat. We looked very different and that helped.'

Burning Spear played two more shows at the Rainbow in late October, again backed by Aswad and with Steel Pulse as support. The night of that final Rainbow appearance, Steel Pulse signed to Island Records, A&R Denise Mills going backstage and offering them a contract on the spot, which they accepted. They accompanied Spear on the rest of his British tour, playing further dates in Bristol, Manchester, Birmingham and Nottingham.

By then, certain UK reggae bands were sharing bills with punk bands. The Roundhouse in Chalk Farm hosted a night called Reggae

Meets Punk in September, featuring the Cimarons, Slaughter & The Dogs and Black Slate, who also appeared with various punk bands at the Vortex on Wardour Street. Delroy Washington, celebrating the release of his latest album *Rasta*, performed at the 100 Club on Oxford Street one night when there was a majority of young white punks in the audience. Journalist Dave Hendley was there and noted that the marriage of punk and reggae was 'causing some strange and pretty ironic situations.' After watching punks shouting 'Jah' and 'Rastafari!' he asked, 'do punks really think they'd be happy in Ethiopia?'

Lee Perry produced the Clash's new single 'Complete Control', which a spokesperson said told the story of 'a conflict between two opposing camps both of which are using the tool of change to further their own beliefs.' Footage from the band's White Riot tour was included in *The Punk Rock Movie*, directed by Don Letts, which had recently made its screen debut at the ICA in central London. What this film lacked technically didn't matter all that much, since it took viewers right to the heart of the action as the Sex Pistols let rip during their show at Islington's Screen on the Green, and also backstage at places like the Roxy.

Six thousand miles away, in Jamaica, fellow director Ted Bafaloukos had been showing rushes of his film *Rockers* to the cast and crew before returning to New York, where it was scheduled to premiere in February '78. As he prepared to leave, President Samora Machel of Mozambique – 'a great African freedom fighter' – arrived on the island and was greeted by crowds of people lining the streets. He and Prime Minister Michael Manley held what was euphemistically billed as 'an anti-imperialist rally' at the National Arena on 8 October, where Machel was awarded the Order of Jamaica and presented with keys to the city. Immaculately dressed in traditional African robes, this charismatic figure spoke eloquently of how Mozambique was embroiled in a civil war, and faced severe pressure from the apartheid government of South Africa. The Mystic Revelations Of Rastafari (now led by Count Ossie's son Time),

United Africa, dread poets Orlando Wong and Michael Smith and a combined schools choir all performed in his honour, and then on 16 October, Jamaica welcomed Cuban leader Fidel Castro on his first visit to the country. Two days later, after having been met by the Governor General and a 21-gun salute, he too was awarded the Order of Jamaica at a massive rally – this time held in Sam Sharpe Square and attended by a 70,000 strong crowd. Castro told them that Cuba would never interfere with the internal affairs of Jamaica or disrespect the sovereign rights of its people. 'However,' he said, 'we know what the people want. They want justice, equality, liberty and dignity, because all people of sound thinking want these.'

Lee 'Scratch' Perry's behaviour was already erratic, but the studied indifference of certain musicians, and the antics of several crazed Rastafarians, would push his patience to the limit. A group of Bobo Ashanti dreadlocks known as the Nyahbinghi Theocracy had recently taken up residence at the Black Ark at Perry's invitation, and their presence had an unsettling effect on him. Singer Robert Palmer, who was signed to Island, passed through soon after Scratch's return to Jamaica, hoping to get tracks finished for his *Double Fun* album. Palmer wasn't an obvious choice of collaborator, and yet he professed admiration for Scratch's production skills. He found it hard to deal with the constant haranguing from members of the Theocracy, though, who thought nothing of interrupting studio sessions and making things uncomfortable for visitors. Scratch intimated that he was powerless to stop them, but the strain was clearly getting to him. Palmer survived to tell the tale – as did Wayne Jobson and members of Native – but there were growing concerns that all was not well at the Black Ark, despite Perry's burgeoning reputation overseas. Paul and Linda McCartney had visited there on 20 June when they'd worked on tracks intended for Linda's debut solo album, but the intensity, drive and enthusiasm that Scratch once had was no longer there. Max Romeo had already left, and the Congos, Junior Murvin and George Faith soon followed.

When Perry had got other people to sing and play overdubs on Bob Marley's 'Punky Reggae Party' the Meditations' Ansel Cridland was among the first he'd called upon. The group had recently completed their second album *Wake Up*, which was again produced by Dobby Dobson. It was a mystery why the Meditations hadn't become more successful, since they were just as talented as most of their rivals, and Ansel was a first-rate songwriter. Island and Virgin both missed out, but their relationship with Dobby ended after they began asking questions about where the money had gone.

'I was paying for airplay in New York City and they thought that because tracks from their album were playing on the radio it had sold a million,' Dobby explained. 'I laughed and said that it was just advertising, but eventually I just gave the album to them. I said, "here, take the record and see how many it is selling for yourselves," and that was the end of it.'

Dennis Bovell experienced similar problems after inviting Sufferers' MC Pebbles to deejay on the 12-inch of Errol Dunkley's 'A Little Way Different.' This was a new version of a song that Errol had originally voiced for Sonia Pottinger, and it was an immediate hit in the UK. Dennis and Aswad's Drummie Zeb built the rhythm, Janet Kay sang harmonies and Julio Finn, US bluesman Billy Boy Arnold's brother, played harmonica. It was Dennis who wrote the lyrics, but the props that Pebbles received from being on that record went to his head and he, too, felt hard done by.

'That was kind of sad, because I had brought him onto the sound system from a young boy,' said Bovell. 'I practically schooled him in the deejay thing, because I was standing right next to him during the recording, telling him the lyrics so he could repeat them in sync with the rhythm. I did all that just to give him a helping hand and he ended up wanting to sue me, yet I was his autocue!'

Matumbi were in a state of flux, despite the success of 'Man In Me.' Trojan wanted new product, and since there wasn't any, they issued *The Best Of Matumbi* after having unearthed a bunch of tracks recorded between 1972-74. The majority of them were unfinished – some even had guide vocals – although the band's cover of the Temptations' 'Law Of The Land', produced by Joe Sinclair, was the genuine article. Everyone knew by then that Dennis Bovell was one of those gifted individuals who could turn his hand to virtually anything musical, writing lyrics, playing instruments and producing and mixing tracks. His star was on the rise, though Eddy Grant had been doing the same kind of thing for even longer, and when he sang 'It's Our Time', he could well have been talking about himself.

That track was taken from his *Message Man* album, which had been three years in the making and heralded a remarkable transition from his previous pop persona into a serious artist. The painting on the sleeve was of a new look Eddy Grant, with dreadlocks, dressed in black leather and looking like he meant business. Indeed, he did, having written all the songs, played every instrument, sung all the vocal parts and produced the whole thing, as well as having masterminded his recent change of direction. Fans of the Equals would have been surprised at tracks like 'Cockney Black', 'Race Hate' and 'Curfew' which were dark, politically aware missives laced with aggression and anger, although the album did include some lighter moments, 'Hello Africa' for example, which he'd recorded in a style no one had a name for at the time. Grant dubbed it 'kaisoul', since it was a fusion of kaiso, which is the traditional word for calypso, and soul. The legendary Lord Shorty then labelled it 'solka' but neither term stuck until the Trinidad and Tobago press came up with the word 'soca.'

In those days it was virtually impossible for any black artist in Britain to earn due recognition for their talents, let alone own their studio and run a successful record label and distribution company. Eddy managed all of that whilst maintaining his solo career and producing other acts such as the Pioneers and his brother Rudy, aka The Mexicano, who had a big hit with 'Move Up Starsky.'

'It was very disappointing,' said Eddy. 'The powers that be didn't know or realise the value of the black population in this country.

In England there had been a reluctance to acknowledge that there was value in the black British people, and it wasn't going to change. I went to see Derek Chinnery, who was in charge of the BBC's music department. My brother and sister insisted that I go and see him, because I'd been speaking to the media quite a lot about how black artists were treated. I was saying how radio DJs would prefer to play a black American's record than develop artists from over here, so I went to see Tim Blackmore over at Capital Radio and told him the same thing. I told them both that they didn't understand our frustration and if they didn't – by dint of their programming – inspire young British black children to recognise their own heroes, then they were going to stunt the development of music in this country. I hope they listened, but it wasn't long after that we had the riots and we started to see policemen having to carry weapons on the street...'

Island finally issued 'Punky Reggae Party' in early December on the flipside of 'Jamming.' The single climbed to number nine in the UK but Chris Blackwell's dislike of 'Punky Reggae Party' was entirely justified. Did Bob Marley really write lines like 'I hope you are hearty, so please don't be naughty for it's a punky reggae party'? If not, why on earth did he agree to sing them? Another reggae song in the British charts that month gifted Joe Gibbs his biggest ever crossover hit. Althea & Donna's 'Uptown Top Ranking' had been topping the charts in Jamaica for weeks, and by Christmas Eve it was number one in the UK as well. The girls had voiced it over the same rhythm as Trinity's 'Three Piece Suit', and the deejay wasn't best pleased. Jealous, he complained that they'd ripped off his idea, but their cut was a lot more accessible. It was extremely catchy, and gawkily delivered by two girls enjoying life as they sashayed down the road in their halter neck tops, hot pants and high heels, or cruised Kingston in their Mercedes Benz – uptown top ranking, indeed, despite their lack of pedigree. Althea Forrest's CV only stretched to a couple of tunes for Derrick Harriott, whilst Donna Reid – the tall one with glasses and an oversize Afro – had no track record at all. They got lucky, basically, but their record was fun, and brought a taste of Jamaican dancehall to mainstream audiences overseas. It even won John Peel's approval, which Dave Henley seized upon in his end-of-year summary for *Black Music*.

'At the moment, reggae is the fashionable thing to be into amongst the punks, so Jamaican musicians find themselves with a bigger white audience than ever before,' he wrote. 'The punks and the rock press, who invented the connection between reggae and punk when they were running out of things to write about, like to think they're well into the heaviest sounds around, yet there is little progress when the likes of John Peel sing the praises of the appalling 'Uptown Top Ranking.' 1977 was supposed to be some big deal as the year when the two sevens clashed. Marcus Garvey had made a prophecy that this year would bring great upheaval and change, though he was only specific in that there would be unrest on the boundary of St Jago De La Vega and Kingston. Somehow the punks and rock press really latched onto this and never let us forget it all year. Unfortunately the musicians and singers couldn't live up to the expectations of Garvey's words. Instead of new powerful music, we were bombarded with Three Piece Suits, Natty BMWs and trivial rhymes about being top ranking – all set to monotonous and unimaginative rhythms. The word seemed to be "play safe, sit back and let the cash roll in." The artists acted like a bunch of clowns, more interested in jewellery and the commercial potential of their "dread" image than the suffering that remains unchanged just a few blocks away.'

CHAPTER NINE

1978: DREAD, BEAT AN' BLOOD

In the New Year, an undercover agent from the Military Intelligence unit of the Jamaican army approached some youths belonging to Chubby Dread's POW Posse – a gang of JLP affiliates based in the Southside district of Central Kingston – and told them he was looking to hire drivers and bodyguards at a rate of JA$300 a day. To prove that his offer was legitimate, he took one of the group to a hotel, where he was introduced to 'the Boss', who showed him four submachine guns and said there was another consignment on its way. The gang member was impressed and given forms for him and his friends to fill in – forms that also required photographs, so that each of them could be issued with driving licenses and security passes. A date was then set for them all to meet the Boss and demonstrate their proficiency with firearms.

They agreed to meet at the Caymanas Golf Club on the morning of 5 January, and at 4.30 a.m. three vehicles duly arrived in Southside; two of them bore a Red Cross insignia, while the other was a green sedan. Ten Southside men were waiting and, after being searched by four undercover security personnel, boarded the vehicles. All was well until it became apparent that they weren't heading for the golf club, but a military firing range in Green Bay, south of Port Henderson.

According to the *Star Report*, once they'd arrived they were met by a man in civilian clothes who persuaded four of the gang members to carry a large box of ammunition to the centre of the range. They were also told to 'bundle together', in case they were spotted by fishermen. The ambush had been staked out well in advance of the youths' arrival. Ten undercover militia were ordered to do the actual killing, and ten others positioned around the perimeter of the range told to pick off anyone who tried to escape. At 5.30 a.m. the first shots rang out, and the four youths who'd carried the box of ammunition were killed instantly. Another was killed after realising that it was a trap, but the five remaining youths were standing too close to the undercover men and so weren't fired upon. Shouts of 'cease fire' were heard, as they ran in a blind panic. One threw himself into the sea whilst the others ran across the limestone craters and cacti of the Hellshire hills. All five escapees managed to get back to Southside somehow.

The ambush had gone badly wrong, but the first uniformed police didn't arrive at the scene until six hours later, when they were told there'd been a shootout with armed youths. A spokesperson for the security forces maintained that survivors were holed up in the area, and some were badly injured. This falsity resulted in a manhunt and search that lasted two days and involved helicopters, police tracker dogs and scores of police and security forces. The police were clearly oblivious to the fact that the youths had been searched before leaving Southside. They also set fire to scrubland around the scene, thus destroying valuable evidence, and then took the victims' bodies to Spanish Town. These police officers were either fed false information, or knowingly fed false information to the media on the day of the murders, since the official story was that fourteen suspicious looking men had been seen going into the hills towards the range. When they were surprised, these men had then allegedly turned their fire on the security forces, and five of them had been killed on the spot during the exchange of gunfire.

Members of the Jamaica Defence Force had been targeted and

killed in the period leading up to the Green Bay killings, strengthening claims that the perpetrators were renegade soldiers looking to avenge the murder of their colleagues. One of the grisliest details to emerge from the inquiry was that the dead men – who all had live rounds of ammunition planted on their persons – had been shot in the head by machine guns. A survivor said that a flashlight had been shone on them as they lay dead or dying and that's when they were shot. One of them was the singer Glenroy Richards, whose last single was 'Wicked Can't Run Away' for Southside producer Glen Brown.

It later transpired that the police involvement in the cover-up had been minimal, but the government's role in what came to be known as the Green Bay Massacre would come under increasing scrutiny. Minister of security Dudley Thompson denied that any Cubans had been involved or that any were attached to the Intelligence unit. He also foolishly declared that 'no angels died at Green Bay', making the situation even worse. Rumours suggesting that leading politicians had been complicit in the murder of opposition supporters no longer seemed so far-fetched. Then, on 10 January, a miracle occurred after representatives of warring gangs from Central and West Kingston met at the intersection of Beeston Street and Oxford Street and called for a truce. A large crowd had gathered to see and hear JLP enforcer Claudie Massop from Tivoli Gardens and Aston 'Bucky' Thompson, a PNP affiliate from Matthews Lane, urge their respective followers to put down their guns and channel their energies into building their communities. The pair were accompanied by a police inspector from Denham Town station, who smiled as several hundred onlookers chanted 'Peace! Peace! Peace!' and then marched through the streets of Hannah Town, Lizard Town and Tivoli Gardens in jubilation.

'There was a carnival atmosphere in West Kingston,' reported the *Guardian*. 'Before yesterday, the political boundaries had been well-defined. If you lived in a certain section you did not go into another without risk. After six in the evening, not even dogs ventured out. The only barking was that of guns. That gathering at Oxford Street and Beeston Street was a sight to gladden the hearts and bring tears to the eyes. People of the ghetto who had been tribalised by politics into boxed-in communities, used to say they had gone to school and played football together on the streets, but after 1967, when the guns came in, they only saw one another over the barrel of the gun. That was their story but since Monday they have lighted peace candles and hugged one another, ending the years of hostility. And yesterday they said their frustrations were lit with hope from the verbal declaration of a peace treaty. As one youth said, "This don't have anything to do with politics. We conscious now. No sense in we a kill off one another, we get together now and that is the key."'

After declaring the truce, Massop and Thompson called a joint meeting with Manley and Seaga and demanded the provision of food, proper sanitation and decent housing for their communities and an end to tribalism. In addition they said that what few government jobs there were should be allocated on merit and not patronage, and that 'the reign of exploitation by self-interested politicians had to stop.'

There was no free ride for people living in government housing projects, even if many of them didn't pay rent or water rates. They paid in other ways instead, called upon for favours, especially when election time came around. They owed allegiance to the politicians and their henchmen, and the same applied to those who worked hard for a living, as well as the ghetto poor – the majority of whom struggled on a daily basis to find enough money to survive. This is the meaning of 'grinding' poverty – it's the kind that sucks the life out of people, that grinds them down to nothing, strips them of their dignity, independence, well-being and so much else besides. With all that comes poor health, a lack of education and general unsuitability for work – decades of disaffection and social neglect having beaten the work ethic out of a lot of ghetto people, especially after being forced to live hand-to-mouth. Children, too, were drawn into this same precarious state of existence as their parents – quite often just their mothers – struggled to care for them. Some attempted to make a profit by buying a packet of chewing gum or cigarettes and then selling the contents one by one, whilst others resorted to prostitution and crime. It's a miracle such people could survive. On top of all that, many were terrorised by gunmen and had to live with the constant threat of violence.

This is why news of a peace treaty was met with such joy. It meant an end – however short-lived – to the fear and intimidation, and offered people a chance to live their lives in relative safety. Days later, 'generals' from both sides of the political divide – including Claudie Massop and PNP henchman Tony Welch – journeyed to London where they met with Bob Marley and told him their idea of staging a concert in Kingston that could raise much-needed funds for regeneration projects in some of the ghetto areas that had been most badly affected by political in-fighting. Marley liked what he heard and gave his backing for a One Love Peace Concert to be held at Kingston's National Stadium on 22 April – the twelfth anniversary of Emperor Haile Selassie I's state visit to Jamaica.

As the Kingston warlords had headed for London, Virgin boss Richard Branson and his party were travelling in the opposite direction. The label had started to get large orders for reggae releases from Nigeria, and according to Virgin co-founder Simon Draper, 'it had become clear that something extraordinary was happening there, and that reggae had suddenly become a massive new fad. That's when Richard went off on his trip to Jamaica with suitcases stuffed full of money, to sign up as many reggae artists as possible. Then we started the Front Line label, so we could put all this material out without flooding Virgin. We had acres of it, and in the end we were chartering Jumbo jets to take all of these records out to Nigeria.'

'They were greedy, because they could see the chance to make lots of money,' Johnny Rotten later told *Sounds*' Vivien Goldman.

Rotten, who'd reverted to his real name of John Lydon, had already quit the Sex Pistols but was still the subject of intense media attention. In his autobiography he wrote how, 'after the Pistols broke up, Branson wanted to sign up a load of reggae bands, and the only white person he knew in the world who knew about reggae was me. I told him I couldn't go there alone so I roped in two associates – Don Letts and Dennis Morris.'

It was blatantly untrue that Branson didn't know any other white people to fill that role, as Virgin staff members Jumbo Vanrenen, Simon Draper, Gaylene Martin and John Varnom all had a great love of reggae and knew a tremendous amount about it, having licensed and worked on a good many releases already. The fact is that Jumbo and Draper, being South African, couldn't get visas for Jamaica, so Branson invited Lydon instead – not as an A&R man, but to keep him from the paparazzi who were tailing his every move. Alas, no one had remembered to get him and Don Letts US entry visas, and upon arriving in Miami they were escorted to their transfer plane by armed guards. They and the rest of Branson's entourage, including Goldman and Virgin director Ken Berry, eventually landed at Kingston airport on 3 February and headed for the Sheraton Hotel in New Kingston, where they had use of an entire floor for a month.

Vivien Goldman once described the Sheraton as a 'somewhat offensive institution, a bland crate of a skyscraper' and 'the last bastion of American imperialism.' It was the same hotel in a scene from *The Harder They Come*, where Jimmy Cliff drives around the grounds in a white convertible. But the Sheraton's veneer of opulence didn't bear close scrutiny since the escalator didn't work, the carpets were worn and there were cracks in the wooden balconies. Guests would sit at round white tables by the pool under a big Sheraton 'S' logo whose reflection could be seen in the water. Potted plants were dotted here and there, whilst the poolside bar hosted a stream of visitors who probably wouldn't have been allowed access in normal circumstances, but were drawn there like moths to a flame by the promise of generous advances for having signed to Virgin's new label.

'It got so that you felt like you were wading through your singles collection every time you went to get a glass of water,' Vivien famously reported in *Sounds*.

'There was an exodus to the Sheraton, and when I say "exodus", I'm not exaggerating,' added Don Letts. 'From our perspective, these guys were legends. They were superstars. But once we got there we began to realise that they might have big names in London or Birmingham, but on the streets of Jamaica they were sufferers. The old guard were still fighting down Rastafari and the colonial legacy was still very much in evidence at the hotel as well. Basically Branson was picking up the bill and they had to go with the flow but there were waiters at the hotel gritting their teeth at seeing all these Rastas lounging by the poolside, drinking Red Stripe and eating good food. It was one of those magical times, though. The Abyssinians would break into some three-part harmonies and then the Gladiators would try and mash them up, I tell you! I-Roy was such a loud and vocal character, as well...

'From what I remember, Richard Branson held his corner. He couldn't understand what was going on when someone spoke in heavy patois, but those guys were looking for a record deal and they weren't stupid. Branson was open to their talent, so there was some common ground there despite the cultural divide, and some of them had already performed in the UK by then. I mean, Richard never ventured out of the hotel, God bless him, but then again, why should he? I'm always telling people that for some Jamaica is a paradise, whereas for others it's a bit of a gamble.'

Whilst Branson rarely ventured into Kingston, his fellow travelers did, despite the volatile surroundings.

'John and I met U-Roy, granddaddy of deejay reggae music,' Don continued. 'You get up with the sun over there, so we'd go round to U-Roy's and get high with him at eight in the morning. U-Roy would make up a big pipe of weed in his back yard. Each cup held a quarter ounce of weed and half an inch of tobacco. I tried to smoke this huge pipe and immediately coughed my guts out. John picked up the pipe and somehow drew the biggest load of smoke. I was ashamed! The guy upstaged me in my roots back yard. U-Roy was saying, "Yes Rotten, cool Rasta."

'One day, Tapper Zukie decided he'd show us the real Jamaica, so he took us to Rema. When we got there we said, "where are all the guns?" because we'd heard that Rema was this really tough place. No sooner had we said that than these guys started pulling guns out from everywhere and John and I were shitting ourselves, because if you were even *seen* with a gun in that time you got indefinite detention. There was all of this political violence going on, which is one of the reasons we spent a lot of time at the hotel. I remember when we arrived at the airport, we were going to hire a car and the man was saying, "don't get a green or a red car because if you drive the wrong colour car in the wrong part of town you're a dead man."'

The JLP's colour was green, and red belonged to the PNP. Even the beer was polarised by politics, with JLP supporters favouring Heineken and their PNP counterparts Red Stripe. Avoiding such coded displays of allegiance could prove difficult, but the Virgin's party trip proved memorable in so many other ways. One day Don accompanied Lydon to the Black Ark, where Lee Perry was attempting another reggae/punk hybrid.

'Some bright spark had the idea of getting Lee Perry to do covers of some Pistols' songs, and sure enough, one day John and I found ourselves in the studio with him as they had a go at reggae versions of songs like 'Anarchy In The UK.' It wasn't so much "dread at the controls", as "bread at the controls." The room was full of ganja smoke, but it wasn't Lee Perry's best work, let's put it that way. Thankfully, those tracks never saw the light of day, but they do exist.'

The two tracks laid that day were 'Submission' and 'Problems', and they're just as bad as Don remembered. Before the Virgin party had left for Jamaica, Jumbo had given Richard Branson a list of records and bands he should try and sign. The Congos' *Heart Of The Congos* was on it, but that deal never happened. Branson thought that he'd made up for this by signing Althea & Donna's album instead, which Jumbo later admitted was a mistake. He felt rather better about I-Roy's *Heart Of A Lion*, which became the first Front Line album in late February 1978, although I-Roy had already done business with Virgin prior to that works outing to Kingston.

'I-Roy was a wonderful character,' remembered Gaylene Martin. 'I just loved I-Roy, and he was very smart too. I remember him carrying this briefcase, and in it was a paper bag stuffed with cash. He was always so well-dressed. He clearly spent a lot of money on clothes, and was such a gentleman.'

Heart Of A Lion was a joint production between I-Roy and Harry J, who also issued an album of I-Roy material produced by Niney called *Hotter Yatta*. That and the Bunny Lee collection *The Godfather* suggested that Virgin had competition, but neither could match Front Line's trailblazer thanks to its superior promotion and distribution, and the deejay's usual diverse mix of lyrics which flitted between reality ('Peace In The City'), low level slackness ('Miss Catty') and culture, as heard on 'Move Up Roots Man', produced by Jack Ruby. I-Roy fans were used to surprises, but it was still a shock when Micron then unleashed *The Ten Commandments* – an album of Bob Marley rhythms, all but one of which came from *Exodus*. The year before, Pete Weston's company had commissioned Canadian band Chalawa to play Marley's *Exodus* album in its entirety, without vocals. Weston then used that same *Exodus Dub* as the basis for I-Roy's set, which must have left the Front Line team wondering what on earth was going to happen next. Situations like that happened because Jamaican artists were prolific and needed to keep recording new songs in order to make a living, and also because Virgin was mainly licensing albums and not actually signing artists, since that would have entailed spending a lot more money and assuming greater responsibility. They'd chosen the cheaper option, and then had to rely on better marketing and distribution to give them the upper hand in any race for sales with other companies releasing albums by the same artists.

The Front Line office was situated above a taxi firm on Woodfield Road, just off the Harrow Road. It was a fair distance from Virgin's main offices in Vernon Yard, just off the Portobello Road, and ganja was smoked openly there, which must have delighted many of their Jamaican visitors. The Gladiators' *Proverbial Reggae* was among the label's first releases, along with albums by Prince Hammer – who Linton Kwesi Johnson described as 'an intelligent, consistent impresario of word music' – Jah Lloyd and U Brown. Count Shelly had sponsored the latter's recent trip to London and his first-ever UK shows at places like Club Noriek and the Four Aces. During that visit the deejay had befriended soundman Ken 'Fat Man' Gordon, who co-produced tracks on *Mr Brown Something*. This alliance didn't last and morale wasn't too good within the Twinkle Brothers' camp either after Norman Grant recorded some of the tracks on *Love* at Channel One with the Revolutionaries, rather than his fellow band members.

'Some of the members of the group didn't like it,' Grant later admitted. 'They thought it was too much hustle. When we recording there, people were stealing food from lorries that had been left there to unload into the shops, so there was a curfew and policemen everywhere. We were being stopped and searched on our way to the studio. It was the right atmosphere to make rebel music!'

In 1977, Derrick Harriott had released an album, *Go Deh Wid Riddim*, that was marketed as if it was a solo outing by Revolutionaries' drummer Sly Dunbar. It wasn't though. It was just some rhythm tracks that Sly had played on, and his debut LP proper was *Simple Sly Man*, which he'd recorded at Channel One after meeting with Richard Branson in February. He and Robbie Shakespeare were a regular pairing by then, although Robbie usually played rhythm guitar or piano with the Revolutionaries, not bass.

Every Thursday they'd play a minimum of a dozen or so rhythms for Joe Gibbs, and then on Fridays and Saturdays they'd do the same for Bunny Lee. In-between they played sessions at Channel One, either for the Hoo Kims or whoever else hired them. Normally a producer would hire the studio, pay the musicians a flat fee and then own the rights to whatever came out of the sessions. The relationship between the Hoo Kim brothers and Sly, who was a linchpin of Channel One's house band, was different since he was given permission to use any of their rhythms for his own album. The overdubbed versions that appear on *Simple Sly Man* turned out to be a lot more imaginative than even Virgin had expected. The 25-year-old drummer even recruited Tyrone Downie to play what he calls 'a talk box' on one track.

'It was something you plugged a keyboard into, then he'd put this thing like a tube in his mouth,' said Sly, 'but Tyrone was a very groovy guy and he and I were born in the same month so whenever we were together anything could happen! We both liked to experiment with different sounds and bring something new to the table – it might be from another culture, because I was always trying to do that. It might just be 1 per cent, but that could still be enough, y'know?'

Althea & Donna appeared on several tracks, including 'A Who Say', whilst Chicago rocker Jimmy Becker played harmonica on 'Nigger Whitey' and former Hitbound single 'Sun Is Shining.' The latter also featured Black Uhuru's Michael Rose. In the aftermath of *Simple Sly Man*, Sly decided to invest some of the advance he got from Virgin in resurrecting the Taxi label, thereby allowing him and Robbie more control over their creative output. They'd chosen that name because Sly traveled around Kingston by taxi and, as Robbie recalled, they got 'a lot of jokes out of that.'

His and Sly's focus was always on the music and they left social commentary and religious proselytising to others. Music was the key that opened all doors and that's how they liked it, but this wasn't an option for many of the artists they worked with, unless they wanted to be considered irrelevant or relegated to the hotel and cabaret circuit. Tapper Zukie had no such qualms – hence the photo on the inner sleeve of his Front Line album *Peace In The Ghetto*, declaring 'Welcome To Rema, Peace And Love Everyone.'

'Is this a dream?' he asked on the opening track. For the first time in over a decade there was peace in areas like Rema, Jungle, Tivoli and Lizard Town, thanks to the likes of Claudie Massop – a young black hero come from the ghetto who according to the lyrics, had been sent to prison many times despite being innocent of any crime. It's fanciful, yes, but the joy in Tapper's song – and also tracks like 'Praise Jah In Gladness' and 'Peace In The City' – was real enough. Bunny Lee, quick-witted as ever, produced this album, which also included 'Tribute To Steve Biko', the South African activist who was cruelly murdered by the security forces in September '77. To coincide with its release, *Sounds* published an article by Vivien Goldman entitled 'Peace Fighter.' Tapper had collected her from the Sheraton in February and taken her to Rema, where he was building a youth centre. Goldman likened Rema to 'a great grey council estate.'

'Dating from the pre-high rise era,' Goldman wrote, 'it's essentially squalid in its very conception. Just one block, then another square block, then another surrounding a great grey courtyard, like a dismally run-down school playground. On the low concrete wall surrounding the estate there's a row of men, doubtless part of Kingston's 60 per cent unemployed, smoking their first spliffs of the day. Well, probably not their first – it's about 11 a.m., and you get up early in Jamaica.'

One of the youths there told her that the troubles had begun in 1972 with Manley's election victory. The PNP had armed their supporters in Jungle, who then began terrorising the people of Rema, aided by rogue police. 'That's how most of my brethren, the youth from Rema, dead up,' he said. 'The police them start shoot up the place, and everybody here have to take cover. We can't defend ourselves. Every day it would continue, they would come in and mash up the people. Pure war and so it was from February 1972 until now...'

Tapper had become an important spokesperson for ghetto people, and it's therefore ironic that his biggest hit from the album was 'Dangerous Woman', written about a troublesome girl who'd given him one headache after another, hence it's alternative title of 'She Want A Phensic.' He hadn't wanted to put it out at first, because of any confusion it might cause – he wanted to be seen as a serious artist – but people loved his descriptive innuendos and it sold well both on Front Line and Tapper's own Stars label in Jamaica. Whilst Front Line did release the occasional single to try and get national airplay for some of its reggae roster, Gaylene Martin says this was 'a complete non-starter.'

'I was trying to get appointments with daytime radio producers and it was impossible. It was like hitting a brick wall,' Martin said. 'John Peel was the exception, and also Janice Long [another Radio 1 presenter] but it was so difficult to get any kind of coverage on daytime radio or in the daily newspapers, because they just wouldn't have anything to do with reggae. They were only interested if there was a scandal of some kind, or if an artist had a Top 10 hit. Also, for a band to do radio or television work here, they had to apply for a visa before entering the country. There was some kind of exchange deal going on between musicians here and from around the world, and so it wasn't as if Jamaican acts could just turn up and do promotional work.'

'Certain journalists were sympathetic and pursued reggae stories and artists,' added Jumbo Vanrenen. 'The *NME*, in particular, which had a weekly circulation of 400,000 at the time, but also *Sounds, Melody Maker* and the *Observer. Black Music* under Chris May was very supportive, and also *Black Echoes*, because I think we had eight records in their Top 10 reggae charts once. That was very useful!'

There's an exception to every rule, of course, and Althea & Donna were it. They'd recently arrived in London for shows and to collect gold and silver discs for 'Uptown Top Ranking', which had sold 500,000 copies to date. This was no mean feat given that the two youngsters had little or no experience of the business and were managed by Donna's father Al Reid, who didn't have any experience either. Jumbo's reservations about the duo turned out to be well-founded since all of their follow-up singles flopped, beginning with the cringe-inducing 'Puppy Dog Song.' The Midas touch had deserted them, although Donna's boyfriend, reggae singer Jacob Miller, had it in abundance. He had two singles in the local charts during February, including 'Peace Treaty Special', whereupon he delighted in an end to tribalism, sang to the melody of a popular marching song. With talk of the truce on everyone's lips, it crashed into the island's Top 10, but Beres Hammond's 'One Step Ahead' was at number one, and would stay on the charts for months. Producer Harold Butler hadn't wanted to release any of the tracks from the *Soul Reggae* album as singles, so Beres and Willie Lindo took matters into their own hands and recorded 'One Step Ahead' specifically for that purpose. Their decision paid off handsomely, and when *Soul Reggae* was repressed, 'One Step Ahead' was added to it.

'From I released that song it's like all of a sudden people started talking about me, but I was just living a small life down here in Jamaica until then,' said Beres. 'It's not like it grew slowly either, because everything happened overnight, and then people started mistaking me for a foreigner! Just because I sang one or two ballads, they were thinking that I wasn't from Jamaica, and that made me unsure. Also I never had any management back then, so I was just fighting the battle all on my own, y' know?'

In late February, the Corporate Area's Peace Committee staged a free show at the Ambassador Youth Training Centre in Trench Town featuring Delroy Wilson, Ruddy Thomas, the Mighty Diamonds and Trinity. He was currently riding high with 'Starsky & Hutch', with lyrics inspired by the American TV series. Judging by 'Premo Ballerina' and tracks from his three – three! – albums for Bunny Lee, Clint Eastwood was more than a match for his brother. 'Premo Ballerina' was one of two Bunny Lee cuts to the *Death In The Arena* rhythm, recorded at Channel One by the Revolutionaries. The other was by Johnny Clarke and sounded more like a dubplate. It was thus entirely in keeping with grassroots' tastes. There were now marked differences between what the Jamaican public loved about their music, and the preferences of many overseas' fans who liked to mythologise what they saw and heard, or view it as entertainment. Michael Epstein of My Father's Place in Long Island knew about such tendencies only too well, because he'd been taking reggae fans down to Jamaica for three years by then.

'We'd all just get crazy!' he said. 'We'd get naked and smoke dope, and that's all we wanted to do, so I decided that we were going to do an international reggae festival in Jamaica.'

The Island Music Festival duly took place over the last weekend in February at the Trelawny Beach Hotel on Jamaica's north coast. Culture and Burning Spear opened on the Friday, Big Youth headlined on Saturday, then Peter Tosh and the Heptones closed on Sunday. There were plenty of tourists there, including the Rolling Stones' Keith Richards and Ron Wood. They watched on as Peter Tosh gave a sterling performance, even when driving rain threatened to put an end to the show. Their interest in Gregory Isaacs had been understandable, given that he was another strong-minded, outlaw-type character with questionable behavioural traits, much like Keith Richards himself. Nothing materialised from it though, and Front Line then stepped in by releasing *Cool Ruler* – an album produced by Gregory, with songs like 'Words Of The Farmer' and 'Uncle Joe' that demonstrated his belief in self-reliance. Like Sly & Robbie, he was determined to keep control over his own affairs, and all of the songs on *Cool Ruler* were self-penned, with the exception of two, one of which was an upbeat cover of John Holt's 'Let's Dance', which sat well with 'Party In The Slum' – an invitation to a ghetto dance that underlined the need for relaxation and enjoyment, even for those enduring hardship. *Cool Ruler* also had more of Gregory's trademark love songs than its predecessor *Mr Isaacs* – 'Native Woman', 'John Public' and 'One More Time', for example – but it was Burning Sounds who issued the matching dubs (on *Slum In Dub*), and another NW London company, Conflict, that released *Extra Classic*, a collection of mostly roots and reality singles from the past two or three years, including the hit 'Mister Cop', produced by Lee Perry. 'Black Against Black' was on it, and also 'Rasta Business', addressed to all those who criticise Rasta without having any understanding of what it represents. In the album's liner notes, Micron's Pete Weston wrote: 'Gregory has a simple formula. He writes the songs and he sings them from his heart, as genuine as the person he is.'

Alvin Ranglin released *The Best Of Gregory Isaacs* amidst this feeding frenzy. Everyone knew that the title was disingenuous, but what can you do? Gregory knew, since in addition to his own African Museum record store he had shares in Cash & Carry – a distribution company on Orange Street that he'd started with Trevor Douglas, aka Leggo Beast. The latter used to work for Dynamic and that's how he came to learn the business. It's also why Big Youth and Bunny Wailer both followed Gregory's example by asking Leggo to help them manage their labels. By involving someone like him, they were able to concentrate on their musical careers. Dennis Brown was another artist who would call upon him for advice from time to time. Dennis had made his debut on UK national television in early March, whilst performing 'Money In My Pocket' on *Top Of The Pops*. This latest Lightning single wouldn't go any higher than number fourteen, but the song vastly improved on the original that Joe Gibbs had released a few years ago. The sound was brighter, thanks to Sly Dunbar's irresistible new drum patterns, and the revamped 'Money In My Pocket' made a sparkling addition to other recent Dennis Brown singles such as 'A True', 'Ain't That Loving You' and 'Girl I've Got A Date.' Gibbs wasn't as creative as Niney, which is why Dennis had been singing so many cover versions of late. There'd also been questions asked concerning Dennis's possible ties with the JLP. That's because he came from a JLP area, got his breaks through a JLP event and worked with Joe Gibbs, who was a well-known JLP supporter. Not only that, but Winston Edwards – who accompanied Dennis when he signed with Lightning – was openly accused of being a CIA agent by *Race Today*'s Darcus Howe, who either had inside information or should have known better.

Despite peace having been declared, there was no escaping politics for most Jamaicans, and especially not those in the public eye. Bob Marley returned to Jamaica 'in a blaze of glory' during the second week of March. He was there to help finalise plans for the forthcoming One Love Peace Concert organised by the Central Peace Council, headed by Claudie Massop and Bucky Marshall, and formed of people representing the eight constituencies in the Corporate Area. James Fox described the 23-year-old Marshall as being, 'small and hawklike and covered with battle scars', whilst Massop was seven years older, 'tall, good looking and wore large felt hats.'

'According to Marshall, the peace movement's demands are stark,' Fox wrote. 'Equal rights and justice, the same weekly pay for everyone, free food programmes, proper sanitation and an attempt at housing. In a severely depressed economy there is not even the mention of employment.'

Massop told him that 'the people are waiting on us now. They look at us as leaders. We have to give them a response so we are asking the government to consider our demands very quickly, because these are the demands of the people.'

The scale of what Fox called 'the ghetto peace miracle' had taken politicians in both parties by surprise. There was a lot of scepticism about it among the security forces, and Michael Manley responded cautiously, as if he was waiting to see what would unfold before making a decisive statement. He and Seaga both realised that if they became too active in the peace process, then it would become compromised. Everyone involved also knew that the truce was fragile, and there was no telling how long the leaders could maintain it.

On 23 March, Island Records released Bob Marley's new album *Kaya*, which some reviewers claimed was 'too soft.' The British public didn't agree, because *Kaya* brought Marley and the Wailers their highest-ever showing on the UK album charts, and after peaking at number four, it would continue to sell steadily throughout the coming months. Yet the songs on it were all recorded during the same sessions as those on *Exodus*, so it was inevitable that *Kaya* wouldn't match up to its predecessor. 'Easy Skanking', 'Is This Love' and 'Satisfy My Soul' served to lighten the rather gloomy mood cast by 'She's Gone', 'Misty Morning' and 'Crisis', and there was ample room for conjecture about what he was saying in certain other songs. There were lines in 'Running Away' for instance, referencing his enforced exile. And was he addressing his would-be assassins in 'Time Will Tell', a song written in Nassau less than a week after the Hope Road shooting, when singing the line about unnamed people thinking they're in heaven, 'but living in hell'?

Steel Pulse's debut single for Island was 'Ku Klux Klan', and there was no ambiguity about that whatsoever.

'There were a lot of things I saw as a kid which a lot of people would just take it in stride but I took it literally,' lead singer David Hinds told Saxon Baird. 'One of the first things that hit me as a child growing up was the assassination of John F. Kennedy, then the assassination of Malcolm X and Martin Luther King Jr. All that planted in my head was, "America – this is a country where they kill people." Then one day I was reading about the Ku Klux Klan. They had a leader named David Duke who was supposed to be coming to the UK to influence leaders of the National Front, a racist political party, and advise them on how to control and contain the blacks that were living in England. That's how I got that specific song going, by imagining all of that happening. I was always in tune with what was going on in the US and the history of it... also by watching movies of these guys running around wearing white cloaks and everything else.'

When Steel Pulse sang it on British television, Hinds had stepped to the mic and said 'this one goes straight to the head of the National Front, and straight to the head of the Ku Klux Klan leader, David Duke.' Two of the members wore white pointed headdresses with slits cut for eyes, like those associated with the Klan, and thousands of viewers must have cheered them on from the safety of their living rooms. Britain had its own group of rebels – one that was every bit as militant and outspoken as their Jamaican counterparts.

Dennis Bovell, who'd produced Steel Pulse's early singles, performed with his band Matumbi at the *Black Echoes Awards* at Stoke Newington's Astra Cinema on 25 March. Also appearing were the Drums Of Rasta, the Blackstones and 15-16-17, who won the award for Best Female Act and were introduced as 'the Three Degrees Of Reggae' by host Castro Brown. The latter was in fine form that night, but he and *Black Echoes'* Paul Phillips would later argue after DEB issued a Various Artists album that not only used the paper's name but also their logo. This dispute was quickly resolved after Castro paid for some advertising, but he was rather less fortunate after crossing Gregory Isaacs. In 1977, DEB had released the *Mr Isaacs* album and brought Isaacs over for some UK dates. Apparently Gregory got annoyed about something Castro had said and lunged at him with a fork, causing a deep wound above his left eye. Another inch lower and DEB's CEO would have been blinded, but he and Dennis Brown remained close, and Castro was all smiles when Dennis won Best Male Singer, then came back on stage to present Tapper Zukie with his award for Best Deejay.

Tapper had arrived from Jamaica earlier that day. He'd been invited to open Patti Smith's three shows at London's Rainbow Theatre starting on 2 April – events that, according to her guitarist Lenny Kaye, 'encapsulated a moment where two different genres with the same sense of apocalyptic vision and revolutionary spirit could go forth and conquer.'

The award winning Castro Brown
© Dave Hendley

The original Congos © Dave Hendley

Dr Alimantado, the best dressed chicken © Dave Hendley

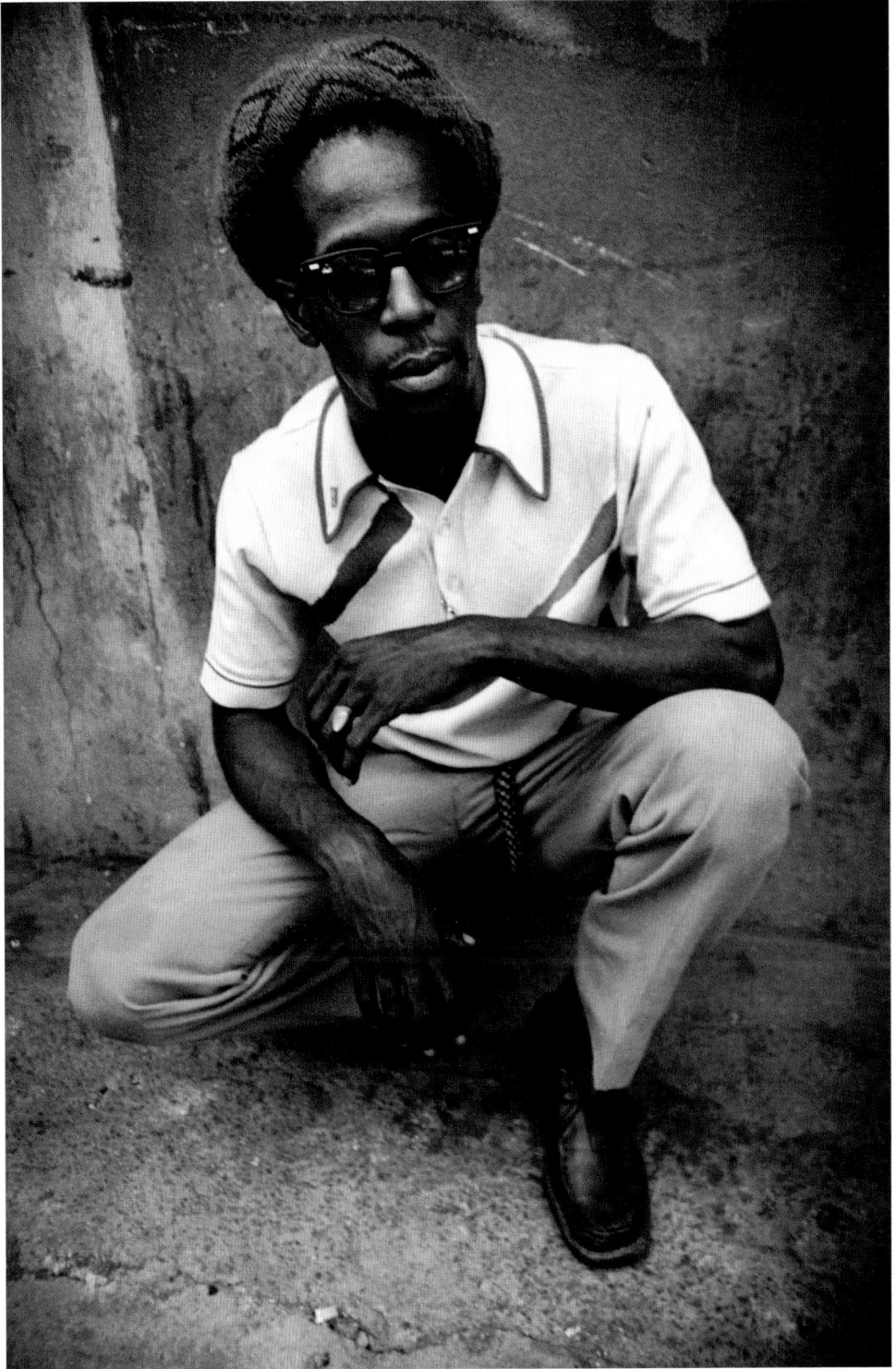
Gregory Isaacs, the Cool Ruler © Dave Hendley

King Tubby the dub master © Dave Hendley

Lee "Scratch" Perry at the Black Ark © Dave Hendley

Marcia Griffiths © Dave Hendley

Tapper Zukie, ghetto superstar © Dave Hendley

Trinity & Dillinger, two bad deejays © Dave Hendley

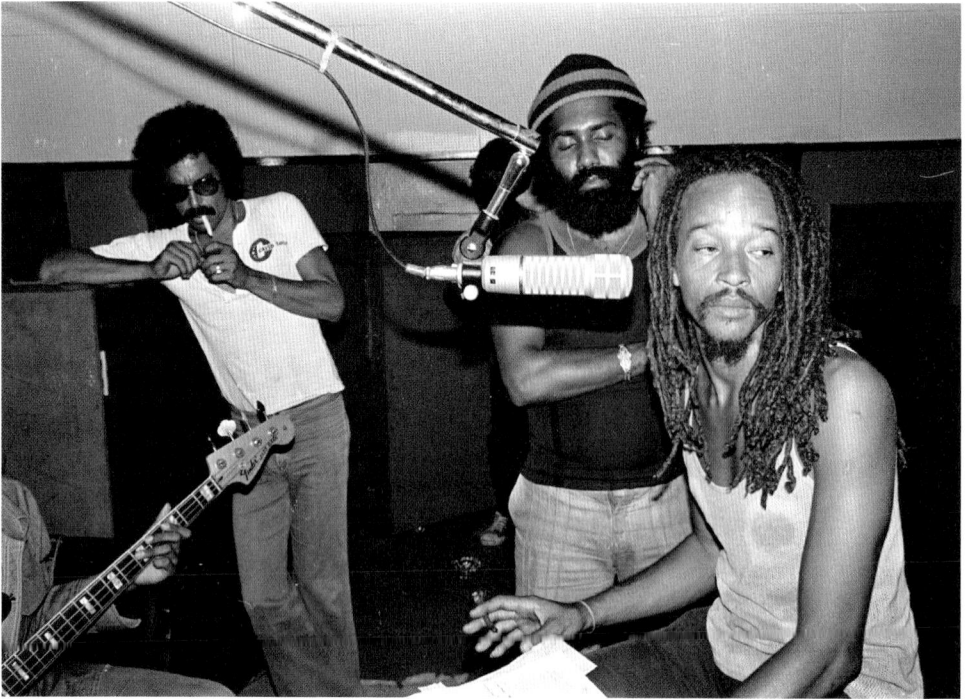
Jack Ruby & Kiddus I © Ted Bafaloukos

Jimmy Cliff in action © Ted Bafaloukos

Leroy "Horsemouth" Wallace, star of Rockers © Ted Bafaloukos

Patti Smith & Burning Spear © Ted Bafaloukos

Randy's record store on North Parade © Ted Bafaloukos

Yabby You, the Jesus Dread © Ted Bafaloukos

Smith's punk credentials were slipping, though, and not only because her latest single 'Because The Night', penned by Bruce Springsteen, was considered too poppy. A journalist with *Sounds* dubbed her 'the harridan of art rock' after she'd kicked photographers, hit someone with a walking stick and acted like 'a real little Hitler' at a press conference held soon after her arrival. 'Who died for your sins, Patti?' he asked, but Tapper wasn't complaining. She and Lenny Kaye reissued 'Viego' on their Mer label after those Rainbow shows, and Zukie also struck a deal with Virgin, who agreed to reissue his *MPLA* album in the wake of Kaye waxing lyrical about songs like 'Pick Up The Rockers', 'Don't Get Crazy' and the title track.

In mid-April it was announced that the Jamaica Tourist Board and Synergy Productions were to co-host the island's first reggae extravaganza to be marketed overseas. Reggae Sunsplash would be held at Jarrett Park in Montego Bay from 23 to 30 June and whilst the line-up hadn't been finalised as yet, names already mentioned included Third World, Toots and the Maytals, Inner Circle, Burning Spear, Dennis Brown, Culture, the Heptones and U-Roy, whose latest album, *Jah Son Of Africa*, opened with a scorching, seven-minute cut to Marley's 'Exodus', again produced by Prince Tony. Jamaican nationals would be able to pre-purchase tickets at special low prices, but the main source of revenue was expected to come from overseas sales of all-inclusive packages comprised of airfare, accommodation and transportation, as well as entry to all music-related events.

If all that was to happen as planned, the promoters had to hope that the peace treaty held and media coverage of any social upheavals didn't deter people from travelling to Jamaica. No sooner had the ink dried on the Sunsplash deal than trouble flared up in central Kingston. Since the peace treaty, people's hopes and expectations had grown, and so too their impatience with the local authorities. Throughout Kingston's West End, from Rema to West Parade, the streets were lined with piles of rotting garbage and

411

there were puddles of sewage underfoot. The smell was unbelievable, and the health risks severe, especially to children. The families forced to live amidst such squalor had appealed for help to members of the Peace Council, who contacted a government minister. His response had left a lot to be desired, and as a consequence a large and hostile crowd gathered in the vicinity of the Spanish Town Road and Coronation Market. Feelings were running high and Edward Seaga, whose constituency it was, got calls to say that people had erected barricades and incidents of looting were taking place. Buses and cars had been overturned and when the police arrived, they came under fire from snipers positioned on nearby buildings. Three looters died and two policemen were injured in the skirmishes that followed, and then matters were even made worse when Seaga told the media that the violence had been started by the police.

An article in the *Gleaner* titled 'Protest From The Ghetto' made the point that such protests were the only mechanism by which poor people could draw attention to their plight, and that 'the massing of thousands of protesting and frustrated poor people inevitably invites vandalism and looting from the more adventurous.'

'The security force overreacted and in fact activated some of the confusion followed but in today's violent Jamaica, who can blame them?' asked the article. 'They are as jumpy and as nervous as any of us. What is left of the leadership of the Peace Movement hardly helps the situation. Some have lost credibility because they are increasingly viewed as puppets manipulated by party figures behind-the-scenes, while others have lost face because jobs, improved amenities and efforts to aid the desperate plight of the ghetto poor have not materialised beyond glib promises and eloquent words. Demonstration and protests are just part of the picture. Almost daily in my experience, grown men and women confront you with tears in their eyes and withered pride because "the pickney them have no food." Children wander the street like stray dogs with nothing to eat. Those of us who have jobs either get consumed by guilt or are terrified with fear that the day will come when some enraged sufferer decides to liberate what little we have. One hears stories of desperate mothers giving away children and some even selling them.'

Poor people in Jamaica didn't believe that anyone cared about them because if they did, then things would change and they wouldn't have to live in fear and poverty. The author of that article believed that Jamaican society was on a collision course 'towards deeper and deeper chasms of social conflict, tensions and confrontation that may make the recent mild disturbances look like a Sunday school picnic.' He pointed out that the government had no answer besides tough rhetoric, and that neither of the main parties had anything tangible to offer in rescuing 'a bankrupt and half-dead economy', and halting the slide towards anarchy. It was a deeply worrying forecast – one that served to underline the urgency of raising much-needed funds for development projects in Kingston's inner cities. This was the prime motivation behind staging the One Love Peace Concert and a lot rested upon the outcome, as everyone involved knew only too well.

During rehearsals for the concert, Bob Marley worked on two new songs, 'Blackman Redemption' and 'Rastaman Live Up.' What's interesting is that he recruited the Meditations, and not the I Three, to sing backing vocals on those tracks.

'We'd sung on 'Punky Reggae Party' before that, but it was still a surprise,' acknowledged Ansel Cridland. 'I was at Chancery Lane, where all the artists and musicians hang out, when Winston and Danny turned up in a taxi and said, "Bob a look fi you." I thought they were joking and said, "Bob Marley? Are you serious?" Them say, "yeah man, 'im give us some money and say that we mustn't stop until we find you." So we went to the Hope Road studio and Lee 'Scratch' Perry was there too. We start to talk and Bob say, "boy, me was there in England when me hear 'Woman Is Like A Shadow' and say, 'which group is this? Because they sound like when the Wailers just a come!" We have a laugh and a talk and then 'im say we have work to do. He start playing 'Blackman Redemption' and 'Rastaman Live Up', and me and Danny work out the harmonies. He was enjoying it, y'know? Then we do 'Buffalo Soldier', and I end up doing harmonies on that too.'

Ansel says they discussed the possibility of the group touring with Marley but there was 'a circling of the wagons' about this. Family Man objected and so it never happened. The Meditations didn't get to perform with them at the concert either, despite Bob having made entreaties on their behalf. This reluctance to indulge him, despite Marley's superstar status, might have been a consequence of the tension surrounding the One Love Peace Concert and fears of another attempt on his life. Don Taylor would later claim that shortly before the One Love concert, he and Bob were told that three of the gunmen involved in the assassination attempt back in December 1976 had been hunted down and captured – not by the police, but ghetto vigilantes. Tek Life, one of Claudie Massop's hitmen, led them to a lonely spot near McGregor Gully, where the men were being held prisoner. All had confessed to taking part in the shooting and admitted the CIA's involvement. It soon became clear that the men were to be killed, but Marley refused to take the gun that was proffered him. Two of the accused were then hanged and the other shot in the head. If there is any truth to this story, it means that both he and Marley were accomplices to murder. It would also lay waste to the notion that Bob Marley was a man of peace, who lived according to the one love philosophy that he so readily expressed in his music.

Film director Theo Bafaloukos was in Kingston for the One Love Peace Concert. He'd just arrived from Los Angeles, where he'd premiered *Rockers* at the International Film Exposition.

'In LA it had played in a big theatre with eight hundred seats. I really wasn't expecting anything, but it was packed! I don't know why that was. Maybe it was due to word of mouth or something

– it certainly didn't come from our own publicity department, who barely knew it existed.'

The only time that *Rockers* was screened in Jamaica prior to general release was at the request of Bob Marley, who watched it at Harry J's studio the night before the concert.

'It was a very heavy atmosphere,' recalled Bafaloukos. 'All these heavy-duty guys from Jungle were there, and also various people actively involved in the Peace Committee. Bob sent for us, and that was actually the film's first-ever audience in Jamaica, period. It was something that I'll never forget, but the reaction was good, which was a big relief, and Bob himself was very cool. He came up to me and said "I like it, but there's just one thing. You should have had Horsemouth wash his dreadlocks in the river." I said, "oh, okay." I mean what can you do? But it was fun...'

Rockers has been described as 'reggae's raw, righteous cinematic masterpiece', whilst the *The New York Times* rated it even more highly than *The Harder They Come*. Apart from Horsemouth, the cast included a dozen or so of the island's leading singers and musicians, including Gregory Isaacs, Burning Spear, Jacob Miller, Dirty Harry, Jack Ruby, Leroy Smart and Robbie Shakespeare. From the minute Horsemouth appears on screen, it's obvious that he's a naturally gifted actor. His real-life wife, children and family home are shown in the film, whilst the studio footage was filmed at Harry J's. To quote the press release, *Rockers* 'starts as a loose interpretation of Vittorio de Sica's *The Bicycle Thief*, and then turns into a reggae interpretation of the *Robin Hood* myth.'

As the story unfolds, so do perceptive observations about Rastafarians, religion, Jamaica's middle class and, of course, the local music industry, although the film is fast-paced, and full of wit and humour. After Horsemouth decides to make some extra money by selling records, he buys a motorcycle so he can take them around the island's shops and sound systems. One of the most memorable scenes occurs when he visits Burning Spear. The drummer's spirit is troubled, and so Spear sits him down by the water's edge and sings to him. It's a spellbinding interlude, and it happened at around seven in the evening, on 7 July 1977 – the day that all the sevens clashed.

'I told the Spear I wanted him to sing a cappella,' explained Bafaloukos, 'and to pick a song that would make him feel comfortable, so he picked 'Jah No Dead.' We filmed it close to Spear's house, because he had wanted to do it there. It was getting late and there must have been about a thousand people stood around, watching us. You don't have too much control in those situations, but you could hear a leaf drop that night, the crowd was so quiet. It's something that I've never experienced before or since. It was magical, it really was.'

There was another scene where Jacob Miller chases Dirty Harry and Horsemouth with a knife after they'd stolen some chicken off his plate. People criticised Bafaloukos for including it, saying that it was derogatory to Rastas, and yet it was Miller's idea to shoot that scene after he'd told the director, 'I want a scene for myself and to do something like I'm messing with some badness, so why don't I sit down and I'm eating, and Dirty Harry and Horsemouth come bother me, then I start chasing them?'

'He wanted to show off his skills with a ratchet or something like that,' remembered Bafaloukos, 'so I said, "okay, we can do that", because it fitted in with the scene I'd been working on anyway.'

Jacob Miller was one of the stars of the One Love Peace Concert, held the following day at the National Stadium. Posters had been plastered on walls all over the city and twenty thousand people attended, with some having arrived early in the afternoon. Tommy Cowan was in charge of logistics, whilst the event itself was produced by the Central Peace Council. Despite it being a fund-raiser, ticket prices had been kept low and security was tight. Jamaican soldiers, dressed in green army uniforms and cradling sub-machine guns, patrolled the venue, and concertgoers were searched for weapons as they filed through the entrance.

The music started at five once Lloyd Parks' We The People band cranked into action behind Culture, Althea & Donna, Trinity, U-Roy (resplendent in a pink suit) and Dennis Brown, who premiered his latest single 'To The Foundation.' He was joined by a dancer dressed in patchwork clothes, whilst U-Roy shared his set with a barefoot Rasta whose dreadlocks had metastasised into large horizontal slabs, and which threatened to unbalance him every time he moved his head. Other acts included the Mighty Diamonds, Ras Michael and the Sons Of Negus, Junior Tucker (billed as 'Jamaica's answer to Michael Jackson'), Big Youth, Dillinger, Leroy Smart and Beres Hammond, who gave his first major stage appearance that day.

It was twilight by the time Inner Circle took the stage and Jacob Miller pulled out all the stops during their performance. He lit up a spliff during 'Tired Fi Lick Weed In A Bush', wore a policeman's hat whilst singing 'Tenement Yard' and introduced members of the Peace Committee to the audience after launching into 'Peace Treaty Special.' He would have upstaged everyone else that day had he not been followed by Peter Tosh and then Bob Marley. Tosh was more outspoken than ever. 'I am not a politician,' he told the crowd, 'I just suffer the consequences.' He too openly smoked ganja – during what else but 'Legalise It' – and made a point of haranguing the prime minister and opposition leader for at least ten minutes, if not longer. 'If it was me alone every police station could a lock up and the policemen go home, yet I and I brethren end up a jail for just a little bit a ganja,' he complained, before angrily calling for equal rights, justice for all and an end to police brutality.

Tosh and Marley were originally scheduled to perform back to back, but at the last minute the I Three went on to cool the vibes a little with their own set. Mick Jagger, who'd been watching from the wings, was heard to mutter, 'just like the United Nations.' Tosh wasn't as natural a showman as Marley, but even Jagger was impressed by his power and fearlessness. It was Bob Marley's night, however, and nothing was going to spoil his and the Wailers' homecoming. Everything about his performance that night oozed international class, the band augmented by horns. Cedric Brooks, fresh from his exploits with United Africa, was part of Marley's horn section that night, along with members of Zap Pow. Their input lifted songs like 'Trench Town Rock', 'Natty Dread' and 'War' to another level, but there was something else, too, which many in the audience felt. It wasn't just the full moon overhead or the thrill of seeing the reggae talisman back on home soil. It was a feeling of disquiet – a collective sense that something significant was about to happen, whether good or bad. It was in the middle of 'Jamming' that Marley called for Michael Manley and Edward Seaga to join him on stage, so they could shake hands and let the people see tangible evidence of their truce. Time seemed to stand still after those words left his lips. Did Bob Marley, a mere singer, really have the power to make that happen? What if they didn't respond? Or only one of them did? It was the ultimate test of Marley's power, though he didn't necessarily see it like that. In his mind, he was just a vessel for God's will to manifest itself, and after making his request he let the music possess him, his arms flailing and body jerking as if controlled by unseen hands. Gradually, shadowy figures arrived on stage. Seaga and his bodyguards were first, then Manley, and when they were stationed either side of him – like 'two thieves flanking Christ', according to Neville Garrick – Marley held their hands above his head with one hand, then stretched out the other whilst uttering 'love, prosperity. Peace and accord. Jah Rastafari. Selassie I.' It was probably the most iconic moment in reggae history, and of Marley's entire career.

In the aftermath, voices whispered that a massacre had been planned for that night, and that Bob knew the only way he could stop the bloodshed was to call up the leaders in the way he did. Others disagree, saying none of what happened was premeditated, but that Marley had acted upon intuition.

'Bob was really, really hurting from that shooting', recalled Marcia Griffiths, who could be heard yelling, 'I hear you brother' when Marley stopped singing and started talking. 'I think his soul was damaged, and that's what convinced him to top it off with a performance like that. Because before the shooting happen, he wasn't dreaming that anybody in Jamaica wanted to hurt him, and so after returning there now, it was like him just use that concert to bring everything back to normal by getting those two political leaders together. Nobody else could have done that, y'know? Only Bob Marley, and it was one of the most beautiful moments ever captured in Jamaica'.

As media reports from the One Love Peace Concert arrived from Jamaica, a hundred thousand people marched the six miles from London's Trafalgar Square to an open air concert at Victoria Park in Hackney as part of a day's programme of events organised by Rock Against Racism and the Anti-Nazi League. UK reggae band Misty In Roots played on a flat-bed truck at the head of the march, which took place on 30 April. They then performed on the same bill as Steel Pulse, the Clash and Tom Robinson Band at the actual concert.

'The punks were just totally against the system,' David Hinds told Saxon Baird. 'One thing the system said it didn't want to do was to promote black music, so the punks said, "you know what? We're going to promote black radio! Say you don't like reggae on the radio? Well, we're going to like reggae!" That's how the punks got amalgamated with Rastafarianism and reggae musicians. Punks supported anything the system was against. The fact that the system didn't play any reggae music led the punks to say, "we're going to be the leading act because we're the 'in' thing right now and we're going to have reggae bands opening for us at these venues." And that's how we got our feet in the door.

'In retrospect, we found out that while whites were appreciating black music coming out of the UK at that time, it wasn't reciprocal in the British black communities. Even to this day, the black communities will never really respond to punk music. They weren't part of that culture, and didn't want to be a part of it either. It was too hard establishing their own music, let alone getting involved in someone else's. The black communities didn't recognise that punk played a very significant role in establishing reggae music in the UK. They'll never see that. They would have to be in the thick of things like ourselves, who were going out into the venues and participating, to see how far the progression has gone and to realise the input that punk had.'

Whilst punks and reggae fans alike were marching in support of Rock Against Racism, Boney M's double A-sided single 'Rivers Of Babylon' b/w 'Brown Girl In The Ring' was at number one in the UK and receiving unparalleled airplay for a record with a Caribbean theme. Boney M were a four-piece vocal group comprised of one male (Bobby Farrell) and three female singers who turned everything they did into a banal singalong. I say 'they' but the band members themselves didn't sing on their records, because session singers did. Yet Boney M were incredibly successful, and their version of the Melodians' hit became the second highest-selling single of all time in the UK. When 'Rivers Of Babylon' began slipping down the charts after five weeks at number one, radio DJs then started playing 'Brown Girl In The Ring' (originally a Jamaican nursery rhyme) in its place, and that went to number two. Boney M would chalk up further number one and number two hits before the end of 1978, securing their status as Britain's most successful black act.

We can safely assume that few punks or dedicated reggae-lovers bought their records, but millions of so-called ordinary British people did. The fact that Boney M were a black group didn't matter. They just made catchy pop records that were easy to sing and dance to, and that pleased people of all ages and ethnic backgrounds. There was also a certain amount of familiarity with the songs, which helped. Was that progress? It's hard to say, but the benchmark for reggae acts hoping to crossover had suddenly become a lot more daunting for most Jamaican artists, who faced the prospect of having to dumb down in order to compete in terms of sales and popular appeal.

Whilst Bob Marley was known to have kept abreast of popular music trends – British journalist John Williams found him listening to the soundtrack to *Saturday Night Fever* once – it's doubtful that he took too much notice of Boney M, despite their dominance of the UK charts. Pinpointing exactly when he played in Tivoli Gardens is another unknown, although I'm guessing that it was during the truce, and a lull in hostilities between Rema and Jungle. He and the Wailers were supposed to begin their next US tour in early May 1978, but the first few shows had to be cancelled, allegedly because Junior Marvin was refused a US visa due to a previous drugs conviction. Marley and the band were primed and ready to go, but had to wait until the Island lawyers straightened things out, so this could well have been when Marley, backed by a pick-up band, ventured into the JLP stronghold.

Soul Syndicate rhythm guitarist Tony Chin was there, and whilst he can't remember the date, he's quite certain of other details.

'Tivoli Garden was a very political place. People didn't go there because you can get killed very easy, by gunshot, but when these people come to you, you can't refuse to play. We didn't want to go but Fully's father said, "listen. You'd better go, because if you don't, those guys will have you down as enemies. They'll think that you're on the other side, so it's better that you go and play." In Jamaica, it was dangerous in those times and Tapper Zukie, he was big in politics, so when he went to see Bob, 'im have to take it. We musicians always try to be neutral in the politics. We have to walk good on both sides, but they had this big concert there. Inner Circle was on the show, and a few other groups, but when it was time for Bob to go on stage, Family Man didn't show up and the keyboard player and drummer, they didn't show up either, so Bob came and asked me and Fully if we could fill in. Fully got scared and said no, so Inner Circle's bass player went and played, Chinna Smith played, and I think Santa played. Touter was on keyboards and Junior Marvin, he played as well, because that was the first time I met him. We didn't rehearse or anything, but Junior was giving me the keys whilst Bob was singing the newer songs, and then I'd give him the keys during the older songs. Man, that was a magical night! That was the last time I performed with Bob, and I'll never forget it.'

On 17 May, the same day that Marley and the Wailers finally left for the US, a man identified as Alton McDowell was shot dead following an incident in Tivoli Gardens. Eyewitnesses said a silver Datsun car drove slowly into the square around 3:30 p.m. and four men jumped out, firing indiscriminately at groups of residents hanging out in the vicinity. McDowell was injured in the head and refused to go with the gunmen, whereupon one of them grabbed him by the front of his shirt and shot him in the chest. He was then thrown into the trunk of the vehicle and driven away. When the police arrived, residents pointed out several bullet holes in nearby buildings and a brand new BMW car belonging to Tapper Zukie that had been punctured by bullets on both sides, badly damaging the bodywork. According to Zukie, he'd gone to Tivoli Gardens to hold talks with members of Third World, who were planning to stage a charity concert there on Labour Day. He was near the square when the shooting began and had run for cover. It wasn't until a detachment of police arrived and started breaking into his car that he identified himself and unlocked it, so they could search it. The officers at the scene said the car had been involved in a shooting incident with Bucky Marshall, who was now wanted on several charges, but the police report later put a different slant on what had happened, and stated that several policemen patrolling Tivoli Gardens were fired on by a group of men with automatic weapons in the vicinity of the Community Centre.

'The police party returned the fire and one man was shot,' the report stated. 'He was then taken to hospital in a serious condition with gunshot wounds to the head and chest and was resting when last seen. Scores of citizens visited the hospital but were later dispersed by the police on guard. Detachments of police carried out searches in Tivoli and the nearby area.'

Tapper wasn't the only reggae artist to drive a flash car. Bob Marley and Family Man both had BMWs, Jacob Miller could be seen driving round Kingston in his Mercedes and Tommy Cowan had a Citroen Pallas. Dawn Ritch, a journalist for the *Gleaner*, noted that the names mentioned above were Rastafarians who felt no guilt about consuming the fruits of their labour.

'A really good car is and will always be a reward for outstanding accomplishment,' she wrote. 'The younger Rastafarians see themselves and all other Jamaicans who try to live justly and are task-orientated as the real beneficiaries of Jamaica. And they call Jamaicans with this new spirit of determination the children of the rainbow.'

Peter Tosh was also a member of this upwardly mobile set of Rasta artists who believed in spreading their righteous message whilst simultaneously reaping reward for their efforts. The Rolling Stones had signed him to their label after his incendiary performance at the One Love Peace Concert, and he'd already laid some tracks at Dynamic for a forthcoming album, aided by Sly and Robbie and the brothers Geoffrey and Mikey Chung. The latter was a staple of Tosh's band Word, Sound & Power and also helped with the arrangements, as well as playing lead and rhythm guitars. The Stones had invited Tosh to open for them on their next US tour, due to start on 11 June. The rehearsals would take place at Bearsville studios in upstate New York, not far from Woodstock. Peter had been there before with Lee Jaffe to discuss a potential record deal with owner Albert Grossman, Bob Dylan's manager. That never materialised, but during his return visit Tosh and his group made themselves at home in Studio B, where they put finishing touches to the *Bush Doctor* album and Peter recorded an impromptu duet with Mick Jagger, a cover of the Temptations' '(You Gotta Walk) Don't Look Back.'

'The whole album was mixed there with Karl Pitterson,' said Sly Dunbar. 'We did overdubs there too. Karl was one of the top engineers at the time and wanted to spearhead the engineering part of

Peter breaking out. Karl had the edge over most of the other engineers in Jamaica at that time, and especially when it came to getting a more international sound. Not just reggae, either, because he was producing a couple of groups as well, like Rico's. He was very good.'

Assistant engineer Chris Anderson recalls Keith Richards overdubbing some guitar parts that weren't used, and a helicopter taking people from the Stones' entourage back and forth to New York at regular intervals. There was a lot of cocaine use – although not by Tosh, his musicians or even Mick Jagger, who Chris said was very focused and knew exactly what he wanted to do. The rapport between Jagger and Tosh at the end of 'Don't Look Back' was adlibbed during one of the only two takes. The horns and female backing vocals on the album were then overdubbed in New York shortly before the tour began.

As Tosh was heading for the big time, the Mighty Diamonds were hosting a launch party at the Sheraton for their latest album, *Planet Earth*. Happily, this new Virgin offering went a long way towards redeeming the mistakes made on *Ice On Fire*, as did matching dub album *Planet Mars Dub*, credited to the Icebreakers, which followed soon afterwards. From the opening bars of 'Where's Garvey' listeners were left in no doubt as to what the Diamonds stood for and the kind of message they wanted to get across. Marcus Garvey had been made Jamaica's first national hero, and yet there was still no sign of his legacy having transformed mainstream society in his homeland. Life in the Kingston ghettos was as tough as ever, hence songs like 'Struggling.' *Planet Earth* contained all original songs, except for 'Sweet Lady' – a former single that deserved wider exposure thanks to its catchy melody and chorus, but failed to get enough airplay. Ultimately, it was a remake of 'Just Can't Figure Out', which they'd first recorded for Bunny Lee, that connected best with reggae audiences. Lead singer Tabby Shaw was almost in tears as he tried to guess his girl's next move on that one, while 'Let The Answer' was quintessential Jamaican lovers rock and 'Only Brothers' featured keyboard-player Touter Harvey, who had so impressed Mick Jagger whilst playing with Inner Circle at the One Love Peace Concert that he was invited to join the Stones for their US tour.

Elsewhere, the Diamonds could have been describing a post-Apocalyptic nightmare when they called out on 'Come Me Brethren.' Then they warned of imminent disaster on 'Planet Earth' itself. The majority of tracks were recorded at Compass Point in Nassau with core members of the Revolutionaries. Whilst a definite improvement on earlier releases, Tabby was still disappointed by the outcome.

'We had built up Channel One by then so everyone wanted to record there, and yet we nah deal with them no more,' he complained in an interview with *Black Echoes'* Simon Buckland. 'Virgin say them nah want no more four-track music. Them say, "a demo that!" Them want sixteen-track and Channel One never have that yet, and that's why we had to go to Nassau.'

Sensing dissatisfaction within the group and also their fanbase, the Hoo Kims wasted no time releasing *Stand Up To Your Judgment* and *Tell Me What's Wrong*, albums recorded with the Revolutionaries that quickly restored the Diamonds' standing with their grassroots audience. *Stand Up To Your Judgment* contrasted roots and reality songs with soulful ballads such as 'Stoned Out Of My Mind', 'I Want To Know', 'Fools Rush In' and 'Country Living', and even the cover art struck the right note by depicting cartoon characters waving M-16 rifles and shouting slogans like 'Death to Capitalism' and 'Death To Yankee Imperialists.' *Tell Me What's Wrong* was its equal in many ways, and the Diamonds' take on the Heptones' 'Love Me Girl' was a massive hit in Jamaica. Both albums were triumphs, but would represent something of a final flowering by the Revolutionaries, as Sly and Robbie were spending more time at Compass Point. Not that you'd know it from the avalanche of albums bearing their name, including *Don't Underestimate The Force* and *Jonkanoo Dub* (issued by Channel One themselves), *Guerrilla Dub* (shared with the Aggrovators) and various others compiled by Linval Thompson, Alvin Ranglin and Sonia Pottinger. The Revolutionaries may have been on their way out, but a ridiculously high proportion of Jamaican releases would still bear their name for months if not years to come.

Leroy Smart, who was one of the stars of *Rockers*, had been the warm-up act at that Mighty Diamonds' launch party. He'd recently returned from a trip to the UK, where he got into a spot of bother. Before leaving for England, Leroy had recorded an album for Bunny Lee, who then licensed it to Count Shelly. Lee told him to check Shelly for royalties when he was in London, but when Leroy did just that, Count Shelly turned him away and said he should check Bunny Lee. Shelly, who was a big man and powerfully built, 'put up a drastic performance', according to Smart, who ran into the street and picked up a bottle to arm himself. He would later claim that he hadn't gone there to cause a disturbance, but he hadn't been prepared to back down either. Eventually the police came and arrested him, and he spent two weeks in jail for assault. Bunny Lee responded as only he could – by cheekily putting out a new Leroy Smart album called *In London Clinker...*

Burning Sounds issued two further albums by the singer after his visit, both self-produced. One of them, *Jah Loves Everyone*, had a painting on the cover of a crowd scene featuring him, a topless blonde, a Russian Cossack, assorted religious figures, a punk, two bandits and Darth Vader. We're assuming that Leroy himself hadn't sanctioned it, but who knows? Togetherness can be expressed in many different ways, and back home in Jamaica, songs written in the wake of the peace treaty were still dominating the local charts. George Nooks was at number one with 'Tribal War' and was kept company by Jacob Miler's 'Peace Treaty Special', Dillinger's 'War Is Over' and Culture's euphoric 'Natty Dread Taking Over.' Culture's follow-up to *Two Sevens Clash* was *Harder Than The Rest*, produced by Sonia Pottinger. The group had defected to her after arguments with Joe Gibbs over money, and the tracks they recorded at Treasure Isle with the Revolutionaries were just as good as its predecessor. Glorious melodies and serious subject matter collided on highlights like 'Stop The Fussing And Fighting', 'Holy Mount Zion', 'Tell Me Where You Get It', 'Vacancy' and 'Iron Sharpening Iron', whilst 'Behold' was a reworking of a song that Joseph Hill first recorded at Studio One. But it was 'Love Shine Bright', radiating such joie de vivre, that epitomised the sound of Culture at that particular moment in time.

Richard Branson had visited Ms Pottinger back in February, when she was busy recording Marcia Griffiths. He did well to sign the Culture album – one of several Front Line albums released during the summer. These included *Jah Son Of Africa* by U-Roy, who the *NME* credited with being 'as important to Jamaica as the Beatles are to Britain' and giving rise to 'the whole sound system cult, skanking and deejay communication.' U-Roy always gave the impression of being humbled by his success. He'd never voiced slack or gun lyrics and didn't engage in disputes with rivals, but chose instead to remain faithful to the Rastafarian principles that he'd first embraced as a teenager. His modesty made a refreshing change from some of the bombast heard elsewhere. Instead, U-Roy liked to remind people of the core values that, to his mind, should forever reside at the heart of the music. That was just one of the reasons why people called him 'the Teacher.' He'd consistently encouraged young talent and had recently launched his own sound system, King Stur Gav, which deejay Ranking Joe and selector Jah Screw operated when U-Roy was away on tour. Ranking Joe was voted most popular deejay for the year in 1977. He and Jah Screw were on Ray Symbolic before they joined King Stur Gav, and their arrival did U-Roy's sound system a lot of good.

Screw, who was from Greenwich Farm, said, 'We actually built Stur Gav. I'm the one who changed the boxes and make lots of other improvements, but U-Roy never give me my credit because when we first went there, it was just some little small box he have – then by the time we leave, he had these big speaker boxes and automatically get the crowd from Ray Symbolic.'

'As it was the best sound going, everybody meet there, but in Jamaica you have politics so it get really horrible,' added Ranking Joe. 'Stur Gav carry the swing and every other week something happen. We played every day except Tuesday, our only rest day, all over Jamaica, but we loved and enjoyed it 'cause the crowd response make we feel it. We were always sure of a crowd, and in those days everything revolved around the sound system. That was the main media in reaching our audience 'cause nuff people couldn't get to a club, which cost too much anyway. And the radio stations, they'd just play certain type of uptown artists like Pluto Shervington, Ernie Smith and Lorna Bennett, or maybe some R&B. Our music was too hardcore, and they didn't want to embrace that. We never had the money to pay these radio station guys, but night after night you had dances keeping all over Jamaica, an' we nah ramp when it came to highlighting certain singers like Sugar Minott, Barry Brown or Johnny Clarke, then once the records dropped in the shops, they would sell like hot cakes.

'Dances in those days were fun. At first they'd be nuff people outside, deciding whether or not to pay and come inside. After they see me come in and start tune up the mic, they start push down the gate and I have to keep them in there, holding a mic from seven in the evening 'til seven the next morning! You might not be saying a lot for some of the time, but you're holding the vibes and responding to the vocals by freestyling with them. You get the people involved that way, and especially if it's a brand new tune that's playing. If the vocal wicked you get applause for that, then it gets turned over and you can get applause for what you do on the version too, 'cause there's nothing sweeter than when you're riding the riddim, and you feel electrified by the crowd when they start bawling "forward!" That means the people are with you, rocking to the music and everything nice, but the sound system itself must be good too, y'know? It can't be like a little joke t'ing, and with joke equipment, cah you have to be able to feel the music too.'

428

Ranking Joe and Brigadier Jerry were now among the deejay frontrunners, and the 18-year-old Ranking Trevor would soon join them. He grew up in Waterhouse and, inspired by U-Roy and Big Youth, started out deejaying on Gold Soul before graduating to King Attorney Hi-Fi, which then changed its name to Socialist Roots in a show of political allegiance to the PNP. He voiced his debut single for Ossie Hibbert, but his breakthrough hit was 'Cave Man Skank', which he voiced for Channel One. In 1977 he was injured in a car crash and had to take time out to recover, but then returned with hits like 'Masculine Gender' and 'Rub A Dub Style', which Front Line included on his *In Fine Style* album. He and Trinity also shared an album called *Three Piece Chicken And Chips*, which Jo Jo Hoo Kim licensed to Cha Cha – a London label with offices on Craven Park Road in Harlesden. Ranking Trevor was a favourite with the Hoo Kims, who recruited him to spice up 12-inch singles by the Jayes and Wailing Souls, whose latest single 'War' was a call for governments to build back nations, rather than engage in hostilities. It was another example of how Rastafarians preferred to direct their anger towards the system – Babylon – rather than individuals or other nationalities.

There were so many new releases flooding out of Jamaica during 1978 that labels such as Cha Cha, Hawkeye, Conflict, Burning Sounds and Third World had their pick of material to license and release. Virgin's bid to outflank the competition led them to reissue albums that had previously appeared in small quantities or been overlooked. Tapper Zukie's *MPLA*, U-Roy's *Version Galore* and Big Youth's *Dreadlocks Dread* all enjoyed a resurgence of interest (and sales) when revived on Front Line. A reviewer in *Melody Maker* likened Big Youth's performance on *Dreadlocks Dread* to 'watching Bela Lugosi beckoning some hapless victim in a Sunday afternoon B horror movie. All the talk you hear nowadays about it being impossible to listen to a toasting album all the way through just doesn't apply to this man.'

He'd obviously been hearing Big Youth's songs not as music, but one long psycho-drama. Previous to that reissue, Trojan had been Big Youth's overseas' label of choice, but his association with them finally came to an end with the release of *Isaiah Prophet Of Old* – another self-produced set that was heavy on Biblical and cultural themes, but light on the rushes of blood and karaoke-style covers that had characterised his previous albums. It was the first Big Youth outing that didn't have at least one big tune that you'd hear regularly played on sound system, but then the rhythms were quite busy and even over-produced in places. 'World In Confusion' was the exception, as Big Youth sent a message to the warmongers. It was reggae as polemic or art, rather than entertainment. In retrospect, *Isaiah Prophet Of Old* would have benefitted from the inclusion of the deejay's recent single 'Green Bay Killing', in which he accused the security forces of murder.

But back to Front Line, because the staff there were on a roll and celebrated by putting out two Prince Far I albums, both produced by the gruff-voiced chanter himself. *Long Life* was recorded at Harry J's with A-list session musicians, whilst *Message From The King* was a more mixed bag credited to Prince Far I and the Arabs. Some of the tracks on the latter were former singles – 'Black Man Land', for example, on which he asked how I and I – the Rasta faithful – can sing their songs in a strange land, whilst others were recorded in the UK with help from Adrian Sherwood, who'd been involved in releasing Far I's *Psalms For I* set two years previously. He was in the car, driving through the cold English countryside, when Far I wrote the lyrics to 'Foggy Road.'

'Prince Far I came to stay at my mum's house and called her "Mummy",' he said, laughing. 'She called him "the Honey Monster" and he'd be there doing Elvis Presley impersonations! He was a real comedian, but after a while he became convinced that people were working black magic on him and was always feeling ill. He was a complex character...'

When Carib Gems had got into difficulties, Adrian and his friend, melodica player Dr Pablo, had launched HitRun with Carol Kalphat's 'African Land' and the debut LP by Creation Rebel, *Dub From Creation*.

'That album sold like a couple of thousand copies,' Adrian said. 'People think that we were selling truckloads of records back then, but we weren't. The thing is, I'd made that whole album for £200, and so those sales figures really weren't that bad. I thought, "wow! This is easy, so maybe I should record someone from Jamaica", but I was literally making records that me and my mates were listening to at home. That's how it went.'

Creation Rebel was the UK's first dedicated dub band, and followed *Dub From Creation* with *Close Encounters Of The Third World*. Their core personnel included keyboard player Clifton 'Bigga' Morrison and guitarist 'Crucial' Tony Philips, who also played in Prince Far I's backing band the Arabs. They accompanied Prince Far I on a live session for John Peel that was broadcast on 16 June, and would be repeated twice more in the coming months. John Peel also played several tracks from *Message From The King* that month, whilst the Arabs later resurfaced on another HitRun release, *Cry Tuff Dub Encounter Chapter 1* – a collection of dub tracks 'given by the inspiration of Prince Far I' and mixed by Adrian, who'd now found his metier.

'Dub really is the domain of the engineer,' he enthused. 'The musicians have done their job, then the engineer shapes something special with his hands and his craft. That's what dub is to me. I always look towards King Tubby as the benchmark, because he showed what was possible by dissembling and reassembling. That's why I say the engineer is like an extra musician, because dub gives us the chance to express ourselves by turning a tune inside-out. I used to spend a lot of time from relatively early on, studying aspects of sound that I liked. I'd plug one thing into another and change things around, searching for something that registered with me, or I'd experiment with outboard sounds and put them through different speakers. I applied all of that to my own productions, and because I was working with authentic reggae people, I never questioned that I was on the right path.'

Adrian was a big fan of Jamaican singer Bim Sherman, whose sweet vocals, devoid of saccharine, were invested with fragile spirituality. He'd first aroused interest two years previously, thanks to a handful of singles on the Scorpio label, including 'Golden Locks.' 1977's tally had yielded 'Mighty Ruler' and 'Tribulation', and led to an album for Lloyd Coxsone's Tribes Man label called *Love Forever*. Bim was from Westmoreland originally but he grew up in Rockfort – an area of East Kingston that he described as 'pure danger.'

'You have to be alert at all times in that kind of environment, and always be prepared to meet with bad minds,' he told me. 'I'm not a fussy person, and I'm not making music to get rich or famous because, no, I don't want that. I would rather know that my music is going out there and reaching people so that they can learn something from it, or it affects them inside so that it will keep them from making war with others. And I just deal with subjects that are real because I want to encourage people to speak their minds, although you need a strong, balanced mind in this world, otherwise you can go totally insane under the pressure!

'I mean, you see broken people by the thousands on the streets, all wondering "where should I go?" and "what should I do?" But it's just down to method, and avoiding the tricks used to keep us in poverty and captivity. That's why I always try to have some roots songs out there for those who need them. Because you can't let people think they own you, otherwise you become just like merchandise for them, and I'm not prepared for that. I'm not ready for that at all!'

The same day that John Peel introduced Prince Far I and the Arabs' live act to BBC listeners, CBS released the latest single by the Clash, 'White Man (In Hammersmith Palais).' Joe Strummer's lyrics namechecking Dillinger, Leroy Smart and Delroy Wilson were inspired by a gig that had taken place a year ago, on 5 June. Delroy was already a regular visitor to the UK, as was Ken Boothe, but then reality is no substitute for mythology. Admiral Ken played during the interval, and the Clash contingent had been disappointed not to hear any current Jamaican hits. Flash-forward twelve months and reggae audiences were listening to new releases by the Wailing Souls ('War'), Jah Thomas, Jimmy Riley ('Majority Rule'), U Brown, Culture ('This Train'), Marcia Griffiths (with a cover of Bob Marley's 'I'm Hurting Inside') and Black Uhuru, who'd gone quiet after recording their album for Prince Jammy. Lead singer Michael Rose had then guested on Sly Dunbar's *Simple Sly Man* album, singing a version of Marley's 'Sun Is Shining.'

'He did another Wailers' song called 'Let Him Go', and a version of 'No, No, No' as well,' Sly explained. 'We were just testing out the sound and putting them out in the marketplace to see what reaction they'd get, and when a lot of people said they liked it I say to him, "You don't really have to do any more covers. We need some original songs", so I gave him some Earth, Wind & Fire, Teddy Pendergrass and Jose Feliciano songs to listen to, and he came back singing 'Shine Eye Girl' and 'Plastic Smile'! I thought, "wow, this is great!" I remember someone saying, "oh, it sounds funny", but I said, "no, let's just go ahead and record it".'

By the time 'Plastic Smile' was released, Sly and Robbie were on tour with Peter Tosh, supporting the Stones and learning how to cope with performing to diehard rock fans. Keyboard-player Touter Harvey didn't last more than a week with the Stones. He'd become overawed by trying to fill Billy Preston's shoes and was replaced in turn by the Faces' Ian McLagan.

'Everybody wanted to open for the Stones,' he said, 'but those stadiums hold fifty thousand people, and there are only twenty-five thousand of them there when the support act's on stage. Out of that number there are only maybe five thousand who are actually listening to the music, and the rest are there to party…'

'A lot of people in America didn't know reggae then and some of the people would get restless,' admitted Sly Dunbar. 'On that first show someone threw a bottle and it was headed straight for the cymbal, but then Peter reach out and catch it, saying, "bumbo-claat!" We'd forgotten this was part of rock'n'roll, but Mick would come out and introduce Peter and make people realise there was a connection, y'know? It wasn't just another band that was playing. The Stones had a connection with us, and things started working better between ourselves and the audiences after that.'

They learnt that to engage with rock audiences, reggae bands had to play with a lot more drive and energy than usual, and having an expressive lead guitarist helped too, as Bob Marley had already discovered. He and the Wailers had played at New York's Madison Square Garden on 17 June, supported by jazz-funk bassist Stanley Clarke, and the night before that Marley had attended a ceremony at the Waldorf Astoria and been awarded a Third World Peace Medal on behalf of '500 million Africans' by the Senegalese youth minister to the UN.

A week or so later, on 23 June, Reggae Sunsplash opened at Jarrett Park in Montego Bay with performances by Dennis Brown, Jacob Miller and Inner Circle. Other highlights included sets by Jimmy Cliff and Joe Higgs on the Saturday, Harold Butler's jazz session on the Wednesday and then Toots and the Maytals' grand-stand finish on the closing Thursday night, when they shared the bill with Althea & Donna, Culture and Beres Hammond.

Jacob Miller was the star of that inaugural Reggae Sunsplash and yet his performance at the One Love Peace Concert was still a source of controversy, even two months later. Prior to Jacob's appearance at Sunsplash, Dudley Thompson, the minister of national security, met with representatives from Synergy and the Jamaica Tourist Board, seeking assurances that the singer's 'disgraceful behaviour' at the Peace concert would not be repeated. Thompson also wrote to the Jamaica Federation of Musicians, warning them that any performers deemed to be guilty of bad behaviour on stage would be prosecuted.

In the wake of Reggae Sunsplash, he'd reported that Jacob Miller 'proceeded not to only flout the law in full view of numerous members of the overseas press, but hurled abominable abuses at senior members of the security forces who were present.' In response, he threatened to close down shows if necessary, and said that the promoters would be held responsible for the artists' behaviour. Such pronouncements raised important security issues, because if the police had dragged Jacob Miller or Peter Tosh off stage at the Peace concert, a riot may have ensued. As a *Gleaner* editorial pointed out, it hadn't been politically expedient to do so at the time, but the situation had become 'a grave embarrassment, and the gate is about to be locked behind the horse.'

Talk of the devil, because on 3 July, Kingston police issued a warrant for the arrest of Peter Tosh when he failed to appear in court on charges of possession of ganja, indecent language and disorderly conduct at Norman Manley International airport. He was still on tour with The Rolling Stones when the warrant was issued, and whilst he had a couple of free days before heading to Detroit, a dressing down by some magistrate simply wasn't on his agenda. Bob Marley and the Wailers were still on the road, too. After finishing the US leg of the *Kaya* tour they played a gig at the New Bingley Hall in the UK, then journeyed onwards to Paris, Ibiza, Denmark, Norway, the Netherlands and finally Belgium. Steel Pulse supported Marley on those European and Scandinavian dates, and David Hinds later told Andy Brouwer they 'learned a lot of discipline on that tour.'

'That's when the doors really started to open for us,' Hinds said. 'It has always been one of the most memorable moments of my career. To play as part of that package exposed Steel Pulse to audiences that literally were in awe of our message. Of course, being formally introduced through Bob Marley helped us tremendously. Playing for audiences, especially those in Paris who saw the force of Steel Pulse and the force of Bob Marley play on the same bill, enabled us to sell out shows every time since then.'

Island Records released the debut Steel Pulse album, *Handsworth*

Revolution, in July. Chris Blackwell hadn't been too sure about the title at first, but had given them free reign of Island's Hammersmith studios and recruited Karl Pitterson, who'd previously worked with all three original Wailers, to oversee production. Karl had quickly connected with what Steel Pulse were all about. According to Basil Gabbidon, he brought clarity, precision and a tighter, more professional feel to their sound, and the vocals in particular. The album railed against racial injustice as experienced in UK inner cities, and was rife with influences derived from Rastafari and the American Civil Rights struggle. The title track was an appeal for unity that alerted listeners to their home locale – a rundown inner city area of Birmingham that was notorious for its high rates of crime, racism and unemployment. Pulse even drew parallels with what was happening in apartheid South Africa, whilst their rebel credentials were writ large on songs like 'Bun Dem', 'Soldiers' and 'Bad Man'. But it was 'Klu Klux Klan' that laid bare their innate militancy.

Astute as ever, Radio 1 DJ John Peel invited them to record a live session for the BBC and the UK music press fell into line as one after that, because the *NME*, *Sounds* and *Melody Maker* all published cover features and photos. Steel Pulse even appeared on *Top of the Pops* during the first week of July, singing 'Prodigal Son.' Whilst that second Island single didn't trouble the national Top 30, the album did better than expected and Steel Pulse were soon attracting black and white fans in droves.

'We had a mixed following – not necessarily in the same way as Bob Marley did, because he attracted everyone, but we drew more students and conscious black people,' said Hinds. 'They loved the honesty within the lyrics, and the stories we told. During the seventies, bands like ourselves and Aswad represented a cry from the youths. We were the first generation of British-born black reggae acts, and we knew what it felt like being under the hammer. We weren't like our parents, content to go into the factories then come home and hide away. We were exposed to the whole vibe of the sixties, learning about our history and trying to get meaningful jobs. We thought we should have the same opportunities as any other British citizens, and to find out that this wasn't the case created real problems. There had to be an outcry, because we'd been told a lie and sold a dream.'

Sometime during 1978, Steel Pulse appeared alongside Jimmy Lindsay, Alton Ellis, Aswad and Matumbi in a film about the British scene called *Reggae In A Babylon*. Michael Riley was still in the band at that point, but would soon be gone. There was talk of him having missed gigs and rehearsals – also conflicts of opinion regarding their musical direction. Island wisely didn't interfere, but concentrated instead on readying albums for release by Burning Spear, Bob Marley, Third World and Ijahman Levi, who made his Island debut with *Haile I Hymn*.

Chris Blackwell had heard Ijahman's singles for Dennis Harris, and asked about the possibility of him recording an album for Island. Ijahman sat in Blackwell's office, playing his ten-string guitar and singing his latest compositions. The Island boss was impressed and offered to pay for recordings in Jamaica. It was unusual for Island to use Joe Gibbs instead of Harry J's or Dynamic, but Ijahman and his team – which included Geoffrey Chung and members of Now Generation – wanted a specific sound, and got it. Island's advertising department called it 'the crossover album of the year', and *Small Axe's* Ray Hurford agreed. He considered *Haile I Hymn* to be 'one of the greatest reggae albums ever made' and wrote how 'time and the evolution of the music have made it possible to fully appreciate the wonderful intricacy of the work.'

'They say I'm a very unique artist,' Ijahman told him. 'I have something special and it takes a special dedication to handle it, which Chris Blackwell provided. He took it within himself to listen to what I was putting out and obviously he was spending money, so he must have an idea about where he's spending it. At the same time, what he did with that dedication was marvellous. It's what bring I to the world as Ijahman, respected in music, and I give thanks. We had an understanding, and for a simple little Rastaman to go into a recording company and deal with the head, it's not very easy, so I give thanks.'

Island issued the opening track – a remake of 'Jah Heavy Load' – as a single, but Ijahman Levi was the epitome of what's known as 'an album artist' and *Haile I Hymn*'s four tracks, two of them lasting over ten minutes, were hardly likely to generate much airplay, despite casting a spell with their sophisticated, multi-layered arrangements. The associate producer on that project was Robert Ash, who'd worked with Eno (*Another Green World*), Stomu Yamashta, Joni Mitchell and Stevie Winwood. His input, like that of Geoffrey Chung's, proved invaluable in making *Haile I Hymn* a listening experience of singular beauty. This style of production would be categorised as 'international reggae', and it was a long way removed from the music's ghetto origins.

Inner Circle were fellow practitioners, and the Lewis brothers owned a house in Kingston's Beverley Hills to prove it, but few expected Bob Marley and Peter Tosh to also attract criticism for supposedly having diluted their music, or chased commercial success at the expense of their Rasta principles. Such dissenters obviously preferred their favourite Jamaican artists to remain musical primitives, unheralded by everyone except themselves. They were elitists, and yet reggae music's leading lights hadn't struggled for years to attain parity with their overseas counterparts only to back down when they got within touching distance of their goals.

Marley and the Wailers had been working their way down America's West Coast before pitching up at Burbank's Starlite Amphitheatre on 21 July. Peter Tosh was there with Mick Jagger and Diana Ross, watching from the side of the stage, but when Marley started to sing 'Get Up Stand Up', he couldn't help himself. Completely unannounced, Tosh strode onto the stage, took the mic and joined in, to Marley's obvious delight.

'When Bob started singing 'Get Up Stand Up' – one of my originals – I just had to get up and go on stage,' Tosh told Arthur

Kitchin. 'Some people didn't know who I was until Bob said, "hey! Is Peter Tosh dat y'know?"'

It was a happy occasion and made even happier by the news that Cindy Breakspeare had given birth to their son Damian, but that night at the Starlite Amphitheatre would be the last time the two original Wailers performed on a stage together.

Meanwhile, at the National Arena in Kingston, a major show had taken place featuring Gregory Isaacs, Leroy Smart, Junior Murvin, the Mighty Diamonds, Meditations and Ras Michael, backed by the Soul Syndicate. The headliner was Dennis Brown, whose *Visions* album had finally been made available in the UK by Lightning Records, followed by his cover of the Heptones' 'Equal Rights.' Dennis's focus was now increasingly split between Joe Gibbs and DEB Music, who had just issued two singles by Junior Delgado – 'Armed Robbery' and 'Tonight' – and announced that the singer's debut album for the label was expected by the end of the year. DEB had also released the Various Artists set *Black Echoes*, which sold well, and *Umoja: Love And Unity*, credited to DEB Players, which didn't, despite Prince Jammy's impressive contributions and Castro Brown's revisionist claims.

'By that time I was going down to Jamaica and we'd be working on things together, like those tracks from the *Umoja* dub album,' Castro said of himself and Dennis Brown. 'We knew they were good tracks. Jah Shaka was playing them hard and they were flaring up with that wicked King Tubby style of mixing and everything. We put out the *Umoja* dub album and that flew out the place, so then we had a next one called *20th Century Dubwise*. That album was far advanced for the time, but we knew what we were doing with the live sound, y' know?'

Castro and his team were creating their own opportunities, whilst north-west London band Tradition, who won Best Single at the *Black Echoes Awards* with the languid lovers rock track 'Breezing', benefitted from having signed to RCA, who'd issued two albums with them so far, *Alternative Routes* and *Tell Your Friends About*

Dub. Tradition were called Special Brew when starting out in 1976. Venture Records had released their debut album *Moving On* a year later, but their true claim to fame would be the cosmic concept album, *Captain Ganja And the Space Patrol*. It was a very British-sounding production and heavily inspired by science fiction. Jamaican dub was often described as sounding like music from another planet, but the explorations from there had a different flavour somehow. The ideas behind them felt more earthy as if they'd sprang from ancient pathways, rather than comic books.

African Dub All-Mighty Chapter 3 was one such example. That album, mixed by Errol Thompson at Joe Gibbs, was a benchmark in the annals of Jamaican dub music. Gibbs had lost Culture to Sonia Pottinger by that point, although you'd never have known it from the adverts promoting Culture's new album *Baldhead Bridge*, declaring 'The Hit Makers Are Back Again!' They were, but not with songs on *Baldhead Bridge*, which had the desultory feel of a cash-in. The strongest track on it was 'Zion Gate', and there were alternative versions to 'Behold' and 'Love Shines Brighter' from *Harder Than The Rest*, but it was the group's latest single on High Note, 'Natty Never Get Weary', that was lighting up the local charts. As July drew to a close, the island's other best sellers included Enos McLeod's 'Money Worries', Ray I's 'Weatherman Skank', Junior Tucker's 'Look Into Your Heart' and Tapper Zukie's 'Oh Lord', which, despite the religious title, was dedicated to 'the little sisters who wind up them bottoms in their shorts.' It was an outburst of joy and surprise, and with an insanely catchy chorus: a 'new Tapper Zukie rocksteady', as promised in the lyrics, voiced over a cut of Gregory Isaacs' 'Storm', and unashamedly populist.

Talking of Gregory, he was a guest artist on the Heptones' show Summer Reggae and Cool Runnings, held at the Epiphany Club in New Kingston on 26 July. Two days later, a delegation from Jamaica left for Havana and the World Festival of Youth and Students, attended by 18,500 people from 145 countries. The motto of the festival was 'For Anti-Imperialist Solidarity, Peace and Friendship.' It was the first time this event had been held in the western hemisphere, and it began with a march through the capital to the Latin American stadium, where the opening ceremony took place. The poets Orlando Wong and Michael Smith were among the Jamaican representatives. Smith was a 24-year-old Kingstonian from a proud working class background. He went to school in Jones Town and Denham Town and had begun writing poems in the late sixties, prompted by a news item that he'd read about Ian Smith's white-minority regime in Rhodesia. His credentials as a revolutionary poet were therefore impeccable. After attending a Social Development Commission workshop, he became a student at the Jamaica School of Drama, which is where he befriended Wong, who'd recently married and adopted the Igbo name Oku Nagba Ozala Onuora, meaning 'a fire or light that burns oppression' (Oku) and 'voice of the people' (Onuora). Close friends like Michael just called him 'Fire', and the two of them often performed at political and cultural events together. That's how Smith's two poems, 'Mi Cyaan Believe It' and 'Roots', became popular, even before he recorded them with Light Of Saba. 'Mi Cyaan Believe It', a sufferer's cry, opened with a description of what it's like to live in a cockroach-infested room whilst struggling to provide for numerous children and grandchildren. He also wrote about the humiliation of having to work for uncaring rich people ('you clean up the dog shit?'), and the hardship caused to a mother of four who obtained work as a domestic and then got pregnant because of the unwelcome attentions of her boss. The litany of woes also included reference to the Orange Street fire, and each verse was punctuated by the line, 'mi cyaan believe it.'

Linton Kwesi Johnson called Michael Smith 'a gifted wordsmith who could deftly negotiate the verbal contours of Jamaican speech, creating memorable poetic discourse that spoke to the conditions of existence for the oppressed and dispossessed in their everyday language. He was essentially a political poet, a people's poet, who wrote about the dehumanisation of the poor and their struggle against poverty and injustice. He wrote with conviction and performed with passion.'

Virgin released Johnson's debut album *Dread, Beat An' Blood*, credited to Poet And The Roots, in July. It was a set based on his poetry that pulled no punches as he spun keenly observed social commentaries involving Britain's disaffected black youth. On the front cover, a young black couple prepare to throw Molotov cocktails at police, and there's a photo of Johnson outside a police station on the back, flanked by officers and addressing the crowd through a megaphone. By the time he signed to Virgin, this former Black Panther was an accomplished poet and committed activist, who wrote for the *Race Today* newspaper as well as various music publications.

'Linton worked for us a marketing consultant, writing ad copy and things like that,' said Jumbo Vanrenen. 'If I'd taken his advice we would have signed the Light of Saba, because the man knew and loved the music, but Simon Draper gave him the money to record his album with Dennis Bovell. We'd originally offered him various dub tapes but he had very definite bass-lines running in the poems and Dennis pulled them out. Vivian Weathers, who we also signed, worked on *Dread, Beat An' Blood*, but I always felt guilty that we didn't do more UK stuff.'

Johnson was born in Chapeltown, Jamaica, but left for London when he was 9 years old. His love of literature began when he'd read the Bible to his grandmother, but then reggae music became an essential ingredient of his own writing.

'I don't know how or why it happened, but from the moment I began to write in the Jamaican language, music entered the poetry,' he told Mervyn Morris. 'There was always a beat or a bass-line going on at the back of my head with the words. And so I developed this style of writing – always with music in mind, always hearing music when I was composing my poetry.'

Initially, he would recite his poetry at schools, libraries and youth clubs around London as part of a loose collective named Rasta Love

442

that included Rasta drummers. A year or so later, *Race Today* published his first collection of poetry, 1974's *Voices Of The Living And The Dead*, which had been dramatised at the Keskidee Centre in Islington the previous summer. It was a very short book consisting of his only play – the title piece – and two poems, 'Youth Of Hope' and 'Five Nights Of Bleeding.' The latter offered vivid testament to five nights 'of horror and bleeding' – war among the rebels and hot heads who blindly practise 'mad blood rituals' in the places where reggae music plays, and 'bad beats tear at your flesh.' No other lyricist had brought the thrills and spills of being in a late night blues dance to life on the printed page with such vibrant clarity, and he did it again in his first collection of poetry *Dread Beat an' Blood*, which Bogle l'Ouverture published in 1975. Several of the songs on his debut album were adapted from poems in that book, including the title track, which begins, 'brothers an' sisters rocking...'

In 'Doun Di Road' he spoke about fratricide – black-on-black violence – whilst 'All Wi Doin Is Defendin' was a war cry, warning that black people had tired of racism and bad treatment and that insurrections would inevitably follow if steps weren't taken to allay the situation. George Lindo and Darcus Howe, who inspired 'Dread Ina Inglan' and 'Man Free' respectively, were both framed for crimes they didn't commit, which is something that producer Dennis Bovell knew about only too well.

'Our generation changed things because we didn't have the kinds of constraints that our parents had,' said Johnson. 'Our parents had mortgages to pay, they had to put us in school and they had to find food. And when a foreman in a factory called them a black bastard sometimes, even if they didn't like it, they would have to put up with it. My generation didn't have to put up with it and we didn't. And it was our generation that began to change things. Not that our parents' generation were Uncle Toms or anything like that. They weren't. I mean, they resisted and fought as they saw fit and as they could. But the responsibilities of having families put a greater constraint on their possibilities for struggle, the kind of constraints that our generation didn't have.

'For example, we would go to certain discos and clubs and find that they had colour bar policies or they had quota policies. I remember we used to go to the Locarno in Streatham and you had to get there by eight o'clock or eight-thirty, because after that no more blacks would be let in. And so we established our own independent cultural institutions, we established the blues dance, which would be held in someone's house on a Saturday night. We established the culture of sound system and gave reggae a local agitation and a name in this country. These things gave us a sense of our own identity, made us feel that we had something going for ourselves that made us proud and strong and independent.'

Johnson and Dennis Bovell made that first album in just three or four days at Gooseberry studios in London's Soho. Johnson had already coined the term 'dub poetry' to describe what deejays like I-Roy were doing in Jamaica. That's because it was spontaneous, improvisatory and had a musical base, and yet he preferred to use the term 'reggae poetry' when discussing his own work – a term that was more literary, perhaps, than that of his Jamaican counterparts, but the degree of commitment, anger, frustration and risk-taking behind it was identical.

By early August the strains on the truce between the JLP and PNP gangs were beginning to show, and when Tapper Zukie was shot in the leg and stomach and taken to hospital, rumours suggested that it had happened because of his involvement in the Peace Treaty movement. Thankfully, his injuries weren't life-threatening, but the incident spurred him into a whirlwind of activity, even as 'Oh Lord' continued selling like hot cakes. His next release on Front Line was the album *Tapper Roots*, which had a photo of a bare-breasted black woman on the cover wearing tribal beadwork, her fists bunched on her hips and her stare aimed straight at the viewer. There was nothing at all seductive or alluring about this image. It was real and in your face, as were songs like 'Green

Bay Murder', 'Don't Shoot The Youth' and 'Simpleton Leave Violence.' Elsewhere, he chanted roots and culture over a cut of the Abyssinians' 'Satta Massagana', co-opted Ray I's best-known hit on 'Rastaman Skank' and flirted with slackness on 'First Street Rock', whilst being sure to include his own Jamaican number one, 'Oh Lord.' Zukie would later claim that this album wasn't finished, and that it was compiled hurriedly after he was shot since Virgin had been pressurising him to deliver a follow-up to *Peace In The Ghetto*. His relationship with Branson's label had become troubled, to say the least. Front Line's Gaylene Martin says that Tapper fell out with Ken Berry and they had to shut down Virgin's New York office for three days after he threatened to go there and kill them. His reputation for violence preceded him, although he later told David Katz that his problems with Virgin came as a result of him demanding that they terminate his contract.

'No disrespect intended, but I heard they was selling a lot of records in South Africa, but those monies wasn't coming back to England. Some people told me they were investing in guns to use against my people in South Africa, so I confront Mr Branson, saying, "I'm a black man and I don't support such things", and that's how me and Virgin mash up. At the time U-Roy was going well for them in Africa, and Culture and I was going well for Virgin in England. But from there no big company would deal with me, so I decide to come back to Jamaica and establish my own thing.'

Richard Branson had assured him that Virgin wasn't involved in any such thing, but Tapper didn't believe him, especially since there were South Africans working for the company. That's when he exited Front Line and continued issuing new releases – both by himself and other artists – on his own Stars label, beginning with *Black Man*. That album contained songs like 'Revolution', 'Poor Man Problem' and 'Leggo Violence', and had a strong message written on the back cover. 'Earth is corrupt,' it said. 'Let's clean it up. All for one and one for all. No failure.' Another album, titled *The Man From Bozrah*, went one better and had liner notes by

Patti Smith. 'Tapper, the extractor, ties it all together,' she wrote. 'Like a playful cat he taps the ravelling ball... sending it into space like a Corvette over Detroit, landing on the throat of the babbling son of ritual...'

A trio of album releases was completed with the dub set *Escape From Hell*. There was a skull on the cover surrounded by flames, which may or may not have reflected something about his state of mind at the time. All this creative endeavour was also motivated by the fact that he'd been hosting a weekly radio show every Sunday lunchtime on RJR throughout the summer, and which had provided him with a platform to promote his own releases. He'd already launched another label called New Stars, reserved for up-and-coming talent like Knowledge, a vocal group from Rema led by Anthony Doyley. Zukie produced their debut single 'Make Faith' and then began work on the album, *Hail Dread*, which he licensed to A&M. The opening track 'What's Yours' lasted over seven minutes. Others included 'Word, Sound And Power', the moody, majestic 'Fools And Their Money', the more upbeat and yet equally cautionary 'Good Luck My Friend' and then 'Zion', which was reminiscent of the Rasta hymns that groups like the Abyssinians and Culture were also making at the time.

We've already learnt that Zukie was a great admirer of Prince Allah, and when he released the singer's debut album *Heaven Is My Roof* he made sure to include the singles 'Funeral', 'Daniel', 'Bosrah' and the title track. Zukie's legacy has been overshadowed by his gangland connections, but his credentials as a producer on Allah's debut were all too evident. It was a masterly set – comparable to what Burning Spear was doing at the time, but lacking the promotion and distribution to help it reach as far. Spear himself had a new album out, called *Marcus Children*, co-produced with the ubiquitous Karl Pitterson and released on Spear's own label. His deal with Island was coming to an end and the parting wouldn't be particularly amicable.

'There was an understanding that such agreements only work

for them, and not for us,' he told me. 'People disrespect and think they can say anything. That's the way they think all the time about Jamaica and Jamaican music. They are always thinking we're stupid and they can do anything and get away with it. That's the way we've been treated, and that's why I do everything myself. I was always conscious of having to build something and to own something and so after Jack Ruby I say to myself that I'm not going to do anything for other people. I have to be doing it for myself because from early on, I saw these record companies come to Jamaica, hear the essence in certain singers' music, work with them, market them, promote them and sell them, so it's our duty now to take it from there and do all of that for ourselves. I always insist that I want to do this and even when I didn't have anything, I still persevered in trying to do it. I go into the studio and I pay for all of my projects. Nobody was giving me money to do these things, because I do them all by myself.'

Its three Island predecessors were great, but *Marcus Children* was arguably Burning Spear's crowning achievement and one of the best seventies reggae albums ever made. From the anguished cries on the opening track 'Marcus Children Suffer' to the powerful testimony that is 'Marcus Say Jah No Dead', Spear was mesmerising throughout. A song cycle, *Marcus Children* stripped the black experience down to just a handful of key precepts, the ideals of socal living and praise of the Creator included. After yearning for the Promised Land on 'Nyah Keith' came a remake of 'He Prayed' called 'Institution' – a hymn-like chant on which he observed that everything in nature has its rightful home, except for mankind; the sadness in this song is almost overpowering whilst 'Marcus Senior' like 'Mister Garvey', was another of his tributes to Jamaica's National Hero. The dream-like qualities of the rhythms, which lift reggae into the rarefied realms of more celebrated works by soul icons like Curtis Mayfield or Marvin Gaye, put the listener into a spell, even when he was singing a simple refrain testifying to the music's global popularity, as on 'Civilize Reggae.'

Island issued that track, backed with 'Social Living', on a 12-inch single. Both sides were over seven minutes in length and this further served to underline the hypnotic quality of the songs, since Spear's approach was to take a simple statement like 'do you know social living is the best' and repeat it many times. What an enduringly strong message that was.

'What could be better than that?' he said, smiling. 'People should socialise with each other. That's how we get to know people and people get to know each other.'

Chris Blackwell's label repackaged *Marcus Children* as *Social Living,* but there was no difference in the choice of songs, some of which had been recorded at Compass Point in the Bahamas. This new studio, rated as the most modern in the Caribbean, was now Karl Pitterson's regular workspace, although several of the Jamaican musicians travelling to Nassau to record there had experienced problems on arriving because they hadn't been able to produce police certificates. This had led people to question why Blackwell – who'd made so much money out of reggae in Jamaica – had felt the need to go to Nassau to build his studio. Such criticism hadn't deterred Richard Branson from thinking about doing something similar, however, because there was talk that he was planning to build a 32-track recording studio in the Virgin Islands.

If there was rivalry between the two men – as opposed to mutual respect – then it was particularly one-sided when it came to music. Chris Blackwell was an astute businessman, but he genuinely lived and breathed music and enjoyed getting to know a range of different artists and musicians, whereas Branson's interests were more far-ranging. Blackwell received a call from Philippe Lerichomme sometime in autumn 1978, informing him that French singer, actor and bon vivant Serge Gainsbourg wanted to record an album in Jamaica. Lerichomme worked for Phonogram, which distributed Island Records in Europe, and he was also Gainsbourg's artistic director.

'Reggae had only just started to get going in France when Serge made *Aux Armes Et Caetera*,' he told Sylvie Simmons. 'I'd been asked to go to a club one Sunday night to listen to a punk group who were due on stage at midnight. So I was in this half-empty club, it was past midnight and the group still hadn't come on. The disc jockey was playing some very hot things in the meantime – punk and some reggae – and it came to me in a flash. It was two in the morning, so I waited a few hours then phoned Serge and said, "we must go to Jamaica and make a reggae album." Serge said, "good idea!" He didn't need any persuasion.'

Gainsbourg had already taken tentative steps towards recording reggae two years earlier on a track called 'Marilou Reggae', but that was nothing compared to what Lerichomme was now planning. After buying a stack of reggae albums and listening to them all, he'd made a note of which musicians he liked and told Blackwell that he wanted to work with Sly and Robbie, who'd only just returned from their US tour with Peter Tosh. It would be the first time that anyone had recorded a French-speaking album in Jamaica and Serge, Philippe and Jane Birkin's father – standing in for his daughter – arrived in Jamaica during September. They booked Dynamic studio for a week – a place that Serge would later describe as 'the most primitive place imaginable, with chickens clucking about on top of the mixing board.'

Dynamic was the top studio in Jamaica, and had hosted the likes of Paul Simon, Eric Clapton and the Rolling Stones. Serge's description was therefore complete nonsense, and possibly racist. Furthermore, he'd written most of the songs on the flight from Paris, so couldn't be said to have approached the project with due diligence.

'It didn't start out too well,' Lerichomme admitted. 'When we arrived the engineer wasn't there and we really couldn't communicate because Jamaicans speak a special kind of English that we couldn't understand. Also, Robbie Shakespeare didn't know which one of us was the singer and kept talking to me, because Serge was older than me and wore a suit. They thought the producer was the star, not that they gave the impression of caring either way.

'It was quite tense, with no one smiling. It was a case of, "let's take the money and run." Serge, to try and ease the atmosphere, tried to talk to them and said, "do you know any French music?" and they started to take the mickey out of us. "French music?" they said. "We're Jamaican." Serge and I looked at each other, crestfallen. This wasn't good, then Sly said, "we know just one piece of French music – a song called 'Je t'aime' which has a girl groaning in it." Serge said in English, "it's me!" and that changed the whole mood. We recorded very, very fast, and when it was done they didn't want to leave. They hung around the studio to hear the playbacks, smoking their enormous spliffs saying "great, brilliant!"'

It's possible that Sly also knew the reggae version by Judge Dread – a Top 10 UK hit in July 1975 – but Gainsbourg and his British actress girlfriend Jane Birkin had recorded their version back in 1969. Serge had originally written it for his then-partner, international pin-up Brigitte Bardot. At the end of 'Je t'aime', Birkin faked an orgasm, and so the record was censored. It was banned across Europe and publicly denounced by the Vatican but still sold seven million copies. Thus began the fruitful, scandal-ridden partnership, both artistic and romantic, of the 36-year-old Gainsbourg and 19-year-old Birkin, which had already been going ten years by the time Serge and assorted Jamaican musicians assembled at Dynamic for those *Aux Armes Et Caetera* sessions.

'Sly and Robbie, Robbie Lyn and Mikey Chung were all there. I think Keith Sterling was there too, and Geoffrey Chung,' said Clive Chin, who accompanied them. 'Before the session started, the French engineer come in now, go into his briefcase and take out some music scores. The man put one in front of Robbie and I hear him say, "what the bloodclaat?" Everybody look 'pon one another and say, "wha' dis?" Mikey and Robbie Lyn, who knew music, said, "they're telling us what to play, which is what they wrote." Robbie said, "but me can't read this bloodclaat. Tell the man to come in and just sing the bloodclaat tune, then we'll know what to play!" I nearly died laughing, but they called in Serge Gainsbourg, set up a mic for him and start to find the bass-line. That guy was so controversial, and the first time I see him I knew he was a big-time joker man. He love his cigarette and him drink, I tell you.'

Sly has confirmed that Gainsbourg drank a lot and smoked endless packs of Gitanes but couldn't recall ever seeing him wear a suit. On the contrary, there are photos of him taken in Jamaica where he's dressed in faded jeans and a ripped T-shirt, looking very relaxed, but who knows? One thing is certain, which is that Gainsbourg was unique, and just didn't behave like a normal person. Everything about him was different, and working with him must have been so strange for the Jamaican singers and musicians who worked on those sessions. It was just as well that few of them, if any, knew any French, and especially when he was considering recording a track that he'd written specially for the trip, entitled 'Nagusa Nagast'. In the original lyrics he refers to Emperor Haile Selassie I as "a dark idiot" but was thankfully convinced to change that description to read "dark idol". Various studio personnel have told of desperately trying not to laugh whenever the Frenchman was at the mic, but there was another side to him that really wasn't all that funny it seems.

In Jamaica, they refer to such people as 'a sample', meaning a one-off. Peter Tosh was another such character, and soon after Gainsbourg's trip to Jamaica, Arthur Kitchin had an article published in the Gleaner titled 'The Volatile Peter Tosh', in which he praised the ex-Wailer for being highly articulate, despite his fondness for expletives. According to Tosh, bad words helped to dispel any evil vibrations that may be present in any given situation.

'Men wouldn't like what I have to say for when I speak, lightning flash and thunder roll and any force, obeah et cetera, can't stand it. No one can come and spy on us and live. The devil has people who even look like you, dreadlocks and write for newspaper who are really writing for him but I don't deal with fear. My struggle is for justice, and I have every missile to deal with all forms of injustice.'

Yet there were members of the Kingston police force who were still smarting at his attempts to humiliate them at the Peace Concert, and who'd been waiting for an opportunity to get revenge. On 19 September, at around ten in the evening, he was standing outside of Aquarius studio waiting for his musicians to arrive, spliff in his hand as always. Suddenly from nowhere, a man who later turned out to be a plainclothes officer approached him, demanding to see what he had in his hand. A scuffle took place, a policeman appeared and Peter was taken to a nearby police station where he was badly beaten – so badly, in fact, that the officers who'd taken part only stopped when they thought he was dead.

'That's what he told me,' said Steel Pulse's David Hinds. 'He told me that he had to play dead. He heard them walking around him and one of them reached for a jug of ice-cold water. They took it out of the fridge and poured it on him but he didn't flinch. The last thing he remembered hearing was this voice saying, "fuck you. I thought you said Rasta can't dead." He had to do that so they would stop beating him, because the more he resisted them and tried to fight them off, the more they beat him.'

There are varying accounts as to how many stitches he needed to have in his head after being taken to a prison hospital. Peter himself said forty-eight, others say twenty, but he would be tormented by frequent headaches thereafter. Less than two weeks after being released on bail he attended Half Way Tree magistrates court with his left hand in a cast and bandages round his head, and pleaded not guilty to charges of smoking ganja, assaulting and wounding a police constable, resisting arrest and using indecent language. He was remanded on bail, until his next court appearance, scheduled for 7 November.

Jacob 'Killer' Miller was the other big name to have angered the authorities.

'Yes, I smoked herbs onstage at the One Love show,' he told the *Gleaner*. 'In fact, every show we have herbs are smoked, so I don't see what the fuss is all about. I was said to have cursed bad words, but I wasn't conscious that I'd used any. People are just afraid of words, sounds and power. Right now the Commissioner of Police, Mr Dudley Thompson, and the prime minister say they are my friends, but I know the people who are my friends and I don't want the heads of government to forget 1972, when the singers, musicians and Selassie's Rod were putting the party into power.'

His latest album was titled *Wanted* in response, and produced by Inner Circle. The back cover of the LP was designed to look like a wanted poster, with descriptions of the Lewis brothers and 'Jacob Matthias Miller, aka The Killer, who is 24 years of age, 5 ft 9 in tall, weighs 200lbs and has no scars or distinguishing marks. He frequents Beverley Hills, Mona and ital food joints. The subject is wanted for smoking the finest lambs bread.'

'Peace Treaty Special' was on it, of course – also the title track, 'Standing Firm' and the pro-marijuana song 'Healing Of The Nation.' The *Gleaner* reporter didn't discuss music with him, but did give an insight into the singer's lifestyle.

'At home, which is sparsely furnished but comfortable and clean, Jacob lounges around between working periods dressed only in a pair of white shorts, revealing his chubby torso which he exposes on stage after working up a sweat. A few friends and spiritual advisers are always present, taking turns cooking ital or mixing fruit juices. Marijuana is smoked freely and plentifully, and visitors, including foreign journalists, are common. Beneath his jocular exterior lies a shrewd and serious personality, bubbling with self-confidence and quiet optimism. Like many of his generation, Jacob praises Rastafari and wears his hair in dreadlocks.

'Along with Inner Circle, he's preparing for another North American tour which is scheduled to get underway shortly.

"Financially I'm still suffering but some gains have been made," he says. "I own a Mercedes Benz and live in Beverly Hills with the group, who I have been living with for the past six years, first at Chelsea Avenue, then Gallery Apartments. I'd like to be rich so I could use the money to help poor people. I'd also like to open a music and commercial school for the less fortunate but talented in the society."'

Touter Harvey had since rejoined Inner Circle's line-up, and spoke about the group as having a split personality.

'Inner Circle itself had that rock and R&B style to it, and played music with more pop appeal, whereas Jacob Miller was like a roots man, and the Fat Man Rhythm Section was more roots as well.'

The latter group had recorded three dub albums to date, all of them produced by the Lewis brothers and released on Tommy Cowan's Top Ranking Sounds. Two of them were mixed by Channel One engineer Maximillian, 'the New Emperor Of Dub', and the identical set of musicians led by Roger and Ian Lewis also played on Israel Vibration's debut album *The Same Song*, which, in addition to the title track, included their former singles 'Why Worry' and 'Lift Up Your Conscience.' Israel Vibration were a vocal trio comprised of Albert 'Apple' Craig, Lascelles 'Wiss' Bulgin and Cecil 'Skelly' Spence, who, to varying extent, all fell victim to the polio epidemic that had swept Jamaica during the fifties and left hundreds of children up to the age of 16 permanently crippled and maimed. Poliomyelitis or 'infantile paralysis' was both cruel and invisible. It was highly contagious, and yet no cure or vaccine was available. A significant number of the children affected had died, or been left fighting for breath in a metal respiratory tank called an 'iron lung.' At that time no one knew what caused polio, which led to widespread fear. People began to theorise about past sins and other such nonsense, and victims were often hounded out of communities in case they passed it on.

After contracting the disease, the members of Israel Vibration were quickly shunted off to the Mona Polio Rehabilitation Centre in Elleston Flats, on the outskirts of Kingston. This was a residential unit where handicapped children received a basic education and were taught vocational skills. Apple was a little older than the others, and just 3 years old when he contracted polio. He was an orphan without parents or any relatives whatsoever, and was sent to a Salvation Army Children's Home called The Nest prior to attending the Rehabilitation Centre. He then spent a year at the Alpha Boys School before returning to Mona and rejoining Skelly and Wiss, who was from Trelawny and called 'Bruck Up' because of his disabilities. Always the rebel, Apple constantly questioned authority and was the first of the trio to embrace Rastafari, which led to him being expelled from the Centre and having to sleep rough in Jamaica's unforgiving capital.

'I was just out on the street and don't really live anywhere, sleeping on the sidewalks, in bushes, old cars and burned down buildings. I go through that for a couple of years, except I used to go back up to the Centre once in a while to look for Skelly, 'cause he and I were very close when I was there. We used to be like brothers, 'cause we all grow together from baby stage. I was out from there for quite a while before Skelly and Wiss leave, so in the meantime I go through many, many things alone, experiencing various hardships and trying to get somewhere in life.

'I used to check Studio One, Treasure Isle, Beverley's Records, Harry J's and Prince Buster, but none of those people would give me a break because my appearance wasn't right. My clothes were dirty and I was barefoot, because I was sleeping in the riverbed and in trees... A lot of things happen, man!'

Wiss was also expelled from the Centre, and he and Apple would sleep in some nearby scrub. Wiss had a job in downtown Kingston but would return to the bushes at night, where a group of them – including Skelly – would rehearse songs in-between reading the Bible and reasoning about Rastafari. Skelly was from Hanover, where he was born in 1952. Like the others, he'd been sent to Mona as an infant. He was called Skelly on account of being skeleton-thin, and would later represent Jamaica at basketball before being dropped from the team after growing dreadlocks. At 16, he left Mona and went to live with an aunt in Cockburn Pen. Music was all around him in such a neighbourhood and, inspired by Roy Richards, he learnt to play harmonica whilst working as a machinist in a car parts factory.

'Tyrone Downie used to live just down the street from me. He was Bob Marley's keyboard player and so he used to let me come to their rehearsal room sometimes and I would sit there quietly whilst they rehearsed. It was all good and very interesting, watching how they approach their songs, y 'know?'

Inspired by the Wailers, he and the other two began writing songs documenting ghetto life and the hardships endured by Rastafarians, who were still shunned in most Jamaican social circles. After auditioning for Channel One they were invited to record but then fell out with the Hoo Kims before anything was released. They voiced their debut single 'Why Worry' for Twelve Tribes producer Hugh Boothe, who also produced two other songs with them, 'Bad Intentions' and 'Jah Jah Time Has Come', that remained unreleased.

'After we leave out of the bush, the Twelve Tribes organisation start to rise up at that time in Jamaica and we get to know some of them,' Skelly said. 'They used to communicate with us and influence us to join up with them and it look to us at last, there were some people in the world who recognise us and were willing to open the door for us, so we join with them and find out that they have music going on within the Twelve Tribes. They had a band, they keep stage shows and we become centre of that whole music t'ing, y'understand? We tear down all the shows them, and them call us the three cripple dreads, seen? It was like a big t'ing, but then the other artists in the Twelve Tribes start to get jealous – them start to give us a big fight, very badly man! It cause a whole heap a t'ing, y' know? We couldn't believe it – not from our Twelve Tribes brethren, because we had a little house in the ghetto by then and brethren from the Twelve Tribes would come there and fling stone. They approach us to beat us up and curse us, telling us we can't enter Zion because we are cursed and say we are crippled because our fathers were great sinners... These are the words that come from many of our Twelve Tribes brethrens, y'understand? And that is how 'The Same Song' came about, because of the fight that was going on. Then they banned us from the performances 'cause some of them went to the Gad man and influence him against us, so we were shut out. That's why we go out and sing 'The Same Song' where we say "whether you a Bobo, whether you a Twelve Tribes, whether you an Orthodox or a Binghi natty dread, we all haffi sing the same song..." We used to say that all of us were calling upon the same Jah, so why must we fight amongst ourselves? Why is it that one man is right and the other man is wrong? That is what made that song powerful, 'cause otherwise them would end up fighting and look like hypocrites! And that song still hold a position, y'understand?'

Augustus Pablo played on their album, and he was also a regular visitor to Lee Perry's Black Ark, where he recorded some of the tracks on *East Of The River Nile*. That was his first instrumental (as opposed to dub) album – one that US reviewer Robert Christgau later described as 'calming, childish and inexplicable.' It was among the first releases on Pablo's new Message label and the title track was a remake of an instrumental produced by Herman Chin Loy, and recorded several years previously. The later version was transcendent, and dated from around the same time that Pablo was producing Tetrack's album *Let's Get Started*. They were a vocal trio from East Kingston featuring Dave Harvey, Paul Mangaroo and Carlton Hines, who wrote the majority of their material.

'I first met Pablo through a guy named Denzil Gooden, who used to sit in on our rehearsals sometimes,' Hines said. 'One day he said, "I can introduce you to Pablo, y' know? Pablo is my good brethren." We said, "okay, let's put together a cassette." I was still at Excelsior school, near where my girlfriend lived, and the music for us was never a career thing. We never said, "we're going to do singing and nothing else." Music for us was a hobby. It was a fun t'ing, and we never had any huge plans for music. We were working class people trying to survive and our focus was more on school. All three of us went to high school and had some tertiary education. Paul was working as a lab technician; after a while Dave became a mechanical engineer and I was working at a bank because I was fortunate enough to go to university where I studied economics.

'There's a song on our album called 'Couldn't Walk Away' which was written whilst I was at Jamaica College. Dave was there studying physics or whatever, but we'd take breaks, and that's when we'd sing some songs. I was there one day and 'Couldn't Walk Away' came to me just like that. I wrote that song in about half an hour. Songs tend to overwhelm me sometimes. Initially I didn't use an instrument, but after meeting Pablo, he gave me a guitar that had previously belonged to Everton Da Silva. I couldn't do anything with it at first but I got myself a chord book and my fingers would *burn*. It was like torture but I start to put some chords together and then the melodies would come, because when I write a song I come with everything. I'm getting the lead and harmony arrangement, I'm hearing bass-lines, horn lines and all type of thing, then when I get in the studio with people who are bass or guitar players, I tend to relax and let them do their thing.'

The group's first song for Pablo was 'I'm Not Satisfied.'

'What was funny about that song is, when we met with Pablo we went to his house first, we gave him the cassette, he listened to it and Pablo is a very laconic type of guy. He doesn't speak a lot, y'know? You have to draw him out, but when he gets going, you can't believe that it's the same Pablo! After he heard the tape he said "come", we jump in the car and went over to Black Ants Lane where the sound system Rockers International was based. His brother Dougie and a guy called Street who lived in Black Ants Lane had that set and Pablo was there, playing us some rhythms and that's how we got *Let's Get Together*, because he said, "I want you to sing this, y' know?" That was the first time we were hearing it, and then he gave us another rhythm and said, "I want you to write something on this." I tried to write something, and 'I'm Not Satisfied' resulted from that.'

Their debut was a concept album, portraying the life and loves of a Jamaican ghetto singer. Carlton has likened it to a documentary, but it remained unheard for almost three years because Pablo didn't have the funds to release it.

'There were all kinds of factors that contributed to that,' Hines explained. 'What people need to understand is that Jamaica was going through a serious social revolution at that time. You had a synthesis going on between uptown and downtown youngsters, and the glue that held those things together was Rastafari because that drew in all different sectors of Jamaican society, and youngsters from all over were expressing their own anti-establishment, anti-colonial viewpoints. That type of environment, it lent itself to a certain kind of vibe, sensitivity, outlook and so on. A certain militancy existed and, if you notice, that was when the music switched to a more predominantly social commentary type of thing. A lot of the artists started to wear dreadlocks and, to my mind, a lot of the work that came out was a very accurate reflection of what was happening in Jamaican society back then.'

The Rockers crew at that time – not counting Pablo's brothers Garth and Dougie – included Jah Bull, Ricky Grant, Delroy Williams, Bunny Brissett, Norris Reid, Lacksley Castell and Hugh Mundell, whose debut album *Africa Must Be Free By 1983* (and matching dub album) was another essential Message release. Some of the rhythms were quite old by the time those albums came out, although they didn't sound all that dated. Steely and Clevie had played their first-ever session together when recording the title track. Clevie was 14 and Steely just 11 when they met up with the other musicians at Harry J's that day. It would prove an auspicious beginning, although the pair went their separate ways soon afterwards. Clevie joined the In Crowd just in time for their debut

LP, *His Majesty Is Coming*, whilst Steely played on Sugar Minott productions like ''51 Storm', 'Man Hungry' and 'River Jordan' for the Black Roots label. Sugar himself had found another gear by then, and for a variety of labels including Channel One, Studio One and Prince Jammy, for whom he voiced the gorgeous ballad 'Never Too Young.' Coxsone did well out of 'Vanity' and 'Peace Treaty Style' but Sugar's biggest hit for the veteran producer was 'Oh Mr DC', which he wrote about being stopped on his way back from the countryside with a stash of collie weed and being admonished by the Deputy Commissioner of Police.

'People in Jamaica make most of their living from selling herb, and in the ghetto where I come from, Maxfield Park, most people sell herb there,' Sugar told Steve Milne. 'Whenever somebody gone to the country to get some herb, the whole area would worry and wonder if he's gonna make it or come home. My friends used to do a lot of these things and they get held often so I decided to make this song like a protest, like a "Legalise It" kind of song "let me survive because this is what make me live." It's not fiction. It's a real thing, and it's happening right now, today.'

Coxsone also released Freddie McGregor's 'Ghetto Child' in 1978, whilst Niney The Observer produced Freddie's cut to Leroy Smart's spine-tingling 'Jah Is My Light.' But it was the trio of songs he recorded with Soul Syndicate's Chinna Smith, including covers of LTD's 'Love Ballad' and Norman Connors' 'You Are My Starship', that marked a turning point in the singer's career. Both demonstrated his mastery of the soul reggae idiom, although Freddie had changed the lyrics of 'You Are My Starship' and transformed it into a ganja song called 'Natural Collie.' It was brilliantly done, and even *sounded* like what a marijuana high feels like. Island were interested in releasing it, but Connors refused to sanction Freddie's adaptation, and so he and Chinna put it out themselves. The other record in that trilogy was 'Mark Of The Beast', an original composition lamenting the influence of Satan, something that Bob Marley also spoke about. There'd been a rise in visits to 56 Hope Road by overseas media people ever since Marley's return to the island, and a reporter from *The New York Times* asked him about the irony involved in having a national music – reggae – that does little more than snipe at the nation.

'Look around you,' Marley replied. 'There's war going on. Right now the devil, him have plenty influence. The devil him strutting everywhere. The government is trampling over the people's sweat and tears. Coming down hard, hard. We're oppressed, so we sing oppressed songs and sometimes people find themselves guilty, and they can't stand the terrible weight of it. Babylon doesn't want peace. Babylon want power, Babylon want to keep the people down. We must fight against the darkness. It is better to die fighting for your freedom than to be a prisoner all the days of your life. It is better that righteousness cover the earth like water cover the sea.'

When the interviewer mentioned 'Burnin' And Lootin'' Bob laughed. 'We're not talking about burning and looting for material goods,' he said. 'We want to burn capitalistic illusions. Anyway, Jamaica just run out of politics today. Me nah deal with politics. Me sing and deal with the truth the best I can. Me sing the songs and hope the people catch the tune and mark the words. People have plenty misunderstanding man. Nothing is important that much. Love life and live, that's all.'

Life in the UK – even for the poor – was very different from that of a third world country, and yet a lot of people of all races felt abandoned by the political system there too, and wanted change. They wanted an end to neglect, discrimination and racism, and faced a growing threat from far right groups like the National Front. Reggae music, like punk, was emblematic of this struggle and it was good to see that audiences had become a lot more diverse as a result. There were increasing numbers of Asian people attending reggae gigs and dances in the London area, and it was a mixed crowd that turned out on 23 September when Aswad, Matumbi and the Cimarons headlined the first International Reggae Festival at London's Alexandra Palace.

Matumbi had recorded their *Seven Seals* album for Harvest at Berry Street studios in May and several of the songs on it – including 'Bluebeat & Ska', 'Empire Road' (written for a UK TV series), 'All Over This World' and 'Hook Deh' – would feature in a live session they did for John Peel in October. Another of the album tracks, 'Rock', was a fabulous semi-instrumental lasting over eleven minutes, complete with wonderful flute. Matumbi weren't concerned with being 'dread.' The music they were making was capable of crossing over, yet still communicated a message and sounded very much like reggae with its heavy bass-lines. Bandleader Dennis Bovell had continued moonlighting outside the band, releasing albums as the 4th Street Orchestra (*Scientific*) and under his own name (*Strictly Dub Wize*), in-between producing hits with Marie Pierre ('Walk Away') and 15-16-17, among others.

The Cimarons were celebrating the release of their *Maka* album for Polydor. There was a lethargic feel about this album that blunted its impact – the songs were stronger on *Live At The Roundhouse*, taped the previous summer – but John Peel had already played several tracks, including 'Loosenin' Out', 'The Word' and 'Willin' (Rock Against Racism)', which keyboardist Carl Levy told *Sounds'* Eric Fuller was 'just a part of the central argument coming through.'

'Racism is different from race consciousness,' Levy continued. 'Racism is abusive and negative. That racialist attitude nullifies the situation where you and I can sit here and smoke a spliff and cool out. If there is a black youth out there with that racialist idea, we will rock against that bloodclaat. Rock Against Racism is a serious thing, because we are living here and we have to benefit from each other.'

The following day another large crowd marched from Hyde Park to Brockwell Park in Brixton. This was another joint promotion organised by Rock Against Racism and the Anti-Nazi League. Aswad were among the bands taking part that day, together with Elvis Costello, Sham 69 and Misty In Roots.

'The punks were there because white people had issues as well,'

Aswad's Tony Gad said. 'There were things they weren't happy with and their argument was that black people were saying what they wanted to say, and so they should do the same thing as well. The message was the same from everyone. It wasn't an argument of just wanting to break down authority, it was more about wanting to get equal treatment. We wanted to get fair treatment and it wasn't just because we were black – all of us wanted fair treatment because we were human beings. Everyone was just against what was going on, basically, and when we talked about certain things in our music, it wasn't just black people who had that problem.'

Aswad's latest single, 'It's Not Our Wish (That We Should Fight)', wasn't about backing down from the struggle, but a failing romance. They were no longer signed to Island, so manager/producer Mikey 'Reuben' Campbell put it out via Grove Music. He was one of the founders of Grove, together with King Sounds and Trevor Bow, who was a close friend of Bob Marley's from Trench Town. He and his group Sons Of Jah had recently released their debut album *Bankrupt Morality* on their own Natty Congo label, whilst King Sounds had followed 'Rock And Roll Lullaby' with 'Spend One Night In Babylon' – a song inspired by visits to Columbo's in Carnaby Street (formerly known as the Roaring Twenties), where Sir Coxsone was the resident sound system.

'Night on top of nights I stand up in there and what I really see vex I,' King Sounds told Penny Reel. 'From it reach two o'clock in the morning when the prostitutes are coming in, I see the formation of Babylon right there. I see where the Father's children get lost in corruption. I see the big bottle of champagne them vainly burst in front of everyone and when everybody get drunk they fight and stab up each other. As a black person me get vexed, because that's not how we're supposed to live in England or anywhere at all. And sometimes when I read what people write about us not being together, I have to agree with it in a sense, seeing such things in places like Columbo's. Because I don't think we come here to be prostitutes, whores and pimps, so 'Spend One Night In A Babylon' come right from that corner...'

It wasn't enough for a reggae artist to deliver a hit. They had to *represent* as well, and Capital Letters' 'Smoking My Ganja' reflected a world that went largely unreported outside of the UK's black communities.

'I'm a wanted man. Running away from the police them. Them want fi charge I for smoking ganja. Some of them come in with their guns. Some of them come with their batons. Some are riding on horses. Some of them are coming with their dogs, just to catch I.'

With its simple but insistent groove, anchored by chopping rhythm guitar and the kind of lively bass-line that would soon become synonymous with the 2 Tone scene, 'Smoking My Ganja' was a masterclass in how to simultaneously make a statement and get people dancing. That song was Wolverhampton band Capital Letters' debut, although their story goes back to the very early seventies. The West Midlands city where they're from had always played second fiddle to neighbouring Birmingham and was renowned for its sound systems, although unemployment was rife and there was little for them to do in Penn Fields except start a band, which is exactly what the founder members did after meeting at a local youth club. That was in 1972, just as *The Harder They Come* was giving many British cinemagoers their first real glimpse of Jamaica. Three of the band members came from there. Percussionist Wenty Stewart aka 'Country' was raised in St Ann and didn't leave for England until he was a teenager. He arrived in 1967, three years after singer/guitarist Danny McKen, otherwise known as 'Teacher', left his home in St Thomas. He started off playing bass, but wanted to sing and play at the same time and so switched to guitar. Fellow guitarist, Hanover-born George Scarlett, took over after the original guitarist, a would-be Casanova called Gilbert, missed one too many rehearsals. After a six-month spell as ABC, the band settled on the Alphabets and, in 1976, made their recording debut with a cover of Errol Dunkley's 'You're Gonna Need Me.' Nothing came out of it except the discovery that there was already a band called the Alphabets, so they changed their name to Capital Letters, whose line-up at the time included Junior Brown (bass), Earl Lynch (keyboards and vocals) and drummer Roderick Harvey, aka 'The Dude.'

'We practised seven days a week in the cellar of this community centre and we had a quarter-inch reel-to-reel running in there non-stop, taping everything we did,' said Danny. "Smoking My Ganja' was the very first song we wrote as Capital Letters. It just happened one night when we were smoking and playing. Every Friday we'd put our money together and see what it could buy us and this particular night it must have been something good because as soon as we lit up, everything just clicked!'

After demoing the song in Wolverhampton, they travelled to London and played it to Greensleeves' Chris Cracknell, who suggested they re-record it at Chalk Farm with Sid Bucknor. This second version of 'Smoking My Ganja' was embraced by punks and reggae fans alike, and stayed on the *Black Echoes'* charts for months. John Peel made it his Record Of The Week and invited them to play a live session which in turn led to wider recognition, not least on the university circuit.

The Greensleeves shop at 44 Uxbridge Road in Shepherd's Bush fast became a major hub for reggae in West London, and it wasn't at all unusual to see visiting reggae stars and producers there, as well as well-known names from the UK.

'When we started the label, it was on the premise that we would operate like a major label and try and do things properly, which was pretty unheard of in the reggae business at the time,' said Chris Cracknell. 'We decided we were going to treat people properly and give them an incentive, so we paid decent advances, went for top quality mastering and sleeve design and accounted to all the right people. We didn't want to stifle people or see them reap little reward. We wanted to encourage them to continue making music and realise that producing records could be a career for them. Ultimately, we wanted everything that we did to reflect our total commitment to the music, and to present reggae in such a way that it could be competitive with any other genre but we never remixed anything, or fell into the trap of trying to make it more accessible for the mainstream market. We didn't go down that path at all.'

Right from the start, Greensleeves allied themselves with the latest musical trends from Jamaica, although not exclusively, as singles by the Reggae Regular and Capital Letters proved. Their first album release was Dr Alimantado's *Best Dressed Chicken In Town*, and if the music itself didn't grab your attention then the sight of a shirtless Alimantado on the front cover, stood in the middle of a Kingston street in broken down shoes with his flies wide open, most probably would have done. He looked like a homeless person – the very opposite of best dressed! Yet Alimantado was also very principled, and knew exactly what he wanted from his career in music. After arriving in London he'd had talks with Dub Vendor and Daddy Kool about them distributing his productions in the UK, but the negotiations had broken down, and that's when he and Greensleeves went into business together.

'Greensleeves' offer wasn't financially viable,' he told David Katz, 'but it offered me a place in a stable company, because at the time there were companies like Virgin willing to spend half a million pounds on promoting Dr Alimantado, but Greensleeves offered to help me set up my own company, to be there when I needed them any time of day and night and to give me any assistance that I needed. I could turn to them, and that was more important to me than half a million pounds at the time.'

The interest from Virgin wasn't hypothetical, because they'd already released 'Slavery Let I Go' on 12-inch by the time his album with Greensleeves came out. Three of the songs on *Best Dressed Chicken In Town* were recorded at Black Ark – the title track, 'Can't Conquer Natty Dreadlocks' and 'Ride On' – whilst others came from sessions at Channel One and Randy's. According to the liner notes, all tracks were 'inspired by Jah feeling inside!' and John Peel obviously agreed, since he played excerpts from it throughout September and October, despite getting letters from some listeners complaining that he played too much reggae.

Rob 'Iron Man' Blackmore from Wolverhampton ('Rock capital of the world') felt much the same. He obviously sensed colonialism in reverse and wrote to one of the main UK music weeklies saying 'I am disgusted with *Sounds* because over the past few weeks the paper has been invaded by Blacks. Nobody likes this rubbish which is pigeon English sung over the same reggae beat. All my fellow rock fans feel the same way and if you do not print this it proves you love Blacks. Why don't you fill *Sounds* with decent groups such as Rainbow, Lizzy, Sabbath, Purple, Floyd, Rush, Priest etc?'

Fortunately, not everyone held the same opinions as Iron Man Blackmore, and with help from John Peel and a handful of other influential club DJs, radio presenters and music journalists, reggae continued selling to fans in the UK who'd never set foot in a blues dance or clubs like the Four Aces and Columbo's, but had developed a taste for the very same releases that sold to black audiences. Greensleeves catered for both these demographics by basically ignoring any distinctions, and just putting out music they believed in. The Wailing Souls' 'War' backed with 'Jah Give Us Life' was Greensleeves' first-ever 12-inch release, featuring songs written by lead singer Winston 'Pipe' Matthews.

'I was asleep and I get up and wrote 'Jah Give Us Life', then I wrote 'War' inside the next hour or so,' he said, laughing. 'They were big songs for me but my girlfriend said, "man, you are different. You get up out of your bed and go and write two songs like that!" During that time the politics war was doing its worst. People were saying, "you can't go here or there because you will get killed", but we were one set of artists that had a good relationship with the rude boys and so they didn't mess with us. We drove anywhere we wanted to go because they know we are not the kind of people who deal with the negative. I had a lot of friends who get caught up in politics – youths that I grew up with in Trench Town – and they all get killed, so if anyone tried to disrespect us we would leave from there because our thing was music and sports. We would play sports in the day and then take up our guitars in the evening. We would eat, smoke, write songs and sing them together... We knew what was happening with politics and all that, because it was all around us, and if you've been raised in the ghetto then you know about suffering. You have to know about hardship and struggle to get that kind of vibe, because that's where reggae music come from and that's why I always say it is the people's music, y'know?'

'Very Well', 'Joy Within Your Heart' and 'Fire Mus Mus Tail' were the Wailing Souls' other big hits from 1978. The group was still working out of Channel One for the most part and that was also where Ranking Joe voiced the songs on his Greensleeves' album *Weakheart Fadeaway*. Prince Tony hardly helped raise standards when issuing a rival LP that was disingenuously titled *The Best Of Ranking Joe*. It wasn't, but that connection had come about because Prince Tony was U-Roy's producer, and Ranking Joe was deejaying on King Sturgav at the time. In Joe's own words, he was a youth whilst U-Roy was the teacher, which may explain why he sounded a bit like him on early hits like 'Mr Finnegan.'

'Me playing on U-Roy's sound was like winning a scholarship or something,' Joe said. 'It was the highest achievement for a deejay at that time working alongside U-Roy, who was the greatest, y'know? You can't pay for that kind of experience, which bring me so much wisdom and knowledge. I was able to eventually stand on my own because of that.'

There's a saying in Jamaica that 'each one teach one', and that certainly applied to deejays. Ranking Joe was only 19 but already had an apprentice of his own called Jah Thomas. He was a few years older and hailed from Rockfort originally, although he grew up between Ghost Town and Trench Town. He had eleven brothers and sisters and sold newspapers from a very young age before working as a mechanic. They called him 'Juke Box' at the repair shop, because he knew all the latest reggae tunes. It wasn't until he moved to Payne Land that he picked up a mic for the first time and, a short while later, recorded his debut 'Midnight Rock' for GGs. By the time he joined Joe and Jah Screw on King Sturgav he was living on Maple View Road and guesting on Soul Imperial and Kilimanjaro, in-between voicing tracks like 'Landlord' for Channel One. Greensleeves licensed his album *Stop Yu Loafin'* from the Hoo Kims and commissioned a young illustrator called Tony McDermott to design the cover. Tony was just 17 and an avid soul fan living in Manchester when Greensleeves' A&R man Chris Cracknell saw his drawings in *Black Echoes* and gave him a call.

'I started drawing cartoons when I was 14, 15, so my main influences were comic book artists,' McDermott said. 'It was just something I was interested in and especially if they had a point to make as well, because the stuff in *Black Echoes* was supposed to be wry and humorous, and that's what had interested Greensleeves. That's how they saw Jah Thomas – as someone who was humorous, and he was.'

That wouldn't have been the first thing anyone said about Keith Hudson. Greensleeves released his 'Bloody Eyes' after hearing it on Hudson's latest LP *Rasta Communication*, for his own Joint International label. The idiosyncratic 'Dark Prince Of Reggae' had released dub versions of these tracks on the previous year's *Brand* but the addition of vocals expounding on Rastafari and the Rastafarian lifestyle took it to another level entirely. There was an eerie atmosphere surrounding songs like 'Felt We Felt The Strain' and 'I'm No Fool', whilst 'Rasta Country' was voiced over a martial, steppers beat that quickly made it a favourite of sound systems like Fat Man and Jah Shaka.

The defunct Pama label had by now morphed into Jet Star Phonographics, based at 155 Acton Lane in Park Royal. It was managed by Carl Palmer and his wife Beverley, with his brothers Harry and Jeff in supporting roles. Jet Star were mainly concerned with distribution and supplying record stores across the country – small independents for the most part like Dub Vendor, situated in a tiny space next to Ladbroke Grove tube station. It was little more than a kiosk, in fact, but one crammed with import 45s and albums and also people, thereby ensuring a lively atmosphere. Customers loved it, and it quickly became a haven for record buyers eager to keep up with the constant flood of releases coming from Jamaica and the UK. Dub Vendor had its origins in a Clapham Junction market stall run by John McGillvray and Chris Lane, who'd been friends since schooldays. They had a shop in Peckham before renting the Ladbroke Grove premises, and started selling reggae records at a time when black British youngsters were searching for identity through the music. In most cases, their parents were from the Caribbean and whilst they often felt stranded between the two cultures, a majority of them looked towards Jamaica when expressing themselves through music, language, fashion, and attitude. This changed with the realisation that their own truth had more value. It made their music different, for sure, but it certainly wasn't any less relevant than whatever was coming from Jamaica.

'It was a peak time for reggae because for a short time we noticed that British reggae was actually outselling the music from Jamaica,' noted McGillvray. 'It was targeted at a specific audience over here because it was influenced by Jamaican reggae, but expressed itself in a slightly different way. You had the roots reggae and the lovers rock, and both those styles came out of the same thing, really. But reggae also had its own infrastructure, and this meant it didn't have to rely upon mainstream radio play and media exposure. If that happened it was a bonus, but you didn't actually need that. We had our own network in place that revolved around record shops, studios, distributors, magazines and a few radio programmes. For instance, when *Black Echoes* came out it proved very useful as a gauge of what was out there, and especially because it was a weekly publication. The charts weren't 100 per cent accurate, but the Top 10 probably was and that certainly helped to spread the music around because before that, the only charts we had were put out by record companies in the form of an advert, selling their own product. If you were in the business then you realised they were just trying to shift stuff they couldn't sell but when you're a 14-year-old white kid and you're fresh to it you wouldn't necessarily know that.'

David Rodigan, who was born in Germany but raised in Oxford, wrote reviews and articles for *Black Echoes* – sometimes under the name Sky Juice – and had recently began co-hosting a Sunday reggae show with Tony Williams on Radio London. The show's title was *B&B* but reggae fans called it *Rice And Peas*, after Jamaica's traditional Sunday dish.

'From very early on, my approach to broadcasting was that you needed to be a companion to the listener,' he wrote in his auto-biography. 'I felt that you were invited into someone's front room, their car or bedroom, and you should behave accordingly. You would never patronise, shout or be demonstrative, because that would be an invasion of their space. You were a guest and you had to remember that.

'One of the problems I had with my early broadcasting was getting to sound more natural and less scripted. For years I continued writing it all down and making precise notes. It reflected not just my love for the music but also the fact that I was incred-ibly nervous. I always felt a need to contextualise the records. I thought that was the responsibility of a broadcaster when dealing with a specialist subject. Jamaican music already had a great history and I wanted it to get all the credit that I thought it deserved – and for that the audience needed all the information.'

Such attention to detail would serve him well as his reputation as a radio presenter grew and he began DJing at places like the Apollo, Bouncing Ball and Streatham's Bali High, where he began his long-time association with Papa Face.

It was around that same time – in late September 1978 – that

Third World's 'Now That We've Found Love' went to number ten in the UK. It's said to have been the only time that another band improved on an O'Jays' song, and the extended 12-inch mix quickly became a firm favourite with club and radio DJs worldwide. This wasn't too much of a surprise since it radiated happiness, made people want to dance and was a perfect synthesis of reggae, pop, soul and disco. Whilst it brought joy to mainstream listeners, there were the inevitable cries of 'sell-out' from hardcore reggae fans. Third World guitarist Cat Coore was no stranger to such criticism, but saw no downside to having taken reggae music to the masses. Stevie Wonder, a big Third World fan, agreed, while *Black Echoes* described them as 'the number one reggae/funk crossover band of all time. They're the only band to fuse the two styles with complete effectiveness and yet not lose that essential vitality of reggae.'

'Now That We've Found Love' was taken from their latest album for Island, *Journey To Addis*, recorded at Compass Point. Lead singer Bunny Rugs was outstanding throughout and the production immaculate thanks to additional input from Alex Sadkin and mixing engineer Stephen Stanley, who the band members knew from his stint at Aquarius. Listening to the title track, inspired by Don Drummond's 'Confucius', one could hear just how far reggae music had come in the past twenty years. The roots of it were still there, but many other influences had come into play more recently, and that allowed the musicians free reign to demonstrate their skills and imagination.

Bunny Wailer's latest single, 'Roots, Radics, Rockers And Reggae', put the message back into the international reggae sound, whilst 'Rockers' was written for the movie soundtrack that Island were about to release. In the main, Bunny's own Solomonic label had become a reliable source of high quality reggae recordings that refused to skimp on anything – not horns, percussion or the latest electronic innovations. All those elements were incorporated into a framework that retained a strong sense of identity – that of a Rastaman living in the modern world, and intent on promoting universal truths. The Abyssinians weren't quite so adventurous but their second album *Arise*, released on Front Line, was a worthy follow-up to *Satta Massagana*. All three members contributed songs and vocals – Linford Manning's 'Jah Loves' is heavenly – but it's when Bernard Collins sings lead that everything seems to fall into place and the Abyssinians really come into their own as heard on 'Wicked Men', 'Let My Days Be Long' and a resplendent 'This Land Is For Everyone', which Virgin nevertheless relegated to the flipside of 'Hey You.'

'Virgin had a lot of things planned when they signed up a lot of artists, but some of them got put on the shelf,' Bernard Collins told David Katz. 'It's like they hide the cultural music from the people. They don't want reggae with true culture. Reggae is black music, the white man really have nothing to do with establishing the culture in it. I myself would never really like a whole heap of money in the business. It is work we are doing to establish the world of Jah Rastafari culture over the years, to show people certain truth for the slavery coming onto this time so they can know themselves. It's about slavery and the day-to-day struggle that I and I go through with our colonial masters. I express certain things to give people cultural faith and strength to keep on. Some of our tracks are dealing with repatriation, because if you are a black man, Africa is where it's at. That's where I and I come from, I and I look fi go back there and show that Africa is for the Africans and we have to organise and centralise ourselves in essentially what is our land. We go to the West Indies under the English, yet we still can't go into England without visas and documentation. It's like we don't live nowhere!'

On 7 October, the *NME* published a photo of Peter Tosh under the caption 'Tosh Brutalised.' He was shown with his arm in a sling and facial injuries as a result of that beating the police had given him in September. Not even The Rolling Stones, those perennial bad boys of rock, could match the former Wailer for rebel status, but he and Mick Jagger's newly released 'Don't Look Back' stuttered

to a halt just outside the UK Top 40 and wasn't the hit everyone had hoped for. Whilst all that was unfolding, prime minister
Michael Manley was awarded a Gold Medal for Distinguished
Service Against Apartheid at the United Nations in New York,
where he received a standing ovation for his acceptance speech.
Jamaica's leader was being deservedly honoured on the world stage
for his support of nations struggling against colonialism, but there
were matters closer to home that needed urgent attention as well,
not least the worsening rates of poverty, unemployment and violent
crime.

'When you born and grow in Jamaica it's like a college a day,'
commented Michael Prophet, then celebrating his debut hit 'Fight
It To The Top.' 'Things is rough on the rock and if you are a
survivor, then you learn and come through, y'know? You will
survive. All those things is experience, and at times it feels like
everything just combines together to form a barrier that you can't
escape from, but I really work on it because I don't wanna trod
down some long, hard road. When a person is gifted no one can
take that away so I take my time and write songs through hard
times and good times...'

Michael was from Clarendon and although he tried – and failed
– to interest Joe Gibbs and Channel One, he successfully auditioned
for Yabby You, who lived nearby. He would go round to the producer's house every evening to practise until one day Yabby took him
back to Channel One where they recorded the 21-year-old's debut
'Praise You Jah Jah.' There was a hurt in Michael's voice that was
unmistakable, and the decision to cover the Heptones' 'Fight To
The Top' was a good one, since everyone knew the original; the
message in it hadn't dated and in the Jamaican dancehalls, fresh
talent was always welcome.

In addition to working with Michael Prophet, Yabby You licensed
a flurry of albums and singles to Grove Music. These included some
of his own, like *Beware Dub*, and also LPs by Wayne Wade (*Dancing
Time*) and Trinity's 'Jesus Dread' single. Grove, as the name

suggests, was based in Ladbroke Grove, whilst Jamaica Sound, who released a lot of Dillinger's output, were in Portobello Road. Burning Sounds was another key outlet for reggae in the UK. They made a splash in 1977 when releasing Gussie Clarke's *Black Foundation Dub* and the Various Artists set *Funny Feelings*, containing Dennis Brown's 'To The Foundation.' That got them noticed and they'd gathered pace since then by licensing material from Winston Riley, Jimmy Riley (*Majority Rule* and *The Explosive Showcase*), Phil Pratt, Jah Lloyd (Mike Brooks' *What A Gathering*) and Linval Thompson, who produced albums by Ranking Dread, Cornel Campbell and Big Joe, and still found time to record three albums of his own – *Love Is The Question, Rocking Vibration* and *I Love Marijuana*, along with his latest single 'Danger In Your Eyes.' Linval was prolific, but Al Campbell had double that number of album releases in 1978 – two self-produced (*Showcase* and *Loving Moods Of*) and one apiece for Phil Pratt and Bunny Lee. Al voiced the other two, *Rainy Days* and *Mr Music Man* for U Brown, whose current hit was 'Weather Balloon.' The first version of that song was produced by Carlton Patterson, who chose Ranking Joe to deejay over the rhythm at first, despite U Brown having popularised those lyrics in the dancehalls. That was a big mistake, because U Brown promptly recut it with a different set of musicians for his own Hit Sound label and it became the biggest hit of his career. Coming into November 1978 there wasn't a sound system in Jamaica – or anywhere else for that matter – that wasn't playing it. It was Bunny Lee who'd initiated U Brown as a producer after giving him a cut of Barry Brown's 'Mr Money Man.' U Brown voiced 'Badness And Madness' on the same rhythm and never looked back. In addition to those albums just mentioned, he pressed up another called *Weather Balloon* that was again self-produced, and that he would soon offer Virgin.

Bunny Lee licensed Barry Brown's eagerly awaited debut album *Showcase* to Third World and it proved well worth the wait. As expected, it was a roots set containing songs like 'Unity Is Strength',

'Mr Money Man' and 'Let Go Jah Jah Children', although anyone browsing through the racks wouldn't know this from looking at the sleeve, which had a painting of a half-naked woman on it. Bunny's latest discovery was coming on strong, as heard on recent singles 'Mafia' and 'Step It Up Youthman', whereas Horace Andy was a champion already, and proved it on his *Sings For You And Yours* set, featuring tracks like 'My Guiding Star', 'Money Is The Root Of All Evil', 'Don't Try To Use Me', 'Better Collie' and the mighty 'Zion Gate', aka 'I Don't Want To Be Outside.' Bunny 'Striker' Lee produced that one, although Horace also voiced an album for Tapper Zukie and was still recording the occasional tune for Everton Da Silva's Hungry Town label. His songs for Striker were imbued with a magisterial power and beauty that distinguished them from virtually everything else he'd done up to that point.

Anyone wanting to hear music like this on Jamaican radio had to tune into JBC on Saturday nights for Mikey Campbell's show *Dread At The Controls.* The DJ sensation from Port Antonio had made his first major public appearance at the Mighty Diamonds' album launch back in May. He'd since embarked on a recording career with the songs 'Barber Saloon' and 'Love The Dread', voiced in a catchy singjay style that was all the rage. Mikey only began broadcasting on the radio in 1977. It was JBC's Ossie Harvey who suggested that he and a girl named Freddie Rodriguez play music every night (except Sundays) from midnight onwards, after the regular programming had finished. Mikey wasn't allowed to speak on air at first as he was just an engineer, and not a presenter. Freddie therefore did the talking, until the station manager changed everything round and Mikey ended up hosting *Dread At The Controls* on his own on Saturday nights. Everything took off from there, despite the station programmers' reservations about what he was playing. The 24-year-old DJ was heavily into reggae music and knew a lot of the Kingston-based artists and producers. He got on especially well with King Tubby, who helped him create an impressive selection of custom-made jingles and dub plates, some of them wildly imaginative. These jingles made him different from every other radio DJ, along with the fact that he would play exclusive music that wouldn't be released for months to come.

'After a while, JBC's management say they were having a board meeting,' he recalled. 'They call me into the meeting and say people are complaining that I'm spoiling up the records. Then they come back again another time and say that I have to stop doing it because people are going to the record store and asking for the ones I play, and not "the other ones." That was another problem right there. I used to write songs when I had a break and I'd go on the mic at stage shows or a dance, but I was never really into making records because then JBC would be thinking that I'm using the radio to promote myself. So most of the time I keep myself out of it because there was so much pressure on me and yet people on the street, they love me, y'know? I won an award for Best Radio Personality of the year in 1978 yet they just play that down and they never really make anything out of it. One time they even told me, "you are playing so much reggae and it's monotonous." That inspired me even more and I get more confidence in myself because I liked what I was doing, and I'd spend a lot of time at different recording studios, getting an idea of what everyone was doing. When I'm not working or I do an early shift and have nothing to do for the whole day, I'd take a bus and go to Tubby's and meet with some of the sound men. I'd see what rhythms them have and what they're dealing with and learn what was happening, y'know what I mean?'

'A lot of things was happening in Jamaica at that time,' Dread told Steve Milne. 'The culture was on an exodus. Everybody wanted to align themselves with some kind of culture, some kind of consciousness, some kind of togetherness, some kind of bonding, spiritually and brotherly and mentally. And Rastafari was really the only choice we had. Every song, every man was singing more about Africa. The Mighty Diamonds and certain other artists would be singing about Africa from the spiritual level, like Junior Byles' 'There's A Place Called Africa.' Certain sounds were prominent within that era. The DJs were not like the ones of today. Those people had to come with conscious lyrics and people wanted to hear that. Then there was Bob Marley around making waves, making an impression, making his presence felt, doing a different kind of reggae. There was Lee Perry – innovative, doing his own kind of Black Ark kind of recording and getting a lot of good international acceptance. There was King Tubby, who was kicking for all the sound systems of the day, making sure that every man have a dub. There were a lot of sounds and there was a lot of dub, so it's like the music was underground. To hear real reggae music in the seventies you had to go underground to listen to it, go to some special dances where King Tubby's would be playing or Tippatone or Jah Love Muzik. Different people were playing different music because it's like them have a different crowd, but what I did on the radio is to utilise the different styles of every sound system operator because I had access to all the dubs, so if one sound was playing a particular dub, me can play the same one. Being on the radio meant that every man used to bring me songs after a while. Originally I had to walk physically and get them, but after a while them start come to me with music and I never turn down none of my brothers or sisters. We just play music and more time I even play it twice. "Lick it back from the top to the very last drop".'

In addition to presenting his radio show, Mikey would deejay alongside Ranking Trevor and U Brown on Socialist Roots from time to time. The first producer to record him was Joe Gibbs, who cut 'Friend And Money' over the 'Money In My Pocket' rhythm. He also recorded songs like 'Home Guard', 'Dread At The Control' and 'School Girl' for Lee 'Scratch' Perry, who Mikey says got the best from him. He and Carlton Patterson, who had the Black & White label, were good friends and worked together on Ray I's 'Weatherman Skank', although it was King Tubby who showed Mikey how to make a record and then get it mixed, mastered, pressed and distributed. That's how Mikey came to record 'Love The Dread' for his own Dread At The Controls label, voiced on a rhythm track that Patterson had given him. In return, Mikey did 'Barber Saloon' for him and it became his breakthrough hit, despite having been voiced in just one take.

Whilst he would continue making records as Mikey Dread, he also produced songs by other artists, beginning with Rod Taylor ('His Imperial Majesty'), Edi Fitzroy, Earl Sixteen and Sugar Minott. Rod Taylor was a youth from Trench Town who was fond of telling people that his mother had given birth to him in the street. ('I drop out on the ground, right on the rock!') He sang with sound systems like Kenyatta, Tippatone and Socialist Roots as a youngster. Coxsone, Joe Gibbs and Channel One all passed on him until Ossie Hibbert spotted him at the Bohemia Club one night and took the schoolboy in the studio to voice his debut 'Bad Man Comes And Goes' and 'Every Little Thing.' Rod also sang in a group called the Aliens, before voicing for Manzie and then causing a stir with 'Ethiopian Kings' for Freedom Sounds.

Meanwhile, in a parallel universe, American civil rights activist the Reverend Jesse Jackson made a public announcement on 30 October in which he gave his backing to a campaign aimed at getting The Rolling Stones' latest single 'Some Girls' banned from airplay and even taken off the group's last album, also called *Some Girls*. This was because of a line saying that black girls just want to get 'fucked all night', which Jackson considered disrespectful to black women. Record buyers were being urged to boycott the Stones' album until those lyrics were deleted or the song withdrawn, although the chances of this happening were slim as the album had been released several months earlier and already topped the US Billboard LP charts. The campaign was therefore a non-starter but then four days later, Rolling Stones Records released Peter Tosh's debut LP for the label, *Bush Doctor*, which arrived amidst minor controversy when some retailers refused to stock it as they thought the scratch and sniff sticker on the cover had ganja in it instead of patchouli. If UK stockists like Boots were embarrassed by their over-hasty reaction, they didn't admit to it, but it was the lukewarm reviews that hurt Peter's cause the most. The music on the album just wasn't militant or roots orientated enough for some. Instead, it was yet another example of a Jamaican artist wanting to prove himself at the highest level, and earn respect from their contemporaries overseas.

'The music Geoffrey and I did with Peter took reggae to a whole different level,' explained Mikey Chung. 'We were getting the full scope – message, a full range of instruments and proper arrangements... The *Bush Doctor* album was such a turning point and that was our intention. We wanted to make an album that could be played alongside anything by Stevie Wonder, Earth, Wind & Fire or Curtis Mayfield... all of that. That was done when I was attending the Jamaica School Of Music, and listening keenly to all of the music of the day. Being a musician, you want to bring yourself to that same level. You don't want to just sit there and think, "oh well, this is Jamaica and so we'll just play a normal kind of rhythm." We wanted to move forward, too, and open our minds to anything new. We were always buying and listening to records in the seventies. We listened to *everything* and Geoffrey, even more than myself, had a real liking for rock music which is how I got introduced to the music of Jimi Hendrix, Santana and a lot of those other American artists. We'd not only listen to singers like Aretha Franklin and Donny Hathaway but also the musicians who played on those records. That's how I came to know of Eric Gale, Cornell Dupree, Chuck Rainey and Richard Tee. We knew those people and we knew the formula. We'd studied how they got a particular sound. Geoffrey and I, we'd been to America and played on sessions there and we knew how things worked. We all learnt a lot from what they did in America, but then those musicians learnt from us too. They'd hear what we did and say, "hey, that's amazing! How did you do that?" We'd show them that feeling had a lot to do with it, and whilst our thing may have sounded simple to people at first, it had real depth to it.'

Peter and Mick Jagger's duet on 'Don't Look Back' was the album's opening track and one of several remakes of songs that Tosh had recorded previously. 'I'm The Toughest', 'Soon Come' and 'Dem Ha Fe Get A Beatin'' were the others. The title track began with a spoken passage, highlighting the health risks associated with smoking tobacco. 'The surgeon general warns cigarette smoking is dangerous. Dangerous, hazard to your health. Does that mean anything to you?' Tosh asked. He then called for marijuana to be legalised and also recognised for its healing properties. That song was said to have been inspired by the herbalist Ras Hu-I of the Theocratic House Of Rastafari. It was educational as well as provocative, whilst 'Stand Firm' implored listeners to live clean, and let their works be seen. Peter had his own spiritual beliefs, and after dismissing Jesus Christ as 'fantasy, a whole pack of ignorancy' – words that were unlikely to endear him to evangelicals – he paid tribute to Marcus Garvey and historic Biblical figures in the lyrics of 'Moses The Prophet.' Finally, 'Creation' was a prayer, complete with celestial chorus, but it was always a gamble presenting rock fans with religious material like that, no matter how well-produced. My own favourite was 'Pick Myself Up' – a hymn to resilience that was reminiscent of Jimmy Cliff's 'Many Rivers To Cross' in some aspects.

Whether it was planned to happen like that or not, Island released Bob Marley and the Wailers' latest album just a week after *Bush Doctor* hit the shelves. *Babylon By Bus* was a double live album culled from shows in Paris, Copenhagen, London and Amsterdam but, try as it might, it simply couldn't measure up to *Live! At The Lyceum*, which may explain why it barely made the UK Top 40, and had all but disappeared from the LP charts by New Year. To compound their error, Island passed on 'Rastaman Live Up' as well as 'Blackman Redemption', and so Marley put them out on Tuff Gong instead. He and Cindy Breakspeare were still very close. He bought her a house near Hope Road after she gave birth to their son Damian and also helped her to set up a local business called Ital Crafts, shared with Donna Coore, wife of Third World's Cat Coore.

'We started from nothing, virtually,' she told the *Gleaner*. 'I started it at my home at the foot of Russell Heights because I had a self-contained cottage that was empty, so it was the perfect spot for a little workshop. We went to Hellshire beach and dug up cactus, we bought clay pots and wrapped them in sisal string that we dyed and sold just whatever we could imagine to do or make. Those were really fun days because there was no pressure, and it was all about creativity.'

Cindy said that Bob would sometimes call round there at three o'clock in the morning while she and Donna were working late to get everything ready for the next day.

'He'd pull up a bench and say "I'm a tradesman, so do you need me to do something?" He'd want to get right into the thick of it and would bring me material from London and all over – stuff that I'd never worked with before. He brought me tons of the most incredible stuff, or maybe tools we could use. That's how he was.'

Marcia Griffiths, who was still working out of Treasure Isle, asked Marley if he could write something for her because there was a rhythm she wanted to voice. Lloyd Lovindeer had brought her a song to sing on it, but she wasn't sure about it and so wanted to find something of her own for the rhythm instead.

'That rhythm was played to quite a few different songwriters including Bob Andy and Bob Marley,' she said. 'I gave Bob Marley a cut of the rhythm and asked if he'd write a song for it. I gave it to Philip James from the Blues Busters who discovered me, and I don't remember who else. Quite a few, but nobody came up with anything, so I took back the rhythm and I loved it so much. It was a dancing rhythm, and then the song started coming to me little by little but it's funny y'know? Because I haven't found one drummer since that song was recorded in the seventies who can reproduce that same pattern. There's hardly any drummer can play that song and yet Sly does it so easily. Every time I do it, I have problems with some drummer and when I run into Sly, I tell him how they just fling away their stick saying, 'me can't play it!' Imagine, because we have all these talents in the one little island'.

What drove it was Sly Dunbar's tumbling drum pattern, which Errol Brown had thankfully kept high in the mix. Marcia denied that 'Stepping Out Of Babylon' was a Rasta song, but her lyrics had the feel of a spiritual as she urged the faithful onwards, out of captivity and towards New Jerusalem. It charted almost immediately once Sonia Pottinger released it on her High Note label during late November, by which time Peter Tosh had left for Europe. He played two nights at the Rainbow Theatre in London on 6 and 7 December, followed by an additional show at the Venue. When Sly and Robbie went into some wild, highly rhythmic live dub midway through these shows, the crowds were ecstatic. It was a highlight of the evening but Peter was consumed by jealousy and didn't like it one bit.

Jimmy Cliff, meanwhile, was headed for Japan. Throughout 1978 he travelled to the Far East, the US, Russia, Britain, France and Egypt, accompanied by his band Oneness, whose all-star line-up included Ernest Ranglin (guitar), Richard Ace (keyboards) and Ghanaian percussionist Rebop Kwaku Baah, who he'd first played with in London during the sixties. Rebop co-wrote 'Stand Up And Fight Back' on Jimmy's latest album *Give Thanx*, co-produced with Bob Johnson, who'd previously worked with Bob Dylan, Aretha Franklin, Johnny Cash and Leonard Cohen, among others. Cliff was Warner Brothers' only reggae artist and he opened his album with nyahbinghi drumming (on 'Bongo Man'), then ran through a gamut of different subjects, moods and styles. En route he explored romantic ins and outs, urged an insurrection, adopted the role of an outlaw ('Wanted Man'), celebrated Africa and called for universal love ('Beyond The Boundaries).'

If he'd ever regretted leaving Island, you'd never have guessed it. Jimmy Cliff wasn't like other Jamaican singers, which is why – as reported earlier – he called himself as 'the thumb.' He acknowledged that his approach was different, and this was both an advantage and disadvantage. On the plus side, he enjoyed major label backing and a greater level of international recognition than most of his contemporaries, but there were other differences too, and not just because he'd chosen Islam over Rastafari. He had an intellectual curiosity that relatively few of his peers could match, and his outlook was so much broader after having traveled so extensively and lived in places like New York, London and Brazil. On the minus side, he was no longer having hits that played in the dances or could be heard blasting out of jukeboxes the length and breadth of the island, which suggested there was a disconnect between what he was doing and what grassroots reggae audiences wanted to hear. He wasn't reaping the benefits from any crossover hits either, because they'd pretty much dried up by that stage. It had been eight years since he last had a song on the UK charts, but it wasn't for lack of trying. One of his most appealing tunes of late had been 'Deal With Life', which he released on his own Sunpower label and suggests the obvious, that we don't have to die before we're stopped living...

It was good advice. But on 9 December came news that the truce agreed upon by warring political factions last January was becoming increasingly unstable. The previous week there had been reports of several shooting incidents with political and gang overtones. At least four youths died and after eleven months of comparative peace, police officials were doubtful that the truce would last much longer. That's because men from Arnett Gardens had declared that they didn't sign any peace treaty, and that they and fellow PNP supporters from Lizard Town and Payne Avenue were going to 'kill off Labourites.' Armed thugs have already succeeded in driving JLP supporters from their homes in Lizard Town, and trouble broke out between rival gangs at a football match in the National Stadium between teams from Tivoli Gardens and Arnett Gardens. During the match Tivoli Gardens supporters sitting in the lower tiers were pelted with orange pulp and abused by opposing fans. Claudie Massop restrained the Tivoli supporters from retaliating but after the match had finished, a group of thugs from Arnett Gardens led by General Starkey had continued to cause trouble. Two cars, one belonging to a Tivoli man were badly damaged and the tyres on Massops car were slashed. The men from Arnett Gardens then fired upon a group of Tivoli supporters who'd stopped to help Massop change his tyres. Peace was eventually restored but everyone could see that General Starkey hadn't been living up to the spirit of the truce since his release from jail, and there were other malcontents who'd been willing to join him in reviving hostilities. Questions were also being asked as to what the Peace Committee had been doing. For instance no one knew for sure what had happened to the profits from the Peace Concert, but at least the money collected on behalf of the Community Peace Fund was said to have been safely put away.

A week after the violence flared up again, American television audiences got their first sight of Peter Tosh when he and Mick Jagger appeared on *Saturday Night Live*. Filming took place at the NBC studios in Rockefeller Plaza, Manhattan, where Peter was booked to perform two numbers. One was 'Bush Doctor', which openly promoted use of ganja – on coast-to-coast US television! – and the other was 'Don't Look Back' featuring Mick Jagger, who was his usual cocky, insouciant self.

'That was a major turning point,' recalled Mikey Chung. '*Saturday Night Live* happened twice every Saturday night. The first show was the rehearsal, and then the second show went out live. It was fascinating watching them do all those sketches and routines in-between doing the set changes. All that happens right before your eyes. It was like a military operation. I never saw Peter get nervous, though, and even if he was, he'd never show it – he'd just get right to it.'

CHAPTER TEN

1979: SOON FORWARD

On 5 January, members of the Theocratic Governmental Order, led by Jah Lloyd, held a Rasta nyahbinghi and remembrance dance in Southside. Five people from there had been killed the year before at the Green Bay firing range, and a survivor from the massacre was at the 'binghi in High Holborn Street Park. Against a backdrop of chanting and drumming, he joined a group of Rastafarians sat around a fire and told them how the youths from Southside had been enticed to Green Bay after being offered well-paid security work, and that none were gunmen with political affiliations.

The day before, Jah Lloyd and his followers had caused a disruption at a reception hosted by the Governor General for members and guests attending a conference organised by the Central Committee of the World Council of Churches. The First Battalion band, the featured attraction, was drowned out by more than a dozen Rastafarians who sang, chanted and played drums on the lawns behind them. Jah Lloyd and his followers acted this way because the Jamaica Council of Churches had excluded all references of the Rastafarians at the conference, despite the Reverend William Watty having declared that they were 'the only religious group that denounced the alliance between established religion and privilege, between theology and colonialisation, and the only people in Jamaica, who in the absolute rejection of the status quo and everything it stands for and the theology which supports it, formulated for themselves an alternative theology, and alternative Christology.'

To suggest there was a battle raging for Jamaica's soul might be too melodramatic, but the voices clamouring for change had been getting louder, and they didn't just belong to those who thought Manley's social revolution hadn't gone fast or far enough, but also opposition forces that were determined to stop it at all costs. In the New Year a branch of the JLP called the National Patriotic Movement orchestrated mass protests across the island as a reaction to the recent increase in petrol prices. There were already shortages of certain foods and basic provisions – soap powder, for example – and a rise in petrol prices would inevitably lead to other increases across the board. To quote newspaper reports, 'Five hundred barricades were thrown up in the streets of Kingston, plus others in Montego Bay, Ocho Rios and other towns. Vehicles were burnt and overturned, tyres slashed and open skirmishes occurred between supporters of the rival parties.'

The protests had started in Kingston's Corporate area on 8 January and, two days later, many petrol stations remained closed and the city had come to a virtual standstill – most motorists having decided to stay at home rather than risk facing the wrath of people mounting the blockades. The following day, on 11 January, a large crowd marched through central Kingston and headed towards Jamaica House, chanting anti-government slogans. They were met at Cross Roads by ranks of police and soldiers who attacked the demonstrators when the situation had quickly got out of hand.

In a televised address the following day, prime minister Michael Manley told Jamaicans that the demonstrations had nothing to do with gas prices. 'This is raw, naked fascism,' he declared. 'This is an attempt to subvert the government, the law and the Constitution for a naked political purpose.' He said the NPM was acting with the full knowledge of the JLP leadership and being used to whip up social unrest. Whatever the truth of his claims, the disturbances all but paralysed Jamaica. Everything closed down – even the power station – and seven people lost their lives in the skirmishes that ensued. Edward Seaga countered by claiming that the PNP had hired thugs to shoot at peaceful demonstrators and that it was all part of a plan to cancel the elections due next year. Yet the cost of living had become unbearably high for many poorer Jamaicans, and no amount of rhetoric could disguise the fact that basic consumer goods were rapidly disappearing from the shops.

Marches and public meetings were banned in the wake of the demonstrations, and so the JLP called for a one day general strike on 19 January, risibly described as 'a national day of peace and justice.' There was little appetite for it, however. Two weeks later, on the evening of 4 February, Peace Treaty organiser Claudie Massop and two of his companions died in a hail of bullets as they returned to Tivoli Gardens from Spanish Town, where they'd been watching a football match. Eyewitnesses said that three motor-cyclists had been tailing Massop's taxi before it was stopped at around 6:40 p.m. at the intersection of Industrial Terrace and Marcus Garvey Drive, where police had laid in wait. The official story told of the men being killed in a shoot-out with the security forces, yet none of them were wanted for any crime and only one revolver – found in the trunk of the car – had been retrieved from the scene. According to the taxi driver, who fled the scene, there were no weapons in the vehicle and the three men were gunned down by the police as they stood with their arms raised above their heads. This detail was later confirmed by the autopsy report, which documented several entry wounds to Massop's armpits. He'd been shot forty times in total, and no officers were hurt in the supposed shootout.

Massop had apparently received death threats from the police, who had resented his role in bringing about the Peace Treaty. The residents of Tivoli Gardens felt otherwise, because several thousand of them, carrying lit candles, marched silently through the streets the night before his funeral to the cemetery adjoining the Ebenezer Methodist Church, where an overnight vigil was kept by the open grave. People sang religious songs and offered prayers to the accompaniment of Rasta drumming, then flocked to Tivoli Gardens Community Centre the following afternoon, where thousands more waited outside and in the surrounding streets. It's estimated that 15,000 people turned out to pay their respects that day, many of whom stayed for the midnight celebrations held at the Community Centre, which was bedecked by black flags. The police had declared a curfew the night before but there was no trouble – only a pervasive air of sorrow. The people of Tivoli Gardens had buried hope along with their charismatic leader, and when the grief subsided, important questions remained. For instance, had Claudie Massop really split from Edward Seaga in recent months as rumours suggested? And did this have any bearing on his death? Also, did his murder and that of the other two men point to the existence of death squads operating within the security forces?

The Peace Treaty was now history, and the euphoria that had generated so many hit songs was but a memory. Jacob Miller, who'd recorded the definitive Peace Treaty anthem, was in London with Inner Circle, performing at the Rainbow Theatre, when Claudie Massop was laid to rest. They were promoting their latest album *Everything Is Great* – their first for Island – but reviews of the LP had been mixed. The title track was pure disco, and rock, soul and funk influences far outweighed any reggae content. Roger Lewis would later blame Chris Blackwell for this supposed change of direction, but Inner Circle always were a showband, one that reserved their hardest-hitting material for Fatman Riddim Section releases, and also outside productions like those for Israel Vibration, Tyrone Taylor ('Africa') and Winston McAnuff, who recorded his album *What The Man A Deal Wid* in just two days after a chance meeting with the Lewis brothers.

Dennis Brown was on the cover of the *NME* in late February and the strapline read 'Money in his pocket, smile on his face.'

That's because 'Money In My Pocket', voiced for Joe Gibbs back in 1974, had just entered the UK charts. The vocals on it had been lifted from the original, but the rhythm was brand new and sounded great. The copies that Gibbs had pressed up a year earlier had soon disappeared, and when demand far exceeded supply, that had opened the door for a bogus 'Money In My Pocket' on Freedom Sounds, which also co-opted the original vocals over a revamped rhythm. Dennis Brown called the people behind that version 'bloodsuckers', because Lightning Records had already licensed the authorised 12-inch of 'Money In My Pocket' for release in the UK. Lightning were a subsidiary of WEA hoping to emulate the success they'd had with Althea & Donna's 'Uptown Top Ranking', but Brown's single fell short of their expectations since it failed to breach the UK Top 10. Alan Davidson, who'd previously worked for EMI, had signed the deal with Joe Gibbs when in charge of Lightning but he left the label shortly after 'Money In My Pocket' charted and set up a new label called Laser, taking Dennis Brown with him.

Laser's first release would be Brown's 'Ain't That Loving You' – a cut of the Johnny Taylor hit that Gibbs had merged seamlessly with Nigger Kojak & Liza's 'There's A Hole In The Bucket' on the 12-inch. Whilst it didn't crossover, 'Ain't That Loving You' was popular in the dancehalls and would reappear on Brown's *Words Of Wisdom* album, again released by Laser. This was another fine set from the former Boy Wonder – one that included 'Money In My Pocket', 'A True' and 'Should I', a recut of 'Cassandra' and cultural songs such as 'So Jah Say', 'Black Liberation', 'Rasta Children' and the title track. Reggae fans were already talking of Dennis Brown as 'the Crown Prince', and in March he was voted Best International Artist at the second *Black Echoes Awards* show in Southgate, North London.

The Royalty Ballroom on Winchmore Hill Road was packed that night. The Heptones, led by their new singer Dolphin 'Naggo' Morris were there, also Errol Dunkley and UK reggae acts Black

Harmony, Tribesman, the Blackstones and Brown Sugar, who won Best Female Act. Errol Dunkley won the award for Best Male Vocalist, and his recent hit 'A Little Way Different' was voted Best Single. Dennis Brown, last year's winner, presented Errol with his award for Best Male Vocalist and then went back onstage with Castro Brown to collect one given them for Best Record label. DEB Music had released twenty 12-inch singles and seven albums over the last twelve months, although Brown told *Black Echoes'* Penny Reel that whilst forthcoming releases by Black Uhuru, Junior Delgado and Earl Cunningham would appear on DEB, his own tracks would be released on Laser. Reel – real name Peter Simon – had recently soured his relationship with Island by painting 'Island Is Babylon' on the wall outside their Hammersmith studio. He called Dennis Brown 'the most popular and most prolific reggae recording artist of the decade', whilst reluctantly conceding that Bob Marley was the best-known name in reggae.

'There is a discrepancy between the public's perception of Bob Marley and his actual standing in the reggae world,' he wrote. 'His elevation to superstar status during the past six years is largely the result of a marketing campaign by Island Records, who promote him like a rock act and perpetuate the myth that he is reggae music's most popular artist, whereas in the sound system dances Bob Marley records are played only intermittently and, in recent years, rarely at all. With Bob Marley presently the focus of media notice as far as reggae is concerned, attention is deflected from all else and, as on previous occasions, the music industry establishment is able to dictate public taste on its own terms. It is also interesting that Bob Marley's recent hits are some of his most bland recordings of all, if at least in keeping with traditional radio fare.'

He wasn't far wrong in some of what he said, and Ken Gordon, owner of Fat Man Hi Fi, no doubt agreed with him. Fat Man won Best Sound System at those *Black Echoes' Awards*, after narrowly missing out the previous year. They were a formidable outfit in terms of weight and power, as well as their musical selection. Ken was close friends with King Tubby, Prince Jammy and Bunny Lee, and therefore didn't lack for prize rhythm tracks or killer dubplates. He was Jamaican like them, and had come to London in 1962 aged 18 at a time when Sir Fanso the Tropical Downbeat ruled Finsbury Park and Tottenham. Ken joined him as a mic man and then started his own sound system after Fanso returned to Jamaica in 1974.

'I started off with Wild Bells, but not for long because then I change it to Fat Man the Imperial Downbeat,' he said. 'The funny thing is, I wasn't even a fat man then. I was slim! It's just that everyone was Sir this or Duke that in those days, and I wanted to be different. That's why I name myself 'Fat Man,' because I didn't fancy any of that...'

The genial Fat Man helped promote reggae music in the UK by playing it on his sound system, opening a record shop on West Green Road and forming his own label, initially called KG Imperial. In spring 1979 his latest production was the dub album *Fatman Dub Contest – Crucial Bunny Versus Prince Jammys*. Jammy was now a recognised mixing engineer in his own right and his style of mixing was heavier than Tubby's, whose jazz sensibilities he eschewed. When Jammy wanted to express tension he didn't concern himself with the interplay between light and shade like Tubby did, but delivered it with a hammer blow – even his backward tape spins had an edge to them. When Jammy was at the mixing-board he'd wield echo, delay and reverb like weapons – basslines would plunge like depth charges and high hats fizzle like live hand grenades, which meant that his other album of 1979, *Kamikazi Dub*, was well-named.

Sir Coxsone was still the number one UK sound in those days, because of their exclusive dub plates and residency at Columbo's on Carnaby Street – described by Penny Reel as being situated 'in a dank, neglected alley in a miserable district behind the big stores of Regent Street, and too far west of the bright Soho lights to attract many visitors either by night or day.'

Coxsone's selector was Denzil Exodus and his playlist in early

1979 would have included lovers rock tracks like Louisa Mark's '6 Sixth Street', Bunny Mahoney's 'Baby I've Been Missing You', Linval Thompson's 'If I Follow My Heart', Ruddy Thomas 'Loving Pauper' and Joy Mack's 'You Had Your Chance.' Lloyd Coxsone's sound still played roots music, but he'd more or less stopped producing records by this time after discovering that dealing with artists was in his own words, 'a life and death t'ing.'

'The thing with the recording business, you can't do it with people who don't understand how it works,' he said. 'You get a lot of aggravation sometimes.'

This was especially true for those who cheated in their business dealings, yet Lloyd's own Tribesman label was still going strong at that point, thanks to Fred Locks' 'Love And Only Love.' Everything about that record was magnificent, and hearing it in a dance through giant speakers was akin to a religious experience.

Jah Shaka was different from other UK sound systems in many ways – not least because he was a one-man band who selected what records to play, operated the amplifiers and mixers, controlled the mic and even played the occasional instrument. His sound system never was a super-powered jukebox, playing all the latest hits from Jamaica, and whilst his selections were more varied than he was often given credit for, he didn't play too many love songs either. The music he played had a spiritual dimension and Shaka dances were places of communion where you could feel part of the human family irrespective of race, class or creed.

'When I started the sound it was in the Black Power era, when we didn't have a media catering for us and we needed sound systems to communicate certain things,' he told me. 'The whole issue was about black consciousness back then, and my sound was formed as a vehicle for this kind of message in order to help people, and to let them know what's really going on.'

Neville Powell, to give him his real name, grew up in South London and had hoped to be a footballer, but music would provide his true calling. As a teenager he lifted speaker boxes for Freddie

Cloudburst, who played in the Lewisham area. Shaka learnt to select playing alongside Freddie in the late sixties, when sounds often stirred a little soul and even Blue Note into the mix. By the time roots reggae and dub had started to take over, he'd joined a sound called Shaka, shared with two friends. Both were jailed soon afterwards, leaving him to run the sound system on his own. This is where the name 'Jah Shaka' came from, and he wore it like a mantle. Several months later his friends were released from jail so he returned their equipment and replaced it with items that he'd had custom-built for himself. For a time those two friends played out as Shaka number two, but there was no mistaking the authentic Jah Shaka as he stood at the control tower, swaying to the warrior beat. By the late seventies he was playing all around London, often sharing the bill with heavyweight sounds such as Fat Man, Coxsone and Jah Tubby's. South-east London was his stronghold but in 1979 he regularly played at Phebes on Amhurst Road in Stoke Newington, where the faithful gathered in near darkness to feel the power of his music.

There was a significant difference between experiencing reggae music of that nature and in such a setting, and what the likes of Third World and Inner Circle were doing. That much was evident, and the more popular the genre became, the more these differences came into focus. Peter Tosh, in the middle of another US tour, told the *Tucson Night Times* that as far as he could see, 'people have been exposed to the leaf and the branch of the music but not its roots. Reggae is a tree,' he said. 'The leaves and the branches are the commercial side, the softer side, but the roots is what you call the political side. You have many people who get to the root but they don't maintain it because of the media that controls the system. This society has a media that makes you and tells you what to say, what to sing, where to sing and how to sing, but no producer or promoter can tell I what to sing or how to sing.'

The paper then made its own comment on reggae – a music it

says 'cuts through politics, ignorance and fear, and is inseparable from life itself in Jamaica.

'Of the vast amount of music made today, so little is vital in interpreting our lives. At its commercial best, music provides us with a nice diversion but is concerned more with external functions – dress, dancing and appearance – than with serious protest for change. Reggae, the music of the people of Jamaica, is the exception in today's market. It is ghetto music with universal appeal – a music born from the suffering of slaves, but believing in the ultimate righteousness of God's ways.'

Four months after its release, Peter Tosh's *Bush Doctor* album was still sitting comfortably in the US Billboard Top 100. It was the singer's biggest-ever seller, his recent performance on *Saturday Night Live* having introduced him to many millions of American television viewers. When he appeared at New York's Bottom Line on 17 March, the place was so full Mick Jagger had to be passed over the heads of the crowd to reach the stage so that he and Peter could sing 'Don't Look Back.' Things were going well for the Bush Doctor, who finally acknowledged that Joe Higgs was the rightful author of 'Stepping Razor' – a song Tosh had recorded on *Equal Rights* three years earlier. Joe received a first payment of $17,000 in backdated royalties as a result, and was able to complete his own album *Unity Is Power* – a fusion of jazz and reggae that he'd recorded at Aquarius in March, co-produced with Synergy's Ronnie Burke. He shared one of the tracks, 'Sons Of Garvey', with Jimmy Cliff, who'd recently appointed Bob Marley's former manager Don Taylor to oversee his affairs. Joe had been touring with Jimmy and the two of them combined brilliantly on this rousing hymn to Marcus Garvey, whose message of self-reliance and shared endeavour was reaffirmed in every line. There was a sophistication in Higgs's music which set it apart, but this didn't necessarily translate into sales or visibility for the man who taught the Wailers and other young Trench Town hopefuls how to sing and harmonise back in the early sixties.

Sangie Davis, who was an active member of the Twelve Tribes, played on that *Unity Is Power* album. Bob Marley had encouraged him to become more involved with what was happening at 56 Hope Road, and especially as the new studio – called Tuff Gong – neared completion. In the second week of April the *Gleaner* ran an article describing Tuff Gong as 'one of the finest studios in the Caribbean.' It was built on the ground floor of the house at No. 56, in a space that had previously been used as bedrooms and a bathroom. An American engineer, Seth Snyder, had designed it and overseen installation of the 24-track MC1500 series console, which was identical to the one at Criteria in Mami.

'With its innumerable, muti-coloured tiny lights, switches and controls, the console resembles the control boards seen only in fictional movies of TV spaceships, and the intimate, subdued lighting and slanted, blue-tinted, double glass panels add to the outer world atmosphere,' reported Arthur Kitchin. 'Other technical features include auxiliary parametric equalisers, compounders, expenders, digital relays, full Dolby system noise reduction, noise gates, harmonisers, etc. Two magnetic tape machines and several speaker boxes complete the control room which has room for further expansion. The main studio has separate booths for a drummer, a solo vocalist, piano and the like. The control room is attractively panelled with light brown Cyprus wood planks, the acoustic flooring executed in matching brown parquet squares. Two rooms of red, gold and green lights dominate the delightfully air-conditioned interior.'

Family Man Barrett proudly announced that it had the best sound in Jamaica, whilst Kitchin predicted that 'as the demand for its modern facilities grows, the studio and its surroundings will probably become the centre of popular music in the Caribbean.'

While Tuff Gong wouldn't be available for public bookings, sessions had already been held there – most notably those for Judy Mowatt's *Black Woman* album, and tracks intended for Bob Marley's next studio album. 'Ambush In The Night', one of those tracks, was written about the assassination attempt, although some of the lyrics also alluded to the street wars that had started up again since the truce ended, and especially those accusing the politicians of bribing people with not only money, but also guns.

Marley and the Wailers had written and worked on songs back in London and during their tours, so there was no shortage of material. The main difference between the new album and *Exodus* – a framed gold disc of which hung in the control room at Tuff Gong – was there were fewer love songs this time around. Instead, the majority of tracks were inspired by cultural issues affecting black people worldwide and not just in Jamaica. This may have been a consequence of the criticism meted out to *Exodus* and *Kaya*, although Marley was a strong enough character to determine his own direction of travel. The other noticeable difference between those two albums and the next was a change of engineer, as Errol Brown was now at Tuff Gong, after having left Treasure Isle. Sonia Pottinger had heavily relied on Brown when recording albums with Culture and Marcia Griffiths and yet according to Brown, she hadn't credited him for having produced them, or paid him appropriately. Marley also called upon the Rass Brass horn section for sessions at Tuff Gong, after they'd impressed with their work on Dennis Brown's *Words Of Wisdom* album. Their line-up was comprised of Dean Fraser (sax), Junior 'Chico' Chin (trumpet) and Ronald 'Nambo' Robinson (trombone). Bob was so delighted with Rass Brass that he asked them come on the road with him, but they'd already promised to tour with Dennis Brown and so weren't available. More's the pity, judging by their performance on 'Wake Up And Live,' which Sangie Davis wrote.

'It's just one line that Bob wrote on it,' Davis explained. 'the one where he sings, "what's the use you live big today and tomorrow you're buried in a casket?" That's the only line Bob wrote. He came by me very early one morning. At that time I was living in Grant's Pen Road and he come to the gate and said, "Sangie, you get your driver's license yet?" I say yes and he said, "Rahtid! Come now. Let's drive!" So he get me to jump in his VW bus and drive, but then just as we reach Constant Spring Road, the road get all bumpy and rocky. They were fixing the road and there were a lot of signs saying Caution, Keep Left and Road Closed… that is where the inspiration come from because out of the blue I just start to sing, "life is one big road with one big sign." Then I say, "don't you complicate your mind… Put your vision to reality", and Bob asked me, "is that something you write?" I say yes and he said, "come, mek me go sing it." When we reach Six Mile now, there was this billboard sign for Andrew's Liver Salts that said, "Wake up and live! Drink Andrew's Liver Salts." That's how the chorus came about, because he'd woken me up and I jump straight up to go with him. I didn't even brush my teeth. I just rinse my mouth with water, spit it out, put on some clothes and run go out there.'

Sangie took his membership of the Twelve Tribes seriously, and hence wove spiritual conviction into his life and music. This was something that Bob Marley admired, so he asked Sangie to take on A&R duties at Tuff Gong. Winning over the Wailers would prove more problematic, however. Family Man refused to play on 'Wake Up And Live', so Val Douglas from the Maytals' band did the honours instead. Family Man's brother Carly didn't care too much for Sangie either, although Junior Marvin apparently wasn't so judgemental.

'There was a lot of fight, even within the Twelve Tribes of Israel,' Sangie admits. 'Bob used to ask me to rehearse it with the group, and some of them never want to play because I was a nobody…'

Marley wrote 'Mix Up' after witnessing what was happening between members of his band and Sangie, who brought in Twelve Tribes' musicians to play on three songs that he'd written – 'Jingling Keys', 'She Used To Call Me Daddy' and 'Babylon Feel This One.'

'Bob voiced the last two but he didn't get around to voice 'Jingling Keys', so after the songs began to circulate everyone think that it's him singing that one but it's actually me because he never find the time to record it.'

'Jingling Keys' has the kind of storyline that we were used to hearing in Bob Marley songs, since it describes a righteous man who finds himself on the wrong side of the law.

'In those days the police would just come and impose a curfew on certain areas, and take everybody down to the jail and lock them up until them prove they were innocent, and especially if they were a Rastaman,' says Davis. 'They would put a lot of charges on you and in those times a Rastaman couldn't take a bus or even a taxi because most times he would be living in the ghetto and nuh man would want go there or pick him up after dark. Even if you had money, you still couldn't rent a vehicle. Them nah give any Rastaman an opportunity, so we'd just have to walk barefoot. People would look upon you like you were something terrible because every Rastaman have him dreadlocks and barely have a pants and shirt. The looks alone turn people off ah you, because you look like a mad man, y'know?'

Bim Sherman had personal experiences of that sort before moving to London. He sang about this on 'Down In Jamdown', produced by Prince Far I, which Adrian Sherwood issued on HitRun in the UK.

'I used to live in some dangerous places where you definitely in with a chance of dying young,' Bim told me. 'It's not as if you grow with a nice house or car, go to high school and blah blah. It's pure danger, and you have to be very, very alert to survive the pressure in those places because sometimes people will judge you wrongly. Maybe they see you standing up at the corner with someone and that get you into some war situation. You have to be careful at all times in that kind of environment, and always be prepared to meet with bad minds and so on. It's rough and tough and there are certain people who need to change their attitude still, Jah know!'

Sherwood also licensed 'Love Jah Only' for HitRun before inviting Bim on the Roots Encounter tour in early April. Prince Far I was the headliner, with a supporting cast of Bim, Jah Woosh and Prince Hammer. Although highly respected because of singles like

'Golden Locks' and 'Lightning And Thunder' – and also his latest LP, *Lovers Leap Showcase* – the 27-year-old singer was still little-known outside of grassroots reggae circles. The exposure gained from touring with Prince Far I was therefore invaluable. Far I's current album was Trojan's *Free From Sin*, recorded at Harry J's and Treasure Isle. This was one of three self-productions, although the other two were both dub sets. Front Line released *Cry Tuff Dub Encounter Part 2* whilst *Dub To Africa*, credited to Prince Far I and the Arabs, was another HitRun title.

Creation Rebel backed all the artists on that UK tour and members of the Clash and other punk bands were in the audience on certain dates as the band played their brand of highly charged reggae music, laced with blistering 'live' dub. Adrian Sherwood produced two albums with them in 1979 – *Rebel Vibrations* for HitRun and *Starship Africa*, which wouldn't appear until a year later. The rhythms on the latter had originally been laid for UK rapper DJ Superstar. Jamaican drummer Lincoln 'Style' Scott and several percussionists then added 'live' overdubs, while Adrian went crazy at the mixing desk. The title track was credited as being 'the soundtrack to a forthcoming motion picture' (which, of course, never materialised).

'That was only the second album I worked on,' Sherwood said. 'It was recorded at Gooseberry studios, and people thought it was a bit weird to be honest.'

The lashings of delay, backward tapes and stereo FX wouldn't have sounded at all out of place on a Jimi Hendrix album. *Starship Africa* wasn't ever likely to pass for Jamaican, but the young producer was already determined to do his own thing and let the music guide him.

'Good music is supposed to have character,' Sherwood explained. 'It's supposed to have all the things that you want in a person – warmth, humour, darkness, excitement and imagination... what you don't want is something that's just playing the game or is methodical. I've learnt that the most important thing is to be true to yourself and make records you care about, but I also love anti-production techniques. I like things like Link Wray and people who play their guitars really loud. I love all of that imbalanced stuff as well, and anything which has a unique, sonic expression to it.'

The album that Serge Gainsbourg recorded in Jamaica, *Aux Armes Et Caetera*, certainly had a unique expression. After it was released in March, one French reviewer described the title track – a reggae arrangement of the French national anthem – as 'repugnant.' The outcry over this album made any controversy generated by 'Je t'aime...' seem trivial by comparison. When 'Aux Armes Et Caetera' aired on French television on April's Fools Day, *Le Figaro* condemned it as an outrage, whilst one journalist called for the chanteur to be stripped of his citizenship.

'He called him a walking pollutoid,' Jane Birkin told Sylvie Simmons, author of *A Fistful Of Gitanes*. 'He said that someone who dared to do the national anthem with a lot of Rastas was poison. Gainsbourg, I remember, was so shocked, he nearly cried. He was mortified but then found it great fun that he was on the news pages, and not the entertainment section.'

The fuss over the title track was just the start, since some of the other tracks were just as contentious. 'Relax Baby Be Cool' was a chat-up routine that unfolded against a backdrop of hooded Klansmen, morgues and blood running through the streets. Gainsbourg summoned up the smell of sex and body odours left behind in seedy hotel rooms on 'Les Locataires', whilst 'Eau Et Gaz A Tous Les Etages' described a man pissing and farting his way upstairs to the bedroom, presumably on his way to meet the subject of 'Lola Rastaquouère' – an under-age Rasta girl who he'd like to 'turn out' (i.e., introduce to prostitution), while rolling his 'poor joint' between her breasts. Bob Marley was reputedly furious at learning that Rita had joined in this 'slackness' but, to quote Simmons, 'hearing a bunch of Jamaicans messing with 'La Marseillaise' was, for the French, the Sex Pistols' 'God Save The

Queen' and Jimi Hendrix's 'Star Spangled Banner' rolled into one, and then some.'

It's interesting to note that the same musicians who played on *Aux Armes Et Caetera* also masterminded the tracks on Peter Tosh's *Mystic Man*, which Rolling Stones Records announced in April, two months before its release. They even took out a full-page advertisement to mark the occasion, which bore the legend 'Don't let disco get you down, keep listening to reggae sounds.'

'We wanted to take Peter to the next level,' said Sly Dunbar. 'We were always trying to add new sounds to reggae, and we decided that every album was going to be different from each other. We said, "well, *Bush Doctor* was like this, and so *Mystic Man* is going to contain this." We weren't going to change anything too drastically but we still wanted to move the music forwards. I'm playing a Simmons electronic drum-kit, which gave that record a fresh sound, and we wanted to have the songs recorded in a certain way, which is why we chose Geoffrey Chung as the engineer. He was a skilled musician himself. He understood where we were trying to go and played a very important part in getting the sound we were hearing in our heads down on tape. We wanted to keep playing reggae, but with that kind of stadium sound with the big tom toms and so on.'

The title track was all about lifestyle, and listed all the things that Tosh didn't indulge in (but members of the Stones did), like champagne, cocaine, morphine, heroin, fried chicken, frankfurters, hamburgers and soda pop. It was a tribute to the ital or Rasta diet, and there was still very poor knowledge of the nutritional value of local foodstuffs in Jamaica. It was the Rastas who used fruit, vegetables and plants of the countryside, and therefore escaped dependence on imported food. Yams, boiled bananas, plantain, callaloo and a wide range of local foodstuffs had been the food of the slaves, but were prepared meticulously by the Rastas who shunned the use of salt, condiments and preserved canned food. Most were vegetarian, although some did eat fish because many of them had made their livelihood as fishermen before redevelopment projects changed much of the Jamaican coastline.

'The Day The Dollar Die' warned of a financial crash; Tosh then switched to nation-building on 'Recruiting Soldiers' and made gloomy predictions on 'Rumours Of War.' In a *Daily Gleaner* article headed 'Peter Tosh – Sleeping Giant Awakens', Arthur Kitchin described the visionary 'Crystal Ball' as 'rockers music at its best with a touch of rhythm and blues, country and western and traditional church music.' The highlight was the eight-and-a-half-minute 'Buk-In-Hamm Palace', which, contrary to the advice about disco, sounded a lot like it. Sly Dunbar had experimented with a similar drum pattern on 'Rasta Fiesta' from his album *Sly, Wicked And Slick*, but 'Buk-In-Hamm Palace' was revolutionary in all aspects, including lyrically.

'Light your spliff, light your chalice,' Tosh urged. 'Make we smoke it in Buk-In-Hamm Palace.'

'Peter was a great believer in spontaneity, and that's how the magic came because many of those hit songs, he'd write them in the studio and then voice them in one take,' explained Mikey Chung. 'A lot of those vocals were done on the first take. Sometimes I saw him sing the lyrics perfectly and if the engineer didn't get it, then he'd refuse to do it again during that session or get nowhere near it, no matter many times he tried. You'd really have to work to get him to do it again. That's why he liked working with Karl Pitterson, because when he was at the board he was always recording. Sometimes you'd say, "okay, ready" and he'd say, "ready? We've finished it already." He'd seen the magic happen and captured it before you'd even noticed, and Geoffrey was very much like that as well. Something invariably happened on that first take that you couldn't get again. Nobody knows why it should be like that but that's what often happens. The magic comes and it's a powerful thing. Peter was a great believer in that.'

Tosh and his band headed back to the US and Canada after the release of *Mystic Man*. After his two concerts at Toronto's

Convocation Hall, one of Toronto's major newspapers published a review with the headline 'Peter Tosh, Merely the Best Reggae Band in the World.'

'With the stage in almost total darkness, the pace was set with the thumping beats of that incomparable bassist Robbie Shakespeare, followed by some double drumming from the boss, Sly Dunbar. From then on, it was reggae music at its best. The gangling Peter Tosh strode onto the stage to a rousing welcome from the 1,700 or so fans and gave the audience plenty to cheer about – he sang, he danced, he slithered along the stage and he skanked. The crowd just lapped it up. They roared when he lit up a 'joint' during one of his big hits, 'Legalise It', and there was little, if anything, he could do no wrong that night. When he began 'Get Up Stand Up' he only had to wave his arms a couple of times and the whole audience rose up, raving and singing along.'

Seconds before British reggae band Misty In Roots launched into 'Mankind' at one of two concerts held at the Cirque Royal in Brussels on 31 March and 1 April, an announcer spoke. 'When we trod this land, we walk for one reason,' he said. 'The reason is to try and help another man think for himself. The music of our hearts is roots music – music which recalls history because without know- ledge of your history, you cannot determine your destiny.'

Misty had been invited to perform at the Counter Eurovision – a radical alternative to the banal annual Eurovision Song contest – by the non-profit organisation CAFIT (*Collectif d'Animation pour la Formation et l'Information des Travailleurs*) under the initiative of Pour Le Socialisme and weekly newspaper *POUR*. Groups of people across Europe were mobilising against a right-wing surge that would see Margaret Thatcher elected to Downing Street and the National Front holding rallies and marching through British streets. Racism, both institutional and otherwise, was rife and Misty in Roots had already played more concerts for Rock Against Racism than any other band, their fierce polemics chanted over hypnotic reggae rhythms that served as some kind of holy union.

It was never just about the music with Misty, and by the time they left for Belgium to play at the Counter Eurovision they'd founded a collective – People Unite In Progress – and started a record label called People Unite, which they used to showcase up-and-coming artists, as well as the band's own releases. Misty's first two singles on People Unite were 'Six One Penny' and 'Oh Wicked Man', a song that opened side two of *Live At Counter Eurovision* and glides along effortlessly, belying the fact that they're invoking judgment on the wicked. 'How Long Jah' was another highlight, with its leaping rhythm and impassioned vocals, whilst 'Ghetto Of The City' despairs all the 'ignorancy, ignorant minds, corrupted and confused. Leading their lives with such vanity...' 'Judas Iscariot' was again accusatory and the sombre mood didn't really change for the remainder of the album, since they were still warning of total destruction on the closing 'Sodom And Gomorra.' They were messengers, as opposed to entertainers, and motivated by goals other than money and fame. You wouldn't see Misty asking the crowd if they feel irie, or telling them to wave their arms in the air and sing along. Yet Misty concerts were rites of passage for student audiences all over Europe during the late seventies, especially after John Peel – who once described *Live At Counter Eurovision* as 'possibly the greatest reggae album of all time' – had started to champion them. He was very influential in spreading the word about this group of Rastas from Southall in West London, who'd started out as Nicky Thomas's backing band four years earlier.

Three weeks after the Brussels shows, on 23 April, the National Front held a general meeting at Southall Town Hall. Ten thousand residents had signed a petition calling for this event to be cancelled, but their entreaties had been ignored. When the day arrived, anti-racism demonstrators arrived from far and wide to make their feelings known. Almost three thousand police, including many on horseback, were drafted in to keep protestors and right-wing extremists apart, but clashes broke out between the police and protestors and as the violence increased, Misty's headquarters at 6

Park View Road, situated just a few blocks away, was used as an impromptu first aid centre.

'There were police horses everywhere, and Special Patrol Group in riot gear,' lead singer Walford 'Poco' Tyson told *Reggae Gist Xtra*. 'There was no way to get out, so everyone came inside... the organisations, the politicians, Indians, local lawyers, everybody. The police let all the politicians out, then all the white people, then the Indians. Then they went inside and beat up all the black people. It was a free-for-all. They smashed up all our equipment, destroyed all our records and beat everyone up.'

Misty's manager, Clarence Baker, was severely beaten and injured during the skirmish, and a local teacher named Blair Peach died from head injuries not too far away. In both cases, the perpetrators were thought to be the Special Patrol Group or SPG – a unit of London's Metropolitan Police responsible for combatting public disorder and terrorism that had been accused of causing more disorder than it prevented. As a result of his injuries, Baker was in a coma for months. Rock Against Racism later organised two benefit concerts at the Rainbow to raise funds for demonstrators who'd been prosecuted. These events, called Southall Kids Are Innocent, featured Misty, Aswad, the Who's Pete Townshend, the Pop Group and UK punk band The Ruts, who started their career with People Unite and honoured Baker in the song 'Jah War.'

Culture had performed to a full capacity Rainbow crowd the week before the Southall demonstration, supported by Tribesman, who had Rico Rodriguez playing trombone that night. Inner Circle were also in town and played a two hour show at the Marquee on Wardour Street, which *Melody Maker* termed 'the most important venue in the history of pop music.' Reggae was well-established on the UK music scene, but its main beneficiaries were by no means restricted to Jamaican acts. A reissue of The Police's 'Roxanne' was hovering on the fringes of the UK Top 10 in late April, and lead singer Sting made no secret of his debt to Caribbean music.

'Reggae's always been part of my DNA,' he later said. 'I've had a large love and respect for it, and also an instinct for it since the seventies, and so actually it's an undercurrent in all of my music. I love that reggae offbeat, and I'm also thinking in the way that a reggae bass player may think. I learnt at the feet of the best, and I stole from them too!'

Bob Marley and the Wailers flew to Japan and played several shows in Tokyo during early April before arriving in Auckland and being given a traditional Māori welcome. It was the first time that a reggae band had visited New Zealand and there was a large turnout at the open-air festival they played at. Meanwhile, Lloydie Coxsone had been to Jamaica hunting for dub plates and hit the jackpot during a visit to Lee 'Scratch' Perry's Black Ark.

'I go there early one morning and say, "Scratch Perry, I want some of the old original tune what you have." And 'im say, "Coxsone. Bwoy me nah 'ave time to look for you, but see that ledge and some tapes up there? Climb and go help yourself to what you can see." So me climb up and take up eight tapes, and I couldn't believe the tunes that were on them. 'Rainbow Country' and 'Natural Mystic' by Bob Marley, 'From Creation' by Colour Red and Max Romeo's 'Iron Shirt'... Those were the tunes that I cut on dubplate from Lee Perry's tape.'

Colour Red's 'From Creation' was in a box with Junior Byles' name written on it, so for years that's who was credited with singing it. Lloydie got a standing ovation after playing his new dub plates at London's Queen's Theatre one night, at a show headlined by U-Roy and Leroy Smart. Keith Stone, the owner of Daddy Kool's record shop, saw the crowd's reaction and went to Jamaica to find the two Bob Marley songs, which he bought from Perry's partner Pauline Morrison in the producer's absence and issued on 12-inch. Marley and Scratch had recorded them at Black Ark using an early drum machine a couple of years earlier, never intending them for release. Whilst they didn't mind Lloydie having them as dubplates for his exclusive use, they were angry that Daddy Kool had pressed up copies for general sale. Keith Stone was sued as a result, but all was not well at the Black Ark, especially after the Congos had flown the coop.

Scratch hadn't taken their departure lightly. He wrote a song about them called 'Evil Tongues' with a line stating there were hypocrites around him pretending to be his friend. He also accused these same people of wanting more money than their songs had actually earned. From there onwards, the Congos' story grew more complicated. It's said the terms of their deal with CBS France required them to appear in a film called *Jamdown*, but no such project materialised. Epic then released *Image Of Africa*, credited to Cedric Myton and the Congos. Whilst their harmonies were exquisite and the lyrical themes typically devout, the lead vocals were a little uneven in places and the production far removed from anything Scratch might have come up with. That said, 'Music Maker' deserved to be a hit in any era, 'Only Jah Know' was prime roots and the lyrics of 'Mister Biggs' another powerful indictment of Jamaica's colonial legacy. There was little wrong with the rest of the album. It's just that it was recorded at Aquarius instead of Black Ark and hadn't benefitted from Scratch's input, which made all the difference.

In 1978, CBS France executive Nadette Duget had taken two Congolese singer/guitarists, Seke Molenga and Kalo Kawongolo, to the Black Ark. Lee Perry welcomed their arrival and the six-track album they recorded together – with the working title of *Monama*, meaning 'rainbow' – was a unique fusion of African and Caribbean styles. Island Records were offered it at the same time as *Heart Of The Congos*, but Chris Blackwell passed on both projects. *Seke Molenga & Kalo Kawongolo* would later appear on Sonafric, a subsidiary of the Paris-based label Sonodisc, around the same time that UK promoter Tony Owens released the album *Lee Perry Presents The Jolly Brothers: Conscious Man*. It was all downhill for Lee Perry thereafter. His intake of herb and white rum rose dramatically and he drew thousands of 'X's everywhere, as if possessed. There were also constant disputes with disgruntled musicians, local hustlers, political gangsters and Rasta organisations wanting financial support until finally he couldn't take the pressure anymore and set fire to the house and studio.

'When I had the Black Ark, I didn't have no peace,' he recalled. 'I nearly lost my life and I couldn't carry the weight anymore. They were parking their cars from one end of the street to the other, just to dip into my pocket. That's why I burn it down, because there was too much pressure. The dream that Rastafari had crumbled, because they only seized on the ideas and not the reality. They didn't know you were not supposed to smoke so much herb in case it crumble your brain...'

Interviews with the Upsetter were always memorable, challenging affairs. One of his former musicians once described how he moved between real and invisible worlds. There was a childlike quality to how he expressed himself that was both endearing and slightly surreal, but then he was an artist in every sense of the word. His unconventional and often bizarre wordplay, dress sense and actions could be interpreted in any number of ways, but that didn't necessarily mean that Lee Perry was mad as some described him.

'Nothing was wrong with Scratch,' said the Meditations' Ansel Cridland, 'although at one time a lot of people were down on him. Every day Scratch was at Black Ark, musicians would come to him and start make noise saying they want money. There was a whole heap a things going on and Scratch bring some Nyahbinghi in the house to come live with him and his family. That create a little more problem again and I watch the whole thing, y'know? Then Lloyd Robinson who sing 'Cuss Cuss' do an album for Scratch and Mojo make a deal to put it out, but then Chris Blackwell come and I don't know what kind of meeting him have with Scratch but the deal with Mojo get called off and Lloyd Robinson was supposed to come there the following day to collect his share of the money. Scratch said to him that the deal is off and Lloyd Robinson never feel good about it. He was mad about it and roll up his shirt sleeves like him was about to fight and Scratch say, "alright. Hear me now, come with me", and Scratch carry him round the back of the studio, put the tape on the machine and press the red button. He wipe off the whole album and said, "you don't have nothing and you don't lose nothing. If anybody loses, it's me!" That's when Scratch start to realise that the only way he can get people off his back is to play mad. When him is around certain people, him talk sensible to them, but when certain other people are around him then he act crazy and it work! Yeah, 'im make it work and nuff people hook into it, but there was nothing wrong with him. He play the game over and over but then he throw out all the tapes on the ground, and he throw paint in the mixing board. At the time now, Scratch's woman take that song 'Rainbow Country' and release it, y'know? That's why Bob Marley call me and said, "tell him to send me the song 'Who Colt The Game' and I will give him a couple of thousand dollars to buy back a mixing board", but when me go to Scratch him say, "tell Bob Marley to keep what 'im have, and me keep what me have." But there was nothing wrong with Scratch. He just play the game. He say, "let me try something now", because if Scratch is a madman, do you think he can go through all these different immigration places and travel the world?'

Scratch later insisted it was those Nyahbinghi Rastafarians that he'd invited to live with him who brought about his demise.

'They were smoking too much herb, then some of them start to smoke crack and that crumbled their brains as well,' he maintained. 'They used to get so high that the more you give them, the more they want. They were sucking me dry, because they have no conscience, so I come to England and live there for four years, and it was pure torment up and down. I wasn't me, but then I learn that there's nothing like show business, and since then everything is much better for me. There are no big bills to pay for musicians and singers, and I don't have to use up any of my time teaching artists how to sing, how to act, or how to behave.'

Members of the Wailers contributed to the Meditations'

Guidance album, playing on tracks like 'Miracles', 'Life Is Not Easy', 'War Mongers', 'Hard Life' and 'Jungle Feeling.' The similarities with the original Wailers' harmonies were striking, although the Meditations had their own identity. Their album was released on Gorgon Records and not Tuff Gong as originally intended – probably because of the same protective ringfence around Marley that had kept Sangie Davis at bay. Freddie McGregor was another artist with ties to 56 Hope Road, although his situation was helped by a romantic involvement with Judy Mowatt and musical involvement on her *Black Woman* album. His latest single 'Sergeant Brown' appeared on the Soul Syndicate label, with Tuff Gong handling distribution. In addition to the studio, record store, Gilly's kitchen and weekly radio programme, Tuff Gong even had its own news- paper for a time, called *Survival*. Within its pages there would be articles about issues affecting black people at home and abroad. Also interviews with people who worked at Tuff Gong, and news of plans for further expansion, whether involving music, or anything else that came under the heading of general livity. Every Friday that Marley was in town hundreds of people would flock to 56 Hope Road seeking financial assistance. The queues to see him would stretch as far as Lady Musgrave Road, several hundred yards away. People would wait patiently for the opportunity to tell him about the bills they had to pay, or the amount of capital they needed to launch certain business ventures. Some would make up stories, knowing that Bob would still give them something. He would just laugh at the more fanciful ones, accepting them for their entertainment value and saying that he got inspiration from them. But for the most part, he helped people survive and improve their lives a little, and that was the whole point.

Helping people who were less fortunate was part of the culture, and Bob Marley wasn't the only Jamaican artist to devote time and energy to good causes.

Cedric Brooks and his African rhythms staged a concert at the

Bellevue Garden Theatre on behalf of workers and patients at Kingston's leading psychiatric hospital, whilst Tapper Zukie did the same for the elderly of Rae Town and adjoining areas. That concert had taken place at the community centre he'd built in Lower First Street, Trench Town with his advance from Virgin. He was now spelling his name 'Tappa' and had his own distribution centre on East Avenue. He also released two self-produced albums in 1979, both for the Stars label. *Earth Running* only had seven tracks and titles such as 'The General,' 'War Is Over', 'Born To Be Black', 'Sinsemilla' and 'Raggamuffin' told their own story, whilst the other one, *Living In The Ghetto*, was a compilation of sorts, and as roots as they come. His biggest hit at this time was a duet with Horace Andy, 'Natty Dread A Weh She Want' – a simple, but very catchy song about a girl who preferred dreadlocked men, which became inescapable in reggae dances for the rest of the year.

'When I was the bodyguard for Bunny Lee, some of the artists who recorded for him would love going around in the ghetto with me,' Zukie told Angus Taylor. 'I was like their protection in the ghetto. That was where me and Horace Andy started to go up and down and I started to record him. But at the time politics was going on in Jamaica and after I made 'Natty Dread A Weh She Want' Horace had to leave Jamaica because people were saying he was recording for politicians. People thought I was a politician in those times but I wasn't, because I am not political minded.'

Michigan & Smiley's 'Rub A Dub Style' was at number one in Jamaica throughout May 1979. The way those two deejays traded lines and bounced off one another was riveting. They had so much style and energy and had raided the Studio One vaults for the rhythm, which was a cut to Alton Ellis's 'I'm Just A Guy.' The pair came from Union Garden in Two Miles and had known each other since their schooldays. Papa Michigan got his name from a tractor (don't ask) whilst General Smiley never smiled and so earned his through default. His grandfather had a sound system but Michigan used to sing in church before deejaying on a sound called Third

World. They were hailed as the first male deejay double act, except Coxsone Dodd had also issued Lone Ranger and Welton Irie's *Big Fight* not too long before. That had been well-received, but Lone Ranger's actual breakthrough arrived courtesy of 'Barnabas Collins'.

Barnabas Collins was a TV vampire who'd starred in the ABC series *Dark Shadows* although the character had first appeared in Canadian author W. E. D. Ross's *Dark Shadows* books. Lone Ranger's song was an instant hit thanks to his descriptive lyrics telling how Collins would leave his coffin at midnight in search of a female victim, his eyes glowing red and fang-like teeth. Once he'd found one he'd then chew her neck 'like a Wrigley's' meaning a chewing gum. Lone Ranger voiced 'Barnabas Collins' for the Synmoie brothers but the tune proved so popular, they couldn't handle it. That's what led to Alvin Ranglin reissuing it on GGs. It then stayed at number one in Jamaica for months, and when Island Records came calling, Ranglin licensed the song to them but didn't tell the brothers or Lone Ranger, who was Jamaican sound system Soul To Soul's regular deejay at the time.

The album that GGs put out, *Barnabas In Collins Wood*, was a hurried affair but entertaining in places, with stories about surprise meetings with Frankenstein, a spacecraft ('UFO') and various duppies ('Obeah Man'). The cover was eye-catching, too, showing the deejay dressed in black and baring fangs, with blood dripping down his chin. Ranglin issued albums by Trinity (*African Revolution*) and the Maytones (*One Way*) around the same time. Both were recorded at Channel One with the Revolutionaries, whose name appeared on a dozen or so albums released in 1979, including *Goldmine Dub, Dawn Of Creation, Burning Dub, Outlaw Dub, Aggrovators Meet The Revolutionaries Part II* and *Revolutionary Sounds*. Dave Hendley wrote an article for *Blues And Soul* about his visit to Channel One that year in which he described the Hoo Kims' studio as 'a Jamaican version of Oxford Circus in the middle of the rush-hour.'

'Along with Joe Gibbs over at Retirement Crescent, it's the focal point of activity for Kingston's musicians – it's the place to hang out,' he wrote. 'In the course of the morning you're likely to see the likes of Sly Dunbar, the Jayes, Leroy Smart (when he's not locked up in a prison cell), Dillinger, Ansel Collins, Lloyd Parks, Bo Pee, I-Roy and even our own Lloydie Coxsone, all passing through to keep up with what's happening. If you're in the music business you have to check how things are down by Channel One. That's because the Channel One sound has dominated reggae in the past two years, with Sly's double drumming. Every producer now has his own variation of the style. Bunny Lee, Joe Gibbs, Niney, Yabby You and even Coxsone Dodd have all used rockers rhythms to good effect, adding their own personal touches along the way.'

Hendley had gone to Jamaica to drum up business for Trojan, but was hampered by Marcel Rodd's insistence on unfair contracts and low advances. This meant that Trojan continually lost out to rival labels like Island, Virgin's Frontline, Greensleeves and Burning Sounds – although in-between launching the *Creation Rockers* series and compiling *Rebel Music*, he did manage to land Prince Far I's *Free From Sin*, the Morwells' *Kingston 12 Tuffie*, the debut album by Marie Pierre, Mikey Dread's *Dread At The Controls* and Sugar Minott's *Ghettology*, which the artist himself dedicated to 'all ghetto youths of the WORLD.' The front cover was taken up by illustrations of foodstuffs, including sugar crystals, canned fruit, syrup, honey, condensed milk, bananas, root ginger and potato chips – items that the majority of ghetto people couldn't afford or even find in their local shops, since food shortages were now the norm. Minott had left Studio One by then and was struggling after going it alone so he called upon Soul Syndicate, told them that he'd pay them 'on trust' and booked time at Channel One. In his formative years, he'd had visions of becoming a balladeer like Nat King Cole or Johnny Mathis, but ended up singing about everyday life in the ghetto instead, hence songs like 'Man Hungry', 'The People Got To Know', 'Walking Through The Ghetto', 'Dreader Than Dread' and 'Africa Is The Black Man's Home.' Interestingly, it was the praise song 'Never Gonna Give Jah Up', voiced at King Tubby's, that became the best-known track from *Ghettology*.

'Prince Jammy was the engineer and he was giving me some time,' Sugar told Miguel Cullen from *clashmusic.com*. 'He said, "okay, you can only have one cut and if you miss, that's it. I can't afford to stop, you only get one chance." So the song started and I had to sing it right through with no mistake. There was a little part where I wanted to try some slow t'ing, but I didn't do that, and that was one of my biggest hits! Nuff pressure helped me and the studio people helped me out a lot, because let's say I had to pay $60, but they would only take $30 from me, y'know?'

Prince Jammy admired Minott's talent and the two worked together on the *Bitter Sweet* album that would appear on several different labels within the next twelve months or so. The opening track 'I'm Not For Sale' was a Ken Boothe song but the remaining seven were all self-penned, and voiced over original rhythms for the most part. 'Never Too Young', sung over a cut of Gregory Isaacs' 'My Only Lover', was the exception. This was the big hit from *Bitter Sweet* and quickly became a staple of blues dances after Jammy had licensed it to Warrior Records in the UK. Other high-lights included the reality songs 'This World' and 'Give The People', whilst 'Be Careful' and 'Right Track' were examples of early dance-hall tunes, as opposed to rockers.

Another of his 1979 albums, *Black Roots*, was the first on Minott's own Black Roots label and generated two of his biggest hits, 'Hard Time Pressure' and 'River Jordan.' He saw Black Roots as being more than just a record company, as he told *Small Axe's* Ray Hurford.

'I get together with James Brown and Keith Hartley and form a company called Black Roots Production and Youth Promotion. The Youth Promotion Organisation is really to help youth from going through the same struggle like me. We team up right as an organ-isation – we hold fund raising dances and get help from sounds like U-Roy's Sturgav and Socialist Roots. We get funds so we can buy shoes and pants for the people of the ghetto that can't afford it. The Youth Promotion, them a band also, but really we don't have any instrument as such, y'know? We use studio instruments instead. Right now we need a whole heap of help, because no one offers any help towards the youth and I really feel for them. The inspiration I keep getting, I can't reject them, you see? Once a thing come into my mind it's hard for me to push that aside, and it will just keep coming back all the while.'

Island licensed *Black Roots* from him for UK release and the advance came in handy, as did the one he received from Dave Hendley when he issued 'Hard Time Pressure' on a Sufferers Heights 12-inch. As well as struggling against poverty, unemployment and discrimination, ghetto youths faced constant police harassment. The title of that song therefore said it all, and more than a few were spared further tribulations because of Minott's interventions. He'd recruited a youngster by the name of Captain Sinbad to deejay on 'Hard Time Pressure.' Real name Carl Dwyer, Sinbad hailed from Three Mile off the Spanish Town Road, where Minott, Leroy Smart, Trinity, Al Campbell and plenty more artists came from.

'My auntie had a little shop where she used to sell pudding and fried fish,' he recalled. 'There was a poco drum in the same yard and everybody would get in the spirit and jump up. That's when I first see how music inspire people, but my father had a little sound system called Mellow Hi-Fi, and that's how I come to love the music as well. He used to keep dances and play out for people and they'd come from all about. After that now, Dillinger come into our area one time. He was a bad youth who go to approved school, but he start to deejay and I say, "wait. This man have lyrics!" Because Dillinger inspire a lot of us, like myself, Ranking Toyan, Jah Thomas and Clint Eastwood...

'How I get to meet Sugar Minott now, it was a Saturday night and me and the guys them sit on the corner, smoke some weed and think about taking in a dance. In those days sound system used to use steel horns and put them up in the treetops, y'know? We hear this music playing in the distance and some man talking on the mic so we walk and follow the music and it take us to a place up near Maxfield Park. When we get there, a little sound a play in this yard and a whole heap a people are there. Sugar Minott was the man playing the music, and he was singing as well. Them times Sugar never make no record yet, he give me a talk on the mic and then says, "hold on there! This deejay a bad!" He says he wants to voice me, and the next day he put me pon a dubplate for his sound system, Sound Of Silence. From deh so, me and Sugar Minott develop a relationship, him carry me a studio and we go and voice 'Hard Time Pressure', ''51 Storm' and quite a few more. I even do an LP for him but some reason it never came out. Sugar used to help nuff people, man. He was good like that, because from you have talent, he'd help make the world know you still.'

Jamaica still had no welfare system to speak of, despite Manley's reforms, and community projects were vital in improving people's lives at ground level. Bertram Brown was doing something similar with Freedom Sounds. Their *Reggae All-Stars* compilation showcased artists like Phillip Fraser, Rod Taylor and Prince Allah, creator of 'Bucket Bottom', a simple, but profound homily that swiftly became a favourite in blues dances in the summer of 1979. Earl Zero was another key Freedom Sounds' artist, whose own album, *Only Jah Can Ease The Pressure*, contained its share of earthy, righteous gems – 'Shackles And Chains', for example.

Earl was the son of Fisherman Zero. That's how the name started, down at Fisherman's Wharf in Greenwich Farm. His father didn't take kindly to the Rasta lifestyle, but his mother was more encouraging and bought him an old guitar, which he practised with his childhood friend Chinna Smith. It was a local shoemaker who financed their first studio session, with Earl singing 'Beautiful Brown Eyes.' Nothing much happened with it and like many of the other local Rastas, the two youths spent most days at the

517

Cornerstone – a large yard where they're meditate, lick the chalice, reason or just get on with daily chores like building fishing traps from chicken wire and mending their nets, since many were fishermen.

Errol 'Don' Mais lived on Fourth Street in Greenwich Town and the first song he produced was Earl's 'Home Sweet Home.' In fact, he'd accompanied Earl to the studio when he voiced 'None Shall Escape The Judgement' for Bunny Lee. He recorded some of the same artists who also voiced for Freedom Sounds on his Roots Tradition label, along with up-and-coming names like Michael Prophet, Little John and Sammy Dread. The Soul Syndicate played on a lot of his and Bertram Brown's recordings, in addition to filling in for the Revolutionaries at Channel One, where they welcomed the Mighty Diamonds back to 'the Channel' on the album *Deeper Roots*, for Virgin's Front Line label. The big hit from it was 'Bodyguard', which started with Mexican-style adlibs before asking who is going to bodyguard Mr Bodyguard himself. This might have been a reference to Manley's recruitment of a home guard, which had been met with mixed reactions. Virgin followed Channel One's example by releasing it as a single, but with 'One Brother Short' on the reverse. 'Blackman' would have worked better, but Little Roy wrote that and the Diamonds obviously wanted to retain the publishing from both sides, which was fair enough. *Deeper Roots* had the added attraction of a bonus dub set, and the group also appeared on albums shared with Trinity and Leroy Smart, produced by Bunny Lee and Gussie Clarke respectively. Outwardly at least, Tabby, Bunny and Judge were back on top, but they were rootless compared to three years before, when Channel One was the crucible of something radically new and exciting for both the Diamonds and everyone around them. Two of their strongest songs for 1979 were 'Identity' and 'Ghetto Living', produced by Joe Gibbs, who also called upon Cornel Campbell to record an album with him and Errol Thompson. The first song that Campbell voiced for them towards it was 'Boxing', followed by seven more including 'Rope

In.' The amount he was paid as an advance was pitiful, though, and when Cornel tried to renegotiate, Gibbs refused and that was the end of their relationship. It was Jack Ruby who made 'Boxing' popular by playing the dubplate on his sound system, and that finally persuaded Gibbs to release it on 45. By the time that happened, Cornel had revoiced both 'Boxing' and 'No Man's Land' for Bunny 'Striker' Lee, who included the latter on the album *Yes I Will* and was in overdrive, as usual. His main outlets were Third World, Live And Love, Gorgon and Attack, and also Brad Osborne's Clocktower Records, based in the Bronx. He put out the mighty *King Of Dub*, which had heavyweight remixes of rhythms like 'Stalag', 'Money Is The Root Of Evil', 'Fittest Of The Fittest' and 'Queen Of The Minstrels' on it. That Bunny managed to maintain the volume of releases – along with the relatively high standards – was astounding. His output during 1979 was again prodigious and included albums by Johnny Clarke, Linval Thompson, Delroy Wilson (four titles, including *True Believer In Love*), George Faith, the Aggrovators, Trinity (*Dreadlocks Satisfaction*), Ken Boothe, Clint Eastwood, Pat Kelly and Barry Brown, whose popularity had rocketed thanks to the *Super Star* and *Step It Up Youthman* LPs, and singles like 'Big Big Pollution' on which he voiced the fears of many ghetto people when lamenting all the 'killing and shooting and robbing and stabbing' that had resumed after the truce ended.

The US market for reggae had improved dramatically since the likes of Marley, Toots, Peter Tosh and Burning Spear had begun touring on a regular basis, and in places such as New York, sound system culture had taken hold in just the same way it had in London and other major UK cities. It would be oversimplifying things to suggest that black audiences preferred the rawer, unfiltered kind of reggae played in blues parties ('dancehall'), whilst the majority of white fans went for the more polished rockers popularised by Marley, Spear and other acts signed to Island Records. True situations are never that well-defined, but the division between the two styles was real, and it was growing. By the end of May 1979 there were several tunes on the Jamaican charts that could easily be classified as dancehall, such as Lone Ranger's number one hit 'Barnabas Collins', Sugar Minott's 'Mr DC', Michigan & Smiley's 'Rub A Dub Style' and Junior Murvin's 'Cool Out Son' – a cut to the 'Real Rock' rhythm produced by Joe Gibbs, and his biggest hit since 'Police And Thieves.' Compare any of those to Eddy Grant's latest release, which raced up the UK charts around the same time, because the contrast between Jamaican dancehall music and its flashy overseas' relative couldn't be more marked. That said, 'Living On The Frontline' wasn't exactly a reggae track, despite the subject matter. It was rather a 'dance floor classic that blended tough lyrics with an electro-sheen, a sense of optimism, and a funk-fired sound', according to the press release, not to mention 'a cult hit in UK clubs.'

Lovers rock was the other sub-genre competing for attention and sales. All it lacked was a crossover hit that would serve as a lightning rod, and one duly arrived in early June when Janet Kay's 'Silly Games' went to number two in the UK national charts. Janet's only previous success – on the reggae market, that is – was a version of Minnie Riperton's 'Loving You' produced by Alton Ellis, who'd been introduced to her by Aswad's Tony Gad. Full name Janet Kay Bogle, she was born in London but raised by Jamaican parents and grew up listening to classic soul and reggae. She was still at secretarial college when voicing 'Loving You', but Delroy Witter released two further songs by her on his D-Roy label, including a cover of Billy Stewart's 'I Do Love You'. Dennis Bovell was musical director on that track, and admired how she sang the high notes. He'd recently seen a TV commercial starring Ella Fitzgerald, who shattered a glass by singing a really high note, and that had led to him writing a song around the same concept.

'After hearing Janet do the Minnie Riperton cover, I told her that I had this song with a really high note in it. I said that if she could make this particular note then she was in, and she did it, although she insisted that Drummie Zeb play drums on the track, which was fine by me. That drum pattern was something I'd invented in my head and I could play it for two seconds, but not for four minutes, otherwise I would have done it myself. But I taught Drummie Zeb the pattern, he jumped on it and he made it his own. But then, when we were halfway through the song, he just stopped. I thought to myself, "what the bloody hell is he doing? I don't want that stop there." But it was a really good take, so we decided to keep it. It tickled me, in fact. I thought it was going to be conducive to every African and West Indian on the planet, and all the Europeans as well, because it was such a poppy tune. I knew that all of those young girls were going to be stood in front of the mirror singing it into their hairbrushes and trying to hit those notes, and the storyline was the reverse of what you'd expect as well, because usually it's the guy who's saying "come on, I like you and I think you like me, so let's stop playing games." But for a young girl to sing that to a guy, saying, "I've been wanting you for so long it's a shame. Every time I see you I get goose bumps and I know you like me as well, so let's stop playing silly games and get on with it" – that was different.'

Dennis Bovell worked on the tracks that he produced at Gooseberry studio in lieu of wages. He was paid in studio time, and that's how records like Marie Pierre's 'Walk Away', Errol Dunkley's A Little Way Different', 'Silly Games' and the Matumbi tracks 'Man In Me' and 'After Tonight' came about. The quality of those productions cannot be denied, and they helped to raise standards where British reggae was concerned.

'To us, lovers rock wasn't a watered-down thing,' confirmed Tony Gad, who played on a good many sessions with Dennis Bovell. 'Those songs had all the chord changes, and that's how we thought music should be. As far as we were concerned, we were playing music that was the equal of what anyone was doing in rock or soul. We valued reggae music just the same, and it wasn't just Caribbean music or cheap music like some people tried to make out.'

Tony Gad and Drummie Zeb worked on new material with Aswad

in-between their sessions with Dennis. The band's forthcoming album *Hulet* would signal the end of their current deal with Island and Tony, who was credited with playing piano, organ and synthesisers, had been made a permanent member at last. Mikey 'Reuben' Campbell was still their manager, and in addition to producing *Hulet*, he oversaw Grove Music's pact with Island Records during the summer. Grove's own releases included a compilation called *The Grove Reggae Collection* and tracks by Yabby You ('Babylon A Fall'), the Prophets, Michael Prophet ('Turn Me Loose'), Claudette Miller, B. B. Seaton ('I'm Aware Of Love') and King Sounds, whose album *Come Zion Side – Happiness* was recorded at Channel One with top Jamaican session musicians.

Trevor Bow's Sons Of Jah had their own label, Natty Congo, but retained close ties with Grove. They recorded their latest album *Burning Black* between Harry J's and Joe Gibbs, and Mikey Campbell then supervised overdubs and mixed it at Free Range studios in London. Tony Gad played on it, and he was joined by Rico Rodriguez, Freddie McGregor, various Wailers and Eddie 'Tan Tan' Thornton, the veteran Jamaican trumpeter who used to play with Georgie Fame at the Flamingo. Trevor Bow knew Bob Marley and the other two original Wailers from when they all lived in Trench Town. His sound was more Jamaican than black British, and this worked against him and the Sons Of Jah in certain respects, since having a foot in both camps meant that they didn't belong in either one.

On 30 May, Trevor's old friend Peter Tosh attended the Half Way Tree Magistrate's Court, where he faced charges that stemmed from the incident that happened outside Aquarius studios last September. The presiding magistrate made not one reference to the brutal beating he'd suffered from the police and, on finding Tosh guilty of possession, fined him $250 or three months' imprisonment. Justice for a Rastaman in Jamaica – even a relatively well-heeled one like Tosh – was hard to come by, and it must have been a relief for him to leave the island and travel to the Netherlands for shows during the first week of June. Mick Jagger, whose divorce from wife Bianca was all over the news, joined him at the Pinkpop Festival. Tosh and his band then left for London and two unforgettable nights at the Rainbow where the response was so good, he was asked to return for two further dates on 21 and 22 June.

Back in Jamaica, JBC Television had launched a new magazine-style programme which they broadcast every Friday evening at 7 p.m. It was produced and presented by Dermot Hussey, who devoted his show to Bob Marley and Tuff Gong International just in time for Marley's headlining performance at Reggae Sunsplash II. His inclusion, as well as the host of other musical talent on show between 3 – 7 July at Jarrett Park in Montego Bay, generated a high degree of overseas and local interest, despite the severe damage caused by a recent hurricane and floods on that western side of the island. It was only the second such event, and the first had proved disappointing, so there was additional pressure on the organisers as a result. The *Gleaner's* Arthur Kitchin was there and reported that the large field inside Jarrett Park 'had been skilfully utilised to accommodate a wide stage decorated by multi-coloured lights and a colourful backdrop.'

'A few thousand seats had been arranged at the front and security was tight, with detachments of soldiers, police, guard dogs and plain clothes police continually patrolling the arena,' Kitchin wrote. 'Several bamboo-framed and thatched huts, reminiscent of the Rastafari 'African Village' erected last August in National Heroes Park, line the perimeter, serving as rustic booths for the many vendors and artisans selling a variety of indigenous products, varying from ital food and drink to ital crafts and jewellery. One notable feature of the festival is the large influx of foreign visitors in town, particularly black Americans and white Europeans, many of whom have been attracted by the promise of fine reggae and Jamaican experiences. Most tend to be the teenagers or mature young people, but there was also a sprinkling of the elderly and small children.'

The opening night featured the finalists of the Jamaica Festival Song competition. Toots and the Maytals headlined the following evening, and on the same bill as Ras Michael and Israel Vibration. The festivities started three hours late the next day, but the seven thousand festivalgoers still got to enjoy the Abyssinians, Lone Ranger and the magnificent Burning Spear, lost in his own utterances, before the proceedings were called to a halt. Jacob Miller and Inner Circle, the scheduled headliners, didn't get to appear, despite Jacob having been seen backstage.

That all happened on the Thursday, the same day that Bob Marley and the Wailers arrived at the Seawind Hotel overlooking Montego Bay. Fans had been camped outside the hotel entrance for hours, hoping to catch a glimpse of him before his appearance the following night, on 6 July. He took to the stage wearing black leather trousers and a sleeveless top in bright Rasta colours with two banners displayed prominently behind him – one featuring the name of the festival and the other declaring 'Welcome to Ting Country' (Ting being a local soft drink). The show itself wasn't especially memorable, but following his performance at the One Love Peace Concert was always going to be near impossible. With a nod to the Jamaicans in the audience, he sang 'Rastaman Live Up' and 'Blackman Redemption' and then previewed 'Ambush In The Night', before closing with a storming rendition of 'Exodus' as his sons Ziggy and Stephen danced on stage.

After sets by Sharon Forrester and the Mighty Diamonds, Third World provided the grand finale on Saturday 7 July with a high energy blend of reggae, rock, disco, Latin-style percussion and soulful lead vocals. Led by the charismatic Bunny Rugs, they did Reggae Sunsplash II proud, but the foreign journalists were there for Marley, whose life and influence continued to be of keen interest. Whoever called him 'the first Third World superstar' knew what they were doing because there was now an aura surrounding Marley that guaranteed headlines wherever he went. Just two weeks after his appearance at Reggae Sunsplash he was at Harvard University in Boston being lauded as 'the man who shares his spiritual power with the world' at the Amandla Festival Of Unity. Nigerian drummer Babatunde Olatunji replaced Seeco on congas in an impressive demonstration of African-style drumming and two more new, as-yet-unreleased songs were premiered during that show – 'Africa Unite' and an electrifying, fifteen minute version of 'Wake Up And Live', the song written by Sangie Davis that the Wailers hadn't wanted to play.

Meanwhile, Peter Tosh had unwittingly found himself as a guest on the same Italian television show as porn queen Ilona Staller, aka Cicciolina. He then gave a powerful performance at the Montreux Jazz Festival in Switzerland, on the same bill as Dennis Brown. Daryl Thompson served the same purpose in Tosh's band as Al Anderson and Junior Marvin did in the Wailers. He was there to add rock bite, but then Word, Sound & Power had the same configuration as Marley's band. Both had two keyboard-players, lead and rhythm guitarists and three backing singers, except the Tamlins were all-male, in contrast to Bob Marley's I Three. The major difference was on drums and bass. The Barrett brothers were the prime architects of roots reggae and the laidback one-drop style that had proved so successful in rebranding reggae music internationally, whereas the rhythms that Sly and Robbie created for Peter were a seething cauldron of high energy rockers, driven by Robbie Shakespeare's attacking, disco-laced bass-lines and Sly's inventive Afrocentric drumming. This was the sound that underpinned songs talking about slavery ('400 Years'), racial identity ('African') and the legalisation of marijuana, since the author of 'Legalise It', 'Bush Doctor' and 'Buk-In-Hamm Palace' was never seen on stage without a spliff. Jamaica had the highest density of ganja smokers in the world, and also the most celebrated strains, like sinsemilla and Lambs bread, grown up in the hills and well out of sight from the police. Peter Tosh was their champion, and in the summer of 1979 he was the most outspoken, uncompromising reggae artist of all, and arguably had the best band.

The support act for his Rainbow shows and the remaining European dates was Steel Pulse. Their second album *Tribute To The Martyrs* had been released in June and was again produced by Karl Pitterson. Island chose to go with 'Sound System' as the lead single but every other song had a strong message, especially 'Jah Pickney – R.A.R.' (which talks about hunting the National Front), 'Uncle George' (dedicated to Soledad brother George Jackson), 'Unseen Guest' (about a lynching) and 'Biko's Kindred Lament.' Lead singer David Hinds wrote all of them except 'Babylon Makes The Rules', and remained unrepentant when Pulse were criticised for not recording songs that were more accessible.

'During the seventies, bands like ourselves and Aswad represented a cry from the youths,' he said. 'We were the first generation of British-born black reggae acts and we knew what it felt like being under the hammer. We were exposed to the whole vibe of the sixties, learning about our history and trying to get meaningful jobs. We thought we had the same opportunities as any other British citizens, and to find out that this wasn't the case created a strong outcry. There had to be an outcry, because we'd been told a lie and sold a dream.

'The industry wasn't ready for our music in a sense, because the punks were rebelling at the same time, so they knew that a revolution was going on among the youths, but they weren't ready to hear it from our standpoint. Radio refused to play us. In those days, Radio 1 were in sole control, and everything hinged on whether they said yes or no. That's why pirate stations had to kick in so hard, because they knew that somebody had to be representing the youth of this country. Also, our counterparts from Jamaica like Bob Marley, Jacob Miller and Burning Spear were talking about Marcus Garvey, slavery days and the historical aspects of our story, so we had to go about finding our own ways to advertise this music in our communities. The birth of the pirate radio stations arose because we musicians had had our backs to a brick wall all those years, and it's *still* there.'

Steel Pulse returned to the UK after touring with Peter Tosh to discover that a band from Coventry, a city not too far from their own hometown of Birmingham, was at number six in the national charts with a raucous fusion of ska and punk called 'Gangsters'. I say ska because the rhythm owed much to Prince Buster's 'Al Capone', but the Specials' take on it was no ordinary cover version – not with its rockabilly guitar licks, snake-charming organ and Terry Hall's ghostly vocals.

Any history of the Specials must start with keyboardist Jerry Dammers – the son of a Coventry clergyman, and someone bassist Horace Panter has described as 'this weird looking bloke with tartan trousers who used to smash things up.' The two met at Lancaster Polytechnic, where, according to the *Guardian*'s Alexis Petridis, Dammers became part of 'a small group who dressed like Teds or skinheads.'

'We used to wreck the hippie parties and play Prince Buster records,' Dammers said. 'I had this band playing dodgy versions of Desmond Dekker's '007', and we used to gob at each other on stage. I was like a forerunner of punk.'

By the mid-seventies he and Panter were back in Coventry, playing covers with the Cissy Stone Band. Jerry soon tired of that and asked Panter and another friend, Lynval Golding, to help him record a few tracks. Though born in Jamaica, Golding had grown up in Gloucester, before learning guitar and moving to Coventry, where he played in local soul and reggae bands. It was Golding who dubbed Panter 'Gentleman' on account of his posh accent, and showed him how to play reggae bass. The line-up then expanded to include drummer Silverton Hutchinson, a 'herb smoker and philosopher' from Barbados who'd played with Lynval in a band called Pharoah's Kingdom featuring Ray King. The latter was well-known on the Midlands soul circuit, and playing with him provided good experience for Golding before Jerry poached the pair for his band Nite Train, which barely survived an ill-advised residency at a Tunisian nightclub. Golding stayed though and suggested they include a few ska tunes in their set, which they trialled at the Bantam pub in Holbrook.

'What really drew me in was the political side of punk, because when Rock Against Racism came about I was immediately attracted to it,' Golding told me. 'I couldn't always understand the music, but the sentiments and the energy behind it were amazing. It brought people together, and it was talking about things that were dear to my heart, which was racism. That's why the Specials had that punk drive and energy, because it was all coming from that and it changed-up the whole music scene. Black and white started converging together into this big melting pot, and the vibe behind a lot of punk was just perfect, although I had black friends say to me, "What are you doing in a punk band? You should be in a roots bands, man!" They could never understand why I wasn't playing roots when that was the music we were all listening to, because you had these British reggae bands who were heavily into politics as well, like Steel Pulse and Misty In Roots. It's just that I was putting the two things together and working on trying to break down barriers, but my black friends, they never got it, really.'

In Dammers and Panter, Golding had found the ideal co-conspirators, and together they began to forge a distinct identity for themselves. Dammers had written a tune called 'Jay Walker' and so the group briefly became the Jaywalkers, before settling on the Coventry Automatics. Tim Strickland was their lead singer, until they recruited the boyish Terry Hall from another Coventry punk band, The Squad. His laconic yet acidic delivery was perfect for the Automatics. Like Panter, he had a typically suburban upbringing, but Hall, aged just 18, also had a razor-sharp wit, and quickly adjusted to his new surroundings. Like Golding, Neville Staple was Jamaican-born. He'd started out as a dancer with Neville & The Boys at the Locarno in Coventry, before deejaying on Jah Baddis, Holyhead Youth Club's resident sound system. With Staple in their line-up, the Automatics' first notable gig was at Tiffany's Ballroom, supporting Ultravox. Soon afterwards, Dammers decided they needed a lead guitarist and reached out to Roderick 'Roddy' Byers, who'd played with him in a band called Gristle and was gigging under the name Roddy Radiation and the Wild Boys, playing rockabilly. He'd got the name 'Radiation' because his face would go bright red after he had a drink. He, too, would have to make adjustments after joining the Automatics, learning to play ska.

Sounds' Adrian Thrills once quoted Jerry as saying that the group had gone back to ska because it was much closer to rhythm and blues, which is where British rock originally came from. Local DJ-turned-A&R man Pete Waterman financed some demo tracks, but the band members weren't too happy with the results, and the gigs hadn't been going too well, either. When the Automatics supported Steel Pulse at Birmingham's Top Rank Suite in early 1978, the sold-out crowd just stood and watched them in silence. Everyone just blanked them, and at another gig in Birmingham around the same time a section of the crowd started chanting racist slogans, accompanied by Nazi salutes. The mood in Britain had grown ugly and such open displays of racism had become more common since the rise of right-wing hate group the National Front. Less than ten years earlier, racist and violent behaviour by skinheads had dealt a serious blow to reggae's mainstream acceptance in the UK. Venues had stopped booking reggae acts for fear of trouble, and the glorious run of crossover hits enjoyed by artists like Desmond Dekker, Jimmy Cliff and others was stopped in its tracks. Skinheads had their origins in the Mods and had adopted the same dress code as the rudies before shaved heads, braces and Doc Martens held sway. The original Jamaican rude boy style suited Golding and Staple, who wore pork pie hats just like their elders and sported loafers, Sta Prest trousers and tonic suits as if in defiance of the Rasta mindset embraced by many other young blacks in the UK. They were exercising their right to be different, except it sent mixed signals and the Coventry Automatics unwittingly attracted a skinhead following, who loved the band's covers of ska and early reggae hits like 'Liquidator' and 'Long Shot Kick The Bucket.'

In summer of 1978 they supported the Clash at Aylesbury Town Hall. It was the first gig of a three-week trek but Clash manager Bernie Rhodes liked them so much he invited them to stay for the rest of the tour. Meanwhile, another band called The Automatics threatened to sue them if they didn't change their name. They became the Special AKA The Automatics after that, just in time for the Clash tour. The Clash's fervent, no-holds-barred perform-ances attracted audiences to match, and, with hindsight, it probably wasn't the best idea to have Sham 69 share the bill on certain dates, just weeks after neo-Nazi skinheads among their following had caused £7,500 worth of damage at a previous gig. The Clash tour was the making of the Special AKA, however, and with Bernie Rhodes behind them, what could go wrong?

Plenty, as it happened, because the French dates that Rhodes booked for them proved disastrous. The band were charged for damages to a hotel caused by the Damned, there were serious transportation issues and Silverton Hutchinson left soon after their return to the UK and was replaced by John 'Brad' Bradbury, a former flatmate of Jerry's whose style had more drive and energy than his predecessor's.

Bradbury was the final piece of the puzzle. The next step was to have another attempt at making a record. The arrival of the punks had heralded an explosion of indie labels aided by distribu-tors like Rough Trade, and this had loosened the major record companies' stranglehold on the industry. Musicians were doing it for themselves and so Dammers approached local character James 'Jimbo' O'Boyle, who lent him £700 to fund a recording session. The resourceful Dammers then designed the 2 Tone label, with its black and white checks, and the drawing of mascot Walt Jabsco, whose name came from a bowling shirt but whose appearance – inspired by an early photo of Peter Tosh – was that of a Jamaican rude boy. 2 Tone was a concept – as well as the name of a record label – that embraced fashion and race at a single stroke. Confidence was therefore high when they booked a session at Coventry's Horizon studios and recorded 'Gangsters' in January 1979. The Special AKA had other tracks, but Dammers wasn't happy with them, the money had run out and he needed something to put on the flipside, so five thousand copies of 'Gangsters' had rolled off the press in March 1979, backed by an instrumental called 'The Selecter' featuring John Bradbury and guitarist Neol Davies. The latter got upset after hearing John Peel credit the track to the Specials and formed a new band called The Selecter, fronted by Pauline Black, more of whom later. Despite Peel's support, 'Gangsters' sold slowly. It wasn't until the Specials signed to Chrysalis (in a deal brokered by new manager Rick Rogers) that it gained any momentum and went into the charts. As part of that arrangement, Chrysalis offered Dammers £1,000 to develop a band of his choice, and that's how The Selecter also got to sign with Chrysalis and record their first three tracks, including 'Too Much Pressure' and 'On My Radio.' For a new musical movement to be birthed in Coventry, rather than cities like London, Manchester, Liverpool or Bristol, was unheard of.

Birmingham was already on the map thanks to Steel Pulse, and local radio presenter Robin Valk had John Lydon on his show at the end of July. Like Tommy Vance before him, he asked Lydon to pick some of his favourite tracks, and among them were reggae releases by Black Uhuru, Gregory Isaacs ('Rock On') and Ken Boothe, and the original cut of Ijahman Levi's 'Jah Heavy Load.' Contentious as ever, the one-time Rotten dismissed the Island Records' recut of that song as 'cocktail jazz.'

Ijahman was at Reggae Sunsplash II and stayed close to Marley throughout. Maybe he considered himself to be of equal stature, and, for a short while, many others did too. Island released his second album *Are We A Warrior* in 1979, which featured five tracks this time, rather than four. 'Moulding' was the standout, a message for singers and players of instruments that urged them to assume

531

responsibility in helping those who cannot help themselves in building a strong foundation.

Bob Marley and the people at Tuff Gong were thinking along the same lines. They were among the sponsors for the third annual Tastees Talent Contest, held in Kingston on 26 July. Sangie Davis was in the crowd that evening as 11-year-old Nadine Sutherland sang and danced her way into the hearts of the judges. She was the first female winner of the competition and won JA$75, three LPS from Record Specialists and one month's supply of Tastees patties. Just days later, she was invited to Tuff Gong where she stood on a chair and recorded her debut single 'Starvation On The Land', as Bob Marley looked on.

Winston Foster had come third at the Tastees show and, according to the *Gleaner*, 'thrilled the crowd with his fancy rhymes' when deejaying his own version of Lone Ranger's 'Barnabas Collins.' He received two weeks' supply of patties, one LP and JA$30 cash, but no record deal. His time would come, though, once the albino Foster had changed his name to Yellowman and began recording for Ruddy Thomas and Channel One.

Despite reggae music's growing popularity overseas, Jamaican audiences liked what they heard of the new dancehall style. The crop of young singers and deejays who'd been voicing fresh tunes on rhythms favoured by sound systems were effectively following in U-Roy's footsteps, and enthusiasm for the crossover music that the likes of Inner Circle and Tosh were making was waning. On 3 August the *Santa Cruz Sentinel* published an article with a headline that asked, 'Is Peter Tosh Really Reggae?' In the text Island Records' Lister Hewan Lowe was quoted as saying 'Peter Tosh is not reggae, he's pop.' On the same page, someone reviewing Tosh's *Mystic Man* album gleefully announced that 'The Rolling Stones are thankfully nowhere to be seen on this disc.' The gates that certain Jamaican artists had worked hard to open for reggae overseas were now closing behind them, leaving them precious little room for manoeuvre.

The dancehall duo Michigan & Smiley had celebrated their chart-topping success with 'Nice Up The Dance' with a show at the InterContinental Hotel ballroom in early August. It was their first performance at a major Kingston venue and was followed by one at the same venue featuring Johnny Osbourne and the up-and-coming Barrington Levy. According to the *Gleaner*, 'the talented but rusty Johnny Osbourne' tried to brighten his performance with some deejaying whilst Barrington Levy was described as 'the newly crowned underground singing star.'

'With some encouragement he took the stage and everyone was glad he did,' the review continued. 'He showed a certain degree of professional knack, cutting songs short and immediately swinging into his next song to cut his performance to a minimum. His 'Shine Eye Gal', 'Collie Weed' and 'Love Is A Two Way Street' are three of the hottest songs around the town, but unluckily he has been denied much radio exposure which is all he needs to make the top.'

The 18-year-old Barrington always was musical, even as a child growing up in Kingston. At the age of 9 he attempted to play a guitar made from a sardine tin, and sang alongside his cousin Everton Dacres in the Mighty Multitudes while still at school. Their debut, 'My Black Girl,' recorded at Federal for Dobby Dobson, didn't go anywhere, so the pair went to Dynamic Sound and voiced a couple of tunes for Barry Biggs and Byron Lee, who renamed them Heckyl & Jeckyl. Barrington, whose biggest influence was Dennis Brown ('because he sings with his heart and not just his lips'), hated the name and wasn't reticent about saying so. The two cousins parted company soon afterwards and Barrington went from dance to dance, looking to practise his singing. One of his favourite sound systems was Burning Spear, where he shared a mic with Leroy Smart, Clint Eastwood and Trinity. His fame soon spread thanks to tapes of these dances circulating on cassette and it wasn't long before he came to the attention of producer Henry 'Junjo' Lawes, who produced Barrington's solo debut, 'A Yah We Deh.' His breakthrough came a little later with 'Collie Weed' – a cut to the 'My Conversation' rhythm that told of him setting off on his bike to buy herb in Maverley. It appeared on Roots From Yard at first before Brooklyn label Jah Life repressed it on 12-inch, and a flood of other singles and albums followed

The reason why the *Gleaner* had described Johnny Osbourne as rusty was that he'd not long returned from Canada, ending his stint with Ishan People. They'd been signed to GRT, but the label went bust, so Johnny decided he'd go back home and see if he could pick up from where he'd left off a decade earlier, after recording 'Come Back Darling' and other hits for Winston Riley. It was meant to be an exploratory visit, but he quickly got caught up in a whirlwind of recording, for the same producer who'd consistently rejected him in the early days.

'Imagine that! For years I would go to Studio One for auditions and I get turned away every time,' said Osbourne, laughing. 'It was only after I decide to go back to Jamaica that I finally got my foot in there, but my career wouldn't have been complete without making any records – even one single 45 – at Coxsone's Studio One label. When I was in Canada I identified some of the rhythms that I wanted to work on, so when I came back I asked Mr Dodd about them and he said that I should go and look for the tapes. I did that – I seek them out, brush them off and then I do some overdubs on them with Pablove Black, Earl 'Bagga' Walker, Horsemouth and Dalton Browne. Dancehall was the thing by then, so I have to do it that way because nobody remembered me. I'd been away too long, but then I make back my name in Jamaica by singing over those rhythms at Studio One.'

His first recordings for Studio One were 'Forgive Them' and 'Jealousy, Heartache And Pain', but it was his *Truth And Rights* album that truly revived his career. The title track opened with lines inspired by the bible although Johnny hadn't embraced Rastafari yet, and was simply soaking up the vibes surrounding the Studio One camp at that time.

'Me and Freddie McGregor were there every day,' he explained.

'Also Jennifer Lara, Devon Russell, Ernest Wilson, Earl Sixteen, the Silvertones and Judah Eskender Tafari, who did 'Jah Light.' We were all brethren there together because that was the same time we started Freddie McGregor's *Bobby Babylon* album as well. Me, Freddie and Jennifer Lara, we moved together. All three of us sang harmonies on *Truth And Rights* and *Bobby Babylon*, as well. We worked in unity and that's what gave those two albums such a nice feeling, because there was harmony between us as friends, and we weren't competing or trying to outdo each other. I didn't even have dreadlocks at the time. I was still searching really, but the songs came out alright because I already had that spiritual feeling inside of me.'

There were only ten tracks on *Truth And Rights* and every one of them was a gem – 'Can't Buy Love', 'We Need Love' and 'Jah Promise' included. Osbourne says the latter was inspired by his boyhood hero, Alton Ellis. Sometimes he'd be preparing to record a song and think about how Alton might approach it, and McGregor was also heavily influenced by some of the great singers that had recorded at Brentford Road before them. His *Bobby Bobylon* set was another landmark Studio One release, thanks to tracks like 'Rasta Man Camp,' 'I Am A Revolutionist', 'We Need More Love', the ska outing 'Gonna Take Over Now' and 'Wine Of Violence' – a cut of 'Undying Love' written by former Clarendonian Ernest Wilson.

Outside of Studio One, Johnny Osbourne began voicing for Prince Jammy and Junjo Lawes, whilst Freddie finished an album that he'd started with Niney The Observer. *Mr McGregor* was recorded at Channel One with the Soul Syndicate and consisted of predominantly roots songs, interspersed with a couple of covers ('Oh No, Not My Baby' and 'Brandy') and a righteous rendition of Little Roy's 'Jah Can Count On I.' He and Niney's cut of 'Rastaman Camp', complete with majestic horns, was less weighty in mood and rhythm than the Studio One version but was still superb, whilst the opening 'We Got Love' was an archetypal sufferers' song.

Freddie McGregor fans – and he gained a lot more of them in 1979 – also took note of his cover of the Interns' Mission Impossible' and a single called 'Sergeant Brown', telling of how a police officer had raided a ganja field, stolen a bag of collie weed and then sold it, leaving the farmer destitute. 'Bring it back, Sergeant Brown,' Freddie demanded.

Devon Russell sang with Cedric Myton in the Bell Stars and also the Tartans, best known for their 1965 hit 'Dance All Night', before the members went their separate ways. Devon sang in a duo with Lloyd Robinson, and the pair recorded 'Bum Ball' for Derrick Morgan, which was an instant hit. After the pair had a falling out, Devon re-voiced 'Bum Ball' with Ernest Wilson for Coxsone, and ended up recording over a dozen solo tracks at Studio One, only two of which came out. Understandably disenchanted, he went off on tour around the Caribbean and lived in Guyana for a while before returning to Jamaica in 1979. By then, he'd embraced Rastafari and was writing roots and culture songs. His lyrics to Jackie Mittoo's 'Drum Song' were inspired by a celestial vision and 'Roots Natty Roots' found him chanting in tandem with the Yoruba Singers over a Gladiators' track. Devon's other songs for Studio One included 'Jah Holds The Key', a cover of Curtis Mayfield's 'People Get Ready' and a stirring cut of 'Darker Shade Of Black' named 'Money Problem.' It was the final flowering of Coxsone's famous label, and everyone who was there at the time made memorable contributions. Jennifer Lara put her stamp on Bob Marley's 'Natural Mystic' and the 21-year-old Ronald Merrills, otherwise known as Judah Eskender Tafari, chalked up several unforgettable tracks, including 'Jah Light' and 'Rastafari Tell You', although he claimed to have recorded two albums' worth of material for Coxsone in total.

There were several former Studio One artists on show at the National Arena on 20 August, at a charity concert organised by the United House Of Elders in aid of the International Year Of The Child. Proceeds from the show went towards the building of a basic school and training centre, and also the Flood Relief Fund. The venue was packed and Bob Marley, Jacob Miller and the I Three all got a great reaction. Burning Spear, who premiered his new song 'African Postman', was also a hit with the crowd, but Toots and the Maytals, Black Uhuru and Third World, who were all originally billed to appear, failed to show. Bob and Rita Marley's children had formed a group called the Melody Makers and proceeds from their debut single 'Children Playing In The Street', written by their father, were also donated to the International Year Of The Child Fund.

In late August, Tuff Gong subsidiary label 56 Hope Road made history by releasing the first-ever Jamaican dub poetry record. Oku, fired up like a wasp in a jar, had voiced 'Reflection In Red' at Harry J studios, backed by members of the Wailers. Opening with sirens gave it the sense that something important was about to unfold, and so it proved, as Oku reiterated a truth that Peter Tosh had previously articulated – that there can be no peace until equal rights and justice prevail. A few months later, Oku met fellow poet Linton Kwesi Johnson, who had been the first to coin the expression 'dub poetry.'

'It was a meeting of spirits and minds and we had a mutual liking of each other,' said Johnson. 'When I met him I felt validated, because I'd been doing this kind of poetry, coming out of the Jamaican oral tradition as well as the reggae tradition, and he was someone who was doing the same thing.'

At the same time that 'Reflection In Red' arrived, Bob Marley and the Wailers' latest single 'Ambush In The Night' was number one on the island's charts. There was no mistaking what this song was about, not with lyrics describing guns being aimed and then fired at him. But it was the observations that politicians were bribing people and trying to belittle people's integrity that hinted at the reasons why he'd been targeted, lifting the lid on Jamaica's corrupt system of government.

In early September, Michael Manley had flown to Havana, where

537

he attended a conference of the so-called non-aligned countries, hosted by Fidel Castro. An editorial in the *Gleaner* described it as 'a festival of anti-imperialism, anti-colonialism and anti-Zionism, where the folk heroes of the hour were a delegation of Sandinista leaders fresh from a recent victory in Nicaragua.' During his speech, Manley denounced imperialism, colonialism, neo-colonialism, racism, fascism and all forms of external domination and exploitation. 'It's a long, hard road,' he warned. 'We have no illusions, but so long as one child cries out in hunger, so long as one mother grieves for lost hopes, so long as Pretoria can strut in arrogance, must we continue to struggle. Our movement is irreversible because our cause is just.'

It's said that the art of politics has a lot to do with optics, and whilst Manley was impressive when lending his voice to issues affecting Third World countries on the world stage, many Jamaicans back home were too busy struggling with a cost of living crisis, food shortages and rising crime rates to care. There were also other indications which suggested that the Manleys had got their priorities wrong. For instance, Beverly Manley had recently come under fire for wearing a mink coat, while the PM was criticised for accepting the gift of a Cadillac at a time when his government had banned the import of such cars. He and his wife were rightly accused of hypocrisy, even as his socialist experiment was increasingly becoming derailed.

Any help for the people was now coming from elsewhere, and Jamaica's musicians were at the forefront of attempts to make that happen. The National Arena was again the venue of choice when the Ethiopian Orthodox Church and the St Terec Haimanot Brotherhood held a two day concert on 22 – 23 September to raise funds for the Church's building fund. The line-up for the opening show featured Third World, Burning Spear, Ras Michael, Big Youth, the Abyssinians and Kiddus I, who was a former member of the Peace Committee and a talented artist, as well as a singer of righteous songs like 'Crying Wolf' and 'Security In The Streets.' He'd helped set up a Rasta commune and craft centre when he was a member of Ras Michael and the Sons Of Negus and was already very community-minded. It was Ras Michael who named him Kiddus I, which means 'saint' or 'blessed one' in Amharic, although Bob Marley used to call him 'Dr Feelgood' – probably because he was renowned for selling ital food and high-grade marijuana.

'We want people to be aware, and we don't divert at all,' he told Angus Taylor. 'We try and maintain that vision and we never deviated, but kept along that path. Because when you have a system that purposely misleads mankind, then information through the written word and news channels is misinformation, so how to read in-between and be aware is important, because the system's not giving you the truth. They don't want you to be aware as them. They always want to step up the ladder and be separated from you. So for the masses, who are the sheep of the world and have been left behind, you need someone who can voice the concerns of the masses, and so that is where we find ourselves as reggae artists. Not dancehall artists, but the reggae music that is really uplifting and trying to highlight matters that affect people in their daily lives. That's why we don't change, because we'd rather help someone who's in a dead end or maybe a cul-de-sac and keep them on the highway. The questions and concern is there, so let people see it. That's the purpose of a singer, writer or poet – to give their critique of the situation as it is, because in the opinion of most leaders, the masses just eat, shit and take up space. But if that's their view, then where is the hope for mankind? Our leaders don't want to share or let others live in a harmonious world. They love wars and confusion because that suits them, but that is our duty as artists – we have to critique them in this time, as singers and players of instruments.'

Bob Marley had already donated JA$10,000 to the Church's building fund. He closed that show after performances by Israel Vibration, Junior Tucker, Light Of Saba, U-Roy, Oku Onoura, I Kong, Rita Marley and the Melody Makers. The only time Marley's

539

dominance was threatened was when Gregory Isaacs strolled on stage singing 'Mr Brown', 'Tune In' and current hit 'Soon Forward.' He'd recently returned from the US and shows at My Father's Place, Club Negril and the Renaissance Ballroom. Nothing had come of the Rolling Stones' interest in him, but maybe he didn't care about that. Virgin was behind his latest album (also called *Soon Forward*) and Cash And Carry were taking care of distribution in the Caribbean. He also had a loyal – and at times fanatical – following, whilst his gift for songwriting remained second to none. *Soon Forward* would be among the last albums released on Virgin's Front Line imprint, and was arguably one of the best. Apart from the title track, it had memorable songs like 'Universal Tribulation', 'Mr Brown', 'Slave Market' and 'Black Liberation Struggle.' The pathos with which he voiced 'Slave Market' cut like a knife, and yet it was a narrative free of anger or bitterness. Instead, we were given truth and certainty – traits born from sufferation, and delivered with consummate restraint.

Restraint is not a word that anyone would associate with Peter Tosh, who performed on the penultimate night of the five MUSE (Musicians United for Safe Energy) concerts held at New York's Madison Square Garden between 19-23 September. 1979 was proving to be an eventful year for the Mystic Man, but any thoughts of him being accepted into the world of rock celebrity were dashed by his appearance that Saturday, on 22 September, which happened to coincide with Jewish New Year or Rosh Hashanah. Tosh, controversial as ever, chose to mark the occasion by dressing in Palestinian robes and lighting up his customary spliff. It was a daring, provocative statement to make on such a day, and in a city with such a large Jewish community. When Asylum Records – owned by David Geffen, who himself was Jewish – later released a three LP boxed set of performances taken from those five MUSE concerts, Peter Tosh was nowhere to be seen or heard. His contribution to the project had been erased, and yet his reasons for having taken part were no doubt sincere. Unlike many other Jamaican reggae artists, he was unafraid to nail his colours to the mast where issues such as apartheid, the decriminalisation of marijuana, police brutality, organised religion and the British monarchy were concerned. He was truly a revolutionary character, guileless and fearless in how he went about making his opinions heard.

Less than two weeks earlier, on 8 September, Tosh had appeared at the Second Annual Tribal Stomp Festival at the Monterey County Fairgrounds in California. The promoters – led by Chet Helms, a legend of the San Francisco scene in the sixties – had boasted that Tribal Stomp would feature the 'heaviest reggae entourage to ever hit the United States.' Yet the only other reggae acts in Monterey that weekend were the Mighty Diamonds, Earl Zero and Soul Syndicate, and the turnout was abysmal. The Clash were there, at the start of only their second US tour, and they played a cover of Willie Williams' 'Armagideon Time' during their encore. Chris Salewicz, writing in *Redemption Song – The Definite Biography Of Joe Strummer*, described it as one of lead singer Strummer's most impassioned performances, 'the palm of his right hand firmly clasped over his right eye, a dramatic piece of mime he'd stolen from Bob Marley.'

Bassist Paul Simonon told Salewicz that he and Joe were always amazed by the way that in reggae, a rhythm could be just lying around. 'It wasn't like, "this is my song." It could be freely used by anybody and they'd just sing over it in their own particular way, depending on what their vision was.'

Jamaica still didn't have proper copyright laws, but the Clash hadn't finished being inspired by reggae music – not by some distance. Patti Smith had, though. The day after the Clash played at Tribal Stomp, she did the biggest show of her career at the Stadium Communale in Florence, Italy, in front of 85,000 people. It was her final concert before retiring to Detroit and a new life with Fred 'Sonic' Smith. Four months earlier she had told the *New York Daily News*, 'I really have no patience at all for so much of the crap in the punk rock scene. New Wave is romantically political but all this shit sticking safety pins in cheeks and all the fucking violence is just a style and a fad. I came into rock as a purist with a motivation to communicate – something I see as man's greatest gift.'

The art of communication takes many forms, and Errol Dunkley's lyrics on his latest hit could have easily been lifted from a Ramones' song because they basically consisted of just four lines repeating how the central character in the song, Fred, was a 'yagga yagga.'

'The words "yagga yagga" or "booga yagga" meant undesirable people,' Bunny Lee explained. 'Those were the words that uptown people used. They didn't want their kids associating with people like that, because they rob and steal. When Errol Dunkley did over John Holt's song and came out on the BBC with that phrase, people were so surprised because a man would say, "I don't want no yagga yagga inside of this place here. Keep them out." From a man start smoke weed and turn Rasta, a lot of people would think he'd gone mad and run him out the place. They'd think the boy had mashed up himself and say, "look how much money me did spend pon him. He should have gone to university, and now him turn fool…"'

Dunkley sang it on *Crackerjack* and *The Basil Brush Show* as well as *Top Of The Pops*, because 'OK Fred' went to number eleven on the UK charts in late September. He was hoping that the follow-up 'Happiness Forgets' would do the same or even better, but that recut of 'A Little Way Different' was his other big-seller from that period.

'I never had a contract with a major company,' said Dunkley, 'but when I had 'OK Fred', I was signed with this French company, and they did a lot for me. They were living up to their agreement and I could see that the record was properly promoted. We did TV shows all over Europe, in Luxembourg, Monte Carlo and Rome. 'OK Fred' even went to number one in France…'

Count Shelly included it on the Third World album *Profile Of Errol Dunkley*, but 'OK Fred' wasn't the only reggae song on the UK charts in late September 1979. When producer Dennis Bovell claimed that Matumbi's 'Point Of View' was 'perfect for the charts', he wasn't joking, even if it did just miss out the UK Top 40. It was commercial to a fault – brimming with melody and doo wop-style harmonies, set to an infectious reggae beat.

'For 'Point Of View' there's no forgiveness,' Bovell said. 'It was being played on Kiss FM in New York, and then WBLS, and the video for that song was the first reggae video to be shown on MTV, but to be fair, it wasn't only the record company that messed up there, because there were all kinds of managerial and internal shenanigans going on. It was strange, because we were booked to do an American tour through EMI, and we were all ready to go, but then the day before the tour was supposed to start, we got word from the record company that it had been cancelled. Maybe EMI thought we were going to create trouble for them in America or something, because we were a bit outspoken at the time. When we finally went there we discovered that 'Point Of View' had been a million-seller over there, and to this day we've seen no accounts regarding that song, even though it was on this hit compilation at the time called *Walk, Don't Boogie*. We never got that sorted out, and that contributed towards the end of us and EMI, because the next thing that happened was that we were booked for the Ivory Coast. We were finally going to get to Africa – we took all the jabs and everything, we were paid in advance, and all that was left to come our way were the airline tickets, which never arrived. What's more, we never heard anymore from the guy who was supposed to be taking us over there.'

Bovell had been busy in the meantime, bridging the divide between reggae and punk.

'The punks liked the idea that you didn't have to be a great singer, and that kind of broke the barrier a bit,' he observed. 'The first band I worked with like that was the Pop Group. I did 'We Are All Prostitutes' and 'She Is Beyond Good And Evil' with them. They were leaning towards reggae because of its militancy and they loved the fact that I knew how to equalise the bass to make it sound monstrous. Also, I was a Hendrix fan, so I knew how to handle distortion and capture it on recordings. After those tracks, Chris Blackwell said to me, "I've just signed the first female punk band and they're called the Slits," so I went to meet them and they said, "oh, we thought Dennis Brown was coming!" It took us maybe nine, ten weeks to do their first album *Cut*, and I let them play everything themselves, except for a few keyboards and percussion. That was because they were going to have go out and play it live. And they liked me for that – for letting them play and just guiding them. A lot of people said to me, "what are you doing that for?" I would say, "we're making some historical sounds", and then, when the album came out, everyone said it was a force to be reckoned with.'

UK reggae DJ David Rodigan's appearances on Radio London resulted in Capital Radio's Tim Blackmore asking him to present a half hour history of reggae as part of Adrian Love's *Music Line*. This in turn led to similar slots on Nicky Horne's Friday night show *Mummy's Weekly*, before 'Rodders' was offered a Saturday night slot called *Roots Rockers Show*, which initially went on air between 8-9 p.m., before shifting to the ten-until-midnight slot. *Roots Rockers* would soon become essential listening for Londoners interested in reggae music. Rodigan played all the songs that mattered, kept fans up-to-date with the latest news from Jamaica and regularly interviewed artists, record producers and musicians whose stories could rarely be heard anywhere else. As well as presenting *Roots Rockers*, the DJ dubbed 'Crazy Baldhead' maintained his acting career, made personal appearances at clubs and venues throughout the UK, was a regular contributor to *Black Echoes* and presented a two-hour show for British Forces Posted Overseas, based in Germany.

Unlike many other radio presenters, Rodigan didn't allow his ego to get the better of him once the red light came on. The music and those who made it took precedence, even as he gave the impression of someone who'd been handed keys to the candy store and couldn't believe their luck. His passion and enthusiasm for reggae was evident, and the excitement he generated on air entirely genuine.

'You have to keep your integrity and be yourself,' he confided. 'The listeners have to believe that you are feeling everything you play, because without that you're a charlatan. As broadcasters we have to stay true to what we believe, and play the kind of music we think represents the essence of the culture, because primarily this music is about understanding. It's music of compassion, and it has always stood up for human rights and justice. Those are some of the things that first attracted me to reggae and that still give me deep joy, along with the melodies and aching vocals, the beautiful love songs, the dub music and people rhyming in time...'

Rodigan had made his first visit to Jamaica in January, which is when Mo Claridge signed Prince Lincoln and the Royal Rasses to Ballistic. The Rasses played their first UK date at the Kensington Nashville on 6 September, but then returned to London the following month to appear on Rodigan's *Roots Rockers* and promote their latest album, *Experience*.

Prince Lincoln had formed the Royal Rasses after leaving Studio One in 1972. The group was originally a quartet comprised of Lincoln, Cedric Myton, Clinton 'Johnny Cool' Hall and Keith 'Cap' Peterkin, but then Cedric then met up with Ashanti Roy and formed the Congos. By then Prince Lincoln had moved out to Hunt's Bay, a coastal area midway between Waterford and Seaview Gardens, where Ras Michael also lived for a time.

'I just chill out there,' Lincoln told me. 'I grew vegetables on my farm and went fishing. I had my own net, and then out of that experience came songs like 'Humanity', 'Kingston 11' and 'San Salvador.' I was sitting by the fire at night with my guitar when I wrote most of those songs, and whilst it only had three strings, I got some beautiful sounds out of it...'

Rodigan had visited him there, and the two became good friends. 'He was a soulful, kind and loving man, softly spoken and very philosophical,' the DJ recalled in his autobiography *Rodigan, My Life In Reggae*.

The Royal Rasses' debut album, *Humanity*, only had seven tracks, most of them having already been released as singles. Prince Lincoln had written, arranged and produced all of them, as well as singing lead vocals in a distinctive high voice and playing guitar. Blessed with lasting greatness, *Humanity* elevated Prince Lincoln to cult status at a time when reggae acts like Bob Marley were beginning to make serious in-roads on the international market. The follow-up *Experience* was another classic set with songs like 'You Gotta Have Love (Jah Love)', 'Nobody Here But Me', 'True Experience' and 'Blessed Are The Meek' upholding the group's reputation for well-crafted, original music with a serious message. The Rasses had begun touring by this point, and the Prince was a compelling frontman, with his flailing dreadlocks and vocal pyrotechnics.

'It's been said that the Rasses' music is outside the idiom and cuts across all musical frontiers,' he explained. 'But then it's very easy to just strum two chords and hum a melody around that. For me, music has to have some form of real creativity in it. Whether it's simple or more complex, it makes no difference. It's got to have that genuine creativity to it, and I can hear music in many different forms all the time in my head. I've never written a song with a pen, I've just sung songs. I think of lyrics and melodies, put them together and that's how it's always been. It's meant to sound like it comes straight from the heart.'

It was whilst living in Cockburn Pen as an adolescent that Prince Lincoln first embraced Rastafari. Israel Vibration's Skelly lived there, too, and spoke of how reggae music helped ghetto people like himself through hard times.

'It help to ease your soul,' he said. 'There might be times when you're hungry and the music feed you. You sing some songs and the music uplift you. Living in the ghetto, it's a thing where you have a lot of artists who sing and that help people to relate on a whole different level. It made living there a little easier, y'know?'

After the success of their first album, Israel Vibration had embarked on a second, *Unconquered People*, which they recorded at Tuff Gong, backed by the Wailers. It was a worthy successor to *The Same Song*, and all three members shared lead vocals and songwriting. Apple Gabriel wrote 'Friday Evening' and there was hunger and deprivation in every note.

'By this time, Talent Corporation mash down and Tuff Gong rise up,' he said. 'There were very few artists there then – just the Melody Makers and Nadine Sutherland as a little girl, and Burning Spear used to record there, too. It was during that time we do the second album for EMI, and Tommy Cowan offered to *lend* us JA$3,000. It was about a year after that we learn he got £15,000, y'understand? He was a greedy man, but we do the album, then Tuff Gong and him have some disagreement over money so them take control over our 24-track tape and everything cork-up pon 'im then. We were there one day and see Bob Marley come in and in front of everybody, take up a big, fat rope and put it round Tommy Cowan's neck saying that him should hang 'is bumbaclaat self. He get vexed 'pon him! Rita Marley, she hang onto the tapes after that, but Tommy Cowan already have the songs mixed on different ones so him make stampers, press up the album and get it released, and we couldn't stop him. 'Im put out 'Friday Evening' as a 45 and that hit, but after months of not getting any money, no royalties or nothing, we decide to stop dealing with him.'

Like Bob Marley, Dennis Brown was born in February. This meant he was a Joseph, according to the Twelve Tribes Of Israel, hence the quote from *Genesis* beginning 'Joseph is a fruitful bough' written on the back of his latest album, *Joseph's Coat Of Many Colours*. Anyone moving in reggae circles during late summer 1979 would have heard tracks from that album playing in dances, cassette players in people's cars, at friend's houses and on the few radio shows that were friendly to reggae in that era. It was the reception given that album, coming after *Visions*, *Wolf And Leopards* and *Words Of Wisdom*, that had compelled people like Penny Reel to insist that Dennis Brown was more popular than Bob Marley in the late seventies, and hearing him open *Joseph's Coat Of Many Colours* with a more urgent version of 'Slave Driver' only served to reinforce such claims. Brown also covered the Paragons' 'Man Next Door' on his and Joe Gibbs' latest tour-de-force and four of the other tracks were released as singles. 'Cup Of Tea' was a eulogy to sharing, whilst 'Together Brothers', voiced on a cut of Junior Murvin's 'Cool Out Son', got pulled up so many times in reggae dances, the lines about stopping the fussing and fighting became permanently imprinted on our consciousness. Songs like those and the repatriation hymn 'Home Sweet Home' had especial relevance to Twelve Tribes members, but weren't exclusive by any means. The same was true of 'Three Meals A Day', which started off sounding like paradise with its description of three meals a day and no rent to pay until the realisation kicked in that he was talking about life behind bars.

Brown had been touring with We The People by the time that album came out. The Rass Brass horn section had turned down the chance of touring with Marley to accompany Brown on his first serious excursion into Europe, and their decision was fully justified. Brown's style of rockers was infectious, and he and We The People put on a tremendous show when they played at the 1979 Montreux Jazz Festival on the same night as Peter Tosh. Laser Records wasted no time in releasing a recording of it on LP and video, and anyone not slayed by that stretched out version of 'Drifter' had better check their pulse... Along with Bob Marley and the Wailers, Dennis Brown was the obvious omission from soundtrack album to *Rockers*, which premiered in Jamaica at the Regal, Kings and State cinemas on 26 September amidst a fanfare of publicity. 'The All Jamaican Movie With The Driving Reggae Beat,' announced the posters. 'See Your Favourite Jamaican Stars Do Their Thing!' The general consensus was that *Rockers*, whilst very different to *The Harder They Come* and directed by a foreigner, was a welcome addition to the cultural life of the island.

'By penetrating the vibrant musical scene which is at the centre of the urban Rastafarian culture, *Rockers* provides a unique perspective on Jamaica today,' wrote a *Gleaner* correspondent. 'Above all, *Rockers* is structured to provide a kaleidoscopic vision of Jamaican music, which has been a staple of life from the days of slavery, gospel, Rasta drumming, calypso, Latin, rhythm and blues and disco, all exist separately and together. In constant stream, this is distributed to the multitude of record shops by daredevil bike riders. The word is spread to inform, inspire, advise and entertain people who possess an advanced oral tradition of communication rooted in Africa.'

Others, most notably Balford Henry, sounded a note of caution.

'Already there have been some rumblings from people like Wallace [Horsemouth] about returns from the picture. There will always be a difficulty, as Perry Henzell found with promoting films of this nature. Do you sell it as a black movie and probably earn the wrath of black Americans who are convinced that such movies are exploitative products produced by white Americans? Or can you sell it as a bi-racial product with enough substance to be rated as a genuine masterpiece? Whatever the outcome, we wish that for a change the Jamaicans who played the important roles will be able to earn some returns and that our foreign exchange situation will benefit from the effort.'

Augustus Pablo has said that he was originally asked to write the soundtrack for *Rockers*. In the end, Bunny Wailer recorded the main theme, and Island padded out the rest of the album with hits by the likes of Inner Circle, Jacob Miller, Junior Murvin ('Police And Thieves'), Gregory Isaacs, the Heptones ('Book Of Rules'), Burning Spear, Peter Tosh ('Stepping Razor'), Third World and Kiddus I, who was filmed voicing 'Graduation In Zion' in a scene from the movie. Bunny had first issued the *Rockers* theme on a Solomonic 12-inch, but then left it off his 1979 album *Struggle*, which contained the single 'Bright Soul' and other songs that demonstrated he'd lost none of his righteous zeal. Witness 'Power

549

Struggle', for instance, or his attempt to incite an insurrection on the title track after telling people they should rise up and 'trample the dragon.'

'The pain from slavery spills over to generations because those people were not given land or money, and they were not given the recognition as human beings so we end up as squatters, right?' he said. 'We end up as people desperate to survive, which explains a lot of the illegitimate stuff, but at the end of the day we finds that it's those at the head of the table that are causing it, because they are the ones doing most of the illegal and unlawful practices. The people making war aren't the ones dying. It's the civilians, because they're the ones losing their lives, their homes and their families, and having to endure famine and want. The leaders of the world need some *judgment*, man. The people are responsible for putting them there but what are they doing in return, other than making people's lives miserable? They *must* get judgment and so up until then, I'm going to be the one blowing the trumpet.'

Bunny was still major league, but his most popular song of 1979 was 'Riding', released on Solomonic and backed by the Roots Radics. This track marked a departure of sorts, as it was recorded in a dancehall style and the lyrics weren't cultural but written about a girl who had persistently rejected his advances. 'Rockers' aside, his Island deal was now over and whilst having his own label gave him autonomy, it meant that his albums and singles would no longer be available in high street shops. Island, meanwhile, had launched their Mango subsidiary in the US. They used it for the Wailing Souls' *Wild Suspense* LP during 1979, which the quartet had recorded at Channel One with a line-up of the Revolutionaries. Former singles 'Bredda Gravalicious' and 'Very Well' were rockers classics, but the Wailing Souls rarely put a foot wrong, and especially on anything led by Pipe Matthews like 'Row Fisherman' and 'We Got To Be Together.'

Virgin's reggae output continued to rival that of Island Records, although the elections that had recently taken place in Nigeria would have serious consequences for Richard Branson's label. The winning National Party put Nigerian interests first, and this affected trade arrangements with other countries, including Britain. The writing was on the wall for Virgin's Front Line label, but their releases in 1979 were generally faultless, if a little worn round the edges. They issued three titles alone by I-Roy, all of which were self-produced. *The General* was the usual mix of humour, keen observation and social commentary and came with a free dub album. The strongest track was the 12-inch single 'Fire On A Wire', on which he lamented the rising cost of living, further exploring similar themes on *World On Fire*. UK author Ray Hurford interviewed him around the time that album came out, and the deejay lost no time in articulating his concerns.

'You wake up and see what's wrong in society – you feel the agony, you feel the pain, the needless suffering... you see the big paper profiteers and the bureaucrats and aristocrats – people in high places. Then you see the poor strewn across space and wonder where we're going. You listen to the radio and television or read the paper and you look at the big leaders trying to kill this one or that one. Survival is the name of the game right now. The days of wine and roses have passed. Jamaica is an island that doesn't need any feasibility study, and the people who were called capitalists are gone. The hassles have gone with them, so we are left to survive, and things go up and up and up but salaries stay the same.'

Front Line's last hurrah also included two albums by Culture – *Cumbolo* and *International Herb*, both produced by Sonia Pottinger and recorded at Treasure Isle with the Revolutionaries. Joseph Hill wrote all the songs, and he too was very preoccupied with what was happening in Jamaica and the world in general. 'Natty Never Get Weary' was the big hit from *Cumbolo*, although 'This Train,' 'They Never Love In This Time', 'Innocent Blood' and 'Down In Jamaica' were just as essential. The title track of 'International Herb' was arguably the most joyous ganja tune ever written, whilst 'Too Long In Slavery' reinforced the notion that little had changed for black people in real terms, and not just in Jamaica but the world over.

'What I can't understand,' Joseph said, 'and I don't think I will ever get to understand, is that the whole world keeps crying out for peace of mind and quiet. That makes a lot of sense. It means people want an end to the guns and Africa needs to be united, Europe needs to be reunited, but how is it that Europe gets united before Africa, when Africa has so much riches? The aid that Europe and America pay out to Africa that's not handouts, that's what's rightfully ours. That can't even begin to compensate for the gold and the diamonds, the mahogany and all those other natural resources that have been ravished away over the centuries. The people are getting hungry now. They're getting angry and it's time for that to stop.'

Those were the last albums Culture recorded for Sonia Pottinger. They'd gone into business with her on the understanding that it was a joint venture. They supplied the songs and she paid the studio expenses, but her accounting left much to be desired, something Marcia Griffiths also discovered after recording two albums for her – *Naturally* and 1979's *Steppin'*, featuring 'Peaceful Woman,' 'Hurting Inside' and current hit 'Steppin' Out Of Babylon.'

U Brown's latest Virgin LP *You Can't Keep A Good Man Down* had exactly the same track-listing as *Weather Balloon*, and neither that nor another self-produced set, *Repatriation*, contained his latest hit, 'Mr Music.' He was one of the hottest deejays on the island, and had an infallible sense of what rhythms to use – a gift he shared with Sly Dunbar whose second solo album *Sly, Wicked And Slick* was recorded at Dynamic for the most part, using members of Word, Sound & Power. That album also included a track called 'Mr Music', but the two were very different. Sly's own productions were all about the groove and finding new sounds that would elevate reggae globally. Third World's *Journey To Addis* was a major influence on his thinking at that time, and also M People's 'Pop Music.'

'It was on that second album where I went and experimented on my own, and came up with different ideas,' he said. 'Even now, people can't believe that album was made in 1979, but all of the tracks were cut in one night because I like just going in the studio and nailing it. I had the vision in my head and the direction I thought it should go in, because I'd been listening to bands like Brass Construction and Kool & The Gang and studying how they operated. They all had strong horn sections but when they sang the chorus they'd keep it simple, and that's what I tried to do with reggae. If you listen to 'Mr Music', there's little to it except for the hook. That's all you need sometimes, because if the sound of the record is good then you're onto a winner.'

Sly's favourite track was 'Rasta Fiesta' – a speeded up cut to Jacob Miller's 'Baby I Love You So' he'd previously versioned with the Professionals on Dennis Brown's 'Repatriation' ('Jubilation Dub'). When he and Chinna Smith were on tour in the UK with Dennis Brown and Big Youth, they'd go to Columbo's in Carnaby Street, where Lloydie Coxsone had demonstrated how the crowd would go mad whenever he played those records. He suggested that Sly recut the rhythm and that's how 'Rasta Fiesta' came about, although the arrangement was slightly different.

'We break it down in the middle,' Sly explained. 'We go right into an African kind of groove, and then Mikey Chung played that slap bass… we had two bass-lines playing on it, in fact, because Robbie played the other one, then Dean came and played that outro on the sax…'

Dean Ivanhoe Fraser grew up in Rema, on Fourth Street. When he was 12, Alfred 'Babe' O'Brien of Jamaica's National Volunteers Youth Organisation began teaching him clarinet. Dean then discovered the saxophone and after starting on tenor, switched to alto. At the age of 15 he played in Sonny Bradshaw's band, absorbing jazz and soul as well as reggae, but mainly playing Top 20 hits. He also played with the Caribs for a while, before making his recording debut on the Revolutionaries' 'Death In The Arena' in

1977. That was when he formed Rass Brass with trombonist Ronald 'Nambo' Robinson and trumpeter Junior 'Chico' Chin, who'd both also been members of the NVYO. After Rass Brass played on Dennis Brown's *Visions* LP, they joined Lloyd Parkes' We The People and toured all over with the young singer. Dean was known as 'Youth Sax' by then and had recorded his first solo album, *Black Horn Man*, for Joe Gibbs. Two more came out in 1979 – *Double Dynamite*, shared with guitarist Willie Lindo and *Pure Horn*, produced by Ossie Hibbert. He was one of reggae music's unsung backroom figures, playing keyboards and supervising auditions at Channel One whilst producing the occasional hit for himself. North-west London label Cha Cha licensed *Pure Horn* for release in the UK, along with Earth & Stone's *Kool Roots*.

Albert Bailey and Clifton Howell had started out as the Officials, but then renamed themselves Earth & Stone around the time they began recording for Channel One in 1975. They were among a number of artists and groups that voiced for the Hoo Kims but failed to get the recognition they perhaps deserved. Hell & Fire and Creole, whose 'Beware Of Your Enemies' became a cult hit, were two other examples – also Stenneth Doyle, aka the Enforcer, and the mysterious group that turned up at the studio one day, recorded 'Kunte Kinte', and then disappeared without trace.

The most successful group to emerge from Channel One in the late seventies was Black Uhuru. Errol Nelson had been a member when they recorded their first album *Love Crisis* for Prince Jammy. He also sang on two further singles – 'Wood For My Fire' and 'Rent Man,' produced by Dennis Brown – before rejoining the Jayes. His place was then filled by America-born Sandra 'Puma' Jones, who'd studied dance in New York with Baba Chuck Davis, creator of the annual celebration DanceAfrica, in addition to obtaining a master's degree at Columbia University. She had thoughts of becoming a social worker until travelling to Jamaica, where a new life awaited her.

'I escaped New York in 1977 after finishing some graduate work and decided that Jamaica would be a great place to look for employment,' she told US radio presenter Doug Wendt, host of *Midnight Dread*. 'I actually went there on vacation, looked around and things seemed feasible… I began to explore some of my other activities in dance and singing that I'd loved for years and everything just hooked up. I was in the right place at the right time and started with Ras Michael and the Sons Of Negus. He wanted to travel and go to the States, but I wanted to deal with Jamaica a little more. Then a common friend introduced me to Ducky and from there we began working together.'

Puma's harmonies, her movements onstage, her Afro-centric clothes and female presence gave Black Uhuru something different and even unique. Her arrival in the group also coincided with a shift in Sly and Robbie's thinking regarding how reggae could better connect with rock audiences, but without losing any of its essential Jamaican character.

'When opening for The Rolling Stones, which we did on many occasions, that was the first time we saw such huge crowds,' Sly said. 'We really got a chance to study their performances and get a grasp on this whole concept of rock'n'roll. That's where we got the idea for that Black Uhuru sound. It came from all the rock concerts that we'd seen, because after we got back to Jamaica we were thinking, "why isn't the reggae music from Jamaica as powerful as rock music when it's being played live? What can we do to really give it a lift and impress a feeling upon people?" That was when Robbie and I tried out a few things and started recording with Black Uhuru. I decided to play with an open snare and we came up with songs like 'Guess Who's Coming To Dinner', 'Shine Eye Gal' and 'Abortion.' But we still felt that it wasn't working so we overdubbed a Syn Drum over it, just to give it a little more kick. We wanted to bring more aggression into reggae music, whilst sticking to a slower pace. Eventually, we realised that we could keep a steady groove even whilst adding all this extra power.'

They'd begun experimenting in this direction on their Channel

One album *Disco Dub*, although needless to say the contents sounded nothing like disco, and whilst Sly & Robbie's name and images were on the cover, the five tracks – including cuts to 'Sidewalk Doctor' and 'No, No, No' – were still credited to the Revolutionaries. It was at this juncture that the Revolutionaries morphed into Sly & Robbie, and all the ingredients that would transform Black Uhuru into Jamaica's first-ever roots rock reggae band clicked into place. As ever, the public would decide whether the new formula was truly successful. Before Black Uhuru's break-through songs made it onto vinyl towards the end of 1979, Sly and Robbie gave dubplates to just a handful of key Jamaican sound systems, Sturgav included.

'U-Roy was really the one who broke Black Uhuru,' confirmed Sly. 'People would go to hear Sturgav and every night they would hear 'General Penitentiary' and songs like that. He was the only one who had them. That's how we did it. And if we give a dubplate to one soundman, then we don't give it to a next one.'

The other lucky recipient was JahLoveMuzik, who got an exclusive mix of 'Leaving To Zion.' Sly and Robbie then licensed an album by the new look Black Uhuru to Delroy Witter, whose D-Roy label was based in Kensal Green, London NW10. The version of *Showcase* he put out was missing 'Shine Eye Gal' and had a photo of the old line-up on the cover, although he later made up for it by issuing 'Shine Eye' on 12-inch – a hit that terrorised reggae dances for many months afterwards with its plunging, heavyweight bass, spooky atmospherics and biting rock guitar courtesy of the Stones' Keith Richards, who went down to Channel One and, according to Sly, 'played like a rocket!'

Sly & Robbie released their own version of *Showcase* (which included 'Shine Eye Gal') on Taxi before licensing to Virgin. It reaped instant acclaim from grassroots fans, but the production duo weren't one-dimensional by any means. They'd had a big hit with Gregory Isaacs' 'Soon Forward' earlier in the year and issued two other singles – Jimmy Riley's 'Love And Devotion' and the

Tamlins' cover of the Eternals' 'Stars' – that also combined a Jamaican lovers rock sound with that extra something that Sly has already alluded to. The perfect example of this was Harold Melvin & The Blue Notes' 'If You Don't Know Me By Now' which had a similar pace as reggae music, but wasn't at all soft.

Beres Hammond had proved his mastery of R&B-styled reggae music on his debut album *Soul Reggae* and quit his role as lead singer with Zap Pow after the band returned from an ill-fated tour of Canada in August. It was at that point he went over to Joe Gibbs and began work on an album entitled *Just A Man*. A write-up in the *Gleaner* had once declared that 'Hammond is no reggae star. He is a first class balladeer who has the ability to earn international respect with the right material.' Gibbs clearly agreed, and produced a well-balanced set with an equal share of slow and up-tempo songs. 'I'm In Love With You' was the lead single, as well as 'the most played R&B song in the dance arena, and a perennial crowd favourite', according to Merritone's Winston Blake.

'I'm In Love With You' took all the accolades, but the title track was a real tearjerker and underlined Hammond's facility for playing on his listeners' emotions. The funky 'I'm Lonely' revolved around the need for forgiveness, whilst two other tracks – 'Do This World A Favour' and 'Keep My Wheel Turning' – showed that he had been keeping close tabs on the latest trends from America.

'It was just natural for some of us to get involved with the music that was happening at that time,' Hammond said. 'We didn't put all our concentration in that area but we still tap into it a little bit, just to assure people that we were there in the mix. I wasn't expecting too much from it, and disco never happened for me because I was never dressed right. You had to have some glitter, and I think my choice of clothes had something to do with it!'

International recognition very nearly did come his way in 1979, after US label A&M – who were also interested in signing Dennis Brown – invited Hammond to Miami, where they hosted a reception for him attended by stars like Betty Wright, Timmy Thomas and K. C. and the Sunshine Band. Such a grand welcome was unexpected, but did nothing to allay Hammond's misgivings about losing his independence.

'There were all these balloons and fancy people... I didn't like how it looked because there were some lawyers there too, getting ready to make me sign, but as they were celebrating I left by a side door and took the next flight to Kingston! They were saying, "where's Beres?" But I was gone by then, and that was it...'

It's rumoured that Beres recorded ten tracks with Isaac Hayes' band in Jamaica around this same time, although the tapes have yet to surface. Had they been released, it's open to debate what difference they would have made to him or the reggae genre, which was constantly being redefined by developments happening both within Jamaica and overseas.

'Remember all those free concerts in the parks, and *Rock Against Racism?*' asked Dennis Bovell. 'I remember Steel Pulse playing with the Stranglers, and the Police supporting Steel Pulse, then Sting started singing like David Hinds and latched onto it so much so that everyone thought he invented it, when it was just another version of Bob Marley, right? Brinsley Forde did the same. David Hinds, Brinsley Forde and Sting were all trying to sound like Bob Marley as far as I was concerned. They were all coming from the same vocal school, and Sting became more popular than any of them, even though he came last!'

The day after The Police's 'Message In A Bottle' went to number one in the UK, the Police embarked on a lengthy US tour. Steel Pulse were supposed to be the support act, but their visas didn't come through on time and so they didn't join the tour until November. A UK tour of a different kind, described as being 'very adventurous and quite ground-breaking' by *Vintagerock*, had criss-crossed the UK several weeks earlier, culminating in a show at London's Rainbow Theatre on 28 September. Headliners were the Slits led by Ari Up, who one reviewer called 'a crazy, wild front-lady, complete with dreads, outlandish outfits and nifty dancing.'

She and the other Slits were promoting their debut album *Cut*, and were 'much more revolutionary than the Pistols and the Clash' according to Viv Albertine, in an interview with the *Guardian's* Caroline Sullivan.

'They were rock bands whereas we were using world music and reggae, filtered through our own musicality. We were like a female Spinal Tap, really. We argued, toured and wanted to make a classic album that never dated.'

They achieved all three objectives, but then their choice of name alone – referencing their vaginas – proved they were capable of anything. They were accompanied by Creation Rebel on that tour, and also avant-garde jazz trumpeter Don Cherry, whose daughter Neneh was friends with the group. Popular music in Britain had always been a melting pot of different styles, thanks to the same collective curiosity that (to a point) had seen the British public embrace blues, jazz, soul, rock and roll, country, electronica and many more genres besides. Punk and reggae, aided by generous Student Union entertainment budgets and support from the music press, were among the latest beneficiaries and this was good news for UK bands like Wolverhampton's Capital Letters, who toured a lot in the late seventies.

'We went to Sweden, and Peter Tosh had been there about two weeks before us, smoking it on stage and all that,' recalled Country. 'When we touch down now, they seize our passports and put police by our door, but it was a waste of time and they didn't find anything. In those days, police think we black people all look the same and so we'd pass our passports round between us and fool them like that. But they come to the club where we were playing, kick the dressing-room door down and we were just sitting there, not moving. We used to get a lot of hassle from the police whenever we played. It was all because of that song 'Smoking My Ganja', but we were just musicians. We weren't selling the stuff or trying to promote it like that. We just wanted the freedom to smoke it for us and for others, y' know?'

The band had recently hired some girl backing singers so they 'could sound just like Bob Marley and the Wailers.' Paulette Hayden and Pauline 'Dell' Spence had joined them at TMC studios in Tooting, South London during the week Capital Letters spent recording their debut album *Headline News*. It was originally going to be called *Smoking My Ganja*, but even Greensleeves paled at that idea, despite the song having stayed on the *Black Echoes'* charts for weeks on end. Most of the songs were about news events or inspired by issues they identified with. 'President Amin', for example, accusing Uganda's president of killing black brothers. He was 'dreader than dread', they warned. It's doubtful that a Jamaican artist would have criticised a black leader in that way, but Capital Letters were simply telling the truth, and that's what made their album so compelling – the bright red vinyl having served as an alarm call for what lay between the grooves. Titles like 'Fire', 'Daddy Was No Murderer' and 'Unemployed' didn't allow so much as a hint of compromise. Jamaican music ruled at the time, and the UK's homegrown reggae acts were long accustomed to living in its shadow. That's what their single 'UK Skanking', voiced over another infectious rhythm, was all about. This was the follow-up to 'Smoking My Ganja' and in Country's own words, 'it touch another nerve' due to the fact that Capital Letters were claiming that reggae from Britain was just as valid as that from Jamaica. Meanwhile, Margaret Thatcher, who'd recently become Britain's first woman prime minister, was waging war on the less fortunate. In response, Capital Letters began writing songs like 'Cheap School Meals' and 'Do We Really Need A Government?' that savaged her administration, and would soon appear on their *Bread And Water* EP.

Right-wing forces were also on the march in Jamaica, literally so, because many of the fifty thousand JLP supporters who had attended a rally led by Edward Seaga on 1 October then paraded through the streets of Kingston, protesting against the government's decision to call in the International Monetary Fund (IMF).

A day after that rally, Island Records released Bob Marley and the Wailers' latest album *Survival*. Marley's next US tour began almost immediately afterwards with a show at the Madison Square Garden in New York, and would include dates at Harlem's famous Apollo Theatre, with soul singer Betty Wright as their support act. The Wailers performed there 25-28 October, playing two shows a day, and were the first reggae act to appear at the hallowed soul venue. People claimed that Marley had deliberately targeted African Americans when writing many of the songs on his new album, but Wailers' guitarist Junior Marvin disputed this when pointing out that songs such as 'Africa Unite' and 'Zimbabwe' were written in support of the African liberation struggle, and that 'So Much Trouble In The World,' 'Babylon System' and the title track sprang from a general discourse that regularly took place within the Wailers' circle.

'Bob was always talking about politics and what was happening in the world, in places like Africa and Jamaica especially,' Marvin said. 'We'd talk about people who were suffering and how we could help with the music. It was like anybody else. Everybody tried to stay in touch with what was happening around us. He was very interested in the latest news, whatever that might be. We'd do Bible reading, of course, because that was the Rasta philosophy, to read a scripture every day.'

'Ambush In The Night' was on that album and also 'Wake Up And Live,' whilst 'Top Rankin'' and 'One Drop' promoted a feeling of togetherness in the face of adversity.

Survival was the first Wailers album to have been recorded at the Tuff Gong studio on Hope Road and art director Neville Garrick's cover designs made a striking impression, with their array of African flags, and illustrations showing how African slaves had been horrifically packed in the ships carrying them to the US and Caribbean. Commercially, the returns from *Survival* proved disappointing. Its highest positions on the UK and US LP charts were number twenty and seventy, respectively, and it failed to qualify for Gold discs in both those territories. Some thought that Marley had been stung into making an album dealing with predominantly black issues because of the criticism aimed at his previous studio album, *Kaya*. Island hinted that they'd been aware of the possible ramifications when changing the title from *Black Survivors* to *Survival*, but many diehard reggae fans considered it Marley's best album to date and were more than happy with his choice of material.

Marley's voluntary abdication from the pop market created space for other reggae-related releases. Less than a week after the arrival of *Survival*, the Specials released their follow-up single 'Rudy, A Message To You', produced by Elvis Costello. The Coventry band had rearranged the title but not the song, which had been a hit for writer Dandy Livingstone more than a decade earlier.

'I did that song in the late sixties for Rita and Benny King,' Livingstone said. 'I wrote it at my parents' home in Leyton. It was just something that came to me one morning after I'd woken up, but I wrote it because of what was happening back in Jamaica with the rudies and in London, too. Back then, the skinheads bought a lot of reggae records and that helped turn them into hits, but the violence part of it, that wasn't for me. That's why I sent a message to them in 'Rudy, A Message To You', because I didn't like the whole skinhead thing, with the bovver boys. I didn't like it at all.'

The Specials' update featured veteran Jamaican trombonist Rico Rodriguez who was so highly thought of by the band that he was invited to tour with them and given joint billing on the 7-inch.

'We discovered that he'd played on the original, and that's how come he played on our version,' Lynval Golding explained. 'I went to his house, and I was shitting myself at the thought of meeting him. I had no idea what to say to him or what a man like him would make of the whole thing, because we were blending the reggae with punk, but he said not to worry, and that everything was cool. He was so easy-going, but that man brought so much to the Specials, because once he'd joined the band, it was like we'd found the blueprint, and from then on, everything just sounded right.'

Jerry Dammers would invite Rico to play on a raft of Two Tone releases thereafter, beginning with the Specials' first album, *The Specials*. They'd recorded it in the basement of a launderette on the Fulham Palace Road in Chelsea and raucous crowd-pleasers like 'Nite Klub' (featuring Chrissie Hynde on backing vocals), 'Little Bitch', punky reggae mash-up 'It's Up To You' and 'Do The Dog' sounded like they went down on tape pretty quickly. A live recording of Toots and the Maytals' 'Monkey Man' added to the general thrills, whilst the lyrics of 'Concrete Jungle' and '(Dawning Of A) New Era' articulated the dangers (irrespective of race) of growing up in Britain's depressed inner cities. Not every track was that frenetic. Recent hit 'A Message To You Rudy' and a cover of Andy & Joey's rocksteady hit 'You're Wondering Now' were cool breezes sent to fan the chest-beating defiance of 'Too Hot' whilst 'Stupid Marriage' took the form of a courtroom drama, much like Prince Buster's 'Judge Dread', with Neville Staple assuming the character of Judge Roughneck.

The Specials went Top 5 in November and would remain in the UK Top 40 for almost a year. The band had really let the genie out the bottle in those sessions, whilst the photo on the album cover – depicting them in tonic suits, shades, button-down shirts and thin ties, with Golding and Staple wearing their trademark pork pie hats – spawned an army of imitators.

2 Tone was no longer just a record label, but home base for Britain's latest youth movement. The Selecter and Madness were also part of 2 Tone and in October, both groups had Top 10 hits in the UK – The Selecter with 'On My Radio' and Madness with a cover of Prince Buster's 'One Step Beyond.' History was made on 8 November when they and the Specials appeared on the same edition of *Top Of The Pops*, a seminal event in British pop. By the end of that year, 2 Tone fever had spread like crazy and the UK was in the grip of a full-blown ska revival fed by some great records

and live performances, a blitz of monochromatic merchandise and extensive radio and television coverage. A joint tour was inevitable, and as winter set in they squeezed in a tour-bus with Walt Jabsco painted on the side and headed for the road. Those UK dates were notorious for the intensity of the music and crowd reaction. The Specials, like the Clash, were renowned for being a people's band. Their fans regularly clambered on stage, crowded round the musicians and turned their performances into a spectacle. All too often these gigs were marred by incidents of violence – not resulting from over-enthusiastic 2 Tone fans, but sections of the audience chanting fascist slogans whilst giving Nazi salutes. The contradictions thrown up by such behaviour beggared belief because on one hand, the majority of people at those shows were dancing to multi-racial bands and singing along with songs promoting racial unity, and yet at the same time – and as part of the very same crowd – far-right thugs were loudly and visibly expressing a mindset that came from the complete opposite end of the spectrum.

Madness were slow to distance themselves from their far-right followers, and there were few complaints when they quit the tour early. In Oldham, security personnel confiscated a number of weapons – mainly knives, but also a home-made mace. There'd been a riot in Huddersfield, where one of the tour's vans was trashed and a film crew terrorised. By the time the Specials hit their stride during 'A Message To You, Rudy' at Brighton Polytechnic, dozens of people were on stage with them, and those that weren't had been thrown back into the crowd by others desperate to seize their own brief time in the spotlight. After the group had fought their way off stage, they discovered angry feminists had blocked the door to their dressing room. These women were incensed that Terry Hall had called music journalist Vivien Goldman 'a stupid cow' after she'd trashed their debut album, but she wasn't alone in dismissing *The Specials*. There were plenty of reggae fans like her who couldn't understand the attraction of hearing punk bands cover classic ska and rocksteady songs when such exciting developments were taking place in Jamaica, and certain reggae figureheads were making such hard-won strides towards international acceptance.

'As black musicians, we've always believed that when it comes to the British media, they would always prefer white people playing the music,' opined Steel Pulse's David Hinds. 'For example, UB40, that's why they were born. Nobody will say it, but *I'll* say it because you had bands like Aswad, Black Slate and ourselves supposedly being shown how to do it by white or mixed-race bands with a white lead singer, and having to take a back seat. The ska revival was built up upon similar lines, yet we all *lived* ska music. It was something that was brought over by our parents, because it reminded them of back home in Jamaica. They wanted to keep up with the latest politics or all the latest dances from back home, and ska was the form of music that was doing it back then, in the sixties. It was something we'd left behind and outgrown, but then all of a sudden, we had a 2 Tone explosion on our hands!

'The music industry disowned us at that stage, because in calling the music something else – namely 2 Tone – they were divorcing bands like us from what was happening. We weren't a part of it, even though it was our roots. A lot of people – especially the white masses within the music industry – were led to believe that the political attributes of the music stopped around that time, not knowing that there were other bands like us still doing it. We spent a lot of time in Europe and the US after that because people in England were saying that reggae was old hat, and were busy giving attention to the ska revival and whatever the punks were dealing with at that time instead.'

The Selecter's Pauline Black once observed that young black people generally try and stay one step ahead and rarely look back, whereas young white people reference a lot and enjoy putting a new spin on retro trends, irrespective of which demographic originated them. That theory is a mite too convenient, but we get the gist. Black herself spans both worlds, as she was born to an

Anglo-Jewish teenage mother and Nigerian father, but was then adopted by a white middle-aged couple and raised in Romford, Essex, a place that was far from reflective of multi-cultural Britain at the time. It wasn't until friends at school introduced her to early reggae hits such as 'Israelites' and 'Long Shot Kick The Bucket' that she developed a taste for Jamaican music and began reading books by radical black intellectuals like Stokely Carmichael and Eldridge Cleaver. In her own words, she turned into 'a sexually confused, racially intolerant loser' – one with well enough defined principles to start a branch of the Workers Revolutionary Party in Leamington Spa before heading for Coventry where she sang folk songs by night and worked as a radiographer by day. It was the Specials' Lynval Golding who introduced her to Neol Davies, founder of The Selecter. The band's other vocalist, Arthur 'Gaps' Hendrickson, arrived a little later.

'His parents were from St Kitts,' explained Black. 'Most of the other musicians in The Selecter were from a Jamaican background, except myself and rhythm guitarist Compton, whose father was from Guyana. We were the odd ones out, if you like, but Gaps grew up with his grandmother until his parents brought him over here to Luton as a teenager, and he was a dancer before joining The Selecter.'

'On My Radio' received a lot of airplay, which was ironic given that Pauline was wagging a finger at legal radio stations with that catchy "just the same old show, on my radio" chorus. She went high as Gaps countered with a deep growl. They looked and sounded great, and the crowd loved them when they played their first major gig supporting the Specials at the Electric Ballroom in Camden. 2 Tone wasn't just a record label for many in the audience, but a statement of intent. Many working class youngsters, black and white, already knew that multiculturalism wasn't anything to fear, and they had more in common – especially sex, music, fashion and sport – than what divided them. Their parents might not share similar backgrounds but this younger generation grew up in the same communities, went to the same schools and faced a lot of the same hardships, including those inflicted by an uncaring government, a hostile media and aggressive police force. They lacked a voice, so when not just one band but several came along with songs they could relate and dance to, and were played by people who looked and talked like them, then it's easy to imagine the excitement this caused. For an all too brief spell it felt like something of real significance was happening before infighting, burnout, commercial pressures and unwelcome attention from racists did their worst.

In November, new 2 Tone signings The Beat released their debut single 'Tears Of A Clown', a cover of Smokey Robinson's Motown classic. They were a multi-racial band from Birmingham fronted by Dave Wakeling (vocals and guitar) and Ranking Roger, a local MC who'd auditioned by running out on stage with them unannounced one night and letting fly with some lyrics. The crowd had loved it and whilst their stay on the label would prove short-lived, 'Tears Of A Clown' made a welcome addition to the 2 Tone soundtrack.

'I liked music that was exciting, but punk was starting to disappear and something was going very wrong with pop,' Wakeling told the *NME*. 'There was just nothing happening and I wanted to create a totally distinct type of music. I was listening to two very distinct types of music, rock and reggae, and watching people's reactions at parties. Those two genres worked really well together. Rock would get people up and dancing and reggae would keep them moving so I brought my two favourite kinds of music together.'

Their own music had irony, insight and honesty, and it was also a good deal of fun. It offered something new, even if that something had been arrived at by combining elements of the past. Reggae in Jamaica had been doing similar by reviving old Studio One rhythms for a new generation of artists to sing and deejay over, but there were important differences between that and the British ska revival. The patois heard on a lot of Jamaican records proved an obstacle for one thing. That's why 'Uptown Top Ranking' had been a hit.

Although delivered in patois, it was of the easily understood variety, whereas deejays in Jamaica often went to the studio right after entertaining a riotous dancehall crowd, and the language and references they used to excite audiences in Kingston were often impenetrable to outsiders – many of whom may not have been familiar with those classic rhythms either. Contrast this with the language heard on 2 Tone releases, which may have incorporated traces of Jamaican patois, but was easily understood by most British people. Also, the old ska hits that the 2 Tone groups had borrowed from weren't obscure, but had been bestsellers and even national chart hits in the UK just a decade earlier. There was an element of familiarity about them and this meant that most fans could relate to what they were singing about, and also the style of music they were playing. It was a recipe for instant recognition and approval, and it was no surprise whatsoever that 2 Tone should prove so successful as the seventies drew to a close.

Reggae's fortunes took a different path as the old guard continued to fall away and Jamaica's new wave struggled to gain traction outside of its heartlands. The latter would become increasingly reliant upon sound systems and pirate radio stations, and have to make do without the support of major labels for the most part. That's because Island Records weren't so interested in dancehall and Virgin's Front Line label hit the rocks, bringing to an end Richard Branson's flirtation with Jamaica. Their absence was felt in various ways, not least financially. Without the promise of paid advertising, leading UK music publications withdrew most of their coverage, and the genre also lost professional expertise after Island and Virgin cut their losses. Jumbo Vanrenen for instance, returned to general A&R duties, although he first he had to deal with the fallout from Virgin having terminated most of the artists' contracts.

'When Prince Far I was dropped in 1979 he was sent a letter, which he signed and sent back,' he said. 'Some months later he turned up in my office with his new recordings. I listened politely and asked where he was going to take them. He hadn't realised that he'd been he dropped and got very angry, with that deep voice of his. I trembled in my boots while he harangued me. That's when he went to Charisma and recorded that song 'Virgin' with words saying that Branson was a pickle he didn't want on his plate, and accusing me of keeping his tape on the shelf...'

Front Line stuck with I-Roy for a while because Dennis Bovell had shown an interest in producing him. The Twinkle Brothers also lasted the distance, but the label's swansong, released in November 1979, was the Gladiators' *Sweet So Till*, which Jumbo dismissed as 'a very bad record.' It was an inglorious end to a label that had released classic albums by the cream of Jamaican (and occasionally British) reggae talent during its brief history. The reason given for its demise was the collapse of the West African market. It's estimated that Virgin shipped two million reggae albums to Nigeria before political changes, mentioned earlier, brought this cosy arrangement to an abrupt halt, bringing the Front Line label down with it. The excitement was over almost as quickly as it had begun and not all of their acts went quietly, as Jumbo explained.

'I felt let down, but we didn't know the business,' Gladiators' bassist Clinton Fearon admitted to Angus Taylor. 'Prince Tony signed a bad thing with them and his way of dealing with it was to go in and cuss to rassclaat! To make a long story short, Prince Tony and Albert Griffiths went to London and cussed and kicked over the table and did not make any good progress at all because we were already holding the blade, so I was disappointed with all of that, and as time went on I realised that it would not get any better. We had somebody to manage the group at that time, but Albert dictated the whole thing and so the brethren couldn't manage anything.'

The lack of a professional infrastructure was a constant problem, and managers, agents and promoters with an appropriate skillset were hard to find. Reggae music had also become plagued by other problems that served to limit its appeal outside of the grassroots market. For example, violence and robbery at concerts had become more commonplace and mainstream promoters began to lose interest. It's not hard to understand why 2 Tone should have been viewed as a welcome alternative by the UK music industry, which more or less relegated Jamaican reggae to an ethnic backwater. There were still plenty of UK- and US-based labels willing to license Jamaican music, but few of them were capable of providing the level of promotion, distribution, good business sense and attention to detail required in generating sales and profile beyond the hardcore market.

Greensleeves, the UK label based in Shepherd's Bush were the exception. After striking up a relationship with producer Henry 'Junjo' Lawes they championed Jamaican dancehall music like the significant and thrilling phenomenon that it really was. They were unafraid to swim against the tide and nail their colours to the mast, whilst treating the artists and producers fairly, and mastering and presenting the music to as high a standard as possible.

'We'd been releasing mainly roots stuff until then and when we started putting out dancehall, a lot of people in the industry said it was rubbish,' Chris Cracknell said with a wry smile. 'We got a lot of fight, because we were the only label that was really pushing that kind of music back then. The rest of the charts was still being dominated by roots or lovers, but when it came to that raw-edged dancehall sound, it was a long time before people began to realise that dancehall music was here to stay, even though it continued to pour out of Jamaica.

'Punk and reggae had gone off together by then and we could see how that came about but we didn't want to be putting out music for the white crossover market. We had the record shop back then, and wanted to keep it real in terms of how we'd always sold music to those members of the Jamaican community who bought from us. We wanted it to be on the button and when Barrington Levy's 'Shine Eye Gal' was released, it sold out so fast that we just couldn't keep up with it! Barrington had this young voice that we'd never heard before and the Roots Radics, who played on Junjo's rhythms, they were fresh out the blocks as well. For us it was like a turning point, because all of a sudden here was something totally new.'

'Junjo Lawes was after dominance,' confirmed Trinity. 'He always wanted the best, but he was quick to see what was happening in the dances, so if an artist went on the mic and tore the place down, then he'd have them in the studio the very next day. That's how it worked back then because sound-systems were the chief means of supplying new talent, and also promotion. Junjo would often record maybe seven or eight albums before offering them for distribution overseas, and in the meantime we'd cut dubplates for the sound systems who might play them for eight, nine months as exclusives before they were released.'

Vinyl and cassettes were the popular formats in those days and producers would license their tracks to different territories, rather than think in terms of worldwide distribution rights. Greensleeves supplied retail outlets throughout Europe with all the latest dancehall releases, most of them produced by Junjo, Jamaican talent scout supreme.

'Junjo would lay tracks with the Roots Radics for his artists, and then deejays would come along and pick out which rhythms they liked before voicing them,' said Chris Cracknell. 'The Roots Radics brought a different flavour, because Sly & Robbie were spending a lot of time touring with first Peter Tosh and then Black Uhuru, so they left this void that was ultimately filled by producers like Junjo, Jah Thomas and Linval Thompson. They were all involved in it together, and there was this real sense of unity between them, even though they were all rivals and wanted that number one spot. Channel One was like a club, because even if certain artists weren't recording there, they'd still go to the studio and hang out. The control room was always full of people, and there were hundreds more outside desperate to get in. It was really exciting and vibrant. Everyone wanted to work there and that in itself placed restrictions

571

upon what music came out, because other producers would always complain that Junjo had booked it solid for a week.'

Barrington Levy's *Bounty Hunter* is often cited as having been the first dancehall album. On the front cover was a drawing of a bounty hunter with automatic rifle holding a flyer depicting a dreadlocks man with the words 'WANTED, DEAD OR ALIVE, NOTORIOUS WOLF IN SHEEP'S CLOTHING. $5,000.'

'This brother named Jah Life, a producer based in Brooklyn, New York had some money and him and Junjo get together and make an album,' said Levy. 'The style what me did have was unique and them feel say it would soon bust, y'know? That was *Bounty Hunter* and my career start take off from there.'

Levy's arrival caused a feeding frenzy within reggae circles. Three albums were released at the same time, and all of them differed from the others to certain extent. The closest to *Bounty Hunter* was *Shaolin Temple*, which Junjo released in Jamaica on Jah Guidance. Those two had seven tracks in common, whereas *Shine Eye Gal*, which appeared on Burning Sounds, rounded up the singer's earliest singles and was again produced by Junjo. The title track was voiced on a cut of a Studio One rhythm made popular by Sugar Minott and is a completely different song to the Black Uhuru hit. The subject is similar – both are about a girl playing the field – but rather than being judgemental, Barrington addressed her with tenderness, like he was really trying to understand her.

People used to call Levy 'the Mellow Canary' when he sang on sound systems, on account of his mellifluous vocal style. The name suited him, and when Greensleeves then released their first album with him, *Englishman* – and with a completely different set of tracks to the other three – it still didn't seem like overkill. *Englishman* was a landmark release, and found him singing over some classic rhythms. Key tracks included 'Don't Fuss Nor Fight,' 'Look Youth Man' and 'Money Makes Friends', but there was undisputed quality in every area – the vocals, production, mixing and the actual playing. Levy made a promotional visit to London in

November 1979. 12-inch mixes of the title track and 'Sister Carol' had been ringing out in reggae dancehalls for weeks before he and *Englishman* arrived. He was Jamaica's most in-demand young singer and he, Junjo, the Roots Radics and Greensleeves all rose to prominence simultaneously.

The Roots Radics were unsure of both Junjo – who many have said was a gunman – and the area around Maxfield Avenue where Channel One was situated. They worried whether they would get paid, and especially upon realising that he wanted them to fill his tape with rhythms. A revolving cast of musicians including Santa Davis, the drummer from the Soul Syndicate, played with bassist Errol 'Flabba' Holt on some of Junjo Lawes' earliest sessions. Yet Flabba had his own crew, shared with Lincoln 'Style' Scott (drums) and Morwells' guitarist Eric 'Bingy Bunny' Lamont, and that also included fellow guitarists Dwight Pinkney and Noel 'Sowell' Bailey and keyboard player Wycliffe 'Steely' Johnson. This was the classic Roots Radics line-up that would take over from the Revolutionaries as the Channel One house band, and played the majority of Junjo Lawes' hit rhythms. When they went in the studio it was with one main objective in mind: to 'mash up the dancehall.' They weren't interested in making crossover hits, appealing to fans of other genres or playing Jamaican style disco music. The Roots Radics were primed to please the most discerning reggae audiences in the world – namely those from Kingston who went to a dance at the weekends to forget their troubles and get transported by the vibes and music experienced in an open air setting under the night sky, flanked by banks of speakers and with an array of entertainers crowded round the control tower.

Linval Thompson was aiming for the same audience, both as a singer and producer. Bunny Lee gave Brad Osbourne an album of Linval Thompson songs to release in the US, but *Cool Down* contained mainly older material, as did *Six Babylon*, which included the hit title track and 'Mr Bossman.' It was the albums Linval licensed to Burning Sounds and Burning Rockers – both owned by the same North London company – that were more representative of where he was at musically and otherwise. *I Love Jah* was a roots set and *Follow My Heart* an album of love songs like recent hits 'Danger In Your Eyes' and 'If I Follow My Heart'. Linval also produced albums by Al Campbell (*Diamonds*), Trinity (*Rock In The Ghetto*) and Ranking Dread, whose 1978 LP *Girls Fiesta* was followed by *Kunta Kinte Roots*, named after Alex Haley's popular book and TV series.

The half-naked black man wearing Zulu gear and holding a leopard skin shield that Karl Finn photographed for the front cover of that album doesn't look much like Ranking Dread, aka Winston Brown. In fact it's difficult imagining that the real Ranking Dread would forfeit his dignity in posing like that, given his background and reputation. Although born in Trelawny, he grew up in the ghetto strongholds of Rema and Tivoli Gardens, where he befriended Claudie Massop and joined the notorious Shower Posse. He was rumoured to have taken part in almost thirty murders by the time he jumped bail and fled to London in 1978, where he deejayed on Sir Coxsone for a while, and recorded for DEB Music. Back in Jamaica he'd previously deejayed on Ray Symbolic, which is where Linval Thompson first saw him, but in future his music career would be greatly overshadowed by his bad boy antics.

General Echo deejayed on Ray Symbolic too, but just for promotional purposes as he was never happier than when holding a mic on his own sound, Echo Tone Hi Fi. Real name Earl Robinson, he was from Fletcher's Land, which is the area below National Heroes Park, a couple of blocks from Orange Street. His debut LP *Rocking And Swing* appeared on Dudley Swaby's Manzie label, and his versatility was evident from the start as he effortlessly chatted lyrics about the International Year Of The Child, girls, the oil crisis and, somewhat improbably, his granny having survived the sinking of the Titanic. Echo was a skilled storyteller, and humorous with it, especially when telling ribald tales. The only slack tune on that first album was 'Foxy Mama', where he mimicked a young boy begging his father's girlfriend to give him 'the same thing' she'd given his Papa the night before. Winston Riley, recognising Echo's talent for tongue-in-cheek rudeness, changed the deejay's name to Ranking Slackness and got him to voice an entire album like that, called *Slackest LP*. It wasn't Echo's finest moment, but gained a certain degree of notoriety. Echo had made his mark and opened the door for other young deejays who liked to chat slackness, including Yellowman and Nigger Kojak.

Kojak & Liza followed 'Hole In The Bucket' with 'Sky Juice' and 'Fist To Fist Rub A Dub', and whilst their vocals wouldn't age too well, the rhythms on those records were timeless. Jah Thomas couldn't miss with his album for Jah Life, *Dance Pon De Corner*, which found him toasting over the same rhythms as used for Barrington Levy's *Bounty Hunter* LP. Just to confuse matters further, Jah Thomas released an album that he'd produced himself called *Dance On The Corner*, and which also featured some Barrington Levy rhythms. One of the tracks – a cut to Lone Ranger's 'Barnabas Collins' called 'Cricket Lovely Cricket' – was the first tune that he'd produced for himself, and was swiftly followed by 'What's Cooking', 'Money Man Skank' and other singles on his Midnight Rock label. It had been a good year for deejays and Errol Scorcher's 'Roach In De Corner' stuck to the Jamaican charts like glue throughout November. Scorcher had previously voiced an album for Channel One (*Rasta Fire*), but the story of him wielding a can of pesticide and attempting to kill a cockroach would come to define his career, and how weird is that?

Ranking Joe was the embodiment of the new wave of Jamaican MCs in many ways, and the album Dennis Brown produced with him was a masterclass in the deejay arts. Brown literally let him loose over the rhythms to some of his recent hits and album tracks including 'Home Sweet Home', 'A Cup Of Tea', 'Slave Driver', 'Bubbling Foundation' and the two songs Black Uhuru did for DEB Music, 'Wood For My Fire' and 'Rent Man.'

'You see that time there?' Joe asked. 'The way we did those

records was like inna a dance! That's how I record them because we just go in the studio, off comes the shirt and lyrics pour out. We do them live, because you're supposed to just let the vibes flow, and that's what created that whole dancehall sound. Professionally, that's where you can tell the ability of an artist,'cause when you're in a dance there's no time to stop and think what to say. There's an audience in front of you and we don't have no script, but we have live lyrics and what could be sweeter than that?'

Sugar Minott's desire to help ghetto youths had witnessed an exodus of raw talent to his premises on Chisholm Avenue, and in addition to recording some of them, he decided to start his own sound system called Youth Promotion. Ranking Joe christened it with a song called 'Youth Promotion' and he also deejayed a cut to Gregory Isaacs' 'Soon Forward' for Sly & Robbie's Taxi label. He and selector Jah Screw had left U-Roy's sound by then and gone back to Ray Symbolic, taking much of Sturgav's crowd with them. They were a winning combination and their role in the development of Jamaican dancehall shouldn't be underestimated. Ray Symbolic later became the first Jamaican sound system to tour the UK, but the owner was tragically killed in a car crash the day before Screw and Ranking Joe had brought the sound back to the island. He would be remembered for furthering the career of several influential deejays, including General Echo, who wasn't the only Jamaican deejay to write lyrics about the International Year Of The Child.

Mikey Dread's 'Proper Education' was both polemic and lament as he mourned the poverty he saw all around him. In it he mourned the sufferation that ghetto children had to endure, which included lack of a proper education. That song was produced by former policeman turned producer Whitfield Henry, aka Witty Reid, and voiced over the same rhythm as David Isaacs' 'Just Like A Sea' – a tune that Mikey often played on JBC.

'When you live in Jamaica you see many of life's changes and go through experiences like poverty, so when it comes to writing a song or putting together music it's already clear what kind of message you should be sending out,' he said. 'You know what you should be doing to make people feel towards those situations. You're doing it to bring about a change and yuh haffi keep your original conceptualisation steadfast inna your mind, then at the first opportunity communicate that to other people who may help you to put it across. In Jamaica we're making music, but it's world music. It reach all over the world so we have to give publicity to the social conditions there man. Talking about the culture is difficult in the fact that there has been no one putting out our kind of music until recently. It's like nobody wanted to hear our original message or stay true to those vibes. Too many people get lost, y'know? And just because of commercialism, really. I'm not condemning other music but we have to maintain that original core of understanding.'

'Proper Education' was a hit in Jamaica and found a place alongside 'Walk Rastafari Way', 'Love The Dread' and 'Barber Saloon' on the deejay's debut album *Evolutionary Rockers*, released on his own Dread At The Controls label. Ever the entrepreneur, Mikey issued a matching dub album called *Dread At The Control Dubwise* he then licensed to Dave Hendley, who also put out Rod Taylor's 'Behold HIM', b/w 'His Imperial Majesty' (produced by Mikey), on a Sufferers Heights 12-inch. Hendley was still working in his capacity as A&R man for Trojan Records at the time, and it was because of him that Trojan released a remixed version of *Evolutionary Rockers* as *Dread At The Controls*, which attracted plenty of attention as Mikey Dread's reputation had already carried across the Atlantic by then. This was also due in part to the single 'Roots Man Revival', which Mikey had recorded at Treasure Isle whilst helping Sonia Pottinger fill the gap left by Errol Brown's departure. That song was a cut to Marcia Griffiths' 'Stepping Out Of Babylon', and whilst it wasn't on any of his albums, it got plenty of exposure on sound system in late 1979, around the same time that he became a fixture on the London reggae scene.

The Clash had just released their double LP *London Calling*, containing songs like 'Guns Of Brixton', 'Lovers Rock' and a cover of Jackie Edwards' 'Revolution Rock.' Mikey Dread knew very little about punk, but it was the Clash's rendition of Willie Williams' 'Armagideon Time', tucked away on the flipside of the 'London Calling', single that first alerted him to them. The band's cover of 'Police And Thieves' had clearly been no fluke, and whilst their reggae productions would have emptied the floor in seconds should any DJ been brave enough to play them in a dance, there was no doubting their sincerity. Mikey Dread would work with both the Clash and UB40, a multi-racial band of avowed socialists from Birmingham who'd only played their first gig less than a year earlier. They hadn't released any music either, which is why the John Peel session they recorded on 12 December wouldn't be broadcast until the New Year, to coincide with the release of their debut single 'Food For Thought.' Lead singer Ali Campbell had originally wanted UB40 to be a dub band, and that influence remained. Together with Brian Travers' jazzy sax-playing, it gave them a different sound to any other reggae outfit. Named after a UK unemployment card, the group was unique and the Pretenders' Chrissie Hynde was quick to appreciate this after watching them perform at the Rock Garden in Covent Garden.

'Chrissie was in the charts with 'Brass In Pocket' and she came down there to see us,' said Brian. 'We were like, "there's that famous bird off the telly!" We had this tiny dressing room and she came in and said, "I love you guys and want you to come on the road with us." We were so excited, but then we looked round and saw this security guy was grappling with a mate of ours. Everyone ended up fighting, someone had got Ali round the neck and Chrissie Hynde was stood there saying, "so we're going to do this tour..." We were all about 19 at the time, but that tour was incredible, and it was amazing to see proper rock stars do their thing every night...'

The diversity of UK reggae was something to celebrate, although most journalists preferred to champion things they already knew about, rather than venture into the unknown – present them with too many variations and they might play divide and rule, pitting one against the others. That's what happened to reggae as the seventies came to an end. The audience began to split into different factions, with some deriding dancehall as being inferior to roots music, and others thinking that 2 Tone and punk had superseded everything else that had led up to that point. Meanwhile, anyone expecting to hear offshoots like those in dancehalls were likely to be disappointed, and national radio in countries like Britain and the US tended to avoid any songs about Rastafari or black history – even those by high profile names like Marley and Tosh.

Linton Kwesi Johnson had turned down the offer of recording more albums for Virgin in the wake of *Dread, Beat & Blood*. Chris Blackwell must have heard about this, because he sent the photographer Dennis Morris to see Linton with an invitation to record for Island, and for double the amount of money he'd got from Branson. Prior to the release of *Forces Of Victory*, Britain's most radical reggae poet had been in America playing dates with Steel Pulse. Watching this slightly built, bespectacled Jamaican intellectual address the crowd, a trilby hat perched on his head and a sheaf of paper in his hand, was a very different kind of experience for many in the audience. Yet the words on those pages cut like a knife, and took the listeners to the very heart of whatever he was talking about.

David Bowie once included *Forces Of Victory* on a list of his twenty-five all-time favourite albums, whilst *AllMusic* called it, 'one of the most important reggae records ever recorded.' Island had chosen wisely when putting an old-fashioned radio mic on the cover, since it was an image reminiscent of war-time broadcasts, and matched the seriousness of what LKJ had to say. Arguably more than any other reggae artist of that period, Johnson gave listeners a ring-side seat on the struggle taking place in the UK between left- and right-wing political groups and the racism affecting British minorities of both personal and institutionalised varieties. It was a time of protests, rioting, marches and street battles, and a repressive government that had all but declared class war against its poorer and most disadvantaged citizens. 'Fite Dem Back' was a battle cry, and had a chorus drenched in dumbed-down irony as he mimicked the ignorance of right-wing thugs. Johnson wasn't afraid to fight, but preferred to do so on his own terms. He was informing parties like the Communists and SWP that black people have to look out for themselves on 'Independent Intavenshan', whilst the title track encouraged us to think – even fleetingly – that triumph was within reach. The main objective, as outlined in 'Reality Poem', was to stay focussed and not become distracted by religion or ideology. It was the procurement and/or defence of our rights that mattered but the track that stood out for many people was 'Sonny's Lettah (Anti-SUS Poem)', written in the form of a letter from a black youth to his mother, explaining that he'd been waiting at a bus stop with his younger brother when a police van had pulled up and three officers got out. The brothers were innocent but, under the SUS law, the police could apprehend anyone they suspected of… well, anything at all, real or imagined. Sonny's brother complained, saying it was an injustice, and when the officers then began beating him, Sonny felt compelled to intervene. In the resulting scuffle, one of the policemen was killed, and Sonny left facing a murder charge.

Rasta and ghetto people in Jamaica were being subjected to such treatment on a daily basis. The Peace Treaty had offered a temporary respite, but since hostilities had recommenced, people living in Kingston's most deprived communities been left bruised and beaten by worsening poverty, political violence, police brutality, corruption and an influx of guns and hard drugs. Jamaica had been brought to its knees and dreams of freedom – collective or otherwise – had crashed to earth, leaving harsh realities in their place. The music slowed accordingly, as if the joy had been squeezed out of it. It became heavy and unrelenting, just like the pressures heaped on the sufferers' heads, and yet at the same time it was invested with tremendous power. Rasta themes and love songs still accounted for the majority of releases, but it was the reality songs that persisted in speaking truth to power, revealing what life was really like in those neighbourhoods.

Michael Manley's decision to call in the IMF to help revive Jamaica's economy had caused splits within the PNP, as well as provoking intense criticism from the opposition, especially after his government failed the IMF's international reserves test by a whopping US$130 million. Manley protested that this failure was due to factors outside of his control, since the costs involved in combatting floods, worldwide inflation, oil price increases and interest rate rises had all proved greater than what had been predicted. Nevertheless the IMF demanded new negotiations and new governmental measures, and this inevitably entailed budget cuts. Manley had promised that 1979 would be a year of economic recovery but it had ended in failure for the IMF programme, and further setbacks for his government. Initially, he'd pinned his hopes on newly inaugurated US president Jimmy Carter – a Democrat – showing him more leniency than either Nixon and Ford, but alarm bells had sounded in the US State Department and Pentagon because of the popular uprisings in Nicaragua and Iran, and also the left-wing coup that had recently taken place in Grenada. Manley's friendship with Fidel Castro was also a significant factor in him being brought to heel. The charismatic leader of the PNP, who'd risen to power promising much needed social reforms, now resembled a dead man walking, and his dream of leading a just and caring island nation was in tatters.

The next election was ten long months away, and almost a thousand lives would be lost during the campaign to determine Jamaica's next leader because of the violence from both sides. Kingston became even more of a powder keg and special police units that all too often acted like death squads increased the pressure on people already beset by more problems than they could bear. For a time at least, reggae singers and deejays would have to be careful about what they said on stage and in the dances, as well as in their songs.

The relative freedom they'd enjoyed in the past now seemed but a fleeting illusion, just like the Peace Treaty. It was a mirage that promised much but couldn't be sustained, and the sense of loss was all too real. The barricades had been stormed but not torn down, warnings had been delivered but not heeded and eyes opened, but not wide enough to bring about lasting change. The new world had failed to materialise. Love and righteousness had not prevailed, despite so many reggae artists having pleaded their cause, and poverty not eradicated. There were still too many children going hungry, too many people living in fear and too many young people being starved of a destination other than jail, cemetery or madhouse. The seventies were supposed to deliver so much after the initial euphoria of Jamaican Independence, but those who needed it most, who'd been born into sufferation and squalor, had been left feeling disenchanted, demoralised and disheartened. They, too, had rejoiced in the national motto 'out of many one people', thinking for once that it also applied to them. It hadn't, and reggae aficionados who later mourned the fact that many Jamaican artists stopped singing about roots and culture after the seventies ended should reflect on how futile such goals had become to people living in the ghettos, where the reggae music these fans appreciated so much had come from. People like them, whose lives had become hardened by desperation and dismay, needed a different soundtrack to see them through the challenging times that lay ahead, just like their counterparts in Britain, America and beyond. With the rise of neo-liberalism and the pain that leaders like Reagan and Thatcher inflicted on the poorer classes, messages of hope and liberation would offer scant comfort. The rules of engagement changed and those artists who didn't adopt a more selfish attitude or take risks faced oblivion. Many of them had to summon great strength and determination in order to make something of their lives, whilst entertaining and uplifting others like themselves. There would be much to admire about eighties' reggae and dancehall, despite the inescapable criticisms of homophobia and misogyny. That same triumph of the human spirit that had informed a great deal of seventies music was still there, empowering the lives of youths with few prospects other than to pick up a mic and articulate whatever was happening in their communities. Artists like them didn't live uptown whilst singing about an Africa that poor people could neither visit nor even imagine. They described ghetto life instead, and with an earthy humour and realism that ordinary people could relate to – that lifted their spirits and helped to alleviate their daily struggles. That's how dancehall originated, and what it returned to when the infrastructure crumbled and many overseas reggae fans looked elsewhere for cultural inspiration. It never fails to amaze me when looking back and seeing to what extent Jamaican music was able to reinvent itself and move from one phase to another – each of them very different from the others.

The seventies were special, though. It was a decade in Jamaican musical history that offered an embarrassment of riches, and a kaleidoscope of different forms, sounds and innovations. It started with the rise of deejays – artists who pioneered the art of chanting rhyming verse on records and sparked off a global love of rapping, since there was no hip hop when the likes of Count Machuki and Sir Lord Comic first strutted their stuff on local sound systems. Jamaican superstars like Desmond Dekker and Jimmy Cliff built on the success of gatecrashers Millie and Prince Buster and a cultural revolution began when Count Ossie took the sounds of nyahbinghi drumming from the shanty towns and Rasta camps to the lawns of Jamaica House and into the consciousness of young rebels such as Bob Marley and the Wailers. It was the decade when proud African descendants fulfilled the dreams of Rastafarian elders who'd suffered persecution and discrimination for so long, and the sufferers stepped out of the shadows to make their voices heard throughout the world via every means available to the singers and players of instruments who'd placed their skills at their disposal.

Shanty towns and ghettos were transformed from burial grounds of poor people's hopes and aspirations into cradles of lyrical and musical brilliance. Great storytellers arose, and also influential thinkers and philosophers, some of whom couldn't read or write. We witnessed the coming of dub, a Jamaican artform where music was freed from all the usual strictures and delivered into the hands of magicians like King Tubby and Lee 'Scratch' Perry, whose ability to manipulate sound would attain near mystical qualities.

That artists like these and others mentioned in these pages were able to achieve all they did at a time of such political turmoil, economic hardship and growing social unrest was nothing short of miraculous. Their hard work, courage and imagination turned the Caribbean island they so proudly represented into one of the most enduring centres of musical influence the world has known, lauded by fans, creatives of all kinds and academics, as well as UNESCO which, in 2018, designated reggae as an 'intangible cultural heritage of humanity.' Can't say fairer than that now, can we?

ACKNOWLEDGEMENTS

'No man is an island, entire of itself...' The truth of John Donne's statement, made famous in reggae by Dennis Brown, becomes all too apparent when writing a book of this nature. The list of people I am indebted to extends far beyond those quoted in these pages, who freely gave of their time and memories. It rightly includes – with special thanks to Sly Dunbar – all the talented artists and musicians whose combined skills brought the reggae music of the seventies to life. Also, not forgetting the journalists writing for Jamaica's *Daily Gleaner* and various media outlets in the UK, US and Canada throughout that decade, who were among the first to appraise what was happening in the dances, clubs and recording studios on both sides of the Atlantic.

This book is dedicated to the memory of the following whose friendship, encouragement and endorsement meant the world to me, namely Aston 'Family Man' Barrett, Castro Brown, Junior Delgado, Alan Douglas, Frederick 'Toots' Hibbert, Bunny 'Striker' Lee and Ronald 'Nambo' Robinson.

I would like to thank Cath, my indispensable first reader; David Barraclough and the team at Omnibus Press, also Chris Wells and the late Paul Phillips at *Echoes Magazine*, who have continued to be an integral part of my reggae journey.

AUTHOR'S SOURCE NOTES

Introduction

Author's interviews with Prince Buster (2007), Chris Blackwell (2022), Derrick Morgan (1992) and Jimmy Cliff (2017).

Peter I, interview with Derrick Morgan, *Reggae Vibes* (2017), Matthew Parker, 'Goldeneye – Where Bond Was Born: Ian Fleming's Jamaica', *Windmill Books* (2015), Stefan Paul, *Reggae Sunsplash* film documentary (1979).

Chapter 1 – Shocks Of Mighty!

Author's interviews with Desmond Dekker (2005), Toots Hibbert (2018), Burning Spear (2022), Marcia Griffiths (2016), Roy Ellis (2017), Dave Barker (2011), Devon Russell (1996), U-Roy (2012), Derrick Harriott (1993), Hopeton Lewis (2009) and Max Romeo (2010).

Uncredited, 'The Skinheads, Greasers And Rudys – England's New, Violent Teen Style', *The Daily Gleaner* (1970), Editorial, 'At Annual National Exhibition - Numerous paintings by Rastafarian artists', *The Daily Gleaner* (1970), Dermot Hussey, 'A Sunday Miracle', *The Daily Gleaner* (1970), Glen Adams, *Wailing Upsetter* (2016), Julian Jingles, 'Bob and Marcia rock House of Chen', *The Daily Gleaner* (1970), Rich Lowe, interview with Dennis Brown, *Reggae*

Directory (1993), Editorial, 'Hundreds seek the coffin and crows', *The Daily Gleaner* (1970), Julian Jingles, 'Round-Up', *The Daily Gleaner* (1970).

Chapter 2 – Another Cycle

Author's interviews with Burning Spear (2009), Bob Andy (2010), Oku Onuora (2017), Sly Dunbar (2012), Dave Barker (2011), Niney The Observer (1993), Patricia 'Miss Pat' Chin (2019), Glenroy Oakley (2012), Alton Ellis (1993), Jimmy Cliff (2012), Clive Chin (2011), Vin Morgan (2016), Marcia Griffiths (2016), Max Romeo (1998) and U-Roy (2012).

Jackie Mittoo, *Wishbone* liner notes, Summus Records (1971), David Katz, interview with Bernard Collins, *Solid Foundation – An Oral History* (2024), *Musical Root 1* (1990), Michael Turner, interview with Donald Manning, *The Beat Vol. 16* (1997), Dr Walter Rodney, *The Groundings With My Brothers*, Bogle-L'Ouverture (1971), Glen Adams, *Wailing Upsetter* (2016), John 'Rabbit' Bundrick, *Diaries* (www.rabbitwho.com), Edward Seaga, 'My Life & Leadership: Hard Road To Travel 1980-2008 Vol. 1', *Macmillan Education* (2010), Paul McCartney (the-paulmccartney-project.com).

Chapter 3 – Every Tongue Shall Tell

Author's interviews with Robbie Lyn (2009), Locksley Gichie (2011), Hux Brown (2009), Jimmy Cliff (2012), Bob Andy (2010), Mitch Graylan (1995), Vivian 'Yabby You' Jackson (1999), Beres Hammond (2016), Brinsley Forde (2011), Dandy Livingstone (2014), Hugh Francis (1999), Robbie Shakespeare (2009), Clive Chin (2011), Junior Dan (2009), Niney The Observer (1999), Big Youth (2001) and Augustus 'Gussie' Clarke (2013).

Glen Adams, *Wailing Upsetter* (2016), Angus Taylor, interview with Mikey Chung, *United Reggae* (2018), Tracy Nicholas' interview with Amy Jacques, *The Daily Gleaner* (1972), Michael Manley, extract from a political rally reprinted in *The Daily Gleaner* (1972), Edward Seaga, 'My Life & Leadership: Hard Road To Travel 1980-2008 Vol. 1', *Macmillan Education* (2010), Musik – Ja Way, interview with Prince Jazzbo, *soundcloud.com/jaway* (2013), Dermot Hussey, 'Rastafari as folk hero', *The Daily Gleaner* (1972), Editorial, 'Premiere of film marred', *The Daily Gleaner* (1972), Ray Connolly, 'The Harder They Come', *Evening Standard* (1972), Joe Sinclair, 'Judge Dread', (trojanrecords.com), Keith Richards, 'Life', W&N (2011), Steve Milne, interview with Big Youth, *Full Watts* (1998).

Chapter 4 – Higher The Mountain

Author's interviews with Wya Lindo (2008), Lloyd Charmers (2006), Ken Boothe (2017), Gregory Isaacs (2006), Errol Dunkley (1998), Augustus 'Gussie' Clarke (2013), Clive Chin (2011), Dennis Bovell (2004), Jimmy Riley (1998), Niney The Observer (1999) and Albert 'Apple' Craig (2011).

Colin McGlashan, 'Reggae, Reggae, Reggae', *Sunday Times Magazine* (1973), Maureen Orth, 'Jamaican Rock – big sound on US Pop Scene,' *Newsweek* (1973), 'Miriam Makeba... in conference', *The Daily Gleaner* (1973), Miriam Makeba, 'My Story', *Penguin* (1989), Bob Andy, liner notes to Ken Boothe's *Black, Gold And Green*, Trojan (1973), David Rodigan, 'My Life In Reggae', *Constable* (2018), David Cavanagh, 'Good Night And Good Riddance', *Faber & Faber* (2016), Chris Lane, review of the Wailers at London's Speakeasy, *Blues And Soul* (1973), Angus Taylor, interview with Big Youth, *United Reggae* (2019), Carl Gayle, interview with I Roy (1973), Ian McCann, interview with Dennis Brown, *Black Echoes* (Unknown) Lee Jaffe, 'Crossroads – Jean Michel

Basquiat', *Rizzoli International Publications* (2022), Angus Taylor, interview with Sylvan Morris, *Reggaeville* (2019), Verena Reckord, liner notes for Cedric ''Im' Brooks' *From Mento To Reggae To Third World Music*, Doctor Bird (1973), Trevor Williams, interview with Dennis Brown, *Reggae Directory* (1993), David Katz, interview with Tapper Zukie, *Red Bull Music Academy* (2015), Peter I, interview with Tapper Zukie, *Reggae Vibes*, (2017), Clement Bushay, liner notes for Tapper Zukie's *Man A Warrior*, Count Shelly, (1973).

Chapter 5 – The Time Has Come

Author's interviews with Watty Burnett (2009), Susan Cadogan (2022), Lloyd Charmers (2010), Bernard 'Touter' Harvey (2009), Bob Andy (2010), Johnny Clarke (1998), Augustus Pablo (1996), Clive Chin (2011), Burning Spear (2009), Sly Dunbar (2012), Winston 'Pipe' Matthews (2020), Junia Walker (2006), Dennis Bovell (2004) and Mikey Chung (2009).

Chris Lane, review of a Big Youth concert, *Blues And Soul* (1974), Angus Taylor, interview with Chris Lane, *United Reggae* (2013), Steve Milne, interview with Big Youth, *Full Watts* (1998), George Terry, 'Eric Clapton: The 1970s Review', DVD (2014), Robert Palmer, interview with Herbie Mann, *The New York Times* (1974), Point Of View: 'What will the Rastafarians do?', *The Daily Gleaner* (1974), Editorial, 'Democratic Socialism For Jamaica', *The Daily Gleaner* (1974).

Chapter 6 – Have You Heard The News?

Author's interviews with Burning Spear (2009), Susan Cadogan (2022), Watty Burnett (2009), Bunny Rugs (2012), Beres Hammond (2016), Sly Dunbar (2022), General Lee (2022), Bunny Lee (2011), Jimmy Cliff (2017), Dennis Bovell (2008), Little Roy (1999), Clive Chin (2012), Gregory Isaacs (2006), Marcia Griffiths (2016), Errol

Brown (2015), Pablo Moses (2023), U-Roy (2012) and Niney The Observer (1999).

Editorial, 'Famine is coming', *The Daily Gleaner* (1975), Roger Steffens, interview with Cindy Breakespeare, *The Beat* (1993), Fitzroy Nation, 'Reggae: What Of The Future?' *The Daily Gleaner* (1975), Mike Flood, 'Review of Brave Warrior', *Sounds* (1975), David Hepworth, 'Uncommon People', *Black Swan* (2018), T 'Boots' Harris, 'King of Reggae – Bob Marley', *The Daily Gleaner* (1975), George Lamming, introduction to 'Rasta and Resistance', *Africa World Press* (1980), Mister Brown, review of Big Youth's *Dreadlocks Dread*, *Sounds* (1975), Bob West, 'Reggae Exemplified', *The Daily Gleaner* (1975), John Ingram, review of Big Youth's 'Wolf In Sheep's Clothing', *Sounds* (1975), Bob West, review of Max Romeo's *Revelation Time*, *The Daily Gleaner* (1975).

Chapter 7 – Heavy Manners

Author's interviews with Michael 'Eppy' Epstein (2010), Sangie Davis (2023), U Brown (1996), Jumbo Vanrenen (2010), Lloyd Charmers (2010), Augustus 'Gussie' Clarke (2013), Ansel Cridland (2022), Bobby Melody (1999), Glen Washington (2001), Joseph Hill (1992), Lee 'Scratch' Perry (2003), Watty Burnett (2009), Max Romeo (2010), Sly Dunbar (2022), Jerry Neville (2023), Angus 'Drummie Zeb' Gaye (2016), John Kpiaye (2004), Dennis Bovell (2004), Anthony Brightly (2014), Bunny Wailer (2009), Cindy Breakspeare (1993) and Marcia Griffiths (2005).

Beverley Manley, 'The Manley Memoirs', *Ian Randle* (2012), Editorial, 'Fires Rage In Rema Area,' *The Daily Gleaner* (1976), Beverley Martyn, 'Sweet Honesty', *Grosvenor House* (2011), Graeme Thomson, 'Small Hours: The Long Night of John Martyn', *Omnibus Press* (2020), Thomas Wright, letter to the editor, *The Daily Gleaner* (1976), Savoy, 'Savoy's stompin' again', *Playboy*

Magazine (1976), Editorial, 'Rastamania hits Britain', *The Daily Gleaner* (1976), Editorial, 'Carifesta 76 Jamaica', *Jamaica Gleaner* (1976), Stephen Davis, 'Fear In Paradise', *New York Times* (1976), Ishmahil Blagrove, 'Carnival', *Abe Books* (2014), Brigadier Jerry, interview with *I Never Knew TV* (2023) and Dan Hedges, review of Bob Andy's *The Music Inside Me, The Daily Gleaner* (1976).

Chapter 8 – When Two Sevens Clash

Author's interviews with Cindy Breakspeare (1993), Roger Mayer (2006), Trinity (2000), Niney The Observer (1999), Clive Chin (2012), Junior Marvin (2011), Theo Bafaloukos (2008), Max Romeo (2010), Andy Bassford (2011), Johnny Osbourne (2023), Watty Burnett (2009), Don Letts (2003), Angus 'Drummie Zeb' Gaye (2016), Chris Blackwell (2022), Chris Cracknell (2001), John Kpiaye (2004), Dennis Bovell (2004), Leonard Dillon (2000), Wesley Tinglin (2016), King Jammy (2013), Vivian 'Yabby You' Jackson (1999), Martin Disney (2023), Chris David (2023), Michael 'Eppy' Epstein (2010), Burning Spear (2022), Dobby Dobson (2012) and Eddy Grant (2008).

Ray Hurford, interview with Bob Andy, 'Fire Burning', *Small Axe Vol. 16* (1983), Jimmy Lindsay on recording 'Easy', *jimmylindsay. co.uk*, Joe Gibbs, liner notes for Culture's *Two Sevens Clash* (1977), Balford Henry, Merry Go Round, *The Daily Gleaner* (1977), David Clayton Thomas, liner notes for Ishan People, *Ishan People* (1977), David Katz, interview with Dr Alimantado, *Solid Foundation – An Oral History* (2024), *More Axe 7* (1989), John Lydon, 'The Johnny Rotten Show: The Punk And His Music', *Capital Radio* (1977), Dave Hendley, 'Earl Zero: Natty Dread in a Greenwich town', *Blues And Soul* (1978), Jah Woosh, liner notes for *Jah Woosh* (1974), Maurice Bottomley, review of Big Youth's 'Riverton City', *Pop Matters* (1977), Greg Whitfield, interview with Keith Levene, *3AM Magazine* (2004), Ray Hurford, interview with Augustus Pablo,

'Tales Of Pablo', *More Axe* (1987), Adam Coxon, interview with Basil Gabbidon, *pennyblackmusic.co.uk*, Dave Hendley, '1977: the beginning of the end?', *Blues And Soul* (1978).

Chapter 9 – Dread, Beat N' Blood

Author's interviews with Don Letts (2003), Gaylene Martin (2010), Sly Dunbar (2011 and 2022), Jumbo Vanrenen (2010), Beres Hammond (2016), Michael 'Eppy' Epstein (2010), Ansel Cridland (2022), Marcia Griffiths (2005), Theo Bafaloukos (2008), Tony Chin (2011), Paul 'Jah Screw' Love (2013), Ranking Joe (2003), Adrian Sherwood (2015), Bim Sherman (1998), Bernard 'Touter' Harvey (2009), David Hinds (1996 and 2010), Castro Brown (1996), Linton Kwesi Johnson (2017), Burning Spear (2022), Clive Chin (2012), Marcia Griffiths (2005), Albert 'Apple' Craig (2011), Cecil 'Skelly' Spence (2015), Carlton 'Tetrack' Hines (2013), Tony 'Gad' Robinson (2016), Danny McKen / Capital Letters (2014), Chris Cracknell (2001), Winston 'Pipe' Matthews (2020), Tony McDermott (2022), John McGillvray (2007), Michael Prophet (1999), Mikey 'Dread' Campbell (1991) and Mikey Chung (2009).

Terry Southern, quotes by Simon Draper and Norman Grant, 'Virgin: A History Of Virgin Records', *A Publishing Company* (2000), John Lydon, 'Rotten. No Irish. No Blacks. No Dogs', *Plexus* (2003), Vivien Goldman, 'Peace Fighter,' Sounds (1978), Pete Weston, liner notes for Gregory Isaacs' *Extra Classic*, Micron (1978), James Fox, 'Rivals declare war', *The Daily Gleaner*, (1978), Saxon Baird, 'Babylon Is Falling: David Hinds on the Early Years of Steel Pulse and His Youth in England', *The World* (2014), Editorial, 'Protest From The Ghetto', *The Daily Gleaner* (1978), Jo-Ann Greene, review of *Rockers* (GOLDMINE), 'Tapper Zukie in Tivoli Gardens', *The Daily Gleaner* (1978), Dawn Ritch, 'An Army Of Performers', *The Daily Gleaner* (1978), Ray Hurford, interview with Ijahman Levi, *Small Axe* (1982), David Katz, interview with

Tapper Zukie, *Red Bull Music Academy* (2015), Patti Smith, liner notes for Tapper Zukie, *The Man From Bozrah*, Mer (1978), Sylvie Simmonds, 'A Fistful Of Gitanes', *Da Capo* (2002), Arthur Kitchin, 'The Volatile Peter Tosh', *The Daily Gleaner* (1978), Dawn Ritch, 'Sundry Stage Antics', *The Daily Gleaner* (1978), Steve Milne, interview with Sugar Minott, *Full Watts Vol 4* (1999), Steve Milne, interview with Mikey Dread, *Full Watts Vol 3* (1999), Interview with Bob Marley, *The New York Times* (1978), Eric Fuller, interview with Carl Levy, *Sounds* (1978), Penny Reel 'Deep Down With Dennis Brown', *Drake Bros* (2000), David Katz, interview with Dr Alimantado, *Solid Foundation – An Oral History* (2024), Rob 'Iron Man' Blackmore, letter to the editor, *Sounds* (1978), David Rodigan, 'My Life In Reggae', *Constable* (2018), David Katz, interview with Bernard Collins, *Solid Foundation – An Oral History* (2024), Jackie Ranston, 'Spotlight on Cindy Breakspeare', *The Daily Gleaner* (1978).

Chapter 10 – Soon Forward

Author's interviews with Ken 'Fat Man' Gordon (2015), Lloyd Coxsone (2015), Jah Shaka (1997), Sangie Davis (2023), Bim Sherman (1998), Adrian Sherwood (2015), Sly Dunbar (2009), Mikey Chung (2009), Lee 'Scratch' Perry (2003), Ansel Cridland (2022), Carl 'Captain Sinbad' Dwyer (2013), Dennis Bovell (2009 and 2022), Tony 'Gad' Robinson (2016), David Hinds (1996), Lynval Golding (2007), Johnny Osbourne (2023), Linton Kwesi Johnson (2017), Bunny Lee (2006), Prince Lincoln Thompson (1996), Albert 'Apple' Craig (2011), Bunny Wailer (2009), Joseph Hill (1992), Beres Hammond (2016), Country / Capital Letters (2014), Junior Marvin (2010), Dandy Livingstone (2014), Pauline Black (2015), Jumbo Vanrenen (2010), Chris Cracknell (2001), Trinity (2000), Ranking Joe (2003), Mikey 'Dread' Campbell (1991), Brian Travers / UB40 (1998).

Editorial, '500 barricades', *The Daily Gleaner* (1979), Penny Reel 'Deep Down With Dennis Brown', *Drake Bros* (2000), Peter Tosh interview, *Tucson Night Times* (1979), Arthur Kitchin, 'Marley's studio: One of the finest in the Caribbean', *The Daily Gleaner* (1979), Sylvie Simmonds, 'A Fistful Of Gitanes', *Da Capo* (2002), Eddy Grant, 'Peter Tosh, merely the best reggae band in the world', *The Daily Gleaner* (1979), Interview with Walford 'Poco' Tyson on *Reggae Gist Xtra* (2023), Angus Taylor, interview with Tapper Zukie, *United Reggae* (2012), Dave Hendley, 'Channel One: Vital Dub', *Blues And Soul* (1979), Sugar Minott, interview with Miguel Cullen, *clashmusic.com* (2010), Sugar Minott, interview with Ray Hurford, *Small Axe* (1979), Arthur Kitchin, 'Reggae Sunsplash II', *The Daily Gleaner* (1979), Alexis Petridis, 'Ska for the madding crowd', *The Guardian* (2002), Lister Hewan Lowe, 'Is Peter Tosh Really Reggae?', *Santa Cruz Sentinel* (1979), Editorial, 'Manley: Non-Aligned Movement will be stronger than ever', *The Daily Gleaner* (1979), Angus Taylor, interview with Kiddus I, *United Reggae* (2016), Chris Salewicz, 'Redemption Song – The Definite Biography of Joe Strummer', *HarperCollins* (2006), David Rodigan, 'My Life In Reggae', *Constable* (2018), Balford Henry, 'Music Round-A-Bout', *The Daily Gleaner* (1979), Ray Hurford, interview with I Roy, *Small Axe 8* (1978), Doug Wendt, interview with Sandra 'Puma' Jones on *Midnight Dread* (1984), Caroline Sullivan, 'How we made Cut (the Slits), *The Guardian* (2013), Interview with Dave Wakeling, 'Not Drowning But Wakeling', *NME* (1982), Angus Taylor, interview with Clinton Fearon, *United Reggae* (2016).

BIBLIOGRAPHY

Bean, J P, *Joe Cocker: With a Little Help from My Friends* (Omnibus Press, 1990)

Black, Pauline, *Black by Design: A 2-Tone Memoir* (Serpent's Tail, 2012)

Blagrove, Ishmahil, *Carnival*, (Abe Books, 2014)

Campbell, Horace, *Rasta and Resistance* (Africa World Press, 1980)

Clapton, Eric, *The Autobiography* (Century, 2007)

De Koningh & Griffiths, Marc, *Tighten Up! The History of Reggae in the UK* (Sanctuary Publishing Ltd, 2004)

De Koningh & Cane-Honeysett, Laurence, *Young, Gifted & Black: The Story of Trojan Records* (Omnibus Press, 2018)

Gimarc, George, *Punk Diary, 1970-79: An Eyewitness Record of the Punk Decade* (Vintage, 1994)

Gray, Marcus, *Last Gang In Town – The Story and Myth of the Clash* (Fourth Estate, 1995)

Hepworth, David, *Uncommon People* (Black Swan, 2018)

Jaffe, Lee, *Crossroads – Jean Michel Basquiat* (Rizzoli International Publications, 2022)

Jaffe, Lee with Steffens, Roger, *One Love – Life with Bob Marley and the Wailers* (W W Norton, 2003)

Johnson, Linton Kwesi, *Time Come: Selected Prose* (Picador, 2023)

Katz, David, *Jimmy Cliff: An Unauthorised Biography* (Macmillan / Signal Books, 2011)

Letts, Don, with Nobakht, David, *Culture Clash – Dread Meets Punk Rockers* (SAF Publishing, 2006)

Lowe, Rich Opre, *The Matador: Lloyd Daley – Sonic Pioneer of Jamaican Music* (Jamaica Way Publishing, 2020)

Lydon, John, *Rotten. No Irish. No Blacks. No Dogs* (Plexus, 2003)

Makeba, Miriam, and Hall, James, *My Story* (Penguin, 1989)

Manley, Beverley, *The Manley Memoirs* (Ian Randle, 2012)

Manley, Michael, *Jamaica: Struggle in the Periphery* (Littlehampton Book Services Ltd, 1982)

Manley, Michael, *Politics of Change* (Andre Deutsch, 1992)

McCann, Ian, *In His Own Words – Bob Marley* (Omnibus Press, 1993)

Martyn, Beverley, *Sweet Honesty*, (Grosvenor House, 2011)

Masouri, John, *Simmer Down – The Early Wailers Story* (Jook Joint Press, 2018)

Masouri, John, *Steppin' Razor – The Life of Peter Tosh* (Omnibus Press, 2013)

Morris, Lee, *2 Tone Before, During & After* (Media House Books, 2020)

Panter, Horace, *Ska'd for Life: A Personal Journey with The Specials* (Pan Books, 2007)

Parker, Matthew, *Goldeneye – Where Bond Was Born: Ian Fleming's Jamaica* (Windmill Books, 2015)

Rachel, Daniel, *Walls Come Tumbling Down: The Music and Politics of Rock Against Racism, 2 Tone and Red Wedge* (Picador, 2017)

Reel, Penny, *Deep Down With Dennis Brown* (Drake Bros, 2000)

Rodigan, David, with Burrell, Ian, *My Life In Reggae* (Constable, 2018)

Salewicz, Chris, *Redemption Song – The Definite Biography of Joe Strummer* (Harper Collins, 2006)

Seaga, Edward, *My Life & Leadership: Hard Road To Travel 1980-2008 Vols 1 & 2* (Macmillan Education, 2010)

Simmonds, Sylvie, *A Fistful Of Gitanes* (Da Capo, 2002)

Southern, Terry, *Virgin: A History Of Virgin Records* (A Publishing Company, 2000)

Staple, Neville, *Original Rude By: From Borstal to The Specials: A Life in Crime & Music* (Aurum, 2009)

Taylor, Don with Henry, Mike, *So Much Things To Say – My Life As Bob Marley's Manager* (Blake, 1995)

Thomas, Michael & Boot, Adrian, *Jamaica: Babylon on a Thin Wire* (Thames & Hudson, 1976)

Thomson, Graeme, *Small Hours: The Long Night of John Martyn* (Omnibus Press, 2020)

Walker, Norman, *Junia Reggae: The Journey from King Street: Volume 1* (Smart Media, 2011)

INDEX

598